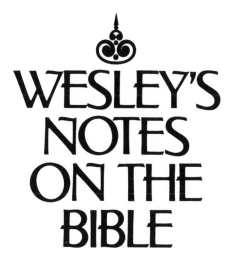

WESLEY'S
NOTES
ON THE
BIBLE

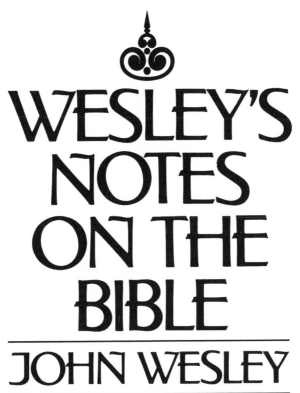

WESLEY'S NOTES ON THE BIBLE

JOHN WESLEY

FRANCIS ASBURY PRESS
of Zondervan Publishing House
1415 Lake Dr. S.E. • Grand Rapids MI 49506

WESLEY'S NOTES ON THE BIBLE
Copyright © 1987 by The Zondervan Corporation
Grand Rapids, Michigan

Francis Asbury Press is an imprint of Zondervan
Publishing House, 1415 Lake Drive, S.E.,
Grand Rapids, Michigan 49506.

Library of Congress Cataloging in Publication Data

Wesley, John, 1703–1791.
   Wesley's notes on the Bible.

    1. Bible—Commentaries—Early works to 1800. I. Schoenhals,
G. Roger. II. Title. III. Title: Notes on the Bible.
BS490.W47   1987   220.7   86-26678
ISBN 0-310-36410-8

Designed by Louise Bauer
Copy-edited by James E. Ruark

Printed in the United States of America

87 88 89 90 91 92 / AH / 10 9 8 7 6 5 4 3 2 1

contents

editor's preface

John Wesley wrote his *Explanatory Notes Upon the Old and New Testaments* during two periods of his life. His work on the New Testament was published in 1755, while his three volumes on the Old Testament were produced and published ten years later, between 1765–66. Together they comprise some 3,682 pages of material.

In the prefaces to both sections, Wesley states that he borrowed freely from various works of his day. For the Old Testament he relied on Matthew Henry and William Poole; his primary source for the New Testament was John A. Bengel. I have included most of both prefaces so that you can read Wesley's rationale in his own words.

When trying to sort out which notes were original with Wesley and which came from the pen of Henry or one of the other sources, I threw up my hands in despair. Such a task would keep one busy for twenty years! But I did check enough to discover that Wesley was highly selective in his borrowing and that he took great liberty to adjust and refine until the adopted words fit his own views or purposes. Even though we may not know which terms or sentences are original with Wesley, we can be reasonably sure that all of them reflect his thinking and convictions.

On the other hand, many of the comments (especially those with pastoral overtones) are obviously constructed out of Wesley's own heart and mind. In addition, his characteristic style comes through repeatedly. He is an exacting writer, closely reasoning his thoughts with an economy of words. And even though some of his sentences travel for one-hundred-plus words, one can easily trace the flow of his ideas. Clearly, his *Notes* are not simply an abridgment of the work of others, but an artful blending of the best of other scholars' work into the stream of his own theological perspectives.

I should note a rather glaring exception to the foregoing remarks. When Wesley comes to the Book of Revelation, he lets Bengel speak for him. He admits as much in his introduction to that book which I have included in full.

One of the reasons for Wesley's commentary, as he explains in his preface to the Old Testament, is to provide something within the financial grasp of the common person. He complained that Henry's exhaustive work was too long, too heavy, too expensive. It is interesting that we face the same "problem" today. To obtain a complete set of Wesley's *Notes,* one would pay well over a hundred dollars. The sheer magnitude of the material may also discourage the modern reader. Hence the production of the current volume: shorter, more condensed, less expensive.

EDITORIAL GUIDELINES

How does one abridge 3,682 pages into the space of the current volume without losing the substance of Wesley? That was my initial question. I answered it by defining and following a set of ten editorial guidelines.

First, I determined to eliminate the biblical text. This freed up considerable space and allowed me to concentrate on the actual notes of the text. Although Wesley's version of the Bible corresponds by and large with the King James (Authorized) Version, he in fact developed his own, based on Greek and Hebrew texts that he considered more reliable than those underlying the King James. Wherever differences occur between them, the wording of the King James is cited in a footnote. This is done to help today's reader who has access to the King James but not to Wesley's own version.

The words and phrases of Scripture that Wesley cites for comment are rendered in italics. When he refers to or quotes from another portion of Scripture during his commentary, those words are given in quotation marks, whether or not—more often not—he has given the Bible reference for them.

Second, while retaining the usage of the King James Version, I attempted to update the language of the notes. Thus I preferred more current spellings of such words as *favour (favor)* and *Saviour (Savior)* and readily changed words that have acquired new meanings during the past two centuries. For example, when Wesley speaks of our "wants," he doesn't mean those things that we desire to have but may not truly need; rather, by our "wants" he means our "needs," things such as our daily bread. I abolished the *thees* and *thous* and other archaic terms. Some long sentences were shortened to give the reader more places to pause. At the same time, I endeavored to retain the flavor and style of Wesley himself.

Third, I decided to provide a comprehensive treatment of the *Notes.* That is, I included something from every chapter of the Bible. In some cases this meant accepting a weak comment just to provide something for a given chapter. I felt, however, that completeness was a worthy end.

Fourth, I selected Wesley's comments proportionately. If he spent more space treating the Book of Ruth than the Book of Jonah, that proportion is reflected in the abridgment. For example, Wesley had far more to say about Genesis than any of the other four books of the Pentateuch. You will find the same proportion in the following pages. Likewise, considerably more space is devoted to Romans than Hebrews.

Fifth, I sought to quote the selected notes in full (where possible and valuable) rather than taking bits and pieces from a greater number of comments. When Wesley expanded on a point, I allowed him to continue.

Sixth, many of Wesley's notes are technical comments about the language or geography or a historical item. These I mostly filtered out, assuming that today's student would want to reach for more recent sources to gain the value of modern discoveries and scholarship. For this abridgment I opted for those things that seem unique to Wesley, thoughts that would not be found in any other commentary.

Seventh, I included every personal reference I could find, every allusion Wesley made to his own life.

Eighth, I watched carefully for theological comments. I recorded his words relating not only to his own doctrinal emphases, but also those written in opposition to such views as unconditional predestination.

Ninth, I recorded every pastoral reference I could find. These heart-to-heart comments contain a devotional tone that reveal some of the special concerns of Wesley.

Finally, I preserved a variety of colorful expressions. Wesley was a masterful writer, and frequently his sentences blossom with the most enchanting constructions.

These ten guidelines, or grids, helped me extract the rich cream of Wesley's *Notes*. We are left with a condensed treasure of insight and inspiration that will not only increase our understanding and appreciation of Wesley, but will motivate us onward in our own pilgrimage of faith.

OBSERVATIONS

Several observations stand out as I look back over my walk through the Bible with Wesley. First, he was uneven in his treatment of Scripture. That is, he gave more attention to some books than to others. Some he treated almost with a cold detachment, while others are filled with the warmth of pastoral concern. Such variance may reflect the particular circumstance of Wesley during the time of composition. He was, after all, preaching some eight hundred sermons a year during the time he produced the Old Testament notes.

A related observation centers on the rather odd fact that Wesley often either skipped or skimmed passages that one would expect him to treat deeply. As Timothy Smith points out, "A quick glance at the notes he wrote on the great texts from which he characteristically preached both the general doctrine of perfect love and the specific call to faith for the experience of it hardly indicates that he had ever preached on those texts, much less proclaimed the promise of entire sanctification from them." Smith concludes that the absence of such treatment reflected Wesley's intention not to duplicate what he had already treated in preaching and print.

During my trek through the material, several themes or special interests seemed to recur. For example, Wesley (especially in the Old Testament) seemed unusually reflective concerning death. One might think he was contemplating his own advancing age or that he had suffered the loss of a close friend or relative.

Another obvious interest was his fellow-clergymen. Again and again he exhorts, warns, and speaks to them. And one also soon- discovers Wesley's "pet peeves." He has strong words for predestinarians, the Roman Catholic Church, and those who are motivated by a passion for wealth. Of the practice of letting a body lie in state before burial, he says, "That stupid, senseless pageantry, that shocking insult on a poor, putrefying carcass was reserved for our enlightened age!" (Luke 16:22).

Wesley's key to understanding the Old Testament is the Messiah of the New Testament. He finds numerous allusions to Christ throughout the Old Testament. His treatment of the Song of Solomon is an intricate interpretation of the woman as the Church, the Bride of Christ.

Wesley's fruitful mind delves into the theological depths of the foreknowledge of God, then turns agilely to an involved discussion of the scriptural prohibitions against eating blood, and in the next breath he is addressing the reader, inquiring about his spiritual needs. He is not shut away in an ivory tower, but dwells in the midst of his readers as both scholar and pastor. "How is it with you?" he inquires in Acts 15:36. In Luke 10:42 he notes that Mary chose the good part, that is, to save her soul. Then he looks out at his reader and asks, "Reader, have you?"

And he speaks to himself as well. In Mark 2:6, after speaking harshly of the scribes who led men into darkness, Wesley prays, "O God, let me never offend one of your simple ones! Sooner let my tongue cleave to the roof of my mouth!" In I Timothy 6:7, where Paul speaks of the perishable wealth of this world, Wesley cries out, "Oh, give me one thing—a safe and ready passage to my own country!"

Wesley brims with conviction. He speaks his mind and challenges his reader. He calls for simplicity of life and ardent faithfulness to Christ.

Often he breaks out in spontaneous prayer. "Lord, may our proud hearts be subdued to the methods of your recovering grace! May we allow you to choose how you will bestow favors which it is our highest interest to receive on any terms!" (John 9:7).

One cannot read Wesley's writings without periodic introspection. He urges it upon us both by the example of his own devotion and by his persistent exhortations. Indeed, more than once I found myself kneeling by my desk, asking God to make me more like Wesley, more fervent in my devotion to Christ.

CONCLUSION

For my primary sources I used two recent reprints of Wesley. The three original volumes of the Old Testament notes (1765) were photographed and printed by Schmul Publishers (Salem, Ohio) in 1975. The two New Testament volumes were published by Baker Book House (Grand Rapids, Michigan) in 1983 from "an undated edition published by The Wesleyan-Methodist Book-Room, London."

In addition, I found two particularly helpful articles in the Bulletin of the Wesleyan Theological Society, the *Wesleyan Theological Journal:* (1) William M. Arnett, *A Study in John Wesley's Explanatory Notes Upon the Old Testament,* vol. 8 (Spring 1973), and (2) Timothy L. Smith, *Notes On the Exegesis of John Wesley's "Explanatory Notes Upon the New Testament,"* vol. 16 (Spring 1981).

Finally, I want to pay tribute to my wife, Sandra, for her encouragement during this lengthy project, and for her diligence in proofreading most of the material. I am also grateful to Joe Allison, Editor of Francis Asbury Press, for his advice and encouragement. Jim Ruark, Senior Editor at Zondervan, deserves special mention for working through the entire manuscript. He is a skillful editor, and his polishing touch enhanced my initial efforts.

I expect that many, many readers will find in this volume not only a source of biblical insight and Wesleyan perspective, but also a devotional work that will challenge them to desire more of that most excellent gift of perfect love.

the old testament

preface to the
old testament

About ten years ago I was prevailed upon to publish *Explanatory Notes Upon the New Testament*. When that work was begun, and indeed when it was finished, I had no design to attempt anything farther of the kind. I had a full determination not to do it, being thoroughly fatigued with the immense labor (had it been only this; though this indeed was but a small part of it) of writing many hundreds of pages.

But this was scarce published before I was importuned to write *Explanatory Notes Upon the Old Testament*. This importunity I have withstood for many years. Over and above the deep conviction I had of my insufficiency for such a work, of my want of learning, of understanding, of spiritual experience, for an undertaking more difficult by many degrees than even writing on the New Testament, I objected that there were many passages in the Old which I did not understand myself, and consequently could not explain to others, either to their satisfaction or my own. Above all, I objected to the lack of time; not only as I have a thousand other employments, but as my day is near spent, as I am declined into the vale of years. And to this day it appears to me as a dream, a thing almost incredible, that I should be entering upon a work of this kind when I am entering into the sixty-third year of my age.

Indeed these considerations, the last in particular, still appear to me of such weight that I cannot entertain a thought of composing a body of Notes on the whole Old Testament. The question remaining was, "Is there already any Exposition which is worth abridging?" Abundantly less time will suffice for this, and less ability of every kind. In considering this question, I soon turned my thought on the well-known Mr. Henry. He is thought by all competent judges to have been a person of strong understanding, of various learning, of solid piety, and much experience in the ways of God. And his exposition is generally clear and intelligible, the thoughts being expressed in plain words.

It is also sound, agreeable to the tenor of Scripture and to the analogy of faith. It is frequently full, giving a sufficient explication of the passages which require explaining. It is in many parts deep, penetrating farther into the inspired writings than most other comments do. It does not entertain us with vain speculations, but is practical throughout. It is usually spiritual too, teaching us how to worship God, not in form only, but "in spirit and in truth."

But it may be reasonably inquired, "If Mr. Henry's exposition be not only plain, sound, full, and deep, but practical, yes, and spiritual too, what need is there of any other? Or how is it possible to mend this, to alter it for the better?" I answer, Very many who have this have no need of any other, particularly those who believe (what runs through the whole work, and will much recommend it to them) the doctrine of absolute, irrespective, unconditional predestination. I do not advise these much to trouble themselves about any other exposition than Mr. Henry's; this is sufficient, through the assistance of the blessed Spirit, to make private Christians "wise unto salvation," and (the Lord applying his word) "thoroughly furnished unto every good work."

But then it is manifest, on the other hand, every one cannot have this exposition. It is too large a purchase: thousands would rejoice to have it; but it bears too high a price. They have not six guineas, the London price, in the world, perhaps from one year's end to another. And if they sometimes have, yet they have it not to spare; they need it for other occasions. However much, therefore, they desire so valuable a work, they must content themselves to go without it.

But suppose they have money enough to purchase, yet they have not time enough to read it. The size is as unsurmountable an objection as the price itself. It is not possible for men who have their daily bread to earn by the sweat of their brows, who generally are confined to their work from six in the morning till six in the evening, to find leisure for reading over six volumes, each containing seven or eight hundred pages. These therefore have need of some other exposition than Mr. Henry's. As excellent as it is in its kind, it is not for their purpose; seeing they have neither money to make the purchase, nor time to read it over.

It is very possible, then, to mend this work, valuable as it is, at least by shortening it. As the grand objection to it is the size, that objection may be removed. They who at present have no possibility of profiting by it, while it is of so great a bulk and so high a price, may then enjoy part, at least, of the same advantage with those who have more money and more leisure. Few, I presume, that have the whole, and leisure to read it, will concern themselves with an extract. But those who cannot have all will, for the present at least, be glad to have a part. And they who complain it is too short may yet serve themselves of it till they can procure the long work.

But I think this valuable work may be made more valuable still by making it plainer as well as shorter. Accordingly what is here extracted from it, which indeed makes but a small part of the following volumes, is considerably plainer than the original. In order to do this, not only all the Latin sentences occasionally interspersed are omitted, but whatever phrases or words are not so intelligible to persons of no education. Those only who frequently and familiarly converse with men that are wholly uneducated can conceive how many expressions are mere Greek to them which are quite natural to those who have any share of learning.

It is not by reading, much less by musing alone, that we are enabled to suit our discourse to common capacities. It is only by actually talking with the vulgar that we learn to talk in a manner they can understand. And unless we do this, what do we profit them? Do we not lose all our labor? Should we speak as angels, we should be of no more use to them than "sounding brass or a tinkling cymbal."

No, I think what is extracted from Mr. Henry's work may in some sense be more sound than the original. Understand me right; I mean more conformable to that glorious declaration, God "willeth all men to be saved, and to come to the knowledge of his truth." And let it not be objected that the making of any alteration with regard to a point of doctrine is a misrepresentation of the author's sense, and consequently an injury done to him. It would be so, if an alteration were made of his words so as to make them bear a different meaning; or if any words were recited as his which he did not write. But neither of these is the case. Nothing is recited here as written by him which he did not write. Neither is any construction put upon his words different from his own. But what he wrote in favor of particular redemption is totally left out. And of this I here give express notice to the reader once for all.

Again: It is possible that a work abundantly shorter than Mr. Henry's may nevertheless be considerably fuller in some particulars. There are many words which he passes over without any explanation at all, as taking it for granted that the reader already knows the meaning. But this is a supposition not to be made; it is an entire mistake. For instance: What does a common man know of an omer or a hin? Why, Moses explains his own meaning: "An omer is the tenth part of an ephah." True; but what does the honest man know of an ephah? Just as much as of an omer.

I suppose that which led Mr. Henry into these omissions, which otherwise are unaccountable, was the desire of not saying what others had said before, Mr. Poole in particular. This is easily gathered from his own words: "Mr Poole's English Annotations are of admirable use, especially for the explaining of Scripture phrases, opening the sense, and clearing of difficulties. I have industriously declined as much as I could what is to be found there" (Preface, p. 6). I wish he had not; or at least that he had given us the same sense in other words.

It is possible likewise to penetrate deeper into the meaning of some Scriptures than Mr. Henry has done. Although in general he is far from being a superficial writer, yet he is not always the same. Indeed if he had been, he must have been more than man, considering the vastness of his work. It was scarce possible for any human understanding to produce such a number of volumes without sinking sometimes into trite reflections, and observations more lively than deep. A stream that runs wide, and covers a large tract of land, will be shallow in some places. If it had been confined within a moderate channel, it might have flowed deep all along.

No, it cannot be denied, there may be an exposition of Scripture more closely practical than some parts of Mr. Henry's are, as well as more spiritual. Even his exposition of the twentieth chapter of Exodus, where one would naturally have expected to find a complete scheme of Christian practice, does not answer that expectation. Nor do I remember that he has anywhere given us a satisfactory account of spiritual religion, of the kingdom of God within us, the fruit of Christ dwelling and reigning in the heart. This I hoped to have found, particularly in the exposition of our Lord's Sermon Upon the Mount. But I was quite disappointed of my hope. It was not by any means what I expected.

I do not therefore intend the following Notes for a bare abridgment of Mr. Henry's exposition. Far from it: I not only omit much more than nineteen parts out of twenty of what he has written, but make many alterations and many additions, well nigh from the beginning to the end. In particular, I everywhere omit the far greater part of his inferences from, and improvement of, the chapter. They who think these the most valuable part of the work may have recourse to the author himself.

I likewise omit the greatest part of almost every note, the substance of which is retained; as it seems to be his aim to say as much, whereas it is mine to say as little, as possible. And I omit abundance of quaint sayings and lively antitheses; as, "God feeds his birds; shall he not feed his babes?" "Pharaoh's princes; his pimps rather." Indeed everything of this kind I have left behind quite untouched; although I am sensible these are the very flowers which numberless readers admire. I doubt not they think these to be the chief beauties of the book. For that very reason I cannot but wish they had never had a place therein; for this is a blemish which is exceedingly catching. He that admires it will quickly imitate it.

I used to wonder whence some whom I greatly esteem had so many pretty turns in preaching. But when I read Mr. Henry, my wonder ceased. I saw they were only copying after him; although many of them probably without designing or even adverting to it. They generally consulted his exposition of their text, and frequently just before preaching. And hence little witticisms and a kind of archness insensibly stole upon them, and took the place of that strong, manly eloquence, which they would otherwise have learned from the inspired writers.

With regard to alterations in what I take from Mr. Henry, I continually alter hard words into easy, and long sentences into short. But I do not knowingly alter the sense of anything I extract from him. I only endeavor in several places to make it more clear and determinate. I have added very largely from Mr. Poole, as much as seemed necessary for common readers, in order to help their understanding of those words or passages which Mr. Henry does not explain.

Actually, from the time that I had more maturely considered Mr. Poole's Annotations on the Bible, which was soon after I had gone through the Book of Genesis, I have extracted far more from him than from Mr. Henry. My constant method, after reading the Bible text, was first to read and weigh what Mr. Poole observed upon every verse, and afterwards to consult Mr. Henry's exposition of the whole paragraph. In consequence of this, instead of short additions from Mr. Poole to supply what was lacking in Mr. Henry, which was my first design, I now only make extracts from Mr. Henry, to supply, so far as they are capable, what was wanting in Mr. Poole. I say so far as they are capable; for I still found it needful to add to both such farther observations as have from time to time occurred to my own mind in reading or thinking on the Scriptures, together with such as I have occasionally extracted from other authors.

Every thinking man will now easily discern my design in the following pages. It is not to write sermons, essays, or set discourses upon any part of Scripture. It is not to draw inferences from the text, or to show what doctrines may be proved thereby. It is this: To give the direct, literal meaning of every verse, of every sentence, and, as far as I am able, of every word in the oracles of God. I design only, like the hand of a dial, to point every man to this; not to take up his mind with something else, however excellent, but to keep his eye fixed upon the naked Bible, that he may read and hear it with understanding. I say again, and I desire it may be well observed, that none may expect what they will not find, it is not my design to write a book which a man may read separate from the Bible, but barely to assist those who fear God in hearing and reading the Bible itself, by showing the natural sense of every part in as few and plain words as I can.

And I am not without hopes that the following Notes may in some measure answer this end, not barely to unlettered and ignorant men, but also to men of education and learning (although it is true, neither these nor the Notes on the New Testament were principally designed for them). Sure I am that tracts writ in the most plain and simple manner are of infinitely more service to me than those which are elaborated with the utmost skill and set off with the greatest pomp of erudition.

But it is no part of my design to save either learned or unlearned men from the trouble of thinking. If so, I might perhaps write volumes too, which usually overlay rather than help the thought. On the contrary, my intention is to make them think, and assist them in thinking. This is the way to understand the things of God: "Meditate thereon day and night"; so shall you attain the best knowledge, even to "know the only true God, and Jesus Christ whom he hath sent." And this knowledge will lead you "to love him, because he hath first loved us"; yes, "to love the Lord your God with all your heart, and with all your soul, and with all your mind, and with all your strength." Will there not then be all "that mind in you which was also in Christ Jesus"? And in consequence of this, while you joyfully experience all the holy tempers described in this book, you will likewise be outwardly "holy as he that hath called you is holy, in all manner of conversation."

If you desire to read the Scriptures in such a manner as may most effectually answer this end, it would be advisable: (1) To set apart a little time, if you can, every morning and evening for that purpose. (2) At each time, if you have leisure, to read a chapter out of the Old, and one out of the New, Testament. If you cannot do this, to take a single chapter, or a part of one. (3) To read this with a single eye, to know the whole will of God, and have a fixed resolution to do it. In order to know his will, you should, (4) Have a constant eye to the analogy of faith, the connection and harmony there is between those grand, fundamental doctrines of original sin, justification by faith, the new birth, inward and outward holiness. (5) Serious and earnest prayer should be constantly used before we consult the oracles of God; seeing "Scripture can only be understood through the same Spirit whereby it was given." Our reading should likewise be closed with prayer, that what we read may be written on our hearts.

(6) It might also be of use, if, while we read, we were frequently to pause and examine ourselves by what we read, both with regard to our hearts and lives. This would furnish us with matter of praise, where we found God had enabled us to conform to his blessed will; and matter of humiliation and prayer, where we are conscious of having fallen short. And whatever light you receive should be used to the uttermost, and that immediately. Let there be no delay. Whatever you resolve, begin to execute the first moment you can. So shall you find this word to be indeed the power of God unto present and eternal salvation.

EDINBURGH
April 25, 1765

GENESIS

CHAPTER 1

1. *In the beginning.* Time began with the creation of those beings that are measured by time. Before the beginning of time there was none but that Infinite Being who inhabits eternity. *The heaven and the earth.* That is, the world, including the whole frame and furniture of the universe. But from what we see of heaven and earth, we may infer the eternal power and godhead of the great Creator. And let our make and place as men mind us of our duty as Christians, which is always to keep heaven in our eye and the earth under our feet.

2. The Creator could have made his work perfect at first, but by this gradual proceeding he would show what is ordinarily the method of his providence and grace. *And darkness was upon the face of the deep.* God did not create this darkness, for it was only the absence of light. The Spirit of God was the first Mover. He *moved upon the face of the waters.* He moved upon the face of the deep, as "the hen gathereth her chicken under her wings," and hovers over them, to warm and cherish them (Matt. 23:37).

3–5. The first of all visible things which God created was *light,* the great beauty and blessing of the universe. Like the firstborn, it does, of all visible beings, most resemble its great parent in purity and power, brightness and beneficence.

He said, *Let there be light.* He willed it, and it was done; *there was light.* Such a copy as exactly answered the original idea in the eternal mind. *God saw the light, that it was good.* It was exactly as he designed it; and it was fit to answer the end for which he designed it.

God divided the light from the darkness. So put them asunder as they could never be joined together. And yet he divided time between them, the day for light and the night for darkness, in a constant succession. Although the darkness was now scattered by the light, yet it has its place because it has its use; for as the light of the morning befriends the business of the day, so the shadows of the evening befriend the repose of the night. God has thus divided between light and darkness, because he would daily remind us that this is a world of mixtures and changes. In heaven there is perpetual light and no darkness; in hell, utter darkness and no light. But in this world they are counter-changed, and we pass daily from one to another; that we may learn to expect the like vicissitudes in the providence of God.

The evening and the morning were the first day. The darkness of the evening was before the light of the morning, that it might set it off and make it shine the brighter.

6–8. We have here an account of the second day's work, the creation of the firmament. *Let there be a firmament.* An expansion, so the Hebrew word signifies, like a sheet spread or a curtain drawn out. This includes all that is visible above the earth, between it and the third heavens, the air, its higher, middle, and lower region, the celestial globe, and all the orbs of light above. It reaches as high as the place where the stars are fixed, for that is called here the firmament of heaven.

God called the firmament Heaven. This is the visible heaven, the pavement of the holy city. The height of the heavens should remind us of God's supremacy and the infinite distance that is between us and him. The brightness of the heavens, and their purity, should remind us of his majesty and perfect holiness. The vastness of the heavens, and their encompassing the earth and influence upon it, should remind us of his immensity and universal providence.

9–13. The third day's work is related in these verses; the forming of the sea and the dry land, and making the earth fruitful. Hitherto the power of the Creator had been employed about the upper part of the visible world; now he descends to this lower world, designed for the children of men, for both their habitation and their maintenance. And here we have an account of the fitting of it for both; the building of their house, and the spreading of their table.

The waters which covered the earth were ordered to retire and be *gathered unto one place* (those hollows which were fitted for their reception). The dry land was *made to appear* and emerge out of the waters and was *called Earth.* Present provision was made by the immediate products of the earth, which in obedience to God's command was no sooner made but it became fruitful.

14–19. This is the history of the fourth day's work, the creating the sun, moon, and stars. *Let there be lights in the firmament of the heaven.* God had said, "Let there be light: and there was light" (v. 3); but that was, as it were, a chaos of light, scattered and confused. Now it was collected and made into several luminaries and so rendered both more glorious and more serviceable. The lights of heaven do not shine for themselves, nor for the world of spirits above; they need them not. They shine for us, and for our pleasure and advantage. Lord, what is man that he should be thus regarded? (Ps. 8:3–4).

He made the stars also. Which are here spoken of only in general; for the Scriptures were written not to gratify our curiosity, but to lead us to God.

20–23. Each day has produced very excellent beings, but we do not read of the creation of any *living creature* till the fifth day. The work of creation not only proceeded gradually from one thing to another, but advanced gradually from that which was less excellent to that which was more so. *God blessed them, saying, Be fruitful, and multiply.* Fruitfulness is the effect of God's blessing and must be ascribed to it. The multiplying of the fish and fowl from year to year is still the fruit of this blessing.

26–28. Here is the second part of the sixth day's work, the creation of man. Observe that man was made last of all the creatures, which was both an honor and a favor to him: an honor, for the creation was to advance from that which was less perfect to that which was more so; and a favor, for it was not fit he should be lodged in the palace designed for him, till it was completely fitted and furnished for his reception. Man, as soon as he was made, had the whole visible creation before him, both to contemplate and to take the comfort of.

Let us make man. Man was to be a creature different from all that had been previously made. Flesh and spirit, heaven and earth must be put together in him, and he must be allied to both worlds. And therefore God himself not only undertakes to make, but is pleased so to express himself, as if he called a council to consider the making of him. *Let us make man*—the three persons of the Trinity consult about it, and concur in it; because man, when he was made, was to be dedicated and devoted to Father, Son, and Holy Ghost.

God's *image* and *after his likeness* are two words to express the same thing. God's image upon man consists: (1) In his nature, not that of his body, for God has not a body, but that of his soul. The soul is a spirit, an intelligent, immortal spirit, an active spirit, herein resembling God, the Father of spirits, and the soul of the world. (2) In his place and authority. Let us make man *in our image,* and *let him have dominion.* As he has the government of the inferior creatures, he is as it were God's representative on earth. Yet his government of himself, by the freedom of his will, has in it more of God's image than his government of the creatures.

(3) And chiefly in his purity and rectitude. God's image upon man consists in knowledge, righteousness, and true holiness (Eph. 4:24; Col. 3:10). He was "upright" (Eccl. 7:29). He had an habitual conformity of all his natural powers to the whole will of God. His understanding saw divine things clearly, and there were no errors in his knowledge. His will complied readily and universally with the will of God, without reluctancy. His affections were all regular, and he had no inordinate appetites or passions. His thoughts were easily fixed to the best subjects, and there was no vanity or ungovernableness in them. And all the inferior powers were subject to the dictates of the superior. Thus holy, thus happy, were our first parents in having the image of God upon them. But how are you fallen, O son of the morning? How is this image of God upon man defaced! How small are the remains of it, and how great the ruins of it! The Lord renew it upon our souls by his sanctifying grace!

God created him *male and female,* Adam and Eve. Adam first out of earth, and Eve out of his side. God made but one male and one female that all the nations of men might know themselves to be "made of one blood" (Acts 17:26), descendants from one common flock, and might thereby be induced to love one another. God, having made them capable of transmitting the nature they had received, said to them, *Be fruitful, and multiply, and replenish the earth.*

God gave to man a dominion over the inferior creatures, *over the fish of the sea, and over the fowl of the air.* Though man provides for neither, he has power over both, much more *over every living thing that moveth upon the earth.* God designed hereby to put an honor upon man that he might find himself the more strongly obliged to bring honor to his Maker.

29–30. We have here the third part of the sixth day's work, which was not any new creation, but a gracious provision of "food to all flesh" (Ps. 136:25). And before the earth was deluged, much more before it was cursed for man's sake, its fruits no doubt, were more pleasing to the taste, and more strengthening and nourishing to the body.

Does God care for oxen? Yes, certainly, he provides food convenient for them; and not for oxen only that were used in his sacrifices, and man's service, but even the young lions and the young ravens are the care of his providence; they ask and have their meat from God.

31. We have here the approbation and conclusion of the whole work of creation. *He saw every thing that he had made.* So he does still. All the works of his hands are under his eye; he that made all sees all. When we come to review our works, we find to our shame that much has been very bad; but when God reviewed his, all was *very good.* Good, for it is all agreeable to the mind of the creator. Good, for it answers the end of its creation. Good, for it is serviceable to man, whom God had appointed lord of the visible creation. Good, for it is all for God's glory; there is that in the whole visible creation which is a demonstration of God's being and perfections, and which tends to beget in the soul of man a religious regard to him.

Very good. Of each day's work (except the second) it was said that it was *good,* but now it is *very good.* For (1) Now man was made, who was the chief of the ways of God, the visible image of the Creator's glory. (2) Now all was made, every part was *good,* but all together *very good.* The glory and goodness, the beauty and harmony of God's works both of providence and grace, as this of creation, will best appear when they are perfected.

The evening and the morning were the sixth day. So that in six days God made the world. We are not to think but that God could have made the world in an instant. But he did it in six days that he might show himself a free agent, doing his own work, both in his own way and

in his own time; that his wisdom, power, and goodness might appear to us and be meditated upon by us the more distinctly, and that he might set us an example of working six days and resting the seventh. And now as God reviewed his work, let us review our meditations upon it; let us stir up ourselves and all that is within us to worship him that made the heaven, earth, and sea, and the fountains of waters. All his works in all places of his dominion bless him, and therefore "bless thou the LORD, O my soul."

CHAPTER 2

1–3. Observe that the heavens and the earth are finished pieces, and so are all the creatures in them. So perfect is God's work that nothing "can be put to it, nor any thing taken from it" (Eccl. 3:14). Observe also that the eternal God, though infinitely happy in himself, yet took a satisfaction in the work of his own hands. He did not *rest* as one weary, but as one well pleased with the instances of his own goodness. He rested on that day and took a satisfaction in his creatures, then sanctified it and appointed us on that day to rest and take a satisfaction in the Creator. His rest is in the fourth commandment made a reason for ours after six days' labor.

The solemn observation of one day in seven as a day of holy rest, and holy work, is the indispensable duty of all those to whom God has revealed his holy sabbaths. These sabbaths are as ancient as the world. The sabbath of the Lord is truly honorable, and we have reason to honor it; honor it for the sake of its antiquity, its great author, and the sanctification of the first sabbath by the holy God himself and, in obedience to him, by our first parents in innocency.

4–7. Man is a little world, consisting of heaven and earth, soul and body. Here we have an account of the original of both, and the putting of both together. Of the other creatures it is said, they were *created* and *made;* but of man, that he was *formed,* which notes a gradual process in the work with great accuracy and exactness.

The body of man is curiously wrought. And the soul takes its rise from the breath of heaven. It came immediately from God; he gave it to be put into the body (Eccl. 12:7), as afterwards he gave the tables of stone of his own writing to be put into the ark. It is by it that man is a *living soul,* that is, a living man. The body would be a worthless, useless carcass if the soul did not animate it.

8–15. Man consisted of body and soul, a body made out of the earth, and a rational immortal soul. We have in these verses the provision that was made for the happiness of both. That part of man which is allied to the world of sense was made happy, for he was put in the paradise of God. That part which is allied to the world of spirits was well provided for, for he was taken into covenant with God.

The inspired penman in this history, writing for the Jews first and calculating his narratives from the infant state of the church, describes things by their outward sensible appearances and leaves us, by further discoveries of the divine light, to be led into the understanding of the mysteries couched under them. There he does not so much insist upon the happiness of Adam's mind as upon that of his outward estate. The Mosaic history, as well as the Mosaic law, has rather the patterns of heavenly things than the heavenly things themselves (Heb. 9:23).

The place appointed for Adam's residence was a garden, not an ivory house. As clothes came in with sin, so did houses. The heaven was the roof of Adam's house, and never was any roof so curiously ceiled and painted. The earth was his floor, and never was any floor so richly inlaid. The shadow of the trees was his retirement, and never were any rooms so finely hung. Solomon's in all their glory were not arrayed like them.

The LORD God planted a garden. We may well suppose it to be the most accomplished place that ever the sun saw, when the all-sufficient God himself designed it to be the present happiness of his beloved creature. The situation of this garden was extremely sweet; it was in *Eden,* which signifies delight and pleasure.

The tree of life also in the midst of the garden. Which was not so much a natural means to preserve or prolong life; but was chiefly intended to be a sign to Adam, assuring him of the continuance of life and happiness, upon condition of his perseverance in innocency and obedience. *The tree of knowledge of good and evil.* So called; not because it had any virtue to beget useful knowledge, but because there was an express revelation of the will of God concerning this tree, so that by it he might know *good and evil.* What is good? It is good not to eat of this tree. What is evil? To eat of this tree. The distinction between all other moral good and evil was written in the heart of man; but this, which resulted from a positive law, was written upon this tree.

17. Thou shalt surely die. That is, you shall lose all the happiness you have in either possession or prospect; and you shall become liable to death and all the miseries that preface and attend it. Not only shall you become mortal, but spiritual death and the forerunners of temporal death shall immediately seize you.

21. *A deep sleep.* So the opening of his side might not be of grievance to him. While he knows no sin, God will take care that he shall feel no pain.

23. *And Adam said, This is now bone of my bones.* Probably it was revealed to Adam in a vision, when he was asleep, that this lovely creature, now presented to him, was a piece of himself and was to be his companion and the wife of his covenant.

24. The sabbath and marriage were two ordinances instituted in innocency; the former for the preservation of the church, the latter for the preservation of mankind. See how necessary it is that children should take their parents' consent with them in their marriage; and how unjust they are to their parents, as well as undutiful, if they marry without it. For they rob their parents of their right to them and interest in them, and alienate it to another fraudulently and unnaturally.

25. *They were both naked.* They needed no clothes for defense against cold or heat, for neither could be injurious to them. They needed none for ornament. "Solomon in all his glory was not arrayed like one of these." They needed none for decency, they were *naked,* and had no reason to be *ashamed.* Blushing is now the color of virtue, but it was not the color of innocence.

CHAPTER 3

1–5. We have here an account of the temptation with which Satan assaulted our first parents, and which proved fatal to them. The devil appeared in the shape of a *serpent.* Multitudes of them fell; but this that attacked our first parents was surely the prince of the devils. Whether it was only the appearance of a serpent or a real serpent, acted and possessed by the devil, is not certain. The devil chose to act his part in a serpent, because it is a *subtle* creature. It is not improbable that reason and speech were then the known properties of the serpent. And therefore Eve was not surprised at his reasoning and speaking, which otherwise she must have been.

That which the devil aimed at was to persuade Eve to *eat* forbidden *fruit.* To do this, he took the same method that he does still: (1) He questions whether it were a sin or not. (2) He denies that there was any danger in it. (3) He suggests much advantage by it. As to the advantage, he suits the temptation to the pure state they were now in, proposing to them not any carnal pleasure, but intellectual delights.

Your eyes shall be opened. You shall have much more of the power and pleasure of contemplation than now you have. You shall fetch a larger compass in your intellectual views, and see farther into things than now you do. *You shall be as gods.* As *Elohim,* mighty gods, not only omniscient but omnipotent too. You shall *know good and evil.* That is, every thing that is desirable to be known. To support this part of the temptation, he abused the name given to this tree. It was intended to teach the practical knowledge of good and evil, that is, of duty and disobedience, and it would prove the experimental knowledge of good and evil, that is, of happiness and misery. But he perverts the sense of it, and uses it to their destruction, as if this tree would give them a speculative knowledge of the natures, kinds, and originals of good and evil. *In the day ye eat thereof,* you will find a sudden and immediate change for the better.

6–8. Satan at length gains his point. God tried the obedience of our first parents by forbidding them *the tree of knowledge,* and Satan does, as it were, join issue with God, and in that very thing undertakes to seduce them into a transgression. Here we find how he prevailed, God permitting it for wise and holy ends.

"The woman being deceived" was ringleader "in the transgression" (I Tim. 2:14). She saw *that the tree was*. It was said of all the rest of the fruit trees in the garden that they were *pleasant to the sight, and good for food*. She imagined a greater benefit by this tree than by any of the rest, that it was a *tree* not only not to be dreaded, but *to be desired to make one wise*, and therein excelling all the rest of the trees. This she *saw*, that is, she perceived and understood it by what the devil had said to her.

She gave also unto her husband with her. It is likely he was not with her when she was tempted. Surely if he had, he would have interposed to prevent the sin. But he came to her when she had eaten, and was prevailed with by her to eat likewise. She gave it to him, persuading him with the same arguments that the serpent had used with her. And to this she added that she herself had eaten of it and found it so far from being deadly that it was extremely pleasant and grateful.

And he did eat. This implied the unbelief of God's word, and confidence in the devil's; discontent with his present state, and an ambition of the honor which comes not from God. He would be both his own carver and his own master, would have what he pleased, and do what he pleased. His sin was in one word, disobedience. Disobedience to a plain, easy, and express command, which he knew to be a command of trial. He sins against light and love, the clearest light and the dearest love that ever sinner sinned against. But the greatest aggravation of his sin was that he involved all his posterity in sin and ruin by it. He could not but know that he stood as a public

person and that his disobedience would be fatal to all his seed. And if so, it was certainly both the greatest treachery and the greatest cruelty that ever was. Shame and fear seized the criminals; these came into the world along with sin and still attend it.

The eyes of them both were opened. The eyes of their consciences; their hearts smote them for what they had done. Now, when it was too late, they saw the happiness they were fallen from and the misery they were fallen into. They saw God provoked, his favor forfeited, his image lost. They felt a disorder in their own spirits, of which they had never before been conscious. They saw a law in their members warring against the law of their minds and captivating them both to sin and wrath. They saw *that they were naked*, that is, stripped, deprived of all the honors and joys of their paradise state, and exposed to all the miseries that might justly be expected from an angry God. They were laid open to the contempt and reproach of heaven and earth and their own consciences. And *they sewed* or platted *fig leaves together* and, to cover at least part of their shame one from another, *made themselves aprons*. See here what is commonly the folly of those that have sinned: they are more solicitous to save their credit before men than to obtain their pardon from God.

They heard the voice of the LORD *God walking in the garden in the cool of the day*. He came to convince and humble them, not to amaze and terrify them. He came not immediately from heaven in their view as afterwards on Mount Sinai, but he came *in the garden*, as one who was still willing to be familiar with them. He came *walking*, not riding on the wings of the wind, but *walking* deliberately, as one slow to anger. He came *in the cool of the day*, not in the night, when all fears are doubly fearful.

Nor did he come suddenly upon them, but they *heard the voice* at some distance, giving them notice of his coming; and probably it was a "still small voice."

And they *hid themselves from the presence of the LORD God*. A sad change! Before they had sinned, if they heard the voice of the Lord God coming towards them, they would have run to meet him. But now God was become a terror to them, and then no marvel they were become a terror to themselves.

9. *Where art thou?* A gracious pursuit in order to gain Adam's recovery. If God had not called to him to reduce him, his condition would have been as desperate as that of the fallen angels.

11. *Hast thou eaten of the tree?* Though God knows all our sins, yet he will know them from us and requires from us an ingenuous confession of them, not that he may be informed, but that we may be humbled. *Whereof I commanded thee* not to eat of it, I your maker, I your master, I your benefactor, *I commanded thee* to the contrary. Sin appears most plain and most sinful in the mirror of the commandment.

13. *What is this that thou hast done?* Will you own your fault? Neither of them does this fully. Adam lays all the blame upon his wife. He not only lays the blame upon his wife, but tacitly on God himself. Eve lays all the blame upon the serpent.

God did not examine the serpent, nor ask him what he had done, but immediately sentenced him, (1) Because he was already convicted of rebellion against God. (2) Because he was to be for ever excluded from pardon; and why should any thing be said to convince and humble him, who was to find no place for repentance?

15. *I will put enmity between thee and the woman.* A perpetual reproach is fastened upon the serpent. He is here

sentenced to be: (1) Degraded and accursed of God. It is supposed, pride was the sin that turned angels into devils, which is here justly punished by a variety of mortifications couched under the mean circumstances of a serpent, crawling on his belly and licking the dust. (2) Detested and abhorred of all mankind. (3) Destroyed and ruined at last by the great Redeemer, signified by the *bruising of his head;* his subtle politics shall be all baffled, his usurped power entirely crushed.

A perpetual quarrel is here commenced between the kingdom of God and the kingdom of the devil among men; war proclaimed between the seed of the woman and the seed of the serpent (Rev. 12:7). It is the fruit of this enmity that there is a continual conflict between God's people and him. Heaven and hell can never be reconciled, no more can Satan and a sanctified soul. There is likewise a continual struggle between the wicked and the good. And all the malice of persecutors against the people of God is the fruit of this enmity, which will continue while there is a godly man on this side of heaven and a wicked man on this side of hell.

A gracious promise is here made of Christ as the deliverer of fallen man from the power of Satan. By faith in this promise, our first parents and the patriarchs before the flood were justified and saved.

Notice is here given of three things concerning Christ: (1) His incarnation, that he should be the seed of the woman. (2) His sufferings and death, pointed at in Satan's bruising his heel, that is, his human nature. (3) His victory of Satan. Satan had now trampled upon *the woman,* and insulted *over her;* but the seed of the woman should be raised up in the fullness of time to avenge her quarrel, and to trample upon *him,* to spoil him, to lead him captive, and to triumph over him (Col. 2:15).

17. *Cursed is the ground for thy sake.* And the effect of that curse is, *Thorns and thistles shall it bring forth unto thee.* The ground or earth, by the sin of man, is made subject to vanity, the several parts of it being not so serviceable to man's comfort and happiness as they were when they were made.

19. *Unto dust shalt thou return.* Your body shall be forsaken by your soul and become itself a lump of dust, and then it shall be lodged in the grave and mingle with the dust of the earth.

21. The beasts whose skins they were must be slain; slain before the eyes of Adam and Eve, to show them what death is. And probably, it is supposed, they were slain for sacrifice, to typify the great sacrifice which in the latter end of the world should be offered once for all. Thus the first thing that died was a sacrifice, or Christ in a figure.

24. God *drove him out.* This signified the exclusion of him and his guilty race from that communion with God which was the bliss and glory of paradise. He might justly have *chased him out of the world* (Job 18:18), but he only chased him out of the garden. He might justly have "cast him down to hell," as the angels that sinned were, when they were shut out from the heavenly paradise (II Pet. 2:4). But man was only sent to *till the ground whence he was taken.* He was only sent to a place of toil, not to a place of torment. He was sent to the ground, not to the grave; to the workhouse, not to the dungeon, not to the prisonhouse; to hold the plough, not to drag the chain. His tilling the ground would be recompensed by his eating its fruits; and his converse with the earth, *whence he was taken,* was improvable to good pur-

poses, to keep him humble and to remind him of his latter end. Our first parents were not abandoned to despair; God's thoughts of love designing them for a second state of probation upon new terms.

CHAPTER 4

3. *In process of time.* At some set time Cain and Abel brought to Adam, as the priest of the family, each of them an offering to the Lord; for which we have reason to think there was a divine appointment given to Adam, as a token of God's favor in spite of their apostasy.

4. *And the* LORD *had respect unto Abel and to his offering,* but to *Cain and to his offering he had not respect.* The Governor of the world, though an absolute sovereign, does not act arbitrarily in dispensing his smiles and frowns. (1) There was a difference in the characters of the persons offering: Cain was a wicked man, but Abel was a righteous man (Matt. 23:35). (2) There was a difference in the offerings they brought. Cain's was only a sacrifice of acknowledgment offered to the Creator; but Abel brought a sacrifice of atonement, the blood which was shed in order to remission, thereby owning himself a sinner, deprecating God's wrath, and imploring his favor in a Mediator. But the great difference was, Abel offered in faith and Cain did not. Abel offered with an eye to God's will as his rule and in dependence upon the promise of a Redeemer. But Cain did not offer in faith, and so it turned into sin to him.

5. *Cain was very wroth, and his countenance fell.* Not so much out of grief as malice and rage. His sullen churlish countenance and down-look betrayed his passionate resentment.

7. *If thou doest well, shalt thou not be accepted?* "God is no respecter of persons"; so that if we come short of acceptance with him, the fault is wholly our own. There is not a damned sinner in hell but, if he had done well as he might have done, had been a glorified saint in heaven.

This verse might also mean that if you repent of your sin, reform your heart and life, and bring your sacrifice in a better manner; you shall yet *be accepted*. See how early the gospel was preached and the benefit of it here offered even to one of the "chief of sinners."

8. Observe, the first that dies is a saint, the first that went to the grave went to heaven. God would secure to himself the first fruits, the firstborn to the dead, that first opened the womb into another world.

9. *And the Lord said unto Cain, Where is Abel thy brother?* God knew him to be guilty; yet he asks him that he might draw from him a confession of his crime. Those who would be justified before God must accuse themselves.

10. The blood is said to cry *from the ground,* the *earth,* which is said (v. 11) to open "her mouth to receive thy brother's blood from thy hand." The earth did, as it were, blush to see her own face stained with such blood; and therefore opened her mouth to hide that which she could not hinder.

11. *And now art thou cursed from the earth.* God could have taken vengeance by an immediate stroke from heaven. But he chose to make the *earth* the avenger of blood; to continue him upon the earth, and not presently to cut him off, and yet to make even that his curse.

16. *And Cain went out from the presence of the Lord.* Those that depart from God cannot find rest anywhere else. When Cain went out from the *presence of the Lord,* he never rested after.

17. Here is an account of Cain's posterity, at least the heirs of his family, for seven generations. His son was Enoch, of the same name, but not of the same character with that holy man that "walked with God."

19. *And Lamech took two wives.* It was one of the degenerate race of Cain who first transgressed that original law of marriage that two only should be "one flesh."

Jabal was a famous shepherd; he delighted much in keeping cattle, and was so happy in devising methods of doing it to the best advantage, and instructing others in them, that the shepherds of those times, and the shepherds of after-times, called him *father.*

Jubal was a famous musician, and particularly an organist, and the first that gave rules for that noble art or science of music.

26. *Then began men to call upon the name of the Lord.* Doubtless God's name was called upon before, but now the worshippers of God began to stir up themselves to do more in religion than they had done. Now men began to worship God, not only in their closets and families, but in public and solemn assemblies.

Cain and those that had deserted religion had built a city and begun to declare for irreligion and call themselves the "sons of men." Those that adhered to God began to declare for him and his worship and called themselves the "sons of God."

CHAPTER 5

1–2. Here we have a brief rehearsal of what was before at large related concerning the creation of man. (1) God created *man.* (2) There was a day in which God *created* man, he was not from eternity; he was not the firstborn, but the junior of creation. (3) God

chose to employ him in making that which was to be the means of his preservation, both for the trial of his faith and obedience, and to teach us that none shall be saved by Christ but those only that "work out their salvation"; we cannot do it without God, and he will not without us. Both the providence of God and the grace of God crown the endeavors of the obedient and diligent.

CHAPTER 7

1. Here is a gracious invitation of Noah and his family into a place of safety, now the flood of waters was coming. *For thee have I seen righteous before me in this generation.* Those are righteous indeed that are righteous before God; that have not only the form of godliness by which they appear righteous before men, who may easily be imposed upon, but the power of it, by which they approve themselves to God who searches the heart.

2. Thanks be to God there are not herds of lions as there are oxen, nor flocks of tigers as there are of sheep.

4. *Yet seven days, and I will cause it to rain.* While Noah told them of the judgment at a distance, they were tempted to put off their repentance. But now he is ordered to tell them that it is at the door. It is common for those that have been careless for their souls during the years of their health, when they have looked upon death at a distance, to be as careless during the days, the seven days of their sickness, when they see it approaching, their hearts being hardened by the deceitfulness of sin.

11. *The six hundredth year of Noah's life* was 1656 years from the creation.

21–23. *All flesh died, all in whose nostrils was the breath of life, of all that was on the dry land, every living sub-stance.* And why so? Man only had done wickedly, and justly is God's hand against him, but "these sheep, what have they done?" I answer: (1) We are sure God did them no wrong. He is the sovereign Lord of all life, for he is the sole fountain and author of it. He that made them as he pleased, might unmake them when he pleased, and who shall say unto him, What are you doing? (2) God did admirably serve the purposes of his own glory by their destruction, as well as by their creation. Herein his holiness and justice were greatly magnified.

By this it appears that he hates sin and is highly displeased with sinners, when even the inferior creatures, because they are the servants of man and part of his possession, and because they have been abused to be the servants of sin, are destroyed with him. It was likewise an instance of God's wisdom. As the creatures were made for man when he was made, so they were multiplied for him when he was multiplied; and therefore, now mankind was reduced to so small a number, it was fit that the beasts should proportionably be reduced, otherwise they would have had the dominion and would have replenished the earth, and the remnant of mankind that was left would have been overpowered by them.

CHAPTER 8

5. *The tops of the mountains were seen.* Like islands appearing above water.

20. *And Noah builded an altar.* Hitherto he had done nothing without particular instructions and commands from God. But altars and sacrifices being already of divine institution, he did not wait for a particular command thus to express his thankfulness.

21. *For the imagination of man's heart is evil from his youth.* He brought it into

the world with him, he was shaped and conceived in it. Now one would think it should follow, therefore, that the guilty race shall be wholly extinguished. No, I will no more take this severe method; for he is rather to be pitied. And it is but what might be expected from such a degenerate race. So that if he be dealt with according to his deserts, one flood must succeed another until all be destroyed.

22. God's providence will carefully preserve the regular succession of times and seasons. To this we owe it, that the world stands, and the wheel of nature keeps its tack. See here how changeable the times are, yet how unchangeable!

CHAPTER 9

3. *Every moving thing that liveth shall be meat.* Before this, man had been confined to feed only upon the products of the earth—fruits, herbs and roots, and all sorts of corn and milk (Gen. 1:29). But the flood having perhaps washed away much of the virtue of the earth, and so rendered its fruits less pleasing and less nourishing, God now enlarged the grant and allowed man to eat flesh, which perhaps man himself never thought of till now.

4. *But flesh with the life thereof, which is the blood thereof, shall ye not eat.* The life of the sacrifice was accepted for the life of the sinner. Blood must not be looked upon as a common thing, but must be "poured out unto the LORD" (II Sam. 23:16). Mr. Henry indeed has a strange conceit, that this is only a prohibition to eat flesh. This does such apparent violence to the text that to mention it is sufficient.

5. *And surely your blood of your lives will I require.* Our own lives are not so our own, that we may quit them at our own pleasure; but they are God's and we must resign them at his pleasure. If

we any way hasten our own deaths, we are accountable to God for it.

6. *By man shall his blood be shed.* That is, by the magistrate, or whoever is appointed to be the avenger of blood. Before the flood, as it should seem by the story of Cain, God took the punishment of murder into his own hands. But now he committed this judgment to men, to masters of families at first, and afterwards to the heads of countries. *For in the image of God made he man.* Man is a creature dear to his Creator, and therefore ought to be so to us. God put honor upon him, let us not then put contempt upon him. Such remains of God's image are still even upon fallen man, that he who unjustly kills a man defaces the image of God and does dishonor to him.

11. *Neither shall there any more be a flood.* God had drowned the world once, and still it is as provoking as ever. Yet he will never drown it any more, for he deals not with us according to our sins.

13. *I do set my bow in the clouds.* The rainbow appears when the clouds are most disposed to wet; when we have most reason to fear the rain prevailing, God shows this seal of the promise that it shall not prevail. The rainbow appears when one part of the sky is clear, which imitates mercy remembered in the midst of wrath, and the clouds are hemmed as it were with the rainbow, that it may not overspread the heavens, for the bow is colored rain, or the edges of a cloud gilded.

21. *And he drank of the wine, and was drunken.* It is highly probable, he did not know the effect of it before.

22. *And Ham saw the nakedness of his father, and told his two brethren.* To have seen it accidentally and involuntarily would not have been a crime. But he pleased himself with the sight.

23. *And Shem and Japheth took a*

garment, and went backward, and covered the nakedness of their father. They not only would not see it themselves, but provided that no one else might see it. Herein they set an example of charity with reference to other men's sin and shame.

26. *The God of Shem.* Shem is sufficiently recompensed for his respect to his father by this, that the Lord himself puts this honor upon him to be his God; which is sufficient recompense for all our services and all our sufferings for his name.

27. *God shall enlarge Japheth, and he shall dwell in the tents of Shem.* His seed shall be so numerous and so victorious that they shall be masters of the tents of Shem, which was fulfilled when the people of the Jews, the most eminent of Shem's race, were tributaries to the Grecians first, and after to the Romans, both of Japheth's seed. This also speaks of the conversion of the Gentiles and the bringing of them into the church.

CHAPTER 10

8. *Began to be a mighty one in the earth.* That is, whereas those that went before him were content to stand upon the same level with their neighbors, Nimrod could not rest in this parity, but he would top his neighbors and lord over them. The same spirit that the giants before the flood were acted by (Gen. 6:4) now revived in him. So soon was that tremendous judgment, which the pride and tyranny of those mighty men brought upon the world, forgotten.

10. *The beginning of his kingdom was Babel.* It does not appear that Nimrod had any right to rule by birth; but either his fitness for government recommended him, or by power and policy he gradually advanced into the throne. See the antiquity of civil government, and particularly that form of it which lodges the sovereignty in a single person.

CHAPTER 11

3−4. *Go to, let us make brick, let us build us a city.* God orders them to scatter. No, say they, we will live and die together. And so they engage themselves and one another in this vast undertaking. That they might unite in one glorious empire, they resolve to build this city and tower, to be the metropolis of their kingdom, and the center of their unity.

5. *And the LORD came down to see the city.* It is an expression after the manner of men, he knew it as clearly as men know that which they come upon the place to view.

6. *Behold, the people is one.* If they continue one, much of the earth will be left uninhabited and these *children of men,* if thus incorporated, will swallow up the little remnant of God's children, therefore it is decreed they must not be one.

7. *Go to, let us go down and there confound their language.* This was not spoken to the angels, as if God needed either their advice or their assistance, but God speaks it to himself, or the Father to the Son and Holy Ghost. God, who when he made man taught him to speak, now made those builders to forget their former language; and to speak a new one, which yet was the same to those of the same tribe or family, but not to others. Those of one colony could converse together, but not with those of another. We all suffer hereby to this day. In all the inconveniences we sustain by the diversity of languages, and all the trouble we are at to learn the languages we have occasion for, we smart for the rebellion of our ancestors at Babel.

As the confounding of tongues divided the children of men and scattered them abroad, so the gift of tongues bestowed upon the Apostles (Acts 2) contributed greatly to the gathering together of the children of God, which were scattered abroad, and the uniting of them in Christ that "with one mind and one mouth" they might "glorify God" (Rom. 15:6).

CHAPTER 12

1. *Get thee out of thy country.* By this precept Abraham was tried whether he loved God better than he loved his native soil and dearest friends, and whether he could willingly leave all to go along with God. His country was become idolatrous, his kindred and his father's house were a constant temptation to him, and he could not continue with them without danger of being infected by them.

By this precept he also was tried whether he could trust God farther than he saw him, for he must leave his own country to go to a *land that I will shew thee.* He must follow God with an implicit faith and take God's word for it in the general, though he had no particular securities given him that he should be no loser by leaving his country to follow God.

2. *I will make of thee a great nation.* This promise was a great relief to Abram's burden, for he had now no child. But it also was a great trial to Abram's faith, for his wife had been long barren, so that if he believe, it must be against hope, and his faith must build purely upon that power which can "out of stones raise up children unto Abraham."

I will bless them that bless thee, and curse him that curseth thee. This made it a kind of league offensive and defensive between God and Abram. Abram

heartily espoused God's cause, and here God promises to interest himself in his. *In thee shall all the families of the earth be blessed.* This was the promise that crowned all the rest, for it points at the Messiah, in whom all the promises are "yea and amen."

4. *So Abram departed.* He "was not disobedient to the heavenly vision." His obedience was speedy and without delay, submissive and without dispute.

7. *And the* LORD *appeared unto Abram.* No place or condition can shut us out from God's gracious visits. Abram is a sojourner, unsettled, among Canaanites, and yet here also he meets with him that lives, and sees him. Enemies may part us and our tents, us and our altars, but not us and our God.

8. *And there he builded an altar unto the* LORD *who appeared to him, and called upon the name of the* LORD. When God appeared to him, then and there he built an altar, with an eye to the God that appeared to him. Thus he acknowledged with thankfulness God's kindness to him in making him that gracious visit and promise. And thus he testified his confidence in and dependence upon the word which God had spoken.

As soon as Abram was got to Canaan, though he was but a stranger and sojourner there, yet he set up, and kept up, the worship of God in his family. And wherever he had a tent, God had an altar and that an altar sanctified by prayer.

10. *And there was a famine in the land.* Now he was tried whether he could trust the God that brought him to Canaan to maintain him there, and rejoice in him as the God of his salvation when the "fig tree shall not blossom."

13. *Say thou art my sister.* The grace Abram was most eminent for was faith, yet he thus fell through unbelief and distrust of the divine providence, even after God had appeared to him twice. Alas, what will become of the willows when the cedars are thus shaken!

18. *What is this that thou hast done?* What an ill thing; how unbecoming a wise and good man! *Why didst thou not tell me that she was thy wife?* Intimating that if he had known that, he would not have taken her. It is a fault, too common among good people, to entertain suspicions of others beyond what there is cause for. We have often found more of virtue, honor, and conscience in some people than we thought there was; and it ought to be a pleasure to us to be thus disappointed, as Abram was here, who found Pharaoh to be a better man than he expected.

CHAPTER 13

3–4. *He went on to Beth-el.* He came *unto the place of the altar,* either to revive the remembrance of the sweet communion he had had with God at that place, or perhaps to pay the vows he had there made to God when he undertook his journey into Egypt.

7. *And the Canaanite and the Perizzite dwelled then in the land.* No doubt the eyes of all the neighbors were upon them, because of the singularity of their religion and the extraordinary sanctity they professed. And notice would soon be taken of this quarrel, and improvement made of it to their reproach by the Canaanites and Perizzites.

17. *Arise, walk through the land.* Enter and take possession, survey the parcels, and it will appear better than upon a distant prospect.

18. *Then Abram removed his tent.* God bid him *walk through the land,* that is, Do not think of fixing in it, but expect to be always unsettled and walking through it to a better Canaan.

CHAPTER 14

1. We have here an account of the first war that ever we read of in Scripture.

18. *Melchizedek.* Many Christian writers have thought that this was an appearance of the Son of God himself, our Lord Jesus, known to Abram at this time by this name. But as nothing is expressly revealed concerning it, we can determine nothing.

20. *And blessed be the most high God.* In all our prayers we must praise God and join hallelujahs with all our hosannas. These are the spiritual sacrifices we must offer up daily and upon particular occasions. God as the most high God must have the glory of all our victories. In them he shows himself higher than our enemies, and higher than we, for without him we could do nothing. *And he gave him tithes of all.* Jesus Christ, our great Melchizedek, is to be humbly acknowledged by every one of us as our king and priest, and not only the tithe of all, but all we have, must be given up to him.

21. *Give me the persons, and take the goods to thyself.* Gratitude teaches us to recompense to the utmost of our power those that have undergone fatigues or been at expense for our service.

CHAPTER 15

1. *Fear not, Abram.* Abram might fear lest the four kings he had routed should rally and fall upon him. No, believe God, *fear not.* Fear not their revenge, nor thy neighbor's envy, I will take care of you. *I am thy shield.* The consideration of this, that God himself is a shield to his people, to secure them from all destructive evils, a shield ready to them, and a shield round about them, should silence all perplexing fears. *And thy exceeding great reward.*

God himself is the felicity of holy souls. He is the "portion of their inheritance and their cup."

6. *And he believed in the* LORD. That is, believed the truth of that promise which God had now made him, resting upon the power and faithfulness of him that made it. *And he counted it to him for righteousness.* That is, upon the score of this he was accepted of God, and by faith he "obtained witness that he was righteous" (Heb. 11:4). This is urged in the New Testament to prove that we are justified by faith without the works of the law (Rom. 4:3; Gal. 3:6), for Abram was so justified while he was yet uncircumcised. If Abram, who was so rich in good works, was not justified by them, but by his faith, much less can we. This faith, which was imputed to Abram for righteousness, had newly struggled with unbelief (v. 2) and, coming off conqueror, it was thus crowned, thus honored.

7. *I am the* LORD *that brought thee out.* He glories in it as an act both of power and grace. *To give thee this land to inherit it.* Not only to possess it, but to possess it as an inheritance, which is the surest title. The providence of God has secret but gracious designs in all its various dispensations. We cannot conceive the projects of Providence, until the event shows what it was driving at.

8. *Whereby shall I know that I shall inherit it?* This did not proceed from distrust of God's power or promise, but he desired this: (1) For the strengthening of his own faith. He believed (v. 6), but here he prays, "Lord, help me against my unbelief." He believed, but he desired a sign, to be treasured up against an hour of temptation. (2) He desired this for the ratifying of the promise to his posterity, that they also might believe it.

9. *Take me an heifer.* Perhaps Abram expected some sign from heaven, but

God gives him a sign upon a sacrifice. Those that would receive the assurances of God's favor must attend instituted ordinances and expect to meet with God in them.

12. *A deep sleep fell upon Abram.* Not a common sleep through weariness or carelessness, but a divine ecstasy, that being wholly taken off from things sensible, he might be wholly taken up with the contemplation of things spiritual. The doors of the body were locked up that the soul might be private and retired and might act the more freely. *And lo, an horror of great darkness fell upon him.* This was designed to strike an awe upon the spirit of Abram and to possess him with a holy reverence. Holy fear prepares the soul for holy joy; God humbles first and then lifts up.

15. *Thou shalt go to thy fathers.* At death we go to our fathers, to all our fathers that are gone before us to the state of the dead, to our godly fathers that are gone before us to the state of the blessed. The former helps to take off the terror of death, the latter puts comfort into it. *Thou shalt be buried in a good old age.* Old age is a blessing, if it be a *good* old age. Theirs may be called a good old age that are old and healthful, not loaded with such distempers as make them weary of life. Theirs may be called a good old age that are old and holy, whose hoary head is "found in the way of righteousness," old and useful, old and exemplary for godliness.

17. *When the sun went down, the sign was given. The smoking furnace* signified the affliction of his seed in Egypt. They were there in the furnace of affliction and laboring in the very fire. They were there in the smoke, their eyes darkened that they could not see to the end of their troubles. The *burning lamp* speaks comfort in this affliction; and this God showed Abram at the same time with the smoking furnace. The lamp notes direction in *the smoke;* God's word was their lamp, a light shining in a dark place. Perhaps too this burning lamp prefigured the pillar of a cloud and fire which led them out of Egypt.

CHAPTER 16

1. We have here the marriage of Abram to Hagar, who was his secondary wife. Herein, though he may be excused, he cannot be justified; for "from the beginning it was not so." And when it was so, it seems to have proceeded from an irregular desire to build up their families, for the speedier peopling of the world. But now we must not do so. Christ has reduced this matter to the first institution, and makes the marriage union to be between one man and one woman only.

4–5. *Hagar* no sooner perceives herself with child, but she looks scornfully upon her mistress; upbraids her perhaps with her barrenness and insults her. Sarah falls upon Abram and very unjustly charges him with the injury, suspecting that he countenanced Hagar's insolence. And as one not willing to hear what Abram had to say, she rashly appeals to God. *The LORD judge between me and thee,* as if Abram had refused to right her. When passion is upon the throne, reason is out of doors and is neither heard nor spoken. Those are not always in the right that are most forward in appealing to God. Rash and bold imprecations are commonly evidences of guilt and a bad cause.

6. *Thy maid is in thy hand.* Those who would keep up peace and love must return soft answers to hard accusations. Husbands and wives particularly should endeavor not to be both angry together.

7. Here is the first mention we have in Scripture of an *angel's* appearance, who arrested her in her flight. It should seem she was making towards her own country, for she was on the way to Shur, which lay towards Egypt. It is a great mercy to be stopped in a sinful way, either by conscience or by Providence.

8. *Whence camest thou?* Consider that you are running away from both the duty you were bound to and the privileges you were blessed with, in Abram's tent. *Whither wilt thou go?* You are running yourself into sin in Egypt. If she returns to that people, she will return to their gods.

11. *Ishmael,* that is, "God will hear." The experience we have had of God's seasonable kindness in distress should encourage us to hope for the like help in the like exigencies. Even there, where there is little cry of devotion, the God of pity hears the cry of affliction. Tears speak as well as prayers.

12. *His hand will be against every man.* That is his sin. *And every man's hand against him.* That is his punishment. Those that have turbulent spirits have commonly troublesome lives. They that are provoking, and injurious to others, must expect to be repaid in their own coin.

13. *Thou God seest me.* You see my sorrow and affliction. This Hagar especially refers to: when we have brought ourselves into distress by our own folly, yet God has not forsaken us. You see the sincerity of my repentance. You see me, if in any instance I depart from you. This thought should always restrain us from sin and excite us to duty.

14. *Well was called Beer–lahai–roi.* The well of him that lives and sees me. It is likely Hagar put this name upon it, and it was retained long after. This was the place where the God of glory manifested the special care he took of a poor woman in distress. Those that are graciously admitted into communion with God, and receive seasonable comforts from him, should tell others what he has done for their souls that they also may be encouraged to seek him and trust in him.

CHAPTER 17

1. *I am the Almighty God.* By this name he chose to make himself known to Abram, rather than by his name Jehovah. Our old English translation reads it here, very significantly, *I am God All-sufficient.* The God with whom we have to do is self-sufficient; he has every thing, and he needs not any thing. And he is enough to us, if we be in covenant with him. We have all in him, and we have enough in him. We have enough to satisfy our most enlarged desires; enough to supply the defect of every thing else and to secure us happiness for our immortal souls.

But the covenant is mutual: *Walk before me, and be thou perfect.* That is, upright and sincere. To walk before God is to set God always before us and to think and speak and act in every thing as those that are always under his eye. It is to have a constant regard to his word as our rule, and to his glory as our end in all our actions. It is to be inward with him in all the duties of religious worship, and to be entire for him in all holy conversation. Upright walking with God is the condition of our interest in his all-sufficiency. If we neglect him, or dissemble with him, we forfeit the benefit of our relation to him. A continual regard to God's all-sufficiency will have a great influence upon our upright walking with him.

7. *And I will establish my covenant.* Not to be altered or revoked; not with you only, then it would die with you; but with your *seed after thee.* And it is not only your seed after the flesh, but your spiritual seed. It is *everlasting* in

the evangelical meaning of it. The covenant of grace is everlasting; it is from everlasting in the counsels of it, and to everlasting in the consequences of it. And the external administration of it is transmitted, with the seal of it, to the seed of believers, and the internal administration of it by the Spirit to Christ's seed in every age. This is a covenant of exceeding great and precious promises.

Here are two promises which indeed are all-sufficient, that God would be *their God.* All the privileges of the covenant, all its joys and all its hopes, are summed up in this. A man needs desire no more than this to make him happy. What God is himself, that he will be to his people: wisdom to guide and counsel them, power to protect and support them, goodness to supply and comfort them. What faithful worshippers can expect from the God they serve, believers shall find in God as theirs. This is enough, yet not all. The second promise reads:

8. *And I will give unto thee* Canaan *for an everlasting possession.* God had before promised this land to Abraham and his seed (15:18). But here it is promised for *an everlasting possession,* as a type of heaven, that everlasting rest which remains for the people of God. As the land of Canaan was secured to the seed of Abraham, according to the flesh; so heaven is secured to all his spiritual seed for a possession truly *everlasting.* The offer of this eternal life is made in the word, and confirmed by the sacraments, to all that are under the external administration of the covenant, and the earnest of it is given to all believers.

16. God reveals the purposes of his goodwill to his people by degrees. God had told Abraham long before that he would have a son, but never until now that he would have a son by Sarah.

17. *Then Abraham fell upon his face,*

and laughed. It was a laughter of delight, not of distrust. Now it was that "Abraham rejoiced to see Christ's day," now "he saw it, and was glad" (John 8:56), for as he saw heaven in the promise of Canaan, so he saw Christ in the promise of Isaac, and said, *Shall a child be born to him that is an hundred years old?* He does not here speak of it as at all doubtful, for we are sure he "staggered not at the promise" (Rom. 4:20), but as wonderful, and that which could not be effected but by the almighty power of God.

18. *And Abraham said unto God, O that Ishmael might live before thee!* This he speaks not as desiring that Ishmael might be preferred before the son he would have by Sarah, but as dreading lest he should be forsaken of God, so he puts up this petition on his behalf. The great thing we should desire of God, for our children, is that they may live before him. That is, that they may be kept in covenant with him and may have grace to walk before him in their uprightness. God's answer to this prayer is an answer of peace. Abraham could not say he sought God's face in vain.

CHAPTER 18

1. This appearance of God to Abraham seems to have had in it more of freedom and familiarity, and less of grandeur and majesty, than those we have thus far read of, and therefore more resembles that great visit which in the fullness of time the Son of God was to make to the world.

2. *And, lo, three men.* These three men were three spiritual heavenly beings, now assuming human shapes, that they might be visible to Abraham and conversable with him. Some think they were all three created angels; others, that one of them was the Son of God.

He *bowed himself toward the ground.* Religion does not destroy but improve good manners and teaches us to honor all men.

12. *Sarah laughed within herself.* It was not a laughter of faith, like Abraham's (17:17), but a laughter of doubting and distrust.

17. *Shall I hide from Abraham that thing which I do?* Thus does God in his councils express himself after the manner of men, with deliberation. "The secret of the LORD is with them that fear him." Those that by faith live a life of communion with God cannot but know more of his mind than other people. They have a better insight into what is present, and a better foresight of what is to come.

19. *For I know him, that he will command his children and his household after him.* This is a bright part of Abraham's character. He not only prayed with his family, but he taught them as a man of knowledge. And he commanded them as a man in authority and was prophet and king, as well as priest, in his own house.

27. *Behold now, I have taken upon me to speak unto the Lord, which am but dust and ashes.* He speaks as one amazed at his own boldness and the liberty God graciously allowed him, considering God's greatness, he is the *Lord,* and his own meanness, but *dust and ashes.* Whenever we draw near to God, it becomes us reverently to acknowledge the vast distance that there is between us and him. He is the Lord of glory, we are worms of the earth.

30. *Oh let not the Lord be angry.* The importunity which believers use in their addresses to God is such that if they were dealing with a man like themselves, they could not but fear that he would be *angry* with them. But he with whom we have to do is God and not man, and he is pleased when he is wrestled with.

CHAPTER 19

8. *I have two daughters.* This was unadvisedly and unjustifiably offered. It is true, of two evils we must chose the less, but of two sins we must choose neither, nor ever do evil that good may come of it.

13. *We will destroy this place.* The holy angels are ministers of God's wrath for the destruction of sinners, as well as of his mercy for the preservation and deliverance of his people.

14. *He seemed as one that mocked unto his sons in law.* They that made a jest of every thing made a jest of that and so perished in the overthrow. Thus many who are warned of the danger they are in by sin make a light matter of it; such will perish with their blood upon their heads.

16. The angels *laid hold upon his hand, and brought him forth.* Herein see *the* LORD *being merciful unto him,* otherwise he might justly have left him to perish, since he was loath to depart. If God had not been merciful to us, our lingering had been our ruin.

17. Return not to sin and Satan, for that is *looking behind* to Sodom. Rest not in the world, for that is *staying in the plain.* And reach towards Christ and heaven, for that is *escaping to the mountain.*

24. *Then the* LORD *rained.* He that is the Savior will be the destroyer of those who reject the salvation.

26. *But his wife looked back from behind him.* She disobeyed an express command. Probably she hankered after her house and goods in Sodom and was loath to leave them. Christ intimates this to be her sin (Luke 17:31–32). She too much regarded her stuff. And her looking back spoke an inclination to go back; and therefore our Savior uses it as a warning against apostasy from our Christian profession.

29. *God remembered Abraham,* and for his sake *sent Lot out of the midst of the overthrow.* God will certainly give an answer of peace to the prayer of faith in his own way and time.

30. *He feared to dwell in Zoar.* He was now glad to go to *the mountain,* the place which God had appointed for his shelter. See in Lot what those bring themselves to at last who forsake the communion of saints for secular advantages.

CHAPTER 20

6. *I withheld thee from sinning against me.* It is God who restrains men from doing the ill they would do; it is not from him that there is sin, but it is from him that there is not more sin, either by his influence on men's minds checking their inclination to sin, or by his providence taking away the opportunity. It is a great mercy to be hindered from committing sin, and God must have the glory of whoever is the instrument.

9. *What have I offended thee?* If I had been your worst enemy, you could not have done me a worse turn, nor taken a more effectual course to be revenged on me. We ought to reckon that those do us the greatest disservice in the world who any way tempt us or expose us to sin, though they may pretend friendship, and offer that which is grateful enough to the corrupt nature.

11. *I thought, Surely the fear of God is not in this place; and they will slay me.* There are many places and persons that have more of the fear of God in them than we think they have. Perhaps they are not called by our name, they do not wear our badges, they do not tie themselves to that which we have an opinion of; and therefore we conclude they have not the fear of God in their hearts!

CHAPTER 21

10. *Cast out this bondwoman.* This was a type of the rejection of the unbelieving Jews, who, though they were the seed of Abraham, yet because they submitted not to the gospel-covenant were unchurched and disfranchised. And that which above any thing provoked God to cast them off was their mocking and persecuting the gospel-church, God's *Isaac,* in his infancy.

13. The casting out of Ishmael was not his ruin. He shall be *a nation, because he is thy seed.* We are not sure that it was his eternal ruin. It is presumption to say that all these who are left out of the external dispensation of God's covenant are excluded from all his mercies. Those may be saved who are not thus honored.

17. *God heard the voice of the lad.* We read not of a word he said; but his sighs and groans cried loud in the ears of the God of mercy. An angel was sent to comfort Hagar, who assures her, God has heard the voice of the lad where he is, though he be in the wilderness; for where we are, there is a way open heavenwards.

18. *Lift up the lad, and hold him in thy hand.* God's readiness to help us when we are in trouble must not slacken but quicken our endeavors to help ourselves. He repeats the promise concerning her son, that he would be *a great nation,* as a reason why she should bestir herself to help him.

33. *And called there on the name of the* LORD. Probably in the grove Abraham planted, which was his oratory, or house of prayer. He kept up public worship, to which probably his neighbors resorted and joined with him. Men should not only retain their goodness wherever they go, but do all they can to propagate it and make others good.

CHAPTER 22

1. *After these things.* After all the other exercises he had had, all the difficulties he had gone through: now perhaps he was beginning to think the storms were blown over. But after all, this encounter comes, which is sharper than any yet. *God did tempt Abraham.* Not to draw him to sin, so Satan tempts; but to discover his graces, how strong they were, that they might be "found unto praise and honor and glory."

Probably he expected some renewed promise, but to his great amazement that which God has to say to him is in short, Abraham, go kill thy son. And this command is given him in such aggravating language as makes the temptation abundantly more grievous. Every word here is a sword in his bones; the trial is steeled with trying phrases. Is it any pleasure to the Almighty that he should afflict? No, it is not; yet when Abraham's faith is to be tried, God seems to take pleasure in the aggravation of the trial.

2. *And he said, Take thy son.* Not your bullocks and your lambs; how willingly would Abraham have parted with them by the thousands to redeem Isaac! Not your servant, no, not the steward of your house. *Thine only son.* Your only son by Sarah. Ishmael was lately cast out, to the grief of Abraham, and now Isaac only was left. And must he go too? Yes, take Isaac, him by name, "thy laughter," that son indeed. Yes, that son *whom thou lovest.* The trial was of Abraham's love to God, and therefore it must be in a beloved son. *And offer him for a burnt offering.* He must not only kill his son, but kill him as a sacrifice, with all that sedateness and composedness of mind with which he used to offer his burnt offering.

3. He left his servants at some

distance off, lest they should have created him some disturbance in his strange oblation. Thus when Christ was entering upon his agony in the garden, he took only three of his disciples with him.

6. Isaac's carrying wood was a type of Christ, who carried his own cross; while Abraham, with a steady and undaunted resolution, carried the fatal knife and fire.

7. *Behold the fire and the wood: but where is the lamb?* This is a teaching question to us all, that when we are going to worship God, we should seriously consider whether we have every thing ready, especially the *lamb for a burnt offering.* Behold, *the fire* is ready; that is, the Spirit's assistance and God's acceptance. The *wood* is ready, the instituted ordinances designed to kindle our affections, which indeed without the Spirit are but like wood without fire, but the Spirit works by them. All things are now ready, but *where is the lamb?* Where is the heart? Is that ready to be offered up to God, to ascend to him as a *burnt offering?*

8. *My son, God will provide himself a lamb.* Christ, the great sacrifice of atonement, was of God's providing. When none in heaven or earth could have found a lamb for that burnt offering, God himself found the ransom.

9. With the same resolution and composedness of mind, Abraham applies himself to the completing of this sacrifice. After many a weary step, and with a heavy heart, he arrives at length at the fatal place. He builds the altar, an altar of earth, we may suppose, the saddest that ever he built. He *lays the wood in order* for Isaac's funeral pile. And now he tells him the amazing news. Isaac, it appears, is as willing as Abraham. We do not find that he made any objection against it. God com-

mands it to be done, and Isaac has learned to submit. Yet it is necessary that a sacrifice be bound. The great Sacrifice, which in the fullness of time was to be offered up, must be bound, and therefore so must Isaac.

Having bound him, he *lays him upon the altar,* and his hand upon the head of the sacrifice. Be astonished, O heavens, at this, and wonder, O earth! Here is an act of faith and obedience which deserves to be a spectacle to God, angels, and men. Abraham's darling, the church's hope, the heir of promise, lies ready to bleed and die by his own father's hands!

Now this obedience of Abraham in offering up Isaac is a lively representation of the love of God to us, in delivering up his only begotten Son to suffer and die for us as a sacrifice. Abraham was obliged both in duty and gratitude to part with Isaac, and parted with him to a friend, but God was under no obligations to us, for we were enemies. Consider also our duty to God in return of that love. We must tread in the steps of this faith of Abraham. God, by his word, calls us to part with all for Christ; all our sins, though they have been as a right hand, or a right eye, or an Isaac. All those things that are rivals with Christ for the sovereignty of our heart. And we must cheerfully let them all go. God, by his providence, which is truly the voice of God, calls us to part with an Isaac sometimes, and we must do it by a cheerful resignation and submission to his holy will.

11. *The angel of the* LORD. That is, God himself, the eternal Word, the Angel of the covenant, who was to be the great Redeemer and Comforter.

12. *Lay not thine hand upon the lad.* God's time to help his people is when they are brought to the greatest extremity. The more eminent the danger is, and the nearer to be put in execution, the more wonderful and the more welcome is the deliverance. *Now I know that thou fearest God.* God knew it before, but now Abraham had given a memorable evidence of it. He need do no more, what he had done was sufficient to prove the religious regard he had to God and his authority. The best evidence of our fearing God is our being willing to honor him with that which is dearest to us, and to part with all to him, or for him.

14. *And Abraham called the name of that place Jehovah–jireh.* "The Lord will provide." Probably alluding to what he had said, "God will provide himself a lamb" (v. 8). This was purely the Lord's doing. Let it be recorded for the generations to come that "the Lord will see." He will always have his eyes upon his people in their straits, that he may come in with seasonable succor in the critical juncture. And that he *will be seen,* in the mount, in the greatest perplexities of his people. He will not only manifest but magnify his wisdom, power, and goodness in their deliverance. Where God sees and provides, he should be seen and praised.

17. *Multiplying I will multiply thy seed.* Abraham has but one son and is willing to part with that one in obedience to God. Well, believe God, you shall be recompensed with thousands and millions. *In blessing I will bless thee.* The gift of the Holy Ghost; the promise of the Spirit was that blessing of Abraham which was to "come on the Gentiles through Jesus Christ" (Gal. 3:14). *Thy seed shall possess the gate of his enemies.* Believers by their faith overcome the world and triumph over all the powers of darkness. *In thy seed.* One particular person that shall descend from you, for he speaks not of many but of one, as the apostle observes (Gal. 3:16). *Shall all the nations of the earth be*

blessed. Christ is the great blessing of the world. Abraham was ready to give up his son for a sacrifice to the honor of God, and on that occasion God promised to give his Son a sacrifice for the salvation of man.

CHAPTER 23

4. *I am a stranger and a sojourner with you.* This was one occasion which Abraham took to confess that he was a stranger and a pilgrim upon earth. The death of our relations should effectually remind us that we are not at home in this world.

7. Abraham returns them thanks for their kind offer with all possible decency and respect. Religion teaches good manners, and those abuse it that place it in rudeness and clownishness.

CHAPTER 24

14. *Let it come to pass.* Abraham prays God that he would make his way plain and clear before him by the concurrence of minute circumstances in his favor. It is the comfort, as well as the belief, of a good man that God's providence extends itself to the smallest occurrences and admirably serves its own purposes by them. And it is our wisdom, in all our affairs, to follow Providence. Yes, it is very desirable, and that which we may lawfully pray for, while in the general we set God's will before us as our rule, that he will, by hints of providence, direct us in the way of our duty and give us indications what his mind is. Thus he guides his people "with mine eye," and leads them in a "plain path."

15. God, in his providence, does sometimes wonderfully own the prayer of faith and gratify the innocent desires of his praying people even in little things, that he may show the extent of his care and may encourage them at all times to seek him and trust in him. Yet we must take heed of being overbold in prescribing to God, lest the event should weaken our faith rather than strengthen it. And the concurrence of providences, and their minute circumstances, for the furtherance of our success in any business ought to be particularly observed with wonder and thankfulness to the glory of God. We have been lacking both in duty and comfort by neglecting to observe Providence.

27. *Blessed be the* LORD *God of my master Abraham.* When God's favors are coming towards us, we must meet them with our praises.

50. *The thing proceedeth from the* LORD. Providence smiles upon it, and we have nothing to say against it. A marriage is then likely to be comfortable when it appears to proceed from the Lord.

57. *Call the damsel, and inquire at her mouth.* As children ought not to marry without their parents' consent, so parents ought not to marry them without their own.

63. Our walks *in the field* are then truly pleasant when in them we apply ourselves to meditation and prayer. We there have a free and open prospect of the heavens above us, and the earth around us, and the hosts and riches of both, by the view of which we should be led to the contemplation of the Maker and Owner of all.

CHAPTER 25

6. *Abraham gave gifts.* It was justice to provide for them; parents that do not that are worse than infidels. He did this *while he yet lived,* lest it should not have been done or not so well done afterwards. In many cases, it is wisdom for men to make their own hands their executors, and what they find to do, to do it while they live.

9. *His sons Isaac and Ishmael buried him.* It was the last office of respect they had to pay to their good father. Some distance there had formerly been between Isaac and Ishmael, but it seems either Abraham had himself brought them together while he lived, or at least his death reconciled them.

20. *And Isaac was forty years old.* Not much is related concerning Isaac, but what had reference to his father while he lived and to his sons afterward. Isaac seems not to have been a man of action, nor much tried, but to have spent his day in quietness and silence.

21. *And Isaac intreated the* LORD *for his wife.* Though God had promised to multiply his family, he prayed for it; for God's promises must not supersede but encourage our prayers and be improved as the ground of our faith. Though he had prayed for this mercy many years, and it was not granted, yet he did not leave off praying for it.

28. *And Isaac loved Esau.* Isaac, though he was not a stirring man himself, yet loved to have his son active. Esau knew how to please him and showed a great respect for him, by treating him often with venison, which won upon him more than one would have thought. But Rebekah loved him whom God loved.

31. *Sell me this day thy birthright.* If we look on Esau's birthright as only a temporal advantage, what he said had something of truth in it, that our worldly enjoyments, even those we are most fond of, will stand us in no stead in a dying hour. They will not put by the stroke of death, nor ease the pangs, nor remove the sting. But being of a spiritual nature, his undervaluing it was the greatest profaneness imaginable. It is egregious folly to part with our interest in God and Christ and heaven for the riches, honors, and pleasures of this world.

CHAPTER 26

2. *The* LORD *said, Go not down into Egypt. Sojourn in this land.* There was a famine in Jacob's days, and God bid him "go down into Egypt" (46:3–4); a famine in Isaac's days, and God bid him not go down; and a famine in Abraham's days, and God left him to his liberty, directing him neither way. Considering that Egypt was always a place of trial to God's people, we gain insight into the different characters of these three patriarchs. Abraham was a man of very intimate communion with God, and to him all places and conditions were alike. Isaac was a very good man, but not cut out for hardship; therefore he is forbidden to go to Egypt. Jacob was inured to difficulties, strong and patient; therefore he must go down into Egypt, that "the trial of his faith might be to praise, and honor, and glory." Thus God proportions his people's trials to their strength.

7. *He said, She is my sister.* So Isaac enters into the same temptation that his father had been once and again surprised and overcome by. It is an unaccountable thing that both these great and good men should be guilty of so odd a piece of dissimulation, by which they so much exposed both their own and their wives' reputation.

24. *Fear not, for I am with thee, and will bless thee.* Those may remove with comfort that are sure of God's presence with them wherever they go.

28. Those whom God blesses and favors have reason enough to forgive those that hate them, since the worst enemy they have cannot do them any real hurt.

CHAPTER 27

1. *He called Esau.* Though Esau had greatly grieved his parents by his marriage, yet they had not expelled him, but it seems were pretty well reconciled to him.

4. *That my soul may bless thee before I die.* Prayer is the work of the soul, and not of the lips only. As the soul must be employed in blessing God (Ps. 103:1), so it must be in blessing ourselves and others. The blessing will not go to the heart if it does not come from the heart.

6. If Rebekah, when she heard Isaac promise the blessing to Esau, had gone to him, and with humility and seriousness put him in remembrance of that which God had said concerning their sons; if she had further showed him how Esau had forfeited the blessing, both by selling his birthright and by marrying strange wives; it is probable Isaac would have been prevailed with to confer the blessing upon Jacob, and needed not thus to have been cheated into it.

19. *And Jacob said, I am Esau.* Who would have thought this plain man could have played such a part? His mother having put him in the way of it, he applies himself to those methods which he had never accustomed himself to, but had always conceived an abhorrence of. But lying is soon learned. I wonder how honest Jacob could so readily turn his tongue to say, *I am Esau thy firstborn.* And when his father asked him, "Art thou my very son Esau?" (v. 24) how could he say, *I have done according as thou badest me,* when he had received no command from his father, but was doing as his mother bid him? How could he say, *Eat of my venison,* when he knew it came not from the field, but from the fold? But especially I wonder how he could have the forehead to father it upon God and to use his name in the cheat.

20. *The LORD thy God brought it to me.* Is this Jacob? It is certainly written not for our imitation, but our admonition. "Let him that standeth take heed lest he fall."

46. *If Jacob take a wife of the daughters of Heth.* As Esau has done. More artifice still. This was not the thing Rebekah was afraid of. But if we use guile once, we shall be very ready to use it again. It should be carefully observed that although a blessing came on his posterity by Jacob's vile lying and dissimulation, yet it brought heavy affliction upon himself, and that for a long term of years. So severely did God punish him personally for "doing evil that good might come."

CHAPTER 28

3–4. Two great promises Abraham was blessed with, and Isaac here entails them both upon Jacob. (1) The promise of heirs, *God make thee fruitful, and multiply thee.* (2) The promise of an inheritance for those heirs, *That thou mayest inherit the land wherein thou art a stranger.*

6. This passage comes in, in the midst of Jacob's story, to show the influence of a good example. Esau now begins to think Jacob the better man and disdains not to take him for his pattern in this particular instance of marrying a daughter of Abraham.

11. *The stones for his pillows* and the heavens for his canopy! Yet his comfort in the divine blessing, and his confidence in the divine protection, made him easy, even when he lay thus exposed. Being sure that his God made him to dwell in safety, he could lie down and sleep upon a stone.

12–13. *The ladder set up on the earth, and the top of it reached to heaven; and*

behold the angels ascending and descending on it; and the LORD stood above it. This might represent the providence of God, by which there is a constant correspondence kept between heaven and earth. The counsels of heaven are executed on earth, and the affairs of this earth are all known in heaven. Providence does his work gradually and by steps. Angels are employed as ministering spirits to serve all the designs of Providence, and the wisdom of God is at the upper end of the ladder, directing all the motions of second causes to his glory.

The angels are active spirits, continually *ascending* and *descending;* they rest not day nor night. They ascend to give account of what they have done, and to receive orders. They descend to execute the orders they have received. This vision gave seasonable comfort to Jacob, letting him know that he had both a good guide and a good guard. Though he was to "wander from his father's house" (20:13), yet he was the care of Providence and the charge of the holy angels.

This might also represent the mediation of Christ. He is this ladder. The foot on earth is his human nature, the top in heaven is his divine nature. Or the former is his humiliation, the latter is his exaltation. All the intercourse between heaven and earth since the fall is by this ladder. Christ is the Way. All God's favors come to us, and all our services come to him, by Christ. If God dwell with us, and we with him, it is by Christ. We have no way of getting to heaven but by this ladder; for the kind offices the angels do us, are all owning to Christ, who has reconciled things on earth and things in heaven (Col. 1:20).

15. *Behold, I am with thee.* Wherever we are, we are safe, if we have God's favorable presence with us. He knew not, but God foresaw what hardships he would meet with in his uncle's service, and therefore promises to preserve him *in all places*. God knows how to give his people graces and comforts accommodated to the events that shall be, as well as to those that are.

16. *Surely the* Lord *is in this place; and I knew it not.* God's manifestations of himself to his people carry their own evidence along with them. God can give undeniable demonstrations of his presence, such as give abundant satisfaction to the souls of the faithful that God is with them of a truth; satisfaction not communicable to others, but convincing to themselves. We sometimes meet with God there, where we little thought of meeting with him. He is there where we did not think he had been, is found there where we asked not for him.

17. *He was afraid.* So far was he from being puffed up. The more we see of God, the more cause we see for holy trembling and blushing before him. Those whom God is pleased to manifest himself to are laid and kept very low in their own eyes, and see cause to fear even "the Lord and his goodness" (Hos. 3:5).

20. *And Jacob vowed a vow.* By religious vows we give glory to God and own our dependence upon him, and we lay a bond upon our own souls to engage and quicken our obedience to him. Jacob was now in fear and distress, and in times of trouble it is seasonable to make vows, or when we are in pursuit of any special mercy (Jonah 1:16; Ps. 66:13–14; I Sam. 1:11; Num. 21:1–3).

If God will be with me, and will keep me. We need desire no more to make us easy and happy wherever we are, but to have God's presence with us, and to be under his protection. It is comfortable in a journey to have a guide in an unknown way, a guard in a dangerous way, to be well carried, well provided for, and to have good company any way. And they that have God with them have all this in the best manner.

And of all that thou shalt give me I will surely give the tenth unto thee. To be spent either upon God's altars, or upon his poor, which are both his receivers in the world. The tenth is a very fit proportion to be devoted to God and employed for him; though as circumstances vary, it may be more or less, as God prospers us.

CHAPTER 29

2. The divine providence is to be acknowledged in all the little circumstances which concur to make a journey or other undertaking comfortable and successful. If, when we are at a loss, we meet with those seasonably that can direct us; if we meet with a disaster, and those are at hand that will help us; we must not say it was by chance, but it was by Providence. Our ways are ways of pleasantness, if we continually acknowledge God in them.

13–14. Laban, though not the best humored of men, bid him welcome, was satisfied in the account he gave of himself, and of the reason of his coming in such poor circumstances. While we avoid the extreme on the one hand of being foolishly credulous, we must take heed of falling into the other extreme of being uncharitably jealous and suspicious.

20. *They seemed to him but a few days, for the love he had to her.* An age of work will be but as a few days to those who love God and long for Christ's appearing.

27. *We will give thee this also.* Hereby he drew Jacob into the sin and snare and disquiet of multiplying wives. He that had lived without a wife to the eighty-fourth year of his age could have been very well content with one. But Laban, to dispose of his two daughters without portions, and to get seven years service more out of Jacob, thus imposed upon him and draws him into such a strait that he had reason for marrying them both.

35. Her fourth she called *Judah,* "Praise," saying, *Now will I praise the LORD.* And this was he of whom, as concerning the flesh, Christ came. Whatever is the matter of our rejoicing ought to be the matter of our thanksgiving. And all our praises must center in Christ, both as the matter of them and as the Mediator of them. He descended from him whose name was praise, for "he is our praise." Is Christ formed in my heart? "Now will I praise the LORD."

CHAPTER 30

1. *Rachel envied her sister.* Envy is grieving at the good of another, and no sin is more injurious both to God, our neighbor, and ourselves. But this was not all: she said to Jacob, *Give me children, or else I die.* A child would not content her; but because Leah has more than one, she must have more too: *Give me children.* Her heart is set upon it. Give them me, *else I die.* That is, I shall fret myself to death. The want of this satisfaction will shorten my days.

Observe here a difference between Rachel's asking for this mercy, and Hannah's (I Sam. 1:10ff.). Rachel envied, Hannah wept. Rachel must have children, and she died of the second; Hannah prayed for this child, and she had four more. Rachel is importunate and peremptory, Hannah is submissive and devout, "If thou wilt" give me a child, I will give him to the Lord. Let Hannah be imitated, and not Rachel. And let our desires be always under the conduct and check of reason and religion.

2. *Am I in God's stead?* Can I give you that which God denies you? He acknowledges the hand of God in the affliction: *He hath withheld the fruit of the womb.* Whatever we want, it is God that withholds it, as sovereign Lord, most wise, holy, and just, that he may do what he will with his own, and is debtor to no man. He never did, nor ever can do, any wrong to any of his creatures.

3. *Behold my maid Bilhah.* At the persuasion of Rachel Jacob took Bilhah her handmaid to wife that, according to the usage of those times, his children by her might be adopted and owned as her mistress's children. Rachel would rather have children by reputation than none at all; children that she might call her own, though they were not so. And as an early instance of her dominion over the children born in her apartment, she takes a pleasure in giving them names that carry in them nothing but marks of emulation with her sister. As if she had overcome her, she calls the first son of her handmaid, *Dan,* "Judgment," saying, *God hath judged me,* that is, given sentence in my favor. In battle, she calls the next *Naphtali,* "Wrestlings," saying, *I have wrestled with my sister, and I have prevailed.* See what roots of bitterness envy and strife are, and what mischief they make among relations!

9. Rachel had done that absurd and preposterous thing of putting her maid into her husband's bed, and now Leah (because she missed one year in bearing children) does the same, to be even with her. See the power of rivalry, and admire the wisdom of the divine appointment, which joins together one man and one woman only.

CHAPTER 31

1. The last chapter began with Rachel's envying Leah; this begins with Laban's sons envying Jacob.

3. *The* L*ORD* *said unto Jacob, Return, and I will be with thee.* Though Jacob had met with very hard usage, yet he would not quit his place until God bid him. He came there by orders from heaven, and there he would stay until he was ordered back.

9. *God hath taken away the cattle of your father, and given them to me.* Thus the righteous God paid Jacob for his hard service out of Laban's estate; as afterwards he paid the seed of Jacob for their service of the Egyptians with their spoils.

19−20. It is certain it was lawful for Jacob to leave his service suddenly. It was not only justified by the particular instructions God gave him, but warranted by the fundamental law of self-preservation, which directs us, when we are in danger, to shift for our own safety, as far as we can do it without wronging our consciences.

Rachel was not so honest as her husband; she stole *her father's images* and carried them away. We are willing to hope that she took them away, not out of covetousness much less for her own use, or out of any superstitious fear lest Laban, by consulting his "teraphim," might know which way they were gone, but with a design to convince her father of the folly of his regard to those as gods which could not secure themselves.

24. *Speak not either good or bad.* The safety of good men is very much owing to the hold God has of the consciences of bad men, and the access he has to them.

30. *Wherefore hast thou stolen my gods?* Foolish man! To call those his gods that could be stolen! Could he expect protection from them that could neither resist nor discover their invaders? Happy are they who have the Lord for their God. Enemies may steal our goods, but not our God.

CHAPTER 32

1. *And the angels of God met him.* In a visible appearance; whether in a vision by day, or in a dream by night, as when he saw them upon the ladder, is uncertain. They met him to bid him welcome to Canaan; a more honorable reception than ever any prince had that was met by the magistrates of a city. They met him to congratulate his arrival and his escape from Laban. They had invisibly attended him all along, but now they appeared, because he had greater dangers before him. When God designs his people for extraordinary trials, he prepares them by extraordinary comforts.

2. *This is God's host.* A good man may, with an eye of faith, see the same that Jacob saw with his bodily eyes. What need we dispute whether he has a guardian angel, when we are sure he has a guard of angels about him?

6. *He cometh to meet thee, and four hundred men with him.* He is now weary of waiting for the days of mourning for his father, and before those come resolves to slay his brother. Out he marches with *four hundred men,* probably such as used to hunt with him, armed no doubt, ready to execute the word of command.

7. *Then Jacob was greatly afraid and distressed.* A lively apprehension of danger may very well conflict with a humble confidence in God's power and promise.

10. *I am not worthy of the least of all the mercies,* much less am I worthy of so great a favor as this I am now suing for. Those are best prepared for the greatest mercies that see themselves unworthy of the least.

11. Lord, *deliver me from Esau: for I fear him.* The fear that quickens prayer is itself pleadable.

12. *Thou saidst, I will surely do thee good.* The best we can say to God in prayer is what he has said to us. God's promises, as they are the surest guide of our desires in prayer and furnish us with the best petitions, so they are the firmest ground of our hopes and furnish us with the best pleas.

13. Jacob, having piously made God his friend by a prayer, is here prudently endeavoring to make Esau his friend by a present. He had prayed to God to deliver him from the hand of Esau. His prayer did not make him presume upon God's mercy, without the use of means.

17–18. He sent him also a very humble message, which he ordered his servants to deliver in the best manner. They must call Esau their *lord,* and Jacob his *servant.* They must especially take care to tell him that Jacob was coming after, that he might not suspect him fled. A friendly confidence in men's goodness may help to prevent the mischief designed us by their badness.

24. Very early in the morning, a great while before day. Jacob had helped his wives and children over the river, and he desired to be private and was *left alone* that he might again spread his cares and fears before God in prayer. While Jacob was earnest in prayer, stirring up himself to take hold on God, an angel takes hold on him. Some think this was a created angel, one of those that "always behold the face of our Father." Rather it was the angel of the covenant, who often appeared in a human shape, before he assumed the human nature. We are told by the prophet (Hos. 12:4) how Jacob wrestled, he "wept, and made supplication"; prayers and tears were his weapons. It was not only a corporal, but a spiritual wrestling by vigorous faith and holy desire.

25. The angel *prevailed not against him.* That is, this discouragement did not shake his faith nor silence his prayer. It was not in his own strength that he wrestled, nor by his own strength that he prevails; but by strength derived from heaven. Job illustrates this (Job 23:6). "Will he plead against me with his great power?" No; had the angel done so, Jacob had been crushed; "but he would put strength in me." And by that strength Jacob had "power over the angel" (Hos. 12:4).

The angel put out Jacob's thigh, to show him what he could do, and that it was God he was wrestling with, for no man could disjoint his thigh with a touch. Some think that Jacob felt little or no pain from this hurt. It is probable he did not, for he did not so much as *halt* until the struggle was over (v. 31); and if so, that was an evidence of a divine touch indeed, which wounded and healed at the same time.

26. *Let me go.* The angel, by an admirable condescension, bids Jacob to let him go, as God said to Moses, "Let me alone" (Exod. 32:10). Could not a mighty angel get clear of Jacob's grapples? He could; but thus he would put an honor upon Jacob's faith and prayer. The reason the angel gives why he would be gone is because *the day breaketh,* and therefore he would not any longer detain Jacob, who had business to do, a journey to go, a family to look after. *And he said, I will not let thee go, except thou bless me.* He resolves he will have a blessing, and rather shall "all his bones be put out of joint" than he will go away without one. Those that would have the blessing of Christ must be in good earnest and be importunate for it.

27. *What is thy name? Jacob* (says he), a "supplanter." Well (says the angel), be never so called any more. You shall be called *Israel,* "a prince with God." He is a prince indeed that is a prince of God; and those are truly honorable that are mighty in prayer. Yet this was not all. Having power with God, he shall have power *with men* too. Having prevailed for a blessing from heaven, he shall, no doubt, prevail for Esau's favor. Whatever enemies we have, if we can but make God our friend, we are well enough. They that by faith have power in heaven have thereby as much power on earth as they have occasion for.

29. *Wherefore is it that thou dost ask after my name?* What good will it do you to know that? The discovery of that was reserved for his deathbed, upon which he was taught to call him "Shiloh." But instead of telling him his name, he gave him his blessing, which was the thing he wrestled for. He *blessed him there,* repeated and ratified the blessing formerly given him. See how wonderfully God condescends to countenance and crown importunate prayer? Those that resolve, though God slay them, yet to trust in him will at length be more than conquerors.

CHAPTER 33

4. *And Esau ran to meet him.* Not in passion but in love. *Embraced him, and fell on his neck, and kissed him.* God has the hearts of all men in his hands and can turn them when and how he pleases. He can of a sudden convert enemies into friends, as he did two Sauls, one by restraining grace (I Sam. 26:21, 25), the other by renewing grace (Acts 9:21). *And they wept.* Jacob wept for joy to be thus kindly received; Esau perhaps wept for grief and shame to think of the ill design he had conceived against his brother.

12. We never find that Jacob and Esau were so loving with one another as they were now. God made Esau not only not an enemy, but a friend.

15. Esau offers some of his men to be his guard and convoy; but Jacob humbly refuses his offer, only desiring he would not take it amiss that he did

not accept it. *What needeth it?* He is under divine protection. Those are sufficiently guarded that have God for their guard and are under a convoy of his hosts, as Jacob was.

CHAPTER 34

25. *They slew all the males.* Nothing can excuse this wretched villainy. It was true Shechem had "wrought folly in Israel" (v. 7) in defiling Dinah, but it ought to have been considered how far Dinah herself had been accessory to it. Had Shechem abused her in her mother's tent, it had been another matter; but she went upon his ground and struck the spark which began the fire. When we are severe upon the sinner, we ought to consider who was the tempter.

30. *I shall be destroyed, I and my house.* Jacob knew indeed that God had promised to preserve his house; but he might justly fear that these vile practices of his children would amount to a forfeiture and cut off the entail. When sin is in the house, there is reason to fear ruin at the door.

CHAPTER 35

1−2. *Arise, go up to Beth−el.* God reminds Jacob of his vow at Beth−el, and sends him to perform it. Jacob had said in the day of his distress, "If I come again in peace, this stone shall be God's house" (28:21−22). God had performed his part, had given Jacob more than bread to eat and raiment to put on. But it would seem he had forgotten his vow, or at least deferred the performance of it. *And dwell there.* That is, Not only go himself, but take his family with him, that they might join with him in his devotions. *Put away the strange gods.* Strange gods in Jacob's family! Could such a family, that was taught the knowledge of the Lord, admit them? Could such a master, to whom God had appeared twice, and oftener, connive at them? *And be clean, and change your garments.* These were ceremonies signifying the purification and change of the heart.

5. *And the terror of God was upon the cities.* Though the Canaanites were much exasperated against the sons of Jacob for their barbarous usage of the Shechemites; yet they were so restrained by a divine power that they could not take this fair opportunity to avenge their neighbors' quarrel. God governs the world more by secret terrors on men's minds than we are aware.

7. *He built there an altar.* And no doubt offered sacrifice upon it, perhaps the tenth of his cattle, according to his vow, "I will give the tenth unto thee."

10. God now confirmed the change of his name. It was done before by the angel that wrestled with him (32:28), and here it was ratified by the divine majesty, to encourage him against the fear of the Canaanites. Who can be too hard for *Israel,* a prince with God?

11. Two things are promised. (1) That he would be the father of a great *nation.* Great in number, *a company of nations shall be of thee.* Every tribe of Israel was a nation, and all the twelve a company of nations. Great in honor and power, *kings shall come out of thy loins.* (2) That he should be master of a good land (v. 12). The land that was given to Abraham and Isaac is here entailed on Jacob and his seed. These two promises had also a spiritual signification, which we may suppose Jacob himself had some notion of; for without doubt Christ is the promised seed, and heaven is the promised land. The former is the foundation, and the latter the top-stone of all God's favors.

14. *And Jacob set up a pillar.* When he was going to Padan–aram he set up that stone which he had laid his head on for a pillar. But now he took time to erect one more stately and durable, probably inserting that stone into it.

17. Rachel had said when she bore Joseph, "The LORD shall add to me another son," which now the midwife remembers and tells her, her words were made good. Yet his did not avail. Unless God commands away fear, no one else can. We are apt in extreme perils to comfort ourselves and our friends with the hopes of a temporal deliverance, in which we may be disappointed. We had better ground our comforts on that which cannot fail us, the hope of eternal life.

18. Jacob buried her near the place where she died. If the soul be at rest after death, the matter is not great where the body lies. In the place where the tree falls, there let it lie.

20. Jacob set up a pillar in remembrance of his joys (v. 14), and here he set up one in remembrance of his sorrows. As it may be of use to ourselves to keep both in mind, so it may be of use to others to transmit the memorials of both.

CHAPTER 36

10. *These are the names.* Observe that only the names of Esau's sons and grandsons are recorded; not their history, for it is the church that Moses preserves the records of, not of those that were without. The elders only that lived by faith "obtained a good report." Nor does the genealogy go any farther than the third and fourth generation, the very names of all after are buried in oblivion. It is only the pedigree of the Israelites who were to be the heirs of Canaan, and of whom were to come the promised seed, and the holy seed, that is drawn out to any length, as far as there was occasion for it, even of all the tribes until Canaan was divided among them, and the royal line until Christ came.

43. Mount Seir is called *the land of their possession.* While the Israelites dwelt in the house of bondage, and their Canaan was only the land of promise, the Edomites dwelt in their own *habitations,* and Seir was in *their possession.* The children of this world have their all in hand, and nothing in hope, while the children of God have often their all in hope, and next to nothing in hand. But, all things considered, it is better to have Canaan in promise than Mount Seir in possession.

CHAPTER 37

2. *Joseph brought unto his father their evil report.* Jacob's sons did that when they were from under his eye, which they would not have done if they had been at home with him. But Joseph gave his father an account of their ill carriage, that he might reprove and restrain them.

3. He *made him a coat of many colors.* Which probably was significant of father honors intended him.

5. Though he was now very young, about seventeen years old, yet he was pious and devout, and this fitted him for God's gracious discoveries to him. Joseph had a great deal of trouble before him, and therefore God gave him this prospect of his advancement, to support and comfort him.

8. *Shalt thou indeed reign over us?* See how truly they interpreted his dream. The event exactly answered this interpretation. See also how scornfully they resented it, *shalt thou* that art but one, *have dominion over us* that are many? You who are the youngest, over us who are elder? The reign of Jesus Christ, our Joseph, is despised and striven against by an unbelieving world, who cannot

endure to think to have "this man to reign over us." The dominion also of "the upright in the morning" of the resurrection is thought of with the utmost disdain.

10. *His father rebuked him.* Probably to lessen the offense which his brethren would take at it. Yet he took notice of it more than he seemed to do.

21. *And Reuben heard it.* God can raise up friends for his people, even among their enemies. Reuben's temper seems to have been soft and effeminate, which had betrayed him to the sin of uncleanness, while the temper of the two next brothers, Simeon and Levi, was fierce, which betrayed them to the sin of murder, a sin of which Reuben startled at the thought.

Joseph was here a type of Christ. Though he was the beloved Son of his Father, and hated by a wicked world; yet the Father sent him out of his bosom to visit us. He came to earth from heaven to seek and save us, yet then malicious plots were laid against him. *He came unto his own,* and his own not only received him not, but consulted, "This is the heir; come, let us kill him." This he submitted to, in pursuance of his design to save us.

25. *They sat down to eat bread.* They felt no remorse of conscience which, if they had, would have spoiled their stomach to their meat. A great force put upon conscience commonly stupefies it, and for the time deprives it both of sense and speech.

28. As Joseph was sold by the contrivance of Judah for twenty pieces of silver, so was our Lord Jesus for thirty, and by one of the same name too, Judas. Reuben, it seems, was gone away from his brethren when they sold Joseph, intending to come round some other way to the pit and to help Joseph out of it. But had this taken effect, what had become of God's purpose concerning his preferment in Egypt? There are many devices of the enemies of God's people to destroy them, and of their friends to help them, which perhaps are both disappointed, as these here; but the "counsel of the Lord that shall stand." Reuben thought himself undone because the child was sold; *I, whither shall I go?* He being the eldest, his father would expect from him an account of him. But it proved they had all been undone, if he had not been sold.

35. *He refused to be comforted.* He resolved to *go down into the grave* mourning. Great affection to any creature does but prepare for so much the greater affliction, when it is either removed from us or embittered to us. Inordinate love commonly ends in immoderate grief.

CHAPTER 38

1. *Judah went down from his brethren.* When young people that have been well educated begin to change their company, they will soon change their manners and lose their good education. They that go down from their brethren, that forsake the society of the seed of Israel and pick up Canaanites for their companions, are going down the hill apace.

14. *She covered her with a veil.* It was the custom of harlots in those times to cover their faces, that though they were not ashamed, yet they might seem to be so. The sin of uncleanness did not then go so bare-faced as it now does.

17. *A kid from the flock.* A goodly price at which her chastity and honor were valued! Had the consideration been thousands of rams, and ten thousand rivers of oil, it had not been a valuable consideration. The favor of God, the purity of the soul, the peace of the conscience, and the hope of heaven are too precious to be exposed to sale at any such rates.

23. *Lest we be shamed.* Either, (1) Lest his sin should come to be known publicly, or (2) Lest he should be laughed at as a fool for trusting a whore with his signet and his bracelets. He expresses no concern about the sin, only about the shame. There are many who are more solicitous to preserve their reputation with men than to secure the favor of God. *Lest we be shamed* goes further with them than "lest we be damned."

CHAPTER 39

1. The Jews have a proverb, If the world did but know the worth of good men, they would hedge them about with pearls. Joseph was sold to an *officer of Pharaoh,* with whom he might get acquainted with public persons and public business, and so be fitted for the preferment he was afterwards designed for. What God intends men for, he will be sure, some way or other, to qualify them for.

2–3. Those that can separate us from all our friends cannot deprive us of the gracious presence of our God. When Joseph had none of his relations with him, he had his God with him, even in *the house of the Egyptian.* Joseph was banished from his father's house, but *the LORD was with him.* It is God's presence with us that makes all we do *to prosper.* Those that would prosper must therefore make God their friend; and those that do prosper must therefore give God the praise.

6. *He knew not ought he had, save the bread which he did eat.* The servant had all the care and trouble of the estate, the master had only the enjoyment of it; an example not to be imitated by any master, unless he could be sure that he had one like Joseph for a servant.

9. *How can I sin against God?* Not only how shall I do it and sin against my master, my mistress, myself, my own body and soul, but *against God?* Gracious souls look upon this as the worst thing in sin, that it is against God, against his nature and his dominion, against his love and his design. They that love God for this reason hate sin.

10. *He hearkened not to her,* so much as to be *with her.* Those that would be kept from harm must keep themselves out of harm's way.

12. When she laid hold on him, he *left his garment in her hand.* He would not stay to parley with the temptation, but flew out from it with the utmost abhorrence, he *left his garment* as one escaping for his life.

20. Our Lord Jesus, like Joseph, was *bound,* and "numbered with the transgressors."

21. *But the LORD was with Joseph, and shewed him mercy.* God "despiseth not his prisoners" (Ps. 69:33). No gates nor bars can shut out his gracious presence from his people. *God gave him favour in the sight of the keeper of the prison.* God can raise up friends for his people even where they little expect them.

CHAPTER 40

1. We should not have had this story of Pharaoh's butler and baker recorded in Scripture if it had not been serviceable to Joseph's preferment. The world stands for the sake of the church and is governed for its good. Two of the great officers of the court having offended Pharaoh are committed to prison. High places are slippery places; nothing more uncertain than the favor of princes. Those that make God's favor their happiness, and his service their business, will find him a better master than

Pharaoh was, and not so extreme to mark what they do amiss.

6. *They were sad.* It was not the prison that made them sad, they were pretty well used to that. It was the dream. God has more ways than one to sadden the spirits of those that are to be made sad. Those sinners that are hardy enough under outward trouble, yet God can find a way to trouble them and take off their wheels, by wounding their spirits and laying a load upon them.

14–15. See what a modest representation he makes of his own case. He does not reflect upon his brethren that sold him, only faith, *I was stolen away out of the land of the Hebrews.* Nor does he reflect on the wrong done him in this imprisonment by his mistress that was his persecutor, and his master that was his judge, but mildly avers his own innocency. *Here also have I done nothing that they should put me into the dungeon.* When we are called to vindicate ourselves, we should carefully avoid as much as may be speaking ill of others. Let us be content to prove ourselves innocent, and not fond of upbraiding others with their guilt.

CHAPTER 41

9. God's time for the enlargement of his people will appear, at last, to be the fittest time. If the chief butler had at first used his interest for Joseph's enlargement and had obtained, it is probable he would have gone back to the land of the Hebrews, and then he had neither been so blessed himself nor such a blessing to his family. But staying two years longer, and coming out upon this occasion to interpret the king's dreams, way was made for his preferment.

16. He gives honor to God: *It is not in me.* God must give it. Great gifts then appear most graceful and illustrious when those that have them use them humbly and take not the praise of them to themselves, but give it to God.

29. See the goodness of God in sending the seven years of plenty before those of famine, that provision might be made accordingly. How wonderfully wisely has Providence, that great housekeeper, ordered the affairs of this numerous family from the beginning! Great variety of seasons there have been, and the produce of the earth sometimes more, and sometimes less. Yet take one time with another, what was miraculous concerning the manna is ordinarily verified in the common course of Providence. "He that gathers much has nothing over, and he that gathers little has no lack" (Exod. 16:18).

30. See the perishing nature of our worldly enjoyments. The great increase of the years of plenty was quite lost and swallowed up in the years of famine. And the overplus of it, which seemed very much, yet did but just serve to keep men alive.

43–44. Where God had been liberal in giving wisdom and other merits, Pharaoh was not sparing in conferring honors. Now this preferment of Joseph was (1) An abundant recompense for his innocent and patient suffering, a lasting instance of the equity and goodness of Providence, and an encouragement to all to trust in a good God. (2) It was also typical of the exaltation of Christ, that great revealer of secrets (John 1:18), or as some translate Joseph's new name, the "Saviour of the world." The brightest glories of the upper world are upon him, the highest trusts lodged in his hand, and all power given him both in heaven and earth. He is gatherer, keeper, and disposer of all the stores of divine grace, and chief ruler of the kingdom of God among men. The work of ministers is to cry before him, *Bow the knee; kiss the Son.*

CHAPTER 42

2. *Get you down thither.* Masters of families must not only pray for daily bread for their families, but must with care and industry provide it.

7. We may well wonder that Joseph, during the twenty years he had been in Egypt, especially during the last seven years that he had been in power there, never sent to his father to acquaint him with his circumstances. It is strange that he who so often went throughout all the land of Egypt never made a step to Canaan to visit his aged father. When he was in the borders of Egypt that lay next to Canaan, perhaps it would not have been above three or four days' journey in his chariot. It is probable conjecture that his whole management of himself in this affair was by special direction from heaven, that the purpose of God concerning Jacob and his family might be accomplished.

9. He *remembered the dreams.* The laying up of God's oracles in our hearts will be of excellent use to us in all our conduct.

18. *I fear God.* You may assure yourselves, I will do you no wrong, I dare not, for I know that as high as I am, there is one higher than I. With those that *fear God* we have reason to expect fair dealing. The fear of God will be a check upon those that are in power, to restrain them from abusing their power to oppression and tyranny.

21. *We are verily guilty concerning our brother.* We do not read that they said this during their three days' imprisonment. But now when the matter was come to some issue, and they saw themselves still embarrassed, they began to relent. Perhaps Joseph's mention of the fear of God put them upon consideration and extorted this reflection.

24. *He took Simeon.* He chose him for the hostage, probably because he remembered him to have been his most bitter enemy, or because he observed him now to be least humbled and concerned. He bound him *before their eyes,* to affect them all.

28, 30. *Their heart failed them, and they were afraid, saying one to another, What is this that God hath done to us?* They knew that the Egyptians abhorred a Hebrew (43:32), and therefore, since they could not expect to receive any kindness from them, they concluded that this was done with a design to pick a quarrel with them, the rather because the *man, the lord of the land,* had charged them as spies. Their own consciences were awake and their sins set in order before them, and this puts them into confusion. When the events of Providence concerning us are surprising, it is good to enquire what it is that God has done and is doing with us.

38. *My son shall not go down with you.* He plainly intimates a distrust of them, remembering that he never saw Joseph since he had been with them; therefore Benjamin shall not go with you.

CHAPTER 43

9. Judah's conscience had lately smitten him for what he had done a great while ago against Joseph. And as an evidence of the truth of his repentance, he is ready to undertake, as far as a man could do it, for Benjamin's security. He will not only not wrong him, but will do all he can to protect him. This is such restitution as the case will admit. When he knew not how he could retrieve Joseph, he would make some amends for the irreparable injury he had done him by doubling his care concerning Benjamin.

11. *If it must be so now,* take your brother. If no corn can be had but upon those terms, we should as good expose him to the perils of the journey as suffer ourselves and families, and Benjamin among the rest, to perish for want of bread. It is no fault, but our wisdom and duty, to alter our resolutions when there is a good reason for so doing. Constancy is a virtue, but obstinacy is not. It is God's prerogative to make unchangeable resolves.

14. *God Almighty give you mercy before the man.* Jacob had formerly turned an angry brother into a kind one with a present and a prayer, and here he sets himself to the same tried method. Those who would find mercy with men must seek it of God. He concludes all with this, *If I be bereaved of my children, I am bereaved.* If I must part with them thus one after another, I acquiesce and say, The will of the Lord be done.

23. *Your God, and the God of your father, has given you treasure in your sacks.* Hereby he shows that he had no suspicion of dishonesty in them; for what we get by deceit we cannot say God gives it us. It appears, by what he said, that by his master's instructions he was brought to the knowledge of the true God, the God of the Hebrews. He directs them to look up to God and acknowledge his providence in the good bargain they had. We must own ourselves indebted to God as our God, and the God of our fathers (a God in covenant with us and them), for all our successes and advantages and the kindnesses of our friends. Every creature is that to us, and no more, than God makes it to be.

29. *God be gracious unto thee, my son.* Joseph's favor, though he was "the lord of the land" (42:30), would do him little good, unless God were gracious to him.

34. *They drank, and were merry.* Their cares and fears were now over, and they eat their bread with joy, concluding they were now upon good terms with "the man, the lord of the country" (42:33). If God accept our works, our present, we have reason to be cheerful.

CHAPTER 44

16. *God hath found out the iniquity of thy servants.* Referring to the injury they had formerly done to Joseph, for which they thought God was now reckoning with them. Even in afflictions wherein we apprehend ourselves wronged by men, yet we must own that God is righteous and finds out our iniquity. We cannot judge what men are by what they have been formerly, nor what they will do, by what they have done. Age and experience may make men wiser and better. They that had sold Joseph yet would not abandon Benjamin.

18. *Then Judah said.* We have here a most pathetic speech which Judah made to Joseph on Benjamin's behalf. Either Judah was a better friend to Benjamin than the rest, and more solicitous to bring him off; or he thought himself under greater obligations to endeavor it than the rest, because he had passed his word to his father for his safe return. His address, as it is here recorded, is so very natural and so expressive of his present passion that we cannot but suppose Moses, who wrote it so long after, to have written it under the special direction of him that "made man's mouth." A great deal of unaffected art and unstudied rhetoric there is in this speech.

Had Joseph been, as Judah supposed, an utter stranger to the family, yet even common humanity could not but be wrought upon by such powerful reasonings as these; for nothing could be said more moving, more tender. It was enough to melt a heart of stone. But to Joseph, who was nearer akin to Benjamin than Judah himself, and who, at this time, felt a greater passion for him and his aged father than Judah did, nothing could be more pleasingly nor more happily said. Neither Jacob nor Benjamin needed an intercessor with Joseph.

CHAPTER 45

1. Judah and his brethren were waiting for an answer and could not but be amazed to discover, instead of the gravity of a judge, the natural affection of a father or brother. *Cause every man to go out.* The private conversations of friends are the most free. When Joseph would put on love, he puts off state, which it was not fit his servants should witness. Thus Christ graciously manifests himself and his loving-kindness to his people, out of the sight and hearing of the world.

2. Tears were the introduction to his discourse. He had dammed up this stream a great while, and with much ado, but now it swelled so high that he could no longer contain, but he *wept aloud,* so that those whom he had forbid to see him could not but hear him. These were tears of tenderness and strong affection, and with these he threw off that austerity with which he had hitherto carried himself towards his brethren; for he could bear it no longer. This represents the divine compassion towards returning penitents, as much as that of the father of the prodigal (Luke 15:20; Hos. 11:8, 9).

3–4. He abruptly tells them, *I am Joseph.* They knew him only by his Egyptian name, "Zaphnath–paaneah," his Hebrew name being lost and forgot in Egypt. But now he teaches them to call him by Joseph. And that they might not suspect it was another of the same name, he explains himself: *I am Joseph your brother*. This would both humble them yet more for their sin in selling him and encourage them to hope for kind treatment. This word, at first, startled Joseph's brethren; they started back through fear, or at least stood still astonished. But Joseph called kindly and familiarly to them, *Come near, I pray you*. Thus, when Christ manifests himself to his people he encourages them to draw near to him with a true heart.

5. *Be not grieved, nor angry with yourselves.* Sinners must grieve and be angry with themselves for their sins; though God by his power bring good out of them, for that is not thanks to the sinner. But true penitents should be greatly affected with it, when they see God bringing good out of evil. Though we must not with this consideration extenuate our own sins, and so take off the edge of our repentance; yet it may do well thus to extenuate the sins of others, and so take off the edge of our angry resentments. Thus Joseph does here. His brethren needed not to fear that he would revenge upon them an injury which God's providence had made to turn so much to his advantage and that of his family. Now he tells them how long the famine was likely to last, "yet five years" (v. 6), and what a capacity he was in of being kind to his relations, which is the greatest satisfaction that wealth and power can give to a good man.

8. Joseph reckoned that his advancement was not so much designed to save a whole kingdom of Egyptians as to preserve a small family of Israelites; for "the Lord's portion is his people." Whatever goes with others, they shall be secured. How admirable are the projects of Providence! How remote its tendencies! What wheels are there within wheels; and yet all directed by the eyes in the wheels, and the Spirit of the living Creature!

9. *Come down unto me, tarry not.* Our Lord Jesus being, like Joseph, exalted to the highest honors and powers of the upper world, it is his will that all that are his should be with him where he is. This is his commandment, that we be with him now in faith and hope and a heavenly conversation. And this is his promise, that we shall be for ever with him.

24. *See that ye fall not out by the way.* He knew they were but too apt to be quarrelsome; what had lately passed, which revived the remembrance of what they had done formerly against their brother, might give them occasion to quarrel. Now Joseph, having forgiven them all, lays this obligation upon them, not to upbraid one another. This charge our Lord Jesus has given to us, that we love one another, that we live in peace, that whatever occurs, or whatever former occurrences are remembered, we fall not out.

For (1) We are brethren, we have all one father. (2) We are *his brethren;* and we shame our relation to him, who is our peace, if we fall out. (3) We are all guilty, verily guilty, and instead of quarreling with one another, have a great deal of reason to *fall out* with ourselves. (4) We are forgiven of God, whom we have all offended, and therefore should be ready to forgive one another. (5) We are *by the way,* a way that lies through the land of Egypt, where we have many eyes upon us, that seek occasion and advantage against us; a way that leads to Canaan, where we hope to be for ever in perfect peace.

CHAPTER 46

2. *And God spake unto Israel in the visions of the night.* Those who desire to keep up communion with God shall find that it never fails on his side. If we speak to him as we ought, he will not fail to speak to us.

3. *I am God, the God of thy father.* That is, I am what you own me to be. You shall find me a God of divine wisdom and power engaged for you. And you shall find me the *God of thy father,* true to the covenant made with him. It seems that Jacob, upon the first intelligence of Joseph's life and glory in Egypt, resolved without any hesitation, "I will go and see him." Yet upon second thoughts he saw difficulties in it. But whatever his discouragements were, this was enough to answer them all, *Fear not to go down into Egypt.*

4. *I will go down with thee into Egypt.* Those that go where God sends them shall certainly have God with them. *And I will surely bring thee up again.* Though Jacob died in Egypt, yet this promise was fulfilled in the bringing up of his body to be buried in Canaan, and in the bringing up of his seed to be settled in Canaan. Whatever low and darksome valley we are called into, we may be confident that if God go down with us, he will surely bring us up again. If he go with us down to death, he will surely bring us up again to glory.

30. *Now let me die.* Not that it was undesirable to live with Joseph and to see his honor and usefulness; but he had so much satisfaction in this first meeting that he thought it too much to desire or expect any more in this world.

CHAPTER 47

3. *What is your occupation?* Pharaoh takes it for granted they had something to do. All that have a place in the world should have an employment in it according to their capacity, some occupation or other. Those that need not work for their bread yet must have something to do to keep them from idleness.

9. Jacob calls his life a *pilgrimage,* looking upon himself as a stranger in this world and a traveler towards another. He reckoned himself not only a pilgrim now that he was in Egypt, a strange country in which he never was before, but his life even in the land of his nativity was a pilgrimage.

10. *And Jacob blessed Pharaoh.* Which was not only an act of civility but an act of piety. He prayed for him, as one having the authority of a prophet and a patriarch. And a patriarch's blessing was not a thing to be despised, no not by a potent prince.

28. Jacob lived seventeen years after he came into Egypt, far beyond his own expectation. Seventeen years he had nourished Joseph, for so old he was when he was sold from him, and now, seventeen years Joseph nourished him.

29. *And the time drew nigh that Israel must die.* Israel, that had power over the angel and prevailed, yet must yield to death. He died by degrees; his candle was not blown out, but gradually burnt down, so that he saw, at some distance, the time drawing nigh.

CHAPTER 48

7. Mention is made of the death and burial of Rachel, Joseph's mother and Jacob's best beloved wife. The removal of dear relations from us is an affliction, the remembrance of which cannot but abide with us a great while. Strong affections in the enjoyment cause long afflictions in the loss.

16. *The Angel which redeemed me from all evil.* A great deal of hardship he had known in his time, but God had graciously kept him from the evil of his troubles. Christ the angel of the covenant is he that redeems us from all evil.

It becomes the servants of God, when they are old and dying, to witness for our God that they have found him gracious.

19. Ephraim *shall be greater*. God, in bestowing his blessings upon his people, gives more to some than to others, more gifts, graces, and comforts, and more of the good things of this life. And he often gives most to those that are least likely. He chooses the weak things of the world, raises the poor out of the dust. Grace observes not the order of nature, nor does God prefer those whom we think fittest to be preferred, but as it pleaseth him.

21. *I die: but God shall be with you, and bring you again.* These words of Jacob furnish us with comfort in the death of our friends. But God shall be with us, and his gracious presence is sufficient to make up the loss. They leave us, but he will never fail us. He will *bring us to the land of our fathers,* the heavenly Canaan, where our godly fathers are gone before us. If God be with us while we stay behind in this world, and will receive us shortly to be with them that are gone before to a better world, we ought "to sorrow not, even as others which have no hope."

22. It may sometimes be both just and prudent to give some children portions above the rest. But a grave is that which we can most count upon as our own in the earth.

CHAPTER 49

1. *Gather yourselves together.* Let them all be sent for to see their father die and to hear his dying words. We cannot tell our children what shall befall them or their families in this world; but we can tell them, from the word of God, what will befall them in the last day of all, according as they carry themselves in the world.

4. *Thou shalt not excel.* No judge, prophet, or prince is found of the tribe of Reuben, nor any person of renown, only Dathan and Abiram, who were noted for their impious rebellion. That tribe, as not aiming to excel, chose a settlement on the other side of Jordan. The character fastened upon Reuben that he was *unstable as water.* His virtue was unstable, he had not the government of himself and his own appetites. His honor consequently was unstable, it vanished into smoke and became "as water spilt upon the ground." Jacob charges him particularly with the sin for which he was disgraced, *thou wentest up to thy father's bed.* It was forty years ago that he had been guilty of this sin, yet now it is remembered against him. Reuben's sin left an indelible mark of infamy upon his family; a wound not to be healed without a scar.

7. *Cursed be their anger.* We ought always in the expressions of our zeal carefully to distinguish between the sinner and the sin, so as not to love or bless the sin for the sake of the person, nor to hate or curse the person for the sake of the sin.

10. *The sceptre shall not depart from Judah, until Shiloh come.* Much of what is said here concerning Judah is to be applied to our Lord Jesus. (1) He is the ruler of all his Father's children, and the conqueror of all his Father's enemies, and he is the praise of all the saints. (2) He is the "Lion of the tribe of Judah," as he is called (Rev. 5:5), who, having "spoiled principalities and powers," went up a conqueror, and couched so as none can stir him up when he "sat down on the right hand of the Majesty."

(3) To him belong *the sceptre,* he is the *lawgiver,* and *unto him shall the gathering of the people be,* as the "desire of all nations" (Hag. 2:7), who being "lifted up from the earth" should "draw

all men unto him" (John 12:32), and in whom the "children of God" that are scattered abroad should meet as the center of their unity (John 11:52). (4) In him there is plenty of all that which is nourishing and refreshing to the soul, and which maintains and cheers the divine life in it. In him we may have "wine and milk," the riches of Judah's tribe, "without money and without price" (Isa. 55:1).

18. *I have waited for thy salvation, O LORD.* If he must break off here, and his breath will not serve him to finish what he intended, with these words he pours out his soul into the bosom of his God, and even breathes it out. The pious ejaculations of a warm and lively devotion, though sometimes they may be incoherent, yet they are not impertinent; that may be uttered affectionately which does not come in methodically. It is no absurdity, when we are speaking to men, to lift up our hearts to God. The salvation he *waited* for was Christ, the promised seed; and heaven, the better country.

20. The God of nature has provided for us not only necessaries but *dainties,* that we might call him a bountiful benefactor. Yet, whereas all places are competently furnished with necessaries, only some places afford *dainties.* Corn is more common than spices. Were the supports of luxury as universal as the supports of life, the world would be worse than it is.

Among God's Israel there is to be found a great variety of dispositions, yet all contributing to the beauty and strength of the body.

23–24. Herein Joseph was a type of Christ: He was *shot at* and *hated,* but borne up under his sufferings, and was afterwards advanced to be the *shepherd* and *stone.* And of the church in general, hell shoots its arrows against her, but heaven protects and strengthens her.

25. *Even by the God of thy father Jacob, who shall help thee.* Our experiences of God's power and goodness in strengthening us are encouragements still to hope for help from him. He that has helped us, will.

33. *And when Jacob had made an end of commanding of his sons.* He addressed himself to his dying work. He put himself into a posture for dying. Having sat upon the bedside to bless his sons, the spirit of prophecy bringing fresh oil to his expiring lamp, when that work was done, he *gathered up his feet into the bed,* that he might lie along, not only as one patiently submitting to the stroke, but as one cheerfully composing himself to rest. He then freely resigned his spirit into the hand of God, the father of spirit. He *yielded up the ghost,* and his separated soul went to the assembly of the souls of the faithful, who after they are delivered from the burden of the flesh are in joy and felicity. He *was gathered unto his people.*

CHAPTER 50

15. *Joseph will peradventure hate us.* While their father lived, they thought themselves safe under his shadow. But now that he was dead, they feared the worst. A guilty conscience exposes men to continual frights. Those that would be fearless must keep themselves guiltless.

17. We are *the servants of the God of thy father.* Not only children of the same Jacob, but worshippers of the same Jehovah. Though we must be ready to forgive all that injure us, yet we must especially take heed of bearing malice towards any that are *the servants of the God* of our fathers. These we should always treat with a peculiar tenderness, for we and they have the same father.

19. *Am I in the place of God?* He in

his great humility thought they showed him too much respect and says to them in effect, as Peter said to Cornelius, "Stand up; I myself also am a man." Make your peace with God, and then you will find it an easy matter to make your peace with me.

21. *Fear not: I will nourish you.* See what an excellent spirit Joseph was of, and learn of him to render good for evil. He did not tell them they were upon their good behavior and he would be kind to them if he saw they carried themselves well. No, he would not thus hold them in suspense, nor seem jealous of them, though they had been suspicious of him. *He comforted them,* and, to banish all their fears, he *spake kindly unto them.* Those we love and forgive we must not only do well for, but speak kindly to.

24. *I die: and God will surely visit you.* To this purpose Jacob had spoken to him (48:21). Thus must we comfort others with the same comforts wherewith we ourselves have been comforted of God, and encourage them to rest on those promises which have been our support.

26. *He was put in a coffin in Egypt.* But not buried till his children had received their inheritance in Canaan (Josh. 24:32). If the soul does return to its rest with God, the matter is not great, though the deserted body find not at all, or not quickly, its rest in the grave. Yet care ought to be taken of the dead bodies of the saints, in the belief of their resurrection. For there is a covenant with the dust which shall be remembered, and a commandment given concerning the bones.

exodus

CHAPTER 1

10. *Come on, let us deal wisely with them; lest they multiply.* When men deal wickedly, it is common for them to imagine that they deal wisely. But the folly of sin will at last be manifested before all men.

12. *But the more they afflicted them, the more they multiplied.* To the grief and vexation of the Egyptians. Times of affliction have often been the church's growing times. Christianity spread most when it was persecuted.

CHAPTER 2

10. *And he became her son.* Those whom God designs for great services he finds out ways to qualify them. Moses, by having his education in a court, is the fitter to be a prince, and king in Jeshurun. By having his education in a learned court (for such the Egyptian then was), is the fitter to be an historian. And by having his education in the court of Egypt, is the fitter to be employed as an ambassador to that court in God's name.

12. *He slew the Egyptian.* By special warrant from heaven (which makes not a precedent in ordinary cases), Moses slew the Egyptian and rescued his oppressed brother. The Jew's tradition is that he did not slay him with any weapon, but as Peter slew Ananias and Sapphira, with the word of his mouth.

14. He challenged his authority: *Who made thee a prince?* A man needs no great authority for giving a friendly reproof; it is an act of kindness. Yet this man interprets it as act of dominion and represents his reprover as imperious and assuming. Thus, when people are sick of good discourse or a seasonable admonition, they will call it preaching, as if a man could not speak a word for God and against sin, but he took too much upon him.

15. God guided Moses to Midian, because the Midianites were of the seed of Abraham and retained the worship of the true God. This allowed Moses to have not only a safe place, but a comfortable settlement among them. And through this country he was afterwards to lead Israel. He came and *sat down by a well*, tired and thoughtful, waiting to see which way Providence would direct him. It was a great change with him, since he was but the other day at ease in Pharaoh's court.

17. *Stood up and helped them.* He loved to be doing justice and appearing in the defense of such as he saw injured. He loved to be doing good. Wherever the providence of God cast us, we should desire and endeavor to be useful. And when we cannot do the good we would, we must be ready to do the good we can.

21. Now this settlement of Moses in Midian was designed by Providence. To shelter him for the present; God will find hiding places for his people in the day of their distress. It was also designed to prepare him for the services he was further designed to do. Egypt accomplished him for a scholar, a gentleman, a statesman, a soldier, all which accomplishments would be afterwards of use to him. But "yet lacketh he one thing," in which the court of Egypt could not befriend him. He that was to do all by divine revelation must know what it was to live a life of communion with God, and in this he would be greatly furthered by the retirement of a shepherd's life in Midian. By the former he was prepared to rule in Jeshurun, but by the latter he was prepared to converse with God in Mount Horeb. Those that know what it is to be alone with God are acquainted with better delights than ever Moses tasted in the court of Pharaoh.

23. *And they cried.* Before God unbound them, he put it into their hearts to cry unto him. It is a sign God is coming towards us with deliverance when he inclines us to cry to him for it.

24–25. *And God heard their groaning.* The groans of the oppressed cry loud in the ears of the righteous God, to whom vengeance belongs; especially the groans of God's children, the burdens they groan under and the blessings they groan after. *And God looked upon the children of Israel.* Moses looked upon them and pitied them, but now God looked upon them and helped them.

CHAPTER 3

4. *When the LORD saw that he turned aside to see it, God called to him.* If he had

carelessly neglected it, it is likely God would have departed and said nothing to him.

5–6. *Put off thy shoes from off thy feet.* The putting off the shoe was then what the putting off the hat is now, a token of respect and submission. We ought to approach God with a solemn pause and preparation; and to express our inward reverence by a grave and reverent behavior in the worship of God, carefully avoiding every thing that looks light or rude. *And Moses hid his face, for he was afraid to look upon God.* The more we see of God, the more cause we shall see to worship him with reverence and godly fear.

8. *I am come down to deliver them.* This deliverance was typical of our redemption by Christ, and in that the eternal Word did indeed come down from heaven to deliver us.

10. *I will send thee.* And the same hand that now fetched a shepherd out of a desert to be the planter of the Jewish church afterwards fetched fishermen from their ships to be the planters of the Christian church, that the excellency of the power might be of God.

11. *Who am I?* The more fit any person is for service, commonly the less opinion he has of himself.

12. *Certainly I will be with thee.* Those that are weak in themselves yet may do wonders, being strong in the Lord and in the power of his might. God's presence puts wisdom and strength into the weak and foolish and is enough to answer all objections.

14. *I AM THAT I AM.* This explains his name "Jehovah" and signifies (1) That he is self-existent; he has his being of himself, and has no dependence upon any other. Being self-existent he cannot but be self-sufficient, and therefore all-sufficient, and the inexhaustible fountain of being and blessing. (2) That he is eternal and unchangeable, always "the same, yesterday, and to-day, and for ever." He will be what he will be, and what he is. (3) That he is faithful and true to all his promises, unchangeable in his word as well as in his nature, and "not a man, that he should lie."

19. *I am sure he will not let you go.* God sends his messengers to those whose obstinacy he foresees, that it may appear he would have them turn and live.

21–22. *Every woman shall* ask (not borrow!) *jewels. And I will give this people favour in the sight of the Egyptians.* God sometimes makes the enemies of his people not only to be at peace with them, but to be kind to them. And he has many ways of balancing accounts between the injured and the injurious, of righting the oppressed, and of compelling those that have done wrong to make restitution.

CHAPTER 4

8. *The voice of the first sign.* God's works have a voice to speak to us, which we must diligently observe.

10. *O my LORD, I am not eloquent.* He was a great philosopher, statesman, and divine, and yet no orator; a man of a clear head, great thought and solid judgment, but had not a voluble tongue, nor ready utterance. Therefore he thought himself unfit to speak before great men and about great affairs. Moses was "mighty in word" (Acts 7:22) and yet not eloquent. What he said was strong, and to the purpose, and distilled "as the dew" (Deut. 32:2), though he did not deliver himself with that readiness, ease, and fineness that some do.

21. *I will harden his heart.* After he has frequently hardened it himself, willfully shutting his eye against the light, I will at last permit Satan to harden it effectually.

24. It seems the sin of Moses was neglecting to circumcise his son, which perhaps was the effect of his being unequally yoked with a Midianite, who was too indulgent of her child, and Moses so of her. *The LORD met him, and,* probably, by a sword in an angel's hand, *sought to kill him.* This was a great change. Very lately God was conversing with him as a friend and now coming forth against him as an enemy.

26. *So he let him go.* The destroying angel withdrew. But still Zipporah cannot forget, but will unreasonably call Moses *a bloody husband,* because he obliged her to circumcise the child. And upon this occasion (it is probable), he sent them back to his father-in-law, that they might not create him any further uneasiness. When we have special service to do for God, we should remove that as far from us as we can, which is likely to be our hindrance: "let the dead bury their dead," but "follow thou me."

28. *Moses told Aaron all.* Those that are fellow-servants to God in the same work should use a mutual freedom and endeavor rightly and fully to understand one another.

CHAPTER 5

2. *Who is the LORD, that I should obey his voice?* Being summoned to surrender, Pharaoh thus hangs out the flag of defiance. Who is Jehovah? I neither know him nor care of him; neither value nor fear him. It is a hard name that he never heard of before, but he resolves it shall be no bugbear to him. Israel was now a despised, oppressed people, and by the character they bore he makes his estimate of their God, and concludes that he made no better figure among the gods than his people did among the nations.

21. *The LORD look upon you, and*

judge. They should have humbled themselves before God, but instead of that they fly in the face of their best friends. Those that are called to public service for God and their generation must expect to be tried not only by the threats of proud enemies, but by the unjust and unkind censures of unthinking friends.

22. *Wherefore hast thou so evil entreated this people?* Even when God is coming towards his people in ways of mercy, yet sometimes he takes such methods that they may think themselves but ill-treated. When they think so, they should go to God by prayer, and that is the way to have better treatment in God's good time.

CHAPTER 6

6, 8. *I will bring you out: I will rid you: I will redeem you: I will bring you into the land* of Canaan; and *I will give it you.* Let man take the shame of his unbelief, which needs such repetitions, and let God have the glory of his condescending grace, which gives us such repeated assurances.

11. *That he let the children of Israel go.* God repeats his precepts before he begins his punishments. Those who have often been called in vain to leave their sins yet must be called again, and again.

29. *Speak all that I say unto thee.* As a faithful ambassador. Those that go on God's errand must not shun to declare the whole counsel of God.

CHAPTER 7

11. Their rods became serpents; probably by the power of evil angels, artfully substituting serpents in the room of the rods, God permitting the delusion to be wrought for wise and holy ends.

13. *And he hardened Pharaoh's heart.* That is, permitted it to be hardened.

20. *The waters that were in the river were turned to blood.* They had strained the river with the blood of the Hebrew children, and now God made that river all bloody. He gave them "blood to drink, for they were worthy" (Rev. 16:6). See the power of God. Every creature is to us what he makes it to be, water or blood. See the mutability of all things under the sun and what changes we may meet with in them. That which is water today may be blood tomorrow; what is always vain may soon become vexatious. And see what mischievous work sin makes! It is sin that turns our waters into blood.

22. *And the magicians did so.* By God's permission *with their enchantments.*

CHAPTER 8

10. The great design, both of judgments and of mercies, is to convince us that *there is none like unto the LORD our God;* none so wise, so mighty, so good; no enemy so formidable, no friend so desirable, so valuable.

15. *But when Pharaoh saw that there was respite, he hardened his heart.* Observe he did it himself, not God, any otherwise than by not hindering.

19. *This is the finger of God.* The power of God. The devil's agents, when God permitted them, could do great things. But when he laid an embargo upon them, they could do nothing. The magicians' inability in this instance showed whence they had their ability in the former instances, and that they had no power against Moses but what was given them from above. But *Pharaoh's heart was hardened.* By himself and the devil.

20. *Rise up early.* Those that would bring great things to pass for God and their generation must rise early and redeem time in the morning.

24. *There came a grievous swarm of flies.* "The prince of the power of the air" has gloried in being Beel–zebub, the god of flies. But here it is proved that even in that he is a pretender and an usurper. For even with swarms of flies God fights against his kingdom and prevails.

28–29. See how ready God is to accept sinners' submissions. Moses promises immediately, *I will intreat the Lord* for you; and that he might see what the design of the plague was, not to bring him to ruin, but to repentance.

CHAPTER 9

3. *The hand of the Lord.* The hand of God is to be acknowledged even in the sickness and death of cattle, or other damage sustained in them; for a sparrow "shall not fall on the ground without our Father." And his providence is to be acknowledged with thankfulness in the life of the cattle, for he "preservest man and beast" (Ps. 36:6).

6. *But of the cattle of the children of Israel not one died.* Does God take care for oxen? Yes, he does, his providence extends itself to the lowliest of his creatures.

10. *Ashes of the furnace.* Sometimes God shows men their punishment. They had oppressed Israel in the furnaces, and now the ashes of the furnace are made as much a terror to them as ever their taskmasters had been to the Israelites.

12. *And the Lord hardened the heart of Pharaoh.* Before, he had hardened his own heart and resisted the grace of God, and now God justly gave him up to his own heart's lusts, to strong delusions, permitting Satan to blind and harden him. Willful hardness is commonly punished with judicial hardness. Let us dread this as the foremost judgment a man can be under on this side of hell.

16. Providence so ordered it that Moses should have man of such a fierce and stubborn spirit to deal with, to make it a most signal and memorable instance of the power God has to bring down the proudest of his enemies.

33–34. *Moses went out of the city.* Not only for privacy in his communion with God, but to show that he could venture abroad into the field, notwithstanding *the hail* and lightning, knowing that every hailstone had its direction from God. Peace with God makes men thunder-proof, for it is the voice of their father. *And spread abroad his hands unto the Lord.* An outward expression of earnest desire and humble expectation. He prevailed with God, but he could not prevail with Pharaoh; *he sinned yet more, and hardened his heart.* The prayer of Moses opened and shut heaven, like Elijah's. And such is the power of God's "two witnesses" (Rev. 11:6). Yet neither Moses nor Elijah, nor those two witnesses, could subdue the hard hearts of men. Pharaoh was frighted into compliance by the judgment, but when it was over, his convictions vanished.

CHAPTER 10

1. These plagues are standing monuments of the greatness of God, the happiness of the church, and the sinfulness of sin. They are standing monitors to the children of men in all ages, not to "provoke the Lord to jealousy" nor to "strive with their Maker." The benefit of these instructions to the world does sufficiently balance the expense.

10. *Let the Lord be so with you, as I will let you go, and your little ones.* Satan does all he can to hinder those that serve God themselves from bringing their children in to serve him. He is a sworn enemy to early piety, knowing how destructive it is to the interests of his kingdom.

17. Pharaoh desires their prayers that *this death only* might be taken away, not this *sin*. He deprecates the plague of locusts, not the plague of a hard heart.

21. It was a total darkness. We have reason to think, not only that the lights of heaven were clouded, but that all their fires and candles were put out by the damp or clammy vapors which were the cause of this darkness. It was also a darkness which might *be felt*, felt in its causes by their finger-ends, so thick were the fogs, felt in its effects (some think) by their eyes which were pricked with pain, and made the more so by their rubbing them.

He poured upon them the fierceness of his anger by sending evil angels among them. Those to whom the devil has been a deceiver, he will at length be a terror.

CHAPTER 11

5. The death of the *firstborn* had been threatened (4:23) but this is at last executed, and less judgments tried which, if they had done the work, would have prevented this. See how slow God is to wrath, and how willing to be met in the way of his judgments, and to have his anger turn away!

8. His proud heart would not yield, no, not to save all the firstborn of his kingdom. Moses was here provoked to a holy indignation, being grieved, as our Savior afterwards, for the "hardness of his heart" (Mark 3:5)

CHAPTER 12

3–14. There was much of the gospel in this ordinance. The paschal lamb was typical. (1) Christ is "our passover" (I Cor. 5:7) and is "the Lamb of God" (John 1:29). (2) It was to be *a male of the first year;* in its prime. Christ offered up himself in the midst of his days. It notes the strength and sufficiency of the Lord Jesus, on whom our help was laid. (3) It was to be *without blemish,* noting the purity of the Lord Jesus, a lamb "without spot" (I Peter 1:19). (4) It was to be set apart four days before, noting the designation of the Lord Jesus to be a Savior, both in the purpose and in the promise. It is observable that as Christ was crucified at the Passover, so he solemnly entered into Jerusalem four days before, the very day that the paschal lamb was set apart.

(5) It was to be slain and *roasted with fire,* noting the exquisite sufferings of the Lord Jesus, even unto death, "the death of the cross." (6) It was to be killed by the whole congregation between the two evenings, that is, between three o'clock and six. Christ suffered in the latter "end of the world" (Heb. 9:26) by the hand of the Jews, the "whole multitude of them" (Luke 23:1, 18). (7) Not *a bone* of it must be broken (v. 46), which is expressly said to be fulfilled in Christ (John 19:33, 36).

The sprinkling of the blood was typical. (1) It was not enough that the blood of the lamb was shed, but it must be sprinkled, noting the application of the merits of Christ's death to our souls. (2) It was to be sprinkled upon the *door posts,* noting the open profession we are to make of faith in Christ, and obedience to him. The mark of the beast may be received in the forehead, or in the right hand (Rev. 13:16), but the seal of the lamb is always in the forehead (Rev. 7:3). (3) The blood thus sprinkled was a means of the preservation of the Israelites from the destroying angel. If the blood of Christ be sprinkled upon our consciences, it will be our protection from the wrath of God, the curse of the law, and the damnation of hell.

The solemn eating of the lamb was typical of our gospel duty to Christ. (1) The paschal lamb was killed not to be looked upon only, but to be fed upon. So we must by faith make Christ ours, as we do that which we eat, and we must receive spiritual strength and nourishment from him, as from our food, and have delight in him, as we have in eating and drinking when we are hungry or thirsty. (2) It was to be all eaten. Those that, by faith, feed upon Christ must feed upon a whole Christ. They must take Christ and his yoke, Christ and his cross, as well as Christ and his crown. (3) It was eaten *with bitter herbs*, in remembrance of the bitterness of their bondage in Egypt. We must feed upon Christ with brokenness of heart, in remembrance of sin. (4) It was to be eaten in a departing posture (v. 11). When we feed upon Christ by faith, we must sit loose to the world and every thing in it.

The feast of *unleavened bread* was typical of the Christian life (I Cor. 5:7–8). Having received Christ Jesus the Lord, (1) We must keep a feast, in holy joy, continually delighting ourselves in Christ Jesus. If true believers have not a continual feast, it is their own fault. (2) It must be a feast of unleavened bread, kept in charity, without the leaven of malice, and in sincerity, without the leaven of hypocrisy. All the old leaven of sin must be put far from us, with the utmost caution, if we would keep the feast of a holy life to the honor of Christ. (3) It was to be *an ordinance for ever*. As long as we live we must continue feeding upon Christ and rejoicing in him always, with thankful mention of the great things he has done for us.

33. *We be all dead men.* When death comes unto our houses, it is seasonable for us to think of our own mortality.

38. *And a mixed multitude went up also with them.* Some perhaps willing to leave their country, because it was laid waste by the plagues. But probably the greatest part was but a rude unthinking mob that followed they knew not why. It is likely when they understood that the children of Israel were to continue forty years in the wilderness, they quit them and returned to Egypt again.

40. *Four hundred and thirty years.* So long the promise God made to Abraham lay dormant and unfulfilled. But now it revived, and things began to work towards the accomplishment of it. The first day of the march of Abraham's seed towards Canaan was four hundred and thirty years (it should seem, to a day) from the promise made to Abraham (Gen. 12:2), "I will make of thee a great nation."

42. This first Passover night was a *night of the LORD, to be much observed.* But the last Passover night, in which Christ was betrayed, was a night of the Lord, much more to be observed, when a yoke heavier than that of Egypt was broke from off our necks, and a land better than that of Canaan set before us. That was a temporal deliverance, to be celebrated *in their generations;* this an eternal redemption to be celebrated world without end.

47. *All the congregation of Israel shall keep it.* And so the new testament passover, the Lord's Supper, ought not to be neglected by any that are capable of celebrating it.

48. No *stranger* that was *uncircumcised* might eat of it. Neither may any now approach the Lord's Supper who have not first submitted to baptism. Nor shall any partake of the benefit of Christ's sacrifice who are not first circumcised in heart.

CHAPTER 13

7. There shall no leavened bread be seen . . . in all thy quarters. Accordingly the Jewish usage was, before the Feast of the Passover, to cast all the leavened bread out of their houses. Either they burnt it, or buried it, or broke it small and threw it into the wind. They searched diligently with lighted candles in all the corners of their houses, lest any leaven should remain. The strictness enjoined in this matter was designed to make the feast the more solemn, and consequently the more taken notice of by the children, who would ask, why is so much ado made? Also, it was designed to teach us how solicitous we should be to put away from us all sin.

17–18. There were many reasons why God led them *through the way of the wilderness of the Red sea.* The Egyptians were to be drowned in the Red Sea, the Israelites were to be humbled and proved in the wilderness (Deut. 8:2). The reason why God did not lead them the nearest way, which would have brought them in a few days to *the land of the Philistines,* was because they were not yet fit for war, much less for war with the Philistines. Their spirits were broken with slavery. The Philistines were formidable enemies. It was convenient they should begin with the Amalekites and be prepared for the wars of Canaan by experiencing the difficulties of the wilderness. God is said to bring Israel out of Egypt as the eagle brings up her young ones (Deut. 32:11), teaching them by degrees to fly.

21. *The LORD went before them.* The Shekinah, or appearance of the divine Majesty, which was a previous manifestation of the eternal Word, who in the fullness of time was to be "made flesh, and dwelt among us." Christ was with the church in the wilderness (I Cor. 10:9). They need not fear missing their way who were thus led, nor being lost who were thus directed. They need not fear being benighted who were thus illuminated, nor being robbed who were thus protected. And they who make the glory of God their end, and the word of God their rule, the Spirit of God the guide of their affections, and the providence of God the guide of their affairs may be confident that the Lord goes before them, as truly as he went before Israel in the wilderness, though not so sensibly.

The pillar *led them the way* in the vast howling wilderness, where there was no road, no track, no way-marks through which they had no guides. When they marched, this pillar went before them, at the rate that they could follow, and appointed the place of their encampment, as infinite Wisdom saw fit. This eased them from care, and secured them from danger, both in moving and in resting. It sheltered them from the heat by day, which at sometimes of the year was extreme. And it gave them light by night when they had occasion for it.

22. He *took not away the pillar of the cloud.* It was a cloud which the wind could not scatter. There was something spiritual in this pillar of cloud and fire. The children of Israel were "baptized unto Moses" in this cloud (I Cor. 10:2). Protection draws allegiance; this cloud was the badge of God's protection, and so became the bond of their allegiance. And it signifies the special conduct and protection which the church of Christ is under in this world.

CHAPTER 14

2, 10. *They were sore afraid.* They knew the strength of the enemy, and their own weakness. Numerous indeed they were, but all on foot, unarmed, undisciplined, dispirited by long servitude, and now pent up, so that they could not escape. On one hand was *Pi–hahiroth,* a range of craggy rocks impassable. On the other hand were *Migdol* and *Baal–zephon,* forts upon the frontiers of Egypt. Before them was the sea, behind them were the Egyptians. So that there was no way open for them but upwards, and thence their deliverance came.

13–14. *Fear ye not.* It is our duty, when we cannot get out of our troubles, yet to get above our fears, so that they may only serve to quicken our prayers and endeavors, but may not prevail to silence our faith and hope. *Stand still,* and think not to save yourselves either by fighting or flying. Wait God's orders, and observe them. Compose yourselves, by an entire confidence in God, into a peaceful prospect of the great salvation God is now about to work for you. *Hold your peace;* you need not so much as give a shout against the enemy. The work shall be done without any concurrence of yours. In times of great difficulty, it is our wisdom to keep our spirits calm, quiet, and sedate, for then we are in the best frame both to do our own work and to consider the work of God.

15–16. *Wherefore criest thou unto me?* We read not of one word he said in prayer, but he lifted up his heart to God, and God well understood and took notice of it. Moses' silent prayer prevailed more with God than Israel's loud outcries. Moses bid them stand still and expect orders from God: and now orders are given. They thought they must have been directed either to the right hand or to the left. No, believe God, speak to them to go forward, directly to the seaside; as if there had lain a fleet of transport ships ready for them to embark in. Let the children of Israel go as far as they can upon dry ground, and then God will *divide* the sea. The same power could have congealed the waters for them to pass over, but infinite wisdom chose rather to divide the waters for them to pass through, for that way of salvation is always pitched upon which is most humbling.

20. The word and providence of God have a black and dark side towards sin and sinners, but a bright and pleasant side towards those who are Israelites indeed.

21. It was a bay, or gulf, or arm of the sea, two or three leagues over. The God of nature has not tied himself to its laws, but when he pleases, dispenses with them, and then the fire does not burn, nor the water flow. This march through the sea was in the night, and not a moonshine night, for it was seven days after the full moon, so that they had no light but what they had from the pillar of fire. This made it the more awful. But where God leads us, he will light us. While we follow his conduct we shall not lack his comforts.

25. They had driven furiously, but now they *drove heavily* and found themselves embarrassed at every step. The way grew deep, their hearts grew sad, their wheels dropped off, and the axletrees failed. They had been flying upon the back of Israel as the hawk upon the dove; but now they cried, *Let us flee from the face of Israel.*

27. Now God got him "honour upon Pharaoh" (v. 17), a rebel to God and a slave to his own barbarous passions. Perfectly lost to humanity, virtue, and all true honor. Here he lies buried in the deep, a perpetual monument of divine justice. Here he went down to the pit, though he was the terror of the mighty in the land of the living.

30. *And Israel saw the Egyptians dead*

upon the sea shore. The Egyptians were very curious in preserving the bodies of their great men, but here the utmost contempt is poured upon all the grandees of Egypt. See how they lie heaps upon heaps, as dung upon the face of the earth.

31. And Israel *feared the* LORD, *and believed the* LORD, *and his servant Moses*. Now they were ashamed of their distrusts and murmurings. And in the mind they were in, they would never again despair of help from heaven; no, not in the greatest straits! They would never again quarrel with Moses, nor talk of returning to Egypt. How well were it for us if we were always in as good a frame as we are in sometimes!

CHAPTER 15

1. *Then sang Moses*. By this instance it appears that the singing of psalms, as an act of religious worship, was used in the church of Christ before the giving of the ceremonial law; therefore it is no part of it, nor abolished with it. Singing is as much the language of holy joy as praying is of holy desire.

25. *And he cried unto the* LORD. It is the greatest relief of the cares of magistrates and ministers, when those under their charge make them uneasy, that they may have recourse to God by prayer. He is the guide of the church's guides, and to the chief shepherd the undershepherds must on all occasions apply themselves.

CHAPTER 16

3. None talk more absurdly than murmurers.

15. *It is manna*. Manna descended from the clouds. It was pleasant food. The Jews say it was palatable to all. It was wholesome food, light of digestion. By this spare and plain diet we are all taught a lesson of temperance, and forbidden to desire dainties and varieties.

19. *Let no man leave of it till the morning*. But let them learn to go to bed and sleep quietly, though they had not a bit of bread in their tent, nor in all their camp, trusting God with the following day to bring them their "daily bread." Never was there such a market of provisions as this, where so many hundred thousand men were daily furnished "without money, and without price." Never was there such an open house kept as God kept in the wilderness for forty years together, nor such free and plentiful entertainment given. And the same wisdom, power, and goodness that now brought food daily out of the clouds does in the constant course of nature bring food yearly out of the earth and gives us "all things richly to enjoy."

34. The manna is called "spiritual meat" (I Cor. 10:3) because it was typical of spiritual blessings. Christ himself is the true manna, the bread of life, of which that was a figure (John 6:49–51). The word of God is the manna by which our souls are nourished (Matt. 4:4). The comforts of the Spirit are "hidden manna" (Rev. 2:17). These comforts from heaven, as the manna did, are the support of the divine life in the soul while we are in the wilderness of this world. It is food for Israelites, for those only that follow the pillar of cloud and fire. It is to be gathered. Christ in the word is to be applied to the soul, and the means of grace used. We must every one of us gather for ourselves. There was manna enough for all, enough for each, and none had too much. So in Christ there is a complete sufficiency, and no superfluity. But they that did eat manna hungered again, died at last, and with many of them God was not well pleased. Whereas they that feed on Christ by faith shall never hunger and shall die no more, and with them God will be for ever well pleased. The Lord evermore give us this bread!

CHAPTER 17

1. They journeyed *according to the commandment of the LORD,* led by the pillar of cloud and fire, and yet they came to a place where there was *no water for them to drink.* We may be in the way of our duty and yet meet with troubles, which Providence brings us into for the trial of our faith.

5. *Go on before the people.* Though they spoke of stoning him. O the wonderful patience and forbearance of God towards provoking sinners! He maintains those that are at war with him and reaches out the hand of his bounty to those that lift up the heel against him. God showed his care of his people in giving them water when they wanted it. He showed his own power in fetching it out of a rock and put an honor upon Moses in appointing the water to flow out upon his smiting of the rock. This fair water that came out of the rock is called "honey and oil" (Deut. 32:13) because the people's thirst made it doubly pleasant, coming when they were in extreme want.

Let this direct us to live in a dependency upon God's providence even in the greatest straits and difficulties. And upon Christ's grace, "that Rock was Christ" (I Cor. 10:4). The graces and comforts of the Spirit are compared to "rivers of living water" (John 7:38). These flow from Christ, and nothing will supply the needs and satisfy the desires of a soul but water out of this rock.

9. *I will stand on the top of the hill with the rod of God in mine hand.* See how God qualifies his people for and calls

them to various services for the good of his church; Joshua fights, Moses prays, and both minister to Israel.

11. The church's cause is ordinarily more or less successful, according as the church's friends are more or less fervent in prayer.

14. In the name of our God we must always lift up our banners. He that does all the work should have all the praise. *Write this for a memorial.* This is the first mention of writing we find in Scripture; and perhaps the command was not given until after the writing of the law on tables of stone.

CHAPTER 18

12. And they did eat bread *before God.* Soberly, thankfully, in the fear of God; and their talk such as became saints. Thus we must eat and drink to the glory of God; as those that believe God's eye is upon us.

24. *So Moses hearkened to the voice of his father-in-law.* When he came to consider the thing, he saw the reasonableness of it and resolved to put it in practice, which he did soon after, when he had received directions from God. Those are not so wise as they would be thought to be, who think themselves too wise to be counseled; for "a wise man will hear, and will increase learning," and not slight good counsel, though given by an inferior.

CHAPTER 19

4. *Ye have seen what I did unto the Egyptians, and how I bare you on eagles' wings.* An high expression of the wonderful tenderness God showed for them. It notes great speed. God not only came upon the wing for their deliverance, but he hastened them out, as it were upon the wing. Also that he did it with great ease, with the strength as well as the swiftness of an eagle. They that "faint not," nor are "weary," are said to "mount up with wings as eagles" (Isa. 40:31). Especially it notes God's particular care of them and affection to them. Even Egypt was the nest in which these young ones were first formed as the embryo of a nation. When by the increase of their numbers they grew to some maturity, they were carried out of that nest.

5. *Then ye shall be a peculiar treasure to me.* Not that God was enriched by them, as a man is by his treasure, but he was pleased to value and esteem them as a man does his treasure. They were precious in his sight. He took them under his special care and protection, as a treasure that is kept under lock and key. He distinguished them from and dignified them above all people, as a people devoted to him and to his service.

6. *A kingdom of priests, a holy nation.* Thus all believers are, through Christ, made to our God "kings and priests" (Rev. 1:6), "a chosen generation, a royal priesthood" (I Peter 2:9).

10. *Sanctify* the people. As Job before sent and sanctified his sons (Job 1:5). *Sanctify them,* that is, call them off from their worldly business and call them to religious exercises, meditation, and prayer, that they may receive the law from God's mouth with reverence and devotion. Two things particularly were prescribed as instances of their preparation: (1) In token of cleaning of themselves from all sinful pollutions, they must *wash their clothes.* Not that God regards our clothes, but while they were washing their clothes, he would have them think of washing their souls by repentance. It becomes us to appear in clean clothes when we wait upon great men; so clean hearts are required in our attendance on the great God. (2) In token of their devoting themselves

entirely to religious exercises, upon this occasion they must abstain even from lawful enjoyments during these days and not come at their wives (v. 15).

13. *The trumpet soundeth long.* Then let them take their places at the foot of the mount. Never was so great a congregation called together and preached to at once as this was here. No one man's voice could have reached so many, but the voice of God did.

CHAPTER 20

1. *God spake all these words.* The law of the Ten Commandments is a law of God's making; a law of his own speaking. God has many ways of speaking to the children of men by his Spirit, conscience, providences; his voice in all which we ought carefully to attend to. But he never spoke at any time upon any occasion so as he spoke the Ten Commandments, which therefore we ought to hear with "the more earnest heed." This law God had given to man before, it was written in his heart by nature. But sin had so defaced that writing that it was necessary to revive the knowledge of it.

2. *I am the* LORD *thy God.* Herein God asserts his own authority to enact this law; and proposes himself as the sole object of that religious worship which is enjoined in the four first commandments. They are here bound to obedience: (1) Because God is the Lord, Jehovah, self-existent, independent, eternal, and the fountain of all being and power. Therefore he has an incontestable right to command us. (2) He was their God, a God in covenant with them. Their God by their own consent. (3) He had brought them *out of the land of Egypt.* Therefore they were bound in gratitude to obey him, because he had brought them out of a grievous slavery into a glorious liberty.

By redeeming them, he acquired a further right to rule them. They owed their service to him to whom they owed their freedom. And thus, Christ, having rescued us out of the bondage of sin, is entitled to the best service we can do him. The four first commandments concern our duty to God (commonly called the first table). It was fit those should be put first, because man had a Maker to love before he had a neighbor to love, and justice and charity are then only acceptable to God when they flow from the principles of piety.

3. The first commandment is concerning the object of our worship, Jehovah, and him only, *Thou shalt have no other gods before me.* The Egyptians and other neighboring nations had many gods, creatures of their own fancy. This law was fixed because of that transgression. And Jehovah being the God of Israel, they must entirely cleave to him, and no other, either of their own invention or borrowed from their neighbors. The sin against this commandment, of which we are most in danger, is giving that glory to any which is due to God only. Pride makes a God of ourselves, covetousness makes a God of money, sensuality makes a God of the belly. Whatever is loved, feared, delighted in, or depended on, more than God, of that we make a god. This prohibition includes a precept which is the foundation of the whole law, that we take the Lord for our God, accept him for ours, adore him with humble reverence, and set our affections entirely upon him. There is a reason intimated in the last words *before me*. It intimates (1) That we cannot have any other god but he will know it. (2) That it is a sin that dares him to his face, which he cannot, will not, overlook.

4–5. The second commandment is concerning the ordinances of worship, or the way in which God will be worshipped, which it is fit he himself should appoint. Here is the prohibition: we are forbidden to worship even the true God by images. First, the Jews (at least after the Captivity) thought themselves forbidden by this to make *any image* or picture whatsoever. It is certain it forbids making any image of God, for to whom can we liken him? (Isa **40**:18, 25). It also forbids us to make images of God in our fancies, as if he were a man as we are. Our religious worship must be governed by the power of faith, not by the power of imagination.

Secondly, they must not *bow down to them,* show any sign of honor to them, much less *serve them* by sacrifice or any other act of religious worship. When they paid their devotion to the true God, they must not have any image before them for the directing, exciting, or assisting their devotion. Though the worship was designed to terminate in God, it would not please him if it came to him through an image. The best and most ancient lawgivers among the heathen forbad that setting up of images in their temples. It was forbidden in Rome by Numa, a pagan prince, yet commanded on Rome by the pope, a Christian bishop. The use of images in the church of Rome, at this day, is so plainly contrary to the letter of this command that in all their catechisms, which they put into the hand of the people, they leave out this commandment, joining the reason of it to the first, and so the third commandment they call the second, the fourth the third, and so on, only to make up the number ten by dividing the tenth into two.

For I the LORD, Jehovah, *thy God am a jealous God,* especially in things of this nature. It intimates the care he has of his own institutions, his displeasure against idolaters, and that he resents every thing in his worship that looks like or leads to idolatry. *Showing mercy unto thousands* of persons, thousands of generations, *of them that love me, and keep my commandments.* As the first commandment requires the inward worship of love, desire, joy, hope, so this requires the outward worship of prayer and praise and solemn attendance on this word. This mercy shall extend to *thousands,* much further than the wrath threatened to those that hate him, for that reaches but to the third or fourth generation.

7. The third commandment is concerning the manner of our worship. We have a strict prohibition: *Thou shalt not take the name of the* LORD *thy God in vain.* Supposing that, having taken Jehovah for their God, they would make mention of his name, this command gives a caution not to mention it *in vain,* and it is still as needful as ever. We take God's name in vain, first, by hypocrisy, making profession of God's name but not living up to that profession. Secondly, by covenant breaking. If we make promises to God and perform not to the Lord our vows, we take his name in *vain.* Thirdly, by rash swearing, mentioning the name of God or any of his attributes in the form of an oath, without any just occasion for it, but to no purpose, or to no good purpose. Fourthly, by false-swearing, which some think is chiefly intended in the letter of the commandment.

Fifth, by using the name of God lightly and carelessly. The profanation of the form of devotion is forbidden, as well as the profanation of the forms of swearing. As also, the profanation of any of those things whereby God makes himself known. *For the* LORD *will not hold him guiltless.* Magistrates that punish other offenses may not think

themselves concerned to take notice of this. But God, who is jealous for his honor, will not connive at it. The sinner may perhaps hold himself guiltless and think there is no harm in it, but God will not *hold him guiltless.* And more is implied, that God will himself be the avenger of those that take his name in vain; and they will find it "a fearful thing to fall into the hands of the living God."

8, 10. The fourth commandment concerns the time of worship. God is to be served and honored daily, but one day in seven is to be particularly dedicated to his honor and spent in his service. *Remember the sabbath day, to keep it holy; . . . in it thou shalt not do any work.* It is taken for granted that the sabbath was instituted before. We read of God's blessing and sanctifying a seventh day from the beginning (Gen. 2:3), so that this was not the enacting of a new law, but the reviving of an old law. First, they are told that is the day they must observe, a seventh after six days' labor. Whether this was the seventh by computation from the first seventh, or from the day of their coming out of Egypt, or both, is not certain. Secondly, they are told how it must be observed. (1) As a day of rest; they were to do no manner of work on this day in their worldly business. (2) As a holy day, set apart to the honor of the holy God, and to be spent in holy exercises. God, by his blessing it, had made it holy; they, by solemnly blessing him, must *keep it holy* and not alienate it to any other purpose than that for which the difference between it and other days was instituted.

Thirdly, who must observe it? *Thou* and *thy son* and *thy daughter.* The wife is not mentioned, because she is supposed to be one with the husband and present with him, and if he sanctify the sabbath, it is taken for granted she will join with him. But the rest of the family is instanced in it; children and servants must keep it according to their age and capacity. In this, as in other instances of religion, it is expected that masters of families should take care, not only to serve the Lord themselves, but that their houses also should serve him. Even the proselyted *strangers* must observe a difference between this day and other days, which, if it laid some restraint upon them then, yet proved a happy indication of God's gracious design, to bring the Gentiles into the church. By the sanctification of the sabbath, the Jews declared that they worshipped the God that made the world, and so distinguished themselves from all other nations, who worshipped gods which they themselves made.

11. God has given us an example of rest after six days of work; he *rested the seventh day*. He took a complacency in himself and rejoiced in the work of his hand, to teach us on that day to take a complacency in him and to give him the glory of his works. The sabbath began in the finishing of the work of creation; so will the everlasting sabbath begin in the finishing of the work of providence and redemption. We observe the weekly sabbath in expectation of that, as well as in remembrance of the former. He has himself *blessed the sabbath day, and hallowed it*. He has put an honor upon it; it is holy to the Lord, and honorable; and he encouraged us to expect from him in the religious observation of that day. Let us not profane, dishonor, and level that with common time what God's blessing has thus dignified and distinguished.

12. We have here the laws of the second table, commonly called the six last commandments, which concern our duty to ourselves and one another, and are a comment upon the second great commandment, "Thou shalt love thy neighbour as thyself." As religion towards God is an essential branch of universal righteousness, so righteousness towards men is an essential branch of true religion. Godliness and honesty must go together. The fifth commandment is concerning the duties we owe to our relations; that of children to their parents is only instanced in *honour thy father and thy mother,* which includes: (1) An inward esteem of them, outwardly expressed upon all occasions in our carriage towards them; "fear" them (Lev. 19:3), "give them reverence" (Heb. 12:9). The contrary to this is mocking at them or despising them. (2) Obedience to their lawful commands; so it is expounded (Eph. 6:1–3), "Children, obey your parents." Come when they call you, go where they send you, do what they bid you, do not what they forbid you; and this cheerfully and from a principle of love. Though you have said you will not, yet afterwards repent and obey.

(3) Submission to their rebukes, instructions, and corrections, not only to the good and gentle, but also to the froward. (4) Disposing of themselves with the advice, direction, and consent of parents, not alienating their property, but with their approbation. (5) Endeavoring in everything to be the comfort of their parents and to make their old age easy to them; maintaining them if they stand in need of support.

13. *Thou shalt not kill.* Thou shalt not do any thing hurtful to the health or life of your own body, or any other's. This does not forbid our own necessary defense, or the magistrates putting offenders to death; but it forbids all malice and hatred to any, for he that "hateth his brother is a murderer."

14. *Thou shalt not commit adultery.* This commandment forbids all acts of uncleanness, with all those desires which produce those acts and war against the soul.

15. *Thou shalt not steal.* This command forbids us to rob ourselves of what we have, by sinful spending, or of the use and comfort of it by sinful sparing; and to rob others by invading our neighbor's rights, taking his goods, or house, or field, forcibly or clandestinely, over-reaching in bargains, not restoring what is borrowed or found, withholding just debts, rents, or wages. And, which is worst of all, to rob the public in the coin or revenue, or that which is dedicated to the service of religion.

16. *Thou shalt not bear false witness.* This forbids speaking falsely in any matter, lying, equivocating, and in any way devising and designing to deceive our *neighbour.* Also, speaking unjustly against our neighbor to the prejudice of his reputation. And (which is the highest offense of both these kinds put together), bearing false witness against him, laying to his charge things that he knows not, either upon oath, by which the third commandment, the sixth, or eighth as well as this are broken. Or in common conversation, slandering, backbiting, tale-bearing, aggravating what is done amiss, and any way endeavoring to raise our own reputation upon the ruin of our neighbor's.

17. *Thou shalt not covet.* The foregoing commands implicitly forbid all desire of doing that which will be an injury to our neighbor; this forbids all inordinate desire of having that which will be a gratification to ourselves. O that such a man's house were mine! Such a man's wife mine! Such a man's estate mine! This is certainly the language of discontent at our own lot, and envy at our neighbor's, and these are the sins principally forbidden here. God give us all to see our face in the glass of this law, and to lay our hearts under the government of it!

20. *Fear not.* That is, Think not that this thunder and fire is designed to consume you. No, it was intended to prove them, to try how they would like dealing with God immediately, without a mediator, and so to convince them how admirably well God had chosen for them in putting Moses into that office. Ever since Adam fled upon hearing God's voice in the garden, sinful man could not bear either to speak to God or hear from him immediately. This was also intended to keep them to their duty and prevent their sinning against God. We must not fear with amazement; but we must always have in our minds a reverence of God's majesty, a dread of his displeasure, and an obedient regard to his sovereign authority.

CHAPTER 21

1. The first verse is the general title of the laws contained in this and the two following chapters. These laws are called *judgments* because their magistrates were to give judgment according to them.

24. *Eye for eye.* The execution of this law is not put into the hands of private persons, as if every man might avenge himself, which would introduce universal confusion. But magistrates had an eye to this rule in punishing offenders and doing right to those that are injured.

CHAPTER 22

6. Men must suffer for their carelessness, as well as for their malice. It will make us very careful of ourselves if we consider that we are accountable not only for the hurt we do, but for the hurt we occasion through inadvertency.

14. Learn hence to be very careful not to abuse any thing that is lent to us. It is not only unjust, but base and disingenuous, we should much rather choose to lose ourselves, than that any should sustain loss by kindness to us.

17. *If her father utterly refuse,* he shall pay money. This shows how ill a thing it is, and by no means to be allowed, that children should marry without their parents' consent.

18. Witchcraft not only gives that honor to the devil which is due to God alone, but bids defiance to the divine providence, wages war with God's government, and puts his work into the devil's hand, expecting him to do good and evil.

21. Those that have themselves been in poverty and distress, if Providence enrich and enlarge them, ought to show a particular tenderness towards those that are now in such circumstances as they were in formerly, now doing to them as they then wished to be done by.

25. *If thou lend.* This law, in the strictness of it, seems to have been peculiar to the Jewish state. But in the equity of it, it obliges us to show mercy to those we have advantage against, and to be content to share with those we lend to in less as well as profit, if Providence cross them. And upon this condition it seems as lawful to receive interest for my money, which another takes pains with and improves, as it is to receive rent for my land, which another takes pains with and improves, for his own use.

29. *The firstborn of thy sons shalt thou give unto me.* And much more reason have we to give ourselves and all we have to God, who "spared not his own Son, but delivered him up for us all."

CHAPTER 23

1. Sometimes we cannot avoid hearing *a false report,* but we must not receive it, we must not hear it with pleasure, nor easily give credit to it.

2. *Thou shalt not follow a multitude to do evil.* General usage will never excuse us in any ill practice. Nor is the broad way ever safer for its being crowded. We must inquire what we ought to do, not what the most do. We must be judged by our master, not our fellowservants. It is too great a compliment to be willing to go to hell for company.

13. *In all things that I have said unto you be circumspect.* We are in danger of missing our way on the right hand and on the left, and it is at our peril if we do, therefore we have need to look about us. A man may ruin himself through carelessness, but he cannot save himself without great care and circumspection. Particularly since idolatry was a sin they were much addicted to, and would be greatly tempted to, they must endeavor to blot out the remembrance of the gods of the heathen, and must disuse all their superstitious forms of speech, and never mention them but with detestation. In Christian schools and academies (for it is in vain to think of reforming the playhouses) it were to be wished that the names and stories of the heathen deities or demons rather were not so commonly and familiarly used.

CHAPTER 24

4. *And Moses wrote all the words of the* LORD. That there might be no mistake; as God dictated them on the mount, where, it is highly probable, God taught him the use of letters. These Moses taught the Israelites, from whom they afterwards traveled to Greece and other nations. As soon as God had separated to himself a peculiar people, he governed them by a written word, as he has done ever since, and will do while the world stands.

6. *The blood* of the sacrifice which the people offered was (part of it) *sprinkled* *on the altar,* which signified the people's dedicating themselves to God and his honor. Thus our Lord Jesus, the Mediator of the new covenant (of whom Moses was a type) having offered up himself a sacrifice upon the cross, that his blood might be indeed the blood of the covenant, sprinkled it upon the altar in his intercession (Heb. 9:12) and sprinkles it upon his church by his word and ordinances and the influences and operations of the Spirit of promise, by whom we are sealed.

16. *A cloud covered the mount six days.* A visible token of God's special presence there, for he so shows himself to us, as at the same time to conceal himself from us, he lets us know so much as to assure us of his power and grace, but intimates to us that we cannot find him out to perfection.

CHAPTER 25

9. When Moses was to describe the creation of the world, though it be such a stately and curious fabric, yet he gave a very short and general account of it. But when he comes to describe the tabernacle, he does it with the greatest niceness and accuracy imaginable. For God's church and instituted religion is more precious to him than all the rest of the world. And the Scriptures were written not to describe to us the works of nature (a general view of which is sufficient to lead us to the knowledge of the Creator), but to acquaint us with the methods of grace and those things which are purely matters of revelation.

16. The tables of the law are called *the testimony,* because God did in them testify his will. The tables of the law were carefully preserved in the ark, to teach us to make much of the word of God and to hide it in our inmost thoughts, as the ark was placed in the Holy of Holies. It intimates likewise the care which divine providence ever did, and ever will take, to preserve the records of divine revelation in the church, so that even in the latter days there shall be "seen in his temple the ark of his testament." (See Rev. 11:19.)

17. The *mercy seat* was the covering of the ark. This propitiatory covering, as it might well be translated, was a type of Christ the great propitiation, whose satisfaction covers our transgressions and comes between us and the curse we deserve.

22. God is said to dwell or sit *between the cherubim,* on the mercy seat (Ps. 80:1), and from thence he here promises for the future to *meet* with Moses and to *commune* with him. Thus he manifests himself, willing to keep up communion with us, by the mediation of Christ.

30. As the ark signified God's being present with them, so the twelve loaves signified their being presented to God. This *bread* was designed to be a thankful acknowledgment of God's goodness to them in giving them their daily bread, a token of their communion with God. This bread on God's table was a type of the spiritual provision which is made in the church, by the gospel of Christ, for all that are made priests to our God.

31. The tabernacle had no windows, all its light was candle light, which notes the comparative darkness of that dispensation, while the Sun of righteousness was not as yet risen, nor had "the dayspring from on high" visited his church. Yet God left not himself without witness, nor them without instruction. The commandment was a lamp, and the law a light, and the prophets were branches from that lamp, which gave light in their several ages. The church is still dark, as the tabernacle was, in comparison with what it will be in heaven. The word of

God is the candlestick, "a light shining in a dark place."

CHAPTER 26

1. The curtains were to be embroidered with *cherubim,* to intimate that the angels of God pitched their tents round about the church (Ps. 34:7). As there were cherubim over the mercy seat, so there were round the tabernacle. There were to be two hangings, five breadths in each, sewed together, and the two hangings coupled together with golden clasps or tacks, so that it might be all "one tabernacle" (v. 6). Thus the churches of Christ, though they are many, yet are one, being "fitly joined together" in holy love and by the unity of the Spirit, so growing into one holy temple in the Lord.

CHAPTER 27

1. As God intended in the tabernacle to manifest his presence among his people, so there they were to pay their devotions to him. Not in the tabernacle itself, into that only the priests entered as God's domestic servants, but in the court before the tabernacle, where, as common subjects, they attended. There *an altar* was ordered to be set up, to which they must bring their sacrifices. And this altar was to sanctify their gifts. From hence they were to present their services to God, as from the mercy seat he gave his oracles to them. And thus a communion was settled between God and Israel.

2. *The horns of it* were for ornament and for use; the sacrifices were bound with cords to the horns of the altar, and to them malefactors fled for refuge. This brazen altar was a type of Christ dying to make atonement for our sins. Christ sanctified himself for his church as their altar (John 17:19) and by his mediation sanctifies the daily services of his people. To the horns of this altar poor sinners fly for refuge and are safe in virtue of the sacrifice there offered.

10. This court was a type of the church, enclosed and distinguished from the rest of the world. The enclosure supported by *pillars,* noting the stability of the church; hung with the clean linen, which is said to be "the righteousness of saints" (Rev. 19:8). Yet this court would contain but a few worshippers. Thanks be to God, now the enclosure is taken down, and there is room for all that in every place call on the name of Christ.

20–21. The *pure oil* signified the gifts and graces of the Spirit, which are communicated to all believers from Christ, the good olive, of whose fullness we receive (Zech. 4:11–12). The priests were to light the lamps and to tend them; *to cause the lamp to burn always,* night and day. Thus it is the work of ministers to preach and expound the Scriptures, which are as a lamp to enlighten the church. This is to be *a statute for ever,* that the lamps of the word be lighted as duly as the incense of prayer and praise is offered.

CHAPTER 28

2. These glorious *garments* were appointed, (1) That the priests themselves might be minded of the dignity of their office. (2) That the people might thereby be possessed with a holy reverence of that God whose ministers appeared in such grandeur. (3) That the priests might be types of Christ, and of all Christians who have the beauty of holiness put upon them.

15. The most considerable of the ornaments of the high priest was this *breastplate,* a rich piece of cloth curiously wrought with gold and purple, two spans long and a span broad. So that, being doubled, it was a span square. In this breastplate, the tribes of Israel were recommended to God's favor in twelve precious stones. Aaron was to bear their names "for a memorial before the LORD continually" (v. 29), being ordained for men, to represent them in things pertaining to God; herein typifying our great High Priest, who always appears in the presence of God for us.

The name of each tribe was engraven in a precious stone, to signify how "precious" in God's sight believers are, and how "honourable" (Isa. 43:4). The high priest had "the names of the children of Israel" (v. 21) both on his shoulders and on his breast, noting both the power and the love with which our Lord Jesus intercedes for us. How near should Christ's name lie to our hearts, since he is pleased to lay our names so near his? And what a comfort is it to us, in all our addresses to God, that the great High Priest of our profession has the names of all his Israel upon his breast, before the Lord, "for a memorial," presenting them to God?

30. *The Urim and Thummim.* Their government was a theocracy. God was their king; the high priest was, under God, their ruler. This Urim and Thummim were his cabinet council. Probably Moses wrote upon the breastplate, or wove into it, these words, Urim and Thummim, to signify that the high priest, having this breastplate, and asking council of God in any emergency, should be directed to those measures which God would own. If he were standing before the ark, probably he received instructions from off the mercy seat, as Moses did (25:22). If he were at a distance from the ark, as Abiathar was when he enquired of the Lord for David (I Sam. 23:6), then the answer was given either by a voice from heaven or by an impulse upon the mind of the high priest, which is perhaps intimated in that expression, he *shall bear the judgment of the children of Israel upon his heart.* This oracle was of great use to Israel; Joshua consulted it (Num. 27:21) and, it is likely, the judges after him. It was lost in the Captivity and never retrieved after.

It was a shadow of good things to come, and the substance is Christ. He is our oracle; by him God, in these last days, makes known himself and his mind to us. Divine revelation centers in him and comes to us through him. He is the light, the true light, the faithful witness. From him we receive the Spirit of truth, who leads into all truth. The joining of the breastplate to the ephod notes that his prophetical office was founded on his priesthood. And it was by the merit of his death that he purchased this honor for himself and this favor for us. It was the Lamb that had been slain that was worthy to "take the book" and to "open the seals" (Rev. 5:9).

38. Aaron must have this upon his *forehead,* that he *may bear the iniquity of the holy things,* and that *they may be accepted before the LORD.* Herein he was a type of Christ, the great Mediator between God and man. Through him what is amiss in our services is pardoned. Even this would be our ruin, if God should enter into judgment with us. But Christ our high priest bears this iniquity; bears it for us, so as to bear it from us. Through him likewise what is good is accepted; our persons, our performances are pleasing to God upon the account of Christ's intercession, and not otherwise. His being "HOLINESS TO THE LORD" (v. 36) recommends all those to the divine favor that believe in him. Having such a high priest, we "come boldly to the throne of grace."

CHAPTER 29

10. There must be a sin offering to make atonement for them. The law made them priests that had "infirmity." Therefore they must first offer for their own sin before they could make atonement "for the people" (Heb. 7:27–28).

35. Now this consecration of the priests was "a shadow of good things to come." (1) Our Lord Jesus is the great high priest of our profession, called of God to be so *consecrated* for evermore, anointed with the Spirit above his fellows, whence he is called Messiah, the Christ; clothed with the holy garments, even with glory and beauty; sanctified by his own blood, not that of bullocks and rams. (2) All believers are spiritual priests, to offer "spiritual sacrifices" (I Peter 2:5) "washed" in the blood of Christ, and so "made priests to our God" (Rev. 1:5–6). They also are clothed with the beauty of holiness and have received the anointing (I John 2:27). His blood, sprinkled upon the conscience, purgeth it from dead works that they may, as priests, serve the living God. The Spirit of God is called the "finger of God" (Luke 11:20 compared with Matt. 12:28), and by him the merit of Christ is effectually applied to our souls, as here Moses "with his finger" was to put the blood upon Aaron (v. 12). It is likewise intimated that gospel ministers are to be solemnly set apart to the work of the ministry with great deliberation and seriousness, both in the ordainers and in the ordained, as those that are employed in a great work and entrusted with a great charge.

36. The altar was also sanctified, not only set apart itself to a sacred use, but made so holy as to *sanctify* the gifts that were offered upon it (Matt. 23:19). Christ is our altar; for our sakes he sanctified himself, that we and our performances might be sanctified and recommended to God (John 17:19).

38. This daily service, a lamb offered upon the altar every morning and every evening, typified the continual intercession which Christ ever lives to make in the virtue of his satisfaction for the continual sanctification of his church. Though he offered himself once for all, yet that one offering thus becomes a continual offering. And this teaches us to offer up to God the spiritual sacrifices of prayer and praise every day, morning and evening, in humble acknowledgment of our dependence on him and our obligations to him.

CHAPTER 30

6. The altar was placed *before the veil*, on the outside of that partition, but *before the mercy seat*, which was within the veil. For though he that ministered at that altar could not see the mercy seat, the veil interposing, yet he must look towards it and direct his incense that way, to teach us that though we cannot with our bodily eyes see the throne of grace, that blessed mercy seat, yet we must in prayer by faith set ourselves before it, direct our prayer, and look up.

10. This altar was purified with the blood of the sin offering put *upon the horns of it* every year, upon the day of *atonement*. (See Lev. 16:18–19). This altar typified the mediation of Christ. The brazen altar in the court was a type of Christ dying on earth; the golden altar in the sanctuary was a type of Christ interceding in heaven. This altar was before the mercy seat, for Christ always appears in the presence of God for us; and his intercession is unto God of "a sweet-smelling savour." And it typified the devotions of the saints, whose prayers are said to be set forth before God as "incense" (Ps. 141:2). As the smoke of the incense ascended, so must our desires, being kindled with the fire of holy love.

This incense was a perpetual incense,

for we must pray always. The lamps were dressed or lighted at the same time that the incense was burnt, to teach us that the reading of the Scriptures (which are our light and lamp) is a part of our daily work and should ordinarily accompany our prayers and praises. The devotions of sanctified souls are well pleasing to God, of a sweet-smelling favor; the prayers of saints are compared to sweet odors (Rev. 5:8), but it is the incense which Christ adds to them that makes them acceptable; and his blood that atones for the guilt which cleaves to our best services. Yet if the heart and life be not holy, even "incense is an abomination" (Isa. 1:13).

12–13. This was that tribute money which Christ paid lest he should offend his adversaries. The tribute to be paid was *an half shekel*, about fifteen pence of our money. In other offerings men were to give according to their ability, but this, which was the *ransom for the soul*, must be alike for all; for the rich have as much need of Christ as the poor, and the poor are as welcome to him as the rich. Hereby they acknowledged that they received their lives from God, that they had forfeited their lives to him, and that they depended upon this power and patience for the continuance of them.

18. Aaron and his sons were to wash their hands and feet at this laver every time they went in to minister. He only shall stand in God's holy place that has "clean hands and a pure heart" (Ps. 24:3–4). And it was to teach us, who are daily to attend upon God, daily to renew our repentance for sin and our believing application of the blood of Christ to our souls for remission.

CHAPTER 31

13. The Jews by observing one day in seven, after six days' labor, testified that they worshipped the God that made the world in six days and rested the seventh. They distinguished themselves from other nations, who having first lost the sabbath, the memorial of the creation, by degrees lost the knowledge of the creator and gave the creature the honor due to him alone.

18. These *tables of stone* were not prepared by Moses, but probably by the ministry of angels. They were *written with the finger of God*. That is, by his will and power immediately, without the use of any instrument. They were written in *two tables,* being designed to direct us in our duty, towards God and towards man.

CHAPTER 32

1. They say, *make us gods, which shall go before us.* Gods! How many would they have? Is not one sufficient? And what good would gods of their own making do them? They must have such gods to go before them as could not go themselves farther than they were carried!

5. And Aaron *built an altar before it* and proclaimed a feast. A feast of dedication; yet he calls it *a feast to the* LORD. For, as brutish as they were, they did not design to terminate their adoration in the image; but they made it for a representation of the true God, whom they intended to worship in and through this image. And yet this did not excuse them from gross idolatry, no more than it will excuse the Romanists, whose plea it is that they do not worship the image, but God by the image; so making themselves just such idolaters as the worshippers of the golden calf, whose feast was a feast to Jehovah, and proclaimed to be so that the most ignorant and unthinking might not mistake it.

6. It was strange that any of the

people, especially so great a number of them, should do such a thing. Had they not, but the other day, in this very place, heard the voice of the Lord God speaking to them out of the midst of the fire, "Thou shalt not make to thyself any graven image?" Yet "they made a calf in Horeb," the very place where the law was given. It was especially strange that Aaron should be so deeply concerned, should make the calf and proclaim the feast! Is this Aaron the saint of the Lord? Is this he that had not only seen, but had been employed in summoning the plagues of Egypt and the judgments executed upon the gods of the Egyptians? What! and yet himself copying out the abandoned idolatries of Egypt? How true is it that the law made them priests which had infirmity and needed first to offer for their own sins.

8. *They have turned aside quickly.* Quickly after the law was given them and they had promised to obey it; quickly after God had done such great things for them and declared his kind intentions to do greater.

12. *Turn from thy fierce wrath.* Israel is dear to Moses, as his kindred, as his charge; but it is the glory of God that he is most concerned for.

14. *And the* LORD *repented of the evil which he thought to do.* See here the power of prayer; God suffers himself to be prevailed with by humble believing importunity. And see the compassion of God towards poor sinners, and how ready he is to forgive.

16. *The writing of God.* Very probably the first writing in the world.

19. *He saw the calf, and the dancing,* and his *anger waxed hot.* It is no breach of the law of meekness to show our displeasure at wickedness. He broke the tables before their eyes (Deut. 9:17), that the sight of it might fill them with confusion when they saw what blessings they had lost. The greatest sign of God's displeasure against any people is his taking his law from them.

23. *They said, . . . Make us gods.* It is natural to us to endeavor thus to transfer our guilt. This was all Aaron had to say for himself, and he had better have said nothing, for his defense did but aggravate his offense; and yet as sin did abound, grace did much more abound.

32. *If not, blot me, I pray thee, out of the book which thou hast written.* That is, out of the Book of Life. If all Israel must perish, I am content to perish with them. Not that Moses absolutely desired this, but only comparatively expresses his vehement zeal for God's glory and love to his people. He thus signifies that the very thought of their destruction and the dishonor of God was so intolerable to him that he rather wishes, if it were possible, that God would accept him as a sacrifice in their stead, and by his utter destruction prevent so great a mischief.

33. *Whosoever hath sinned, him will I blot out of my book.* The soul that sins shall die, and not the innocent for the guilty.

CHAPTER 33

11. *And the* LORD *spake unto Moses face to face, as a man speaketh to his friend.* Which intimates not only that God revealed himself to Moses with greater clearness than to any other of the prophets, but also with greater expressions of particular kindness than to any other. He spake not as a prince to a subject, but as a man to his friend, whom he loves and with whom he takes sweet counsel.

17. *I will do this thing also that thou hast spoken.* See the power of prayer! See the riches of God's goodness! See in type the prevalence of Christ's intercession, which he ever lives to make for all those that come to God by him! And the ground of that prevalence is purely in his own merit, it is because *thou hast found grace in my sight.*

18–19. *Shew me thy glory,* said Moses; I will show thee *my goodness,* said God. God's goodness is his glory; and he will have us to know him by the glory of his mercy, more than by the glory of his majesty. And I *will be gracious to whom I will be gracious.* In bestowing his gifts, he is not debtor to any nor accountable to any. All his reasons for mercy are fetched from within himself, not from any merit in his creatures, and I *will shew mercy on whom I will shew mercy.* For his grace is always free. He never damns by prerogative, but by prerogative he saves.

22. *I will put thee in a cleft of the rock.* In that he was to be sheltered from the dazzling light and devouring fire of the glory of God. This was the rock in Horeb, out of which water was brought, of which it is said, "That Rock was Christ" (I Cor. 10:4). It is in the clefts of this rock that we are secured from the wrath of God, which otherwise would consume us. God himself will protect those that are thus hid. And it is only through Christ that we have the knowledge of the glory of God. None can see that to their comfort but those that stand upon this rock and take shelter in it.

23. *And I will take away mine hand.* Speaking after the manner of men. *And thou shalt see my back parts.* The face in man is the seat of majesty, and men are known by their faces. In them we take a full view of men. That sight of God Moses might not have, but such a sight as we have of a man who is gone past us, so that we only see his back. Now Moses was allowed to see this only; but when he was a witness to Christ's transfiguration, he saw his face shine as the sun.

CHAPTER 34

1. Though Christ has redeemed us from the curse of the law, yet not from the command of it, but still we are under the law to Christ. When our Savior in his Sermon on the Mount expounded the moral law and vindicated it from the corrupt glosses with which the scribes and Pharisees had broken it, he did in effect renew the tables and make them *like the first.* That is, he reduced the law to its primitive sense and intention.

5–7. *And proclaimed the name of the* LORD. He had made himself known to Moses in the glory of his self-existence and self-sufficiency when he proclaimed that name, I AM THAT I AM. Now he makes himself known in the glory of his grace and goodness and all-sufficiency to us. The proclaiming of it notes the universal extent of God's mercy. He is not only good to Israel, but good to all. The God with whom we have to do is a great God. He is Jehovah, the Lord, that has his being of himself and is the fountain of all being; Jehovah-El, the Lord, the strong God, a God of almighty power himself and the original of all power. This is prefixed before the display of his mercy to teach us to think and to speak even of God's goodness with a holy awe, and to encourage us to depend upon these mercies. He is a good God. His greatness and goodness illustrate each other. That his greatness may not make us afraid, we are told how good he is; and that we may not presume upon his goodness, we are told how great he is.

Many words are here heaped up to acquaint us with and convince us of God's goodness. First, he is *merciful.* This speaks of his pity and tender compassion, like that of a father to his children. This is put first because it is the first wheel in all the instances of

God's goodwill to fallen man. Second, he is *gracious*. This speaks both freeness and kindness. It speaks him not only to have compassion to his creatures, but a complacency in them and in doing good to them; and this of his own goodwill, not for the sake of anything in them. Third, he is *longsuffering*. This is a branch of God's goodness which our wickedness gives occasion for. He is long-suffering, that is, he is slow to anger and delays the executions of his justice, he waits to be gracious and lengthens out the offers of his mercy.

Fourth, he is *abundant in goodness and truth*. This speaks plentiful goodness; it abounds above our deserts, above our conception. The springs of mercy are always full, the streams of mercy always flowing. There is mercy enough in God, enough for all, enough for each, enough for ever. It speaks promised goodness, goodness and truth put together, goodness engaged by promise. Fifth, he is *keeping mercy for thousands*. This speaks mercy extended to thousands of persons and is never exhausted. It speaks mercy entailed upon thousands of generations, even to those upon whom the ends of the world are come; the line of it is drawn parallel with that of eternity itself.

Sixth, he is *forgiving iniquity and transgression and sin*. He forgives offenses of all sorts, iniquity, transgression, and sin, multiplies his pardons, and with him is plenteous redemption. He is a just and holy God. For, (1) He *will by no means clear the guilty*. He will not clear the impenitently guilty, those who go on still in their trespasses; he will not clear the guilty without satisfaction to his justice. (2) He is *visiting the iniquity of the fathers upon the children*. Especially for the punishment of idolaters. "Neither will he keep his anger for ever," but visits to *the third and fourth generation* only, while he

keeps *mercy for thousands*. This is God's name for ever, and this is his memorial unto all generations.

10. *Behold, I make a covenant.* When the covenant was broken, it was Israel that broke it. Now as it comes to be renewed, it is God that makes it. If there be quarrels, we must bear all the blame; if there be peace, God must have all the glory.

11. *Observe that which I command thee.* We cannot expect the benefit of the promises unless we make conscience of the precepts.

21. *Thou shalt rest,* even *in earing time and in harvest.* The most busy times of the year. All worldly business must give way to that holy rest. Harvest work will prosper the better for the religious observation of the sabbath day in harvest time. Hereby we must show that we prefer our communion with God before either the business or the joy of harvest.

29. *The skin of his face shone.* This time of his being in the mount he heard only the same he had heard before. But he saw more of the glory of God, which having with "open face" beheld, he was in some measure "changed into the same image." This was a great honor done to Moses, that the people might never again question his mission or think or speak slightly of him. He carried his credentials in his very countenance. Some think as long as he lived he retained some reminders of this glory, which perhaps contributed to the vigor of his old age. That eye could not wax dim which had seen God, nor that face wrinkle which had shone with his glory.

33. And Moses *put a veil upon his face.* It was beauty veiled, gold in the mine, a pearl in the shell. But thanks be to God, by the gospel, the veil is taken away from off the old testament. Yet still it remains upon the hearts of those who shut their eyes against the light.

34. When he *went in before the* LORD, . . . *he took the veil off.* Every veil must be thrown aside when we go to present ourselves unto the Lord. This signified also, as it is explained (II Cor. 3:16), that when a soul turns to the Lord, "the veil shall be taken away," that with open face it may behold his glory.

CHAPTER 35

2. *On the seventh day.* You must not strike a stroke, no, not at the tabernacle work; the honor of the *sabbath* was above that of the sanctuary.

21. *Every one whom his spirit made willing.* What they did, they did cheerfully. They were willing; and it was not any external inducement that made them so, but their spirits. It was from a principle of love to God, and his service; a desire of his presence with them by his ordinances; gratitude for the great things he had done for them; and faith in his promises of what he would do further.

CHAPTER 36

2. *And Moses called Bezaleel.* Those are to be called to the building of the gospel tabernacle whom God has by his grace made in some measure fit for the work and free to it. Ability and willingness, with resolution, are the two things to be regarded in the call of ministers.

35. The *veil* made for a partition between the holy place and the most holy signified the darkness and distance of that dispensation compared with the New Testament, which shows us the glory of God more clearly and invites us to draw near to it. And it signifies the darkness and distance of our present state in comparison with heaven, where we shall "ever be with the Lord" and "see him as he is."

CHAPTER 37

1–9. In these verses we have an account of the making of *the ark* with its glorious and significant appurtenances, *the mercy seat* and *the cherubims.* Consider these three together, and they represent the glory of a holy God, the sincerity of a holy heart, and the communion that is between them by a Mediator. It is the glory of a holy God that he dwells between the cherubim, that is, is continually attended by the blessed angels, whose swiftness was signified by the wings of the cherubim, and their unanimity in their services by their faces being one towards another. It is the character of an upright heart that, like the ark of the testimony, it has the law of God hid and kept in it. By Jesus Christ the great propitiation there is reconciliation made between us and God. He interposes between us and God's displeasure; and through him we become entitled to God's favor.

10. Though here was a *table* furnished, it was only with shewbread, bread to be looked upon, not to be fed upon, while it was on the table, and afterwards only by the priests. But to the table Christ has spread in the new covenant all good Christians are invited guests, and to them it is said, Eat, O friends, come eat of my bread. What the law gave but a sight of at a distance, the gospel gives the enjoyment of.

17. This *candlestick,* which was not of wood overlaid with gold, but all *beaten work* of *pure gold* only, signified that light of divine revelation with which God's church upon earth (which is his tabernacle among men) has always been enlightened, being always supplied with fresh oil from Christ the good olive (Zech. 4:2–3). The Bible is a golden candlestick, it is of pure gold; from it light is diffused to every part of

God's tabernacle, that by it the spiritual priests may see to do the service of his sanctuary. The candlestick has not only its *bowls* for necessary use, but its *knops*[1] *and flowers* for ornament. There are many things with which God saw fit to beautify his word, which we can no more give a reason for than for these knops and flowers, and yet must be sure they were added for good purpose. Let us bless God for this candlestick, have an eye to it continually, and dread the removal of it "out of its place!"

CHAPTER 38

1. *The altar of burnt offering.* On this all their sacrifices were offered. Christ was himself the altar to his own sacrifice of atonement, and so he is to all our sacrifices of acknowledgment. We must have an eye to him in offering them, as God has in accepting them. **8.** This *laver* signified the provision that is made in the gospel for cleaning our souls from the pollution of sin by the merit of Christ, that we may be fit to serve the holy God in holy duties. **9.** *And he made the court.* The walls of the court were like the rest, curtains, or hangings. This represented the state of the Old Testament church, it was a garden enclosed; the worshippers were then confined to a little compass. But the enclosure being of curtains only intimated that the confinement of the church to one particular nation was not to be perpetual. The dispensation itself was a tabernacle-dispensation, movable and mutable, and in due time to be taken down and folded up, when the place of the tent should be enlarged and its cords lengthened to make room for the Gentile world. **24.** The raising of the gold by

voluntary contribution, and of the silver by way of tribute, shows that either way may be taken for the defraying of public expenses, provided that nothing be done with partiality.

CHAPTER 39

1. The priest's garments are called here *cloths of service*. Those that wear robes of honor must look upon them as clothes of service; for those upon whom honor is put, from them service is expected. Holy garments were not made for men to sleep in, but to do service in, and then they are indeed for glory and beauty. These also were shadows of good things to come, but the substance is Christ. He is our great high priest. He put upon him the clothes of service when he undertook the work of our redemption; arrayed himself with the gifts and graces of the Spirit, which he received not by measure; charged himself with all God's spiritual Israel, bore them on his shoulder, carried them in his bosom, and presented them in "the breastplate of judgment" unto his Father. And, lastly, he crowned himself with holiness to the Lord, consecrated his whole undertaking to the honor of his Father's holiness. And all true believers are spiritual priests. The clean "linen" (vv. 2ff.), with which all their clothes of service must be made, is "the righteousness of saints." And "HOLINESS TO THE LORD" (v. 30) must be so written upon their foreheads that all who converse with them may see they wear the image of God's holiness. **32.** *Thus was all the work . . . finished.* In not much more than five months. Though there was a great deal of fine work, such as used to be the work of

---

[1] (37:17) Knobs or protuberances.

time, embroidering and engraving, not only in gold but in precious stones, yet they went through with it in a little time, with the greatest exactness imaginable. The workmen were "taught of God" and so were kept from making blunders which would have retarded them.

43. *And Moses blessed them.* He not only praised them, but prayed for them. He blessed them as one having authority. We read not of any wages Moses paid them for their work, but his blessing he gave them. For though ordinarily the labor be worthy of his hire, yet in this case they cared for themselves. The honor and comfort of God's tabernacle among them would be recompense enough. And they had their meat from heaven on free-cost, for themselves and their families, and their raiment waxed not old upon them. So that they neither needed wages nor had reason to expect any. But indeed this blessing in the name of the Lord was wages enough for all their work. Those whom God employs he will bless, and those whom he blesses, they are blessed indeed. The blessing he commands is life for evermore.

CHAPTER 40

34–35. As when God had finished this earth, which he designed for man's habitation, he made man and put him in possession of it; so when Moses had finished the tabernacle, which was designed for God's dwelling place among men, God came and took possession of it.

And the glory of the LORD filled the tabernacle. The Shekinah now made an awful entry into the tabernacle, passing through the outer part of it into the most holy place and there seating itself between the cherubim. It was in light and fire and, for all we know, in no other wise that the Shekinah made itself visible. With these the tabernacle was now filled. Yet as before with the bush, so now the curtains were not consumed, for to those who have received the anointing, the majesty of God is not destroying. Yet now so dazzling was the light, and so dreadful was the fire, that *Moses was not able to enter into the tent of the congregation,* at the door of which he attended, until the splendor was a little abated and *the glory of the LORD* retired within the veil.

But what Moses could not do, our Lord Jesus has done, whom God caused to draw near and approach, and he as "the forerunner is for us entered" and has invited us to come boldly even to the mercy seat. He was able to enter into the holy place "not made with hands." He himself is the true tabernacle, filled with the glory of God, even with that divine grace and truth which were figured by this fire and light. In him the Shekinah took up its rest for ever, "for in him dwelleth all the fulness of the Godhead bodily."

Leviticus

CHAPTER 1

2. *An offering unto the* LORD. There are many kinds of sacrifices here prescribed, some by way of acknowledgment to God for mercies either desired or received; others by way of satisfaction to God for men's sins. Others were mere exercises of devotion. And the reason why there were so many kinds of them was partly a respect to the childish state of the Jews, who by the custom of nations and their own natural inclinations were much addicted to outward rites and ceremonies, that they might have full employment of that kind in God's service and thereby be kept from temptations to idolatry. And partly to represent as well the several perfections of Christ, the true sacrifice, and the various benefits of his death, as the several duties which men owe to their Creator and Redeemer, all which could not be so well expressed by one sort of sacrifice.

Of the flock. Or, "of the sheep," though the Hebrew word contains both the sheep and goats. Now God chose these creatures for his sacrifices, either (1) In opposition to the Egyptian idolatry, to which many of the Israelites had been used and were still in danger of revolting to again, that the frequent destruction of these creatures might bring such silly deities into contempt. Or, (2) Because these are the fittest representations both of Christ and of true Christians, as being gentle, and harmless, and patient, and useful to men. Or, (3) As the best and most profitable creatures, with which it is fit God should be served, and which we should be ready to part with, when God requires us to do so. Or, (4) As things most common, that men might never lack a sacrifice when they needed or God required it.

3. *A burnt sacrifice.* Strictly so called, such as was to be all burnt, the skin excepted. For every sacrifice was burnt, more or less. The sacrifices signified that the whole man, in whose stead the sacrifice was offered, was to be entirely offered or devoted to God's service; and that the whole man did deserve to be utterly consumed, if God should deal severely with him. And the sacrifices directed us to serve the Lord with all singleness of heart, and to be ready to offer to God even such sacrifices or services wherein we ourselves should have no part or benefit. *Without blemish.* To signify that God should be served with the best of every kind. And that man, represented by these sacrifices, should aim at all perfection of heart and life, and that Christians should one day attain to it (Eph. 5:27).

At the door. In the court near the door, where the altar stood (v. 5). For here it was to be sacrificed, and here the people might behold the oblation of it. And this further signified that men could have no entrance, neither into the earthly tabernacle, the church, nor into the heavenly tabernacle of glory, but by Christ, who is the door (John 10:7, 9) by whom alone we have access to God.

4. *He shall put his hand*. Both his hands (8:14, 18; 16:21). Whereby he signified that he willingly gave it to the Lord; and that he judged himself worthy of that death which it suffered in his place. It signified that he laid his sins upon it with an eye to him upon whom God would lay the iniquity of us all (Isa. 53:6) and that together with it he did freely offer up himself to God. *To make atonement*. Sacramentally; as directing his faith and thoughts to that true propitiatory sacrifice which in time was to be offered up for him. And although burnt offerings were commonly offered by way of thanksgiving; yet they were sometimes offered by way of atonement for sin, that is, for sins in general, as appears from Job 1:5; but for particular sins there were special sacrifices.

5. *Sprinkle the blood*. Which was done in a considerable quantity, and whereby was signified (1) That the offerer deserved to have his blood spilt in that manner. (2) That the blood of Christ should be poured forth for sinners, and that this was the only means of their reconciliation to God and acceptance with him.

9. *But his inwards*[1] *shall he wash*. To signify the universal and perfect purity both of the inwards, or the heart, and of the legs, or ways or actions, which was in Christ and which should be in all Christians. And he washed not only the parts now mentioned, but all the rest, the trunk of the body and the shoulders. *A sweet savour*. Not in itself, for so it rather caused a stink, but as it represented Christ's offering up himself to God as a sweet-smelling savor.

11. *Northward*. This might design the place of Christ's death both more generally in Jerusalem, which was in the sides of the north (Ps. 48:2), and more specifically on Mount Calvary, which was on the northwest side of Jerusalem.

14. *Turtledoves*. These birds were appointed for the poor who could not bring better. And these birds are preferred before others, partly because they were easily gotten, and partly because they are fit representations of Christ's chastity, and meekness, and gentleness, for which these birds are remarkable.

16. *With his feathers*. Or, with its dung or filth, contained in the crop and in the guts. *On the east*. Of the tabernacle. Here the filth was cast because this was the remotest place from the Holy of Holies, which was in the west end. This was to teach us that impure things and persons should not presume to approach God, and that they should be banished from his presence.

CHAPTER 2

1. *A meal offering*.[2] This was of two kinds, the one joined with other offerings (Num. 15:4, 7, 10), which was prescribed, together with the measure or proportion of it. The other, of which this place speaks, was left to the offerer's goodwill both for the thing and for the quantity. And the matter for this offering was things without life, as

---

[1] (1:9) That is, "its inwards."
[2] (2:1) KJV: "meat offering," but Wesley gives the better reading.

meal, corn, or cakes. Now this sort of sacrifices were appointed (1) Because these are things of greatest necessity and benefit to man, and therefore it is right that God should be served with them and owned and praised as the giver of them. (2) In condescension to the poor, that they might not lack an offering for God, and to show that God would accept even the smallest services when offered with a sincere mind. (3) These were necessary provisions for the feast, which was to be presented to God, and for the use of the priests, who were to attend upon these holy ministrations.

He shall pour oil. This may note the graces of the Holy Ghost, which are compared to oil, and anointing with it (Ps. 45:7; I John 2:20), and which are necessary to make any offering acceptable to God. *Frankincense.* Manifestly designed as Christ's satisfaction and intercession, which is compared to a sweet odor (Eph. 5:2).

2. *A sweet savour unto the* LORD. And so are our spiritual offerings, which are made by the fire of holy love, particularly that of almsgiving. With such sacrifices God is well pleased.

11. *No leaven.* Namely, in that which is offered of free will; for in other offerings it might be used (Lev. 7:13; 23:17). This was forbidden, partly to remind them of their deliverance out of Egypt, when they were forced through haste to bring their meal or dough (which was the matter of this oblation) unleavened; partly to signify what Christ would be, and what they should be, pure and free from all error in the faith and worship of God, and from all hypocrisy, and malice or wickedness, all which are signified by leaven.

Nor any honey. Either (1) Because it has the same effect with leaven in paste or dough, making it flour, and swelling. Or (2) In opposition to the sacrifices of the Gentiles, in which the use of honey was most frequent. Or (3) To teach us that God's worship is not to be governed by men's fancies and appetites but by God's will.

13. *Salt.* To signify that incorruption of mind and sincerity of grace which in Scripture is signified by salt (Mark 9:49; Col. 4:6) and which is necessary in all them that would offer an acceptable offering to God.

16. *Made by fire.* The fire denotes that fervency of spirit which ought to be in all our religious services. Holy love is the fire by which all our offerings must be made, else they are not of a sweet savor to God.

CHAPTER 3

1. *A peace offering.* This was an offering for peace and prosperity and the blessing of God, either (1) Obtained, and so it was a thank offering. Or (2) Desired, and so it was a kind of supplication to God. Burnt offerings had regard to God, as in himself the best of beings, and therefore were wholly burned. But peace offerings had regard to God as a benefactor to his creatures, and therefore were divided between the altar, the priest, and the offerer.

2. *At the door.* Not on the north side of the altar, where the burnt offering was killed, as also the sin offering and the trespass offering, but on the very entrance of the court where the brazen altar stood, which place was not so holy as the other. It was more remote from the Holy of Holies, and the ashes of the sacrifices were to be laid here. And the reason of this difference is not obscure, both because part of this sacrifice was to be waved by the hands of the offerer (Lev. 7:30) who might not come into the court; and because this offering was not so holy as the others, which were to be eaten only by the priest, whereas part of these were eaten by the offerer.

17. *Fat.* Was forbidden. (1) To preserve the reverence of the holy rites and sacrifices. (2) That they might be taught hereby to acknowledge God as their Lord, and the Lord of all the creatures, who might reserve what he pleased to himself. (3) To exercise them in obedience to God and self-denial and mortification of their appetites, even in those things which probably many of them would much desire.

Blood. Was forbidden partly to maintain reverence to God and his worship; partly out of opposition to idolaters, who used to drink the blood of their sacrifices; partly with respect to Christ's blood, thereby manifestly signified. God would not permit the very shadows of this to be used as a common thing. Nor will he allow us, though we have the comfort of the atonement made, to assume to ourselves any share in the honor of making it.

CHAPTER 4

2. *Through ignorance.* Or error, either not knowing his act to be sinful, as appears by comparing verses 13 and 14, or not considering it, but falling into sin through the power of some sudden passion or temptation, as the Hebrew word signifies (Ps. 119:67). *Things which ought not to be done.* The words may be rendered, "in" or "about every," or "any of the commandments of the Lord which should not be done"; or, "which concerns things that should not be done," namely, in any negative commands. (And there is great reason why a sacrifice should be more necessary for these than for other sins, because affirmative precepts do not so strictly and constantly bind men as the negative do.)

3. *If the priest.* That is, the high priest, who only was anointed after the first time. His anointing is mentioned because he was not complete high priest until he was anointed. *Do sin.* Either in doctrine or practice, which it is here supposed he may do. And this is noted as a character of imperfection in the priesthood of the law, whereby the Israelites were directed to expect another and better high priest, even one who is "holy, harmless, and separate from sinners" (Heb. 7:26).

According to the sin of the people. In the same manner as any of the people do; which implies that God expected more circumspection from him than from the people. But the words may be rendered "to the guilt of the people," which may be mentioned as an aggravation of his sin, that by it he commonly brings sin and guilt and punishment upon the people, who are infected or scandalized by his example.

4. *On the head.* To testify both his acknowledgment of his sin and his faith in God's promise for the expiation of his sins through Christ, whom that sacrifice typified.

5. *To the tabernacle.* Into the tabernacle; which was not required nor allowed in any other sacrifice, possibly to show the greatness of the high priest's sin, which needed more than ordinary diligence in him, and favor from God to expiate it.

6. *Seven times.* A number much used in Scripture as a number of perfection. It is here prescribed, to show that his sins needed more than ordinary purgation and more exercise of his faith and repentance, both which graces he was obliged to join with that ceremonial rite.

12. *Shall he carry forth.* Not the priest himself, which would have defiled him, but by another whom he shall appoint for that work. Without the camp. To signify either (1) The abominable nature of sin, especially in high and holy persons, or when it overspreads a whole people. Or (2) The removing of the guilt or punishment of that sin from the people. Or (3) That Christ should suffer without the camp or gate.

17. *And sprinkle it.* It was not to be poured out there, but sprinkled only; for the cleansing virtue of the blood of Christ was sufficiently represented by sprinkling. It was to be sprinkled *seven times.* Seven is a number of perfection, because God made the world in six days, and rested the seventh. This signified the perfect satisfaction Christ made and the complete cleansing of our souls thereby.

24. *It is a sin offering.* And therefore to be killed where the burnt offering is killed; whereby it is distinguished from the peace offering, which was killed elsewhere.

26. *It shall be forgiven.* Both judicially, as to all ecclesiastical censures or civil punishment; and really, upon condition of repentance and faith in the Messiah to come.

CHAPTER 5

2. *If it be hidden from him.* If he do it unawares, yet that would not excuse him, because he should have been more circumspect to avoid all unclean things. Hereby God designed to awaken men to watchfulness against, and repentance for, their unknown or unobserved sins.

3. *When he knoweth.* As soon as he knows it, he must not delay to make his peace with God. Otherwise *he shall be guilty* for this violation and contempt of God's authority and command.

5. *In one of these things.* In one of the three aforementioned cases, either by sinful silence, or by an unclean touch, or by rash swearing. *He shall confess.* Before the Lord in the place of public worship. And this confession is not to

be restrained to the present case, but by a parity of reason and comparing of other Scriptures, to be extended to other sacrifices for sin, to which this was a constant companion.

10. *Shall make an atonement.* Either declaratively, he shall pronounce him to be pardoned; or typically, with respect to Christ.

15. *Through ignorance.* For if a man did it knowingly, he was to be cut off (Num. 15:30).

CHAPTER 6

2. *If a soul sin.* This sin, though directly committed against man, is emphatically said to be done against the Lord, not only in general, for so every sin against man is also against the Lord, but in a special sense, because this was a violation of human ˙society, whereof God is the author and president and defender. And because it was a secret sin, of which God alone was the witness and judge. And because God's name was abused in it by perjury.

5. *In the day.* It must not be delayed, but restitution to man must accompany repentance towards God. Wherever wrong has been done, restitution must be made, and until it is made to the utmost of our power we cannot look for forgiveness; for the keeping of what is unjustly got avows the taking. And both together make but one continued act of unrighteousness.

12. *It shall not be put out.* The fire coming down from heaven was to be perpetually preserved and not allowed to go out. Partly that there might be no occasion or temptation to offer strange fire. And partly to teach them whence they were to expect the acceptance of all their sacrifices, even from the divine mercy, signified by the fire that came down from heaven, which was an usual token of God's favorable acceptance.

13. Thus should we keep the fire of holy love ever burning in our hearts.

CHAPTER 7

13. *Leavened bread.* Because this was a sacrifice of another kind than those in which leaven was forbidden, this being a sacrifice of thanksgiving for God's blessings, among which leavened bread was one. Leaven indeed was universally forbidden (Lev. 2:11), but that prohibition concerned only things offered and burnt upon the altar, which this bread was not.

16. *A vow.* Offered in performance of a vow, the man having desired some special favor from God and vowed the sacrifice to God if he would grant it.

34. *Wave breast and heave shoulder.* The breast or heart is the seat of wisdom, and the shoulder of strength for action; and these two may denote that wisdom and power which were in Christ our high priest and which ought to be in every priest.

CHAPTER 8

3. *All the congregation.* The elders who represented all, and as many of the people as would and could get together, that all might be witnesses both of Aaron's commission from God and of his work and business.

12. *He poured.* In a plentiful manner, as appears from Psalm 133:2; whereas other persons and things were only sprinkled with it. His unction was to typify the anointing of Christ with the Spirit, which was not given by measure to him. A measure of the same anointing is given to all believers.

33. *He.* Either God or Moses; for the words may be spoken by Moses, either in God's name or in his own; Moses speaking of himself in the third person, which is very common in Scripture.

CHAPTER 9

3. *A sin offering.* For the people, for whose sin a young bullock was required (4:15). But that was for some particular sin; this was more general for all their sins. Besides, there being an eye here to the priest's consecration and entrance into his office, it is no wonder if there be some difference in these sacrifices from those before prescribed.

7. *For thyself, and for the people.* The order is very observable, first for yourself, otherwise you are unfit to do it for the people. Hereby God would teach us both the deficiency of this priesthood and how important it is that God's ministers should be in the favor of God themselves, that their ministrations may be acceptable to God and profitable to the people.

17. *Besides the burnt sacrifice.* Which was to be first offered every morning; for God will not have his ordinary and stated service swallowed up by extraordinary.

22. *Aaron lifted up his hands.* Which was the usual rite of blessing. By this posture he signified both whence he expected the blessing and his hearty desire of it for them. *And blessed them.* And this blessing was an act of his priestly office, no less than sacrificing. And herein he was a type of Christ, who came into the world to bless us and, when he was parting from his disciples, lifted up his hands and blessed them. Yes, and in them his whole church, of which they were the elders and representatives.

23. *And blessed the people.* Prayed to God for his blessing upon them, as this phrase is explained (Num. 6:23ff.), and particularly for his gracious acceptance of these and all succeeding sacrifices, and for his signification thereof by some extraordinary token. *And the glory of the* LORD. Either a miraculous brightness shining from the cloudy pillar (Exod. 16:10), or a glorious and visible discovery of God's gracious presence and acceptance of the present service.

24. *And there came a fire.* In token of God's approbation of the priesthood now instituted, and the sacrifices offered, and consequently of others of the nature. And this fire now given was to be carefully kept, and not allowed to go out (6:13), and therefore was carried in a peculiar vessel in their journeys in the wilderness. *They shouted.* As wondering at, rejoicing in, and blessing God for this gracious discovery of himself and his favor. This also was a figure of good things to come. Thus the Spirit descended in fire upon the apostles, so ratifying their commission as this does that of the priests. And the descent of this holy fire into our souls, to kindle in them devout affections and such an holy zeal as burns up all unholiness, is a certain token of God's gracious acceptance.

CHAPTER 10

1. *Strange fire.* Fire so called because it was not taken from the altar, as it ought, but from some common fire.

2. *From the LORD.* From heaven, or rather from the sanctuary. *Devoured them.* Destroyed their lives; for their bodies and garments were not consumed. Thus the sword is said to devour (II Sam. 2:26). Thus lightning many times kills persons without any hurt to their garments.

3. *The LORD spake.* Though the words be not recorded in Scripture, where only the heads of discourses are contained, yet it is probable they were uttered by Moses in God's name. However, the sense of them is in many places. *I will be sanctified.* This may note either (1) Their duty to sanctify God,

to demean themselves with such care and reverence and watchfulness as becomes the holiness of the God whom they serve; whence he leaves them to gather the justice of the present judgment. Or (2) God's purpose to sanctify himself, to manifest himself to be an holy and righteous God by his severe and impartial punishment of all transgressors, however near they are to him.

4. *Moses called Mishael.* For Aaron and his sons were employed in their holy ministrations, from which they were not called for funeral solemnities. *Out of the camp.* Where the burying places of the Jews were, that the living might neither be annoyed by the unwholesome scent of the dead nor defiled by the touch of their graves.

6. *Uncover not your heads.* That is, give no signification of your sorrow; mourn not for them. Partly lest you should seem to justify your brethren and tacitly reflect upon God as too severe. And partly lest thereby you should be diverted from or disturbed in your present service, which God expects to be done cheerfully. *But bewail the burning.* Not so much in compassion to them, as in sorrow for the tokens of divine displeasure.

7. *The oil of the LORD is upon you.* You are persons consecrated peculiarly to God's service, which therefore it is just you should prefer before all funeral solemnities.

9. *Do not drink wine.* It is not improbable that the sin of Nadab and Abihu was owing to this very thing. But if not, yet drunkenness is so odious a sin in itself, especially in a minister, and most of all in the time of his administration of sacred things, that God saw fit to prevent all occasions of it. And hence the devil, who is God's ape, required this abstinence from his priests in their idolatrous service.

17. *God hath given it to you.* As a

reward of your service, whereby you expiate, bear, and take away their sins, by offering those sacrifices by which God though Christ is reconciled to the penitent and believing offerers.

20. He rested satisfied with his answer. It appeared that Aaron sincerely aimed at pleasing God; and those who do so will find he is not extreme to mark what is done amiss.

CHAPTER 11

1. From the laws concerning the priests, he now comes to those which belong to all the people. God spake to both of them because the following matters belonged to both: the priest was to direct the people about the things forbidden or allowed, where any doubt or difficulty arose; and the magistrate was to see the direction followed.

2. *These are the beasts.* Though every creature of God be good and pure in itself, yet it pleased God to make a difference between clean and unclean, which he did in part before the flood (Gen. 7:2), but more fully here for many reasons. (1) To assert his own sovereignty over man, and all the creatures which men may not use but with God's permission. (2) To keep up the wall of partition between the Jews and other nations, which was very necessary for many great and wise purposes. (3) That by bridling their appetite in things in themselves lawful, and some of them very desirable, they might be better prepared and enabled to deny themselves in things simply and grossly sinful. (4) For the preservation of their health, some of the creatures being forbidden, though used by the neighboring nations, of unwholesome nourishment, especially to the Jews, who were very obnoxious to leprosies. To teach them to abhor that filthiness and all those ill qualities for which some of these creatures are noted.

3. *Clovenfooted.* That is, divided into two parts only. This clause is added to explain and limit the former, as appears from verse 26, for the feet of dogs, cats, etc., are parted or cloven into many parts. *And cheweth the cud.* That is, the meat once chewed, out of the stomach in the mouth again, that it may be chewed a second time for better digestion. And this branch is to be joined with the former, both properties being necessary for the allowed beasts. But the reason for this must be resolved into the will of the lawgiver; though interpreters guess that God would hereby signify their duties, by the first, that of discerning between good and evil; and by the latter, that duty of recalling God's word to our minds and mediating upon it.

8. *Shall ye not touch.* Not to eat, as may be gathered by comparing this with Genesis 3:3. But since the fat and skins of some of the forbidden creatures were useful for medicinal and other good purposes, and were used by good men, it is not probable that God would have them cast away. Thus God forbade the making of images (Exod. 20), not universally, but for the worshipping of them, as Christian interpreters agree.

9. *Fins and scales.* Both of them; such fishes being more cleanly and more wholesome food than others. The names of them are not particularly mentioned, partly because most of them lacked names, the fish not being brought to Adam and named by him as other creatures were; and partly because the land of Canaan had not many rivers, nor a great store of fish.

11. *Unto you.* This clause is added to show that they were neither abominable in their own nature, nor as food of other nations; consequently when the partition wall between Jews and Gentiles was taken away, these distinctions of meat were to cease.

13. *Among the fowls.* In general, it may be observed that the fowls forbidden in diet are all either ravenous and cruel, or such as delight in the night and darkness, or such as feed upon impure things. And so the significance of these prohibitions is to teach men to abominate all cruelty or oppression and all works of darkness and filthiness.

20. *All fowls that creep.* Flying things that crawl or creep upon the earth, and so degenerate from their proper nature and of a mongrel kind, which may intimate that apostates and mongrels in religion are abominable in the sight of God.

27. *Upon his paws.* That is, which has feet divided into several parts like fingers, as dogs, cats, apes, and bears.

40. *He that eateth.* Unwittingly, for if he did it knowingly, it was a presumptuous sin against an express law (Deut. 14:21) and therefore punished with cutting off.

44. *Ye shall be holy.* By this he gives them to understand that all these cautions about eating or touching these creatures was not for any real uncleanness in them, but only that by the diligent observation of these rules they might learn with greater care to avoid all moral pollutions, and to keep themselves from all filthiness of flesh and spirit and from all familiar and intimate converse with notorious sinners.

45. *That bringeth you up out of the land of Egypt.* This was a reason why they should cheerfully submit to distinguishing laws who had been so honored with distinguishing favors.

46. *This is the law.* It was so, as long as the Mosaic dispensation lasted. But under the gospel we find it expressly repealed by a voice from heaven (Acts 10:15). Let us therefore bless God that to us every creature of God is good and nothing to be refused.

CHAPTER 12

1. From uncleanness contracted by the touching or eating of external things, he now comes to that uncleanness which arises from ourselves.

2. *Seven days.* Not for any filthiness which was either in the conception or in bringing forth, but to signify the universal and deep pollution of man's nature, even from birth and from conception.

8. The morality of this law obliges women who have received mercies from God in child bearing with all thankfulness to acknowledge his goodness to them, owning themselves unworthy of it, and (which is the best purification) to continue in faith and love and holiness, with sobriety.

CHAPTER 13

4. *Seven days.* For greater assurance; to teach ministers not to be hasty in their judgments, but diligently to search and examine all things beforehand.

6. *He shall wash his clothes.* Though it was no leprosy, to teach us that no sin is so small as not to need to be washed by the blood of Christ, which was the thing designed by all these washings.

31. *No black hair.* For had that appeared, it had ended the doubt, the black hair being a sign of soundness and strength of nature, as the yellow hair was a sign of unsoundness.

45. *His clothes shall be rent.* In the upper and fore parts, which were most visible. This was done partly as a token of sorrow, because though this was not a sin, yet it was an effect of sin and a sore punishment, whereby he was cut off both from converse with men and from the enjoyment of God in his ordinances. And partly it was done as a warning to others to keep at a due distance from him whenever he came. *His head bare.* Another sign of mourning. God would have men though not overwhelmed with, yet deeply sensible of his judgments. *A covering on his upper lip.* Partly as another badge of his sorrow and shame, and partly for the preservation of others from his breath or touch. *Unclean, unclean.* As begging the pity and prayers of others, and confessing his own infirmity, and cautioning those who came near him to keep at a distance from him.

46. *He shall dwell alone.* Partly for his humiliation; partly to prevent the infection of others; and partly to show the danger of converse with spiritual lepers or notorious sinners.

47. Leprosy in garments and houses is unknown in these times and places, which is not strange, there being some diseases peculiar to some ages and countries. And that such a thing was among the Jews cannot reasonably be doubted. For if Moses had been a deceiver, a man of his wisdom would not have exposed himself to the contempt of his people by giving laws about that which their experience showed to be but a fiction.

48. *In the warp or woof.* If the significance of these words be doubtful now, as some of those of the living creatures and precious stones are confessed to be, it is not material to us, this law being abolished. It suffices that Jews understood these things by frequent experience.

CHAPTER 14

3. *Healed* by God. For God alone did heal or cleanse him really, the priest only declaratively.

4. *Two birds.* The one to represent Christ as dying for his sins, the other to represent him as rising again for his purification or justification. *Scarlet.* A thread of wool of a scarlet color to represent both the leper's sinfulness, and the blood of Christ, and the happy change of the leper's color and complexion, which before was loathsome, now sprightly and beautiful. *Hyssop.* The fragrant smell of which signified the cure of the leper's ill scent.

5. *In an earthen vessel.* That is, over running water put in an earthen vessel. Thus the blood of the bird and the water were mixed together, partly for the convenience of sprinkling, partly to signify Christ, who came by water and blood (I John 5:6). The *running water,* that is, spring or river water, by its liveliness and motion did fitly signify the restoring of liveliness to the leper, who was in a manner dead before.

12. *A trespass offering.* To teach them that sin was the cause of leprosy and of all diseases, and that these ceremonial observations had a further meaning, to make them sensible of their spiritual diseases that they might fly to God in Christ for the cure of them.

14. *Priest shall put it.* To signify he was now free to hear God's word in the appointed places, and to touch any person or thing without defiling it, and to go wherever he pleased.

15. *The oil.* As the blood signified Christ's blood by which men obtained remission of sins, so the oil noted the graces of the spirit by which they are renewed.

25. The priest shall put the blood upon the extremities of the body, to include the whole. And some of the oil was afterwards put in the same places upon the blood. That blood seems to have been a token of forgiveness, the oil of healing. For God first forgiveth our iniquities and then healeth our diseases. When the leper was anointed, the oil must have blood under it, to signify that all the graces and comforts of the spirit, all his sanctifying influences, are owing to the death of Christ. It is by his blood alone that we are sanctified.

36. *All be not made unclean.* It is observable, neither the people nor the household stuff were polluted until the leprosy was discovered and declared by the priest, to show what great difference God makes between sins of ignorance and sins against knowledge.

57. *To teach.* To direct the priest when to pronounce a person or house clean or unclean. So it was not left to the priest's power or will, but they were tied to plain rules, such as the people might discern no less than the priest.

CHAPTER 15

18. Though in some special cases relating to the worship of God, men were to forbear the use of the marriage bed, yet to affirm that the use of it in other cases did generally defile the persons is contrary to the whole current of Scripture, which affirms the marriage bed to be undefiled (Heb. 13:4), to the practice of the Jews, which is a good comment upon their own laws, and to the light of nature and reason.

31. The grand reason of all these laws was to separate the children of Israel from their uncleanness. Hereby they were taught their privilege and honor, that they were purified unto God a peculiar people. For that was a defilement to them which was not so to others. They were also taught their duty, which was to keep themselves clean from all pollutions.

CHAPTER 16

4. *The linen coat.* It is observable, the high priest did not now use his peculiar

and glorious robes, but only his linen garments, which were common to him with the ordinary priests. The reason was because this was not a day of feasting and rejoicing, but of mourning and humiliation, at which times people were to lay aside their ornaments.

8. *For the* LORD. For the Lord's use by way of sacrifice. Both this and the other goat typified Christ; this in his death and passion for us, that in his resurrection for our deliverance.

14. *Upon the mercy seat.* To teach us that God is merciful to sinners only through and for the blood of Christ. With his face eastward, or upon the eastern part, toward the people, who were in the court which lay eastward from the Holy of Holies, which was the most western part of the tabernacle. This signified that the high priest in this act represented the people, and that God accepted it on their behalf.

15. *Then shall he kill the goat.* He went out of the Holy of Holies, and killed it, and then returned again with its blood. And whereas the high priest is said to be allowed to enter into that place but once a year, that is to be understood but one day in a year, though there was occasion of going in and coming out more than once upon that day.

16. *Because of the uncleanness of Israel.* For though the people did not enter into that place, yet their sins entered and would hinder the effects of the high priest's mediation on their behalf, if God was not reconciled to them. *In the midst of their uncleanness.* In the midst of a sinful people, who defile not themselves only, but also God's sanctuary. And God hereby showed them how much their hearts needed to be purified, when even the tabernacle, only by standing in the midst of them, needed this expiation.

21. *All the iniquities.* He mentioned

iniquities, transgressions, and sins to note sins of all sorts; and that a free and full confession was to be made; and that the smallest sins needed, and the greatest sins were not excluded from, the benefit of Christ's death here represented. *Upon the head.* Charging all their sins and the punishment due to them upon the goat, which though only a ceremony, yet being done according to God's appointment and manifestly pointing at Christ upon whom their iniquities and punishments were laid (Isa. 53:5–6), it was available for this end. And hence the heathens took their custom of selecting one beast or man, upon whom they laid all their imprecations and curses, and whom they killed as an expiatory sacrifice for their sins and to prevent their ruin. *A fit man.* That is, of years and discretion, who may be trusted with this work. *Into the wilderness.* Which signified the removal of their sins far away both from the people and out of God's sight. And here the goat being neglected by all men and exposed to many hazards from wild beasts, which were numerous there, might further signify Christ's being forsaken both by God and by men, even by his own disciples, and the many dangers and sufferings he underwent. The Jews write that this goat was carried to the mountain called Azazel, which the goat is so called (v. 10), and that there he was cast down headlong.

34. *This shall be an everlasting statute.* By which were typified the two great gospel privileges: remission of sins and access to God, both which we owe to the mediation of the Lord Jesus.

CHAPTER 17

4. *The tabernacle.* This was appointed in opposition to the heathens, who sacrificed in all places; to cut off occasions of idolatry; to prevent the people's usurpation of the priest's office, and to signify that God would accept of no sacrifice but through Christ and in the Church. But though men were tied to this law, God was free to dispense with his own law, which he did sometimes to the prophets (I Sam. 7:9; 11:15). *He hath shed blood.* He shall be punished as a murderer. The reason is, because he shed that blood which, though not man's blood, yet was precious, being sacred and appropriated to God, and typically the price by which men's lives were ransomed.

7. *Unto devils.* So they did not directly or intentionally, but by construction and consequence, because the devil is the author of idolatry and is eminently served and honored by it. And as the Egyptians were notorious for their idolatry, so the Israelites were infected with their leaven (Josh. 24:14; Ezek. 20:7; 23:2–3). *A-whoring.* Idolatry, especially in God's people, is commonly called whoredom because it is a violation of that covenant by which they were peculiarly betrothed or married to God.

10. *I will set my face.* I will be an enemy to him and execute vengeance upon him immediately; because such a person probably would do this in private, so that the magistrate could not know nor punish it. Write that man undone, forever undone, against whom God sets his face.

CHAPTER 18

5. *He shall live in them.* Not only happily here, but eternally hereafter. This is added as a powerful argument why they should follow God's commands rather than men's examples, because their life and happiness depend upon it. And though in strictness and according to the covenant of works, they could not challenge life for so doing—except their obedience was universal, perfect, constant, and perpetual, and therefore no man since the fall could be justified by the law—yet by the covenant of grace this life is promised to all that obey God's commands sincerely.

18. *Neither shalt thou take a wife to her sister.* Perhaps this text does not simply forbid the taking one wife to another, but the doing it in such a manner or for such an end that he may vex or punish or revenge himself of the former; which probably was a common motive among that hard-hearted people to do so.

21. *Pass through the fire.* This was done, either by burning them in the fire, or by making them pass between two great fires, which was a kind of consecration of them to that god. *Molech.* Called also "Milcom," an idol chiefly of the Ammonites.

29. *Cut off.* This phrase is to be understood variously, of either ecclesiastical or civil punishment, according to the differing natures of the offenses for which it is inflicted.

CHAPTER 19

2. *Be ye holy.* Separated from all the forementioned defilements, and entirely consecrated to God and obedient to all his laws. *I am holy.* Both in my essence and in all my laws, which are holy and just and good.

3. *His mother.* The mother is put first, partly because the practice of this duty begins there, mothers by perpetual converse being sooner known to their children than their fathers; partly because this duty is commonly neglected to the mother, upon whom children have not so much dependence as they have upon their father. And this *fear* includes the two great duties of reverence and obedience.

And keep my sabbaths. This is added to show that, whereas it is enjoined to parents that they should take care that the sabbath be observed both by themselves and their children, it is the duty of children to fear and obey their parents in this matter. But that, if parents should neglect their duty herein or by command, counsel, or example draw them to pollute the sabbath, the children in that case must keep the sabbath and prefer the command of God before the commands of their parents.

14. *Before the blind.* To make them fall. Under these two particulars are manifestly forbidden all injuries done to such as are unable to right or defend themselves. Of whom God here takes the more care, because they are not able to secure themselves.

17. *Thou shalt not hate.* As you do, in effect, if you do not rebuke him. *Thy brother.* The same as *thy neighbour,* that is, every man. If your brother has done wrong, you shall neither divulge it to others, nor hate him and smother that hatred by sullen silence. Nor flatter him therein, but shall freely and in love tell him of his fault. *And not suffer sin upon him.* Not permit him to lie under the guilt of any sin which you by rebuking him, and thereby bringing him to repentance, could free him from.

19. *Thou shalt not let thy cattle gender.* This was prohibited, partly to restrain the curiosity and boldness of men, who might attempt to amend or change the works of God; partly that by the restraint here laid even upon brute-creatures men might be taught to abhor all unnatural lusts; partly to teach the Israelites to avoid mixtures with other nations, either in marriage or in religion, which also may be signified by the following prohibitions.

26. *Neither shall ye use enchantment.* It was unpardonable in them to whom were committed the oracles of God that they ask counsel of the devil. And yet worse in Christians, to whom the Son of God is manifested, to destroy the works of the devil. For Christians to have their fortunes told or to use charms for the cure of diseases is an intolerable affront to the Lord Jesus, a support of idolatry, and a reproach both to themselves, and to that worthy name by which they are called. *Nor observe times.* Superstitiously, esteeming some days lucky, others unlucky.

31. Wizards. Them that have entered into covenant with the devil, by whose help they foretell many things to come and acquaint men with secret things. (See Lev. 20:27; Deut. 18:11; I Sam. 28:3, 7, 9; II Kings 21:6.)

CHAPTER 20

3. *I will set my face against that man.* Deal with him as an enemy and make him a monument of my justice. *And to profane my name.* Partly by despising it themselves, partly by disgracing it to others and giving them occasion to blaspheme it and to abhor the true religion.

4. *Hide their eyes.* Wink at his fault, and forbear to accuse and punish him.

12. *Confusion.* By perverting the order which God has appointed, and making the same offspring both his own child and his grandchild.

15. *Slay the beast.* Partly for the prevention of monstrous births, partly to blot out the memory of so loathsome a crime.

17. In this and several following verses, "uncovering nakedness" plainly appears to mean not marriage, but fornication or adultery.

20. *They shall die childless.* Either shall be speedily cut off lest they can have a child by that incestuous conjunction. If this seem a less crime than most of the

former incestuous mixtures, and therefore the magistrate forbear to punish it with death; yet they shall either have no children from such an unlawful bed, or their children shall die before them.

27. *A man or a woman that hath a familiar spirit . . . shall surely be put to death.* They that are in league with the devil have in effect made a covenant with death. And so shall their doom be.

CHAPTER 21

1. *Among his people.* None of the priests shall touch the dead body, or assist at his funeral, or eat of the funeral feast. The reason for this law is evident, because by such pollution they were excluded from converse with men, to whom by their function they were to be serviceable upon all occasions, and from the handling of holy things. And God would hereby teach them, and in them all successive ministers, that they ought entirely to give themselves to the service of God. Yes, to renounce all expressions of natural affection and all worldly employments, so far as they are impediments to the discharge of their holy services.

2. *Near to him.* Under which general expression his wife seems to be comprehended, though she be not expressed. And hence it is noted as a peculiar case that Ezekiel, who was a priest, was forbidden to mourn for his wife (Ezek. 24:16ff.). These exceptions God makes in condescension to human infirmity, because in such cases it was very hard to restrain the affections. But this allowance concerns only the inferior priest, not the high priest.

11. *Go in.* Into the chamber or house where they lie. This and many other rites here prescribed were from hence translated by the heathens into their use, whose priests were put under the same obligations.

13. *In her virginity.* Or, a virgin, partly because as he was a type of Christ, so his wife was a type of the church, which is compared to a virgin; and partly for greater caution and assurance that his wife was not a defiled or deflowered person. Most of these things are forbidden to all the priests; and here to the high priest, to show that he also, and he especially, is obliged to the same cautions.

17. *That hath.* In parts, any notorious deformity or imperfection in his body. The reason for this is (1) Partly typical that he might more fully represent Christ, the great High Priest, who was typified both by the priest and sacrifice, and therefore both were to be without blemish. (2) Partly moral, to teach all Christians and especially ministers of holy things what purity and perfection of heart and life they should labor after, and that notorious blemishes in the mind or conversation render a man unfit for the ministry of the gospel. (3) And partly prudential, because such blemishes were apt to breed contempt of the person; and consequently, of his function, and of the holy things wherein he ministered.

For this reason, such persons as have notorious defects or deformities are still unfit for the ministry. Except where there are eminent gifts and graces, which vindicate a man from the contemptibleness of his bodily presence. The particular defects here mentioned, I shall not enlarge upon, because some of the Hebrew words are diversely interpreted, and because, the use of these things being abolished, the knowledge of them is not necessary.

18. *A flat nose.* Most restrain this word to the nose and to some great deformity relating to it. But according to others, it signifies more generally a person who lacks some member or members, because the next word

[*superfluous*], to which it is opposed, signifies one that has more members than he should.

CHAPTER 22

12. *A stranger.* Yet the priest's wife, though of another family, might eat. The reason for the difference is because the wife passes into the name, state, and privileges of her husband, from whom the family is denominated.

CHAPTER 23

11. *He shall wave the sheaf before the* LORD. In the name of the whole congregation, which as it were sanctified to them the whole harvest and gave them a comfortable use of all the rest. For then we may eat our bread with joy, when God has accepted our works. And thus should we always begin with God; begin our lives with him, begin every day with him, begin every work and business with him: "seek ye first the kingdom of God."

21. *An holy convocation.* A sabbath or day of rest, called Pentecost; which was instituted, (1) Partly in remembrance of the consummation of their deliverance out of Egypt by bringing them to the mount of God, or Sinai, as God had promised, and of that admirable blessing of giving the law to them on the fiftieth day and forming them into a commonwealth under his immediate government. And (2) Partly in gratitude for the further progress of their harvest, as in the Passover they offered a thank offering to God for the beginning of their harvest. The perfection of this feast was the pouring out of the Holy Spirit upon the apostles on this very day, in which the law of faith was given, fifty days after Christ our Passover was sacrificed for us. And on that day the apostles, having themselves

received "the firstfruits of the Spirit," begat three thousand souls through the word of truth, as the first fruits of the Christian church.

27. *Afflict your souls.* With fasting and bitter repentance for all, especially their national sins, among which no doubt God would have them remember their sin of the golden calf. For as God had threatened to remember it in aftertimes to punish them for it, so there was great reason why they should remember it to humble themselves for it.

29. *Whatsoever soul.* Of either the Jewish nation, or religion. Hereby God would signify the absolute necessity which every man had of repentance and forgiveness of sin, and the desperate condition of all impenitent persons.

32. *Ye shall celebrate your sabbath.* The Jews are supposed to begin every day, and consequently their sabbaths, at the evening, in remembrance of the creation, as Christians generally begin their days and sabbaths with the morning in memory of Christ's resurrection.

34. *Of tabernacles.* Of tents or booths or arbors. This feast was appointed to remind them of that time when they had no other dwellings in the wilderness, and to stir them up to bless God, as well for the gracious protection then afforded them, as for the more commodious habitations now given them. It was to excite them to gratitude for all the fruits of the year newly ended, which were now completely brought in.

38. *Your gifts.* Which, being here distinguished from the free-will offerings made to the Lord, may note what they freely gave to the priests over and above their firstfruits and tithes or other things which they were enjoined to give.

42. *In booths.* Which were erected in their cities or towns, either in their streets or gardens or the tops of their houses. These were made flat and therefore were fit for the use.

44. *The feasts of the LORD.* We have reason to be thankful that the feasts of the Lord are not now so numerous, nor the observance of them so burdensome and costly; but more spiritual and significant, and surer and sweeter earnests of the everlasting feast at the last ingathering, which we hope to be celebrating to eternity.

CHAPTER 24

2. *To cause the lamps to burn.* The seven lamps made all one lamp. In allusion to which, the Blessed Spirit is represented (Rev. 4:5) by "seven lamps of fire before the throne." For there are diversities of gifts, but one Spirit.

8. *By an everlasting covenant.* By virtue of that compact made between me and them, by which they were obliged to keep this among other commands and, they so doing, I am obliged to be their God and to bless them. And this may be here called an everlasting covenant, not only because it was to endure as long as the Jewish polity stood, but also because this was to stand everlastingly, or continually, and therefore the new cakes were first brought before the old were taken away.

17. *That killeth.* This law is repeated here to prevent the mischievous effects of men's striving together, which as here it caused blasphemy, so it might in others lead to murder.

23. *Stone him with stones.* This blasphemer was the first that died by the law of Moses. Stephen, the first that died for the gospel, died by the abuse of the law. The martyr and the malefactor suffered the same death; but how vast the difference between them!

CHAPTER 25

2. *Keep a sabbath.* That is, enjoy rest and freedom from plowing and tilling. *Unto the* LORD. In obedience and unto the honor of God. This was instituted, (1) For the assertion of God's sovereign right to the land, in which the Israelites were but tenants at God's will. (2) For the trial of their obedience. (3) For the demonstration of his providence as well as in general towards men, and especially towards his own people. (4) To wean them from inordinate love and pursuit of worldly advantages, and to encourage them to depend upon God alone and upon God's blessing for their subsistence. (5) To put them in mind of that blessed and eternal rest provided for all good men.

4. *A sabbath of rest unto the land.* They were neither to do any work about it, nor expect any harvest from it. All yearly labors were to be intermitted in the seventh year, as much as daily labors on the seventh day.

9. *The jubilee.* Signified the true liberty from our spiritual debts and slaveries to be purchased by Christ, and to be published to the world by the sound of the gospel. *In the day of atonement.* A very fit time, that when they fasted and prayed for God's mercy to them in the pardon of their sins, then they might exercise their charity to men in forgiving their debts. And to teach us that the foundation of all solid comfort must be laid in repentance and atonement for our sins through Christ.

10. *The fiftieth year.* This law was not at all unjust, because all buyers and sellers had an eye to this condition in their bargains; but it was expedient in many regards, as (1) To remind them that God alone was the Lord and proprietor both of them and of their lands, and they only his tenants; a point which they were very apt to forget. (2)

That hereby inheritances, families, and tribes, might be kept entire and clear until the coming of the Messiah, who was to be known by other things, so by the tribe and family out of which he was to come. And this accordingly was done by the singular providence of God until the Lord Jesus did come. Since which time those characters are miserably confounded: which is no small argument that the Messiah is come.

(3) To set bounds both to the insatiable avarice of some, and the foolish prodigality of others, that the former might not wholly and finally swallow up the inheritances of their brethren, and the latter might not be able to undo themselves and their posterity for ever, which was a singular privilege of this law and people.

12. *It shall be holy.* So it was, because it was sequestered in great part from worldly employments and dedicated to God, and to the exercise of holy joy and thankfulness. And because it was a type of that holy and happy jubilee which they were to expect and enjoy under the Messiah.

25. *If any of his kin come.* Or, If the redeemer come, being near akin to him, who in this was an eminent type of Christ, who was made near akin to us by taking our flesh that he might perform the work of redemption for us.

30. *It shall not go out.* The reasons before alleged for lands do not hold in such houses. There was no danger of confusion in tribes or families by the alienation of houses. The seller also had a greater propriety in houses than in lands, as being commonly built by the owner's cost and diligence, and therefore had a fuller power to dispose of them. Besides, God would hereby encourage persons to buy and possess houses in such places, as frequency and fullness of inhabitants in cities was a great strength, honor, and advantage to the whole land.

36. *Or increase.* All kinds of usury are in this case forbidden, whether of victuals or of money or of any thing that is commonly lent by one man to another upon usury or upon condition of receiving the thing lent with advantage and overplus. If one borrow in his necessity, there can be no doubt but this law is binding still. But it cannot be thought to bind where money is borrowed for purchase of lands, trade, or other improvements. For there it is reasonable that the lender share with the borrower in the profit.

42. *They are my servants.* They, no less than you, are members of my church and people. Such as I have chosen out of all the world to serve me here and to enjoy me hereafter, and therefore are not to be oppressed, neither are you absolute lords over them to deal with them as you please.

43. *Fear thy God.* Though you do not fear them who are in your power and unable to right themselves, yet fear that God who has commanded you to use them kindly, and who can and will avenge their cause if you oppress them.

CHAPTER 26

4. *Rain.* Therefore God placed them not in a land having such rivers as the Nile, to water it and make it fruitful, but in a land which depended wholly upon the rain of heaven, the key whereof God kept in his own hand so that he might the more effectually oblige them to obedience, in which their happiness consisted.

6. *The sword.* That is, war, as the sword is often taken. It shall not enter into it nor have passage through it, much less shall your land be made the seat of war.

12. *I will walk among you.* As I have done, both by my pillar of cloud and fire and by my tabernacle, which have walked or gone along with you in all your journeys and stayed among you in all your stations, to protect, conduct, instruct, and comfort you. And I will own you for that peculiar people which I have singled out of mankind, to bless you here and to save you hereafter.

13. *Upright.* Heads lifted up, not pressed down with a yoke. It notes their liberty, security, confidence, and glory.

15. *Break my covenant.* Break your part of that covenant made between me and you, and thereby discharge me from the blessings promised by me.

19. *The pride of your power.* That is, your strength of which you are proud, your numerous and united forces, your kingdom, yes, your ark and sanctuary. I will make your heaven as iron. The heavens shall yield you no rain, nor the earth fruits.

29. *The flesh of your sons.* Through extreme hunger. (See Lam. 4:10.)

30. *High places.* In which you will sacrifice after the manner of the heathens. The carcasses of your idols. So he calls them, either (1) To signify that their idols, however glorious in their eyes, were in truth but lifeless and contemptible carcasses. Or, (2) To show that their idols should be so far from helping them that they should be thrown down and broken with them, and both should lie together in a forlorn and loathsome state.

39. *Pine away.* Be consumed and melt away by degrees through diseases, oppressions, griefs, manifold miseries.

41. *If they accept.* The meaning is, if they sincerely acknowledge the righteousness of God and their own wickedness, and patiently submit to this correcting hand; if with David they are ready to say, it is good for them that they are afflicted, that they may learn God's statutes and yield obedience to them for the future, which is a good evidence of true repentance.

42. *I will remember my covenant.* So as to make good all that I have promised in it. For words of knowledge or remembrance in Scripture commonly denote affection and kindness. *I will remember the land.* Which now seems to be forgotten and despised, as if I had never chosen it to be the peculiar place of my presence and blessing.

44. *For I am the* LORD *their God.* Therefore neither the desperateness of their condition nor the greatness of their sins shall make me wholly make void my covenant with them and their ancestors, but I will in due time remember them for good, and for my covenant's sake return to them in mercy. For this place the Jews take great comfort and assure themselves of deliverance out of their present servitude and misery. And from this and such other places, St. Paul concludes that the Israelite nation, though then rejected and ruined, should be gathered again and restored.

46. *These are . . . the laws which the* LORD *made between him and the children of Israel.* Hereby his communion with his church is kept up. He manifests not only his dominion over them, but his favor to them, by giving them his law. And they manifest not only their holy fear, but their holy love by the observance of it. And thus it is made between them rather as a covenant than as a law.

CHAPTER 27

4. *Thirty shekels.* Less than the man's price, because she is inferior to him both in strength and serviceableness.

5. *Five years old.* At which age they might be vowed by their parents, as appears from I Samuel 1, though not by themselves. And the children were obliged by their parents' vow, which is not strange considering the parents' right to dispose of their children so far as is not contrary to the mind of God.

16. *Of his possession.* That is, which is his by inheritance, because particular direction is given about purchased lands (v. 22). And he said, *part* of it, for it was unlawful to vow away all his possessions, because thereby he disabled himself from the performance of many duties and made himself burdensome to his brethren.

21. *The possession shall be the priest's.* For their maintenance. Nor is this repugnant to that law that the priests should have no inheritance in the land (Num. 18:20), for that is only spoken of the tribe of Levi in general, in reference to the first division of the land, wherein the Levites were not to have a distinct part of land, as other tribes had. But this does not hinder, but some particular lands might be vowed and given to the priests, either for their own benefit or for the service of the sanctuary.

32. *Under the rod.* Either, (1) The tither's rod, it being the manner of the Jews in tithing to cause all their cattle to pass through some gate or narrow passage, where the tenth was marked by a person appointed for that purpose and reserved for the priest. Or, (2) The shepherd's rod, under which the herds and flocks passed, and by which they were governed and numbered. (See Jer. 33:13; Ezek. 20:37).

34. *These are the commandments, which the* LORD *commanded Moses.* This has reference to the whole book. Many of these commandments are moral; others ceremonial and peculiar to the Jewish economy; which yet are instructive to us, who have a key to the mysteries that are contained in them. Upon the whole, we have cause to bless God that we are not come to mount Sinai, that we are not under the dark shadows of the law, but enjoy the clear light of the gospel.

The doctrine of our reconciliation to

God by a Mediator is not clouded with the smoke of burning sacrifices, but cleared by the knowledge of "Christ, and him crucified." And we may praise him that we are not under the yoke of the law, but under the sweet and easy instructions of the gospel, which pronounces those the true worshippers that "worship the Father in spirit and in truth," by Christ only, who is our priest, temple, altar, sacrifice, purification, and all.

NUMBERS

CHAPTER 1

2. *Take ye the sum.* This is not the same counting as that of Exodus 38:26. They were for different ends; that one was to tax them for the charges of the tabernacle; this one was for other ends. (1) Partly that the great number of the people might be known to the praise of God's faithfulness, in making good his promises of multiplying them, and to their own encouragement. (2) Partly for the better ordering their camp and march, for they were now beginning their journey.

And, (3) Partly that this account might be compared with the other in the close of the book, where we read that not one of all this vast number, except Caleb and Joshua, were left alive. This was a fair warning to all future generations to take heed of rebelling against the Lord. It is true, the sums and numbers agree in this and that computation, which is not strange, because there was not much time between the two numberings, and no eminent sin among the people in that interval, whereby God was provoked to diminish their numbers.

33. *Ephraim.* Above 8,000 more than Manasseh, towards the accomplishment of that promise (Gen. 48:20) which the devil in vain attempted to defeat by stirring up the men of Gath against them (I Chron. 7:21–22).

37. *Thirty and five thousand.* The smallest number, except one, though Benjamin had more immediate children than any of his brethren (Gen. 46:21), whereas Dan had but one immediate son (Gen. 46:23), yet now his number is the biggest but one of all the tribes and is almost double to that of Benjamin. Such great and strange change God easily can, and frequently does, make in families (I Sam. 2:5). And therefore let none boast or please themselves too much in their numerous offspring.

50. *The tabernacle of testimony.* So called here (and Exod. 38:21) because it was made chiefly for the sake of the ark of the testimony, which is often called "the testimony."

51. *That cometh nigh.* The *stranger* elsewhere is one of another nation, here one of another tribe. So as to do the offices mentioned in verse 50.

CHAPTER 2

2. It is observable, those tribes were placed together that were nearest of kin to each other. Judah, Issachar, and Zebulun were the three youngest sons of Leah, and Issachar and Zebulun would not grudge to be under Judah, their elder brother. Reuben and Simeon would not be content with their place. Therefore Reuben, Jacob's eldest son, is chief of the next squadron. Simeon doubtless is willing to be under him. And Gad, the son of Leah's handmade, is fitly added to him, in Levi's room. Ephraim, Manasseh, and Benjamin are all the posterity of Rachel. Dan the eldest son of Bilhah leads the rest. To them are added the two younger sons of the handmaids. So much of the wisdom of God appears even in these smaller circumstances!

3. *Judah.* This tribe was in the first post, and in their marches led the van, not only because it was the most numerous, but chiefly because Christ, "the lion of the tribe of Judah," was to descend from it. Yea, from the loins of Nahshon, who is here appointed the chief captain of it.

17. *In the midst.* This is not to be understood strictly, but largely. For in their march they were divided, and part of that tribe marched next after Judah (Num. 10:17), and the other part exactly in the midst of the camp.

18. *Ephraim.* Who is here preferred before his brother, according to the prophecy (Gen. 48:19–20).

31. *The camp of Dan.* The strongest camp next after Judah, and therefore he comes in the rear, as Judah marched in the front, that the tabernacle might be best guarded where there was most danger.

CHAPTER 3

12. *The firstborn.* Who were God's property (Exod. 13:12), and to whom the administration of holy things was formerly committed, which now was taken away from them, either because they had forfeited this privilege by joining with the rest of their brethren in the idolatrous worship of the calf, or because they were to be mainly concerned in the distribution and management of the inheritances which now they were going to possess, and therefore could not be at leisure to attend upon the service of the sanctuary.

15. *From a month old.* Because at that time the firstborn, in whose stead the Levites came, were offered to God. And from that time the Levites were consecrated to God and were, as soon as capable, instructed in their work. Elsewhere they are numbered from twenty-five years old, when they were entered as novices into part of their work (Num. 8:24), and from thirty years old, when they were admitted to their whole office.

27. *Of Kohath.* This family had many privileges above the others; of that were Moses and Aaron and all the priests. They had the chief place about the tabernacle, and the care of the most holy things here, and in the land of Canaan they had twenty-three cities, which were almost as many as both their brethren received. Yet the posterity of Moses were not at all dignified or distinguished from other Levites. So far was he from seeking any advantage or honor for his own family.

39. *Twenty and two thousand.* If the particular numbers mentioned in verses 22, 28, 34 be put together, they make 22,300. But the odd 300 are omitted here, either according to the use of the holy Scripture, where in such great numbers small sums are commonly neglected, or, because they were the firstborn of the Levites, and therefore belonged to God already, and so could not be given to him again instead of the other firstborn. If this number of firstborn seem small to come from 22,000 Levites, it must be considered that only such firstborn are here named as were males, and such as continued in their parents families, not such as had erected new families of their own.

Add to this that God so ordered things by his wise providence for many weighty reasons, that this tribe should be much the least of all the tribes, as is evident by comparing the number of the other tribes, from twenty years old (Num. 1) with the number of this from a month old. Therefore it is not strange if the number of their firstborn be less than in other tribes.

CHAPTER 4

3. *From thirty.* This age was pre-scribed as the age of full strength of body and therefore most proper for their laborious work of carrying the parts and vessels of the tabernacle, and of maturity of judgment, which is necessary for the right management of holy services. (Whence even John and Christ entered not upon their ministry until that age.) Indeed their first en-trance upon their work was at their twenty-fifth year, when they began as learners, and acted under the inspection and direction of their brethren; but in their thirtieth year they were com-pletely admitted to a full discharge of their whole office.

But David, being a prophet, and particularly directed by God in the affairs of the temple, made a change in this matter, because the magnificence of the temple, and the great multitude of sacred utensils and sacrifices, required a greater number of attendants than for-merly was necessary.

31–32. The death of the saints is represented to us as the taking down of the tabernacle. The immortal soul, like the most holy things, is first covered and taken away, carried by angels un-seen, and care is taken also of the body, the skin and flesh, which are as the curtains, the bones and sinews, which are as the *bars* and *pillars*. None of these shall be lost. Commandment is given

concerning the bones, a covenant made with the dust. They are in safe custody and shall be produced in the great day, when this tabernacle shall be set up again and these vile bodies made like the glorious body of Jesus Christ.

CHAPTER 5

6. *Against the* LORD. Which words may be added to show that such inju-ries done to men are also sins against God, who has commanded justice to men as well as religion to himself.

7. *They shall confess their sin.* They shall not continue in the denial of the fact, but give glory to God and take shame to themselves by acknowledging it. *And add.* Both as a compensation to the injured person for the lack of his goods so long, and as a penalty upon the injurious dealer, to discourage others from such attempts.

12. *If any man's wife.* This law was given partly to deter wives from adul-terous practices, and partly to secure wives against the rage of their hard-hearted husbands, who otherwise may upon mere suspicions destroy them, or at least put them away. There was not like fear of inconveniences to the hus-band from the jealousy of the wife, who had not that authority and power and opportunity for the putting away or killing the husband, as the husband had over the wife.

15. *Then shall the man bring his wife unto the priest.* Who first strove to persuade her to own the truth. If she did, she was not put to death (which must have been if it had been proved against her) but only was divorced and lost her dowry. *Her offering.* By way of solemn appeal to God, whom hereby she desired to judge between her and her husband, and by way of atonement to appease God, who had for her sins stirred up her husband against her.

Bringing iniquity to remembrance. Both to God before whom she appeared as a sinner, and to her own conscience if she was guilty; and, if she were not guilty of this, yet it reminded her of her other sins, for which this might be a punishment.

18. *Before the LORD.* Before the tabernacle with her face towards the ark. *Uncover the woman's head.* Partly that she might be made sensible how manifest she and all her ways were to God; partly in token of her sorrow for her sin, or at least for any cause of suspicion which she had given. *In her hands.* That she herself might offer it and thereby call God to be witness of her innocence. *Bitter.* So called either from the bitter taste which the dust gave it, or from the bitter effects of it upon her, if she were guilty.

22. *Amen, amen.* That is, so let it be if I be guilty. The word is doubled by here as an evidence of her innocence, and ardent desire that God would deal with her according to her desert.

23. *In a book.* That is, in a scroll of parchment, which the Hebrews commonly call a book. *Blot them out.* Or scrape them out and cast them into *bitter water.* Whereby it was signified that if she was innocent, the curses should be blotted out and come to nothing. If guilty, she should find in her the effects of this water which she drank, after the words of this curse had been scraped and put in.

31. *Guiltless.* Which he should not have been, if he had either indulged her in so great a wickedness and not endeavored to bring her to repentance, or cherished suspicions in his breast and thereupon proceeded to hate her or cast her off. Whereas now, whatsoever the consequence is, the husband shall not be censured for bringing such curses upon her, or for defaming her, if she appear to be innocent.

CHAPTER 6

2. *A vow of a Nazarite.* Whereby they sequestered themselves from worldly employments and enjoyments, that they might entirely consecrate themselves to God's service, and this either for their whole lifetime or for a less and limited space of time.

3. *Nor eat . . . grapes.* Which was forbidden him for greater caution to keep him at further distance from wine.

5. *No razor.* Nor scissors nor other instrument to cut off any part of his hair. This was appointed, (1) Partly as a sign of his mortification to worldly delights and outward beauty. (2) Partly as a testimony of that purity which hereby he professed, because the cutting off the hair was a sign of uncleanness, as appears from verse 9. (3) Partly that by the length of his hair he might be constantly reminded of his vow. And, (4) Partly that he might reserve his hair entirely for God, to whom it was to be offered.

9. *He shall shave his head.* Because his whole body, and especially his hair, was defiled by such an accident, which he ought to impute either to his own heedlessness or to God's providence so ordering the matter, possibly for the punishment of his other sins, or for quickening him to more purity and detestation of all dead works, whereby he would be defiled.

14. *A sin offering.* Whereby he confessed his misdeeds, in spite of the strictness of his vow and all the diligence which he could use, and consequently acknowledged his need of the grace of God in Christ Jesus the true Nazarite. *For peace offerings.* For thankfulness to God, who had given him grace to make and in some measure to keep such a vow. So he offered all the three sorts of offerings that he might so far fulfill all righteousness and profess his obligation to observe the will of God in all things.

18. *At the door.* Publicly, that it might be known that his vow was ended and therefore he was at liberty as to those things from which he had restrained himself for a season, otherwise some might have been scandalized at his use of his liberty.

20. *May drink wine.* And return to his former manner of living.

24. *Bless thee.* Bestow upon you all manner of blessings, temporal and spiritual. *Keep thee.* That is, continue his blessings to you, and preserve you in and to the use of them; keep you from sin and its bitter effects.

25. *Shine upon thee.* Alluding to the shining of the sun upon the earth, to enlighten and warm and renew the face of it. The Lord love you, and make you know that he loves you. We cannot but be happy if we have God's love; and we cannot but be at ease if we know that we have it.

26. *Lift up his countenance.* That is, look upon you with a cheerful and pleasant countenance, as one that is well pleased with you and your services. *Peace.* Peace with God, with your own conscience, and with all men; all prosperity is comprehended under this word.

27. *Put my name.* Shall call them by my name, shall recommend them to me as my own people, and bless them and pray unto me for them as such; which is a powerful argument to prevail with God for them.

CHAPTER 7

89. *To speak with him.* To consult God upon occasion. *The mercy seat.* Which Moses standing without the veil could easily hear. And this seems to be added in this place to show that when men had done their part, God was not lacking in the performance of his part and promise. God's speaking thus to Moses by an audible voice, as if he had been clothed with a body, was an earnest of the incarnation of the Son of God, when in the fullness of time the Word should be made flesh and speak in the language of the sons of men. That he who spoke to Moses was the Eternal Word was the belief of many of the ancients. For all God's communion with man is by his Son, who is "the same yesterday, and to-day, and for ever."

CHAPTER 8

2. *When thou lightest the lamps.* The priests lit the middle lamp from the fire of the altar. And the rest, one from another; signifying that all light and knowledge comes from Christ, who has the seven spirits of God, signified by the "seven lamps of fire."

7. *Shave all their flesh.* This external rite signified the cutting off of their inordinate desire of earthly things, and that singular purity of heart and life which is required in the ministers of God.

19. *To do the service of the children of Israel.* To serve God in their stead, to do what otherwise they had been obliged to do in their own persons. *To make an atonement.* Not by offering sacrifices, which the priests alone might do, but by assisting the priests in that expiatory work, and by a diligent performance of all the parts of their office, whereby God was pleased both with them and with the people. *That there be no plague.* This is added as a reason why God appointed them to serve in the tabernacle, that they might guard it and not allow any of the people to come near it, or meddle with holy things, which if they did would certainly bring a plague upon them.

CHAPTER 9

7. *An offering.* Which if we neglect, we must be cut off, and if we keep it in these circumstances, we must also be cut off. What shall we do?

18. The motion or stay of the cloud is fitly called *the commandment of the* LORD, because it was a sign of God's will and their duty.

21. *When the cloud abode.* This is repeated again and again, because it was a constant miracle and because it is a matter we should take particular notice of, as highly significant and instructive. It is mentioned long after by David (Ps. 105:39) and by the people of God after their captivity (Neh. 9:19). And the guidance of this cloud is spoken of, signifying the guidance of the Blessed Spirit (Isa. 63:14). "The Spirit of the LORD caused him to rest: and so didst thou lead thy people."

And thus, in effect, does he guide all those who commit their ways unto the Lord. So that they may well say, Father, thy will be done! Dispose of me and mine as you please. Here I am, waiting on my God, to journey and rest at the commandment of the Lord. What you will, and where you will; only let me be yours and always in the way of my duty.

CHAPTER 10

2. *Two trumpets.* For Aaron's two sons. Though afterwards the number of the trumpets was much increased, as the number of the priests also was.

10. *In the day of your gladness.* Days appointed for rejoicing and thanksgiving to God for former mercies, or deliverances. *Your solemn days.* Your stated festivals. *For a memorial.* That God may remember you for good to accept and bless you. God then takes pleasure in our religious exercises,

when we take pleasure in them. Holy work should be done with holy joy.

31. *Thou mayest be to us instead of eyes.* To direct and guide us. For though the cloud determined them to a general place, yet many particulars might be unknown to Moses, wherein Hobab, having long lived in those parts, might be able to advise him as concerning the conveniences of water for their cattle, concerning the safety or danger of the several parts, by reason of serpents or wild beasts or enemies in the parts adjoining to them, so that they might guard themselves better against them.

Or, this is to be understood of his directing them not so much in their way, as about great and difficult matters, wherein the counsel he had from God did not exclude the advice of men, as we see in Hobab's father, Jethro (Exod. 18). And it is probable this was the wise son of a wise father.

33. *The ark . . . went before them.* Although in their stations it was in the middle, yet in their marches it went before them. And the cloud was constantly over the ark whether it stood or went. Therefore the ark is said to go before and direct them, not as if the ark could be seen of all the camps, which being carried only upon men's shoulders was impossible. But because the cloud, which always attended upon the ark and did, together with the ark, constitute one sign of God's presence, did lead and direct them.

34. *By day.* And by night too, as was expressed before. So we must learn to compare places of Scripture and to supply the defects of one out of another, as we do in all authors.

CHAPTER 11

1. *Complained.* Or, "murmured," the occasion whereof seems to be their last three days' journey in a vast howling wilderness, and thereupon the remembrance of their long abode in the wilderness, and the fear of many other tedious journeys, whereby they were likely to be long delayed from coming to the land of milk and honey, which they thirsted after.

5. *Freely.* Either without price, for fish was very plentiful and fishing was there free, or with a very small price. And this is the more probable because the Egyptians might not taste of fish, nor of the leeks and onions, which they worshipped for gods, and therefore the Israelites might have them upon cheap terms.

8. The nature and use of manna is here particularly described, to show the greatness of their sin in despising such excellent food.

10. *In the door of his tent.* To note they were not ashamed of their sin.

11. *Not found favour.* Why did you not hear my prayer, when I desired you would excuse me and commit the care of this unruly people to some other person?

14. *Alone.* Others were only assistant to him in smaller matters. But the harder and greater affairs, such as this unquestionably was, were brought to Moses and determined by him alone.

15. *My wretchedness.* My torment, arising from the insuperable difficulty of my office and work of ruling this people, and from the dread of their utter extermination, and the dishonor which thus will accrue to God and to religion, as if, not I only, but God also were an impostor.

16. *To be the elders.* Whom you by experience discern to be elders not only in years and name, but also in wisdom and authority with the people. And according to this constitution, the Sanhedrin, or great council of the Jews, which in after-ages sat at Jerusalem and was the highest court of the judgment among them, consisted of seventy men.

17. *I will come down.* By my powerful presence and operation. I *will put it upon them.* That is, I will give the same Spirit to them which I have given to you. But as the Spirit was not conveyed to them from or through Moses, but immediately from God, so the Spirit or its gifts were not by this means impaired in Moses. The Spirit is here put for the gifts of the Spirit and particularly for the spirit of prophecy, whereby they were enabled, as Moses had been and still was, to discern hidden and future things and resolve doubtful and difficult cases, which made them fit for government. It is observable that God would not, and therefore men should not, call any persons to any office for which they were not sufficiently qualified.

18. *Sanctify yourselves.* "Prepare to meet thy God, O Israel," in the way of his judgments. Prepare yourselves by true repentance, that you may either obtain some mitigation of the plague or, while your bodies are destroyed by the flesh you desire and eat, your souls may be saved from the wrath of God. "Sanctifying" is often used for "preparing" (Jer. 6:4; 12:3). *In the ears of the* LORD. Not secretly in your closets, but openly and impudently in the doors of your tents, calling heaven and earth to witness.

24. *The seventy men.* They are called "seventy" from the stated number, though two of them were lacking, as the apostles are called "the twelve" (Matt. 26:20) when one of that number was absent. *Round about the tabernacle.* Partly that the awe of God might be imprinted upon their hearts, that they might more seriously undertake and more faithfully manage their high employment, but principally, because that was where God manifested himself and therefore there he would bestow his Spirit upon them.

25. *Rested upon them.* Not only moved them for a time, but took up his settled abode with them, because the use and end of this gift was perpetual. *They prophesied.* Presented the word and works of God in a marvelous manner, as the prophets did. So this word is used in I Samuel 10:5–6; Joel 2:28; and I Corinthians 14:3. Yet they were not hereby constituted teachers, but civil magistrates, who together with the spirit of government received also the spirit of prophecy as a sign and seal, both to themselves and to the people, that God had called them to that employment.

29. *Enviest thou for my sake?* Are you grieved because the gifts and graces of God are imparted to others besides me? So we ought to be pleased that God is glorified and good done, though to the lessening of our own honor.

31–32. *A wind from the* LORD. An extraordinary and miraculous wind, both for its vehemence and for its effects. *Two cubits high.* Not as if the quails did cover all the ground two cubits high for a day's journey on each side of the camp, for then there had been no place left where they could *spread them all abroad for themselves round about the camp.* But the meaning is that the quails came and fell down round and about the camp for a whole day's journey on each side of it, and that in all that space they lay here and there in great heaps, which were often two cubits high.

33. *A very great plague.* Probably the pestilence. But the sense is, before they had finished eating their quails, which lasted for a month. Why did God so sorely punish the people's murmuring for flesh here, when he spared them after the same sin (Exod. 16)? Because this was a far greater sin and aggravated with worse circumstances; proceeding not from necessity, as that did when as yet they had no food, but from mere wantonness when they had manna constantly given them. It was committed after large experience of God's care and kindness, after God had pardoned their former sins and had in a solemn and terrible manner made known his laws to them.

CHAPTER 12

2. *By us.* Are not we prophets as well as he? So Aaron was made (Exod. 4:15–16), and so Miriam is called (Exod. 15:20). Moses has debased and mixed the holy seed, which we have not done. Why then should he take all power to himself and make rulers as he pleases without consulting us?

3. *Meek.* This is added as the reason why Moses took no notice of their reproach and why God did so severely plead his cause. Thus was he fitted for the work he was called to, which required all the meekness he had. And this is often more tried by the unkindness of our friends than by the malice of our enemies. Probably this commendation was added, as some other clauses were, by some succeeding prophet. How was Moses so meek when we read of his anger? But this only proves that "the law made nothing perfect."

6. *Among you.* If you be prophets, yet know there is a difference among prophets, nor do I put equal honor upon all of them.

8. *Mouth to mouth.* That is, distinctly, by an articulate voice. Immediately, not by an interpreter nor by shadows and representations in his fancy, as it is in visions and dreams; and familiarly. *The similitude.* Neither the face nor essence of God, which no man can see and live (Exod. 33:20), but some singular manifestation of his glorious presence (Exod. 33:11, 20). The Son of God appeared to him in a human shape, which he took up for a time that he might give him a foretaste of his future incarnation.

9. *He departed.* The removal of God's presence from us is the saddest token of his displeasure. And he never departs until we by our sin and folly drive him from us.

14. *Spit in her face.* That is, expressed some eminent token of indignation and contempt, which was this (Job 30:10; Isa. 1:6). So though God healed her according to Moses' request, yet he would have her publicly bear the shame of her sin and be a warning to others to keep them from the same transgression.

CHAPTER 13

16. *Jehoshua.* Or "Joshua," includes a promise of salvation, "He shall save." Joshua is the same name as Jesus, of whom Joshua was a type. He was the Savior of God's people from the power of Canaan, Christ from the powers of hell.

25. *They returned . . . after forty days.* It is a wonder the people had patience to stay forty days when they were just ready to enter Canaan, under all the assurances of success they could have from the divine power, proved by a constant series of miracles that had attended them. But they distrusted God and chose to be held in suspense by their own counsels rather than to rest upon God's promise! How much do we stand in our own light by unbelief?

30. *Caleb.* Together with Joshua, as is manifest from chapter 6:7, 30. But Caleb alone is here mentioned, possibly because he spoke first and most, which he might better do because he might be presumed to be more impartial than Joshua, who being Moses' minister might be thought to speak only what he knew his master would like. *Stilled the people.* Which implies either that

they had begun to murmur, or that by their looks and carriage they discovered the anger which boiled in their breasts.

Before Moses. Or, "towards Moses," against whom they were incensed as the man who had brought them into such sad circumstances. *Let us go up at once and possess it.* He does not say, Let us go up and conquer it. He looks on that to be as good as done already. But, Let us go up and *possess* it! There is nothing to be done but to enter without delay and take the possession which our great Lord is now ready to give us. Thus difficulties that lie in the way of salvation vanish away before a lively faith.

CHAPTER 14

3. *The LORD.* From instruments they rise higher and strike at God, the cause and author of their journey. By this we see the prodigious growth and progress of sin when it is not resisted.

4. *Into Egypt.* Stupendous madness! Who could give protection against the hazards and provision against all the lacks of the wilderness? Could they expect either God's cloud to cover and guide them, or manna from heaven to feed them? Who could conduct them over the Red Sea? Or, if they went another way, who should defend them against those nations whose borders they were to pass? What entertainment could they expect from the Egyptians whom they had deserted and brought to so much ruin?

5. *Fell on their faces.* As humble and earnest suppliants to God, the only refuge to which Moses resorted in all such straits, and who alone was able to govern this stiff-necked people. *Before all the assembly.* That they might awake to apprehend their sin and danger when they saw Moses at this prayers, whom God never failed to defend, even with the destruction of his enemies.

9. *Only rebel not ye against the LORD.* Nothing can ruin sinners but their own rebellion. If God leaves them, it is because they drive him from them, and they die because they will die.

10. *Appeared.* When they reflected upon God, his glory appeared not to silence their blasphemies. But when they threatened Caleb and Joshua, they touched the apple of his eye, and his glory appeared immediately. They who faithfully expose themselves for God are sure of his special protection.

24. *He had another spirit.* Was a man of another temper, faithful and courageous, not affected by that evil spirit of cowardice, unbelief, but by the Spirit of God. *Fully.* Universally and constantly, through difficulties and dangers, which made his partners halt.

32. *Your carcases.* See with what contempt they are spoken of, now they had by their sin "made themselves vile"! The mighty men of valor were but carcasses, now the Spirit of the Lord was departed from them. It was very probable upon this occasion that Moses wrote the ninetieth psalm.

34. *Each day for a year.* So there should have been forty years to come, but God was pleased mercifully to accept of the time past as a part of that time.

38. *But Joshua . . . and Caleb . . . lived still.* Death never misses his mark nor takes any by oversight who are designed for life, though in the midst of those that are to die.

39. *And the people mourned greatly.* But it was now too late. There was now no place for repentance. Such mourning as this there is in hell; but the tears will not quench the flames.

CHAPTER 15

2. *I give unto you.* Will certainly give you in spite of this great provocation. And for their better assurance of this he repeats and amplifies the laws of sacrifices, whereby through Christ he would be reconciled to them and theirs upon their repentance.

32. *Upon the sabbath day.* This seems to be added as an example of a presumptuous sin. For as the law of the sabbath was plain and positive, so this transgression of it must needs be a known and wilful sin.

34. *What should be done.* That is, in what manner he was to be cut off, or by what kind of death he was to die, which therefore God here particularly determines. Otherwise it was known in general that sabbath breakers were to be put to death.

41. *I am the LORD your God.* Though I am justly displeased with you for your frequent rebellions, for which also I will keep you forty years in the wilderness, yet I will not utterly cast you off, but will continue to be your God.

CHAPTER 16

3. For whatever they intended, they seem not now directly to strike at Moses for his supreme civil government, but only for his influence in the disposal of the priesthood. *Ye take too much.* By perpetuating the priesthood in yourselves and family, with the exclusion of all others from it.

4. *Upon his face.* Humbly begging that God would direct and vindicate him. Accordingly God answers his prayers and strengthens him with new courage and confidence of success.

8. *Ye sons of Levi.* They were of his own tribe; rather, they were of God's tribe. It was therefore the worse in them thus to mutiny against God and against him.

9. *To minister unto them.* So they were the servants both of God and of the church, which was an high dignity, though not sufficient for their ambitious minds.

11. *Against the* LORD. Whose chosen servant Aaron is. You strike at God through Aaron's sides.

19. *Against them.* And it seems by this that the people were generally incensed against Moses, and inclined to Korah's side. *The glory of the* LORD *appeared.* In the cloud, which then shone with greater brightness and majesty as a token of God's approach and presence.

41. *On the morrow.* Prodigious wickedness and madness so soon to forget such a terrible instance of divine vengeance! *The people of the* LORD. So they call those wicked wretches and rebels against God. Though they were but newly saved from sharing in the same punishment, and the survivors were as brands plucked out of the burning, yet they fly in the face of Moses and Aaron, to whose intercession they owe their preservation.

46. *Incense.* Which was a sign of intercession and was to be accompanied with it. *Go quickly unto the congregation.* He went with the incense to stir up the people to repentance and prayer to prevent their utter ruin. This he might do upon this extraordinary occasion, having God's command for his warrant, though ordinarily incense was to be offered only in the tabernacle.

48. *The living.* Whereby it may seem that this plague, like that fire in chapter 11:1, began in the uttermost parts of the congregation and so proceeded to destroy one after another in an orderly manner, which gave Aaron occasion and direction so to place himself as a mediator to God on their behalf.

CHAPTER 17

4. *Before the testimony.* That is, before the ark of the testimony, close by the

ark. *I will meet with you.* And manifest my mind to you, for the ending of this dispute.

12. *We perish.* Words of consternation, arising from the remembrance of these severe and repeated judgments for the threatening of death upon any succeeding murmurings, and from the sense of their own guilt and weakness, which made them fear lest they should relapse into the same misdeeds and thereby bring the vengeance of God upon themselves.

13. *Near.* Nearer than he should do; an error which we may easily commit. Will God proceed with us according to his strict justice, until all the people be cut off?

CHAPTER 18

6. *To you they are given as a gift.* We are to value it as a great gift of the divine bounty to have those joined to us that will be helpful and serviceable to us in the service of God.

7. *As a service of gift,* which I have freely conferred upon you, and you alone. And therefore let no man henceforth dare either to charge you with arrogance in appropriating this to yourselves, or to invade your office.

19. *A covenant of salt.* A durable and perpetual covenant. It is so called here (and II Chron. 13:5), either because salt is a sign of incorruption, as being of singular use to preserve things from corruption; or, because it is ratified on their part by salt, which is therefore called "the salt of the covenant," for which the priests were obliged to take care, that it should never be lacking from any meal offering (Lev. 2:13). And this privilege conferred upon the priests is called a covenant because it is given them conditionally, upon condition of their service and care about the worship of God.

20. The reason of this law was (1) Partly because God would have them wholly devoted to his service and therefore free from worldly encumbrances. (2) Partly because God had abundantly provided for them otherwise, by tithes and firstfruits and oblations. And, (3) partly by this means being dispersed among the several tribes, they might have the better opportunity for teaching and watching over the people.

21. *The tenth.* For the tithes were all given to the Levites, and out of their tithes the tenth was given to the priests.

CHAPTER 19

2. *Red.* A fit color to shadow the bloody nature of sin and the blood of Christ, from which this water and all other rites had their purifying virtue. No blemish. A fit type of Christ. *Upon which never came yoke.* Whereby may be signified, either that Christ in himself was free from all the yoke or obligation of God's command, until for our sakes he put himself under the law; or that Christ was not forced to undertake our burden and cross, but did voluntarily choose it. He was bound and held with no other cords but those of his own love.

4. *Before the tabernacle.* Or, "towards the tabernacle." This signified his presenting this blood before the Lord by way of atonement for his and the people's sins, and his expectation of acceptance and pardon only from God and from his mercy seat in the tabernacle. And this typified the satisfaction that was made to God by the death of Christ, who "through the eternal Spirit offered himself without spot to God" and did as it were sprinkle his own blood before the sanctuary, when he said, "Father, into thy hands I commend my spirit."

5. *Burn the heifer.* To signify the sharp and grievous sufferings of Christ for our sins.

7. *Shall be unclean.* Partly to teach us the imperfection of the Levitical priesthood, in which the priest himself was defiled by some parts of his work, and partly to show that Christ himself, though he had no sin of his own, yet was reputed by men and judged by God as a sinful person, by reason of our sins which were laid upon him.

9. *It is a purification for sin.* This was a type of that purification for sin which our Lord Jesus made by his death.

12. *On the third day.* To typify Christ's resurrection on that day by which we are cleansed or sanctified.

17. *Running water.* Waters flowing from a spring or river, which are the purest. These manifestly signify God's Spirit, which is often compared to water and by which alone true purification is obtained. Those who promise themselves benefit by the righteousness of Christ, while they submit not to the influence of this Spirit, do but deceive themselves; for they cannot be purified by the ashes otherwise than in the running water.

CHAPTER 20

2. *No water.* This story, though like that of Exodus 17, is different from it, as appears by many circumstances. It is a great mercy to have plenty of water; a mercy which if we found the want of, we should own the worth of.

3. *Before the* Lord. Suddenly, rather than to die such a lingering death. Their sin was much greater than that of their parents, because they should have taken warning by their misdeeds and by the terrible effects of them which their eyes had seen.

12. *Ye believed me not.* But showed your infidelity. Which they did, either by smiting the rock and that twice, which is emphatically noted, as if he doubted whether one smite would have done it, whereas he was not commanded to smite so much as once, but only to speak to it; or by the doubtfulness of these words (v. 10), "Must we fetch water out of the rock?" which implies a suspicion of it, whereas they should have spoken positively and confidently to the rock to give forth water. And yet they did not doubt of the power of God, but of his will, whether he would gratify these rebels with this further miracle after so many of the like kind.

To sanctify me. To give me the glory of my power in doing this miracle, and of my truth in punctually fulfilling my promise, and of my goodness in doing it in spite of the people's perverseness. *In the eyes of the children of Israel.* This made their sin scandalous to the Israelites, who of themselves were too prone to infidelity. To prevent the contagion, God leaves a monument of his displeasure upon them and inflicts a punishment as public as their sin.

16. *An angel.* The Angel of the Covenant, who first appeared to Moses in the bush and afterward in the cloudy pillar, who conducted Moses and the people out of Egypt and through the wilderness.

17. *The wells.* No man's property ought to be invaded under color of religion. Dominion is founded in Providence, not in Grace.

23. *And the* LORD *spake unto Moses and Aaron.* So these two dear brothers must part! Aaron must die first; but Moses is not likely to be long after him. So that it is only for a while, a little while, that they are separated.

24. *Because ye rebelled.* This was one but not the only reason. God would not have Moses and Aaron carry the people into Canaan for this reason also, to signify the insufficiency of the Mosa-

ical law and Aaronical priesthood to make them perfectly happy, and the necessity of a better; and to keep the Israelites from resting in them, so as to be taken off from their expectation of Christ.

27. *In the sight of all the congregation.* That their hearts might be more affected with their loss of so great a pillar, and that they all might be witness of the translation of the priesthood from Aaron to Eleazar.

28. *And Moses stripped Aaron.* And death will strip us. Naked we came into the world; naked we must go out. We shall see little reason to be proud of our clothes or ornaments or marks of honor if we consider how soon death will strip us of all our glory and take the crown off from our head. Presently after he was stripped of his priestly garments, he laid him down and died. A good man would desire, if it were the will of God, not to outlive his usefulness. Why should we covet to continue any longer in this world than while we may do God and our generation some service?

CHAPTER 21

3. *They utterly destroyed them.* Neither Moses nor the whole body of the people did this, but a select number sent out to punish that king and people, who were so fierce and malicious that they came out of their own country to fight with the Israelites in the wilderness. And these, when they had done this work, returned to their brethren in the wilderness. But why did they not all now go into Canaan and pursue this victory? Because God would not permit it, there being several works yet to be done; other people must be conquered, the Israelites must be further humbled and tried and purged, Moses must die, and then they shall enter, and that in a more glorious manner, even over Jordan which shall be miraculously dried up to give them passage.

5. *Against God.* Against Christ, their chief conductor, whom they tempted (I Cor. 10:19). Thus contemptuously did they speak of manna, whereas it appears it yielded excellent nourishment, because in the strength of it they were able to go so many and such tedious journeys.

6. *Fiery serpents.* There were many in this wilderness which, having been until now restrained by God, are let loose and sent among them. They are called fiery from their effects, because their poison caused an intolerable heat and burning and thirst, which was aggravated with this circumstance of the place, that here was no water (v. 5).

8. *When he looketh.* This method of cure was prescribed that it might appear to be God's own work and not the effect of nature or art; and that it might be an eminent type of our salvation by Christ. The serpent signified Christ, who was "in the likeness of sinful flesh," though without sin, as this brazen serpent had the outward shape but not the inward poison of the other serpents. The pole resembled the cross upon which Christ was lifted up for our salvation; and looking up to it designed our believing in Christ.

14. *The book of the wars of the LORD.* This seems to have been some poem or narration of the wars and victories of the Lord, either by or relating to the Israelites. This may be asserted without any prejudice to the integrity of the Holy Scripture, because this book does not appear to have been written by a prophet or to be designed for a part of the canon, which yet Moses might quote, as St. Paul does some of the heathen poets. And as St. Luke assures us that many did write a history of the

things done and said by Christ (Luke 1:1) whose writings were never received as canonical, the like may be conceived concerning this and some few other books mentioned in the Old Testament.

16. *I will give them water.* In a miraculous way. Before they prayed, God granted and presented them with the blessings of goodness. As the brazen serpent was the figure of Christ, so is this well a figure of the Spirit, who is poured forth for our comfort, and from him flow "rivers of living waters."

18. *With their staves.* Probably as Moses smote the rock with his rod, so they struck the earth with their staves as a sign that God would cause the water to flow out of the earth where they smote it, as he did before out of the rock. Perhaps they made holes with their staves in the sandy ground, and God caused the water immediately to spring up.

29. *People of Chemosh.* The worshippers of Chemosh; so the god of the Moabites was called. He, that is, their god, has delivered up his own people to his and their enemies; nor could he secure even those that had escaped the sword, but suffered them to be carried into captivity. The words of this and the following verse seem to be not a part of that triumphant song made by some Amoritish poet, which seems to be concluded at verse 28, but of the Israelites making their observation upon it. And here they scoff at the impotence not only of the Moabites, but of their God also, who could not save his people from the sword of Sihon and the Amorites.

30. Though you feeble Moabites, and your god too, could not resist Sihon, we Israelites, by the help of our God, have shot with success and victory *at them,* at Sihon and his Amorites.

CHAPTER 22

5. *Balaam.* Called a prophet (II Peter 2:16) because God was pleased to inspire and direct him to speak the following prophecies. Indeed many of the Jewish writers say that Balaam had been a great prophet who, for the accomplishment of his predictions and the answers of his prayers, had been looked upon justly as a man of great interest with God. However, it is certain that afterwards, for his covetousness, God departed from him.

6. *Curse* them for my sake and benefit; use your utmost power, which you have with your gods, to blast and ruin them. *We may smite them.* You by your imprecations, and I by my sword.

8. *This night.* The night was the time God used to reveal his mind by dreams. *The LORD.* The true God, whom he here mentions, either for his own greater reputation, as if he consulted not with inferior spirits, but with the supreme God. Or, rather, because this was Israel's God, and the only possible way of ruining them was by engaging their God against them. When the Romans and other heathens went to besiege any city, they used enchantments to call forth that god under whose peculiar protection they were.

9. *What men are these with thee?* He asks this that Balaam, by repeating the thing in God's presence, might be convinced and ashamed of his sin and folly in offering his service in such a business. And for a foundation to the following answer.

22. *Because he went.* Because he went of his own accord, with the princes of Moab, and did not wait until they came to call him, which was the sign and condition of God's permission, but rather himself rose and called them. The apostle describes Balaam's sin here to be that he ran greedily into an error for reward (Jude 11).

28. *Opened the mouth.* Conferred upon her the power of speech and reasoning for that time.

29. *Balaam said.* Balaam was not much terrified with the ass's speaking, because perhaps he was accustomed to converse with evil spirits who appeared to him and discoursed with him in the shape of such creatures. Perhaps he was so blinded by passion that he did not consider the strangeness of the thing.

33. *I had slain thee.* I had slain you alone, and not her, therefore her turning aside and falling down was wholly for your benefit, not for her own, and your anger against her was unjust and unreasonable.

CHAPTER 23

10. *Of the righteous.* Of this righteous and holy people. The sense is, they are not only happy above other nations in this life, and therefore in vain should I curse them; but they have this peculiar privilege, that they are happy after death. Their happiness begins where the happiness of other people ends. And therefore I heartily wish that my soul may have its portion with theirs when I die. Was not God now again striving with him, not only for the sake of Israel, but his own soul?

21. *The shout of a king.* That is, such joyful and triumphant shouts as those with which a people congratulate the approach and presence of their King when he appears among them upon some solemn occasion, or when he returns from battle with victory. This expression implies God's being their King and ruler, and their abundant security and confidence in him.

22. The sense is, Israel is not now what he was in Egypt; a poor, weak, dispirited, unarmed people, but high and strong and invincible. *An unicorn.* The word may mean either a rhinoceros or a strong and fierce kind of wild goat. But such a creature as a unicorn, as commonly painted, has no existence in nature.

23. *Against Jacob.* Nor against any that truly believe in Christ. *What hath God wrought!* How wonderful and glorious are those works which God is now about to do for Israel! These things will be a matter of discourse and admiration to all ages.

CHAPTER 24

3. The *eyes* of his mind, which God had opened in a peculiar and prophetical manner, whence prophets are called "Seers" (I Sam. 9:9). It implies that before he was blind and stupid, having eyes but not seeing nor understanding.

17. *I shall see him.* Or, I have seen or do see the Star and Sceptre, as it here follows; that is, a great and eminent prince, which was to come out of Israel's loins, the Messiah, as both Jewish and Christian interpreters expound it, who most eminently and fully performed what is here said, in destroying the enemies of Israel or of God's church, here described under the names of the nearest and fiercest enemies of Israel. And to him alone agrees the foregoing verb properly, *I shall see him,* in my own person, as "every eye shall see him," when he comes to judgment. *Not now.* Not yet, but after many ages. *A star.* A title often given to princes and eminent persons, and particularly to the Messiah (Rev. 2:28; 22:16). *A sceptre.* That is, a scepter-bearer, a king or ruler, even that scepter mentioned in Genesis 49:10.

18. *A possession.* Which was also foretold in Genesis 25:23, in part fulfilled (II Sam. 8:14; I Chron. 18:13), but more fully by Christ (Amos 9:12; Obad. 18), who shall subdue and possess all his enemies; here signified

by the name of Edom, as Jacob or Israel, his brother, signifies all his church and people.

19. *Out of Jacob.* Out of Jacob's loins. *He that shall have dominion.* David, and especially Christ.

20. That victory was an earnest and firstfruit of the large harvest of victories which the Israelites should in due time get over all their enemies.

21. *Thy nest.* Your dwelling place, so called, either because it was in a high place, as nests commonly are; or in allusion to their name, for *ken* in Hebrew signifies a nest.

23. *Who shall live.* How calamitous and miserable will the state of the world be when the Assyrian, and after him the Chaldean, shall overturn all these parts of the world? Who will be able to keep his heart from fainting under such grievous pressures? How few will escape the destroying sword?

24. Although the Assyrian and Chaldean empire was subdued by the Medes and Persians, yet the chief afflictions of that people came from two hands, both beyond the sea and brought to them by ships; first from the Grecians under Alexander and his successors, by whom that people were grievously oppressed and wasted; then from the Romans, who subdued all the Grecian empire, one great part whereof were the Assyrians largely so called. Thus Balaam, instead of cursing the church, curses Amalek, the first, and Rome, the last enemy of it.

CHAPTER 25

1. *Shittim.* This was their last station, whence they passed immediately into Canaan. This is noted as a great aggravation of their sin, that they committed it when God was going to put them into the possession of their long-expected land. *Whoredom.* Either because they prostituted themselves to them upon condition of worshipping their god, or because their filthy god was worshipped by such filthy acts.

12. *My covenant of peace.* That is, "the covenant of an everlasting priesthood," as it is expounded (v. 13), which is called a covenant of peace, partly with respect to the happy effect of this heroical action of his, whereby he made peace between God and his people; and partly with regard to the principal end of the priestly office, which was constantly to do that which Phinehas now did, even to mediate between God and men, to obtain and preserve his own and Israel's peace and reconciliation with God. This he did by offering up sacrifices and incense and prayers to God on their behalf, as also by turning them away from iniquity, which is the only peace breaker, and by teaching and pressing the observation of that law, which is the only bond of their peace.

13. *An everlasting priesthood.* To continue as long as the law and commonwealth of the Jews did. But this promise was conditional and therefore might be made void by the misdeeds of Phinehas' sons, as it seems it was. Thereupon a like promise was made to Eli of the line of Ithamar, that he and his should walk before the Lord, namely, in the office of high priest "for ever," which also for his and their sins was made void (I Sam. 2:30). And the priesthood returned to Phinehas' line in the time of Solomon (I Kings 2:26–27, 34).

CHAPTER 26

2. *Take the sum.* They were numbered twice before (Exod. 30:11–12; Num. 1:1–2). Now they are numbered a third time to demonstrate the faithfulness of God, both in cutting all those off whom he had threatened to cut off

(14:29) and in a stupendous increase of the people according to his promise, in spite of all their sins and the sweeping judgments inflicted upon them. And to prepare the way for the equal division of the land, which they were now going to possess.

14. *Twenty and two thousand and two hundred.* No tribe decreased so much as Simeon's. From fifty-nine thousand and three hundred it sunk to twenty-two thousand and two hundred, little more than a third part of what it was. One whole family of that tribe (Ohad, Exod. 6:15) was extinct in the wilderness. Some think most of the twenty-four thousand, cut off by the plague for the iniquity of Peor, were of that tribe, for Zimri, a ringleader in that iniquity, was a prince of that tribe. Simeon is not mentioned in Moses' blessing (Deut. 33). And the lot of that tribe in Canaan was inconsiderable, only a canton out of Judah's lot (Josh. 19:9).

22. *The families of Judah.* About two thousand more than they were (1:27), whereas the foregoing tribes were all diminished.

34. *Fifty and two thousand and seven hundred.* Whereas they were but thirty-two thousand and two hundred (1:35). They are now increased above twenty thousand, according to that prophecy in Genesis 49:22.

43. *Threescore and four thousand and four hundred.* All from one son and family, whereas of Benjamin, who had ten sons and five families, there were only forty-five thousand and six hundred, to show that the increase of families depends singly upon God's blessing and good pleasure.

65. *Not left a man.* Only of the Levites, who being not guilty of that sin did not partake of their judgment.

CHAPTER 27

2. *By the door of the tabernacle.* Near which it seems was the place where

Moses and the chief rulers assembled for the administration of public affairs, which also was very convenient, because they had frequent occasion of recourse to God for his direction.

13. *Thou also shalt be gathered unto thy people.* Moses must die. But death does not *cut him off;* it only *gathers him to his people,* brings him to rest with the holy patriarchs that were gone before him. Abraham, Isaac, and Jacob were his people, the people of his choice, and to them death gathered him.

15. *And Moses spake unto the LORD.* Concerning his successor. We should concern ourselves both in our prayers and in our endeavors for the rising generation, that God's kingdom may be advanced among men when we are in our graves.

20. *Put some of thine honour.* You shall not now use him as a servant, but as a brother and your partner in the government, that the people, being used to obeying him while Moses lived, might do it afterward the more cheerfully.

22. *And Moses did as the LORD commanded him.* It had been little to resign his honor to a son of his own. But with his own hands, first to ordain Eleazar high priest, and now Joshua chief ruler, while his own children had no preferment at all, but were left in the rank of common Levites; this was more to his glory than the highest advancement of his family could have been. This shows him to have had a principle which raised him above all other lawgivers, who always took care to establish their families in some share of the greatness they themselves possessed.

CHAPTER 28

2. *Command the children of Israel.* God here repeats some of the former laws about sacrifices, not without great reason. (1) Partly because they had been generally discontinued for thirty-eight years together. (2) Partly because the generation to which the former laws had been given about these things was wholly dead, and it was fit the new generation should be instructed about them, as their parents were. (3) Partly to renew their testimonies of God's grace and mercy in spite of their frequent forfeitures by their rebellion. And, (4) Principally because they were now ready to enter into that land in which they were obliged to put these things in practice.

23. *In the morning.* And that in the evening too, as is evident from other Scriptures. But the morning sacrifice alone is mentioned, because the celebration of the feast began with it, and principally because this alone was doubtful, whether this might not be omitted when so many other sacrifices were offered in the morning, whereas there was no question but the evening sacrifice should be offered when there were none other to be offered.

CHAPTER 29

7. *Afflict your souls.* Yourselves, by fasting and abstinence from all delightful things, and by compunction for your sins and the judgments of God, either deserved by you or inflicted upon you.

12. *Seven days.* Not by abstaining so long from all servile work, but by offering extraordinary sacrifices each day. This was the Feast of Tabernacles. And all the days of their dwelling in booths, they must offer sacrifices. While we are in these tabernacles, it is our interest as well as duty to keep up our communion with God. Nor will the unsettledness of our outward condition excuse our neglect of God's worship.

CHAPTER 30

13. *To afflict the soul.* Herself by fasting, by watching, or the like. And these words are added to show that the husband had this power not only in those vows which concerned himself or his estate, but also in those which might seem only to concern her own person, or body; and the reason is, because the wife's person or body being the husband's right, she might not do anything to the injury of her body without his consent.

CHAPTER 31

17. *The little ones.* Which they were forbidden to do to other people (Deut. 20:14) except the Canaanites, to whom this people had equalled themselves by their horrid crimes; and therefore it is not strange nor unjust that God, the supreme Lord of all men's lives, who as he gives them so may take them away when he pleases, did equal them in the punishment. *Every woman.* Partly for punishment, because the guilt was general, and though some of them only did prostitute themselves to the Israelites, yet the rest made themselves accessory by their consent or approbation; and partly for prevention of the like mischief from such an adulterous generation.

50. We should never take any thing to ourselves in war or trade of which we cannot in faith consecrate a part to God, who "hates robbery for burnt offering." But when God has remarkably preserved and succeeded us, he expects we should make some particular return of gratitude to him.

CHAPTER 32

23. *Your sin.* The punishment of your sin. Sin will certainly find out the

sinner sooner or later. It concerns us therefore to find our sins out that we may repent of them and forsake them, lest our sins find us out to our confusion and destruction.

42. *Nobah.* Who, though not elsewhere named, was doubtless an eminent person of the tribe of Manasseh. It is observable that these tribes, as they were placed before the other tribes, so they were displaced before them. They were carried captive by the king of Assyria some years before the other tribes. Such a proportion does Providence frequently observe in balancing prosperity and adversity.

CHAPTER 33

2. *And Moses wrote their goings out.* When they set out, God ordered him to keep a journal of all the remarkable occurrences in the way, that it might be a satisfaction to himself and an instruction to others. It may be of use to Christians to preserve an account of the providences of God concerning them, the constant series of mercies they have experienced, and especially those turns which have made some days of their lives more remarkable.

4. *Upon their gods.* Their false gods, namely those beasts which the brutish Egyptians worshipped as gods, which were killed with the rest, for the firstborn both of men and beasts were then killed. Probably their images likewise were thrown down, as Dagon afterward before the ark.

52. *Drive out.* Not by banishing, but by destroying them. *Pictures.* Which seem to have been stones curiously engraved and set up for worship.

CHAPTER 34

2. There was a much larger possession promised them if they were obedient, even to the river Euphrates. But this, which is properly Canaan, lay in a very little compass. It is but about a hundred and sixty miles in length, and about fifty in breadth. This was that little spot of ground in which alone for many ages God was known. But its littleness was abundantly compensated by its fruitfulness. Otherwise it could not have sustained so numerous a nation. See how little a share of the world God often gives to his own people! But they that have their portion in heaven can be content with a small pittance of this earth.

17. *Eleazar.* Who was to act in God's name, to cast lots, to prevent contentions, to consult with God in cases of difficulty, to transact the whole business in a solemn and religious manner.

CHAPTER 35

6. *Cities for refuge.* Or, of escape for manslayers. And these cities are assigned among the Levites, (1) Partly because they might be presumed to be the most proper and impartial judges between manslayers and willful murderers. (2) Partly because their presence and authority would more effectually bridle the passions of the avenger of blood who might pursue him there. And, (3) Perhaps to signify that it is only in Christ (whom the Levitical priests represented) that sinners find refuge and safety from the destroyer.

12. *Before the congregation.* Before the judges or elders who were appointed in every city for the decision of criminal cases, who were to examine, and that publicly before the people, whether the murder was willful or casual.

19. *He shall slay him.* Either by himself, as the following words show, for it is a permission that he may do it without offense to God or danger to himself; or by the magistrate, from whom he shall demand justice.

25. *He shall abide in it.* Be confined to it, partly to show the hatefulness of murder in God's account by so severe a punishment inflicted upon the very appearance of it, and partly for the security of the manslayer, lest the presence of such a person and his conversation among the kindred of the deceased might occasion reproach and bloodshed.

27. *Not be guilty.* Not liable to punishment from men, though not free of guilt before God. This God ordained to oblige the manslayer to abide in his city of refuge.

CHAPTER 36

8. *The inheritance of his fathers.* This law was not general to forbid every woman to marry into another tribe, as may be reasonably concluded from the practice of so many patriarchs, kings, priests, and other holy men who have married women of other tribes, sometimes of other nations, but restrained to heiresses or such as were likely to be so. But if they had brethren, they were free to marry into any tribe, so that if their brethren died, the inheritance went from them to the next of kin of their father's tribe and family. And the principal reason why God was solicitous to preserve tribes and families unmixed was that the tribe and family too, out of which the Messiah was to come and by which he should be known, might be evident and unquestionable.

∂euteronomy

CHAPTER 1

16. *The stranger.* That converses or deals with him. To such God would have justice equally administered as to his own people, partly for the honor of religion, and partly for the interest which every man has in matters of common right.

17. *Respect persons.* That is, do not give sentence according to the outward qualities of the person, as he is poor or rich, your friend or enemy, but purely according to the merit of the case. For this reason some of the Grecian lawgivers ordered that the judges should give sentence in the dark where they could not see men's faces.

31. *Bare thee.* Or carried thee, as a father carries his weak and tender child in his arms, through difficulties and dangers, gently leading you according as you are able to go and sustaining you by his power and goodness.

32. *Ye did not believe the* LORD. So they "could not enter in because of unbelief." It was not any other sin that shut them out of Canaan, but their disbelief of that promise, which was typical of gospel grace. This signifies that no sin will ruin us but unbelief, which is a sin against remedy, and therefore without remedy.

34. *Your words.* That is to say, your murmurings, and your unthankful, impatient, distrustful, and rebellious speeches.

44. *As bees.* As bees which, being provoked, come out of their hives in great numbers and with great fury pursue their adversary and disturber.

CHAPTER 2

6. *Buy meat.* For though the manna did yet rain upon them, they were not forbidden to buy other meats when they had opportunity, but only were forbidden greedily to hunger after them when they could not obtain them. *Buy water.* For water in those parts was scarce, and therefore private persons did severally dig pits for their particular use.

29. *As the children of Esau.* They did permit them to pass quietly by the borders, though not through the heart of their land, and in their passage the people sold them meat and drink, being it seems more kind to them than their king would have had them. And therefore they here ascribe this favor not to the king, though they are now treating with a king, but to the people, *the children of Esau.*

30. *Hardened his spirit.* That is, allowed it to be hardened.

CHAPTER 3

14. *Unto this day.* This must be put among those passages which were not written by Moses, but added by those holy men who digested the books of Moses into this order and inserted some few passages to accommodate things to their own time and people.

23. *I besought the LORD.* We should allow no desire in our hearts which we cannot in faith offer unto God by prayer.

24. *Thou hast begun to shew thy servant thy greatness.* Lord, perfect what you have begun. The more we see of God's glory in his works, the more we desire to see. And the more we are affected with what we have seen of God, the better we are prepared for further discoveries.

25. *Let me go over.* For he supposed God's threatening might be conditional and reversible, as many others were.

28. *He shall go over.* It was not Moses, but Joshua (or Jesus) who was to give the people rest (Heb. 4:8). It is a comfort to those who love mankind, when they are dying and going off, to see God's work likely to be carried on by other hands, when they are silent in the dust.

CHAPTER 4

7. *So nigh.* By glorious miracles, by the pledges of his special presence, by the operations of his grace, particularly by his readiness to hear our prayers, and to give us those aids which we call upon him for.

8. *So righteous.* Whereby he implies that the true greatness of a nation does not consist in pomp or power or largeness of empire, as commonly men think, but in the righteousness of its laws.

12. *No similitude.* No resemblance or representation of God, whereby either his essence or properties or actions were represented, such as were usual among the heathens.

14. *Statutes and judgments.* The ceremonial and judicial laws which are here distinguished from the moral, or the Ten Commandments.

15. *In Horeb.* God, who in other places and times did appear in the fashion of a man, now in this most solemn appearance, when he comes to give eternal laws for the direction of the elites in the worship of God and in their duty to men, purposely avoids all such representations, to show that he abhors all worship of images, or of himself by images of whatever kind, because he is the invisible God and cannot be represented by any visible image.

28. *Ye shall serve gods.* You shall be compelled by men, and given up by me to idolatry. So that very thing which was your choice shall be your punishment; it being just and usual for God to punish one sin by giving men up to another.

29. *If from thence thou shalt seek the LORD.* Whatever place we are in, we may *from thence* seek him. There is no part of the earth which has "a great gulf fixed" between it and heaven.

37. *In his sight.* Keeping his eye fixed upon him, as the father does on his beloved child.

CHAPTER 5

5. *Between the LORD and you.* As a mediator between you, according to your desire. *The word of the LORD.* Not the Ten Commandments, which God himself uttered, but the following statutes and judgments.

7. There being little said concerning the spiritual sense of the Ten Commandments in the notes on the Exodus

20, I think it needful to add a few questions here, which the reader may answer between God and his own soul. *Thou shalt have none other gods before me.* Have you worshipped God in spirit and in truth? Have you proposed to yourself no end besides him? Has he been the end of all your actions? Have you sought for any other happiness than the knowledge and love of God? Do you experimentally[1] know the only true God, and Jesus Christ whom he has sent? Do you love God? Do you love him with all your heart, with all your soul, and with all your strength; so as to love nothing else but in that manner and degree which tends to increase your love of him? Have you found happiness in God? Is he the desire of your eyes, the joy of your heart? If not, thou hast other gods before him.

8. *Thou shalt not make any graven image.* Have you not formed any image of God in your mind? Have you always thought of him as a pure spirit, whom no man has seen nor can see? And have you worshipped him with your body as well as with your spirit, seeing both of them are God's?

11. *Thou shalt not take the name of the* Lord *thy God in vain.* Have you never used the name of God, unless on solemn and weighty occasions? Have you then used it with the deepest awe? Have you duly honored his word, his ordinances, his ministers? Have you considered all things as they stand in relation to him and seen God in all? Have you looked upon heaven as God's throne? Upon earth as God's footstool? On every thing therein as belonging to the great king? On every creature as full of God?

12. *Keep the sabbath day to sanctify it.* Do you do no work on this day which can be done as well on another? Are you peculiarly careful on this day to avoid all conversation which does not tend to the knowledge and love of God? Do you watch narrowly over all that are "within thy gates" that they too may keep it holy? And do you try every possible means to bring all men, wherever you are, to do the same?

16. *Honour thy father and thy mother.* Have you not been irreverent or undutiful to either? Have you not slighted their advice or not cheerfully obeyed all their lawful commands? Have you loved and honored their persons? Supplied their needs and concealed their infirmities? Have you wrestled for them with God in prayer? Have you loved and honored your prince, and avoided as fire all speaking evil of "the ruler of thy people"? Have you that are servants done all things as unto Christ, not with eye service, but in singleness of heart? Have you who are masters behaved as parents to your servants, with all gentleness and affection? Have you all obeyed them that watch over your souls and esteemed them highly in love for their work's sake?

17. *Thou shalt not kill.* Have you not tempted any one to what might shorten his life? Have you tempted none to intemperance? Have you allowed none to be intemperate under your roof or in your company? Have you done all you could in every place to prevent intemperance of all kinds? Are you guilty of no degree of self-murder? Do you never eat or drink anything because you like it, although you have reason to believe it is prejudicial to your health? Have you constantly done whatever you had reason to believe was conducive to it? Have you not hated your neighbor in

---

[1] (5:7) That is, "experientially."

your heart? Have you reproved him that committed sin in your sight? If not, you have in God's account hated him, seeing you "suffer sin upon him."

Have you loved all men as your own soul? As Christ loved us? Have you done unto all men, as in like circumstances you would they should do to you? Have you done all in your power to help your neighbors, enemies as well as friends? Have you labored to deliver every soul you could from sin and misery? Have you shown that you love all men as yourself by constant, earnest endeavor to fill all places with holiness and happiness, with the knowledge and love of God?

18. *Neither shalt thou commit adultery.* If you have not been guilty of any act of uncleanness, has your heart not looked on a woman so as to lust after her? Have you not betrayed your own soul to temptation, by eating and drinking to the full, by needless familiarities, by foolish talking, by levity of dress or behavior? Have you used all the means which Scripture and reason suggest to prevent every kind and degree of unchastity? Have you labored by watching, fasting, and prayer to "possess [thy] vessel in sanctification and honour"?

19. *Neither shalt thou steal.* Have you seriously considered that these houses, lands, money, or goods, which you are used to calling your own, are not your own, but belong to another, even God? Have you ever considered that God is the sole proprietor of heaven and earth? The true owner of everything therein? Have you considered that he has only lent them to you? That you are but a steward of your Lord's goods? And that he has told you expressly the uses and purposes for which he entrusts you with them? Namely, for furnishing first yourselves and then as many others as you can with the things needful for life

and godliness? Have you considered that you have no right at all to apply any part of them to any other purpose? And that if you do, you are as much a robber of God as any can be a robber of you?

20. *Neither shalt thou bear false witness against thy neighbour.* Have you not been guilty of evil speaking? Of needlessly repeating the real fault of your neighbor? If I see a man do an evil thing and tell it to another, unless from a full and clear conviction that it is necessary to mention it just then, for the glory of God, the safety or good of some other person, or for the benefit of him that has done amiss; and unless I then do it only so far as is necessary to these ends, that is evil speaking. O beware of this! It is scattering abroad arrows, firebrands, and death.

21. *Neither shalt thou covet . . . any thing that is thy neighbour's.* The plain meaning of this is, you shall not desire any thing that is not your own, any thing which you have not. Indeed why should you? God has given you whatever tends to your one end, holiness. You can not deny it without making him a liar; and when anything else will tend thereto, he will give you that also. There is therefore no room to desire any thing that is really good for you. Would you have more money, more pleasure, more praise still? Why, this is not good for you. God has told you so by withholding it from you. O give yourself up to his wise and gracious disposal!

22. *Out of the midst of the fire, of the cloud, and of the thick darkness.* That was a dispensation of terror designed to make the gospel of grace the more welcome and to be a specimen of the terrors of the judgment day.

29. *O that there were such an heart in them.* A heart to fear God and keep his commandments for ever! The God of heaven is truly and earnestly desirous of the salvation of poor sinners. He has given abundant proof that he is so. He gives us time and space to repent. By his mercies He invites us to repentance and waits to be gracious. He has sent his Son to redeem us, published a general offer of pardon, promised his Spirit to those that pray for him. And he has said Yes and sworn that he has no pleasure in the death of a sinner.

CHAPTER 6

5. *And thou shalt love the* LORD *thy God with all thine heart.* Is this only an external commandment? Can any then say that the Sinai covenant was merely external? *With all thine heart.* With an entire love. The whole stream of our affections must run towards him. O that this love of God may be shed abroad in our hearts!

8. *Thou shalt bind them.* You shall give all diligence and use all means to keep them in your remembrance, as men often bind something upon their hands or put it before their eyes to prevent forgetfulness of a thing which they much desire to remember.

16. *Ye shall not tempt.* Not provoke him, as the following instance explains. Sinners, especially presumptuous sinners, are said to tempt God, that is, to make a trial of God, whether he be so wise as to see their sins, so just and true and powerful as to take vengeance on them, concerning which they are very apt to doubt because of the present impunity and prosperity of many such persons.

17. *Ye shall diligently keep.* Negligence will ruin us. But we cannot be saved without diligence.

25. *It shall be our righteousness.* We shall be owned and pronounced by God to be righteous and holy persons if we sincerely obey him, otherwise we

shall be declared to be unrighteous and ungodly.

CHAPTER 7

8. *The* LORD *loved you.* It was his free choice without any cause or motive on your part.

15. *The evil diseases of Egypt.* Diseases are God's servants, which go where he sends them and do what he bids them.

24. *There shall no man be able to stand.* This promise is made on condition of their performance of their duty, which they neglecting justly lose the benefit of it.

CHAPTER 8

2. *To know.* That you might discover to yourself and others that infidelity, inconstancy, hypocrisy, and perverseness, which lay hid in your heart; the discovery whereof was of singular use both to them and to the church of God in all succeeding ages. It is good for us likewise to remember all the ways both of God's providence and grace by which he has led us through the wilderness, that we may trust him and cheerfully serve him.

5. *As a man chasteneth.* That is, unwillingly, being constrained by necessity; moderately, in judgment remembering mercy; and for your reformation, not your destruction.

10. *Bless the* LORD. Some only praise him for your food; which is a debt both of gratitude and justice, because it is from his providence and favor that you receive both your food and refreshment and strength by it.

16. *That he might humble thee.* By keeping you in constant dependence upon him for every day's food, and convincing you what an impotent, helpless creature you are, having nothing whereon to subsist, and being supported wholly by the alms of divine goodness from day to day. The mercies of God, if duly considered, are as powerful a means to humble us as the greatest afflictions, because they increase our debts to God and manifest our dependence upon him. And by making God great, they make us little in our own eyes.

CHAPTER 9

1. *Mightier than thyself.* This he adds that they might not trust to their own strength, but wholly rely upon God's help for the destroying of them, and after the work was done, might ascribe the glory of it to God alone and not to themselves.

5. *Not for thy righteousness.* Neither for your upright heart nor holy life, which are the two things which God above all things regards. And consequently he excludes all merit. And surely they who did not deserve this earthly Canaan could not merit the kingdom of glory.

6. *Stiffnecked.* Rebellious and perverse, and so destitute of all pretense of righteousness. And thus our gaining possession of the heavenly Canaan must be ascribed to God's power, not our own might, and to God's grace, not our own merit. In him we must glory.

10. *With the finger of God.* Immediately and miraculously, which was done not only to procure the greater reverence to the law, but also to signify that it is the work of God alone to write this law upon the tables of men's hearts.

17. *I . . . brake them before your eyes.* Not by an unbridled passion, but in zeal for God's honor and by the direction of God's Spirit, to signify to the people that the covenant between God and them contained in those tables was broken, and they were now cast out of God's favor and could expect nothing from him but fiery indignation.

CHAPTER 10

2. *I will write on the tables.* Though the tables were broken, because they broke his commandment, they were now renewed in proof that his wrath was turned away. And thus God's writing his law in our inward parts is the surest proof of our reconciliation to him.

9. *The LORD is his inheritance.* That is, the Lord's portion, namely tithes and offerings, which belong to God, are given by him to the Levites for their subsistence, from generation to generation.

11. *Take thy journey before the people.* It was fit that he who had saved them from ruin by his intercession should have the conduct and command of them. And herein he was a type of Christ, who, as he "ever liveth to make intercession for [us]," so has "all power in heaven and in earth."

15. *To love them.* He shows that God had no particular obligation to their fathers, any more than to other persons or people, all being equally his creatures, and that his choice of them out of and above all others proceeded only from God's good pleasure.

17. *Regardeth not persons.* Whether Jews or Gentiles, but deals justly and equally with all sorts of men. And as whosoever fears and obeys him shall be accepted, so all incorrigible transgressors shall be severely punished, and you no less than other people. Therefore do not flatter yourselves as if God would bear with your sins because of his particular kindness to you or to your fathers.

CHAPTER 11

11. *Of hills and valleys.* And therefore much more healthful than Egypt was, which as it was enriched, so it was annoyed with the Nile, which overflowed the land in summertime and thereby made the country both unpleasant and unhealthful. And health being the greatest of all outward blessings, Canaan must therefore needs be a more desirable habitation than Egypt.

18. *Lay up.* Let us all observe these three rules. (1) Let our hearts be filled with the word of God. *Lay up these my words in your heart,* as in a storehouse, to be used upon all occasions. (2) Let our eyes be fixed upon the word of God. *Bind them* for a *sign upon your hand,* which is always in view, and *as frontlets between your eyes,* which you cannot avoid the sight of. (3) Let our tongues be employed about the word of God, especially with our children, who must be taught this as far more needful than the rules of decency or the calling they are to live by.

CHAPTER 12

5. *To put his name there.* That is, to set up his worship there, and which he shall call by his name, as his house or his dwelling place. Namely, where the ark should be, the tabernacle or temple; which was first Shiloh and then Jerusalem. There is not one precept in all the law of Moses so largely inculcated as this, to bring all their sacrifices to that one altar. And how significant is that appointment? They must keep to one place in token of their belief that "there is one God, and one mediator between God and men." It not only served to keep up the notion of the unity of the godhead, but the one only way of approach to God and communion with him in and by his Son.

12. *Your daughters.* Hence it appears that, though the males only were obliged to appear before God in their solemn feasts, yet the women also were permitted to come.

CHAPTER 13

3. *Thou shalt not hearken unto the words of that prophet.* Not receive his doctrine, though the sign come to pass. For although when such a sign or wonder foretold did not follow or come to pass it was a sign of a false prophet, yet when it did come to pass, it was not sufficient sign of a true one, especially in such a case. There are many things which may be wrought by evil spirits, God so permitting it for wise and just reasons, not only for the trial of the good, but also for the punishment of ungodly men.

6. *Thy daughter.* Your piety must overcome both your affection and your compassion to the weaker sex. The father and mother are here omitted because they are sufficiently contained in the former examples.

9. *Thou shalt surely kill him.* Not privately, which pretense would have opened the door to innumerable murders, but by procuring his death by the sentence of the magistrate. You shall cast the first stone at him, as the witness was to do.

16. *For the* LORD. For the satisfaction of God's justice, the maintenance of his honor and authority, and the pacification of his offended majesty.

CHAPTER 14

1. *Ye shall not cut yourselves.* Which were the practices of idolaters, both in the worship of their idols, in their funerals, and upon occasion of public calamities. Is not this like a parent's charge to his children, playing with knives, "Do not cut yourselves!" This is the intention of those commands, which obliges us to deny ourselves. The meaning is, Do yourselves no harm! And as this also is the design of cross providences, to remove from us those things by which we are in danger of doing ourselves harm.

27. *Thou shalt not forsake him.* You shall give him a share in such tithes or in the product of them.

CHAPTER 15

8. *Open thine hand wide.* That is, deal bountifully and liberally with him.

9. *Beware.* Suppress the first risings of such uncharitableness.

10. *Thine heart shall not be grieved.* That is, you shall give, not only with an open hand, but with a willing and cheerful mind, without which your very charity is uncharitable and not accepted by God.

11. *The poor shall never cease.* God by his providence will so order it, partly for the punishment of your disobedience, and partly for the trial and exercise of your obedience to him and charity to your brother.

15. *The LORD thy God redeemed thee.* And brought you out with riches, which because they would not, God gave you as a just recompense for your service; and therefore you shall follow his example and send out your servant furnished with all convenient provisions.

CHAPTER 16

6. *There.* Namely, in the court of the tabernacle or temple. This he prescribed, partly that this great work might be done with more solemnity in such manner as God required; partly, because it was not only a sacrament but also a sacrifice, and because here was the sprinkling of blood, which is the essential part of a sacrifice; and partly to design the place where Christ, the true Passover or Lamb of God, was to be slain.

15. *Thou shalt surely rejoice.* In God

and the effects of his favor, praising him with a glad heart.

CHAPTER 17

3. *The host of heaven.* Those glorious creatures which are to be admired as the wonderful works of God, but not to be set up in God's stead.

14. *When thou . . . shalt.* He only foresees and foretells what they would do, but does not approve of it. For when they did this thing for this very reason, he declares his utter dislike of it (I Sam. 8:7).

15. *Thy brethren.* Of the same nation and religion; because such a person was most likely to maintain true religion, and to rule with righteousness, gentleness, and kindness to his subjects; and that he might be a fit type of Christ their supreme King, who was to be one of their brethren.

18. *Out of that.* Out of the original, which was carefully kept by the priests in the sanctuary, that it might be a perfect copy, and that it might have the greater influence upon him, coming to him as from the hand and presence of God.

19. *All the days of his life.* It is not enough to have Bibles, but we must use them, yes, daily. Our souls must have constant meals of that manna which, if well digested, will afford them true nourishment and strength.

20. *That his heart be not lifted up.* He intimates that the Scriptures, diligently read, are a powerful means to keep him humble, because they show him that, though he be a king, he is subject to an higher monarch, to whom he must give an account of all his administrations and receive from him his sentence agreeable to their quality, which is sufficient to abate the pride of the haughtiest person in the world.

CHAPTER 18

14. *Hath not suffered thee so to do.* Has not allowed you to follow these superstitious and diabolical practices as he has allowed other nations to do, but has instructed you better by his word and Spirit, and will more fully instruct you by a great prophet.

15. *A prophet . . . like unto me.* Christ was truly and in all commendable parts like him, in being both a prophet and a king and a priest and mediator, in the excellence of his ministry and work, in the glory of his miracles, in his familiar and intimate converse with God.

CHAPTER 19

9. *If thou shalt keep all these commandments.* But the Jewish writers themselves own that, the condition not being performed, the promise of enlarging their coast was not fulfilled, so that there was no need for three more cities of refuge. Yet the holy, blessed God, say they, did not command it in vain, for in the days of Messiah the Prince they shall be added. They expect it in the letter; but we know it has in Christ its spiritual accomplishment. For the borders of the Gospel-Israel are enlarged according to the promise; and in "the LORD our righteousness," refuge is provided for all that by faith fly to him.

21. *Eye for eye.* What punishment the law allotted to the accused, if he had been convicted, the same shall the false accuser bear.

CHAPTER 20

5. *What man.* This and the following exceptions are to be understood only of a war allowed by God, not in a war commanded by God, not in the approaching war with the Canaanites,

from which even the bridegroom was not exempted, as the Jewish writers note.

19. *Thou shalt not destroy.* Which is to be understood of a general destruction of them, not of the cutting down some few of them as the convenience of the siege might require.

CHAPTER 21

3. *Which hath not drawn in the yoke.* A type of Christ, who was under the yoke, but what he had voluntarily taken upon himself.

11. *Hast a desire unto her.* Or, "hast taken delight in her." Which may be a modest expression for lying with her, and seems probable, because it is said (v. 14) that he had "humbled her."

12. *She shall shave her head.* In token of her renouncing her heathenish idolatry and superstition, and of her becoming a new woman and embracing the true religion.

14. *Thou shalt not make merchandise of her.* Make gain of her, either by using her to your own servile works, or by prostituting her to the lusts or to the service of others.

15. *Two wives.* This practice, though tolerated, is not hereby made lawful; but only provision is made for the children in that case.

19. *His father and his mother.* The consent of both is required to prevent the abuse of this law to cruelty. And it cannot reasonably be supposed that both would agree without the son's abominable and incorrigible wickedness, in which case it seems a righteous law, because the crime of rebellion against his own parents did so fully signify what a pernicious member he would be in the commonwealth of Israel, who had dissolved all his natural obligations. *Unto the elders.* Which was a sufficient caution to preserve children from the malice of any hard-hearted parents, because these elders were first to examine the case with all exactness and then to pronounce the sentence.

23. *He . . . is accursed of God.* This curse is here appropriated to those that are hanged to signify that Christ should undergo this execrable punishment and be made a curse for us (Gal. 3:13), which though it was to come in respect to men, yet was present unto God.

CHAPTER 22

1. *Thy brother's.* Any man's. *Thou shalt not . . . hide thyself.* Dissemble or pretend that you do not see them; or pass them by as if you had not seen them.

5. *Shall not wear.* This is forbidden, both for decency sake, that men might not confound those sexes which God has distinguished; that all appearance of evil might be avoided, such change of garments carrying a manifest sign of effeminence in the man, of arrogance in the woman, of lightness and petulance in both; and to cut off all suspicions and occasions of evil, which this practice opens a wide door to.

7. *Let the dam go.* Partly for the bird's sake, which suffered enough by the loss of its young; for God would not have cruelty exercised towards the brute creatures. And partly for men's sake, to restrain their greediness, that they should not monopolize all to themselves, but leave the hopes of a future seed for others.

8. *A battlement.* The Jews say that by the equity of this law they are obliged, and so are we, to fence or remove every thing whereby life may be endangered, as wells or bridges, lest if any perish through our omission, their blood be required at our hand.

12. *Fringes.* Or "laces," or "strings," partly to bring the commands of God

to their remembrance (Num. 15:38), and partly as a public profession of their nation and religion, whereby they might be distinguished from strangers, so that they might be more circumspect to behave as became the people of God, and that they should own their religion before all the world.

27. *The betrothed damsel cried.* Which is in that case to be presumed; charity obliging us to believe the best until the contrary be manifest.

CHAPTER 23

1. *He that is wounded.* A phrase denoting an eunuch. He shall not be admitted to honors and offices either in the church or in the commonwealth of Israel. Nor is it strange that eunuchs are excluded from government, both because such persons are commonly observed to lack that courage which is necessary for a governor, because as such persons ordinarily were despicable, so the authority in their hands was likely to be exposed to the same contempt.

6. *Thou shalt not seek their peace.* That is, make no contracts either by marriages or leagues or commerce with them, but rather constantly keep a jealous eye over them, as enemies who will watch every opportunity to ensnare or disturb you. Each particular Israelite is not hereby forbidden to perform any office of humanity to them, but the body of the nation are forbidden all familiar conversation with them.

7. *Thou wast a stranger.* It is ordinary with men that one injury blots out the remembrance of twenty courtesies. But God does not deal so with us, nor will he have us to deal so with others, but commands us to forget injuries and to remember kindnesses.

13. *Cover.* To prevent the annoyance of ourselves or others; to preserve and exercise modesty and natural honesty; principally that by such outward rites they might be inured to the greater reverence of the Divine Majesty, and the greater caution to avoid all real and moral uncleanness.

18. *The hire of a whore.* This is opposed to the practice of the Gentiles, who allowed both such persons and the oblations they made out of their infamous gains. And some of them kept lewd women, who prostituted themselves in the temples, to the honor of their false gods, and offered part of their profit to them. *The price of a dog.* It seems to mean of a whoremonger or sodomite. Such are called dogs (Rev. 22:15). And it is not improbable they are called so here. From these God would not accept of any offering.

CHAPTER 24

1. *Let him write.* This is not a command as some of the Jews understood it, nor an allowance and approbation, but merely a permission of that practice for prevention of greater mischiefs, and this only until "the time of reformation," until the coming of the Messiah when things were to return to their first institution and purest condition.

4. *Defiled.* Not absolutely, as if her second marriage were a sin, but with respect to her first husband, to whom she is as a defiled or unclean woman, that is, forbidden things. Forbidden things are accounted and called "unclean" (Judg. 13:7), because they may no more be touched or used than an unclean thing.

5. *One year.* That their affections may be firmly settled so as there may be no occasions for the divorces last mentioned.

12. *Thou shalt not sleep.* But restore it before night, which intimates that he should take no such thing for pledge, without which a man cannot sleep.

13. *Bless thee.* Bring down the blessing of God upon you by his prayers. For though his prayers, if he be not a good man, shall not avail for his own behalf, yet they shall avail for your benefit.

16. *Not be put to death.* For though God visits the father's sins upon the children (Exod. 20), yet he will not allow men to do so.

CHAPTER 25

3. *Forty stripes.* It seems not superstition, but prudent caution when the Jews would not exceed thirty-nine stripes, lest through mistake or forgetfulness they should go beyond their bounds, which they were commanded to keep.

5. *One of them die.* Any of them, for the words are general, and the reason of the law was to keep up the distinction of tribes and families, so that the Messiah might be discovered by the family from which he was appointed to proceed; and also of inheritances, which were divided among all the brethren, the firstborn having only a double portion. *Stranger.* To one of another family.

9. *Loose his shoe.* As a sign of his resignation of all his right to the woman and to her husband's inheritance. For as the shoe was a sign of one's power and right (Pss. 60:8; 108:9), so the parting with the shoe was a token of the alienation of such right.

CHAPTER 26

11. *Thou shalt rejoice.* You shall thus be enabled to take comfort in all your employments, when you have sanctified them by giving God his portion. It is the will of God that we should be cheerful not only in our attendance upon his holy ordinances, but in our enjoyment of the gifts of his providence. Whatever good thing God gives us, we should make the most comfortable use of it we can, still tracing the streams to the fountain of all consolation.

CHAPTER 27

4. *Mount Ebal.* The mount of cursing. Here the law is written to signify that a curse was due to the violators of it, and that no man could expect justification from the works of the law by sentence whereof all men are justly accused as being all guilty of the transgression of it in one kind and degree or other. Here the sacrifices are to be offered to show that there is no way to be delivered from this curse but by the blood of Christ, which all these sacrifices did typify, and by Christ's being made a curse for us.

12. *Upon mount Gerizim.* These words may be rendered "beside" or "near to" Mount Gerizim. There were in Canaan two mountains that lay near together, with a valley between, one called Gerizim, the other Ebal. On the sides of these which faced each other, all the tribes were to be drawn up, six on a side, so that in the valley they came near each other, so near that the priests standing between them might be heard by them that were next to them on both sides. Then one of the priests, or perhaps more, at some distance from each other pronounced with a loud voice one of the curses following. And all the people who stood on the foot and side of Mount Ebal (those farther off taking the signal from those who were nearer), said, "Amen!" Then the contrary blessing was pronounced, "Blessed is he that doth so or so." To which all who stood on the foot and side of Mount Gerizim said, "Amen!"

15. *Cursed.* The curses are expressed, but not the blessings. "For as many as are of the works of the law are under the curse." But it was an honor reserved for Christ to bless us; to do "what the law could not do." So in his Sermon on the Mount, the true Mount Gerizim, we have blessings only. *Amen.* It is easy to understand the meaning of *Amen* to the blessings. But how could they say it to the curses? It was both a profession of their faith in the truth of it, and an acknowledgment of the equity of these curses. So that when they said, *Amen,* they did in effect say not only it is certain it shall be so, but it is just it should be so.

26. *Confirmeth not.* Or, "performeth not." To this we must all say, "Amen!" Owning ourselves to be under the curse, and that we must have perished for ever if Christ had not "redeemed us from the curse of the law" by "being made a curse for us."

CHAPTER 28

2. *Overtake thee.* Those blessings which others greedily follow after, and never overtake, shall follow after you and shall be thrown into your lap by special kindness.

3. *In the city, and . . . in the field.* How constantly must we depend upon God, both for the continuance and comfort of life! We need him at every turn. We cannot be safe if he withdraw his protection, nor easy if he suspends his favor. But if he bless us, go where we will, it is well with us.

15. *Overtake thee.* So that you shall not be able to escape them, as you shall vainly hope and endeavor to do. There is no running from God, but by running to him; no flying from his justice, but by flying to his mercy.

20. *Rebuke.* Namely, from God, not so much in words as by his actions, by cross providences, by sharp and sore afflictions.

28. *Blindness.* Of mind, so that they shall not know what to do. *Astonishment.* They shall be filled with wonder and horror because of the strangeness and soreness of their calamities.

29. *Grope at noonday.* In the most clear and evident matter you shall grossly mistake. *Thy ways.* Your counsels and enterprises shall be frustrated and turn to your destruction.

34. *Thou shalt be made for the sight of thine eyes.* Quite put out of the possession of their own souls. Quite bereaved of all comfort and hope, and abandoned to utter despair. They that walk by sight and not by faith are in danger of losing reason itself when all about them looks frightful, and their condition is bad indeed.

45. *Moreover all these curses.* It seems Moses was foretelling their captivity in Babylon, by which even after their return they were brought to the low condition mentioned in verse 44. But in the following he foretells their last destruction by the Romans. And this destruction, more dreadful than the former, shows that their sin in rejecting Christ was more provoking to God than idolatry itself and left them more under the power of Satan. For their captivity in Babylon cured them effectually of idolatry in seventy years. But under this last destruction, they continue above sixteen hundred years incurably averse to the Lord Jesus.

46. *A wonder.* It is amazing that a people so incorporated should be so universally dispersed. And that a people scattered in all nations should not mix with any but, like Cain, be fugitives and vagabonds and yet so marked as to be known.

49. *As the eagle flieth.* Not only swiftly, fiercely, and greedily, as the eagle to its prey; but also strongly and irresistibly. This may be understood of the Romans, who did come *from far, from the end of the earth,* more truly and literally than the Chaldeans, and may allude to the eagle which was in the ensigns.

57. *She shall eat them.* This was fulfilled more than once, to the perpetual reproach of the Jewish nation. Never was the like done either by Greek or Barbarian. See the fruit of being abandoned by God!

63. *To destroy you.* His indignation against you will be so great that it will be a pleasure to him to take vengeance on you. For though he does not delight in the death of a sinner in itself, yet he does delight in glorifying his justice upon incorrigible sinners, seeing the exercise of all his attributes must please him, else he were not perfectly happy.

68. *Into Egypt.* Which was literally fulfilled under Titus when multitudes of them were carried there in ships and sold for slaves. And this expression seems to remind them of that time when they went over the sea without ships, God miraculously drying up the sea before them, which they would now have occasion sadly to remember. *No man shall buy you.* Either because the number of your captives shall be so great that the market shall be glutted with you; or because you shall be so loathsome and contemptible that men shall not be willing to have you for slaves. And this was the condition of the Jews after the destruction of Jerusalem, as Josephus the Jew has left upon record. Let us all learn therefore to "stand in awe and sin not."

CHAPTER 29

4. *Yet the* LORD. That is, you have perceived and seen them with the eyes of your body, but not with your minds and hearts. You have not yet learned rightly to understand the word and works of God so as to know them for your good, and to make a right use of them, and to comply with them. Although the hearing ear and the seeing eye be the workmanship of God, yet their lack of his grace was their own fault and the just punishment of their former sins. The present case was like theirs in Isaiah's time, who first shut their own eyes and ears that they might not see and hear, and would not understand; and then by the righteous judgment of God had their eyes and ears closed that they should not see and hear, and understand. God's readiness to do us good in other things is a plain evidence that if we have not grace, that best of gifts, it is our own fault and not his. He would have gathered us, and we would not.

CHAPTER 30

10. *If thou shalt hearken.* This is added to warn them that they should not receive the grace of God in vain, and to teach them that the grace of God does not discharge man's obligation to his duty, nor excuse him for the neglect of it. It is observable that Moses calls God *the* LORD *thy God* twelve times in verses 1 to 10. In the threatenings of the former chapter, he is all along called *the* LORD, a God of power and a judge of all. But in the promises of this chapter, *the* LORD *thy God,* a God of grace and in covenant with you.

11. *This commandment.* The great command of loving and obeying God, which is the sum of the law, of which yet he does not here speak as it is in itself, but as it is modified and accompanied with the grace of the gospel. The meaning is that, though the practice of God's laws be now far from us

and above our strength, yet, considering the advantage of gospel grace whereby God enables us to do our duty, it is near and easy to us who believe. And so this well agrees with Romans 10:6ff., where St. Paul applies this place to the righteousness of faith.

19. *Choose life.* They shall have life that choose it. They that choose the favor of God and communion with him shall have what they choose. They that come short of life and happiness, just thank themselves only. They had had them, if they had chosen them, when they were put to their choice. But they die, because they will die.

20. *That thou mayest love the* LORD *thy God.* Here he shows them in short what their duty is: To love God as the Lord, a being most amiable, and as their God, a God in covenant with them. As an evidence of their love, to *obey his voice* in every thing, and by constancy in this love and obedience, *to cleave unto him* all their days. And what encouragement had they to do this? *For he is thy life, and the length of thy days.* He gives life, preserves life, restores life, and prolongs it, by his power, though it be a frail life, and by his presence, though it be a forfeited life. He sweetens life by his comforts, and completes all in life everlasting.

CHAPTER 31

17. *Hide my face.* Withdraw my favor and help. Whatever outward troubles we are in if we have but the light of God's countenance, we are safe. But if God hide his face from us, then we are undone.

21. *Their imaginations.* Inclinations to idolatry, which they do not check as they ought; and some of them do not only cherish it in their hearts, but as far as they can and dare secretly practice it, as may be gathered from Amos 5:25 and Acts 7:43.

26. *Take this book.* Probably the very same book which (after having been some way misplaced) was found in the house of the Lord in the days of Josiah and publicly read by the king himself, for a witness against a people who were then almost ripe for ruin.

CHAPTER 32

4. *The Rock.* As for the stability of his nature and invincibleness of his power, so for his fixedness and immutability in his counsels and promises and ways; so that if there shall be a sad change in your affairs, remember that this proceeds from yourselves and from the change of your ways towards God, and not from God, "with whom is no variableness, neither shadow of turning" (James 1:17). *A God of truth.* Constant to his promises. You cannot accuse him of any unfaithfulness to this day.

6. *O foolish people and unwise.* Fools and double fools! Fools indeed, to disoblige one on which you so entirely depend. Who has bewitched you? To forsake your own mercies for "lying vanities"! *Bought thee.* That has redeemed you from Egyptian bondage. *Made thee.* Not only in general by creation, but in a peculiar manner by making you his peculiar people. *Established.* Renewed and confirmed his favor to you, and not taken it away, which you have often provoked him to do.

10. *In the waste howling wilderness.* In a place destitute of all the necessities and comforts of life, which also was a type of that desolate and comfortless condition in which all men are before the grace of God finds them out. Here, instead of the voices of men, nothing is heard but the howlings and yellings of ravenous birds and beasts.

11. *On her wings.* That is, gently and tenderly and safely too, as if she carried them not in her claws for fear of hurting them, but upon her wings. Some say the eagle usually carries her young ones upon her wings.

12. *Did lead him.* When they were shut up in Egypt as in their nest, whence they dared not venture to fly nor stir, he taught and encouraged and enabled them to fly out from that bondage, he dealt tenderly with them, bearing with their infirmities, keeping them from all harms.

13. *Out of the rock.* This being a land flowing with honey, where the bees made honey in the holes of rocks, or in the trees that grew upon or among the rocks.

17. *Unto devils.* Unto idols, which the devils brought into the world in opposition to God, and by which the devils often manifested themselves to men, gave them answers, and received their worship. The Gentiles pretended to worship God in those idols, and the devils which inspired them deluded the nations with pretenses that they were a sort of lower gods.

18. *Of the Rock.* Of God, one of whose titles this is, or of Christ, who is called the "rock" (I Cor. 10:4), whom the Israelites tempted.

24. *With hunger.* With famine, which burns and parches the inward parts and makes the face "black as a coal" (Lam. 4:8).

35. *At hand.* So the Scripture often speaks of those things which are at many hundred years distance, to signify that though they may be afar off as to your measures of time, yet in God's account they are near, they are as near as can be, when the measure of their sins is once full; the judgment shall not be deferred.

43. *Rejoice.* He calls upon the nations to rejoice and bless God for his favors, and especially for the last wonderful deliverance which shall be given to the Jews, when they shall be converted to the gospel in the last days. Which they have all reason to do because of that singular advantage which all nations will have at that time and upon that occasion.

48. *That selfsame day.* Now that he had finished his work, why should he desire to live a day longer? He had indeed formerly desired and prayed that he might go over Jordan. But now he is entirely satisfied and says more of that matter.

51. *Because ye trespassed.* God reminds him of the sin he had committed long before. It is good for the holiest of men to die repenting, even of their early sins.

52. *Yet thou shalt see the land.* And see it as the earnest of that "better country," which is only seen with the eye of faith. What is death to him who has a believing prospect and a steadfast hope of eternal life?

CHAPTER 33

2. *And rose up.* He appeared or showed himself, as the sun does when it rises. *With ten thousands of saints.* That is, with a great company of holy angels (Ps. 68:17; Dan. 7:10) which attended upon him in this great and glorious work of giving the law, as may be gathered from Acts 7:53 and Galatians 3:19. *From his right hand.* Which both wrote the law and gave it to men. An allusion to men who ordinarily write and give gifts with their right hand. *A fiery law.* The law is called fiery because it is of a fiery nature purging and searching and inflaming, to signify that fiery wrath which it inflicts upon sinners for the violation of it, and principally because it was delivered out of the midst of the fire.

3. *People.* The tribes of Israel. The sense is, this law, though delivered with fire and smoke and thunder, which might seem to portend nothing but hatred and terror, yet in truth was given to Israel in great love, as being the great means of their temporal and eternal salvation. Yes, he embraced the people, and laid them in his bosom! So the word signifies, which speaks not only the dearest love, but the most tender and careful protection.

4. *Moses.* He speaks this of himself in the third person, which is very unusual in the Hebrew language.

5. *He was king in Jeshurun.* Moses was their king not in title, but in reality, being, under God, their supreme governor and lawgiver.

7. *From his enemies.* You will preserve this tribe in a special manner, so that his enemies shall not be able to ruin it, as they will do other tribes, and that for the sake of the Messiah who shall spring out of it.

16. *Him that was separated from his brethren.* Joseph's brethren separated him from them by making him a slave, and God distinguished him from them by making him a prince.

Many a time had God appeared to Moses; but now that he is just dying, he seems to have the most pleasing remembrance of the first time that he saw the visions of the Almighty. It is here God declared himself "the God of Abraham, Isaac, and Jacob," and so confirmed the promise made to the father, that promise which our Lord shows reaches as far as the resurrection and eternal life.

26. *There is none.* These are the last words that ever Moses wrote, perhaps the greatest writer that ever lived upon the earth. And this man of God, who had as much reason to know both as ever any mere man had, with his last breath magnifies both the God of Israel and the Israel of God. *Riding upon the* *heaven* denotes the greatness and glory in which God manifests himself to the upper world and the use he makes of the influences of heaven and the products of the clouds in bringing to pass his own counsels in this lower world. All these he manages and directs, as a man does the horse he rides upon.

27. *The eternal God.* He who was before all worlds, and will be when time shall be no more. *Is thy refuge.* Or, "thy habitation or mansion house" (so the word signifies) in whom you are safe, at ease, and at rest, as a man is in his own house. Every true Israelite is at home in God; the soul returns to him and reposes in him. And they that make him their habitation shall have all the comforts and benefits of a habitation in him. *And underneath are the everlasting arms.* The almighty power of God, which protects and comforts all who trust in him in their greatest straits and distresses. *Destroy them.* Giving you not only a commission, but strength to put it in execution. And has he not given the same commission and the same strength to believers to destroy all sin?

29. Those in whose hearts is the excellence of holiness have God himself for their shield and sword. They are defended by "the whole armour of God." His word is their sword, and faith their shield. *And thou shalt tread upon their high places.* Their strongholds, palaces, and temples. Thus shall the God of peace tread Satan under the feet of all believers, and that shortly.

CHAPTER 34

1. *And Moses went up.* When he knew the place of his death, he cheerfully mounted a steep hill to come to it. Those who are well acquainted with another world are not afraid to leave this. When God's servants are sent for out of the world, the summoned ones go up and die!

4. *I have caused thee to see it.* For though his sight was good, yet he could not have seen all Canaan, a hundred and sixty miles in length and fifty or sixty in breadth, if his sight had not been miraculously assisted and enlarged. He saw it at a distance. Such a sight the Old Testament believers had of the kingdom of the Messiah. And such a sign believers have now of the glory that shall be revealed. Such a sight have we now of the knowledge of the glory of the Lord, which shall cover the earth. Those who come after us shall undoubtedly enter into that promised land; which is a comfort to us, when we find our own carcasses falling in this wilderness.

5. And it was more his honor to be *the servant of the LORD,* than to be king in Jeshurun. Yet he dies. Neither his piety nor his usefulness would exempt him from death. God's servants must die, that they may rest from their labors, receive the recompense, and make room for others. But when they go, they go to serve him better, to "serve him day and night in his temple." The Jews say, God sucked his soul out of his body with a kiss. No doubt he died in the embraces of his love.

6. *He.* The Lord buried him either immediately or by the ministry of angels, whereof Michael was the chief or prince. *Of his sepulchre.* Of the particular place where he was buried, which God hid from the Israelites to prevent their superstition and idolatry, to which he knew their great proneness. And for this very reason the devil endeavored to have it known and contended with Michael about it (Jude 9). God takes care even of the dead bodies of his servants. As their death is precious, so is their dust. Not one grain of it shall be lost, but the covenant with it shall be remembered.

12. *Moses* was greater than any other

prophet of the Old Testament. By Moses God gave the law and molded and formed the Jewish church. By the other prophets he only sent particular reproofs, directions, and predictions. But as far as the other prophets came short of him, our Lord Jesus went beyond him. "Moses . . . was faithful . . . as a servant; . . . but Christ as a son." His miracles more illustrious, his communion with the Father more intimate; for he is in his bosom from eternity. Moses lies buried; but Christ is sitting "at the right hand of God," and "of the increase of his government and peace there shall be no end."

Joshua

CHAPTER 1

2. *Now therefore arise.* Let not the withering of the most useful hands be the weakening of ours. When God has work to do, he will either find or make instruments fit to carry it on. *Moses my servant* is dead; but God the master is not. He lives for ever.

6. *Be strong and of a good courage.* Joshua, though a person of great courage and resolution, whereof he had given sufficient proof, yet needs these exhortations. This, partly because his work was great and difficult and long, and in a great measure new. And partly because he had a very low opinion of himself, especially if compared with Moses; and remembering how perverse and ungovernable that people were, even under Moses, he might very well suspect the burden of ruling them would be too heavy for his shoulders.

7. *Commanded thee.* Remember that though you are the commander of my people, yet you are my subject and obliged to observe all my commands. *To the right hand or to the left.* That is, in any kind or upon any pretense; which plainly shows that God's assistance promised to him and the Israelites was conditional and might justly be withdrawn upon their breach of the conditions.

8. *Out of thy mouth.* That is, you shall constantly read it, and upon occasion discourse of it, and the sentence which shall come out of your mouth shall in all things be given according to this rule. *Day and night.* That is, diligently study, and upon all occasions consider what is God's will and your duty. The greatness of your place and employments shall not hinder you from this work, because this is the only rule of all your private actions and public administrations.

9. *I commanded thee.* I whom you are obliged to obey. I who can carry you through all I put you upon. I of whose faithfulness and almighty power you have had large experience.

16. Thus must we swear allegiance to our Lord Jesus, as the captain of our salvation.

CHAPTER 2

1. *To spy.* It is evident Joshua did not do this out of distrust. It is probable he had God's command and direction in it for the encouragement of himself and his army.

3. Probably Israel had but one friend in all Jericho. And God directed them to her! Thus what seems to be most accidental is often overruled, to serve the great ends of Providence. And those who acknowledge God in their ways, he will guide them with his eye.

4. *And hid them.* This is justly mentioned as a great and generous act of faith (Heb. 11:31), for Rahab apparently ventured her life upon a steadfast persuasion of the truth of God's word and promise given to the Israelites. *Whence they were.* Her answer contained in these and the following words was false and therefore unquestionably sinful; though her intention was good therein. But it is very probable, she being a heathen might think that an officious lie is not unlawful.

12. *True token.* Either an assurance that you will preserve me and mine from the common ruin; or a token which I may produce as a witness of this agreement, and a means of my security. This is all that she asks. But God did for her more than she could "ask or think."

14. *For yours.* We will venture our lives for the security of yours.

CHAPTER 3

4. *Ye have not passed this way heretofore.* While we are here, we must expect unusual events and to pass ways that we have not passed before. And much more when we pass through the valley of the shadow of death. But if we have the assurance of God's presence, what have we to fear?

9. *The* LORD *your God.* Who is now about to give a proof that he is both *the* LORD, the omnipotent governor of heaven and earth and all creatures; and *your God,* in covenant with you, having a tender care and affection for you.

10. *Ye shall know.* By experience and sensible evidence. *The living God.* Not a dull, dead, senseless God, such as the gods of the nations are; but a God of life and power and activity to watch over you and work for you. *Among you.*

Is present with you to strengthen and help you.

13. *The ark of the* LORD. That it may appear this is the Lord's doing in pursuance of his covenant made with Israel.

16. *Against Jericho.* Here God carried them over because this part was, (1) The strongest, as having in its neighborhood an eminent city, a potent king, and a stout and warlike people. (2) The most pleasant and fruitful, and therefore more convenient both for the refreshment of the Israelites after their long and tedious marches, and for their encouragement.

17. *Stood firm.* That is, in one and the same place and posture; their feet neither moved by any waters flowing in upon them, nor sinking into any mire, which one might think was at the bottom of the river.

CHAPTER 4

9. *Twelve stones.* These stones are not the same as those which a man could carry upon his shoulder (v. 5). They might be very much larger; and being set up in two rows one above another might be seen, at least when the water was low, especially where it was shallow as it was ordinarily, though not at this time when Jordan overflowed all its banks. Add to this that the waters of Jordan are very clear; therefore, these stones might be seen in it, either by those who stood upon the shore, because the river was not broad; or by those that passed in boats. *Unto this day.* This might be written, either (1) By Joshua, who probably wrote this book near twenty years after this was done. Or, (2) By some other holy man divinely inspired who inserted this and some such passages both in this book and in the writings of Moses.

10. *Hasted.* That is, passed over with

haste, an argument of their fear or weakness of their faith; as on the contrary, the priests are commended that they stood firm and settled in their minds as well as in the posture of their bodies.

23. It greatly magnifies later mercies to compare them with former mercies; for hereby it appears that God is "the same yesterday, and to-day, and for ever."

CHAPTER 5

1. *Melted.* They lost all their courage and dared not attempt anything upon the Israelites; not without God's special providence, that the Israelites might quietly participate in the two great sacraments of their church, circumcision and the Passover, and thereby be prepared for their high and hard work, and for the possession of the holy and promised land; which would have been defiled by an uncircumcised people.

2. *The second time.* He calls this a second circumcision, not as if these same persons had been circumcised before, but with respect to the body of the people, whereof one part had been circumcised before and the other at this time, which is called a second time in relation to some former time wherein they were circumcised.

7. *Circumcised.* Which God would have done, (1) As a testimony of God's reconciliation to the people and that he would not further impute their parent's rebellion to them. (2) Because the great impediment of circumcision was now removed—their continued travels, and frequent and uncertain removal. (3) To prepare them for the approaching Passover. (4) To distinguish them from the Canaanites, into whose land they were now come. (5) To ratify the covenant between God and them, whereof circumcision was a sign and seal to assure

them that God would now make good his covenant in giving them this land. And (6) To oblige them to perform all the duties to which that covenant bound them, as soon as they came into Canaan (Exod. 12:25; Lev. 23:10; Num. 15:2).

8. *Whole.* Free from that pain and soreness which circumcision caused. It was indeed an act of great faith to expose themselves to so much pain and danger too, in this place where they were hemmed in by Jordan and their enemies.

10. *The passover.* Which was their third Passover. The first was in Egypt (Exod. 12), the second at Mount Sinai (Num. 9), the third here; for in their wilderness travels these and all other sacrifices were neglected (Amos 5:25).

12. *The manna ceased.* Which God now withheld to show that manna was not an ordinary production of nature, but an extraordinary and special gift of God to supply their necessity. And because God would not be prodigal of his favors by working miracles where ordinary means were sufficient.

13. *A man.* One in the appearance of a man. *Drawn.* In readiness to fight, not, as Joshua thought, against him, but for him and his people.

14. Now this person is not a created angel, but the Son of God, who went along with the Israelites in this expedition as their chief and captain. And this appears, (1) By his acceptance of adoration here, which a created angel dared not receive (Rev. 22:8–9). (2) Because the place was made holy by his presence (Josh. 5:15), which was God's prerogative (Exod. 3:5). (3) Because he is called the Lord (Josh. 4:2). *My lord.* I acknowledge you for my Lord and captain, and therefore wait for your commands which I am ready to obey.

15. The very same orders which God gave to Moses at the bush when he was sending him to bring Israel out of Egypt, he here gives to Joshua for the confirming of his faith, that as he had been with Moses, so he would be with him.

CHAPTER 6

5. *The wall.* Not all of it; which was unnecessary and might have given the people better opportunity of escaping, but only a considerable part where the Israelites might fitly enter; for Rahab's house was not overthrown (v. 22).

God chose this way to try the faith and obedience of the people; whether they would observe a precept which to human policy seemed foolish, and believe a promise which seemed impossible to be performed; whether they could patiently bear the reproaches of their enemies, and patiently wait for the salvation of God. Thus by faith, not by force, the walls of Jericho fell down.

6. *Rams' horns.* Of basest matter and dullest sound, that the excellence of the power might be of God.

10. *Ye shall not shout.* Because shouting before the time appointed would be ineffectual, and so might give them some discouragement and their enemies reason for insulting.

16. *Shout.* To testify your faith in God's promise and thankfulness for this glorious mercy, to encourage yourselves and brethren, and to strike a terror into your enemies.

17. *To the LORD.* Partly because the first fruits were appropriated to God, partly lest the soldiers being glutted with the spoil of this rich city should grow sluggish in their work, and partly to strike the greater terror into the rest of their enemies.

21. *Young and old.* Being commanded to do so by the sovereign Lord of every man's life; and being informed by God before that the Canaanites were abominably wicked and deserved the severest punishments. As for the infants, they were guilty of original sin, and otherwise at the disposal of their creator; but if they had been wholly innocent, it was a great favor to them to take them away in infancy, rather than reserve them to those dreadful calamities to which those who survived them were liable.

27. *The word of the LORD was with him.*[1] (So the Chaldee.) Even Christ himself, the same that was with Moses. Nothing makes a man appear more truly great than to have the evidences of God's presence with him.

CHAPTER 7

1. *Against the children of Israel.* Why did God punish the whole society for this one man's sin? All of them were punished for their own sins, whereof each had a sufficient proportion. But God took this occasion to inflict the punishment upon the society, partly because many of them might be guilty of this sin, either by coveting what Achan actually did, or by concealing his fault, which it is probable could not be unknown to others; or by not sorrowing for it and endeavoring to purge themselves from it. Partly to make sin the more hateful; as being the cause of such dreadful judgments. And partly to oblige all the members of every society to be more circumspect in ordering their own actions, and more diligent to prevent the misdeeds of their brethren, which is a great benefit to them and to the whole society.

9. *Thy great name.* The name of God

---

[1](6:27) KJV: "The LORD was with Joshua."

is a great name, above every name. And whatever happens, we ought to pray that this may not be polluted. This should be our concern more than any thing else. On this we should fix our eyes. And we cannot urge a better plea than this, Lord, *what wilt thou do unto thy great name?* Let God in all be glorified, and then welcome his whole will!

13. And it is a marvelous thing that Achan did not on this occasion acknowledge his crime. But this is to be imputed to the heart-hardening power of sin, which makes men grow worse and worse; to his pride, being loath to take to himself the shame of such a mischievous and infamous action; and to his vain conceit, whereby he might think others were guilty as well as he and some of them might be taken and he escape.

15. *In Israel.* That is, among the church and people of God who had such excellent laws to direct them, and such an all-sufficient and gracious God to provide for them, without any such unworthy practices. It was sacrilege. It was invading God's rights and converting to a private use that which was devoted to his glory, which was to be thus severely punished for a warning to all people in all ages, to take heed how they rob God.

19. *My son.* So Joshua calls him, to show that this severe inquisition and sentence did not proceed from any hatred to his person, which he loved as a father does his son and as a prince ought to do each of his subjects.

21. *When I saw.* He accurately describes the progress of his sin, which began at his eyes, which he permitted to gaze upon them, which inflamed his desire, and made him covet them; and that desire made him take them; and having taken, resolve to keep them; and to that end hide them in his tent.

22. *And they ran.* Partly longing to free themselves and all the people from the curse under which they lay; and partly that none of Achan's relations might get there before them and take away the things.

24. *His sons, and his daughters.* Their death was a debt they owed to their own sins, which debt God may require when he pleases. And he could not take it in more honorable circumstances than these, that the death of a very few in the beginning of a new empire and of their settlement in the land might be useful to prevent the death of many thousands who took warning by this dreadful example; whom, if the fear of God did not, yet the love of our own and of their dear children's lives would restrain them from such pernicious practices.

His oxen, and his asses, and his sheep. Which, though not capable of sin nor of punishment, properly so called, yet as they were made for man's use, so they are rightly destroyed for man's good; and being daily killed for our bodily food, it cannot seem strange to kill them for the instruction of our minds, that hereby we might learn the contagious nature of sin, which involves innocent creatures in its plagues; and how much sorer punishments are reserved for man, who having a law given to him, and that excellent gift of reason and will to restrain him from the transgressions of it, his guilt must needs be unspeakably greater, and therefore his sufferings more severe and terrible.

CHAPTER 8

29. *Hanged on a tree.* Joshua dealt more severely with the kings of Canaan than with the people, because the abominable wickedness of that people was not restrained and punished (as it should have been), but countenanced and encouraged by their evil examples; and because they were the principal authors of the destruction of their own people by engaging them in an obstinate opposition against the Israelites.

30. *Mount Ebal.* God's altar was to be but in one place (Deut. 12:13–14), and this was appointed to be Mount Ebal (Deut. 27:4–5). This seems most proper that in that place where the curses of the law were denounced against sinners, there might also be the tokens and means of grace and peace and reconciliation with God, for the removing of the curses and the procuring of God's blessing to sinners.

CHAPTER 9

2. *Together.* O that Israel would learn this of Canaanites, to sacrifice private interests to the public good and to lay aside all animosities among themselves, that they may cordially unite against the common enemy!

14. In every business of importance we should take God along with us, and by the word and prayer consult him. Many a time our affairs miscarry, because we *asked not counsel at the mouth of the Lord.* Did we acknowledge him in all our ways, they would be more safe, easy, and successful.

23. *Ye are cursed.* You shall not escape the curse of God which by divine sentence belongs on all the Canaanites; but only change the quality of it. You shall feel that curse of bondage which is proper to your race by virtue of that ancient decree (Gen. 9:25).

25. *Unto thee.* We refer ourselves to you and your own piety and honesty and faithfulness to your word and oath. If you will destroy your humble suppliants, we submit. Let us in like manner submit to our Lord Jesus and refer ourselves to him; saying, *We are in thine hand: as it seemeth good and right unto thee to do unto us, do.* Only save our souls; give us our lives for a prey; and let us serve you just as you will!

CHAPTER 10

9. *Came suddenly.* Though assured by God of the victory, yet he uses all prudent means. It is true God had promised that he would without fail deliver the enemies into his hand. Yet God's promises are intended not to slacken, but to quicken our endeavors. "He that believeth shall not make haste" to anticipate Providence; but does make haste to attend it with a diligent, not a distrustful speed.

12. It may seem that the sun was declining, and Joshua, perceiving that his work was great and long and his time but short, begs God to lengthen the day, and that the sun and moon might stop their course. He mentions two places, *Gibeon* and *Ajalon,* not as if the sun stood over the one and the moon over the other, which is absurd, especially these places being so near the one to the other; but partly to vary the phrase, as is common in poetical passages. And partly because he was in his march in the pursuit of his enemies, to pass from Gibeon to Ajalon.

He begs that he may have the help of longer light to pursue them, and to that end that the sunlight stand still, and the moon also. Not that he needed the moon's light, but because it was fit either that both sun and moon should go or that both should stand still to prevent disorder in the heavenly bodies. The prayer is thus expressed with authority, because it was not an ordinary prayer, but the prayer of a prophet divinely inspired at this very time for this purpose. And yet it intimates to us the prevalence of prayer in general, and may remind us of that honor put upon prayer, "concerning the work of my hands command ye me."

13. *The sun stood.* Here is no mention of the moon because the sun's standing was the only thing which Joshua desired and needed; and the moon's standing he desired only by accident to prevent irregularity in the motions of those celestial lights. And if it seem strange to anyone that so wonderful a work should not be mentioned in any heathen writers, he must consider that it is confessed by the generality of writers, heathen and others, that there is no certain history or monument in heathen authors of anything done before the Trojan war, which was a thousand years after Joshua's time; and that all time before that is called by the most learned heathens the uncertain, unknown, or obscure time.

14. This stupendous miracle was designed for something more than to give Israel light to destroy the Canaanites. It was designed to convince and confound those idolaters who worshipped the sun and moon by demonstrating that these also were subject to the command of the God of Israel; as also to signify that in the latter days, when the world was covered with darkness, "the sun of righteousness," even our Joshua, should arise and be the true light of the world. To which we may add that when Christ conquered our enemies upon the cross, the miracle wrought on the sun was the reverse of this. It was then darkened as if gone down at noon. For Christ needed not the light of the sun to complete his victory, so he "made darkness pavilions round about him."

16. *A cave.* A place of the greatest secrecy; but there is no escaping the eye or hand of God.

21. *None moved his tongue.* Not only their men of war could not find their hands, but they were so confounded that they could not move their tongues in way of insult. They were silenced as well as conquered.

27. Thus that which they thought would have been their shelter was made their prison first and then their grave. So shall we surely be disappointed in whatever we flee to from God.

40. And hereby was typified the final destruction of all the impenitent enemies of the Lord Jesus, who having slighted the riches of his grace, must for ever feel the weight of his wrath.

CHAPTER 11

18. And God would have the land to be conquered gradually for many weighty reasons. (1) Lest the sudden extirpation of those nations should have made a great part of the land desert and thereby have increased the number of wild beasts (Deut. 7:22). (2) Lest being done suddenly and easily, it should soon be forgotten and despised, as the nature of man is apt to do in those cases. (3) That by long exercise the Israelites might grow skillful in the art of war. (4) For the trial and exercise of their patience and courage and trust in God. (5) To oblige them to the greater care to please God, whom they yet need for their help against their enemies.

20. *To harden their hearts.* It was the design of God's providence not to soften their hearts to a compliance with the Israelites, but to give them up to their own animosity, pride, confidence, and stubbornness. So that their abominable and incorrigible wickedness might be punished, and that the Israelites might not be mixed with them, but be entire among themselves in the possession of the land.

23. God had promised to "drive out nations from before [them]." And now the promise was fulfilled. Our successes and enjoyments are then doubly comfortable when we see them flowing to us from the promise. This is *according to all that the LORD said*. Our obedience is acceptable when it has an eye to the precept. And if we conscientiously execute our duty, we need not question the performance of the promise.

CHAPTER 12

6. *Smite.* Fresh mercies must not drown the remembrance of former mercies. Nor must the glory of the present instruments of good to the church diminish the just honor of those that went before them. Joshua's services were confessedly great. But let not those under Moses be forgotten. Both together proclaim God to be the Alpha and Omega of his people's salvation.

24. What a fruitful land must Canaan then be, which could subsist so many kingdoms! And yet at this day it is one of the most barren and despicable countries in the world. Such is the effect of the curse it lies under, since its inhabitants rejected the Lord of glory.

CHAPTER 13

1. It is good for those who are *stricken in years* to be remembered that they are so; that they may be quickened to do the work of life and to prepare for death which is coming on apace.

6. *Will I drive out.* The promise of driving them out *from before the children of Israel* supposes that the Israelites must use their own endeavors, must go up against them. If Israel through sloth or cowardice let them alone, they are not likely to be driven out. We must go forth on our Christian warfare, and then God will go before us.

CHAPTER 14

2. *By lot.* This course God ordained, partly to prevent discontents, enmities, and quarrels among the tribes, and partly to demonstrate the truth and wisdom of his providence, by which alone those parts fell to each of them, which Jacob long since, and Moses lately, foretold.

8. *I wholly followed the LORD.* Which self-commendation is justifiable, because it was necessary as being the ground of his petition. Therefore it was not vain-glory in him to speak it; no more than it is for those who have God's spirit witnessing with their spirits, that they are the children of God, humbly and thankfully to tell others for their encouragement what God has done for their souls.

10. *Forty and five years.* Whereof thirty-eight years were spent in the wilderness, and seven since they came into Canaan. The longer we live, the more sensible we should be of God's goodness to us in keeping us alive. And of his care in prolonging our frail lives, his patience in prolonging our forfeited lives. And shall not the life thus kept by his providence be devoted to his praise?

11. Moses had said that at eighty years old even our "strength [is] labour and sorrow." But Caleb was an exception to this rule. At eighty-five years old his strength was still ease and joy. This he got by following the Lord fully.

CHAPTER 15

1. *The lot.* For the general understanding of this, it must be known, (1) That casting lots was transacted with great seriousness and solemnity, in God's presence, with prayer and appeal to him for the decision of the matter. (2) That although exact survey of this land was not taken until 18:4−5, yet there was and must needs be a general description of it, and a division thereof into nine parts and a half. Which, as far as they could guess, were equal either in quantity or quality. (3) That the lot did not at this time so unchangeably determine each tribe that their portion could neither be increased or diminished; as is manifest because after Judah's lot was fixed, Simeon's lot was taken out of it (19:9), though after the land was more distinctly known and surveyed, it is likely the bounds were more certain and fixed.

(4) That the lot determined only in general what part of the land belonged to each tribe, but left the particulars to be determined by Joshua and Eleazar. For the manner of this, it is likely there were two pots, into one of which were put the names of all the tribes, each in a distinct paper, and into the other the names of each portion described. Then Eleazar, or some other person, drew first the name of one of the tribes out of one pot, and then the name of one portion out of the other, and that portion was appropriated to that tribe. And with respect to these pots, in the bottom of which the papers lay, these lots are often said to come up, or come forth.

2. Every sea is salt, but this had an extraordinary saltiness, the effect of that fire and brimstone which destroyed Sodom and Gomorrah.

16. *To wife.* Which is to be understood with some conditions, as, if he were one who could marry her by God's law. And if she were willing; for though parents had a great power over their children, they could not force them to marry any person against their own wills.

CHAPTER 16

5. It is no wonder if some of these descriptions are dark to us at this distance of time; there having been so many alterations made in places, and so many circumstances, being now altogether undiscoverable. But this much is certain, that all the descriptions here mentioned were then evident to the Israelites, because these were the foundation of all the possessions which then they took and peaceably possessed in succeeding ages.

CHAPTER 17

6. *The daughters.* Not less than the son, so the sex was no bar to their inheritance.

15. *A great people.* He retorts their own argument; seeing you are a great and numerous people, turn your complaints into action and enlarge your borders by your own hand, to which you may confidently expect God's assistance.

16. *Chariots of iron.* Not all made of iron but armed with iron, not only for defense, but for offense also, having as it were scythes and swords fastened to them, to cut down all that stood in their way.

CHAPTER 18

1. *Shiloh.* The name given to the Messiah in dying Jacob's prophecy, intimating to the Jews that Shiloh who would be a greater and more perfect tabernacle.

11. *And the children of Joseph.* Wherein we see the wisdom of Divine Providence, this being the only place in which that prophecy (Deut. 33:12) could have been accomplished. Providence cast Benjamin next to Joseph on the one hand, because Benjamin was the only brother to Joseph, and next to Judah on the other hand, that this tribe might hereafter unite with Judah in an adherence to the throne of David and the temple at Jerusalem.

CHAPTER 19

28. *Zidon.* Called great for its antiquity and riches and glory. The city either was not given to the Israelites or at least was never possessed by them. Not without a singular providence of God that they might not by the opportunity of so good a port be engaged in much commerce with other nations; from which, together with wealth, that great corrupter of mankind, they might contract their errors and vices.

49. *The children of Israel.* That is, they are said to give it, because the whole land was given to Joshua and Eleazar and the princes as joint trustees, acting in the name and for the good of the people. So that even Joshua could take nothing without their gift.

CHAPTER 20

2. *Cities of refuge.* Designed to typify the relief which the gospel provides for poor, penitent sinners and their protection from the curse of the law and the wrath of God, in our Lord Jesus, to whom believers fly for refuge.

7. *And they appointed.* Concerning these cities note, (1) That they were all upon mountains that they might be seen at a great distance, and so direct those who fled to them. (2) That they were seated at convenient distance one from another for the benefit of the several tribes; for Kadesh was in the north, Hebron in the south, and Shechem between them.

(3) That they all belong to the Levites; partly that these cases might be more impartially examined and justly determined by them who are presumed best able to understand the law of God and most obliged to follow it and not to be biased by any affection or corrupt interest; and partly, that their reputation with the people and their good

counsels might lay a restraint upon revengeful persons who might be inclined to follow the manslayer and endeavor to kill him there. It was likewise an advantage to the poor refugee that when he might not go up to the house of the Lord, yet he had the servant of God's house with him to instruct him and pray for him and help to make up for the lack of public ordinances.

CHAPTER 21

2. *The LORD commanded.* Observe that the maintenance of ministers is not an arbitrary thing, left purely to the good will of the people. No, as the God of Israel commanded that the Levities should be provided for, so has the Lord Jesus ordained (and a perpetual ordinance it is) "that they which preach the gospel should live of the gospel."

45. *All came to pass.* Such an acknowledgment as this, here subscribed by Joshua in the name of all Israel, we afterward find made by Solomon; and all Israel did in effect say amen to it (I Kings 8:56). The inviolable truth of God's promise, and the performance of it to the uttermost, is what all believers in Christ have been always ready to bear their testimony to. And if in any thing it has seemed to come short, they have been as ready to take all the blame to themselves.

CHAPTER 22

4. Though their affections to their families could not but make them very desirous to return, yet like good soldiers they would not move until they had orders from their general. So, though we desire to be at home with Christ ever so much, yet we must stay here until our warfare is accomplished, wait for a due discharge, and not anticipate the time of our removal.

22. The multiplying of his titles and the repetition of these words show their zeal and earnestness in this matter. *Save us not.* You, O Lord, to whom we have appealed, and without whom we cannot be saved and preserved, save us not from any of our enemies nor from the sword of our brethren. It is a sudden apostrophe to God, usual in such vehement speeches.

25. *Cease from fearing the LORD.* For they that are cut off from public ordinances usually by degrees lose all religion. It is true that the form and profession of godliness may be kept without the life and power of it. But the life and power will not long be kept without the form and profession of it.

31. *Hand of the LORD.* That is, from the wrathful and dreadful judgments of God, by avoiding that sin which would have involved both you and us in a most bloody war; you have delivered us from the evils we feared. He that prevents an approaching disease or mischief does as truly deliver a man from it as he that cures or removes it after it has been inflicted.

CHAPTER 23

7. *Name of their gods.* To wit, unnecessarily and familiarly, lest the mention of them breed discourse about them and so by degrees begin to the approbation and worship of them. It is a pity that among Christians the name of the heathen gods are so commonly used, especially in poems. Let those names which have been set up in rivalship with God be forever loathed and lost. *Nor bow.* Neither give them any inward reverence or outward adoration. Here is an observable gradation whereby he shows what notable progress sin usually makes and what need there is to look to the beginnings of it, forasmuch as a civil and common conversation with their persons was likely to bring them, and indeed did actually bring them by insensible steps to the worship of their gods. So it is no wonder if some things, not simply and in themselves evil, be forbidden by God, as here the naming of their gods is, because they are occasions and introductions to evil.

14. *Of all the earth.* That is, of all flesh, or of all men; the way which all men go; I am about to die, as all men must. To die is to go on a journey, a journey to our faraway home. And Joshua himself, though he could so ill be spared, cannot be exempted from this common lot. He takes notice of it, that they might look on these as his dying words and regard them accordingly.

16. It will aggravate their perdition that the land from which they shall perish is a good land, and a land which God himself had given them. And which therefore he would have secured to them if they had not thrown themselves out of it.

"Thus the goodness of the heavenly Canaan," says Mr. Henry, "and the free and sure grant God has made of it, will aggravate the misery of those that shall forever be shut out and perish from it. Nothing will make them see how wretched they are, so much as to see how happy they might have been." Might have been! What? On the supposition of absolute decrees? How happy might a person not elected have been? And if he was elected, how could he be wretched for ever? What art of man can reconcile these things? Again, shall any of the elect perish for ever? Or has God made to any others a free and sure grant of the heavenly Canaan? If not, how can the misery of those that perish be aggravated by a free and sure grant which they never had any share in?

CHAPTER 24

1. *All the tribes of Israel.* Namely, their representatives. *Shechem.* To the city of Shechem, a place convenient for the purpose, not only because it was a Levitical city, and a city of refuge, and a place near Joshua's city; but especially for the two main ends for which he summoned them there. (1) For the solemn burial of the bones of Joseph and the rest of the patriarchs, for which their place was designed. (2) For the solemn renewing of their covenant with God; which in this place was first made with Abraham (Gen. 12:6–7) and afterwards renewed by the Israelites at their first entrance into the land of Canaan, between the two mountains of Ebal and Gerizim (8:30ff.), which were very near Shechem. And therefore this place was most proper both to remind them of their former obligations to God and to engage them to a further ratification of them.

Before God. He had taken a solemn farewell before; but as God renewed his strength, he desired to improve it for their good. We must never think our work for God done until our life is done.

7. *Your eyes.* He speaks this to the elders (v. 1), who were so not only by power and dignity, but many of them by age. And there being now not sixty years past since those Egyptian plagues, it is very probable that a considerable number of those present had seen those things in Egypt and, being not twenty years old, were exempted from that dreadful sentence passed upon all who were older (Num. 14).

15. *Choose you.* Not that he leaves them to their liberty, whether they would serve God or idols; for Joshua had no such power himself, nor could give it to any other; and both he and they were obliged by the law of Moses to give their worship to God only and to forebear all idolatry in themselves and severely to punish it in others. But it is a powerful insinuation whereby he both implies that the worship of God is so highly reasonable, necessary, and beneficial; and the service of idols so absurd, vain, and pernicious, that if it were left free for all men to take their choice, every man in his right wits must needs choose the service of God before that of idols; and provokes them to bind themselves tighter to God by their own choice.

We will. But know this, if you should all be so base and brutish as to prefer senseless and impotent idols before the true and living God, it is my firm purpose that I, and my children and servants (as far as I can influence them), shall be constant and faithful to the Lord. And that, whatever others do. They that resolve to serve God must not start at being singular in it. They that are bound for heaven must be willing to swim against the stream and must do, not as most, but as the best do.

19. *Ye cannot.* He speaks not of an absolute impossibility (for then both his resolution to serve God himself and his exhortation to them had been vain), but of a moral impossibility or a very great difficulty, which he alleges not to discourage them from God's service, but to make them more considerate in obliging themselves and more resolved in answering their obligations. The meaning is, God's service is not, as you seem to fancy, a slight and easy thing, but it is a work of great difficulty and requires great care and courage and resolution.

And when I consider the infinite purity of God, that he will not be mocked or abused; and your proneness to superstition and idolatry, even during the life of Moses, and in some of you, while I live, and while the obligations which God had laid upon you in this land are fresh in remembrance; I cannot but fear that after my decease you will think the service of God burdensome, and therefore will cast it off and revolt from him, if you do not carefully avoid all occasion of idolatry.

Will not forgive. If you who own yourselves his people and servants shall willfully transgress his ways, he will not let this go unpunished in you as he does in other nations. Therefore consider what you do when you take the Lord for your God. Weigh your advantages and inconveniences together; for if you be sincere and faithful in God's service, you will have admirable benefits by it; so if you be false to your professions and forsake him whom you have so solemnly avouched to be your God, he will deal more severely with you than with any people in the world.

20. *Will turn.* That is, he will alter his course and the manner of his dealing with you, and will be as severe as ever he was kind and gracious. He will repent of his former kindnesses, and his goodness abused will be turned into fury.

32. One reason why Joshua called all Israel to Shechem might be to attend Joseph's bones to the grave. So that he now delivered as it were both Joseph's funeral and his own farewell sermon. And if it was in the last year of his life, the occasion might well remind him of his own death now at hand. For he was just of the same age with his illustrious ancestor, who died being "an hundred and ten years old" (Gen. 50:26).

33. While Joshua lived, religion was kept up under his care and influence, but after he and his contemporaries were gone, it swiftly went to decay. How well is it for the gospel church that Christ, our Joshua, is still with it by his Spirit; and will be always, even "unto the end of the world"!

JUDGES

CHAPTER 1

1. *Asked the* LORD. Being assembled together at Shiloh, they enquired of the high priest by the Urim and the Thummin. *Against the Canaanites first.* Finding their people multiplying exceedingly, and consequently the necessity of enlarging their quarters, they renew the war. They do not enquire who shall be captain general to all the tribes; but what tribe shall first undertake the expedition, that by their success the other tribes may be encouraged to make the like attempt upon the Canaanites in their several lots.

2. *Judah.* The tribe of Judah is chosen for the first enterprise because they were both most populous and so most needing enlargement; and the most valiant and therefore most likely to succeed. For God chooses fit means for the work which he designs. Moreover, the Canaanites were numerous and strong in those parts and therefore to be suppressed before they grew too strong for them.

19. *Could not drive.* Because of their unbelief, whereby they distrusted God's power to destroy those who had chariots of iron; and so gave way to their own fear and sloth, whereby God was provoked to withdraw his helping hand.

CHAPTER 2

1. *An angel.* Christ the angel of the covenant, often called "the angel of the LORD," to whom the conduct of Israel out of Egypt into Canaan is frequently ascribed. He alone could speak the following words in his own name and person; whereas created angels and prophets universally usher in their message with "Thus saith the LORD," or some equivalent expression. And this angel having assumed the shape of a man, it is not strange that he imitates the motion of a man and comes as it were from Gilgal to the place where now they were. By which motion he signified that he was the person that brought them to Gilgal, the first place where they rested in Canaan, and there protected them so long, and from there went with them to battle and gave them success.

16. *Raised up.* By inward inspiration and excitation of their hearts and by outward designation testified by some extraordinary action. *Judges.* Supreme magistrates, whose office it was, under God and by his particular direction, to govern the commonwealth of Israel by God's laws and to protect and save them from their enemies, to preserve and purge religion, and to maintain the liberties of the people against all oppressors.

18. *It repented the LORD.* That is, the Lord changed his course and dealing with them, as penitent men use to do; removed his judgments and returned to them in mercy.

CHAPTER 3

2. *Teach them war.* That by the neighborhood of such warlike enemies they might be purged from sloth and security and obliged to accustom themselves to martial exercises, and to stand continually upon their guard, and consequently to keep close to that God whose assistance they had so great and constant need of.

10. *Came upon him.* With extraordinary influence, endowing Othniel with singular wisdom and courage, and stirring him up to this great undertaking.

13. *City of palm trees.* That is, Jericho. Not the city which was demolished, but the territory belonging to it.

23. *Went forth.* With a composed countenance and gait, being assured that God, who by his extraordinary call had put him upon that enterprise, would by his special providence carry him through it.

31. *An ox goad.* As Samson did a thousand with a jawbone of an ass: both being miraculous actions, and not at all incredible to him that believes in a God who could easily give strength to effect this. It is no matter how weak the weapon is if God direct and strengthen the arm.

CHAPTER 4

4. *A prophetess.* As there were men-prophets, so there were also women-prophetesses, as Miriam (Exod. 15:23), Huldah (II Kings 22:14), and many others; but the word "prophets" or "prophetesses" is ambiguous, sometimes being used of persons extraordinarily inspired by God and endowed with the power of working miracles and foretelling things to come; and sometimes of persons endowed with special gifts or graces for the better understanding and discoursing about the word and mind of God.

6. *Hath not the LORD.* That is, assuredly God has commanded you; this is not the fancy of a weak woman, which peradventure you may despise, but the command of the great God by my mouth.

8. *I will not go.* Barak's offer to go with Deborah shows the truth of his faith, for which he is praised (Heb. 11:32). But his refusal to go without her shows the weakness of his faith, that he could not trust God's bare word, as he ought to have done, without the pledge of the presence of his prophetess.

21. *A nail of the tent.* Wherewith they used to fasten the tent, which consequently was long and sharp. This might seem a very bold attempt, but it must be considered that she was encouraged to it by observing that the heavens and all the elements conspired against him as one devoted to destruction. In the following song, Deborah does not commend Jael's words (v. 18), "Turn in my LORD, . . . fear not"; but only her action. Touching which, this one fact may abundantly suffice to stop the mouths of objectors.

It cannot be denied that every discourse which is recorded in Scripture is not divinely inspired because some of them were uttered by the devil; others by holy men, but mistaken. This being so, the worst that any can infer from this place is that this song, though indited by a good woman, was not divinely inspired, but only composed by a person transported with joy for the deliverance of God's people but subject to mistake; who therefore, out of zeal to commend the instrument of so great a deliverance, might overlook the indirectness of the means, and commend that which should have been disliked.

And if they further object that it was composed by a prophetess and therefore must be divinely inspired, it may be replied that every expression of a true prophet was not divinely inspired; as is evident from Samuel's mistake concerning Eliab, whom he thought to be the Lord's anointed (I Sam. 16:6). This is said upon supposition that Jael acted deceitfully in this affair. But if we suppose, which is much more likely, that Jael fully intended to afford Sisera the shelter and protection which he sought of her, but was afterwards by the immediate direction of heaven ordered to kill him, the whole difficulty vanishes, and the character both of Jael and of Deborah remains unimpeached.

CHAPTER 5

4. The prophetess, beginning to praise God for the present mercies, takes her rise higher and begins her song with the commemoration of the ancient deliverances afforded by God to his people, the rather because of the great resemblance this had with them in the miraculous manner of them.

5. *Sinai.* She slides into the mention of a more ancient appearance of God for his people in Sinai; it being usual in Scripture repetitions of former actions to put many together in a narrow compass.

9. *My heart is toward.* I honor and love those who, being the chief of the people in wealth and dignity, did not withdraw themselves from the work, as such usually do; but exposed themselves to the same hazards and joined with their brethren in this noble but dangerous attempt.

12. *Awake.* Stir up yourself and all that is within you to admire and praise the Lord. This work needs and well deserves the utmost liveliness and vigor of soul.

16. *Why abodest.* Why were you so unworthy and cowardly that you would not engage yourself in so just, so necessary, and so noble a cause, but did prefer the care of your sheep and your own ease and safety before this generous undertaking? Reuben thought neutrality their wisest course, being very rich in cattle (Num. 32:1). They were loath to run the hazard of so great a loss by taking up arms against so potent an enemy as Jabin. And the bleatings of their sheep were so loud in their ears that they could not hear the call of Deborah and Barak.

19. *No gain.* They fought without pay, whether from mere hatred of the Israelites and a desire to be revenged upon them, or from a full hope and confidence of paying themselves abundantly out of Israel's spoils.

20. *From heaven.* By thunder and lightning and hailstones, possibly mingled with fire. *The stars.* Raising these storms by their influences, which they do naturally.

21. *Trodden down.* You, O Deborah, though but a weak woman, have by God's assistance subdued a potent enemy. Such abrupt speeches are frequent in poetical Scriptures.

23. *The angel.* She signifies that this curse proceeded not from her ill-will towards that place, but from divine inspiration; and that if all the rest of the song should be taken but for the breathings of a pious soul but liable to mistake, yet this branch of it was immediately directed to her by the Lord, the angel of the covenant. *Of the LORD.* Of the Lord's people. For God takes what is done for or against his people as if it was done to himself. The cause between God and the mighty, the principalities and powers of the kingdom of darkness, will not admit of a neutrality.

31. *In his might.* When he first rises and so goes on in his course, which he does with great might, even "as a strong man that runneth a race," and no creature can stop or hinder him; even so irresistible let your people be. Such shall be the honor and such the joy of all that love God in sincerity, and they shall shine for ever "as the sun in the kingdom of their father."

CHAPTER 6

5. *Without number.* That is, so many that it was not easy to number them. And not in a regular army to engage, but in a confused swarm to plunder the country. Yet Israel, being forsaken of God, had not spirit to make headway against them; God fighting against them with those very terrors with which otherwise he would have fought for them.

8. *A prophet.* We have reason to hope that God is designing mercy for us if we find he is by his grace preparing us for it.

10. *Not obeyed my voice.* He intends to bring them to repentance. And our repentance is then genuine when the sinfulness of sin, as disobedience to God, is that in it which we chiefly lament.

14. *Have not I sent thee?* I do hereby give you command and commission for this work. God's fitting men for his work is a sure evidence of his calling them to it.

21. *Consumed the flesh.* By which he showed himself to be no man that needed such provisions, but the Son of God; and by this instance of his omnipotence gave him assurance that he both could and would consume the Midianites.

26. *And offer.* Gideon was no priest, nor was this the appointed place of sacrifice; but God can dispense with his own institutions, though we may not; and his call gave Gideon sufficient authority.

31. *He that will plead.* He that shall further plead for such a god as this deserves to die for his folly and impiety. It is not probable that this was all which he said for his son; but it is usual in Scripture to give only short hints of things which were more largely discoursed.

34. *The Spirit of the* LORD *came.* Inspiring him with extraordinary wisdom and courage and zeal to vindicate God's honor and his country's liberty. The Hebrew is, "The Spirit of the LORD clothed Gideon"; clothed him as a robe to put honor upon him; clothed him as a coat of mail to put a defense upon him. Those are well clad that are thus clothed.

40. *And God did so.* See how tender God is, even of the weak; and how ready to condescend to their infirmities! These signs were very expressive. They are going to engage the Midianites. Could God distinguish between a small fleece of Israel and the vast floor of Midian? Yes, by this token it appears that he can. Is Gideon desirous that the dew of divine grace might descend on himself in particular? He sees the fleece wet with dew to assure him of it. Does he desire that God will be as the dew to all Israel? Behold all the ground is wet!

CHAPTER 7

2. *Too many.* This may help us to understand those providences which sometimes seem to weaken the church of Christ. Its friends are too many, too mighty, too wise, for God to work deliverance by them. God is taking a course to lessen them, that he may be exalted in his own strength.

7. *His place.* That is, to his own home. By this further distinction it was proved that none should be made use of, but (1) Men who were hardy, who could endure fatigue without complaining of thirst or weariness. (2) Men who were hasty, that thought it long until they were engaged with the enemy, and so just wetted their mouth and away, not staying for a full draught. Such as these God chooses to employ that are not only well affected, but zealously affected to his work.

CHAPTER 8

1. *Why hast thou.* Why have you neglected and despised us in not calling us in to your help, as you did other tribes? These were a proud people, puffed up with a conceit of their number and strength and the preference which Jacob gave them above Manasseh, of which tribe Gideon was, who by this act had seemed to advance his own tribe and to depress theirs.

6. *Are the hands.* Are you so foolish to think with your three hundred faint and weary soldiers to conquer and destroy a host of fifteen thousand men? Thus the bowels of their compassion were shut up against their brethren. Were these Israelites! Surely they were worshippers of Baal, or in the interest of Midian.

27. Though Gideon was a good man, and did this with an honest mind, and a desire to set up religion in his own city and family; yet there seem to be many sins in it. (1) Superstition and will-worship, worshipping God by a device of his own, which was expressly forbidden. (2) Presumption, in wearing, or causing other priests to wear, this kind of ephod, which was peculiar to the high priest. (3) Transgression of a plain commandment, of worshipping God ordinarily but at one place and one altar (Deut. 12:5, 11, 14). (4) Making a division among the people. (5) Laying a stumbling block, or an occasion of idolatry before that people, whom he knew to be too prone to it.

32. *A good old age.* His long life being crowned with the continuance of honor, tranquillity, and happiness.

33. *As soon as.* Whereby we see the temper of this people, who did no longer cleave to God than they were in a manner constrained to it, by the presence and authority of their judges.

CHAPTER 9

10. *Fig tree.* Gideon refused this honor, both for himself and for his sons; and the sons of Gideon, whom Abimelech had slain upon pretense of their affecting the kingdom, were as far from such thoughts as their father.

14. *Bramble.* Or thorn, fitly representing Abimelech, the son of a concubine and a person of small use and great cruelty.

29. *Increase thine army.* I desire not to surprise you at any disadvantage; strengthen yourself as much as you can and come out into the open field, that you and I may decide it by our arms.

53. *Millstone.* Such great stones no doubt they carried up with them, whereby they might defend themselves or offend those who assaulted them. Here the justice of God is remarkable in suiting the punishment to his sin. He slew his brethren upon a stone (v. 5), and he loses his own life by a stone.

CHAPTER 10

6. *Forsook the LORD.* They grew worse and worse and so ripened themselves for ruin. Before they worshipped God and idols together; now they forsake God and wholly cleave to idols.

8. The cases of Jair and Samson seem

to be much alike. For as it is said of Samson that "he judged Israel in the days [of the tyranny] of the Philistines twenty years" (Judg. 15:20), by which it is evident that his judicature, and their dominion, were contemporary; the like is to be conceived of Jair, that he began to judge Israel, and endeavored to reform religion, and purge out all abuses; but being unable to effect this through the backwardness of the people, God would not enable him to deliver the people, but gave them up to this sad oppression; so that Jair could only determine differences among the Israelites, but could not deliver them from their enemies.

14. *Chosen.* You have not been forced to worship those gods by your oppressors; but you have freely chosen them before me.

15. *Do thou unto us.* Do not give us up into the hands of these cruel men, but chastise us with your own hand as much as you please, if we be not more faithful and constant to you than we have been.

16. *They put away.* This was an evidence of the sincerity of their sorrow, that they did not only confess their sins, but also forsake them. *His soul.* He acted towards them like one that felt their sufferings. He had pity upon them, quite changed his carriage towards them, and punished their enemies as sorely as if they had grieved and injured his own person.

CHAPTER 11

1. *Son of a harlot.* That is, a bastard. And though such were not ordinarily to "enter into the congregation of the LORD" (Deut. 23:2), yet God can dispense with his own laws and has sometimes done honor to base-born persons, so far that some of them were admitted to be the ancestors of the Lord Jesus Christ.

9. *Shall I.* Will you really make good this promise? Jephthah was so solicitous in this case, either from his zeal for the public good, which required that he should be so; or from the law of self-preservation, that he might secure himself from his brethren; whose ill-will he had experienced and whose injuries he could not prevent if, after he had served their ends, he had been reduced to his private capacity.

10. *The LORD be witness.* "The LORD be an hearer"; so the Hebrew word is. Whatever we speak, it concerns us to remember that God is a hearer!

16. *The Red sea.* Unto which they came three times. Once (Exod. 13:18), again a little after their passage over it, and a third time, long after, when they came to Ezion–geber, which was upon the shore of the Red Sea, from whence they went to Kadesh. Of this third time he speaks here.

29. *Spirit of the LORD came.* Endued him with a more than ordinary courage and resolution.

36. *Do to me.* Do not for my sake make yourself a transgressor; I freely give my consent to your vow.

37. *Bewail.* That I shall die childless, which was esteemed both a curse and a disgrace for the Israelites, because such were excluded from that great privilege of increasing the holy seed and contributing to the birth of the Messiah.

39. *Did with her.* Jephthah's daughter was not sacrificed, but only devoted to perpetual virginity. This appears, (1) From verses 37–38 where we read that she bewailed not her death, which had been the chief cause of lamentation if that had been vowed, but her virginity. (2) From this (v. 39) where, after he had said that he *did with her according to his vow,* he adds, by way of declaration of the matter of that vow, and *she knew no man.* It is probably conceived that the Greeks, who used to steal sacred histories and turn them into fables, had from this history their relation of Iphigenia (which may be put for Jephtigenia) sacrificed by her father Agamemnon, which is described by many of the same circumstances wherewith this is accompanied.

40. *The daughter of Jephthah.* It is really astonishing that the general stream of commentators should take it for granted that Jephthah murdered his daughter! But, says Mr. Henry, "We do not find any law, usage or custom, in all the Old Testament, which doth in the least intimate that a single life was any branch or article of religion." And do we find any law, usage, or custom there which does in the least intimate that cutting the throat of an only child was any branch or article of religion? If only a dog had met Jephthah, would he have offered up that for a burnt offering? No, because God had expressly forbidden this. And had he not expressly forbidden murder? But Mr. Poole thinks the story of Agamemnon's offering up Iphigenia took its rise from this. Probably it did. But then let it be observed, Iphigenia was not murdered. Tradition said that Diana sent a hind in her stead, and took the maid to live in the woods with her.

CHAPTER 12

3. *Put my life.* That is, I exposed myself to the utmost danger; as a man that carries a brittle and precious thing in his hand, which may easily either fall to the ground or be snatched from him.

6. *There fell.* Not in that place, but in that expedition, being slain either in the battle or in the pursuit or at Jordan. See the justice of God! They had gloried that they were Ephraimites. But how soon are they afraid to own their country? They had called the Gileadites fugitives. And now they are in good

earnest become fugitives themselves. He that rolls the stone or reproach unjustly on another, it may justly return upon himself.

9. *Took in.* That is, took them home for wives to his sons. What a difference between this and his predecessor's family! Ibzan had sixty children and all married. Jephthah had but one, and she dies unmarried. Some are increased, others diminished. All is the Lord's doing.

15. It is strange that in the history of all these judges there is not so much as one mention of the high priest or of any other priest or Levite appearing either for council or action in any public affair, from Phinehas to Eli, which may well be computed two hundred and fifty years. Surely this intimates that the institution was chiefly intended to be typical, and that the benefits which were promised by it were to be chiefly looked for in its antitype, the everlasting priesthood of Christ, in comparison of which that priesthood had no glory.

CHAPTER 13

3. *The angel.* The Son of God, yet distinguished from the Lord, because he appeared here in the form of a servant, as a messenger sent from God. The great Redeemer did in a particular manner concern himself about this typical redeemer.

5. *Begin to deliver.* And the deliverance shall be carried on and perfected by others. God chooses to carry on his work gradually and by several hands. One lays the foundation of a good work, another builds, and perhaps a third brings forth the top stone.

18. *Secret.* Hidden from mortal men. This was the angel of the covenant, the Son of God.

CHAPTER 14

2. *To wife.* Herein he is an example to all children, conformable to the fifth commandment. Children ought not to marry nor to move toward it without the advice and consent of their parents. Parents have a property in their children as parts of themselves. In marriage this property is transferred. It is therefore not only unkind and ungrateful, but palpably unjust to alienate this property without their concurrence. Whosoever thus "robbeth his father or his mother [stealing himself from them who is nearer and dearer to them than their goods], and yet saith, It is no transgression, the same is the companion of a destroyer" (Prov. 28:24).

3. *Get her.* This action of Samson's, though against common rules, seems to be warranted by the direction of God (mentioned in the following words), which was known to Samson, but not to his parents. *Pleaseth me.* Not so much for her beauty as for the design mentioned in the next verse.

5. *His father and his mother.* Who accompanied him, either because they were now acquainted with his design; or to order the circumstances of that action which they saw he was set upon.

18. *If ye had not.* If you had not employed my wife to find it out, as men plow up the ground with a heifer, thereby discovering its hidden parts; he calls her heifer because she was joined with him in the same yoke.

19. *The spirit of the* LORD *came.* Though he had constant strength and courage, yet that was exceedingly increased upon special occasions by the extraordinary influences of the Spirit of God. *To Ashkelon.* Either to the territory or to the city itself, where he had both strength and courage enough to attempt what follows; and upon the doing hereof they were doubtless struck with such terror that everyone sought only to preserve himself, and none dared pursue him. *He went.* Without his wife. It were well for us if the unkindnesses we meet with from the world and our disappointments therein have this good effect on us, to oblige us to return by faith and prayer to our heavenly father's house.

CHAPTER 15

2. *Hated her.* Because you deserted her. But this was no sufficient cause; for he should have endeavored a reconciliation and not have disposed of another man's wife without his consent.

3. Although this may look like an act of private revenge, yet it is plain Samson acted as a judge (for so he was) and as an avenger of the public injuries of his people.

4. *Foxes.* It is not said that Samson caught them all, either at one time or by his own hands. For being so eminent a person, and the judge of Israel, he might require assistance of as many persons as he pleased. These creatures were the fittest for the purpose, being very fearful of fire and having such tails as the firebrands might most conveniently be tied to; and not going directly forward, but crookedly, whereby the fire would be dispersed in more places. *And put.* That the foxes might not make too much haste, nor run into their holes, but one of them might delay another and so continue longer in the places where they were to do execution.

6. The Philistines had threatened to burn her and her father's house with fire. To avoid this she betrayed her husband. And now the very thing she feared comes upon her!

12. *Bind thee.* Why not rather, to fight under your banner? Because sin dispirits men; no, it infatuates them, and hides from their eyes the things that belong to their peace.

13. *And they bound him.* Thus was he a type of Christ, who yielded himself to be bound, yes and led "as a lamb to the slaughter." Never were men so besotted as these men of Judah, except those who thus treated our blessed Savior.

14. *Loosed.* This typified the resurrection of Christ by the power of the Spirit of holiness. In this he loosed the bands of death, it being impossible he should be held by them. And thus he triumphed over the powers of darkness, which had shouted against him.

18. One would have thought that the men of Judah would meet him with bread and wine; but they so little regarded him that he is fainting for want of a draught of water! Thus are the greatest slights often put upon those that do the greatest services.

CHAPTER 16

1. *And saw.* Going into a house of public entertainment to refresh himself. He there saw this harlot accidentally; and by giving way to look upon her, was ensnared. (See Gen. 3:6.)

2. O that all who indulge any unholy desire might see themselves thus surrounded and marked for destruction by their spiritual enemies! The more secure they are, the greater their danger.

3. It may seem strange that Samson immediately after so foul a sin should have courage and strength from God for so great a work. But first, it is probable that Samson had in some measure repented of his sin and begged of God pardon and assistance. Secondly, the singular strength and courage was not in itself a grace, but a gift, and it was such a gift as did not so much depend on the disposition of his mind, but on the right ordering of his body,

by the rule given to him and others of that order.

4. *Loved.* Probably as a harlot. Because the dreadful punishment now inflicted upon Samson for this sin, whom God spared for the first offense, is an intimation that this sin was not inferior to the former.

7. *Samson said.* Samson is guilty both of the sin of lying, and of great folly in encouraging her inquiries, which he should at first have checked. But as he had forsaken God, so God had now forsaken him, otherwise the frequent repetition and vehement urging of this question might easily have raised suspicion in him.

18. *And brought money in their hand.* See one of the bravest men then in the world bought and sold, as a sheep for the slaughter. How does this instance sully all the glory of man, and forbid the strong man ever to boast of his strength!

20. *Wist not.* Many have lost the favorable presence of God and are not aware of it. They have provoked God to withdraw from them; but are not sensible of their loss.

21. *Grind.* As slaves used to do. He made himself a slave to harlots, and now God suffers men to use him like a slave. Poor Samson, how you are fallen! How your honor is laid in the dust. Woe unto him, for he has sinned! Let all take warning by him carefully to preserve their purity. For all our glory is gone when the covenant of our separation to God, as spiritual Nazarites, is profaned.

28. *Samson called.* This prayer was not an act of malice and revenge, but of faith and zeal for God, who was there publicly dishonored; and justice, in vindicating the whole common-wealth of Israel, which was his duty, as he was judge. And God, who hears not sinners and would never use his omnipotence to gratify any man's malice, did manifest by the effect, that he accepted and owned his prayer as the dictate of his own Spirit. I conceive this prayer was made with an audible voice, though he knew they would entertain it only with scorn and laughter.

30. *Let me die.* This is no encouragement to those who wickedly murder themselves. For Samson did not desire or procure his own death voluntarily, but by mere necessity. He was by his office obliged to seek the destruction of these enemies and blasphemers of God and oppressors of his people; which in these circumstances he could not effect without his own death. Moreover, Samson did this by divine direction, as God's answer to his prayer manifests, and that he might be a type of Christ, who by voluntarily undergoing death destroyed the enemies of God and of his people.

Nothing fills up the measure of the iniquity of any person or people faster than mocking or misusing the servants of God; yes, though it is by their own folly that they are brought low. Those know not what they do, nor whom they affront, that make sport with a good man.

CHAPTER 17

6. God raised up judges to rule and deliver the people when he saw fit. And at other times for their sins he suffered them to be without them, and such a time this was. And therefore they ran into that idolatry from which the judges usually kept them; as appears by that solemn and oft-repeated passage in this book, that after the death of such or such a judge, the people forsook the Lord and turned to idols.

8. *To sojourn.* For employment and a livelihood; for the tithes and offerings, which were their maintenance, not

being brought into the house of God, the Levites and priests were reduced to straits.

10. *A father.* That is, a priest, a spiritual father, a teacher or instructor. He pretends reverence and submission to him; and what is lacking in his wages, he pays him in titles.

13. *Do me good.* I am assured God will bless me. So blind and grossly partial he was in his judgment to think that one right circumstance would answer for all his substantial errors in making and worshipping idols against God's express command, in worshipping God in a forbidden place by a priest illegally appointed.

CHAPTER 18

6. *Before the* LORD. That is, your design is under the eye of God; that is, under his care, protection, and direction. This answer he either feigns to gratify their humor, or did indeed receive from the devil, who transformed himself into an angel of light and in God's name gave them answers, and those not sometimes very true, which God allowed for the trial of his people. But it is observable that his answer was, as the devil's oracles usually were, ambiguous and such as might have been interpreted either way.

20. *Was glad.* Being wholly governed by his own interest.

24. *What have I.* I value nothing I have in comparison of what you have taken away. Which zeal for idolatrous trash may shame multitudes that call themselves Christians and yet value their worldly conveniences more than all the concerns of their own salvation. Is Micah thus fond of his false gods? And how ought we to be affected toward the true God? Let us reckon our communion with God our greatest gain; and the loss of God the sorest loss. Woe unto us if he depart! For what have we more?

CHAPTER 19

2. *Went away.* Either for fear of punishment, or because her heart was alienated from him; wherein not only she sinned, but her father by connivance at her sin and neglect of just endeavors for his reconciliation to her husband.

3. *Friendly.* To offer her pardon and reconciliation.

15. *To lodge.* Though they were soft and effeminate in other respects, yet they were hardhearted to strangers, and at that time there were no public houses in that country.

26. *Fell down.* Namely, dead; killed partly with grief of heart, and partly with excessive abuse. Thus the sin she formerly chose (v. 2) is now her destruction; and though her husband pardoned her, God would punish her, at least as to this life.

CHAPTER 20

21. *Destroyed.* Why would God let them have so great a loss in so good a cause? Because they had many and great sins reigning among themselves and they should not have come to so great a work of God with polluted hands, but should have pulled the beam out of their own eye before they attempted to take that out of their brother Benjamin's eye. And because they did not, God does it for them, bringing them through the fire that they might be purged from their dross; it being probable that the great God who governs every stroke in battle did so order things that their worst members should be cut off, which was a great blessing to the whole commonwealth. And God would hereby show that "the race is not to the swift, nor the battle to the strong." We must never lay that weight on an arm of flesh which only the Rock of Ages will bear.

28. *The* LORD *said.* When they sought God after the due order and truly humbled themselves for their sins, he gives them a satisfactory answer.

29. *Liers in wait.* Though they were assured of the success by a particular promise, yet they do not neglect the use of means; as well knowing that the certainty of God's promises does not excuse, but rather require man's diligent use of all fit means for the accomplishment of them.

48. If this seem harsh and bloody, either it may be ascribed to military fury; or perhaps it may be partly justified, from that command of God in a parallel case (Deut. 13:15) and from that solemn oath by which they had devoted to death all that came not up to Mizpeh (Judg. 21:5), which none of the Benjamites did.

CHAPTER 21

6. *Repented.* Not for the war, which was just and necessary, but for their immoderate severity in the execution of it. That is no good divinity which swallows up humanity. Even necessary justice is to be done with compassion.

15. *The* LORD. The Benjamites were the only authors of the sin, but God was the chief author of the punishment, and the Israelites were but his executioners.

19. *A feast.* Probably the Feast of Tabernacles, which they celebrated with more than ordinary joy. And that feast was the only season at which the Jewish virgins were allowed to dance. But even this was not mixed dancing. No men danced with these daughters of Shiloh. Nor did the married women so forget their gravity as to join with them. However, their dancing thus in public made them an easy prey. Whence Bishop Hall observes, "The ambushes of evil spirits carry away many souls from dancing to a fearful desolation."[1]

23. *And took them wives.* That is, each man his wife. By which we may see they had no very favorable opinion of polygamy, because they did not allow it in this case, when it might seem most necessary for the reparation of a lost tribe. *Repaired.* By degrees, increasing their buildings as their number increased.

25. *Right in his own eyes.* What wonder was it, then, if all wickedness overflowed the land?

---

[1] (21:19) Probably Joseph Hall (1574–1656), bishop of Norwich. In other writings and letters, Wesley makes reference to the same "Bishop Hall."

Ruth

CHAPTER 1

1. *In the land.* Canaan. It must be early, for Boaz was born of Rahab. So Christ descended from two Gentile mothers.

2. Naomi signifies "my amiable or pleasant one." Mahlon and Chilion signify "sickness" and "consumption." Probably they were sickly children and not likely to be long-lived. Such are the products of our pleasant things, weak and infirm, fading and dying.

4. *Took them wives.* Either these were proselytes when they married them, or they sinned in marrying them and therefore were punished with short life and lack of offspring.

5. It is God alone who is able to comfort those who are thus cast down.

11. *Your husbands.* According to the ancient custom (Gen. 38) and the express law of God (Deut. 25:5), which doubtless she had acquainted them with before, among other branches of the Jewish religion.

13. *It grieveth me.* That you are left without the comfort of husbands or children; that I must part with such affectionate daughters; and that my circumstances are such that I cannot invite you to go along with me. For her condition was so meager at this time that Ruth, when she came to her mother's city, was forced to glean for a living. It is with *me* that God has a controversy. This language becomes us when we are under affliction; though many others share in the trouble, yet we are to hear the voice of the rod as if it spoke only to us. But did not she wish to bring them to the worship of the God of Israel? Undoubtedly she did. But she would have them first consider upon what terms, lest having "set their hand to the plow" they should look back.

14. *Kissed.* Departed from her with a kiss. Bade her farewell for ever. She loved Naomi, but she did not love her so well as to quit her country for her sake. Thus many have a value for Christ and yet come short of salvation by him because they cannot find in their hearts to forsake other things for him. They love him and yet leave him because they do not love him enough, but love other things better.

15. *Unto her gods.* Those who forsake the communion of saints will certainly break off their communion with God. This she said to try Ruth's sincerity and constancy, and that she might intimate to her that if she went with her, she must embrace the true religion.

17. *There will I be buried.* Naomi and she having joined souls, she desires they may mingle dust, in hopes of rising together and remaining together for ever.

18. *Left speaking unto her.* See the power of resolution! Those who are half-resolved are like a door ajar, which invites a thief. But resolution shuts and bolts the door, and then the devil flees from us.

CHAPTER 2

3. *Her hap.* It was a chance in reference to second causes, but ordered by God's providence. God wisely orders small events, even those that seem altogether contingent. Many a great affair is brought about by a little turn, fortuitous as to men, but designed by God.

4. *Said.* They expressed their piety even in their civil conversation and worldly transactions; which now so many are ashamed of.

8. *Maidens.* Not by the young men, to avoid both occasion of sin and matter of scandal. Herein he shows his piety and prudence.

10. *Fell.* The humblest posture of reverence, either civil when performed to men, or religious when to God.

12. *Wings.* That is, protection and care. An allusion either to hens, which protect and cherish their young ones under their wings; or to the wings of the cherubim, between which God dwelled.

13. *Though I be not.* I humbly implore the continuance of your good opinion of me, though I do not deserve it, being a person more lowly, needy, and obscure, a stranger, and one born of heathen parents, and not of the holy and honorable people of Israel, as they are.

14. *She sat.* Not with or among them, but at some little distance from them as one inferior to them. It is no disparagement to the finest hand to be reached forth to the needy.

19. *Where hast thou gleaned to-day?* It is a good question to ask ourselves in the evening, "Where have I gleaned today?" What improvements have I made in grace or knowledge? What have I learned or done which will turn to account?

21. She tells what kindness Boaz had showed her; but not how he had commended her. Humility teaches not only not to praise ourselves, but also not to be forward in repeating the praise which others have given us.

CHAPTER 3

1. *Rest.* A life of rest and comfort and safety under the care of a good husband.

2. *Threshingfloor.* Which was in a place covered at the top, but open elsewhere, whither Ruth might easily come. And this work of winnowing corn was usually ended with a feast.

4. *Uncover his feet.* Remove the clothes that were upon his feet; thereby to awaken him. *Will tell thee.* What course you shall take to obtain that marriage which belongs unto you.

9. *Spread . . . thy skirt.* That is, take me to be your wife and perform the duty of a husband to me.

13. *Perform.* Take you to wife, to raise up seed to his brother. Bishop Hall sums up the matter thus: "Boaz, instead of touching her as a wanton, blesses her as a father, encourages her as a friend, promises her as a kinsman, rewards her as a patron, and sends her away laden with hopes and gifts, no less chaste, but more happy than she came. O admirable temperance, worthy the progenitor of him, in whose lips and heart there was no guile!"

14. *Let it not.* He takes care to preserve not only his conscience before

God, but his reputation, and hers also, among men.

16. *Who art thou.* This is not a question of doubting, but of wonder, as if she had said, Are you in very deed my daughter? I can hardly believe it! How came you here in this manner and thus early?

CHAPTER 4

3. *Naomi.* Both Naomi and Ruth had an interest in this land during their lives, but he mentions only Naomi because all was done by her direction; lest the mention of Ruth should raise a suspicion of the necessity of his marrying Ruth before he had given his answer to the first proposition.

5. *To raise.* To revive his name, which was buried with his body, by raising up a seed to him to be called by his name.

6. *Mar.* Either because having no children of his own, he might have one, and but one son by Ruth, who, though he should carry away his inheritance, yet would not bear his name but the name of Ruth's husband; and so by preserving another man's name, he should lose his own. Or, because as his inheritance would be but very little increased by this marriage, so it might be much diminished by being divided among his many children, which he possibly had already and might probably have more by Ruth.

7. *Gave it.* He who relinquished his right to another plucked off his own shoe and gave it to him. This was symbolic and a significant and convenient ceremony, as if he said, Take this shoe with which I used to go and tread upon my land, and in that shoe you enter upon it and take possession of it.

13. *Took Ruth.* Which he might do, though she was a Moabite, because the prohibition against marrying such is to be restrained to those who continue heathens; whereas Ruth was a sincere proselyte and convert to the God of Israel. Thus he that forsakes all for Christ shall find more than all with him.

15. *Better to thee than seven sons.* See how God sometimes makes up the lack of those relations from whom we expected most comfort, in those from whom we expected least! The bonds of love prove stronger than those of nature.

I samuel

CHAPTER 1

2. *Two wives.* As many had in those ages, though it was a transgression of the original institution of marriage. And it is probable that Elkanah took his second wife, namely, Peninnah, because Hannah was barren.

3. This is the first time in Scripture that God is called *the LORD of hosts,* or armies. Probably Samuel was the first who used this title of God, for the comfort of Israel at the time when their armies were few and feeble and those of their enemies many and mighty.

5. *Shut up her womb.* Yet Elkanah did not withdraw his love from her. To abate our just love to any relation for the sake of any infirmity which they cannot help is to add affliction to the afflicted.

12. *Continued.* Hebrew: "multiplied to pray." By which it appears that she said much more than is here expressed. And the same way you are to judge of the prayers and sermons of other holy persons recorded in Scripture, which gives us only the sum and substance of them. This consideration may help us much to understand some passages of the Bible.

16. *Count not.* Thus when we are unjustly censured, we should endeavor not only to clear ourselves, but to satisfy our brethren by giving them a just and true account of that which they misunderstood.

18. *Sad.* Her heart being cheered by the priest's comfortable words, and especially by God's Spirit setting them home upon her and assuring her that both his and her prayers would be heard, it quickly appeared in her countenance.

28. *Lent him.* But not with a purpose to require him again. Whatever we give to God may upon his account be said to *be lent* to him, that though we may not recall it, yet he will certainly repay it, to our unspeakable advantage.

CHAPTER 2

2. *There is none holy.* None so perfectly, unchangeably, and constantly holy. *None beside.* Not only none is so holy as you are, but in truth *there is none [holy] beside thee;* namely, entirely or independently, but only by participation from you.

9. *Feet.* That is, the steps or paths, their counsels and actions; he will *keep;* that is, both uphold that they may not fall into ruin; and direct and preserve from wandering and from those fatal errors that wicked men daily run into. *Silent.* Shall be put to silence. They who used to open their mouths wide against heaven and against the saints shall be so confounded with the unexpected disappointment of all their hopes, and with God's glorious appearance and operations for his people, that they shall have their mouths quite stopped.

10. *His anointed.* His king. This may respect Christ, the singular anointed one of God and the special king of his people.

17. *Abhorred.* But we know the validity and efficacy of the sacraments does not depend on the goodness of those that administer them. It was therefore folly and sin in the people to think the worse of God's institutions. But it was the much greater sin of the priests which gave them occasion so to do.

21. *Grew.* Not only in age and stature, but especially in wisdom and goodness. *Before the* LORD. Not only before men, who might be deceived, but in the presence and judgment of the all-seeing God.

23. *He said.* Eli's sin was not only that he reproved them too gently, but that he contented himself with a verbal rebuke and did not restrain them, inflicting those punishments upon them which such high crimes deserved by God's law and which he, as judge and high priest, ought to have done without respect of persons.

25. They had now sinned away their day of grace. They had long hardened their hearts. And God at length gave them up to a reprobate mind and "determined to destroy" them (II Chron. 25:16).

35. *Anointed.* Before Jesus Christ, who is the main scope and design not only of the New, but of the Old Testament, which in all its types and ceremonies represented him; and particularly, the high priest was an eminent type of Christ and represented his person and acted in his name and stead.

CHAPTER 3

1. *Open vision.* God did not impart his Mind by way of vision or revelation openly or to any public person, to whom others might resort for satisfaction, though he might privately reveal himself to some pious persons for their particular direction. This is premised as a reason why Samuel understood not when God called him once or twice.

13. *Restrained them not.* He contented himself with a cold reproof and did not punish and effectually restrain them. They who can, and do not, restrain others from sin make themselves partakers of the guilt. Those in authority will have a great deal to answer for if the sword they bear be not a terror to evildoers.

18. *It is the* LORD. This severe sentence is from the sovereign Lord of the world, who has an absolute right to dispose of me and all his creatures; who is in a special manner the ruler of the people of Israel, to whom it properly belongs to punish all my offenses; whose chastisement I therefore accept.

CHAPTER 4

3. *The ark.* That great pledge of God's presence and help, by whose conduct our ancestors obtained success. Instead of humbling themselves for and purging themselves from their sins, for which God was displeased with them, they take an easier and cheaper course and put their trust in their ceremonial observances, not doubting but that the very presence of the ark would give them the victory.

5. *Shouted.* From their great joy and confidence of success. So formal Christians triumph in external privileges and performances; as if the ark in the camp would bring them to heaven, though the world and the flesh reign in the heart.

13. Beside being a calamity to all Israel, it was a particular loss to Shiloh, for the ark never returned there. Their candlestick was removed out of its place, and the city sunk and came to nothing.

18. *He fell.* So fell the high priest and judge of Israel! So fell his heavy head, when he had lived within two of a hundred years. So fell the crown from his head, when he had judged Israel forty years. Thus did his sun set under a cloud. Thus was the wickedness of those sons of his, whom he had indulged, his ruin. Thus does God sometimes set marks of his displeasure on good men, that others may hear and fear. Yet we must observe, it was the loss of the ark that was his death, and not the slaughter of his sons. He says in effect, Let me fall with the ark. Who can live when the ordinances of God are removed? Farewell all in this world, even Life itself, if the ark be gone!

20. *Fear not.* Indeed the sorrows of her travail would have been forgotten, "for joy that a [child was] born into the world." But what is that joy to one that feels herself dying? None but spiritual joy will stand us in stead then. Death admits not the relish of any earthly joy; it is then all flat and tasteless. What is it to one who is lamenting the loss of the ark? What can give us pleasure if we want God's word and ordinances? Especially if we want the comfort of his gracious presence and the light of his countenance?

CHAPTER 5

4. *Cut off.* The *head* is the seat of wisdom; the *hands* the instruments of action. Both are cut off to show that he had neither wisdom nor strength to defend himself or his worshippers.

9. *Secret parts.* In the inwards of their hinder parts, which is the worst kind of hemorrhoids as all physicians acknowledge, both because its pains are far more sharp than the other; and because the malady is more out of the reach of remedies.

CHAPTER 6

18. It is desirable to see the ark in its habitation, in all the circumstances of solemnity. But it is better to have it on a great stone and in the fields of the wood than to be without it. The intrinsic grandeur of divine ordinances ought not to be diminished in our eyes by the lowliness and poverty of the place where they are administered.

20. *Who is able.* That is, to minister before the ark where the Lord is present. Since God is so severe to mark what is amiss in his servants, who is sufficient to serve him? It seems to be a complaint or expostulation with God concerning this great instance of his severity. *And to whom.* Who will dare to receive the ark with so much hazard to themselves? Thus, when the word of God works with terror on men's consciences, instead of taking the blame to themselves they frequently quarrel with the word and endeavor to put it from them.

CHAPTER 7

3. *Spake.* To all the rulers and people too, as he had occasion in his circuit, described below, mixing exhortation with repentance, with his judicial administrations. *If.* If you do what you profess; if you are resolved to go on in that which you seem to have begun. *With all your hearts.* Sincerely and in good earnest. *Put.* Out of your houses, where some of you keep them; and out of your hearts, where they still have an interest in many of you.

6. *Poured it out.* As an external sign,

whereby they testified both their own filthiness and need of washing by the grace and Spirit of God and blood of the covenant, and their sincere desire to pour out their hearts before the Lord in true repentance, and to cleanse themselves from all filthiness of flesh and spirit. *Before the* LORD. That is, in the public assembly, where God is in a special manner present.

7. *Afraid.* Being a company of unarmed persons unfit for battle. When sinners begin to repent and reform, they must expect Satan will muster all his forces against them and set his instruments at work to the uttermost to oppose and discourage them.

8. *Cease not.* We are afraid to look God in the face because of our great wickedness. Do therefore intercede for us, as Moses did for his generation. They had reason to expect this, because he had promised to pray for them, had promised them deliverance from the Philistines, and they had been observant of him in all that he had spoken to them from the Lord. Thus they who receive Christ as their lawgiver and judge need not doubt of their interest in his intercession. O what a comfort is it to all believers that he never ceases, but always "appears in the presence of God" for us.

15. *Samuel judged.* For though Saul was king in Samuel's last days, yet Samuel did not cease to be a judge, being so made by God's extraordinary call, which Saul could not destroy; and therefore Samuel did sometimes upon great occasions, though not ordinarily, exercise the office of judge after the beginning of Saul's reign; and the years of the rule of Saul and Samuel are joined together (Acts 13:20–21).

17. *Built an altar.* That by joining sacrifices with his prayers, he might the better obtain direction and assistance from God upon all emergencies. And this was done by prophetical inspiration, as appears by God's acceptance of the sacrifices offered upon it. As the patriarchs did, he built an altar where he lived. And that not only for the use of his own family, but for the good of the country who resorted to it.

CHAPTER 8

1. *Old.* And so unfit for his former travels and labors. He is not supposed to have been now above sixty years of age. But he had spent his strength and spirits in the fatigue of public business; and now if he thinks to shake himself as at other times, he finds he is mistaken. Age has cut his hair. They that are in the prime of their years ought to be busy in doing the work of life; for as they go into years, they will find themselves less disposed to it and less capable of it.

3. *Took bribes.* It has often been the grief of holy men that their children did not tread in their steps. So far from it, that the sons of eminently good men have been often eminently wicked.

5. *A king.* Their desires exceed their reasons, which extended no further than to the removal of Samuel's sons from their places, and the procuring some other just and prudent assistance to Samuel's age.

6. *Displeased.* Because God was thus dishonored by that distrust of him, and that ambition and itch after changes which were the manifest causes of this desire; and because of that great misery which he foresaw the people would hereby bring upon themselves.

7. *Hearken.* God grants their desire in anger, and for their punishment.

20. *Be like.* What stupidity! It was their happiness that they were unlike all the other nations (Num. 23:9; Deut. 33:28), as in other glorious privileges, so especially in this, that the Lord was their immediate king and lawgiver. But they will have a king to *go out before* them, and to *fight battles*. Could they desire a battle better fought from them than the last was, by Samuel's prayers and God's thunders? Were they fond to try the chance of war at the same uncertainty that others did? And what was the issue? Their first king was slain in battle; and so was Josiah, one of the last and best.

CHAPTER 9

6. *Honourable man.* Acquaintance with God and serviceableness to the kingdom of God make men truly honorable.

7. *A present.* Presents were then made to the prophets, either as a testimony of respect; or as a grateful acknowledgment; or for the support of the prophets themselves; or of the sons of the prophets; or of the persons in want known to them.

21. *The smallest.* For so indeed this was, having been all cut off except six hundred (Judg. 20), from which blow they never recovered, and therefore they were scarce reckoned as an entire tribe, but only as a remnant of a tribe; and being ingrafted into Judah, in the division between the ten tribes and the two, they in some sort lost their name and together with Judah were accounted but one tribe.

CHAPTER 10

1. *Poured it.* Which was the usual rite in the designation, as of priests and prophets, so also of kings, whereby was signified the pouring forth of the gifts of God's Spirit upon him, to fit him for the administration of his office. These sacred unctions, then used, pointed at the great Messiah, or Anointed One, the king of the church and "High Priest of our profession," who was anointed with the oil of the Spirit without measure above all the priests and princes of the Jewish church.

5. *Prophets.* By prophets he understands persons that wholly devoted themselves to religious studies and exercises. For the term of prophesying is not only given to the most eminent act of it, foretelling things to come, but also to preaching and to the making or singing of psalms or songs of praise to God. And they that wholly attended upon these things are called "sons of the prophets," who were commonly combined into companies or colleges, that they might more conveniently assist one another in God's work. This institution God was pleased so far to honor and bless that sometimes he communicated unto those persons the knowledge of future things.

6. *Another man.* That is, you shall be suddenly endowed with another spirit, filled with the skill of divine things, with courage, and wisdom, and magnanimity, and other qualifications befitting your dignity.

12. *Who is.* Who is the father of all these prophets, among whom Saul now is one? Who is it that instructs and inspires them but God? They have it not from their parents, nor from their education, but by inspiration from God, who, when he pleases, can inspire Saul or any other man with the same skill. And therefore wonder not at this matter, but give God the glory of it.

24. *None like him.* As to the height of this bodily stature, which was in itself commendable in a king, and some kind of indication of great endowments of mind. *God save the king.* Hereby they accept him for their king and promise subjection to him. None will be losers in the end by their humility and modesty. Honor, like the shadows, follows them that flee from it, but flees from them that pursue it.

27. *No presents.* As subjects in those times used to do to their kings. This was an evidence both of his humility and the mercifulness of his disposition. So Christ held his peace in the day of his patience. But there is a day of recompense coming.

CHAPTER 11

5. Good magistrates are in pain if their subjects are in tears.

7. *Sent them.* Wisely considering that the sight of men's eyes does much more affect their hearts than what they only hear with their ears. *Fear.* A fear sent upon them by God, that they should not dare to deny their help. The fear of God will make men good subjects, good soldiers, and good friends to their country. They that fear God will make conscience of their duty to all men, particularly to their rulers.

CHAPTER 12

1. *Said.* This is another instance of Samuel's great wisdom and integrity. He would not reprove the people for their sin in desiring a king while Saul was unsettled in his kingdom; lest, through their accustomed levity, they should as hastily cast off their king as they had passionately desired him, and therefore he chooses this season for it. Because Saul's kingdom was now confirmed by an eminent victory; and because the people "rejoiced greatly," applauded themselves for their desires of a king, and interpreted the success which God had given them as a divine approbation of those desires. Samuel therefore thinks fit to temper their joys and to excite them to that repentance which he saw lacking in them, and which he knew to be necessary to prevent the curse of God upon their new king and the whole kingdom.

12. *Your king.* That is, when God was your immediate king and governor, who was both able and willing to deliver you, if you had cried to him, whereof you and your ancestors have had plentiful experience; so that you did not at all need any other king; and your desire of another was a manifest reproach against God.

15. *Your fathers.* Who lived under the judges; and you shall have no advantage by the change of government, nor shall your kings be able to protect you against God's displeasure. We mistake if we think we can evade God's justice by shaking off his dominion. If we will not let God rule us, yet he will judge us.

18. *Samuel.* Who had such power and favor with God. By this thunder and rain, God showed them their folly in desiring a king to save them, rather than God or Samuel, expecting more from an arm of flesh than from the arm of God or from the power of prayer. Could their king *thunder* with a voice like God? Could their prince command such forces as the prophet could by his prayers? Likewise he intimates that however serene their condition was now (like the weather in wheat harvest), yet if God pleased, he could soon change the face of their heavens and "persecute them with his tempest."

21. *Vain things.* So idols are called (Deut. 32:21; Jer. 2:5), and so they are, being mere nothings, having no power in them, no influence upon us, nor use or benefit to us.

22. *His great name's sake.* That is, for his own honor, which would suffer much among men if he should not preserve and deliver his people in eminent dangers. *To make.* Out of his own free grace, without any merit of yours, and therefore he will not forsake you, except you thrust him away.

CHAPTER 13

6. *Strait.* Notwithstanding their former presumption that if they had a king, they should be free from all such straits. And hereby God intended to teach them the vanity of confidence in men; and that they did not one jot less need the help of God now than they did when they had no king. And probably they were the more discouraged, because they did not find Samuel with Saul. Sooner or later men will be made to see that God and his prophets are their best friends.

14. "But was it not hard to punish so little a sin so severely?" It was not little. Disobedience to an express command, though in a small matter, is a great provocation. And indeed, there is no little sin, because there is no little God to sin against. In general, what to men seems a small offense, to him who knows the heart may appear a heinous crime. We are taught hereby how necessary it is that we "wait on God continually." For Saul is sentenced to lose his kingdom for lack of two or three hours' patience.

CHAPTER 14

6. *Uncircumcised.* So he calls them, to strengthen his faith by this consideration, that his enemies were enemies to God; whereas he was circumcised and therefore in covenant with God, who was both able and engaged to assist his people. *It may be.* He speaks doubtfully. For though he felt himself stirred up by God to this exploit, and was assured that God would deliver his people, yet he was not certain that he would do it at this time and in this way.

10. *A sign.* Jonathan, not being assured of the success of this exploit, desires a sign and, by the instinct of God's Spirit, pitches upon this. Many such motions and extraordinary impulses there were among great and good men in ancient times. Observe that God has the governing of the hearts and tongues of all men, even of those that know him not, and serves his own purposes by them, though they mean not so, neither do their hearts think so.

13. *They fell.* For being endowed with extraordinary strength and courage, and having with incredible boldness killed the first they met with, it is not strange if the Philistines were both astonished and intimidated. God also struck them with a panic, and infatuated their minds, and possibly put an evil spirit among them, which in this universal confusion made them conceive that there was treachery among themselves and therefore caused them to sheathe their swords in one another's bowels.

15. *Trembling.* He that made the heart knows how to make it tremble. To complete their confusion, even *the earth quaked;* it shook under them and made them fear it was just going to swallow them up. Those who will not fear the eternal God, he can make afraid of a shadow.

33. *Transgressed.* He sees their fault, but not his own, in giving the occasion of it.

39. *Answered.* None of those who saw Jonathan eating informed against him, because they were satisfied that his ignorance excused him, and from their great love to Jonathan, whom they would not expose to death for so small an offense.

42. *Jonathan.* God so ordered the lot; not that he approved Saul's execration (v. 24) or his oath that the transgressor should die (v. 39); nor that he would expose Jonathan to death; but that Saul's folly might be chastised when he saw what danger it had brought upon his son; and that Jonathan's innocency might be cleared.

44. *For thou.* We have no proof that Saul did not act in this whole affair from a real fear of God.

CHAPTER 15

1. *Hearken.* You have committed error already, now regain God's favor by your exact obedience to what he commands.

3. *Slay.* Which was not unjust, because God is the supreme Lord of life and can require his own when he pleases; infants likewise are born in sin and therefore liable to God's wrath. Their death also was rather a mercy than a curse, as being the occasion of preventing their sin and punishment.

6. *Shewed kindness.* When destroying judgments are abroad, God takes care to separate the precious from the vile. It is then especially dangerous to be found in the company of God's enemies. The Jews have a saying, "Woe to a wicked man, and to his neighbour."

11. *Repenteth.* Repentance implies grief of heart and change of counsels and therefore cannot be in God; but it is ascribed to God when God alters his method of dealing and treats a person as if he did indeed repent of the kindness he had showed him. *Is turned back.* Therefore he did once follow God. Otherwise it would have been impossible that he should turn *back from following* him.

22. *Sacrifice.* Because obedience to God is a moral duty, constantly and indispensably necessary; but sacrifice is but a ceremonial institution, sometimes unnecessary, as it was in the wilderness. And sometimes it is sinful, when it is offered by a polluted hand or in an irregular manner. Therefore your gross disobedience to God's express command is not to be compensated with sacrifice.

24. *I have transgressed.* It does by no means appear that Saul acts the hypocrite herein, in assigning a false cause of his disobedience. Rather, he nakedly declares the thing as it was.

25. *Pardon my sin.* Neither can it be proved that there was any hypocrisy in this. Rather, charity requires us to believe that he sincerely desired pardon, both from God and man, as he now knew he had sinned against both.

26. *I will not.* This was no lie, though he afterwards returned, because he spoke what he meant; his words and his intentions agreed together, though afterwards he saw reason to change his intentions. (See Gen. 19:2–3.) This may relieve many perplexed consciences who think themselves obliged to do what they have said they would do, though they see just cause to change their minds.

31. *Turned.* First, that the people might not, upon pretense of this sentence of rejection, withdraw their obedience to their sovereign; whereby they would both have sinned against God and have been as sheep without a shepherd. Secondly, that he might rectify Saul's error and execute God's judgment upon Agag.

33. *Hewed.* This he did by divine instinct and in pursuance of God's express command, which being sinfully neglected by Saul is now executed by Samuel. But these are no precedents for private persons to take the sword of justice into their hands. For we must live by the laws of God and not by extraordinary examples.

CHAPTER 16

1. *I have provided.* This phrase is very emphatic and implies the difference between this and the former king. Saul was a king of the people's providing; he was the product of their sinful desires.

But this is a king of my own providing, "to fulfil all my will," and to serve my glory.

6. This I take to be the person I am sent to anoint: wherein yet Samuel was mistaken, as other prophets sometimes were, when they hastily spoke their own thoughts, before they had consulted God.

11. And God so ordered it by his providence that David's choice might plainly appear to be God's work, and not Samuel's or Jesse's. "David" signifies "beloved"; a fit name for so eminent a type of the Beloved Son.

13. *The Spirit.* That is, he was immediately endowed with extraordinary gifts of God's Spirit, as strength, and courage, and wisdom, and other excellent qualities which fitted him for and put him upon noble attempts.

14. *Departed.* God took away that prudence, courage, and alacrity, and other gifts wherewith he had qualified him for his public employment. *From the* LORD. That is, by God's permission, who delivered him up to be buffeted of Satan. *Troubleth.* Stirred up in him unruly and tormenting passions, as envy, rage, fear, or despair. He grew fretful, peevish, discontented, timorous and suspicious, frequently starting and trembling.

16. *Be well.* And the success confirms their opinion. For although music cannot directly have an influence upon an evil spirit to drive him away; yet, because the devil, as it seems, had not possession of him, but only made use of the passions of his mind and humors of his body to molest him; and because it is manifest that music has a mighty power to qualify and sweeten these and to make a man sedate and cheerful; it is not strange, if the devil had not that power over him when his mind was more composed which he had when it was disordered; as the devil had less

power over lunatics in the decrease than in the increase of the moon (Matt. 17:15, 18).

And seeing music prepared the Lord's prophets for the entertainment of the good Spirit (II Kings 3:15), why might it not dispose Saul to the resistance of the evil spirit? And why might not the cheering of his heart in some measure strengthen him against those temptations of the devil which were fed by his melancholy humor? And by this means, David, without any contrivance of him or his friends, is brought to court soon after he was anointed to the kingdom. Those whom God designs for any service, his providence will concur with his grace to prepare and qualify them for it.

18. *Prudent.* Wonder not that David was so suddenly advanced from a poor shepherd to so great a reputation; for these were the effects of that Spirit of the Lord which he received when he was anointed.

21. *And he loved him greatly.* So there was something good in Saul still. He had not lost all, though he had lost the kingdom.

CHAPTER 17

1. The enemies of the church are watchful to take all the advantages, and they never have greater advantage than when her protectors have provoked God's Spirit and prophets to leave them.

4. *Six cubits.* At least nine feet, nine inches high. And this is not strange; for besides the giants mentioned in Scripture, Herodotus, Diodorus Siculus, and Pliny make mention of persons seven cubits high.

11. *Afraid.* This may seem strange, considering the glorious promises and their late experience of divine assistance. And where was Jonathan, who in the last war had so bravely engaged a whole army of the Philistines? Doubtless he did not feel himself so stirred up of God as he did at that time. As the best, so the bravest of men are no more than what God makes them. Jonathan must sit still now, because this honor is reserved for David.

28. *Naughtiness.* Your false confidence, vain-glory, and curiosity. See the folly and wickedness of envy! How groundless its jealousies are, how unjust its censures, how unfair its representations. God preserve us from such a spirit!

29. *A cause.* Is this giant invincible? Is our God unable to oppose him and subdue him? However, David is not deterred from his undertaking by the hard words of Eliab. They that undertake public services must not think it strange if they be opposed by those from whom they had reason to expect assistance, but must humbly go on with their work in the face, not only of their enemies' threats, but of their friends' slights, suspicions, and censures.

32. *Let no man's heart fail.* A little shepherd, come but this morning from keeping sheep, has more courage than all the mighty men of Israel! Thus does God often do great things for his people by the weak things of the world.

48. *Ran.* So far was he from fear!

49. *Forehead.* Probably the proud giant had lift up that part of his helmet which covered his forehead, in contempt of David and his weapons, and by the singular direction of Providence.

51. The stone threw him down to the earth and bereaved him of sense and motion; but there remained some life in him, which the sword took away, and so completed the work. God is greatly gloried when his proud enemies are cut off with their own sword.

CHAPTER 18

1. *Loved him.* For his excellent virtues and endowments, which shone both in his speeches and actions; for the service he had done to God and to his people; and for the similarity of their age and qualities.

10. *The evil spirit.* His fits of frenzy returned upon him. The very next day after he conceived envy at David, the evil spirit was permitted by God to seize him again. Such is the fruit of envy and uncharitableness.

18. In these expressions David shows not only his humility, but also his wisdom, in discovering so deep a sense of his own lowliness that Saul might see how far he was from aspiring at the kingdom.

CHAPTER 19

8. They who are paid for doing good yet must not "be weary in well doing," remembering how bountiful a benefactor God is, even to the evil and unthankful.

9. *The evil spirit.* David's successes against the Philistines revived Saul's envy, and the devil watched the opportunity, as he had done before.

20. *Over them.* To instruct and direct them in those holy exercises. For although they prophesied by divine inspiration, yet they were both to prepare themselves for it beforehand, and to make good improvement of it afterwards, in both which they needed Samuel's counsel and assistance.

23. *The Spirit.* It came upon him in the way; whereas it came not upon his messengers until they came to the place. Hereby God would convince Saul of the vanity of his designs against David, and that in them he fought against God himself.

CHAPTER 20

8. *A covenant of the* LORD. That is, a solemn covenant, not lightly undertaken but seriously entered into, in the name and fear of God and in his presence, calling him to be the witness of our sincerity therein and the avenger of faithlessness in him that breaks it.

16. *A covenant.* The covenant which before was personal, he now extends to the whole house of David, expecting a reciprocal enlargement of it on David's side, which doubtless he obtained.

33. *To smite him.* Saul seemed to be in great care that Jonathan should be established in his kingdom; and now he himself aims at this life! What fools, what worse than savage beasts does anger make us?

CHAPTER 21

1. *Alone.* For though David had some servants (vv. 4–5) whom Jonathan probably had sent to a place appointed, yet they were left at another place; as David himself affirms (v. 2). And David was now alone, as also he was when he fled to Achish. He who had been suddenly advanced to the highest honor is as soon reduced to the desolate condition of an exile. Such changes are there in this world, and so uncertain are its smiles.

2. *The king.* This seems to be a plain lie extorted from him by fear. But it was pernicious to all the priests there. Whence David afterwards declares his repentance for this sin of lying (Ps. 119:29).

9. *None like that.* Because it not only served him for his use, for he was a strong and tall man and one that could wield that sword, but was also a pledge of God's favor to him. Whenever he looked upon it, it would be a support to his faith by reminding him of what God had already done.

10. *To Achish.* A strange action; but it must be considered that Saul's rage was so great, his power also, and diligence in hunting after him that he despaired of escaping any other way; and a desperate disease produces a desperate remedy. The king-elect is here an exile; anointed to the crown and yet forced to flee his country. So do God's providences sometimes run counter to his promises, for the trial of our faith and the glorifying of his name in accomplishing his counsels, notwithstanding the difficulties that lie in the way.

12. *Was sore afraid.* Perhaps he was the more apprehensive because he wore Goliath's sword, which was probably well known at Gath. He now learned by experience what he afterward taught us (Ps. 118:9), "It is better to trust in the LORD than to put confidence in man."

15. *Mad men.* It is highly probable, Achish was aware that this madness was counterfeit. But being desirous to preserve David, he speaks as if he thought it real.

CHAPTER 22

3. *Till I know.* He expresses his hopes very modestly, as one that had entirely cast himself upon God and committed his way to him, trusting not in his own arts or arms, but in the wisdom, power, and goodness of God.

8. *That all.* See the nature of jealousy, and its arts of wheedling, to extort discoveries of things that are not.

10. *He enquired.* David charges him with the sin of lying (Ps. 52:3), and it is not improbable that he told many lies not here expressed.

19. *Both men.* In all the life of Saul, there is no wickedness to be compared to this. He appears now to be wholly under the power of that evil spirit which had long tormented him. And this destruction could not but go to the heart of every pious Israelite and make them wish a thousand times they had been content with the government of Samuel.

CHAPTER 23

1. When princes begin to persecute God's people and ministers, let them expect nothing but vexation on all sides.

16. *And strengthened.* He comforted and supported him against all his fears, by reminding him of God's infallible promises made to him, and his singular providence, which before had and still would be with him.

27. *A messenger.* The wisdom of God is never at a loss for ways and means to preserve his people.

CHAPTER 24

2. *Rocks.* Which the wild goats used to delight in and climb over. These very rocks are exceedingly steep and full of precipices and dangerous to travelers, as an eyewitness has left upon record. And yet Saul was so transported with rage as to venture himself and his army here, that he might take David, who, as he thought, would judge himself safe and therefore be secure in such inaccessible places.

13. *Wickedness.* That is, wicked men will do wicked actions, among which this is one, to kill their sovereign lord and king; and therefore, if I were so wicked a person as your courtiers represent me, I should make no conscience of laying violent hands upon you.

16. *Wept.* From the sense of his sin against God, and his base carriage to David. He speaks as one quite overcome with David's kindness, and as one that relents at the sight of his own folly and ingratitude.

17. *More righteous than I.* He ingenuously acknowledged David's integrity and his own iniquity.

19. *The LORD reward thee.* Because he thought himself not able to recompense so great a favor, he prays God to recompense it.

CHAPTER 25

1. *Lamented him.* They have hard hearts who can bury their faithful ministers with dry eyes and are not sensible of the loss of them who have prayed for them and taught them the way of the Lord.

17. *Cannot speak.* But he flies into a passion.

22. *Enemies of David.* That is, unto David himself. But because it might seem ominous to curse himself, therefore instead of David, he mentions David's enemies. But is this the voice of David? Can he speak so unadvisedly with his lips? Has he been so long in the school of affliction, and learned no more patience therein? Lord, "what is man?" And what need have we to pray, "Lead us not into temptation."

24 This whole speech of Abigail shows great wisdom. By an absolute submitting to mercy, without any pretense of justification, of what was done (but rather with aggravation of it), she endeavors to work upon David's generosity, to pardon it. And there is hardly any head of argument, whence the greatest orator might argue in this case, which she does not manage to the best advantage.

28. *Sure house.* Will give the kingdom to you and to your house for ever, as he has promised you. And therefore let God's kindness to you make you gentle and merciful to others; do not sully your approaching glory with the stain of innocent blood; but consider that it is the glory of a king to pass by offenses; and that it will be your loss to cut off such as will shortly be your subjects. *Evil hath not.* Though you have been charged with many crimes, by Saul and others, yet your innocence is evident to all men. Do not therefore by this cruel act justify your enemies' reproaches, or blemish your great and just reputation.

33. *From coming.* Which I had sworn to do. Hereby it plainly appears that oaths whereby men bind themselves to any sin are null and void; and as it was a sin to make them, so it is adding sin to sin to perform them.

36. *Told him nothing.* As he was then incapable of admonition, his reason and conscience being both asleep.

37. *His heart died.* He fainted away through the fear and horror of so great a mischief, though it was past. As one who, having in the night galloped over a narrow plank, laid upon a broken bridge, over a deep river, when in the morning he came to review it, was struck dead with the horror of the danger he had been in.

CHAPTER 26

7. *Came.* That is, to Saul's host. It might seem a bold and strange attempt; but it may be considered, (1) That David had a particular assurance that God would preserve him to the kingdom. (2) That he had a special instinct from God to this work; and possibly God might inform him that he had cast them into a deep sleep, that he might have this second opportunity of manifesting his innocence towards Saul.

21. *My soul.* This second instance of David's tenderness wrought more upon Saul than the former. He owns himself melted and quite overcome by David's kindness to him. *My soul was precious in thine eyes,* which I thought had been odious. He acknowledges he had acted

against God's law, *I have sinned;* and against my own interest, *I have played the fool,* in pursuing him as an enemy, who was indeed one of my best friends. And herein *I have erred exceedingly,* have wronged both you and myself. Nothing can be more full and ingenuous than this confession. God surely now touched his heart. And he promises to persecute him no more. Nor does it appear that he ever attempted it.

25. *Blessed.* And this, it seems, was their last interview. After this they saw each other no more.

CHAPTER 27

1. *I shall now perish.* But this was certainly a very great fault in David, for (1) This proceeded from gross distrust of God's promise and providence; and that after such repeated demonstrations of God's peculiar care over him. (2) He forsakes the place where God had settled him (22:5) and given him both assurance and experience of his protection there. (3) He voluntarily runs upon that rock, which he cursed his enemies for throwing him upon (26:19), and upon many other snares and dangers, as the following history will show; and deprives the people of the Lord of those encouragements which he might have given them in case of a battle. But God hereby designed to withdraw David from the Israelites, that they might fall by the hand of the Philistines without any reproach or inconvenience to David.

4. *Sought no more again for him.* At their meeting Saul's heart was deeply wounded, and he had said, "Return, my son David." Be with me as in time past. Nor have we the least proof that he would have sought for him again with any other design.

6. *Unto this day.* This and some such clauses seem to have been added after the main substance of the several books was written.

10. *David said.* These and the following words are ambiguous, and contrary to that simplicity which became David, both as a prince and as an eminent professor of the true religion.

CHAPTER 28

5. *Trembled.* Had he kept close to God, he needed not fear all the armies of the Philistines.

11. This practice of divination by the dead, or the souls of dead persons, was very common among all nations.

12. *Saw Samuel.* The words are express, *the woman saw Samuel,* instead of the spirit whom she expected to see, God ordering it so for his own glory. *She cried with a loud voice.* Terrified and astonished, and thereby easily conjectured whom she had been talking with.

13. *Gods.* That is, a god, and divine person, glorious, and full of majesty and splendor, exceeding not only mortal men, but common ghosts. She used the plural number, *gods,* either after the manner of the Hebrew language, which commonly uses that word of one person; or after the language and custom of the heathens.

15. *Called Samuel.*[1] Happy had it been, if he had called Samuel sooner, or rather the God of Samuel! It was now too late; destruction was at hand, and God had determined it should not be stayed.

19. *To-morrow shalt thou and thy sons be with me.*

"What do these solemn words
    portend?
A gleam of hope, when life shall end.
Thou and thy sons, tho' slain shall be
Tomorrow in repose with me.

Not in a state of hellish pain
If Saul with Samuel doth remain;
Not in a state of damned despair,
If loving Jonathan is there."

20. *Fell.* As if the archers of the Philistines had already hit him, and *there was no strength in him,* to bear up against these heavy tidings. Especially, as we cannot doubt, but all his past sins were now brought to his remembrance. And what authority has any man to affirm that he felt no contrition all this time?

CHAPTER 29

4. *Make this fellow.* Herein the wise and gracious providence of God appeared, both in helping him out of those difficulties, out of which no human wit could have extricated him, but he must have been an ungrateful person either to the one or the other side; and moreover in giving him the happy opportunity of recovering his own and his all from the Amalekites, which had been irrecoverably lost if he had gone into this battle. And the kindness of God to David was the greater, because it had been most just for God to have left David in those distresses into which his own sinful counsel had brought him.

8. *David said.* This was deep dissimulation and flattery, no way to be justified. No one knows how strong a temptation they are in to compliment and dissemble, which they are in who attend great men.

11. *Rose up early.* David did not then know how necessary this was for the relief of his own city. But God knew it well, and sent him there accordingly. On how many occasions may he say, "What I do thou knowest not now; but thou shalt know hereafter"?

---

[1] (28:15) Wesley inserts "called," which is not in KJV.

CHAPTER 30

4. *Wept.* It is no disparagement to the boldest, bravest spirits to lament the calamities of friends or relations.

6. *Encouraged himself.* That is, in this that the all-wise and all-powerful Lord was his God by covenant and special promise and fatherly affection, as he had showed himself to be in the whole course of his providence towards him. It is the duty of all good men, whatever happens, to encourage themselves in the Lord their God, assuring themselves that he both can and will bring light out of darkness.

8. *He answered.* Previously, God answered more slowly and gradually (23:11–12), but now he answers speedily and fully at once, because the business required haste. So gracious is our God, that he considers even the degree of our necessities and accommodates himself to them.

13. But he paid dear for this cruelty, for this was the occasion of the ruin of him and all their company. And God by his secret providence ordered the matter thus for that very end. So that there is no fighting against God, who can make the smallest accidents serviceable to the production of the greatest effects.

23. *My brethren.* He uses his authority to overrule them; but manages it with all sweetness, though they were such wicked and unreasonable men calling them brethren; not only as of the same nation and religion with him, but as his fellow-soldiers. What God has freely imparted to us, we should not unkindly and injuriously withhold from our brethren.

24. *Part alike.* A prudent and equitable constitution, and therefore practiced by the Romans, as Polybius and others note.

CHAPTER 31

2. *Jonathan.* David's dear friend; God so ordering it for the further exercise of David's faith and patience; and that David might depend upon God alone for his crown and receive it solely from him and not from Jonathan; who doubtless, had he lived, would have speedily settled the crown upon David's head. There was also a special providence of God in taking away Jonathan (who of all Saul's sons seems to have been the fairest for the crown), for preventing divisions, which might have happened among the people concerning the successor; David's way to the crown being by this means made the more clear.

13. This book began with the birth of Samuel and ends with the death of Saul. The comparing these together will teach us to prefer the honor that comes from God before all the honors of the world.

II samuel

CHAPTER 1

19. *How.* How strangely! How suddenly! How universally!

20. *Tell it not.* This is not a precept, but a poetical wish.

23. It is observable that David speaks not a word here of his piety; but only commends him for those things which were truly in him. A fit pattern for all preachers in their funeral commendations.

26. *Distressed.* That is, for the loss of you. For besides the loss of a true friend, which is inestimable, he lost him who both could and undoubtedly would have given him a speedy, quiet, and sure possession of the kingdom. Whereas now he met with long and troublesome interruptions. *Of women.* That is, that love wherewith they love their husbands or children; for their affections are usually more ardent than men's.

CHAPTER 2

1. *Enquired.* By Urim. Thus David begins at the right end and lays his foundation in God's counsel and assistance.

4. *Anointed.* This they did upon just grounds, because not only was the kingdom promised to that tribe, but David was designed and anointed by God, whose will both they and all Israel were obliged to obey. And they resolved not to neglect their duty though they saw that the other tribes would. Yet their modesty is observable in that they make him king of Judah only, and not of all Israel. And therefore there was need of a third anointing to the kingdom over all Israel, which he had (5:3). The first anointing (I Sam. 16:13) was only a designation of the person who should be king, not an actual inauguration of him to the kingdom.

5. *Kindness.* This respect and affection. For as it is an act of inhumanity to deny burial to the dead, so it is an act of mercy and kindness to bury them.

14. *And play.* That is, show their prowess and dexterity in fighting together. He speaks like a vain-glorious and cruel man and a soldier of fortune that esteemed it a sport to see men wounding and killing one another. So this he designed, partly for their mutual recreation and trial of skill, and partly that by this occasion they might be engaged in a battle. He is unworthy the name of a man who is thus prodigal of human blood.

32. *In Bethlehem.* The rest they buried in the field of battle, but Asahel in the sepulcher of his father. Thus are distinctions made upon earth even between the dust of some and of others. But in the resurrection no difference will be made but between good and bad, which will remain for ever.

CHAPTER 3

5. *Eglah.* This is added either because she was of obscure parentage and was known by no other title but her relation to David; or because this was his first and most proper wife, best known by her other name of Michal, who, though she had no child by David after she scoffed at him for dancing before the ark (6:23), yet might have one before that time. And she might be named the last because she was given away from David and married to another man. Six sons in seven years. Some have had as numerous an offspring, and with much more honor and comfort, by one wife. And we know not that any of the six were famous; but three were very infamous.

12. Thus God overrules the passions of wicked men to accomplish his own wise and holy purposes. And who then dare contend with that God who makes even his enemies do this work and destroy themselves?

14. *My wife.* Who, though she was taken from me by force and constrained to marry another, yet is my rightful wife. David demands her both for the affection he still retained to her and upon a political consideration that she might strengthen his title to the kingdom.

30. *Abishai.* For though Joab only committed the murder, yet Abishai was guilty of it because it was done with his consent, counsel, and approbation.

33. *As a fool.* That is, as a wicked man. It is a sad thing to die *as a fool dieth,* as they do that any way shorten their own days; and indeed all who make no provision for another world.

38. *Know ye not.* But how little, how lowly are they made by death who were the terror of the mighty in the land of the living.

39. *Too hard.* That is, too powerful. They have so great a command over all the soldiers and so great favor with the people that I cannot punish them without apparent hazard to my person and kingdom. Especially now when all the tribes, except Judah, are in a state of opposition against me. But although this might give some color to the delay of their punishment, yet it was a fault that he did not do it within some reasonable time, because this indulgence proceeded from a distrust of God's power and faithfulness, as if God could not make good his promise to him against Joab and all his confederates. And because it was contrary to God's law, which requires the punishment of willful murderers. It was therefore wicked policy, yes, cruel pity that spared him. If the law had had its course against Joab, it is probable the murder of Ishbosheth, Amnon, and others had been prevented.

CHAPTER 4

4. *Had a son.* This history is inserted as that which encouraged these men to commit wicked murder, because Saul's family was now reduced to a low ebb; and if Ishbosheth was dispatched, there would be none left but a lame child, who was altogether unfit to manage the kingdom, and therefore the crown must necessarily come to David by heir act and deed; for which they promised themselves no small recompense.

12. *David commanded.* And such they will meet with who think to serve the Son of David by cruelty or injustice; who, under color of religion, outrage or murder their brethren, supposing that they do God service. However men may now canonize such methods of serving the church, Christ will let them know another day that Christianity was not designed to destroy humanity. And they who thus think to merit heaven shall not "escape the damnation of hell."

CHAPTER 5

13. *David took*. This may well be reckoned among David's miscarriages, the multiplication of wives being expressly forbidden to the king (Deut. 17:17). It seems to have been his policy that hereby he might enlarge his family and strengthen his interest by alliances with so many considerable families. But all these did not preserve him from coveting his neighbor's wife. Rather they inclined him to it; for men who have once broken the fence will wander carelessly.

21. *Images*. When the ark fell into the hand of the Philistines, it consumed them. But when these images fell into the hands of Israel, they could not save themselves from being consumed.

22. *And spread themselves*. The expression intimates that they were very numerous and made a very formidable appearance. So we read (Rev. 20:9) of the church's enemies going "up on the breadth of the earth." But the wider they spread themselves, the fairer mark they are for God's arrows.

CHAPTER 6

3. *They set*. Being taught and encouraged to do so by the example of the Philistines, who did so without any token of God's displeasure upon them for so doing. But they did not sufficiently consider that God might wink at the Philistines because they were ignorant of God's laws; and yet be angry with them for the same thing because they knew, or might have known, the law of God which commanded the priests to bear it upon their shoulders. But their present transports of joy, and the happy change of their affairs and their greedy desire of having the ark of God removed, made them inconsiderate.

5. *Played before the* LORD. Public joy should always be as *before the* LORD with an eye to him and terminating in him. Otherwise it is no better than public madness and the source of all manner of wickedness.

7. *He died*. This may seem very severe, considering that his intention was pious and his transgression not great. But besides that, men are improper judges of the actions of God. And his judgments are always just, though sometimes obscure.

10. Obed–edom knew what slaughter the ark had made among the Philistines and the Bethshemites. He saw Uzzah struck dead, yet invites it to his house and opens his doors without fear, knowing it was a favor of death only to them that treated it ill. "O the courage," says Bishop Hall, "of an honest and faithful heart! Nothing can make God otherwise than amiable to him; even his justice is lovely."

11. *The* LORD *blessed*. The same hand that punished Uzzah's presumption rewarded Obed–edom's humble boldness. None ever had, or ever shall have, reason to say that it is in vain to serve God. Piety is the best friend to prosperity. His household, too, shared in the blessing. It is good living in a family that entertains the ark; for all about it will fare the better for it.

20. *Bless his household*. Ministers must not think that their public performances will excuse them from family worship. But when they have blessed the public assembly, they are to return and bless their own household. And none is too great to do this. It is the work of angels to worship God and therefore certainly can be no disparagement to the greatest of men.

22. *More vile than thus.* The more we are vilified for well doing, the more resolute therein we should be, binding our religion the closer to us.

CHAPTER 7

3. *Nathan said.* Nathan hastily approves it before he had consulted God about it, as both he and David ought to have done in a matter of so great moment. And therefore Nathan meets with this rebuke and he is forced to acknowledge his error and recant it. For the holy prophets did not speak all things by prophetic inspiration, but some things by a human spirit.

12. *And when.* When the time of the life shall expire. This phrase implies that his days shall be prolonged to the usual course of nature and not cut off in the midst by any violent or untimely death. *I will set.* I will set up in your throne your posterity, first Solomon, and then others successively, and at last the Messiah. So the following words may be understood as part of his posterity in general, part of Solomon, and part of Christ only, according to the different nature of the several passages.

13. *He shall.* This is meant literally of Solomon, who alone built the material house or temple; but ultimately of Christ, who is the builder of God's spiritual house or temple. *For my name.* That is, for my service and glory. *For ever.* This is not meant of Solomon, for his kingdom was not for ever. But it is to be understood of David's posterity in general and with special respect to Christ, in whose person the kingdom was to be lodged for ever.

14. *His father.* I will carry myself towards him as a father, with all affection, and I will own him as my son. This is intended both of Solomon, as a type of Christ, and of Christ himself, as is evident from Hebrews 1:5. *If he commit.* This applies only to Solomon and some others of David's posterity; but not to Christ, who never committed iniquity as Solomon did, who therein was no type of Christ. Therefore, this branch is terminated in Solomon; whereas in those things wherein Solomon was a type of Christ, the sense passes though Solomon to Christ.

16. *Before thee.* Your eyes in some sort beholding it; for he lived to see his wise son, Solomon, actually placed in the throne with reputation and general applause, which was in itself a good presage of the continuance of the kingdom in his family. And being considered, together with infallible certainty of God's promise to him and his, gave him good assurance thereof; especially considering that he had his eyes and thoughts upon the Messiah (Ps. 110:1), whose day he saw by faith, as Abraham did (John 8:56), and whom he knew that God would raise out of the fruit of his loins to sit on his throne, and that for ever. And so the eternity of his kingdom is rightly said to be before him.

20. *What can David say.* Neither in a way of gratitude and praise can words express my obligations to you, nor my sense of these obligations. What can I ask of you more than you have freely done? *Thou knowest.* You know my deep sense of your favors and my obligations to you. And my condition and necessities, what I do or may need hereafter; and as you know this, so I doubt not you will supply me.

27. *This prayer.* That prayer that is found in the tongue only will not please God. It must be *found in his* *heart.* That must be lifted up and poured out before God.

29. *Continue for ever.* When Christ for ever sat down on the right hand of God, and received all possible assurance that his seed and throne should be as the days of heaven, then this prayer was abundantly answered.

CHAPTER 8

3. *As he went.* David, remembering the grant which God had made to his people of all the land as far as Euphrates, and having subdued his neighboring enemies, went to recover his rights and establish his dominion as far as Euphrates.

4. *Seven hundred.* Or, seven hundred companies of horsemen, that is, in all seven thousand; as it is in I Chronicles 18:4, there being ten in each company. *Houghed.*[1] That is, cut the sinews of their legs, that they might be useless for war.

14. *The LORD preserved.* All David's victories were typical of the success of the gospel over the kingdom of Satan, in which the Son of David rode forth, "conquering and to conquer," and will reign until he has brought down all opposing rule, principality, and power.

CHAPTER 9

5. *Machir.* This Machir appears to have been a generous man who entertained Mephibosheth out of mere compassion, not of disaffection to David. For afterwards we find him kind to David himself when he fled from Absalom. David now little thought that the time would come when he himself should need his assistance. Let us be forward to give, because we know not what we ourselves may sometime want.

8. *Bowed himself.* It is good to have the heart humbled under humbling providences.

CHAPTER 10

4. *Cut off.* This was worse than the former, because the Israelites wore no breeches, and so their nakedness was uncovered.

19. *And served them.* And thus at length was fulfilled the promise made to Abraham, and repeated to Joshua, that the borders of Israel should extend as far as the river Euphrates. The Son of David sent his ambassadors, his apostles and ministers, to the Jewish church and nation. But they treated them very shamefully, as Hanun did David's, mocking them, abusing them, killing them. And this it was that filled the measure of their iniquity and brought upon them ruin without remedy.

CHAPTER 11

2. *Arose from off his bed.* Where he had laid and slept for some time. The bed of sloth often proves the bed of lust.

3. *Sent and inquired.* Instead of suppressing that desire which the sight of his eyes had kindled, he seeks rather to feed it. He first inquires who she was; that if she were unmarried, he might make her either his wife or his concubine.

4. *Took her.* From her own house into his palace, not by force but by persuasion. *Lay with her.* See how all the way to sin is downhill! When men begin, they cannot soon stop themselves.

9. *The servants.* With the king's

---

[1] (8:4) KJV: "Hocked."

guard. This he did by the secret direction of God's wise providence, who would bring David's sin to light.

15. *He wrote.* So far is David from repenting that he seeks to cover one sin with another. How are the beginnings of sin to be dreaded! For who knows where it will end? David has sinned, therefore Uriah must die! That innocent, valiant, gallant man who was ready to die for his prince's honor must die by his prince's hand. See how "fleshly lusts war against the soul," and what devastations they make in that war! How they blind the eyes, sear the conscience, harden the heart, and destroy all sense of honor and justice!

27. *The mourning.* Which was seven days. Nor could the nature of the thing admit of longer delay lest the too early birth of the child might discover David's sin. *Bare him a son.* By which it appears that David continued in the state of impenitence for many months; and this in spite of his frequent attendance upon God's ordinances. This is an eminent example of the corruption of man's nature, of the deceitfulness of sin, and of the tremendous judgment of God in punishing one sin by delivering a man up to another.

CHAPTER 12

1. *The LORD sent.* When the ordinary means dies not awaken David to repentance, God takes an extraordinary course. Thus the merciful God pities and prevents him who had so horribly forsaken God.

5. *Shall surely die.* It is observable that David now, when he was most indulgent to himself and to his own sin, was most severe and even unjust to others; as appears by this passage and the following relation (v. 31), which

was done in the time of David's impenitent continuance in his sin.

7. *Thus saith the LORD God.* Nathan now speaks, not as a petitioner for a poor man, but as an ambassador from the great God.

9. In all this he *despised the word of the LORD* (so it is in the Hebrew).[2] Not only his commandment in general, but the particular word of promise which God had before sent him by Nathan, that he would "build him an house"; which sacred promise if he had had a due value for, he would not have polluted his house with lust and blood.

13. *I have sinned.* How serious this confession was we may see in Psalm 51.

17. *He would not.* This excessive mourning did not proceed simply from the fear of the loss of the child, but from a deep sense of his sin and the divine displeasure manifested herein.

20. *And came.* That is, to the tabernacle to confess his sin before the Lord, to own his justice in this stroke, to deprecate his just displeasure, to acknowledge God's rich mercy in sparing his own life; and to offer sacrifices as were required in such cases.

23. *I shall go to him.* Into the state of the dead in which he is, and into heaven where I doubt not I shall find him.

24. *His wife.* Who was now much dejected both for her former sin and for the loss of the child.

25. *Because of the LORD.* Either because of the Lord's love to him, or because the Lord commanded him to do so.

31. It is probable David exercised this cruelty while his heart was hardened and impenitent, and when he was bereaved of that good Spirit of God, which would have taught him more mercy.

---

[2](12:9) KJV: "Commandment" instead of "word."

CHAPTER 13

12. *Force.* You should abhor it if I were willing; but to add violence is abominable.

13. *Fools.* That is, contemptible to all the people, whereas now you are heir apparent of the crown.

16. *Greater than the other.* This she might truly say because, though the other was in itself a greater sin, yet this was an act of greater cruelty and a greater calamity to her because it exposed her to public infamy and contempt. And besides, it turned a private offense into a public scandal, to the great dishonor of God and of his people and especially of all the royal family.

20. *Been with thee.* Behold and imitate the modesty of Scripture expressions. *Brother.* Therefore you must forgive and forget the injury; therefore your disgracing of him will be a blot to us all; therefore you will not get right from David against him because he is as near and dear to him as you; therefore your dishonor is the less, because you were not abused by any lowly person but by a king's son; therefore this evil must be borne because it cannot be avenged. And thus he covers his design of taking vengeance upon him at the first opportunity.

21. *Wroth.* With Amnon; whom yet he did not punish least so severely as he should, either from the consciousness of his own guilt in the like kind, or for that foolish indulgence which he often showed to his children.

22. *Spake.* That is, he said nothing at all to him about that business. He neither debated it with him, nor threatened him for it, but seemed willing to pass it by with brotherly kindness.

27. *Pressed him.* It is strange that his urgent desire of Amnon's company raised no suspicion in so wise a king.

But God allowed him to be blinded, that he might execute his judgments upon David and bring upon Amnon the just punishment of his lewdness.

29. *Commanded.* Now the threatened sword is drawn in David's house, which will not depart from it. His eldest son falls by it through his own wickedness, and his father by his connivance is accessory to it.

39. *Go forth.* And could not be recalled, to visit him or to send for him. What amazing weakness was this! At first he could not find it in his heart to do justice to the ravisher of his sister. And now he can almost find it in his heart to receive into favor the murderer of his brother. How can we excuse David from the sin of Eli, who honored his sons more than God?

CHAPTER 14

11. *Remember.* Remember the LORD, in whose name you have made me this promise, and who will be a witness against you if you break it.

13. *Faulty.* By your word and promise and oath given to me for my son, you condemn yourself for not allowing the same equity towards your own son. It is true, Absalom's case was widely different from that which the woman of Tekoah had supposed. But David was too well affected to him to mark that difference, and was more desirous than she could be to apply that favorable judgment to his own son, which he had given concerning hers.

15. *The people.* The truth is, I was even forced to this bold address to you by the disposition of your people, who are discontented at Absalom's perpetual banishment; lest, if Absalom by his father-in-law's assistance invade the land, the people who have a great kindness for him, and think he is very hard used, should take up arms.

16. *My son.* Implying that her life was bound up in the life of her son and that she could not outlive his death (and supposing that it might be David's case also, and would therefore touch him in a tender part, though it were not proper to say it expressly); and thereby suggesting that the safety and comfort of the people of Israel depended upon Absalom's restitution.

22. *Fulfilled.* But it seems David had no power to dispense with God's laws, nor to spare any whom God appointed him to destroy. For the laws of God bound the kings and rulers as well as the people of Israel. How justly did God make this man, whom he had so sinfully spared, a scourge to him?

25. *Beauty.* This is noted as the occasion of his pride and of the people's affection to him.

32. *Kill me.* For it is better for me to die than to lack the sight and favor of my dear father. Thus he insinuates himself into his father's affections by pretending such respect and love to him. It seems that by this time Absalom, having so far recovered his father's favor, began to grow upon him and take so much confidence as to stand upon his own justification, as if what he had done had been no iniquity, at least not such as to deserve death. See how easily wise parents may be imposed on by their children when they are blindly fond of them.

33. *Kissed.* Did the heart of a father prevail to reconcile him to an impenitent son? And shall penitent sinners question the compassion of him who is the Father of mercy?

CHAPTER 15

11. *Called.* Such as Absalom had picked out as fit for his purpose; such as were of some reputation with the king and people, which would give a countenance to his undertaking and give occasion to people at first to think that this was done by his father's consent, as being now aged and infirm and willing to resign the kingdom to him. It is no new thing for good men to be made of use by designing men to put a respectability upon ill practices.

16. *After him.* Or, "on foot," which the king chose to do, to humble himself under the hand of God, to encourage his companions in this hard and comfortless march, and to move compassion in his people towards him.

20. *Mercy.* Since I am now unable to recompense your kindness and fidelity to me, my hearty prayer to God is that he would show to you his mercy in blessing you with all sorts of blessings, and his faithfulness in making good all these promises which he has made, not to Israelites only, but to all true-hearted proselytes, such as you are.

21. *Will thy servant be.* He is a friend indeed who loves at all times and will cleave to us in adversity. Thus should we cleave to the Son of David, that "neither death, nor life . . . shall be able to separate us from [his] love."

23. *Kidron.* The very same brook that Christ passed over when he entered upon his sufferings (John 18:1).

26. *Let him do.* That we may not complain of what is, let us see God's hand in all events. And that we may not be afraid of what shall be, let us see all events in God's hand.

30. *Barefoot.* In testimony of his deep sorrow and humiliation and shame for his sins.

37. *Absalom came.* How soon do royal cities and royal palaces change their masters? But we look for "a kingdom which cannot be moved."

CHAPTER 16

21. *Go.* This counsel he gave, partly to avenge the injury done to Bathsheba, the daughter of Eliam (11:3), who was "the son of Ahithophel" (23:34), and principally for his own and the people's safety, that the breach between David and Absalom might be irreparable. But by this we may observe the character of Absalom's party, how abominably wicked they were, whom such a scandalous action tied the faster to him. And we may further learn how corrupt the body of the people was, how ripe for that judgment which is now hastening to them.

22. *The top.* Of the king's palace, the very place whence David had gazed upon Bathsheba (11:2). So that his sin was legible in the very place of his punishment. *Israel.* Who saw him go into the tent and thus concluded that he lay with them, as he had designed to do. God had threatened by Nathan that for his defiling Bathsheba, David's own wives should be defiled in the face of the sun. This is now fulfilled: "The LORD is righteous"; and no word of this shall fall to the ground.

CHAPTER 17

2. *And I will.* That such a wretch as Absalom should aim at his father's throat is not strange. But that the body of the people to whom David had been so great a blessing should join with him in it is amazing. But the finger of God was in it. Let not the best of parents, or the best of princes, think it strange if they are injured by those who should be their support and joy, when they (like David) have provoked God to turn against them.

14. *Absalom and all.* Be it observed, to the comfort of all that fear God, he turns all men's hearts as the rivers of water. He "standeth in the congregation of the mighty," has an overruling hand in all counsels, and a negative voice in all resolves, and laughs at men's projects against his children.

23. *Hanged himself.* See here contempt poured upon the wisdom of man! He that was more renowned for policy than ever any man was, played the fool with himself more than ever any man did. See likewise honor done to the justice of God! "The wicked is snared in the work of his own hands."

29. *In.* Having been *in the wilderness.* Thus God sometimes makes up to his people that comfort from strangers which they are disappointed of in their own families.

CHAPTER 18

5. *Deal gently.* "What means," says Bishop Hall, "this ill-placed mercy? Deal gently with a traitor? Of all traitors with a son? And all this for thy sake, whose crown, whose blood he hunts after? Even in the holiest parents nature may be guilty of an injurious tenderness. But was not this done in type of that immeasurable mercy of the true King of Israel, who prayed for his murderers, Father, forgive them! Deal gently with them for my sake!" Yes, when God sends an affliction to correct his children, it is with this charge, *Deal gently [with them] for my sake;* for he knows our frame.

9. *His head.* In which probably he was entangled by the hair of the head, which being very long and thick might easily catch hold of a bough, especially when the great God directed it. Either he wore no helmet, or he had thrown it away as well as his other arms, to hasten his flight. Thus the matter of his pride was the instrument of his ruin.

33. *My son.* This he might speak from a deep sense of his eternal state, because he died in his sins, and because David himself had by his own sins been the occasion of his death. But it seems rather to be the effect of strong passion, causing him to speak "unadvisedly with his lips."

CHAPTER 19

13. *Of Joab.* Who, besides his other crimes, had lately exasperated the king by his murder of Absalom, contrary to David's express command. And therefore the king, having now the opportunity of another person who had a greater interest than Joab, gladly complies with it, that so he might both chastise Joab for his faults and rescue himself from the bondage in which Joab had held him.

22. *King.* Is not my kingdom, which was in a manner wholly lost, just now restored and assured to me? And when God has been so merciful to me in forgiving my sin, shall I show myself revengeful to Shimei? Shall I sully the public joy and glory of this day with an act of such severity? Or shall I alienate the hearts of my people from me, now that they are returning to me?

35. *I am.* My senses are grown dull and incapable of relishing the pleasures of a court. I am past taking pleasures in delicious tastes or sweet music and other such delights. I am through age both useless and burdensome to others, and therefore most improper for a court life.

37. *That I may die in mine own city.* That my bones may, with little ado, be carried to the place of their rest. The grave is ready for me; let me go and get ready for it, go and die in my nest.

40. *Half.* Whereas the men of Judah came entirely and unanimously to the king, the Israelites of the other tribe came in but slowly, and by halves, as being no less guilty of the rebellion than the tribe of Judah; but not encouraged to come in by such a gracious message as they were. And this is here mentioned as the occasion both of the contention here following and of the sedition (ch. 20).

CHAPTER 20

8. *It fell.* Things having (it is likely) been so contrived by Joab that upon the least motion of his body, his sword should drop out and he might take it up without raising Amasa's suspicion.

16. *Then cried a wise women.* It seems none of all the men of Abel offered to face Joab. No, not even when they were reduced to extremity. But one woman saved the city. Souls know no difference of sex; many a manly heart is lodged in a female breast. Nor is the treasure of wisdom the less valuable for being lodged in the weaker vessel.

21. *His head.* Which she undertook because she knew the present temper of the citizens, and soldiers too. And it is not unlikely that this woman might be a governess in that city. For although this office was commonly performed by men, yet women were sometimes employed in the government; as we see in Deborah, who judged Israel (Judg. 4:4).

23. *Over all the host.* The good success of this and of the former expedition, under the conduct of Joab, had so fixed his interest in the army, and others of David's fastest friends, that the king could not without danger displace him.

CHAPTER 21

1. *Then.* The things related here and in chapter 24 are by the best interpreters conceived to have been done long before Absalom's rebellion.

10. *Until water.* Until they were taken down; which was not to be done until God had given rain as a sign of his favor and a means to remove the famine, which was caused by the lack of it. Thus she let the world know that her sons died not for any sin of their own, not as stubborn and rebellious sons, whose eye had despised their mother, but for their father's sin; and therefore her mind could not be alienated from them by their hard fate.

11. *David.* Who heard it with so much approbation that he thought fit to imitate her piety, being by her example provoked to do what before he had neglected, to bestow an honorable interment on the remains of Saul and Jonathan, and with them, upon those that are now put to death, that the honor done to them herein might be some comfort to this disconsolate widow.

CHAPTER 22

This chapter is inserted among the Psalms, no. 18, with some little variation. It is here as it was composed for his own closet; there, as it was delivered to the chief musician for public service. The inspired writer, having largely related David's deliverances in this and the foregoing book, thought fit to record this sacred poem as a memorial of all that had been before related.

CHAPTER 23

1. *Last words.* Not simply the last that he spoke, but the last which he spoke by the Spirit of God, assisting and directing him in an extraordinary manner. When we find death approaching, we should endeavor both to honor God and to profit others with our last words. Let those who have had experience of God's goodness and the pleasantness of the ways of wisdom, when they come to finish their course, leave a record of those experiences and bear their testimony to the truth of the promise. *Psalmist.* He who was eminent among the people of God for composing sweet and holy songs, to the praise

of God and for the use of his church in after ages; these seem not to be the words of David, but of the sacred penman of this book.

4. *Shall be.* These words are a further description of the king's duty, which is not only to rule with justice and piety, but also with sweetness and gentleness and condescension to the infirmities of his people; to render his government as acceptable to them, as is the sunshine in a clear morning, or the tender grass which springs out of the earth by the warm beams of the sun after the rain.

5. *Covenant.* Notwithstanding all our transgression whereby we have broken covenant with God, yet God, to whom all my sins were known, was graciously pleased to make a sure covenant, to continue the kingdom to me and to my seed for ever (7:16) until the coming of the Messiah, who is to be my son and successor, and whose kingdom shall have no end. *Ordered.* Ordained in all points by God's eternal counsel; and disposed by his wise and powerful providence, which will overrule all things, even the sins of my house so far, that although he punished them for their sins, yet he will not utterly root them out, nor break his covenant made with me and mine.

Salvation. Both my own eternal salvation, and the preservation of the kingdom to me and mine. *Although* God as yet has not made my house or family to grow; that is, to increase, or to flourish with worldly glory as I expected; yet this is my comfort, that God will inviolably keep this covenant. But this refers also to the covenant of grace made with all believers.

This is indeed an *everlasting covenant,* from everlasting in the contrivance of it, and to everlasting in the continuance and the consequence of it. It is *ordered,* well ordered *in all things;* admirably well, to advance the glory of God and the honor of the mediator, together with the holiness and happiness of believers. It is *sure,* and therefore sure because well ordered; the promised mercies are sure, on the performance of the conditions. It is *all my salvation;* nothing but this will save me, and this is sufficient. Therefore it should be *all my desire.* Let me have an interest in this covenant, and I have enough that I desire no more.

12. LORD *wrought.* However great the bravery of the instruments is, the praise of the achievement is to be given to God. These men fought, but God "wrought great victory."

16. *Would not.* Lest by gratifying himself upon such terms he should seem either to set too high a price upon the satisfaction of his appetite, or too low a price upon the lives of his soldiers. *Poured it.* As a kind of drink offering and acknowledgment of God's goodness in preserving the lives of his captains in so dangerous an enterprise. And to show that he esteemed it as a sacred thing, which it was not fit for him to drink.

20. *Pit.* Where he put himself under a necessity either of killing or being killed. *Of snow.* When lions are most fierce, both from the sharpness of their appetite in cold seasons, and from want of provisions.

39. *Thirty and seven.* Here are but thirty-six named. Either therefore one must be supplied whose name is not expressed among the three second worthies; or Joab is comprehended in the number as being the lord general of all. All the good soldiers of Jesus have their names better preserved than even these. For they are "written in heaven," in "the Lamb's book of life." This honor have all his saints.

CHAPTER 24

2. *May know.* This expression points at David's sin in this matter, that he numbered them, not by direction from God, but out of mere curiosity, pride, and vain-glory; accompanied with a confidence in the numbers of his people. All which sins were so manifest that not only God saw them, but even Joab and the captains of the host.

14. *And let me not fall.* True, "it is a fearful thing, to fall into the hands of the living God"! Fearful indeed for those who have by their impenitence shut themselves out from his mercy. But a penitent dares cast himself into God's hand, knowing that *his mercies are great.*

16. *Angel.* Who appeared in the shape of a man with a sword in his hand (I Chron. 21:16) in order to convince them more fully that this was no natural plague, but inflicted immediately by the hand of God. This was on Mount Moriah. In the very same place where Abraham, by a countermand from heaven, was stayed from slaying his son, this angel by a like countermand was stayed from destroying Jerusalem. It is for the sake of the great sacrifice that our forfeited lives are preserved from the destroying angel.

17. *What have they done.* Done? They have done much amiss. It was their sin as well as his own which provoked God to leave David to himself to do as he did. Yet as became a penitent, he is severe on his own faults, while he extenuates theirs. *Against me.* Wherein David shows his piety and fatherly care of his people, and that he was a type of Christ.

1 KINGS

CHAPTER 1

2. *Virgin.* Whose natural heat is fresh and wholesome, and not impaired with bearing or breeding of children. The same counsel does Galen give for the cure of some cold and dry distempers. *Stand.* That is, minister unto him, or wait upon him, in his sickness as occasion requires. *Lie in thy bosom.* As his wife; for that she was so may appear by many arguments. (1) Otherwise this had been a wicked course; which therefore neither his servants dared have prescribed, nor would David have used, especially being now in a dying condition. (2) It appears from this phrase of "lying in his bosom," which is everywhere in Scripture mentioned as the privilege of a wife. (3) This made Adonijah's crime in desiring her to wife so heinous in Solomon's account, because he saw that by marrying the king's wife he designed to revive his pretense to the kingdom.

11. *Nathan spake.* Being prompted to it, both by his piety in fulfilling the will of God declared to him concerning Solomon's succession (II Sam. 7:13) and by his prudence, knowing that Adonijah hated him for being the principal instrument of Solomon's advancement.

29. *Out of all distress.* The words contain a grateful acknowledgment of the goodness of God to him in bringing him safe through the many difficulties which had lain in his way, and which he now mentions to the glory of God (as Jacob when he lay dying), thus setting to his seal, from his own experience, that "the LORD redeemeth the soul of his servants."

31. *Live for ever.* Though I desire your oath may be kept and the right of succession confirmed to my son, yet I am far from thirsting after your death, and should rather rejoice if it were possible for you to live and enjoy your crown for ever.

48. *Blessed.* It is a great satisfaction to good men, when they are going out of the world, to see their children rising up in their stead, to serve *the LORD God* and their generation; and especially to see "peace upon Israel," and the establishment of it.

CHAPTER 2

2. *I go the way.* Even the sons and heirs of heaven must go the way of all the earth, of all who dwell thereon. But they walk with pleasure in this way, "through the valley of the shadow of death." Prophets, yes, kings must go this way to brighter light and honor than prophecy or sovereignty.

8. *I will not.* The words are, "The king said unto Shimei, Thou shalt not die. And the king sware unto him" (II Sam 19:23). The oath, we see, was absolute. It was not, "I will not put thee to death now"; or, "*I will not put thee to death with the sword.*" But who can reconcile his charge to Solomon with this oath? Surely, considering the time of that charge, this is, next to the matter of Uriah, the greatest blemish in all David's life.

26. *Because.* Thus Solomon shows respect to his sacred function. He mixes mercy with justice, and requites Abiathar's former kindness to David; hereby teaching princes that they should not write injuries in marble and benefits in sand, as they have been too often observed to do.

CHAPTER 3

1. *Pharaoh.* As being a powerful neighbor, whose daughter doubtless was first instructed in and proselyted to the Jewish religion. It seems this was designed by God to be a type of Christ, calling his church to himself and to the true religion, not only out of the Jews, but even out of the Gentile world.

3. *Yet.*[1] Although he miscarried in the matter of high places, yet in the general his heart was right with God.

7. *Child.* So he was in years; not above twenty years old; and thus (which he principally intends) he was raw and unexperienced, as a child, in state affairs.

9. *An understanding heart.* Whereby I may both clearly discern and faithfully perform all the parts of my duty; for both these are spoken of in Scripture as the effects of a good understanding. And he that lives in the neglect of his duties, or the practice of wickedness, is called a "fool," and one void of understanding. *Discern.* Namely, in causes and controversies among my people; that I may not through mistake or prejudice or passion give wrong sentences and call evil good, or good evil. Absalom, who was a fool, wished himself a judge. Solomon, who was a wise man, trembles at the undertaking. The more knowing and considerate men are, the more jealous they are of themselves.

15. *Burnt offerings.* Chiefly for the expiation of his and his people's sin, through the blood of Christ, manifestly signified in these sacrifices. *Peace offerings.* Solemnly to praise God for all his mercies, and especially for giving him quiet possession of the kingdom, and for his glorious appearance to him in the dream, and for the promise therein made to him, and the actual accomplishment of it.

16. *Harlots.* Or, victuallers; for the Hebrew word signifies both. Yet that they are unmarried persons seems probable, both because there is no mention of any husbands, whose office it was, if there were any such, to contest for their wives; and because they lived a solitary life in one house.

CHAPTER 4

25. *Under his vine.* Enjoying the fruit of his own labor with safety and comfort. Under these two trees, which were most used and cultivated by the Israelites, he understands all other fruit-bearing trees and all other comforts. And they are brought in as sitting or dwelling under these trees, partly for recreation or delight in the shade; and partly for the comfort or advantage of the

---

[1] (3:3) KJV: "And" instead of "yet."

fruit; and thus, to note their great security, not only in their strong cities but even in the country, where the vines and fig trees grew, which was most open to the incursions of their enemies.

29. *Largeness of heart.* Vastness of understanding, a most comprehensive knowledge of all things both divine and human.

32. *Proverbs.* That is, short and deep and useful sentences, whereof a great part are contained in the books of Proverbs and Ecclesiastes. *Songs.* Of which the chief and most divine are in the Canticles.

33. *Trees.* That is, of all plants, of their nature and qualities; all which discourses are lost, without any impeachment of the perfection of the Holy Scriptures; which were not written to teach men philosophy or physics, but only to make them wise unto salvation. *From the cedar tree.* That is, from the greatest to the least.

34. Let those who magnify the modern learning above that of the ancients produce such a treasury of learning, anywhere in these later ages, as that of which Solomon was master. Yet this puts an honor upon human learning, that Solomon is praised for it, and recommends it to the great ones of the earth as well worthy their diligent search. In all this Solomon was a type of Christ, "in whom are hid all the treasures of wisdom and knowledge."

CHAPTER 5

6. *They.* That is, your servants. And this assistance which these Gentiles gave to the building of Solomon's temple was a type of the calling of the Gentiles, that they should be instrumental in building and constituting Christ's spiritual temple.

11. *Gave Hiram.* Either, first, for

sustenance to the workmen during the years wherein they were employed in the cutting down and hewing of timber. Or, for the yearly support of the king's house during the specified time. Thus by the wise disposal of Providence, one country has need of another, and is benefited by another, that there may be a mutual correspondence and dependence to the glory of God our common Parent.

17. *Great stones, costly stones.* Marble and porphyry, or other stones of great size and value. *The foundation.* Where they could not afterwards be seen; and therefore that this was done is mentioned only as a point of magnificence, except it was intended for a type or mystical significance of the preciousness of Christ, who is the foundation of the true temple, the church of God.

CHAPTER 6

1. *Four hundred and eightieth.* Allowing forty years to Moses, seventeen to Joshua, two hundred ninety-nine to the Judges, forty to Eli, forty to Samuel and Saul, forty to David, and four to Solomon before he began the work, we have just the sum of four hundred and eighty. So long it was before that holy house was built, which in less than four hundred and thirty years was burnt by Nebuchadnezzar. It was thus deferred, because Israel had by their sins made themselves unworthy of this honor; and because God would show how little he values external pomp and splendor in his service. And God ordered it now, chiefly to be "a shadow of good things to come."

7. *Made ready.* Hewed, and squared, and fitted exactly according to the direction of the architect. *Neither hammer.* So it was ordered, partly for the ease and convenience of carriage; partly for the magnificence of the work, and commendation of the workmen's skill and diligence; and partly for mystical significance. And as this temple was a manifest type both of Christ's church upon earth and of the heavenly Jerusalem; so this circumstance signified, as to the former, that it is the duty of the builders and members of the church, as far as in them lies, to take care that all things be transacted there with perfect peace and quietness; and that no noise of contention, division, or violence be heard in that sacred building. And for the latter, that no spiritual stone, no person, shall bear a part in that heavenly temple unless he be first hewed, squared, and made ready for it in this life.

12. *If.* God expresses the condition upon which his promise and favor is suspended; and by assuring him thereof in case of obedience, he plainly intimates the contrary upon his disobedience. Thus he was taught that all the charge he and the people had in erecting this temple would neither excuse them from obedience to the law of God, nor shelter them from his judgments in case of disobedience.

19. *Prepared.* That is, adorned and fitted it for the reception of the ark. Solomon made everything new but the ark. That with its mercy seat was still the same that Moses made. This was the token of God's presence, which is with his people, whether they meet in tent or temple, and changes not with their condition.

38. Now let us see what this temple typifies. (1) Christ himself is the true temple. He spoke of "the temple of his body"; and in him "dwelleth all the fulness of the godhead." In him all the Israel of God meet, and through him have "access with confidence" to God. (2) Every believer is a living temple in whom the Spirit of God dwells. We are wonderfully made by the divine provi-

dence, but more wonderfully made anew by the divine grace. And as Solomon's temple was built on a rock, so are we built on Christ.

(3) The church is a mystical temple, enriched and beautified, not with gold and precious stones, but with the gifts and graces of the Spirit. Angels are ministering spirits which attend the church and all the members of it on all sides. (4) Heaven is the everlasting temple. There the church will be fixed and no longer movable. The cherubim there always attend upon the throne of glory. In the temple there was no noise of axes or hammers; everything is quiet and serene in heaven. All that shall be stones in that building must here be fitted and made ready; but be hewn and squared by the divine grace, and so made ready for a place in that temple.

CHAPTER 7

21. *Jachin.* Jachin signifies "he"; that is, God shall establish his temple and church and people; and Boaz signifies "in it," or rather, "in him [to answer the 'he' in the former name] is strength." So these pillars, being eminently strong and stable, were types of that strength which was in God, and would be put forth by God to defend and establish his temple and people if they were careful to keep the conditions required by God on their parts.

49. *Candlesticks.* Which were ten, according to the number of the tables, whereas Moses made but one. This signifies the progress of the light of sacred truth, which was now grown clearer than it was in Moses' time, and should shine brighter and brighter until the perfect day of gospel light.

CHAPTER 8

10. *The cloud.* The usual token of God's glorious presence. *Filled.* In testimony of his gracious acceptance of this work and their service; and to foster an awe and reverence in them, and in all others, when they approach God.

12. *Then spake.* Perceiving both priests and people struck with wonder at this darkness, he reminds them that this was no sign of God's disfavor, as some might possibly imagine; but a token of his approbation and special presence among them.

27. *But will.* Is it possible that the great, and high, and lofty God should stoop so low as to take up his dwelling among men? *Contain.* For your essence reaches far beyond them, being omnipresent. *Much less.* This house therefore was not built as if it were proportionable to your greatness, or could contain you, but only that therein we might serve and glorify you.

30. *In heaven.* Which he adds to direct them in their addresses to God in this temple, to lift up their eyes above it, even to heaven, where God's most true and glorious dwelling place is.

33. *Confess.* Give glory to your name, by acknowledging their sins, and by justice; and by accepting the punishment of their iniquity; and by trusting to your power and goodness alone for their deliverance.

36. *Give rain.* The order of Solomon's prayer is very observable; first and chiefly, he prays for their repentance and forgiveness, which is the chief blessing and the only solid foundation of all other mercies. And then he prays for temporal mercies, thereby teaching us what to desire principally in our prayers; which also Christ has taught us in his perfect prayer, wherein there is but one petition for outward, and all the rest are for spiritual blessings.

38. *The plague.* His sin, which may be called *the plague of his own heart,* in opposition to the other plagues here mentioned; so the sense is, who by

their afflictions are brought to a true and serious sense of their worse and inward plague of their sins, which are most fitly called "the plague of the heart," because that is both the principal seat of sin and the fountain whence all actual sins flow.

43. *Calleth to thee for.* Agreeable to your will and word. It is observable that his prayer for the strangers is more large and comprehensive than for the Israelites; that thereby he might both show his public spiritedness and encourage strangers to the worship of the true God. Thus early were the indications of God's favor toward the sinners of the Gentiles. As there was then one law for the native and for the stranger, so there was one gospel for both.

44. *Shall pray.* Whereby he instructs them, that they should not trust to either the strength or justice of their arms, but only to God's help and blessing. *Toward the house.* For to it they were to turn their faces in prayer; to profess themselves worshippers of the true God, in opposition to idols; and to strengthen their faith in God's promises and covenant, the tables of which were contained in that house. Soldiers in the field must not think it enough that others pray for them; they must pray for themselves. And they are here encouraged to expect a gracious answer. Praying should always go along with fighting.

55. *He stood.* He spoke this standing, to be the better heard, and because he blessed as one having authority. Never were words more pertinently spoken; never was a congregation dismissed with that which was more likely to affect them and to abide with them.

56. *Blessed.* This discharge he gives in the name of all Israel, to the everlasting honor of the divine faithfulness and the everlasting encouragement of all those that build upon the divine promises.

58. *Incline.* That he may not only bless us with outward prosperity, but especially with spiritual blessings; and that as he has given us his word to teach and direct us, so he would by his Holy Spirit effectually incline us to obey it.

61. *Be perfect.* Let our obedience be universal, without dividing; upright, without dissembling; constant, without declining.

CHAPTER 9

21. *Those.* He used them as bondmen and imposed bodily labors upon them. "But why did not Solomon destroy them as God had commanded, when now it was fully in his power to do so?" The command of destroying them (Deut. 7:2) did chiefly, if not only, concern that generation of Canaanites who lived in or near the time of the Israelites' entering into Canaan. And that command seems not to be absolute but conditional, and with some exception for those who should submit and embrace the true religion, as may be gathered both from Joshua 11:19 and from the history of the Gibeonites. For if God's command had been absolute, the oaths of Joshua and of the princes could not have obliged them, nor dispensed with such a command.

CHAPTER 10

1. *Name of the* LORD. That is, concerning God; the name of God being often put for God; concerning his deep knowledge in the things of God. For it is very probable she had, as had many other heathens, some knowledge of the true God and an earnest desire to know more concerning him.

2. *All that was in her heart.* Of all the doubts and difficulties wherewith her mind was perplexed.

5. She saw the manner of his offering sacrifices to the Lord; which doubtless she would not neglect to see, and in the ordering of which she might discern many aspects of excellent wisdom, especially when she had so excellent an interpreter as Solomon to inform her of the reasons of all the circumstances of that service. *No more spirit.* She was astonished and could scarcely determine whether she really saw these things, or whether it was only a pleasant dream.

8. *Happy.* With much more reason may we say this of Christ's servants: "Blessed are they that dwell in thy house: they will be still praising thee."

16. The Roman magistrates had rods and axes carried before them, in token of their power to correct the bad; but Solomon, shields and targets, to show he took more pleasure in his power to defend and protect the good.

CHAPTER 11

3. *Seven hundred wives.* God had particularly forbidden the kings to multiply either horses or wives (Deut. 17:16–17). We saw (10:29) how he broke the former law, multiplying horses. And here we see how he broke the latter, multiplying wives. David set the example. One ill act of a good man may do more mischief than twenty of an evil man. Besides, they were "strange women," of the nations which God had expressly forbidden them to marry. And to complete the mischief, he "clave unto these in love," was extravagantly fond of them. Solomon had much knowledge; but to what purpose, when he knew not how to govern his appetites?

4. *Turned away his heart.* Not that they changed his mind about the true God and idols, which is not credible; but they obtained from him a public indulgence for their worship, and possibly persuaded him to join with them in the outward act of idol worship; or at least, in their feasts upon their sacrifices, which was a participation of their idolatry.

5. *Milcom.* Called also "Moloch."

8. *And sacrificed.* See what need those have to stand upon their guard who have been eminent for religion. The devil will set upon them most violently; and if they go astray, the reproach is the greater. It is the evening that commends the day. Let us therefore fear lest, having run well, we come short.

25. *An adversary.* But what hurt could Hadad or Rezon have done to so powerful a king as Solomon if he had not by sin made himself lowly and weak? If God be on our side, we need not fear the greatest adversary. But if he be against us, he can make us fear the least; yes, "the grasshopper shall be a burden."

39. *Not for ever.* There shall a time come when the seed of David shall not be molested by the kingdom of Israel, but that kingdom shall be destroyed, and the kings of the house of David shall be uppermost, as it was in the days of Asa, Hezekiah, and Josiah. And at last the Messiah shall come, who shall unite together the broken sticks of Judah and Joseph, and rule over all the Jews and Gentiles too.

40. *Shishak.* Solomon's brother-in-law, who yet might be jealous of him or alienated from him, because he had taken so many other wives to his sister, might cast a greedy eye upon the great riches which Solomon had amassed together and upon which, presently after Solomon's death, he laid violent hands (II Chron. 12:9).

43. Did Solomon repent before he died? This seems to be put out of dispute by the Book of Ecclesiastes,

written after his fall; as is evident, not only from the unanimous testimony of the Hebrew writers, but also from the whole strain of that book, which was written long after he had liberally drunk of all sorts of sensual pleasures and sadly experienced the bitter effects of his love of women (Eccl. 7:17ff.). This makes it more than probable that, as David wrote Psalm 51, so Solomon wrote this book as a public testimony and profession of his repentance.

CHAPTER 12

1. Out of a thousand wives and concubines, he had but one son to bear his name, and he a fool! Is not sin an ill way of building up a family?

4. And Solomon having so grossly forsaken God, it is no wonder if he oppressed the people.

15. *From the LORD.* Who gave up Rehoboam to so foolish and fatal a mistake, and alienated the people's affections from him; and ordered all circumstances by his wise providence to that end.

16. *In David.* In David's family and son. We can expect no benefit or relief from him, and therefore we renounce all commerce with him and subjection to him. *To their tents.* Let us forsake him and go to our own homes, there to consider how to provide for ourselves.

19. *Rebelled.* Their revolt was sinful, as they did not do this in compliance with God's counsel, but to gratify their own passions.

26. *Said.* Reasoned within himself. The phrase discovers the fountain of his error, that he did not consult with God, who had given him the kingdom; as in all reason and justice and gratitude he should have done; nor believed God's promise (11:38), but his own carnal policy.

28. *Calves.* In imitation of Aaron's

golden calf and of the Egyptians, from whom he was lately come. And this he the rather presumed to do because he knew the people of Israel were generally prone to idolatry; and that Solomon's example had strengthened those inclinations exceedingly. *Behold thy gods.* Not as if he thought to persuade the people that these calves were that very God of Israel who brought them out of Egypt; which was so monstrously absurd and ridiculous that no Israelite in his right wits could believe it, and had been so far from satisfying his people that this would have made him both hateful and contemptible to them. But his meaning was that these images were visible representations by which he designed to worship the true God of Israel.

30. *A sin.* That is, an occasion of great wickedness, not only of idolatry, which is called sin by way of eminence; nor only the worship of the calves, wherein they pretended to worship the true God; but also of the worship of Baal, and of the utter desertion of the true God; and of all sorts of impiety.

CHAPTER 13

2. *Josiah.* Which being done above three hundred years after this prophecy plainly shows the absolute certainty of God's providence and foreknowledge even in the most contingent things. For this was in itself uncertain and wholly depended upon man's will, both as to the having of a child and as to the giving it this name. Therefore God can certainly and effectually overrule man's will whichever way he pleases; or else it was possible that his prediction should have been false, which is blasphemous to imagine. Whoever is sent on God's errand must not fear the faces of men. It was above three hundred and fifty years ere this prophecy was fulfilled.

Yet it is spoken of as sure and nigh at hand. For a thousand years are with God as one day.

9. *Eat no bread, nor drink water.* In that place or with that people. Whereby God declares how detestable they were in God's eyes, because they were vile apostates from the true God and embraced this idol worship against the light of their own consciences, merely to comply with the king's humor and command.

11. *An old prophet.* One to whom, and by whom, God did sometimes impart his mind, as it is manifest from verses 20 and 21; and one that had a respect to the Lord's holy prophets and gave credit to their predictions. But whether he was a good man may be doubted, seeing we find him in a downright lie (v. 18). And although a holy prophet may possibly have continued in the kingdom of Israel, he would never have gone from his own habitation to dwell at Bethel, the chief seat of idolatry, unless with design to preach against it; which it is evident he did not. His sons seem to have been present at and to have joined with others in that idolatrous worship.

22. *Shall not.* Is it not strange that the lying prophet escapes, while the man of God is so severely punished? Certainly there must be a judgment to come, when these things shall be called over again, and when those who sinned most and suffered least in this world will receive according to their works.

24. *Slew him.* "But why does God punish a good man so severely for so small an offense?" His sin was not small, for it was a gross disobedience to a positive command. And it cannot seem strange if God should bring this deserved death upon him in this manner to accomplish his own glorious designs, to vindicate his own justice from the imputation of partiality; to assure the truth of his predictions, and thereby provoke Jeroboam and his idolatrous followers to repentance; and to justify himself in all his dreadful judgments which he intended to inflict upon Jeroboam's house and the whole kingdom of Israel.

31. *When I am dead.* Though he was a lying prophet, yet he desired to die the death of a true prophet. Gather not my soul with the sinners of Bethel, but with the man of God.

34. *Sin.* His obstinate continuance in his idolatry after such warnings was the utter ruin of all his family. They betray themselves effectually who endeavor to support themselves by any sin.

CHAPTER 14

8. *David.* Though he fell into some sins, yet first he constantly persevered in the true worship of God; for which you are revolted. Secondly, he heartily repented of and turned from all his sins, whereas you are obstinate and incorrigible.

9. *Images.* Namely, the golden calves; not as if they thought them to be *other gods* in a proper sense (they still pretended to worship the God of their fathers), but because God rejected their whole worship and, however they accounted it, he reckoned it a manifest defection from him and a giving in to *other gods,* or "devils," as they are called (II Chron. 11:15), whom alone they served and worshiped therein, whatever pretenses they had to the contrary.

13. *Shall mourn.* For the loss of so worthy and hopeful a person, and for the sad calamities which will follow his death, which possibly his moderation, wisdom, and virtue might have prevented. So they should mourn, not simply for him, but for their own loss in him.

16. *Who made.* He was not content with his own sin, but was the great author of drawing others into sin and of corrupting and undoing the whole kingdom. Therefore God would never forgive him, but upon all occasions mentions him with this eternal brand of infamy upon him.

18. *Mourned.* And justly; not only for the loss of a hopeful prince, but because his death plucked up the floodgates at which an inundation of judgments broke in.

21. *Ammonitess.* None can imagine how fatal and how lasting are the consequences of being unequally yoked with an unbeliever.

22. *In the sight of the* LORD. In contempt and defiance of him and the tokens of his special presence. *Jealousy.* As the adulterous wife provokes her husband by breaking the marriage covenant.

23. *Under every green tree.* The people were universally corrupted; which is prodigious, all things considered, and is a clear evidence of the greatness and depth of the original corruption of man's nature.

24. *Abominations.* They dishonored God by one sin, and then God left them to dishonor themselves by another.

CHAPTER 15

5. *Save only.*[2] This and the like phrases are not to be understood as exclusive of every sinful action, but only of a habitual and continued apostasy from God, as the very phrase of "turning aside" from God or from his commands does constantly imply. And

---

[2](15:5) That is, "except" or "but only."

thus it is most true. For David's other sins were either sudden and transient acts, soon repented of and blotted out, as in the cases of Nabal and Achish; or they were mistakes of his judgment, which was not fully convinced of the sinfulness of such actions. But that which concerned Uriah's wife was a designed and studied sin, long continued in, defended with a succession of other sins, presumptuous, and scandalous to his government and to the true religion.

14. *Was perfect.* That is, he sincerely and constantly adhered to the worship of God. Though he could not hinder the people from using the high places, yet he entirely devoted himself to the worship of God in the manner and place prescribed by him.

18. *Sent them.* Wherein he committed three great faults, among many others. First, he alienated things consecrated to God without necessity. Secondly, he did this out of distrust of that God whose power and goodness he had lately experienced. Thirdly, he did this for an ill intent, to hire him to the breach of his league and covenant with Baasha (v. 19) and to take away part of that land which by right and by the special gift of God belonged to the Israelites.

21. Asa met with success in this ungodly course as good men sometimes meet with disappointment in a good cause and course. So there is no judging of causes by events.

23. *Nevertheless.* In spite of the great things he had done and the glory and prosperity which he enjoyed, he felt the effects of human infirmity and of his own sins.

30. *Because.* So that same wicked policy which he used to establish the kingdom in his family proved his and their ruin; which is very frequently the result of ungodly counsels.

CHAPTER 16

2. *Forasmuch.* If Baasha had done this in obedience to God's command and with a single design to execute God's vengeance threatened against him, it had been no more a sin than Jehu's act in killing his master King Jehoram upon the same account (II Kings 9). But Baasha did this merely to gratify his own pride, covetousness, or malice (v. 7).

22. *Died.* A violent death in the battle, but not until after a struggle of some years. But why in all these confusions of the kingdom of Israel did they never think of returning to the house of David? Probably because the kings of Judah assumed a more absolute power than the kings of Israel. It was the heaviness of the yoke that they complained of when they first revolted from the house of David. And it is not unlikely that the dread of that made them averse to it ever after.

31. *Jezebel.* A woman infamous for her idolatry, cruelty, sorcery, and filthiness. *Baal.* The idol which the Sidonians worshipped, which is thought to be Hercules. And this idolatry was much worse than that of the calves, because in the calves they worshipped the true God; but in these, false gods or devils.

34. *Hiel the Bethelite.* Who lived in Bethel, the seat and sink of idolatry, with which he was thoroughly leavened.

CHAPTER 17

1. *Elijah.* The most eminent of the prophets, who is here brought in, like Melchizedek, without any mention of his father or mother or beginning of his days; like a man dropped out of the clouds and raised by God's special providence as a witness for himself in this most degenerate time. And this, that by his zeal, courage, and miracles he might give some check to their various and abominable idolatries and some reviving to that small number of the Lord's prophets and people who yet remained in Israel. He seems to have been naturally of a rough spirit. And rough spirits are called to rough services. His name signifies, "my God Jehovah is he"; he that sends me and will own me and bear me out.

4. *Have commanded.* Or, "shall command." That is, effectually move them by instincts which shall be as forcible with them as a law or command is to men. God is said to command both brute creatures and senseless things when he causes them to do the things which he intends to effect by them. *The ravens.* Which he chooses for this work, to show his care and power in providing for the prophet by those creatures which are noted for their greediness; that by this strange experiment he might be taught to trust God in those many and great difficulties to which he was to be exposed. God could have sent angels to minister to him, but he chose winged messengers of another kind to show he can serve his own purposes as effectually by the lowliest creatures as by the mightiest. Ravens neglect their own young and do not feed them; yet when God pleases, they shall feed his prophet.

9. God's providing for his prophet, first by an unclean bird; then by a Gentile whom the Jews esteemed unclean, who was a presage of the calling of the Gentiles and rejection of the Jews. So Elijah was the first prophet of the Gentiles.

12. *She said.* Therefore, though she was a Gentile, yet she owned the God of Israel as the true God. What a poor supporter was this likely to be? She had no fuel but what she gathered in the streets, and nothing to live upon herself but a handful of meal and a little oil! To her Elijah is sent that he might live upon Providence, as much as he had done when the ravens fed him.

15. *Many days.* A long time, even above two years before the following event about her son happened. And surely the increase of her faith, to such a degree as to enable her thus to deny herself and trust the promise, was as great a miracle in the kingdom of Grace as the increase of her oil in the kingdom of Providence. Happy are they who can thus against hope believe and obey in hope.

16. *Wasted not.* See how the reward answered the service. She made one cake for the prophet and was repaid with many for herself and her son. What is laid out in charity is set out to the best interest and upon the best securities.

20. *He cried.* A prayer full of powerful arguments. You are *the* LORD who can revive the child. You are *my God;* therefore you will not deny me. She is a *widow;* add not affliction to the afflicted; deprive her not of the support and staff of her age. She has given me kind entertainment; let her not fare the worse for her kindness to a prophet whereby wicked men will take occasion to reproach both her and religion.

22. *Into him again.* This plainly supposes the existence of the soul in a state of separation, and consequently its immortality. Probably God might design by this miracle to give an evidence of this for the encouragement of his suffering people.

CHAPTER 18

1. *Will send.* According to your word and prayer which you shall make for it. Thus God takes care to maintain the honor of his prophet, and in judgment remembers mercy to Israel for the sake of the holy seed yet left among them, who suffered in this common calamity.

2. *Elijah went.* Wherein he shows a strong faith, resolute obedience, and invincible courage, that he dared at God's command to run into the mouth of this raging lion.

4. *Prophets.* This name is not only given to such as are endowed with an extraordinary spirit of prophecy, but to such ministers as devoted themselves to the service of God in preaching, praying, and praising God. *Bread and water.* See how wonderfully God raises up friends for his ministers and people where one would least expect them!

17. *Ahab said.* Have I at last met with you, O disturber of my kingdom, the author of this famine and all our calamities?

18. *He answered.* These calamities are not to be imputed to me, but to your and your father's wickedness. He answered him boldly because he spoke in God's name and for his honor and service.

20. *Ahab sent.* He complied with Elijah's motion, because the urgency of the present distress made him willing to try all means to remove it; from a curiosity of seeing some extraordinary events; and principally, because God inclined his heart.

21. *And said.* Why do you walk so lamely and unevenly, being so unsteady in your opinions and practices, and doubting whether it is better to worship God or Baal?

24. *By fire.* That shall consume the sacrifice by fire sent from heaven, which the people knew the true God used to do. It was a great condescension in God that he would permit Baal to be a competitor with him. But thus God would have every mouth to be stopped and all flesh become silent before him. And Elijah doubtless had a special commission from God, or he dared not have put it to this issue. But the case was extraordinary, and the judgment upon it would be of use not only then, but in all ages.

Elijah does not say, "The God that answers by water," though that was the thing the country needed. But the God *that answereth by fire, let him be God;* because the atonement was to be made before the judgment could be removed. The God therefore who has power to pardon sin, and so to signify that by consuming the sin offering, must needs be the God who can relieve us against the calamity.

26. *They leaped upon.* Or, "beside" the altar; or, "before" it. They used some superstitious and disorderly gestures, either pretending to be acted upon by the spirit of their god and to be in a kind of religious ecstasy, or in way of devotion to their god.

28. *Cut themselves.* Mingling their own blood with their sacrifices; as knowing by experience that nothing was more acceptable to their Baal (who was indeed the devil) than human blood; and hoping thereby to move their god to help them. And this indeed was the practice of many heathens in the worship of their false gods.

29. *Prophesied.* That is, prayed to and worshipped their god.

36. Lord *God of.* Hereby he shows faith in God's ancient covenant and also reminds the people of their relation both to God and to the patriarchs.

37. *Hast turned.* Let them feel so powerful a change in their hearts that they may know it is your work.

39. *He is the God.* He alone; and Baal is a senseless idol. And they double the words to note their abundant satisfaction and assurance of the truth of their assertion.

40. *Slew them.* As these idolatrous priests were manifestly under a sentence of death, passed upon such by the sovereign Lord of life and death, so Elijah had authority to execute it, being a prophet and an extraordinary minister of God's vengeance.

44. *Like a man's hand.* Great blessings often rise from small beginnings, and showers of plenty from a cloud of a span long. Let us therefore never "despise the day of small things," but hope and wait for greater things from it.

46. *Ran before Ahab.* To show how ready he was to honor and serve the king, that by this humble and self-denying carriage it might appear what he had done was not from envy or passion, but only from a just zeal for God's glory. And that by his presence with the king and his courtiers he might animate and oblige them to proceed in the reformation of religion. And to demonstrate that he was neither ashamed of nor afraid for what he had done, but dared venture himself in the midst of his enemies.

CHAPTER 19

2. *Jezebel sent.* She gives him notice of it beforehand; partly out of the height of her spirit as scorning to kill him secretly; partly out of her impatience until she had breathed out her rage; and principally from God's all-disposing providence, that he might have an opportunity of escaping.

7. Wherever God's children are, they are still under their Father's eye.

9. *Unto a cave.* Perhaps the same one where Moses was hid when the Lord passed before him and proclaimed his name.

12. *A still small voice.* To intimate that God would do his work in and for Israel in his own time, "not by might, nor by power, but by my spirit" (Zech. 4:6), which moves with a powerful, yet with a sweet and gentle gale.

18. *Seven thousand.* Either, definitely so many; or rather, indefinitely, for so many thousands; the number of seven being often used for a great number.

20. *Ran.* Being powerfully moved by God's Spirit to follow Elijah and to give himself up wholly to his function. *For what.* Either, first, to hinder you from performing that office; the employment to which I have called you does not require an alienation of your heart from your parents nor the total neglect of them. Or, secondly, to make such a change in you that you should be willing to forsake your parents, lands, and all that you may follow me. Whence comes this marvelous change? It is not from me who did only throw my mantle over you, but from a higher power, even from God's Spirit, who has changed your heart and consecrated you to your prophetical office; which therefore it concerns you vigorously to execute and wholly to devote yourself to it.

21. *The instruments.* That is, with the wood belonging to the plow, to which more was added as occasion required. But that he burned to show his total relinquishing of his former employment. He showed how willingly and joyfully he forsook all his friends, that he might serve God in that high and honorable employment. It is of great advantage to young ministers to spend some time under the direction of those who are aged and experienced; and not to think much, if occasion be, to minister unto them. Those who would be fit to teach must have time to learn; those should first serve who may hereafter rule.

CHAPTER 20

7. *Seeketh mischief.* Though he pretended peace upon these terms propounded, it is apparent by those additional demands that he intends nothing less than our utter ruin.

22. *Mark, and see.* Consider what is necessary for you to do by way of preparation. The enemies of the children of God are restless in their malice, and though they may take some breathing time for themselves, they are still "breathing out threatenings and slaughter" against the church. It therefore concerns us always to expect our spiritual enemies and to mark and see what we do.

30. This might possibly happen through natural causes, but most probably was effected by the mighty power of God sending some earthquake or violent storm which threw down the walls upon them; or doing this by the ministry of angels. By this he showed that he was the God of the plains as well as of the mountains; and that he could as effectually destroy them in their strongest hold as in the open fields; and make the very walls, to whose strength they trusted for their defense, to be the instruments of their ruin.

31. *He will save thy life.* This encouragement have all poor sinners, to repent and humble themselves before God. The God of Israel is a merciful God; let us rent our hearts and return to him.

32. *My brother.* I do not only pardon him, but honor and love him as my brother. What a change is here! From the height of prosperity to the depth of distress. See the uncertainty of human affairs! Such turns are they subject to, that the spoke of the wheel which is uppermost now may soon be the lowest of all.

36. *Slew him.* We cannot judge of the case. This man might be guilty of many other heinous sins unknown to us but known to God; for which God might justly cut him off. God chose to cut

him off upon this occasion that by the severity of this punishment of a prophet's disobedience, proceeding from pity to his brother, he might teach Ahab the greatness of his sin in sparing him through foolish pity, whom by the laws of religion, justice, and prudence he should have cut off.

42. *Thy life.* "What was the great sin of Ahab in this action for which God so severely punished him?" The great dishonor hereby done to God was in allowing so horrid a blasphemer to go unpunished, which was contrary to an express law (Lev. 24:16). And God had delivered him into Ahab's hand for his blasphemy, as he promised to do (v. 28), by which act of his providence, compared with that law, it was most evident that this man was appointed by God to destruction. But Ahab was so far from punishing this blasphemer that he does not so much as rebuke him, but dismisses him upon easy terms and takes not the least care for the reparation of God's honor. And the people were punished for their own sins, which were many and great; though God took this occasion to inflict it.

CHAPTER 21

13. Let us commit the keeping of our lives and comforts to God; for innocence itself will not always be our security.

19. *Saying.* You have murdered an innocent man; and instead of repenting for it have added another piece of injustice and violence to it. And you are going confidently and cheerfully to reap the fruit of your wickedness.

20. *Sold thyself.* You have wholly resigned yourself to be the bondslave of the devil, as a man who sells himself to another is totally in his master's power. *To work evil.* Impudently and contemptuously. Those who give themselves up to sin will certainly be found out, sooner or later, to their unspeakable amazement.

24. *Him that dieth.* Punishments after death are here most insisted on. And these, though affecting the body only, yet undoubtedly were designed as figures of the soul's misery in an after state.

29. *Humbleth himself.* His humiliation was real, though not lasting, and accordingly pleasing to God. This discovers the great goodness of God and his readiness to show mercy. It teaches us to take notice of that which is good even in the worst of men. It gives a reason why wicked persons often prosper; God rewards what little good is in them. And it encourages true penitence. If even Ahab goes to his house reprieved, doubtless they shall go to their houses justified.

CHAPTER 22

2. *Came down.* It is strange that so good a man would be so closely connected with a king revolted from the worship of God! But Jehoshaphat appears to have been of too easy a temper, which betrayed him to many inconveniences.

5. *Enquire.* A good man, wherever he goes, will take God along with him, will acknowledge him in all his ways, and will look to him for success. And wherever he goes, he ought to take his religion along with him and not be ashamed to own it, even among those who have no kindness for it.

14. *Said.* What answer God shall put into my mouth. Bravely resolved! And as became one who had an eye to a greater king than either of these.

18. The greatest kindness we can do to one who is walking in a dangerous way is to tell him of his danger.

19. *The host.* The angels, both good and bad, one possibly on his right, the other on his left hand. Nor is it strange that the devils are called *the host of heaven* if you consider, first, that their original seat was in heaven. Secondly, if you consider that the name of "heaven" is often given to all that part of the world which is above the earth, and among the rest, to the air and where the devil's residence and dominion lies (Eph. 2:2). And that both "Michael and his angels" and "the dragon and his angels" are said to be and to "wage war in heaven" (Rev. 12:7).

34. No armor is proof against the darts of divine vengeance. Case the criminal in steel and it is all one; "he that made him can make his sword to approach unto him." And that which to us seems altogether casual comes by the determinate counsel of God.

53. *His father.* Most unhappy parents who thus help to damn their own children's souls!

II Kings

CHAPTER 1

8. *An hairy man*. His garment was rough and hairy, such as were worn by eminent persons in Greece in ancient times; and were the proper habit of the prophets. *Girdle*. As John the Baptist also had; that by his very outward habit he might represent Elijah, in whose spirit and power he came.

13. *Besought*. Expressing both reverence to his person and a dread of God's judgments. There is nothing to be got by contending with God. If we would prevail with him it must be by supplication. And those are wise who learn submission for the fatal consequences of obstinacy in others.

CHAPTER 2

1. *Would take up*. It is supposed (though not expressly revealed) that Elijah flourished about twenty years before he was translated, body and soul, to heaven, only undergoing such a change as was necessary to qualify him as an inhabitant in that world of spirits. By translating him, God gave in that dark and degenerate age a very sensible proof of another life, together with a type of the ascension of Christ and the opening of the kingdom of heaven to all believers.

7. *To view*. To observe this great event, Elijah's translation to heaven, which they expected every moment; and whereof they desired to be spectators, not to satisfy their own curiosity, but that they might be witnesses of it to others.

8. *Smote the waters*. When God will take his children to himself, death is the Jordan which they must pass through. And they find a way through it, a safe and comfortable way. The death of Christ has divided those waters, that the ransomed of the Lord may pass over.

9. *A double portion*. But though Elisha desired no more, yet God gave him more than he desired or expected; and he seems to have had a greater portion of the gifts of God's Spirit than even Elijah had.

11. *A chariot of fire*. In this form the angels appeared. The souls of all the faithful are carried by an invisible guard of angels into the bosom of Abraham. But to Elijah, who was to carry his body with him, this heavenly guard appeared visibly. Not in human shape, though so they might have borne him in their arms, but in the form of a chariot and horses that he may ride in state, may ride in triumph, like a prince, like a conqueror. See the readiness of the angels to do the will of God even in the lowliest services for the heirs of salvation! Thus he who had burned with holy zeal for God and his honor was now conveyed in fire into his immediate presence.

13. *That fell.* God so ordering it for Elisha's comfort and the strengthening of his faith, as a pledge, that together with Elijah's mantle his Spirit should rest upon him. And Elijah himself was gone to a place where he needed not the mantle, either to adorn him, to shelter him from weather, or to wrap his face in.

15. *Elisha was taken from the plough.* Yet, when they perceive that God is with him and that this is the man whom he delights to honor, they readily submit to him as their head and father, as the people to Joshua when Moses was dead.

23. *Unto Bethel.* To the other school of prophets to inform them of Elijah's translation and his succession to the same office; and to direct, comfort, and establish them. *Children.* Or, "young men," as this Hebrew word often signifies. *The city.* Bethel was the mother city of idolatry, where the prophets planted themselves that they might bear witness against it and dissuade the people from it; though, it seems, they had but small success there. *Baldhead.* So they mock his natural infirmity, which is a great sin. The repetition shows their heartiness and earnestness, that it was no sudden slip of their tongue, but a scoff proceeding from a rooted impiety and hatred of God and his prophets. And very probably it was their usual practice to jeer the prophets as they went along the streets, that they might expose them to contempt and, if possible, drive them out of their town. Had the abuse done to Elisha been the first offense of the kind, they might not have been so

severely punished. But mocking the messengers of the Lord was one of the crying sins of Israel.

24. *Cursed them.* Nor was this punishment too great for the offense, if it be considered, (1) That their mocking proceeded from a great malignity of mind against God. (2) That they mocked not only a man, and an ancient man whose very age commanded reverence, and a prophet, but even God himself and that glorious work of God, the assumption of Elijah into heaven. (3) That they might be guilty of many other heinous crimes which God and the prophet knew, and were guilty of idolatry, which by God's law deserved death. (4) That the idolatrous parents were punished in their children. And (5) That if any of these children were more innocent, God might have mercy upon their souls. And then this death was not a misery but a real blessing to them that they were taken away from that education which was most likely to expose them not only to temporal but to eternal destruction.

In the name. Not from any revengeful passion, but by the motion of God's Spirit and by God's command and commission. God did this, partly for the terror and caution of all other idolaters and profane persons who abounded in that place; partly to vindicate the honor and maintain the authority of his prophets; and particularly of Elisha, now especially in the beginning of his sacred ministry.

CHAPTER 3

14. *Jehoshaphat.* Whom I reverence and love for his piety. It is good being with those who have God's favor and the love of his people. Wicked men often fare the better for the friendship and society of good men.

15. *Minstrel.* One who can sing and

play upon a musical instrument. This he requires that his mind, which had been disturbed at the sight of wicked Jehoram, might be composed; and that he might be excited to more fervent prayer whereby he was prepared to receive the prophetic inspiration. Those who desire communion with God must keep their spirits quiet and serene. All hurry of spirit and all turbulent passions make us unfit for divine visitations.

CHAPTER 4

6. *The oil stayed.* To teach us that we should not waste any of his good creatures; and that God would not work miracles unnecessarily. We are never in straits in God and in his power and bounty and in the riches of his grace. All our straitness is in ourselves. It is our faith that fails, not his promise. Were there more vessels, there is enough in God to fill them, enough for all, enough for each.

10. *On the wall.* That he may be free from the noise of family business and enjoy that privacy which, I perceive, he desires for his prayers and meditations. *A bed.* He will not be troublesome or chargeable to us. He cares not for rich furniture or costly entertainment and is content with bare necessaries.

16. *Do not lie.* Do not delude me with vain hopes. She could not believe it for joy.

21. *Bed of the man of God.* Being apt to believe that he who so soon took away what he had given would restore what he had taken away. By this faith "women received their dead raised to life." In this faith she makes no preparation for the burial of her child, but for his resurrection.

26. *It is.* So it was in some respects because it was the will of a wise and good God and therefore best for her.

When God calls away our dearest relations by death, it becomes us to say, it is well both with us and them. It is well, for all is well that God does. All is well with them who are gone if they are gone to heaven. And all is well with us who stay behind if by the affliction we are furthered in our way there.

33. *Shut the door.* Upon himself and the dead child, that he might pray to God without distraction and might more freely use those means which he thought fit.

34. *Waxed warm.* Not by any external heat, which could not be transmitted to the child's body by such slight touches of the prophet's body, but from a principle of life which was already infused into the child and by degrees enlivened all the parts of his body.

35. *He . . . walked.* He changed his postures for his own necessary refreshment and walked to and fro, exercising his mind in prayer to God. *And went.* Repeating his former actions to teach us not to be discouraged in our prayers if we be not speedily answered. *Opened his eyes.* So the work begun in the former verse is here perfected. Although miracles were for the most part done in an instant, yet sometimes they were done by degrees.

CHAPTER 5

10. *Elisha sent.* Which he did, partly to exercise Naaman's faith and obedience; partly for the honor of his religion, that it might appear he sought not his own glory and profit, but only God's honor and the good of men.

16. *He refused.* Not that he thought it unlawful to receive presents, which he did receive from others, but because of the special circumstances of the case; this being much for the honor of God that the Syrians should see the generous piety, the kindness of his ministers and servants, and how much they despised all that worldly wealth and glory which the prophets of the Gentiles so greedily sought after.

20. *Gehazi.* One would expect that Elisha's servant should have been a saint. But we find him far otherwise. The best men, the best ministers, have often had those about them that were their grief and shame.

26. What a folly is it to presume upon sin in hopes of secrecy? When you go aside into any bypath, does not your own conscience go with you? No, does not the eye of God go with you? What then avails the absence of human witnesses?

27. Those who get money by any way displeasing to God make a dear purchase. What was Gehazi profited by his two talents when he lost his health, if not his soul, for ever?

CHAPTER 6

16. *They.* Angels, unspeakably more numerous; God, infinitely more powerful.

17. *He saw.* Fire is both dreadful and devouring. That power which was engaged for Elisha could both terrify and consume the assailants. Elijah gave a specimen of divine justice when he called for flames of fire on the heads of his persecutors to consume them. Elisha gives a specimen of divine mercy in heaping coals of fire on the heads of his persecutors to melt them.

33. *Evil.* This dreadful famine, which is now so extreme that women are forced to eat their own children. *The Lord.* Has inflicted it, and (for ought I see) he will not remove it. All penal evil is of the Lord, as the first cause and sovereign judge. And this we ought to apply to particular cases. If all evil, then this evil which we are groaning under.

Whoever are the instruments, God is the principal agent. *What should I.* You bid me wait upon God for help; but I perceive I may wait long enough before deliverance comes. I am weary with waiting, I can wait no longer.

CHAPTER 7

7. *Fled.* None of them had so much sense as to send scouts to discover the supposed enemy, much less courage enough to face them. God can, when he pleases, dispirit the boldest and make the stoutest heart to tremble. They that will not fear God, he can make them fear at the shaking of a leaf. Perhaps Gehazi was one of these lepers, which might occasion his being taken notice of by the king (8:4).

20. *And so it fell out.* See how heinously God resents our distrust of his power, providence, and promise! Whenever God promises the end, he knows where to provide the means.

CHAPTER 8

1. *The Lord.* Has appointed to bring a famine. This expression intimates that all afflictions are sent by God and come at his call or command. *Seven years.* A double time to the former famine under Elijah, which is but just, because they were still incorrigible under all the judgments of God and the powerful ministry of Elisha.

8. Among other instances of the change of men's minds by affliction or sickness, this is one: that it often gives them other thoughts of God's ministers and teaches them to value those whom they before hated and despised.

13. *King.* And when you shall have power in your hand, you will discover that bloody disposition and that hatred against God's people which now lies hid from others and possibly from yourself.

19. *Alway.* Until the coming of the Messiah; for so long, and not longer, this succession might seem necessary for the making good of God's promise and covenant made with David. But when the Messiah was once come, there was no more need of any succession, and the scepter might and did without any inconvenience depart from Judah and from all the succeeding branches of David's family, because the Messiah was to hold the kingdom for ever in his own person, though not in so gross a way as the carnal Jews imagined.

CHAPTER 9

7. *I may avenge.* That they were idolaters was bad enough; yet that is not mentioned here. The controversy God has with them is for being persecutors. Nothing fills the measure of the iniquity of any prince so as this does, nor brings a surer or sorer ruin.

11. *Mad fellow.* They perceived him to be a prophet by his clothing, gestures, and manner of speech. And these profane soldiers esteemed the prophets madmen. Those that have no religion commonly speak of those that are religious with disdain, and look upon them as crack-brained. They said of our Lord, "He is beside himself"; of St. Paul, that "much learning doth make thee mad." The highest wisdom is thus represented as folly, and they that best understand themselves, as men beside themselves.

21. *Portion of Naboth.* The very sight of that ground was enough to make Jehu triumph and Joram tremble. The circumstances of events are sometimes so ordered by divine providence as to make the punishment answer the sin, as face answers face in a mirror.

CHAPTER 10

18. *Jehu . . . said.* These words, being manifestly false and spoken with a design to deceive, cannot be excused, this being an unmovable principle, that we must not do the least evil that the greatest good may come.

29. *Jehu departed not.* So it is plain that his religion was but superficial. Otherwise it would not have given way to his policy.

CHAPTER 11

2. *They hid.* Now was the promise made to David bound up in one life. And yet it did not fail. Thus to the Son of David will God, according to his promise, secure a spiritual seed; which though sometimes reduced to a small number, brought very low and seemingly lost, yet will be preserved to the end of time. It was a special providence that Joram, though a king, a wicked king, married his daughter to Jehoiada, a priest, a holy priest. This some might think a disparagement to the royal family, but it saved the royal family from ruin. For Jehoiada's interest in the temple gave her an opportunity to preserve the child; and her interest in the royal family gave him an opportunity of setting him on the throne. See what blessings they lay up in store for their families who marry their children to those who are wise and good.

12. *Testimony.* The book of the law which he put into the king's hand to remind him of his duty at his entrance upon his kingdom, which was to read and write out that holy book (Deut. 17:18) and to govern himself and his kingdom by it. The law of God being frequently and most properly called a *testimony* because it is a witness of God's will and man's duty.

CHAPTER 12

4. *And Jehoash said.* Remembering that he owed his preservation and restoration to the temple and that he was made by God the guardian of his temple, he now takes care to repair it.

20. *And slew Joash.* We are told in the Chronicles that his murdering the prophet, Jehoiada's son, was the provocation. In this, however unrighteous they were, yet the Lord was righteous. And this was not the only time that he let even kings know it was at their peril if they touched his anointed or did his prophets any harm. Thus fell Joash, who began in the Spirit and ended in the flesh. And indeed, God usually sets marks of his displeasure upon apostates, even in this life.

CHAPTER 13

14. *Fallen sick.* He lived long; for it was sixty years since he was first called to be a prophet. It was a great mercy to Israel and especially to the sons of the prophets that he was continued so long as a burning and a shining light. Elijah finished his testimony in the fourth part of that time. God's prophets have their day set them, long or shorter, as infinite wisdom sees fit. But all the latter part of his time, from the anointing of Jehu, which was forty-five years before Joash began his reign, we find no mention of him or of anything he did until we find him here upon his deathbed.

23. *Had compassion.* The slowness of God's process against sinners, even when they remain impenitent, must be construed to the advantage of his mercy, not to the impeachment of his justice.

CHAPTER 14

4. *High places.* It is hard to get clear of those corruptions which by long usage have gained prescription.

8. *Sent.* This challenge he sent from self-confidence and from a desire to advance his glory. But he that is fond either of fighting or going to law will probably be the first to repent of it.

10. *Glory.* Content yourself with that glory and let not your ambition betray you to ruin.

29. *Jeroboam.* It was in the reign of this Jeroboam that Hosea began to prophesy, and he was the first to write his prophecies. Amos prophesied at the same time, soon after Micah, and then Isaiah in the days of Ahaz and Hezekiah. Thus God never left himself without witness, but in the darkest ages of the church raised up some to be burning and shining lights to their own age, by their preaching and living; and a few by their writings to reflect light upon us on whom the ends of the world are come.

CHAPTER 15

13. *Full month.* That dominion seldom lasts long which is founded in blood and falsehood.

30. *Twentieth year.* The meaning is that he began his reign in the twentieth year after the beginning of Jotham's reign; or, which is the same thing, in the fourth year of Ahaz, son of Jotham.

33. *Reign.* Alone; he had reigned before this as his father's deputy.

CHAPTER 16

7. *Sent messengers.* But was it because there was no God in Israel that he sent to the Assyrian for help? The sin itself was its own punishment. For though it served his present turn, yet he made but an ill bargain, seeing he not only impoverished himself, but enslaved both himself and his people.

14. *And put.* So he put God's altar out of its place and use! A bolder stroke than the very worst of kings had before given to religion.

15. Having thrust it out from the use for which it was instituted, which was to sanctify the gifts offered upon it, he pretends to advance it above its institution, which it is common for superstitious people to do. But to overdo is to underdo. Our wisdom is to do just what God has commanded.

CHAPTER 17

6. *Carried Israel away.* There, we have reason to think, after some time they were so mingled with nations that they were lost, and "the name of Israel [was] no more in remembrance." They who forgot God were themselves forgotten, and they who studied to be like the nations were buried among them. Thus ended Israel as a nation. When we read of their entry into Canaan under Hoshea, the son of Nun, who would have thought that such would be their exit under Hosea, the son of Elah?

Yet we find James writing "to the twelve tribes . . . scattered abroad." So that though we never read of the return of those who were carried captive, nor have any ground to believe that they still remain a distinct body in some remote corner of the world, yet a remnant of them did escape and will remain until "all Israel shall be saved."

13. *Seers.* To whom he declared his mind by revelations and visions, and by whom he published it, bearing witness from heaven to their doctrine by eminent and glorious miracles.

14. *Hardened.* Refused to submit their neck to the yoke of God's precepts. A metaphor from stubborn oxen that will not bow to the yoke.

15. *Vanity.* Idols; so called because of their nothingness, impotency, and unprofitableness. And by the long worship of idols they were made like them, vain, sottish, and senseless creatures.

16. *Left all.* They grew worse and worse; from a partial disobedience to some of God's laws, they fell by degrees to a total apostasy from all.

20. *All the seed of Israel.* All the tribes of Israel; first one part of them, and now the rest. But this extends not to every individual person of these tribes; for many of them moved into the kingdom of Judah and were associated with them.

21. *A great sin.* So the worship of the calves is called, to meet with that idle conceit of the Israelites, who esteemed it a small sin, especially when they were forced to it by severe penalties; which yet he shows did not excuse it from being a sin, and a great sin too.

34. *Unto this day.* That is, until the time when this book was written, above three hundred years in all, until the time of Alexander the Great when they were prevailed upon to cast away their idols. *They fear not.* Though they pretended to fear and serve both the Lord and idols, yet in truth they did not and do not fear or worship the Lord, but their own calves or other vain inventions. And God will not accept that false worship which they pretend to give to the true God.

CHAPTER 18

19. *Thus saith.* But what are the greatest men when they come to compare with God, or when God comes to contend with them?

21. *This bruised reed.* Whoever trusts in man leans on a broken reed; but God is the rock of ages.

22. *Is not.* Thus boldly he speaks of the things which he understood not, judging the great God by their petty gods; and of God's worship by the vain fancies of the heathens, who measured piety by the multitude of altars.

25. *Am I.* He neither owned God's

word nor regarded his providence; but he forged this to strike a terror into Hezekiah and the people.

CHAPTER 19

1. *Rent his clothes.* Great men must not think it any disparagement to them to sympathize with the injured honor of the great God.

3. *The children.* We are like a poor travailing woman in great extremity, having no strength left to help herself and to bring forth her infant into the world. We have attempted to deliver ourselves from the Assyrian yoke; and had carried on that work to some maturity, and as we thought, brought it to the birth; but now we have no might to finish. We have begun a happy reformation and are hindered by this insolent Assyrian from bringing it to perfection.

21. *Virgin.* So he calls Zion, or Jerusalem, because she was pure in good measure from that gross idolatry with which other people were defiled, which is called spiritual whoredom. And to signify that God would defend her from the rape which Sennacherib intended to commit upon her with no less care than parents do their virgin daughters from those who seek to force and deflower them.

27. *I know.* Although you do not know me, yet I thoroughly know you and all your designs and actions, all your secret contrivances in the place of *thy abode,* in your own kingdom and court; and the execution of your designs abroad, what you intend in *thy going out,* and with what further thoughts you come in or return to your own land.

28. *My hook.* What a comfort it is that God has a hook in the nose and a bridle in the jaws of all his and our enemies.

31. *The zeal.* Although when you reflect upon yourselves and consider either your present fewness, weakness, or your great unworthiness, they may seem too great a blessing for you to expect; yet God will do it from the zeal which he has both for his own name and for the good of his undeserving people.

35. *Angel.* Such an angel as destroyed the firstborn of Egypt.

36. *So Sennacherib.* The manner of the expression intimates the great disorder and distraction of mind he was in.

37. *Was worshipping.* The God of Israel had done enough to convince him that he was the only true God. Yet he persists in his idolatry. Justly then is his blood mingled with his sacrifices, who will not be convinced by so dear-bought a demonstration of his folly in worshipping idols.

CHAPTER 20

3. *Wept.* For that horror of death which is and was common to men, especially in the times of the Old Testament, when the grace of God in Christ was not so fully manifested as now it is. And for the distracted condition in which the church and state were then likely to be left, through the uncertainty of the succession to the crown.

6. *Fifteen years.* We have not an example of any other who was told beforehand just how long he should live. God has wisely kept us at uncertainties that we may be always ready.

11. *Degrees.* These degrees were lines in the dial. But whether each of these lines or degrees noted an hour, or half an hour, or a quarter of an hour is uncertain. But the sun itself went back, and the shadow with it. This miracle was noted by the Babylonians, who, having understood that it was done for

Hezekiah's sake, sent to enquire into the truth and manner of it (II Chron. 32:31).

13. *Shewed.* Which he did through "the pride of his heart" (II Chron. 32:25–26), being lifted up by the great honor which God had done him in working such glorious miracles for his sake, and by the great respects rendered to him from many princes and now by this great Babylonian monarch. So hard a matter is it even for a good man to be high and humble.

19. *Good is.* I heartily submit to this sentence as being both just and merciful. True penitents, when they are under divine rebukes, call them not only just but good; not only submit to but accept the punishment of their iniquity. So Hezekiah did, and by this it appeared he was indeed humbled for the pride of his heart.

CHAPTER 21

9. *More evil.* Partly because they were not content with those idols which the Canaanites worshipped, but either invented or borrowed from other nations many new idols. And partly because as their light was far more clear, their obligations to God infinitely higher, and their helps against idolatry much stronger than the Canaanites had; so their sins, though the same in kind, were unspeakably worse in respect of these dreadful aggravations.

16. *His sin.* His idolatry, which is called sin by way of eminence. The tradition of the Jews is that Manasseh caused Isaiah to be sawn asunder.

21. *He walked.* Amon revived that idolatry which Manasseh in the latter end of his reign had put down. Those who set bad examples, if they repent themselves, cannot be sure that they whom their example has drawn into sin will repent. It is often otherwise.

CHAPTER 22

8. *The book.* That original *book of the law of the LORD,* given or written by the hand of Moses (II Chron. 34:14), which by God's command was put beside the ark (Deut. 31:26) and probably taken from there and hid by the care of some godly priest.

11. *The words.* The dreadful condemnations against them for the sins still reigning among the people. If Josiah had seen and read it before, which seems more probable, yet the great reverence which he justly bare to the original book and the strange, remarkable, and seasonable finding of it had awakened and quickened him to a more serious and diligent consideration of all the passages contained in it. And that it was still preserved!

Yes, what a providence that the whole book of God is preserved to us. If the Holy Scriptures had not been of God, they would not be in existence today. God's care of the Bible is a plain proof of his interest in it.

14. *College.* Where the sons of the prophets, or others who devoted themselves to the study of God's word, used to meet and discuss of the things of God and receive the instructions of their teachers.

15. *The man.* She used no compliments. *Tell the man that sent you.* Even kings, though gods to us, are men to God and shall be so dealt with; for with him there is no respect of persons.

19. *Tender.* He trembled at God's word. He was grieved for the dishonor done to God by the sins of his people. He was afraid of the judgments of God which he saw coming on Jerusalem. This is tenderness of heart.

CHAPTER 23

2. It seems he read it himself. Josiah did not think it beneath him to be a reader, any more than Solomon did to be a preacher and David to be even "a doorkeeper" in the house of God. All people are concerned to know the Scripture; and all in authority, to spread the knowledge of it.

3. *Stood.* They declared their consent to it and their concurrence with the king in that act, which possibly they did by standing up, as the king himself stood when he took it. It is of good use, with all possible solemnity, to oblige ourselves to our duty. And he that bears an honest heart does not startle at assurances.

7. *Sodomites.* Sodomy was a part of idol worship, being done to the honor of some of their idols and by the appointment of those impure and diabolical spirits which were worshipped in their idols.

8. *The governor.* This circumstance is noted to show Josiah's great zeal and impartiality in rooting out all monuments of idolatry without any respect to those great persons who were concerned in them.

12. *The top.* Upon the roof of the king's house. They were so caught up with their idols that they were not content with all their public high places and altars, but made others upon their housetops for the worship of the heavenly bodies.

14. *Men.* Of the idolatrous priests which he caused to be taken out of their graves (v. 18). As he carried the ashes of the images to the graves to mingle them with dead men's bones to the places where the images had been, that both ways idolatry might be rendered loathsome. Dead men and dead gods were indeed much alike and fit to go together.

16. *Himself.* Josiah's care and zeal was so great that he would not trust his officers with these things, but would see them done with his own eyes.

22. *Such a passover.* None of the kings had taken such care to prepare themselves, the priests, and people, and accurately to observe all the rites, and diligently to purge out all uncleanness, and to renew their covenant with God. And undoubtedly God was pleased to recompense their zeal in destroying idolatry with uncommon tokens of his presence and favor. All this concurred to make it such a Passover as had not been even in the days of Hezekiah.

25. *No king.* For his diligent study in God's law and his exact care, unwearied industry, and fervent zeal in rooting out idolaters, and all kinds and appearances of idolatry, not only in Judah, but in Israel also. And in the establishment of the true religion in all his dominions, and in the conforming of his own life and his people's (as far as he could), to the holy law of God; though Hezekiah might excel him in some particulars.

26. *Notwithstanding.* Because though the king was most hearty in his repentance and acceptable to God, and therefore the judgment was delayed for this time, yet the people were generally corrupt and secretly averse to Josiah's pious reformation. This appears from the complaints of the prophets, especially Jeremiah and Zephaniah, against them. And by the following history, wherein we see that as soon as Josiah was gone, his children, the princes, and the people suddenly and greedily returned to their former abominations.

29. *Slew.* Gave him his death wound there, though he did not die until he came to Jerusalem. *Seen him.* When he fought with him, or in the first onset. It does not appear that Josiah had any clear call to engage in this war; possibly he received his death wound as a punishment for his rashness.

CHAPTER 24

12. *Went out.* Yielded up himself and the city into his hands; and this by the counsel of Jeremiah, and to his own good. Had he made his peace with God and taken the method that Hezekiah did in the like case, he needed not to have feared the king of Babylon, but might have held out with courage, honor, and success. But lacking the faith and piety of an Israelite, he had not the resolution of a man.

20. *Came to pass.* Thus the people's sins were the true cause why God gave them wicked kings whom he allowed to do wickedly, that they might bring the long-deserved and threatened punishment on themselves and their people.

CHAPTER 25

3. Now they eat their own children for want of food (Lam. 4:3). Jeremiah in this extremity earnestly persuaded the king to surrender, but his heart was hardened to his destruction.

7. *Slew.* Though they were but children, that this spectacle, the last he was to behold, might leave a remaining impression of grief and horror upon his spirit. And in slaying his sons they in effect declared that the kingdom was no more, and that neither he nor any of his breed were fit to be trusted; therefore not fit to live.

8. *Months.* So the Chaldeans did not put all to fire and sword as soon as they had taken the city; but about a month after, orders were sent to complete the destruction of it. The space God gave them to repent after all the foregoing days of his patience. But in vain; they still hardened their hearts. Therefore, execution is awarded to the utmost.

9. *Burnt the house of the LORD.* One of the apocryphal writers tells us that Jeremiah got the ark out of the temple

and conveyed it to a cave in Mount Nebo (II Macc. 2:4–5). But this is like the other tales of that author, who has no regard either to truth or probability. For Jeremiah was at this time a close prisoner. By the burning of the temple God would show how little he cares for the outward pomp of his worship when the life and power of religion are gone. For about four hundred and thirty years the temple of Solomon had stood. And it is observed by Josephus that the second temple was burnt by the Romans, the same month and the same day of the month that the first temple was burnt by the Chaldeans.

12. *Left of the poor.* So while the rich were prisoners in a strange land, the poor had liberty and peace in their own country! Thus Providence sometimes humbles the proud and favors them of low degree.

21. *Out of their land.* This completed their calamity, about eight hundred and sixty years after they were put in possession of it by Joshua.

24. *Sware.* Assured them by his promise and oath that they should be kept from the evils which they feared. This he might safely swear because he had not only the king of Babylon's promise, but also God's promise delivered by Jeremiah. And it might seem that a fair prospect was opening again. How soon was the scene changed! This hopeful settlement is quickly dashed in pieces, not by the Chaldeans, but by some of themselves.

30. *All the days of his life.* Let none say they shall never see good again because they have long seen little but evil. The most afflicted know not what blessed turn providence may yet give to their affairs.

1 chronicles

CHAPTER 1

1. The great promise of the Messiah was transmitted from Adam to Seth, from him to Shem, from him to Eber, and so to the Jewish nation who were instructed above all nations with that sacred treasure until the promise was performed and the Messiah was come. And then that nation was made "not a people."

14. *The Jebusite.* The names which follow until verse 17 are not the names of particular persons, but of people or nations.

28. *The sons of Abraham.* All nations but the seed of Abraham are already shaken off from this genealogy. Not that we conclude no particular persons of any other nation but this found favor with God. Multitudes will be brought to heaven "out of every nation," and we may hope there were many, very many people in the world whose names were in the book of life, though they did not spring from the loins of Abraham.

54. *These are the dukes of Edom.* Let us, in reading these genealogies, consider the multitudes which have gone through the world, have successively acted their parts in it, and retired into darkness. All these and all theirs had their day. Many of them made a mighty noise in the world until their day came to fall, and their place knew them no more. The paths of death are trodden paths. How soon are we to tread them?

CHAPTER 2

6. *Dara.* If these be the same who are mentioned as the sons of Machol (I Kings 4:31), either the same man had two names (Zerah and Machol), as was usual among the Hebrews; or one of these was their immediate father and the other their grandfather. These are named because they were the glory of their father's house. When the Holy Ghost would magnify the wisdom of Solomon, he said, he "was wiser than" these four men. That four brothers should be so eminent was a rare thing.

CHAPTER 3

16. *Zedekiah.* This was another Zedekiah. How seldom has a crown gone in a direct line, from father to son, as it did here for seventeen generations! This was the recompense of David's piety. About the time of the captivity, the lineal descent was interrupted and the crown went from a nephew to an uncle, a foretaste of the glory's departing from that house.

CHAPTER 4

9. *Honourable.* For courage and for fervent piety. She records this that it might be a memorandum to herself to be thankful to God as long as she lived for bringing her through that sorrow. And a memorandum to him that she bore him into a vale of tears, in which he might expect "few days and full of trouble." And the sorrow in his name might serve to put a seriousness upon his spirit.

23. *The king.* Of Babylon; esteeming it a greater honor to serve that earthly monarch in the meanest employments than to serve the King of Kings in his temple.

40. *Fat pasture.* Those who thus dwelt (as we do) in a fruitful country, and whose land is wide and quiet and peaceable, have reason to feel indebted to that God who appoints the bounds of our habitation.

CHAPTER 5

10. *They made war.* Thus God did for his people as he promised them. He cast out the enemy from before them by little and little and gave them their land as they had occasion for it.

22. *Was of God.* Undertaken in his fear and carried on in a dependence on him. Then we may expect to prosper in any enterprise, and then only when we take God along with us.

CHAPTER 6

54. *Castles.* Thus called, not only because they were walled and well guarded by the country, but because they and their possessions were in a particular manner the care of divine providence. As God was their portion, so God was their protector. And a cottage will be a castle to those who abide under the shadow of the Almighty.

CHAPTER 7

23. *Bare a son.* Thus the breach was in some measure repaired by the addition of another son in his old age. When God thus restores comfort to his mourners, he makes glad according to the days wherein he afflicted; setting the mercies over against the crosses, we ought to observe the kindness of his providence. Yet the joy that a man was born into his family could not make him forget his grief. For he gives a melancholy name to his son, Beriah, that is, "in trouble." For he was born when the family was in mourning. It is good to remember the affliction and the misery which are past, that our souls may be humbled within us.

CHAPTER 8

28. *Heads of the fathers.* Particular notice is taken of these, that others at their return from captivity might be induced to settle there, too, which it seems few were willing to do, because it was the post of danger. Many great and mighty nations were then upon earth, and many illustrious men in them whose names are buried in perpetual oblivion, while the names of multitudes of the Israel of God are here carefully preserved in everlasting remembrance. This is a figure of God's writing the names of his spiritual Israel in the Lamb's book of life.

CHAPTER 9

4. *Ammihud.* That there is so great a diversity of names between this catalogue and that of Nehemiah 11 may be ascribed to two causes. (1) To the custom of the Hebrews, who frequently gave several names to one person. (2) To the change of times; for here they are named who came up at the first return, while many of those in Nehemiah might be such as returned afterward and came and dwelt, either instead of the persons here named or with them.

21. Before the temple was built they had a lowly and movable tent which they made use of in the meantime. They who cannot yet have a temple, let them be thankful for a tabernacle and make the best use of it. Never let God's work be left undone for the lack of a place to do it in.

33. *Chambers.* So that they might be ready to come whenever they were called to the service of God in the tabernacle. *Free.* From all trouble and employment, that they might wholly attend upon the proper work. *That work.* Either composing or ordering sacred songs; or actually singing, or teaching others to sing them. *Day and night.* Continually, and particularly in the morning and evening, the two times appointed for solemn service. Thus was God continually praised, as it is fit he should be who is continually doing us good.

CHAPTER 10

1. *The men of Israel fled.* Thus princes sin and the people suffer for it. No doubt there was enough in them to deserve it. But that which divine justice had chiefly an eye to was the sin of Saul. Great men should especially take heed of provoking God's wrath. For if they kindle that fire, they know not how many may be consumed by it for their sakes.

10. *Temple of Dagon.* If we give not God the glory of our successes, even Philistines will rise up in judgment with us and condemn us. Shall Dagon have

so great a place in their triumphs and the true God be forgotten in ours?

14. *Enquired not.* He did in some sort, but not in a right manner, not humbly and penitently, not diligently and importunately, not patiently and perseveringly. Nor till he was brought to the last extremity. And then it was too late.

CHAPTER 11

10. *Mighty men.* Yet David ascribed his success not to the hosts he had, but to the Lord of Hosts; not to the mighty men that were with him, but to the mighty God whose presence with us is all in all.

18. *Would not drink of it.* That water which he thought too precious for his own drinking he "poured out to the LORD" for a drink offering. If we have anything better than something else, let God, who is the best and should have the best, be honored with it.

CHAPTER 12

2. *Even.* Of Saul's own tribe. Who were moved here by God's Spirit, by the conscience of their duty to David, and by their observation of God's departure from Saul and of his special presence with David.

18. *The spirit.* Not only the saving graces, but other heroical and generous motions are ascribed to God's Spirit, which here stirred up in him a more than ordinary greatness of mind and resolution.

33. *Double heart.* They were sincerely loyal to David and did not pretend to be for him while in their hearts they favored Saul's family. And none had any separate interests, but all were for the public good.

CHAPTER 13

3. *For.* The ark was then neglected, and most of the people contented themselves with going to Gibeon and offering sacrifices there, not caring that the ark, the soul of the tabernacle, was in another place. As soon as David had power in his hand, he would use it for the advancement of religion. It ought to be the first care of those who are enriched or preferred to honor God with their honors and to serve him and the interests of his kingdom among men with their wealth and power.

10. *Put his hand.* Let the case of Uzza warn us to take heed of presumption or rashness with regard to holy things; and not to think that a right intention will justify a wrong action.

11. *Perez-uzza.* That is, the breach of Uzza. Let David's displeasure on this occasion caution us to watch over our spirit lest when God reproves us, instead of submitting to God, we quarrel with him. If God be angry with us, shall we dare to be angry with him?

14. *And the* Lord *blessed.* Let this encourage us to welcome God's ordinance into our houses, believing the ark is a guest no one shall lose by. Nor let it be the less precious to us for its being to others a rock of offense.

CHAPTER 14

David is confirmed in his kingdom (vv. 1–2); his wives and children are listed (vv. 3–7); and we are told of his victories over the Philistines (vv. 8–17).

CHAPTER 15

20. *On Alamoth.* Or, "with Alamoth," which is thought to be the name of an instrument of music; or of a certain tune or note or part in music.

The certain significance of it is not now known; and the like may be said of Sheminith (v. 21).

21. *To excel.* Which word may be added to note the excellence of that instrument or part of music; or that there was a greater extension or elevation of the voice than in the former. This way of praising God by musical instruments had not been in use before this time. But David instituted it by divine direction and added it to the other ordinances of that dispensation.

22. *For song.* He was the moderator of the music, instructing them when and how to lift up their voices or change their notes or make their stops.

26. *Helped.* Encouraging them in their work with some comfortable sign of his presence with them. In all our religious exercises we must derive help from heaven. God's ministers who bare the vessels of the Lord have special need of divine help in their ministrations, that God may be glorified thereby and the people edified.

CHAPTER 16

4. *To thank and praise.* All our rejoicings should express themselves in thanksgivings to him from whom all our comforts are received.

35. *From the heathen.* This psalm or prayer was made by David for the use of the church, not only in that present time but in future ages in which David foresaw, by the spirit of prophecy, that the Israelites would forsake God and for their apostasy be dispersed among the heathens. In the midst of our praises we must not forget to pray for those servants of God who are in distress. When we are rejoicing in God's favors we should remember our afflicted brethren and pray for their deliverance as our own. We are members one of another.

37. *He left.* He appointed them their work and station there. Indeed, no incense was burnt there, nor sacrifices offered because the altars were not there. But David's prayers were directed "as incense; and the lifting up of [his] hands as the evening sacrifice." So early did spiritual worship take place of ceremonial.

40. *Which he commanded Israel.* These must be kept up because, however in their own nature they were inferior to prayer and praise, yet as they were types of the mediation of Christ, the observance of them was of mighty importance.

42. *Of God.* Appropriated to the worship of God, not such as they used on other occasions. Between common mirth and holy joy there is a vast difference. And the limits and distances between them must be carefully kept.

CHAPTER 17

14. *Kingdom.* In God's kingdom in a large and general sense. And this, as well as the former phrase, singularly belongs to the Messiah, who was not only to be the king of Israel, but also of all nations. This is an intimation of that great mystery which is more fully revealed in the New Testament, namely, that Christ is the head or king of all God's church, consisting of Jews and Gentiles and of all nations; and indeed of all creatures, all which is God's kingdom and by him given to his Son, our blessed Lord.

16. *Who am I.* We have here David's solemn address to God in answer to his gracious message. How humbly does he here abase himself and acknowledge his own unworthiness! How highly does he advance the name of God and admire his condescending favor! With what devout affections does he magnify the God of Israel! With what assurance

does he build upon the promise! What an example is this of believing, fervent prayer! The Lord enable us all thus to seek him.

18. *The honour of thy servant.* The honor God puts upon his servants by taking them into covenant and communion with himself is so great that they need not, they cannot, desire to be more highly honored.

27. *Blessed for ever.* David's prayer concludes as God's promise did (v. 14), with that which is for ever. God's word looks at things eternal. And so should our desires and hopes.

CHAPTER 18

David conquers the Philistines, the Moabites, the king of Zobah, and the Syrians (vv. 1–8). David makes the king of Hamath and the Edomites pay tribute (vv. 9–13). David's court and kingdom flourish (vv. 14–17).

CHAPTER 19

19. *His servants.* Let those who have in vain stood it out against God be thus wise. Let them become *his servants*; for they are undone if they remain his enemies.

CHAPTER 20

8. *They fell.* We need not fear great men against us while we have the great God for us.

CHAPTER 21

1. *Satan stood.* Standing is the accuser's posture before men's tribunals. And therefore the Holy Scripture (which speaks of the things of God after the manner of men to bring them down to our capacities) elsewhere represents Satan in this posture.

3. God commonly punishes the people for the sins of their rulers, because they are for the most part guilty of their sins in one kind or other; or at least God takes this occasion to punish people for all their sins.

14. *There fell.* He was proud of the number of his people, but God took a course to make them fewer. Justly is that which we are proud of taken from us or embittered to us.

26. *By fire.* The sign of God's acceptance. The fire that might justly have fastened on the sinner fastened upon the sacrifice and consumed it. Thus Christ was made sin and a curse for us, and it pleased the Lord to bruise him that through him God might be to us, not a consuming fire, but a reconciled Father.

CHAPTER 22

5. *Prepared.* And good reason because it was intended for the honor of the great God and was to be a type of Christ in whom all fullness dwells and in whom are hid all treasures.

8. *Shed blood.* Not that wars are simply unlawful, but to teach us that the church (whereof the temple was an illustrious type) should be built by Christ, "the Prince of Peace" (Isa. 9:6), and that it should be gathered and built up, "not by might, nor by power, but by my spirit" (Zech. 4:6) and by the preaching of the gospel of peace. David therefore was less fit for that service than one who had not been called to such bloody work. Likewise, by setting him aside for this reason, God showed how precious human life is to him.

16. The sense of God's presence must not slacken our endeavors; because he is with us, we must *arise therefore, and be doing.* Then he will be with us even to the end. Work out your salvation, and God will work in you.

CHAPTER 23

2. To declare God's mind and his own will, that Solomon should be his successor. And to acquaint them with those directions which he had received from God by the Spirit.

CHAPTER 24

5. *By lot.* That the disposal thereof might be of the Lord and so all contention be prevented, as no man could be charged with partiality, nor could any say they had wrong done them. In like manner Matthias was chosen to the apostleship by lot with prayer. "And I know not," says Mr. Henry, "but it might be still used in faith, in parallel cases, as an instituted ordinance."

CHAPTER 25

1. *Workmen.* Of the persons employed in this sacred work. This good work it seems Samuel revived, but did not live to bring it to perfection. Let each in his day do what he can for God, though he cannot carry it so far as he would. When we are gone, God can raise up others to build on our foundation and bring forth the top stone.

CHAPTER 26

5. And a great blessing it is to have many children when they are like these, eminent in the service of God.

31. *Fortieth year.* His last year in which he made all the orders of families and officers recorded in these chapters. We should be so much the more diligent in doing good, "as ye see the day approaching." If we live not to enjoy the fruit of our labors, let us not grudge it to them that come after us.

CHAPTER 27

31. *All these.* It is observable, here are no officers for state, none for sport, no master of the ceremonies, or of the hounds, but all for substance, agreeable to the simplicity and plainness of those times. David was a great soldier, a great scholar, and a great prince. And yet a great husband of his estate. Those magistrates who would have their subjects industrious must themselves be examples of application to business.

33. *The king's counsellor.* The person whose counsel in matters of state the king most prized and followed. *Companion.* Of his friend (II Sam. 15:37), the person whom he trusted with his secrets, and whose conversation was most pleasant and acceptable to him. Observe that a cunning man was his counselor; but an honest man was his friend.

CHAPTER 28

2. *Footstool.* A house for the ark is here presented as a *house for the footstool of our God.* Heaven is his throne. The earth and the most magnificent temples thereon are but his footstool. So much difference is there between the manifestations of his glory in the upper and in the lower world!

6. *My house.* So was he a figure of him who was to come, who is both the founder and the foundation of the gospel-temple.

7. *At this day.* As he has begun. This promise is absolute with regard to the Messiah, but conditional with regard to Solomon. If we are constant in our duty, then, and not otherwise, we may expect the continuance of his favor.

8. *Keep and seek.* Keep those commands which you know, and *seek for,* or search into, what you are yet ignorant of, that you may distinctly understand the whole will of God and seriously give yourselves to the practice of it. God's commandments cannot be kept without great care.

9. *Searcheth.* If you do only put on a profession of religion to please me, or if your obedience to God be insincere, you may indeed deceive me; but you cannot deceive him, for he searches the motions of your heart.

10. *Be strong.* Take courage to break through all difficulties. Without this we can do no work of God as we ought.

12. *By the spirit.* All the particulars of the tabernacle built by Moses were suggested to him by God's Spirit, and it is not credible that God would use less care and exactness in the building of this far more glorious and durable work. All this, it seems, was given him in writing, probably by the ministry of an angel.

The temple was to be a sacred thing, a type of Christ, of his church, and of heaven. Therefore it was not to be contrived by man's invention, but to be framed by divine institution. So Christ, the true temple, the church, and the gospel-temple are all framed according to the divine counsels and the plan laid before the world began.

18. *Refined gold.* Purer than any of the rest. For that was typical of the intercession of Christ, than which nothing can be more pure and perfect.

19. *In writing.* God revealed this to some man of God who put it into writing to David. Or God, as it were, by his own hand (wherewith he wrote the Ten Commandments), wrote these things upon the table of his mind.

20. *My God.* Whom I have chosen and served, who has all along been with me and prospered me, I recommend you to him. He will be with you to strengthen, direct, and prosper you. The God who owned our fathers and carried them through the services of their day will, in like manner, if we are faithful to him, go along with us in our day and will never fail us. God never leaves any unless they first leave him.

CHAPTER 29

2. *My might.* Work for God must be done with all our might, or we shall bring nothing to pass in it.

5. *To consecrate.* To offer an offering, as I have done. Hebrew: "To fill his hand unto the Lord." They that engage themselves in the service of God will have their hands full. There is work enough for the whole man in that service.

9. *Great joy.* To see the work, which his heart was so much set upon, likely to go on. It is a great reviving to good men, when they are leaving the world, to see those they leave behind zealous for the work of God.

10. The nearer we come to the land of everlasting praise, the more we should speak the language and do the work of that world.

14. *Of thine.* We return only what we have received and therefore only pay a debt to you. The more we do for God, the more we are indebted to him for the honor of being employed in his service and for grace enabling us in any measure to serve him.

18. *Keep this for ever.* Since it is from your grace that your people have such willing minds, continue that grace to them that they may persist in the same generous disposition towards you and your worship.

29. *The book.* In the chronicles of the kingdom which were written by Nathan and Gad, who were not only prophets but historiographers, out of which either they or some other prophets took by the direction of God's Spirit such passages as were most important and useful for the church in succeeding ages.

II Chronicles

CHAPTER 1

8. The eminence of those who went before us, and the obligation that lies upon us to keep and carry on the good work they were engaged in, should quicken our prayers for wisdom and grace that we may do the work of God in our day as faithfully as they did in theirs.

12. *Neither.* Those who make this world their end come short of the other, and frequently of this, too. But those who make the other world their end shall not only obtain that, but shall have as much as is convenient of this world in their way.

CHAPTER 2

6. *Contain.* When I speak of building a house for our great God, let none think I mean to comprehend God within it, for he is infinite.

CHAPTER 3

14. *The veil.* The inner veil before the most holy place. This denoted the darkness of that dispensation and the distance at which the worshippers were kept. But at the death of Christ this veil was rent; for through him we are brought nigh and have boldness, or liberty, not only to look, but "to enter into the holiest."

CHAPTER 4

16. *His father.* He is so called because Solomon usually called him by that name, out of that great respect which he had for him and for his excellent art and service which he did for him. It was usual to call great artists and inventors of things by this name.

CHAPTER 5

5. *The ark.* The ark was a type of Christ and a token of the presence of God. That gracious promise, "Lo, I am with you alway, even unto the end of the world," does in effect bring the ark into our religious assemblies if we claim it by faith and prayer. And this we should be earnest for. The temple itself, if Christ leave it, is a desolate place.

14. *Glory of the Lord.* And this beautified it more than all the gold with which it was overlaid or the precious stones with which it was garnished. Yet even that was no glory in comparison to the glory of the gospel dispensation.

CHAPTER 6

9. *But thy son.* Thus one sows and another reaps. And let not the wisest of men think it any disparagement to pursue the good designs which those who went before them had laid.

14. *O Lord.* By this prayer the temple of Solomon is made a figure of Christ, the great Mediator through whom we are to offer up all our prayers and to expect all God's favors, and to whom we are to have an eye in every thing we have to do with God.

21. *They shall make.* He asks not that God would help them without their praying for themselves, but that God would help them in answer to their prayers. Even Christ's intercession does not supersede but encourage our supplications.

42. *The mercies.* Those which you have promised to David and to his house for ever. And thus may we plead with an eye to Christ, who is called David (Hos. 3:5). Lord, remember his merits and accept us in account of them. Remember the promises of the everlasting covenant which are called "the sure mercies of David" (Isa. 55:3). This must be all our desire, all our hope, all our prayer, and all our plea; for it is all our salvation.

CHAPTER 7

1. *The fire.* In token of God's acceptance of his prayer. The surest evidence of God's acceptance of our prayers is the descent of his holy fire upon us. As a further token that God accepted Solomon's prayer, the glory of the Lord filled the house. The heart that is filled with a holy awe and reverence of the divine glory, to which God manifests his greatness and (which is no less his glory) his goodness, is thereby owned as a living temple.

CHAPTER 8

14. *Man of God.* A prophet inspired by God in these matters, whose commands therefore are the commands of God.

CHAPTER 9

8. *For the Lord.* In the Lord's name and stead, in a special manner because he sat in God's own throne and ruled over God's peculiar people and did in an eminent manner maintain the honor of God in his land and in the eyes of all the world. Those mercies are doubly sweet in which we can taste the kindness and good will of God as our God.

31. *And Solomon slept.* We have here Solomon in his throne and Solomon in his grave; for the throne could not secure him from the grave. Here is he stripped of his pomp, and leaving all his wealth and power; not to one whom he knew not "whether he shall be a wise man or a fool," but one he knew would be a fool! This was not only "vanity," but "vexation of spirit."

CHAPTER 10

7. *If thou be kind.* Moderate counsels are generally best. Gentleness will do what violence will not do. Good words cost nothing but a little self-denial, and yet they purchase great things.

16. *See to thine own house.* When public affairs are in a ferment, violent proceedings make matters worse. Many have been driven to the mischief they did not intend by being too severely dealt with.

CHAPTER 11

14. No secular advantages whatever should detain us where we are in danger of making shipwreck of faith and a good conscience.

17. *So they strengthened the kingdom of Judah.* Not only by the addition of so many persons to it, but by their piety and prayers they procured a blessing upon the kingdom which was a sanctuary to them. They made him strong *three years;* for so long he served God. But when he forsook God, none could strengthen him. We retain our strength as long as we cleave to God and our duty, and no longer.

And Solomon. This honorable mention of Solomon as a pattern of piety is a considerable evidence of his true repentance before his death.

CHAPTER 12

7. Those who acknowledge God is righteous in afflicting them shall find him gracious.

14. *Did evil.* Though he humbled himself for a season, yet he quickly relapsed into sin because his heart was not right with God.

CHAPTER 13

12. *The LORD.* You have not only us for your enemies, but God, even the God whom your fathers served. It is folly to fight against the God of almighty power. But it is base ingratitude to fight against your father's God.

15. *Gave a shout.* It is unspeakable comfort that no stratagem or ambush can cut off our communication with heaven. To the cry of prayer they added the shout of faith, and so became more than conquerors.

20. *The LORD struck him.* He escaped the sword of Abijah; but God struck him. There is no escaping his sword.

CHAPTER 14

6. *The land had rest.* Those have rest indeed to whom God gives rest; peace indeed to whom Christ gives peace. We find by experience that it is good to seek the Lord. While we pursue the world we meet with nothing but vexation.

CHAPTER 15

1. *Spirit of God.* Both to instruct him what to say and to enable him to say it plainly and boldly.

15. *All Judah rejoiced at the oath.* The times of renewing our covenant with God should be times of rejoicing. It is an honor and happiness to be in bonds with God. And the closer, the better.

CHAPTER 16

9. *Done foolishly.* It is a foolish thing to lean on a broken reed when we have the rock of ages to rely upon.

12. *Sought not.* He did not humble himself before God, but put his confidence in the skill and faithfulness of his physicians. His making use of physicians was his duty, but his trusting in them, and expecting that from them which was to be had from God only, was his sin and folly. The help of every creature must be used with an eye to the Creator and in dependence on him who makes every creature, without whom the most skillful and faithful are physicians of no value.

CHAPTER 17

10. *Fear of the LORD fell.* Just concluding from his singular piety that God would eminently appear for him, for even the heathens could not but observe that the kings of Judah were either prosperous or unhappy, according as they served God or forsook him.

CHAPTER 18

4. *Enquire.* This we should do whatever we undertake by particular, believing prayer, by an unbiased consulting of the Scriptures and our own consciences, and by a close regard to the hints of Providence.

21. *Lying spirit.* See the power of Satan! One lying spirit can make four hundred lying prophets. And thus he frequently becomes a murderer by being a liar and destroys men by deceiving them.

26. *This fellow.* How frequently has this been the lot of faithful ministers, to be hated and ill treated merely for being true to God and just and kind to the souls of men! But that day will declare who is in the right and who is in the wrong, when Christ appears to the unspeakable consolation of the persecuted and the everlasting confusion of their persecutors.

31. *Cried out.* Either to his friends to help, or to his enemies to let them know he was not the king of Israel; or to God, and not in vain; for *God moved* the captains *to depart from him.* Many are moved in a manner unaccountable both to themselves and others; but an invisible power moves them.

34. *He died.* What can hurt those whom God will protect? And what can shelter those whom God will destroy? Jehoshaphat is saved in his robes; Ahab is killed in his armor.

CHAPTER 19

3. *Good things.* Good works proceeding from an honest heart, which God more regards than this particular error. And therefore, though he will chasten you, yet he will not utterly destroy you.

4. *And brought them.* Many probably had revolted to idolatry when they saw the king so intimate with idolaters. Therefore he thought himself doubly obliged to do all he could to reduce them. If we truly repent of sin, we shall do our utmost to repair the damage we have done to religion or the souls of others.

6. *The LORD.* You represent God's person to whom judgment belongs; you have your commission from God and not from man only. And your administration of justice is not only for man's good, but also for God's honor and service.

7. *Wherefore.* And therefore you who are in God's stead and do his work and must give an account to him, must imitate God.

CHAPTER 20

12. *Wilt thou not judge them?* Will you not give sentence against them and execute it upon them? The justice of God is the refuge of those who are wronged.

13. *Little ones.* Whom they used to present before the Lord in times of great distress to stir up themselves to more fervent prayers, their eyes being upon their harmless and tender children, and to move God to compassion because God has declared that he will be prevailed with by such methods as these.

22. *To sing.* So acceptable are the fervent prayers of God's people to God, and so terrible to their enemies.

28. *Unto the house.* To renew their praises in the court of the temple, the proper and usual place for it. Praising God must not be the work of a day only, but our praises, when we have received mercy, must be often repeated as our prayers were when we were in pursuit of it. Every day we must bless God as long as we live, and while we have any being we must praise him, spending our time in that work in which we hope to spend our eternity.

CHAPTER 21

20. *Desired.* This is an emphatic expression, because it is usual with men to desire the deaths of some persons whom afterward they lament and heartily wish they were alive again. But for this ungodly and unhappy prince, the people did not only in his lifetime wish his death but afterwards did not repent of those desires.

CHAPTER 22

4. *His father.* Who, while he lived, seduced his son himself and made other evil counselors unnecessary.

CHAPTER 23

21. *Rejoiced.* The majority of the people rejoiced. The rest were quiet and made no opposition. When the Son of David is enthroned in the soul, all therein is quiet and springs of joy are opened.

CHAPTER 24

16. They buried him among the kings with this honorable epitaph (perhaps inscribed on his gravestone), that *he had done good in Israel.* But the little religion that Joash had was all buried in his grave. See how great a judgment to any prince or people that the death of a holy, useful man is!

18. *Left.* The king and princes that awhile ago so zealously repaired the temple now forsook the temple. So inconstant a thing is man! So little confidence is to be put in him!

CHAPTER 25

2. *But not.* He was not an enemy to religion, but a cool and indifferent friend. He was not a man of serious piety, for his heart was not whole with God.

7. *Let not.* It is comfortable to employ those whom we have reason to

hope have an interest in heaven, but dangerous associating with those from whom the Lord is departed.

16. *Art thou.* Who are you that presume to direct my affairs without my commission? The secure sinner perhaps values himself on having silenced his reprovers and monitors. But what comes of it? It is a plain indication he is marked out for ruin. They who are deaf to reproof are ripening themselves for destruction.

17. *He took advice.* But with whom? Not with the prophet, but with his flattering statesmen. It is good to take advice, but it should be of them who are fit to advise us.

CHAPTER 26

21. He thrust himself into the temple of God where the priest only had admission. And for that he was thrust out of the very courts of the temple into which the lowliest of his subjects might enter. He invaded the dignity of the priesthood to which he had no right and is for that deprived of the royal dignity to which he had an undoubted right.

CHAPTER 27

2. *He did.* We must not imitate those we have the greatest esteem for any further than we should. Their failings must be warnings to us to walk more circumspectly.

CHAPTER 28

6. *Forsaken.* Ahaz walked in the ways of the kings of Israel, and God chose the king of Israel for his scourge. It is just with God to make them a plague to us whom we have made our patterns or partners in sin.

10. *To keep under.* It ill becomes

sinners to be cruel. Show mercy to them, for you are undone unless God shows you mercy.

19. *Low.* As high as they were before in wealth and power. They who will not humble themselves under the word of God will be humbled by his judgments.

22. *That king Ahaz.* That monster and reproach of mankind, that unteachable and incorrigible prince whom even grievous afflictions made worse, which commonly make men better. This is he whose name deserves to be remembered and detested forever.

CHAPTER 29

4. Those who begin with God begin at the right end of their work; and it will prosper accordingly.

8. *Hissing.* To such calamities as all who see and hear of shall be astonished, and hiss at those who by their own sin and folly have brought such miseries upon themselves. When we are under the rebukes of God's providence, it is good for us to enquire whether we have not neglected God's ordinances and whether that be not the controversy he has with us.

17. *The first day.* A happy beginning of the new year! Thus should every year begin with the reformation of what is amiss and the purging away of all the defilements contracted the foregoing year.

19. *Sanctified.* Though the vessels of the sanctuary may be profaned for a while, God will find a time and a way to sanctify them. Neither his ordinances nor his obedient people shall be allowed to fail forever.

21. *Sanctuary.* They thought it not enough to lament and forsake their sins, but they brought a sin offering. Even our repentance and reformation will not obtain pardon but through

Christ, who was made sin—that is, a sin offering—for us.

27. *The song.* The psalms composed by David and Asaph. Even sorrow for sin must not put us out of tune for praising God. By faith we must even then rejoice in the Lord our righteousness, and our prayers and praises must ascend with his offering, to be accepted only in virtue of it.

36. *Rejoiced.* It was a very great and sudden change that the people, who but the other day were so ready to comply with wicked Ahaz in his idolatrous prescriptions, were now free and forward in God's service. By this it plainly appeared to be the work of God changing their hearts by his Holy Spirit.

CHAPTER 30

12. *The hand of God.* God by the power of his grace inclined their hearts to a unanimous compliance with God's and the king's will.

15. *Ashamed.* Their negligence and remissness being upbraided by the general forwardness of the people. The zeal we observe in others should make us ashamed of our own coldness and quicken us not only to do our duty, but to do it with our might.

19. The great thing required in our attendance on God's ordinances is that we prepare our heart to seek him, that the inward man be engaged, and that we make heart work of it. All is nothing without this.

CHAPTER 31

4. *Encouraged.* Freed from worldly cares and distractions and enabled to give up themselves entirely to the serious study of God's law and to the instruction and direction and quickening of the people.

8. *Blessed the* LORD. Both for giving such plentiful provisions to his land and for giving his people such liberal hearts. And they praised the people for their forwardness and faithfulness in it.

CHAPTER 32

1. *After.* An emphatic preface, signifying that in spite of all his zeal for God, God saw fit to exercise Hezekiah with a sore trial. And God ordered it at this time that he might have an opportunity of showing himself strong on the behalf of his returning people. It is possible that we may be in the way of our duty and yet meet with trouble and danger. God permits this for the trial of our confidence in him and the manifestation of his care over us.

21. *The* LORD *sent an angel.* The Jewish comment says the word of the Lord sent Gabriel to do this execution and that it was done with lightning and on the Passover night, the same night wherein the firstborn in Egypt were slain.

31. *Wonder that was done.* Either the destruction of the Assyrians, or the going back of the sun. These miracles were wrought to alarm and awaken a stupid, careless world, and to turn them from dumb and lame idols to the living God. *God left him.* To himself and allowed Satan to try him that he might know he had infirmities and sins as well as virtues. O what need have great men, good men, and useful men to study their own follies and infirmities and to beg earnestly of God that he would hide pride from them!

CHAPTER 33

12. *Besought.* It becomes sinners to humble themselves before that God whom they have offended. It becomes sufferers to humble themselves before him who corrects them and to accept the punishment of their iniquity.

17. *Still.* Manasseh could not carry the reformation so far as he had carried the corruption. It is an easy thing to debauch men's manners; but not so easy to reform them again.

CHAPTER 34

3. *Young.* In the sixteenth year of his age; when he was entering into the age of temptation and had the administration of his kingdom wholly in his own power, and none to restrain him. Even then he begins to be religious in good earnest.

19. *Rent his clothes.* Were the things contained in Scripture new to us, as they were here to Josiah, surely they would make deeper impressions upon us than they commonly do. But they are not the less weighty, and therefore should not be the less regarded, because they are well known.

33. *Even to serve.* The repetition shows that this was the only thing his heart was set upon. He aimed at nothing in all he did but to engage them to God and their duty.

CHAPTER 35

3. Ministers must look upon themselves as servants both to Christ and to the people for his sake. They must take care and take pains and lay themselves out to the utmost, both for the honor and glory of God and for the benefit of his people, not as having dominion over their faith, but as helpers of their holiness and joy.

20. *After all.* When he and his people hoped that God was reconciled and the foundation of a lasting happiness laid, their hopes were quickly blasted. So much are men often mistaken in their judgments about the designs of God's providence.

22. *Hearkened not.* How can we think to prosper in our ways if we do not acknowledge God in them!

25. *To this day.* In all their succeeding lamentations for their public calamities, they remembered Josiah's death as their first and fatal blow, which opened the floodgates to all other miseries.

CHAPTER 36

15. *Sending.* God sent them many prophets and messages, some at the very beginning of their apostasy and others afterward, until the very day of their captivity.

16. *No remedy.* Because the people would not repent and God would not pardon them.

21. *Sabbaths.* Many a time had they ploughed and sowed their land in the seventh year when it should have rested. And now it lay unploughed and unsown for ten times seven years. Yet even this might encourage them to hope that they should in due time return to it again. Had others come and taken possession of it, they might have despaired of ever recovering it. But while it lay desolate, it, as it were, waited for them and refused to acknowledge any other owners.

EZRA

CHAPTER 1

6. *Strengthened their hands.* God can, when he pleases, incline the hearts of strangers to be kind to his people. Yes, he can make those strengthen their hands who formerly weakened them.

CHAPTER 2

1. *The province.* Of Judah. And he calls it thus emphatically to remind himself and his brethren of that sad change which their sins had made among them, that from an illustrious, independent, and formidable kingdom, they were fallen to be an obscure, servile, and contemptible province, first under the Chaldeans and now under the Persians.

21. *Beth–lehem.* So these were the remainders of the inhabitants of that city. So little was Bethlehem "among the thousands of Judah"! Yet from here the Messiah will arise.

62. *Genealogy.* The Jews were generally very exact in their genealogies from their own choice and interest, that they might preserve the distinctions of the several tribes and families; which was necessary both to make out their titles to offices or inheritances and to govern themselves thereby in the matter of marriages and from the special provi-

dence of God, so that it might be certainly known of what tribe and family the Messiah was born.

63. It appears that the Urim and Thummim were lost in the destruction of the city and temple, though the Jews fed themselves with hopes of recovering them, but in vain. And by the lack of that oracle they were taught to expect the great oracle, the Messiah.

65. *Women.* For women as well as men were employed in this exercise in the temple service.

CHAPTER 3

3. *For fear.* So they made the more haste, lest they should be hindered. Apprehension of dangers should quicken us in our duty. Have we many enemies? We have the more need to have God for our friend and to keep up our correspondence with him.

5. *Offering.* The morning and evening sacrifice. The law required much, but they offered more; for though they had little wealth, they had much zeal. Happy are they that bring with them out of the furnace of affliction such a holy heat as this!

11. *Sang.* That everlasting hymn, which will never be out of date and to which our tongue should never be out of tune, the burden of Psalm 136.

Whatever our condition is, let it be owned that God is good, and whatever fails, his mercy fails not.

13. *Could not discern.* This mixture of sorrow and joy is a representation of this world. In heaven all are singing and none sighing. In hell all are wailing and none rejoicing. But here on earth we can scarce *discern the noise of the shout of joy from the noise of the weeping.* So let us learn to "rejoice with them that rejoice, and weep with them that weep." Meantime, let us ourselves "weep, as though [we] wept not; and . . . rejoice, as though [we] rejoiced not."

CHAPTER 4

3. Take heed whom you are partners with and on whose hand you lean. While we trust God with an absolute confidence, we must trust men with a prudent caution.

23. See what need we have to pray, not only for kings, but for all in authority under them. The quietness of our lives depends much on the integrity and wisdom of inferior magistrates as well as the supreme.

CHAPTER 5

2. *Helping.* Encouraging the people to work by their presence and assurance of success. It is supposed that the work had stopped about fifteen years. The first chapter of Haggai is the best comment on these two verses.

8. *Great God.* And indeed thus far the greater part of the Samaritans agreed with them.

CHAPTER 6

12. *Destroy.* Though this temple was at length most justly destroyed by the righteous hand of God, yet perhaps the Romans, who were the instruments of that destruction, felt the effects of this curse. For that empire sensibly declined ever after until it was wholly destroyed.

22. *Joyful.* He had given them both cause to rejoice and hearts to rejoice. God is the fountain whence all the streams of true joy flow.

CHAPTER 7

10. *To teach.* The order of things in this verse is very observable. First he endeavors to understand God's law and word, and that not for curiosity or ostentation, but in order to practice it. Next he consciously practices what he did understand, which made his doctrine much more effectual. And then he earnestly desires and labors to instruct others that they also might know and do it.

27. *Blessed.* Ezra cannot proceed in his story without inserting this thankful acknowledgment of God's goodness to him and the people.

28. *As the hand.* If God gives us his hand, we are bold and cheerful. If he withdraws it, we are weak as water. Whatever service we are enabled to do for God and our generation, God must have all the glory of it.

CHAPTER 8

18. *By the good hand.* If ministers have been lacking and the vacancies are well supplied, let us ascribe it to *the good hand of our God,* qualifying them for the service, inclining them to it, and opening a door for them.

21. *Afflict ourselves.* For our sins; and so be qualified for the pardon of them. When we are entering on any new condition of life, our care should be to bring into it none of the guilt of the sins of our former condition. When we are in any imminent danger, let us make our peace with God, and then nothing can hurt us.

35. *Sin offering.* For it is the atonement that secures every mercy to us, which will not be truly comfortable unless iniquity be taken away and our peace made with God.

CHAPTER 9

4. All good people ought to own those who appear and act for God against vice and profaneness. Every one that fears God ought to stand by them and do what he can to strengthen their hands.

6. *Our.* He includes himself in the number of the transgressors, because he himself was guilty of many sins. And because the princes and priests and so many of the people had done this, the guilt had now become national.

8. *A little space.* It is but a little while since God has delivered us, and yet we are already returned to our sin.

CHAPTER 10

1. *There assembled.* The account of his grief and public expressions thereof in the court before the temple was in an instant dispersed over all the city and brought a great company together. See what a happy influence the example of great ones may have upon their inferiors!

2. *We.* He said "we" in the name of the people and their several families, and his own among the rest. For this man's name is not in the following catalogue, but there we have his father, *Jehiel,* and his father's brethren, five other sons of his grandfather *Elam* (v. 26). It was an evidence of his great courage and good conscience that he dared so freely discharge his duty, whereby he showed that he honored God more than his nearest and dearest relations.

44. *Had children.* This implies that most of their wives were barren. Which came to pass by God's special providence in order to manifest his displeasure against such matches, and that the putting them away might not be encumbered with too many difficulties. One would think this grievance altogether removed. Yet we meet with it again (Neh. 13:22). Such corruptions are easily and insensibly brought in, though not easily purged out. The best reformers can but do their endeavor. It is only the Redeemer himself who, when he cometh to Zion, will effectually "turn away ungodliness from Jacob."

nehemiah

CHAPTER 1

11. *To fear thy name.* Those who truly *desire to fear [his] name* shall be graciously accepted of God. *This man.* The king, who is but a man, and therefore his heart is wholly at your disposal. Favor with men is then comfortable when we see it springing from the mercy of God.

CHAPTER 2

2. *Sad.* His fasting joined with inward grief had made a sensible change in his countenance.

3. *Why should.* All the grievances of the church, but especially its desolations, ought to be matter of grief to all good people, to all who have a concern for God's honor and are of a public spirit.

CHAPTER 3

1. *Rose.* Began the work. Ministers should be foremost in every good work, animating others by their example as well as doctrine.

5. Let not nobles think anything beneath them by which they may benefit their country. What is their nobility good for but that it places them in a higher and larger sphere of usefulness?

20. *Earnestly.* He did his work with eminent diligence and fervency; which is here noted to his commendation. And it is probable that this good man's zeal provoked many to take the more pains and make the more haste.

30. *The sixth son of Zalaph.* It seems his five elder brethren put not their hands to the work. But in doing that which is good, we need not stay to see our betters go before us.

CHAPTER 4

14. *Looked.* He looked up, engaged God for him, and put himself and his cause under the divine protection. That was his way and should be ours. All his cares, all his griefs, all his fears he spread before God. *Great and terrible.* You think your enemies are great and terrible. But what are they in comparison to God? Especially in opposition to him?

17. *A weapon.* This is to be taken figuratively, being a proverbial speech, as when they say of a man pretending kindness, "he carries bread in one hand, and a stone in another." Thus must we "work out [our] own salvation," with "the weapons of our warfare" in our hands. For in every duty we must expect opposition from our spiritual enemies.

CHAPTER 5

10. *Exact.* As a just recompense for our pains and care of the public good, to which we wholly devote ourselves, even to the neglect of all our private concerns. But I freely remit my own right and therefore you also ought to do so, seeing I lay no burden upon you but what I am willing to bear a part of upon my own shoulders.

15. *Their servants.* Ruled them with rigor and cruelty; which fault of the servants is charged upon their masters because they did not restrain them. He had an awe of God's mercy and a fear of offending him. Those who truly fear God will not dare do anything cruel or unjust. And this is not only a powerful, but an acceptable principle both of justice and charity.

CHAPTER 6

4. *Four times.* We must never be overcome by the greatest importunity to do anything ill or imprudent. But when we are attacked with the same temptation, we must resist it with the same reason and resolution.

9. *Strengthen my hands.* A good prayer when we are entering on any particular service or conflict in our Christian warfare.

11. *As I.* I, the chief governor, upon whose presence the very life of the whole city and nation in a great measure depends; I who have professed such resolution and courage and confidence in God; I who have had such eminent experience of God's assistance, of his calling me to this employment, and carrying me through it when our danger was greater than it now is. Shall I now dishonor God and religion, and betray the people and city of God by my cowardice?

14. *My God.* This prayer we are not to imitate.

CHAPTER 7

5. *God put into mine heart.* Whatever good motion is in our minds, we must acknowledge it to come from God. What is done by human prudence is to be ascribed to the direction of divine providence.

CHAPTER 8

10. *Your strength.* Rejoicing in God and serving him with cheerfulness and thankfulness, which is your duty always but now especially, will give you that strength both of mind and body which you greatly need, both to perform all the duties required of you and to oppose all the designs of your enemies.

13. *The Levites.* Choosing rather to confess their ignorance than vainly to pretend to more knowledge than they had. Wherein they show both humility and serious godliness, that they were more careful to learn their duty than to preserve their reputation.

CHAPTER 9

13. *Good statutes.* The moral and judicial precepts were all founded on natural equity. And even the ceremonial were tokens of God's goodness, being types of gospel-grace.

33. *Thou art just.* It becomes us, when we are under the rebukes of Providence, be they ever so sharp or ever so long continued, still to justify God and to affirm that we are punished less than our iniquities deserve.

CHAPTER 10

29. *Their nobles.* The common people agreed with the nobles in this good work. Great men never look so great as when they encourage religion and are examples of it. And they would by that, as much as anything, encourage the most valuable of their inferiors, who would cleave to them closer than they can imagine. Observe that their nobles are called *their brethren;* for in the things of God, rich and poor, high and low meet together.

31. *On the sabbath.* They who covenant to keep all the commandments of God must particularly covenant to keep the sabbath holy. For the profanation of this is a sure inlet to all manner of profaneness.

CHAPTER 11

36. *Divisions.* Thus were they settled free and comfortably, though few and poor. And they might have been happy but for that general lukewarmness with which they are charged by the prophet Malachi, who prophesied about this time; and in whom prophecy ceased for some ages until it revived in the great prophet.

CHAPTER 12

30. *Purified themselves.* They who would be instrumental to sanctify others must sanctify themselves and set themselves apart for God with purity of mind and sincerity of intention.

43. *The children rejoiced.* And their hosannas were not despised, but are recorded to their praise. All who share in public mercies ought to join in public thanksgivings.

44. The sure way of ministers to gain an interest in the affections of their people is to wait on their ministry, to devote to it their whole time, thought, and strength.

47. When what is contributed for the support of religion is given with an eye to God, it is sanctified and will "cause the blessing to rest in thine house," and all who are therein.

CHAPTER 13

22. *Mercy.* Whereby he intimates that, though he mentioned his good works as things with which God was well pleased and which he had promised to reward, yet he neither did nor dared trust to their merit or his own worthiness; but when he had done all, he judged himself an unprofitable servant and one who needed God's infinite mercy to pardon all his sins and particularly those infirmities and corruptions which adhered to his good deeds.

25. *Cursed.* This and the following punishments were justly inflicted upon them because this transgression was contrary both to a plain law of God and to their own late solemn covenants.

31. *For good.* This may well be the summary of our petitions. We need no more to make us happy but this.

esther

CHAPTER 1

6. *Beds.* For in those eastern countries, they did not then sit at tables as we do, but rested or leaned upon beds or couches.

8. *The law.* According to this law which the king had now made, none should compel another to drink more than he pleased. How does this heathen prince shame many who are called Christians, who think they do not make their friends welcome unless they make them drunk!

9. *The women.* While the king entertained the men. For this was the common custom of the Persians, that men and women did not feast together.

CHAPTER 2

13. *Desired.* For ornament, or by way of attendance. And it should be observed that everyone whom the king took to his bed was his wife of a lower rank, as Hagar was Abraham's, so that it would have been no sin or dishonor to Esther, though she had not been made queen.

CHAPTER 3

7. *They cast Pur.* The diviners cast lots according to the custom of those people, what day and what month would be most lucky, not for his success with the king (of which he made no doubt), but for the most effectual extirpation of the Jews. Wherein appears both his implacable malice and unwearied diligence in seeking vengeance of them with so much trouble to himself, and God's singular providence in disposing the lot to that time that the Jews might have space to get the decree reversed.

CHAPTER 4

14. *From another place.* This was the language of strong faith, "against hope [believing] in hope." *Who knoweth.* It is probable that God has raised you to this honor for this very season. We should, every one of us, consider for what end God has put us in the place where we are. And when an opportunity arises to serve God and our generation, we must take care not to let it slip.

CHAPTER 5

3. *It shall be even given.* God in his providence often prevents the fears and outdoes the hopes of his servants.

8. *To-morrow.* I will acquaint you with my humble request. She did not present her petition at this time, but delayed it until the next morning. This she did, either because she was a little daunted with the king's presence, or because she would further engage the king's affection to her and would also intimate to him that her petition was of a more than ordinary nature. But principally, she did this by direction of divine providence, which took away her courage of utterance for this time that she might have a better opportunity for it the next time by that great accident which happened before it.

10. *Refrained.* From taking present vengeance upon Mordecai, which he might easily have effected either by his own or any of his servants' hands without any fear of inconvenience to himself. But herein God's wise and powerful providence appeared in disposing Haman's heart, contrary to his own inclination, and making him, as it were, to put fetters upon his own hands.

12. *Am I.* Thus he makes that matter of glorying which was the occasion of his utter ruin. So ignorant are the wisest men, and subject to fatal mistakes, rejoicing when they have most cause for fear and sorrowing for those things which tend to produce joy and comfort.

CHAPTER 6

1. *Sleep.* How vain are all the contrivances of foolish man against the wise and omnipotent God, who has the hearts and hands of kings and all men perfectly at his disposal and can by such trivial accidents (as they are accounted) change their minds and produce such terrible effects.

CHAPTER 7

3. *My life.* It is my only request that you would not give me up to the malice of that man who designs to take away my life. Even a stranger, a criminal, shall be permitted to petition for his life. But that a friend, a wife, a queen should have occasion to make such a petition was very affecting.

5. *Who.* The expressions are short and doubled, as proceeding from a discomposed and enraged mind. Ahasuerus is amazed at that wickedness of which he himself was guilty. For he consented to the bloody edict. So that Esther might have said, "Thou art the man!"

6. *Afraid.* And it was time for him to fear when the queen was his prosecutor, the king his judge, and his own conscience a witness against him. And the surprising turns of providence that very morning could not but increase his fear.

CHAPTER 8

8. *Reverse.* For this reason he could not recall the former letters because they were irrevocable by the law of the Medes and Persians. How much more prudent is our constitution, that no law whatever can be established as to be unrepealable? It is God's prerogative not to reverse and to say what can never be altered.

9. *Then.* Which was more than two months after the former decree. All which time God allowed the Jews to lie under the terror of this dreadful day, that they might be more thoroughly humbled for, and purged from, those many and great sins under which they lay.

Also, that they might be convinced of their great sin and folly in the many offers they had had of returning to their native country, by which means, being dispersed in the several parts of this vast dominion, they were likely to be easy prey to their enemies, whereas their brethren in Judea were in a better capacity to preserve themselves. And also, for the greater illustration of God's glorious power, wisdom, and goodness in giving his people such an admirable and unexpected deliverance.

11. *Both little ones and women.* Which is here added to strike the greater terror into their enemies; and according to the laws and customs of this kingdom, whereby children were punished for their parents' offenses. Yet we read nothing in the execution of this decree of the slaughter of women and children, nor is it probable they would kill their innocent children.

CHAPTER 9

10. *But.* Because they would leave it to their children that it might appear what they did was not done out of malice or covetousness, but out of mere necessity and by that great law of self-preservation.

12. *What.* In which doubtless many more were slain. So that I have fully granted your petition. And yet, if you have anything further to ask, I am ready to grant it.

CHAPTER 10

2. *Chronicles.* These are lost long since and buried in oblivion, while the sacred writings remain throughout the world. When the kingdoms of men, monarchs, and their monarchies are destroyed, "and their memorial is perished with them," the kingdom of God among men and the records of that kingdom shall remain "as the days of heaven."

JOB

CHAPTER 1

3. *The greatest*. That lived in those parts. The account of his piety and prosperity comes before the account of his afflictions, to show that neither of these will secure us from the common, no, nor from the uncommon calamities of human life.

5. Parents should be particular in their addresses to God for the several branches of their family. They should pray for each child according to his particular temper, genius, and disposition.

6. *Before*. Before his throne, to receive his commands and to give him an account of their negotiations. But you must not think that these things are to be understood literally. It is only a parabolic representation of that great truth that God by his wise and holy providence governs all the actions of men and devils. It being usual with the great God to condescend to our shallow capacities and to express himself, as the Jews phrase it, "in the language of the sons of men." And it is likewise intimated that the affairs of earth are much the subject of the counsels of the unseen world. That world is dark to us, but we lie open to it.

12. *Behold*. It seems strange that God should give Satan such a permission as this. But he did it for his own glory, for the honor of Job, for the explanation of Providence, and for the encouragement of his afflicted people in all ages.

21. *Return thither*. I shall be as rich when I die as I was when I was born and therefore have reason to be contented with my condition, which also is the common lot of all men. Into the lap of our common mother, the earth, as the weary child lays its head in its mother's bosom. We go out of the world naked; the body does, though the sanctified soul goes clothed (II Cor. 5:3). Death strips us of all our enjoyments; clothing can neither warm nor adorn a dead body. *Taken*. He has taken away nothing but his own and what he so gave that he reserved the supreme disposal of in his own hand. And what is it to me, by what hand he that gives resumes what he gave?

22. *Charged*. The Hebrew reads, "not imputed folly to God." So far was he from blaspheming God that he did not entertain any dishonorable thought of God, as if he had done anything unworthy of his infinite wisdom, justice, or goodness, but heartily acquiesced in his good pleasure and in his righteous, though sharp, proceedings against him. Discontent and impatience do in effect impute folly to God.

Against the working of these we should watch carefully, acknowledging that God has done well, but we have done foolishly.

CHAPTER 2

3. *Movedst.* This, as the rest of this representation, is not to be understood literally. But the design is to signify both the devil's restless malice in promoting man's misery and God's permission of it for wise and holy ends.

6. *In thine hand.* If God did not chain up the roaring lion, how soon would he devour us! As far as he permits the wrath of Satan and wicked men to proceed against his people he will make it turn to his praise and theirs, and the remainder thereof he will restrain. Job, in being thus maligned of Satan, was a type of Christ. He had permission to "bruise his heel," to "touch his bone and his flesh"; yes, and his life also, because by dying he was to do what Job could not do, to "destroy him that had the power of death."

8. If God lay him among the ashes, there he will contentedly sit down. A low spirit becomes us in low circumstances and will help to reconcile us to them.

9. *Then said his wife.* Whom Satan spared, to be a troubler and tempter to him. It is his policy to send his temptations by the hands of those who are dear to us. We must, therefore, watch carefully that we be not drawn to any evil by them whom we love and value the most.

Die. I see you are set on blessing God; you bless God for giving, and you bless God for taking away, and you are still blessing God for your loathsome diseases; and he rewards you accordingly, giving you more and more of that kind of mercy for which you bless him. Go on, therefore, in your generous course, and bless God, and die as a fool dies.

10. *Shall we.* Shall we poor worms give laws to our supreme Lord and oblige him never to afflict us? And shall not those great and manifold mercies, which from time to time God has given us, compensate these short afflictions? Ought we not to bless God for those mercies which we did not deserve, and contentedly endure those corrections which we do deserve? And if we receive so much good for the body, shall we not receive some good for our souls? That is, some affliction whereby we may be made "partakers of his holiness"? Let murmuring, therefore, as well as boasting, be for ever excluded.

CHAPTER 3

1. *His day.* He does not proceed so far as to curse God, but makes the devil a liar. But although he does not break forth into direct reproaches of God, yet he makes indirect reflections upon his providence. His curse was sinful, both because it was vain, being applied to a thing which was not capable of blessing and cursing, and because it cast a blame upon God for bringing that day and for giving him life on that day.

20. *Light.* Life is called light because it is pleasant and serviceable for walking and working. And this light is said to be given us because it would be lost if it were not daily renewed to us by a fresh gift.

22. *Glad.* To be thus impatient of life for the sake of the trouble we meet with is not only unnatural in itself, but ungrateful to the giver of life, and shows a sinful indulgence of our own passion. Let it be our great and constant care to get ready for another world. And then let us leave it to God to order the circumstances of our removal.

24. *Before*. All the time I am eating I fall into sighing and weeping because I am obliged to eat and to support this wretched life, and because of my uninterrupted pains of body and of mind, which do not afford me one quiet moment. *My roarings*. My loud outcries, more befitting a lion than a man. *Poured out*. With great abundance, irresistible violence, and incessant continuance, as waters flow in a river or as they break the banks and overflow the ground.

25. *Feared*. Even in the time of my prosperity I was full of fears, considering the variety of God's providences, the changeableness of this vain world, God's justice, and the sinfulness of all mankind. And these fears of mine were not in vain, but are justified by my present calamities.

CHAPTER 4

12. He does not pretend to have understood it fully; but something of it he perceived. How "little a portion is heard of [God]"! How little do we know of him in this world.

13. Visions differed from dreams in that God imparted his mind to men in dreams when asleep, but in visions when they were awake. These visions sometimes happened by day, but most frequently by night.

17. Those who find fault with the directions of the divine law, the dispensations of the divine grace, or the disposal of the divine providence make themselves *more just* and *pure* than God; who, being their maker, is their Lord and owner, and the author of all the justice and purity that is in man.

19. We stand but upon the dust. Some have a higher heap of dust to stand upon than others. But still it is the earth that keeps us up and will shortly swallow us up.

21. *Their excellency*. Whatever is commonly considered excellent in men, all their natural, moral, and civil accomplishments, such as high birth, great riches, power, and wisdom; these are so far from preserving men from perishing that they perish themselves together with those houses of clay in which they are lodged. *Without wisdom*. Even without having attained that only wisdom for which they came into the world. Shall such lowly, weak, foolish, sinful, dying creatures as this pretend to be "more just than God? . . . more pure than his maker?" No; instead of quarreling with his afflictions, let him admire that he is out of hell.

CHAPTER 5

2. *Killeth*. A man's wrath and impatience prey upon his spirit and so hasten his death; and provoke God to cut him off.

9. *Marvellous things*. The works of nature are mysteries. The most curious searches come far short of full discoveries. And the works of Providence are still more deep and unaccountable.

10. *Rain*. There is something wonderful, as indeed there is in the rise of it from the earth, in the strange hanging of that heavy body in the air, and in the distribution of it as God sees fit. And how much more in the hidden paths of divine providence?

17. *Happy*. Various and great happiness belong to that man *whom God correcteth*. The reason is plain, because afflictions are pledges of God's love which no man can buy too dear; and are necessary to purge out sin and thereby to prevent infinite and eternal miseries. *Despise not thou*. Reverence the chastening of the Lord. Have a humble, awesome regard to his correcting hand, and study to understand the design of it.

18. *For he.* God's usual method is first to humble and then to exalt. And he never makes a wound too great, too deep for his own cure.

20. *He shall.* These things he utters with more confidence, because the rewards or punishments of this life were more constantly distributed to men in the Old Testament according to their good or bad behavior than they are now. And because it was his opinion that great afflictions were the certain evidences of wickedness; and consequently, that great deliverances would infallibly follow upon true repentance.

26. *Full age.* In a mature and old, but vigorous age, as the word implies. It is a great blessing to live to a full age and not to have the number of our years cut short. Much more, to be willing to die, to come cheerfully to the grave. And to die seasonably, just in the bedtime, when our souls are ripe for God.

CHAPTER 6

4. *Drinketh.* Exhausts and consumes my soul. *In array.* They are like a numerous army, who invade me on every side. This was the sorest part of his calamity, wherein he was an eminent type of Christ who complained most of the sufferings of his soul. "Now is my soul troubled." "My soul is exceeding sorrowful." "My God, my God, why hast thou forsaken me?" Indeed, trouble of mind is the sorest trouble. "A wounded spirit who can bear?"

11. *That.* As desirous of death as Job was, yet he never offered to put an end to his own life. Such a thought will never be entertained by any who have the least regard to the law of God and nature. No matter how uneasy the soul's confinement in the body may be, it must by no means break the prison, but wait for a fair discharge.

14. *But.* But you have no pity for your friend, a plain evidence that you are guilty of what you charged me with, even of the lack of the fear of God. The least which those that are at ease can do for them who are pained is to pity them, to feel tender concern for them, and to sympathize with them.

15. *Brethren.* "Friends," for though Eliphaz only had spoken, the other two showed their approbation of his discourse. *Dealt deceitfully.* Adding to the afflictions which they said they came to remove. And it is no new thing, for even brethren to deal deceitfully. It is, therefore, our wisdom to cease from man. We cannot expect too little from the creature, or too much from the Creator.

CHAPTER 7

3. *Nights.* He mentions nights, because that is the saddest time for sick and miserable persons. The darkness and solitude of the night being of themselves uncomfortable, and giving them more opportunity for solemn and sorrowful reflections.

7. He turns his speech to God. Perhaps observing that his friends grew weary of hearing it. If men will not hear us, God will. If men cannot help us, he can. For his arm is not shortened, neither is his ear heavy.

11. *Therefore.* Since my life is so vain and short and, when once lost, without all hope of recovery, I will plead with God for pity before I die. I will not smother my anguish within my breast, but will ease myself by pouring out my complaints.

12. *That.* That you should guard and restrain me with such heavy and unexampled miseries? We are apt in our affliction to complain of God as if he laid more upon us than there is occasion for.

20. *Sinned.* Although I am free from those crying sins, for which my friends suppose you have sent this judgment upon me, yet I freely confess I am a sinner and therefore obnoxious to your justice.

21. *Pardon.* Seeing you are so gracious to others, why may not I hope for the same favor from you?

CHAPTER 8

11. *Can.* The hypocrite cannot build his hope without some false, rotten ground, any more than the rush can grow without mire.

20. *Behold.* God who will not *help the evildoers,* will not *cast away* a good man, though he may be cast down. Yet it may be he will not be lifted up in this world. And therefore, Bildad could not infer that if Job was not restored to temporal prosperity, he was not a good man. Let us judge nothing before the time, but wait until the secrets of all hearts are revealed and the present difficulties of providence solved to universal and everlasting satisfaction.

CHAPTER 9

4. *He.* He is infinitely wise and searches all men's hearts and ways, and discovers a multitude of sins which men's shortsighted eyes cannot see. And therefore he can charge them with innumerable evils where they thought themselves innocent, and he sees far more malignity than men could discern in their sins.

Hardened himself. Obstinately contended with him. The devil promised himself that Job, in the day of his affliction, would curse and speak ill of God. But instead of that he sets himself to honor God and speak highly of him. As ill pained as he is, and as much as he is taken up with his own miseries, when he has occasion to mention the wisdom and power of God, he forgets his complaints and pours out a flood of eloquence on that glorious subject.

16. *Yet.* I could not believe that God had indeed granted my desire, because I am still full of the tokens of his displeasure; and therefore should conclude that it was but a pleasant dream and not a real thing.

21. I could not own nor plead before God the integrity of my soul, but would only make supplication to my judge. I would abhor or condemn my life. I would not trust to the integrity either of my soul and heart or of my life so as to justify myself before the pure and piercing eyes of the all-seeing God.

26. *Eagle.* Which flies swiftly, especially when in the sight of his prey. See here how swift the motion of time is! It is always upon the wing, hastening to its period. What little need have we of pastimes! What great need to redeem time, which runs out, runs on so fast toward eternity! And how vain are the enjoyments of time which we may be deprived of, even while time continues! Our day may be longer than our sunshine; and when that is gone, it is as if it had never been.

CHAPTER 10

4. *Eyes of flesh.* No. Eyes of flesh cannot see in the dark. But darkness hides not from God. Eyes of flesh are but in one place at a time and can see but a little way. But "the eyes of the LORD are in every place," and "run to and fro throughout the whole earth." Eyes of flesh will shortly be darkened by age and shut up by death. But the eyes of God are ever the same, nor does his sight ever decay.

12. *Preserved.* You have done great things for me, given me life and the blessings of life, and daily deliverances.

And will you now undo all that you have done? And shall I who have been such an eminent monument of your mercy now be a spectacle of your vengeance?

13. *Hid.* Both your former favors and your present frowns. Both are according to your own will and therefore undoubtedly consistent, however they seem. When God does what we cannot account for, we are bound to believe that there are good reasons for it *hid in thine heart.* It is not with us or in our reach to assign the cause; but *I know that this is with thee.*

20. *Cease.* My life is short and of itself hastens to an end. There is no need that you should grudge me some ease for so small a moment.

CHAPTER 11

2. *Answered.* Truly, sometimes it should not. Silence is the best confrontation of impertinence and puts the greatest contempt upon it.

6. *Secrets.* The secret wisdom of God is infinitely greater than that which is revealed to us by his word or works. The greatest part of what is known of God is the least part of those perfections that are in him.

CHAPTER 12

2. When wise and good men die, it is a comfort to think that wisdom and goodness do not die with them. It is folly to think that there will be a great, irreparable loss of us when we are gone, since God has "the residue of the spirit" and can raise up others more fit to do his work.

16. *The deceived and the deceiver are his.* Wholly subject to his disposal. He governs the deceiver and sets bounds to his deceits, how far they shall extend.

He also overrules all this to his own glory and the accomplishment of his righteous designs of trying the good and punishing wicked men by giving them up to believe lies. Yet God is not the author of any error or sin, but only the wise and holy governor of it.

CHAPTER 13

19. *The ghost.* My grief would break my heart if I should not give it vent.

23. *My sin.* That I am a sinner I confess; but not that I am guilty of such crimes as my friends suppose. If it be so, do, O Lord, discover it.

CHAPTER 14

2. *Flower.* The flower is fading, and all its beauty soon withers and is gone. The *shadow* is fleeting, and its very being will soon be lost in the shadows of night. Of neither do we make any account, in neither do we put any confidence.

10. *Man.* Two words are here used for man. "Geber," a mighty man, though mighty, dies; "Adam," a man of earth, returns to it. Before death he is dying daily, continually wasting away. In death, he *giveth up the ghost,* the spirit returns to God who gave it. After death, *where is he?* Not where he was; his place knows him no more. But is he no where? Yes, he is gone to the world of spirits, gone into eternity, gone, never to return to this world!

13. *The grave.* The grave is not only a resting place, but a hiding place to the children of God. He hides them in the grave, as we hide our treasure in a place of secrecy and safety. *Hide me* there, not only from the storms of this life, but for the glory of a better.

CHAPTER 15

4. *Restrainest prayer.* You do by your words and principles, as far as in you lie, banish prayer out of the world by making it useless and unprofitable to men.

22. *Believeth not.* When he falls into trouble, he despairs of deliverance, by reason of his guilty conscience.

30. *His mouth.* And this expression intimates with how much ease God subdues his enemies. His word, his blast; one act of his will is sufficient.

CHAPTER 16

10. *Gaped.* Opened their mouths wide against me. In all this, Job was a type of Christ. These very expressions are used in the predictions of his sufferings (Ps. 22:13; Mic. 5:1).

11. *The wicked.* And thus Christ was *delivered into the hands of the wicked* by the determinate counsel of God.

13. *His archers.* Whoever are our enemies, we must look on them as God's archers and see him directing the arrow.

CHAPTER 17

1. *The graves.* He speaks of the sepulchers of his fathers, to which he must be gathered. The graves where they are laid are ready for me also. Whatever is unready, the grave is ready for us. It is a bed soon made. And if the grave be ready for us, it concerns us to be ready for the grave.

8. *Yet.*[1] In spite of all these sufferings of good men, and the astonishment which they cause, he shall the more zealously oppose those hypocrites who make these strange providences of God an objection to religion.

13. I endeavor to make it easy by keeping my conscience pure, by seeing Christ lying in this bed, and by looking beyond it to the resurrection.

16. We must shortly be *in the dust,* under *the bars of the pit,* held fast there until the general resurrection. All good men, if they cannot agree now, will there *rest together.* Let the foresight of this cool the heat of all contenders and moderate the disputers of this world.

CHAPTER 18

4. *Forsaken.* Shall God give over the government of the earth for your sake to prevent your complaints and clamors? Shall the counsels of God, which are more immovable than rocks, and the whole course of his providence be altered to comply with your desires?

CHAPTER 19

10. *Tree.* Which being once plucked up by the roots will never grow again. Hope in this life is a perishing thing. But the hope of good men, when it is cut off from this world, is but removed like a tree, transplanted from this nursery to the garden of God.

13. *Estranged.* As we must eye the hand of God in all the injuries we receive from our enemies, so likewise in all the slights and unkindnesses we receive from our friends.

23. *My words.* The words which I am now about to speak. And that which Job wished for, God granted him. His words are written in God's book; so that wherever that book is read, there shall this glorious confession be declared for a memorial of him.

25. *For.* This is the reason of his confidence in the goodness of his cause

---

[1](17:8) KJV: "And."

and his willingness to have the matter between him and his friends published and submitted to any trial, because he had a living and powerful Redeemer to plead his cause and to give sentence for him. *My redeemer.* In whom I have particular interest. The Hebrew word *goel,* here used, properly signifies Jesus Christ. For this word is primarily used of the next kinsman, whose office it was to redeem, by a price paid, the sold or mortgaged estate of his deceased kinsman, to avenge his death, and to maintain his name and honor by raising up seed to him.

All which most fitly agrees to Jesus Christ, who is our nearest kinsman and brother, as having taken our nature upon him. He has redeemed that everlasting inheritance which our first parents had utterly lost, by the price of his own blood. And he has revenged the death of mankind upon the great contriver of it, the devil, by destroying him and his kingdom. And he has taken a course to preserve our name, our honor, and ourselves to eternity. And it is well observed that after these expressions we meet not with such impatient or despairing passages as we had before; which shows that they had inspired Job with new life and comfort.

27. *See.* No wonder he repeats it again, because the meditation of it was most sweet to him. *Another.* For me or in my stead. I shall not see God by another's eyes, but by my own, and by these selfsame eyes in this same body which now I have. *Though.* This I do confidently expect, though the grave and the worms will consume my whole body.

CHAPTER 20

12. *Hide.* As an epicure does a sweet morsel, which he keeps and rolls about his mouth that he may longer enjoy the pleasure of it.

23. *Rain.* This phrase denotes both the author of his plagues, God, and the nature and quality of them, that they shall come upon him like rain with great vehemence so that he cannot prevent or avoid it.

26. *Secret.* In those places where he confidently hopes to hide himself from all evil. Even there God shall find him out.

27. *Earth.* All creatures upon earth shall conspire to destroy him. If the God of heaven and earth be his enemy, neither heaven nor earth will show him any kindness, but all the host of both are, and will be, at war with him.

CHAPTER 21

4. *Is.* I do not make my complaint to, or expect relief from, you or from any men, but from God only. I am pouring forth my complaints to God.

22. *Teach.* How to govern the world? For so you do while you tell him that he must not afflict the godly nor give the wicked prosperity. That he must invariably punish the wicked and regard the righteous in this world. No, he will act as sovereign, and with great variety in his providential dispensations.

25. *Another.* So there is a great variety of God's dispensations. He distributes great prosperity to one and great afflictions to another, according to his wise but secret counsel.

26. *Alike.* All these worldly differences are ended by death, and they lie in the grave without any distinction; so that no man can tell who is good and who is bad by events which befall them in this life. And if one wicked man die in a palace and another in a dungeon, they will meet in the congregation of the dead and damned; and the worm that dies not and the fire that is not quenched will be the same to both.

This makes those differences inconsiderable and not worth perplexing ourselves about.

34. *How.* Why then do you seek to comfort me with vain hopes of recovering my prosperity, seeing your grounds are false, and experience shows that good men are often in great tribulation while the vilest of men prosper?

CHAPTER 22

3. God needs not us or our services. We are undone, forever undone without him. But he is happy, forever happy without us.

4. *Reprove.* Punish you. Because he is afraid lest if he should let you alone, you would grow too great and powerful for him. Surely no. As your righteousness cannot profit him, so our wickedness can do him no hurt.

21. *Him.* With God, renew your acquaintance with God by prayer, and repentance for all your sins, and true humiliation under his hand, and hearty compliance with all his commands, and diligent care to serve and enjoy him. It is our honor that we are made capable of this acquaintance; our misery that by sin we have lost it; our privilege that through Christ we may return to it; and our unspeakable advantage to renew and cultivate it.

CHAPTER 23

5. *Know.* If he should reveal to me any secret sins for which he contends with me, I would humble myself before him and accept the punishment of my iniquity.

7. *Delivered.* From the damnatory sentence of God. This and some such expressions of Job cannot be excused from irreverence towards God, for which God afterwards reproves him and Job abhors himself.

CHAPTER 24

13. *Light.* As well the light of reason and conscience, as the light of divine revelation, which was then in good measure imparted to the people of God and shortly after committed to writing.

18. *Swift.* That is, he quickly passes away with all his glory, *as the waters* which never stay in one place, but are always hastening away.

23. *Yet.* His eyes are upon their ways; although God gives them such strange successes, yet he sees and observes them all and will in due time punish them.

CHAPTER 25

1. Perhaps Bildad and the rest now perceived that Job and they did not differ so much as they thought. They owned that the wicked might prosper for a while. And Job owned that they would be destroyed at the last.

6. *Worm.* Lowly, vile, and impotent. Proceeding from corruption and returning to it. *The son.* For "miserable man" in the last branch he here puts *the son of* any man to show that this is true even of the greatest and best of men. Let us then wonder at the condescension of God in taking such worms into covenant and communion with himself!

CHAPTER 26

5. *Dead things.* Job, having censured Bildad's discourse, proceeds to show how little he needed his information in that point. Here he shows that the power and providence of God reaches not only to the things we see, but also to the invisible parts of the world. It extends not only to the heavens above and their inhabitants, and to men upon earth, but also to such persons or things as are under the earth or under the waters; which are out of our sight and reach, yet not out of the reach of divine providence.

God's dominion is over all men, yes, even the dead, and the worse of them, who, though they would not own God nor his providence while they lived, yet now are forced to acknowledge and feel that power which they despised and bitterly mourn under the sad effects of it in their infernal habitations.

6. *Hell.* Is in his presence and under his providence. Hell itself, that place of utter darkness, is not hid from his sight.

11. *Pillars.* Perhaps the mountains, which by their height and strength seem to reach and support the heavens.

14. *His power.* His mighty power is aptly compared to thunder in regard to its irresistible force and the terror which it causes to wicked men.

CHAPTER 27

7. *Let.* I am so far from practicing evil that I abhor the thoughts of it. If I wished to be avenged of my enemy, I could wish him no greater mischief than to be a wicked man.

22. *Would fain flee.* He earnestly desires to escape the judgments of God, but in vain. Those who will not be persuaded to fly to the arms of divine grace, which are now stretched out to receive them, will not be able to flee from the arms of divine wrath, which will shortly be stretched out to destroy them.

23. *Clap.* In token of their joy at the removal of such a public pest by way of astonishment. And in contempt and scorn, all which this gesture signifies in Scripture use.

CHAPTER 28

1. *Surely.* In the last chapter, Job spoke of God's various providences toward wicked men and showed that God does sometimes, for a season, give them prosperity but afterwards calls them to a sad account. He also showed that God does sometimes prosper the wicked all their days, so they live and die without any visible token of God's displeasure when, on the contrary, good men are exercised with many calamities. Perceiving that his friends were scandalized at these methods of divine providence and denied the thing because they could not understand the reason of such dispensations, Job, in this chapter, declares that this is one of the depths of divine wisdom, not discoverable by any mortal man; and that although men had some degree of wisdom whereby they could search out many hidden things, as the veins of silver and gold, yet this was a wisdom of a higher nature and out of man's reach. The caverns of the earth he may discover, but not the counsels of heaven.

12. *Shall wisdom.* Man has one kind of wisdom, to discover the works of nature and to perform the operations of art; as for that sublime wisdom which consists of the knowledge of God and ourselves, no man can discover this but by the special gift of God.

21. *Hid.* The line and plummet of human reason can never fathom the abyss of the divine counsels. Who can account for the maxims, measures, and methods of God's government? Let us then be content not to know the future events of providence until time reveals them; and not to know the secret reasons of providence until eternity brings them to light.

22. *Death.* Though they cannot give an account of it themselves, yet there is a world on which these dark regions border where we shall see it clearly. Have patience, says death. I will fetch you shortly to a place where even this wisdom shall be found. When the veil of flesh is rent and the interposing clouds are scattered, we shall know what God does, though we know not now.

24. *For.* He, and he only, knows it, because his providence is infinite and universal, reaching to all places and times, past, present, and to come. The most knowing men have narrow understandings, and the wisdom, justice, and beauty of God's works are not fully seen until all the parts of them be laid together.

25. *Winds.* God manages them all by weight, appointing to every wind that blows its season, its proportion, its bounds, when and where, how much, and how long each shall blow.

28. *Fear of the* LORD. True religion. Which consists of two branches, doing good and forsaking evil. The design of Job in this close of his discourse is not only to reprove the boldness of his friends in prying into God's secrets and passing such a rash censure upon him and upon God's carriage towards him; but also to vindicate himself from the imputation of hypocrisy by showing that he had ever esteemed it to be his best wisdom to fear God and to depart from evil.

CHAPTER 29

18. *Multiply.* See how apt even good men are to set death at a distance from them!

CHAPTER 30

10. *Spit.* Not literally, for they kept far from him, but figuratively, they use all manner of reproachful expressions even to my face. Herein also we see a type of Christ, who was thus made "a reproach of men and despised of the people."

23. *House appointed.* The grave is a narrow, dark, cold house, but there we shall rest and be safe. It is our home, for it is our mother's lap and in it we are gathered to our fathers. It is a house appointed for us by him who has appointed the bounds of all our habitations. And it is *appointed for all living.* It is the common receptacle for rich and poor. We must all be brought there, and that shortly.

24. *To the grave.* The hand of God's wrath will not follow me beyond death. I shall then be safe and at ease. Though most men cry and are frightened while they are dying, while the body is sinking into destruction, yet I desire it. I have nothing to fear therein, since "I know that my redeemer liveth."

CHAPTER 31

6. *Let me.* I desire nothing more than to have my heart and life weighed in just balances and searched out by the all-seeing God.

7. *Heart.* If I have let my heart loose to covet forbidden things which my eyes have seen. Commonly sin enters by the eye into the heart.

12. *Destruction.* Lust is a fire in the soul. It consumes all that is good there, the convictions, the comforts. It lays the conscience waste. It consumes the body, consumes the substance, roots out all the increase. It kindles the fire of God's wrath which, if not quenched by the blood of Christ, will burn to the lowest hell.

23. *I could not.* I knew myself unable either to oppose his power or to bear his wrath. Even good men have need to restrain themselves from sin, with the fear of *destruction from God.* Even when salvation from God is a comfort to us, yet destruction from God should be *a terror to me.*

35. This shows that Job did not live

before letters were in use. And undoubtedly the first letters were those written on the two tables by the finger of God. He wishes that his friends, who charged him with hypocrisy, would draw up the charge in writing.

CHAPTER 32

22. *I know not.* The more closely we eye the majesty of God as our maker, and the more we dread his wrath and justice, the less danger shall we be in of a sinful fearing or flattering of men.

CHAPTER 33

14. *Twice.* When one speaking does not awaken men, God is graciously pleased to give them another admonition. Though he will not gratify men's curiosity in enquiring into his hidden judgments, yet he will acquaint them with their duty. God speaks to us by conscience, by providence, and by ministers.

17. *Pride.* And God by this means is said to *hide pride from man,* because by these glorious representations of his divine majesty to man he takes him away from the admiration of his own excellence; and brings him to a sight of his own weakness and to a humble and ready submission to his will.

23. *To shew.* To direct him to the right way he may please God and procure that mercy which he thirsts after; which is not by quarreling with God, but by a humble confession and supplication for mercy through Christ the Redeemer.

24. *I have found a ransom.* Although I might justly destroy him, yet I will spare him, for I have found out a way of ransoming sinners from death, which is the death of my Son, the redeemer of the world, and through him I will pardon them who repent and cry for mercy. Observe how God glories in the invention! *I have found,* I have found *a ransom,* a ransom for poor, undone sinners! I, even I, am he who has done it.

30. *To bring.* That he may save men from being for ever miserable and make them for ever happy. "Lord, what is man, that thou shouldest thus visit him? This should engage us to comply with God's designs, to work with him for our own good, and not to counter-work him. And this will render those who perish inexcusable that so much was done to save them, and they would not be healed." So writes Mr. Henry. Excellent words! But how much did God do to save them? Did he ever do anything to save them? Did he ever design to save them? If not, how does that which was never done, no, nor designed, "render them inexcusable"?

CHAPTER 34

13. *Who.* Who or where is his superior who made the world and then delivered the government of it to God? God himself is the sole creator, the absolute Lord of all, and therefore cannot do unjustly. Because the Creator and Lord of the world must have all possible perfections in himself; and among others, perfect justice.

17. *Govern.* Elihu's argument is the same as that of Abraham (Gen. 18:25) and that of Paul (Rom. 3:5–6). If God be unrighteous, how shall he judge or govern the world? And the argument is undeniable; if God were unjust, there would be nothing but injustice and confusion in the world, whereas we see there is a great deal of justice administered in the world. All this must proceed from him who is the fountain of all justice and rule and authority. And he who makes men just, shall he be unjust?

CHAPTER 35

10. *Maker.* Who alone made me and who only can deliver me. Who when our condition is ever so dark and sad can turn our darkness into light; can quickly put a new song in our mouth, a thanksgiving unto our God.

11. *Who.* God has given men what he has denied to beasts, wisdom to know God and themselves. Therefore, they are inexcusable for not using that wisdom by calling on God in the time of trouble.

14. *Trust.* Instead of murmuring, repent of what is past, humble yourself under God's hand, wait patiently in his way until deliverance comes. For it will certainly come if you do not hinder it.

CHAPTER 36

5. *Wisdom.* His strength is guided by wisdom and therefore cannot do anything unbecoming God or unjust to his creatures.

22. *Behold.* God is omnipotent and therefore can either punish you far worse, or deliver you if you do repent. He is also infinitely wise, and as none can work like him, so none can teach like him. Therefore, do not presume to teach him how to govern the world. None teaches with such authority and convincing evidence, with such condescension and compassion, with such power and efficacy as God does. He teaches by the Bible, and that is the best book; by his Son, and he is the best master.

25. *It.* The power, and wisdom, and greatness of God are so manifest in all his works that all who are not stupid must see and acknowledge it.

26. *Neither.* He is eternal, as in his being, so in all his counsels; which therefore must be infinitely above the comprehension of short-lived men.

27. *For.* Having affirmed that God's works are incomprehensibly great and glorious, he now proves it from the most common works of nature and providence. And hence he leaves it to Job to consider how much more deep and inconceivable the secret counsels of God must be.

CHAPTER 37

12. *Turned.* The clouds are carried about to this or that place. Not by chance (though nothing seems to be more casual than the motions of the clouds), but by his order and governance.

14. *Consider.* If there be so much matter of wonder in the most obvious works of God, how wonderful must his secret counsels be?

CHAPTER 38

2. *Counsel.* God's counsel. For the great matter of the dispute between Job and his friends was concerning God's counsel and providence in afflicting Job; which Job had endeavored to obscure and misrepresent. This first word which God spoke struck Job to the heart. This he repeats (42:3) as the arrow that struck fast in him.

14. *To the seal.* Have you seen or do you know the place and state of the dead; the depths and bowels of that earth in which the majority of dead men are buried? Death is a grand secret. We know not when or by what means we shall be brought to death; by what road we must go the way whence we shall not return. We cannot describe what death is; how the knot is untied between soul and body, or how the spirit goes. With what dreadful curiosity does the soul launch out into an untried abyss? We have no communication with souls, nor any acquaintance with their state. It is an unknown, undiscovered region to which they are removed. While we are here in a world of sense, we speak of the world of spirits as blind men do of colors. When we arrive there we shall be amazed to find how much we were mistaken.

19. *Dwelleth.* Has its constant and settled abode. Whither goes the sun when it departs from this hemisphere? Where is the tabernacle and the chamber in which he is supposed to rest? And seeing there was a time when there was nothing but gross darkness upon the face of the earth, what way came light into the world? Which was the place where light dwelled at that time, and whence was it fetched? Whence came that orderly constitution and constant succession of light and darkness? Was this your work? Or were you privy to it, or a counselor, or assistant in it?

27. *To spring forth.* Until now God has put such questions to Job as were proper to convince him of his ignorance. Now he comes to convince him of his impotence. As it is but little that he can know, and therefore he ought not to arraign the divine counsels; so it is but little he can do, and therefore he ought not to oppose divine providence.

31. *Bind.* Restrain or hinder them. *Pleiades.* The seven stars, which bring in the spring. *Bands.* By which it binds up the air and earth, by bringing storms of rain and hail or frost and snow. *Orion.* This constellation rises in November and brings in winter. Both summer and winter will have their course? God indeed can change them when he pleases, can make the spring cold, and so *bind the sweet influences of the Pleiades,* and the winter warm, and so *loose the bands of Orion;* but we cannot.

32. *Bring forth.* Can you make the stars in the Southern signs arise and appear? *Arcturus.* Those in the northern. *His sons.* The lesser stars, which are

placed round about them and attend upon them as children upon their parents.

CHAPTER 39

26. *Fly.* So strongly, constantly, unweariedly, and swiftly. *South.* At the approach of winter, when wild hawks fly into warmer countries, as being impatient of cold. The birds of the air are proofs of the wonderful providence of God, as well as the beasts of the earth.

27. *Mount.* Flies directly upward until she be out of your sight; which no other bird can do.

29. *Her eyes.* Her sight is exceedingly sharp and strong, so that she is able to look upon the sun with open eyes, and to behold the smallest prey upon the earth or sea when she is mounted out of our sight.

CHAPTER 40

1. *Answered.* Having made a little pause to try what Job could answer. This is not said to be spoken out of the whirlwind, and therefore some think God said it in a still, small voice, which wrought more upon Job (as upon Elijah) than the whirlwind did. Though Job had not spoken any thing, yet God is said to answer him. For he knows men's thoughts and can return a fit answer to their silence.

10. *Deck.* Seeing you make yourself equal, yes, superior to me; take to yourself my great power, come and sit in my throne, and display your divine perfections in the sight of the world.

15. *Behemoth.* Very learned men take the leviathan to be the crocodile, and the behemoth to be the river-horse; which may fitly be joined with the crocodile, both being well known to Job and his friends, as being frequent in the adjacent parts, both amphibious, living and preying both in the water and upon the land.

19. *The chief.* He is one of the chief of God's works, in regard of its great bulk and strength.

CHAPTER 41

25. *Purify.* Those who ordinarily live in the neglect of God, "they cry unto the LORD in their trouble," and endeavor to purge their consciences from the guilt of their sins.

34. *King.* He can tame both the behemoth and leviathan, as strong and stout-hearted as they are. This discourse concerning them was brought in to prove that it is God only who can look upon proud men and abase them, bring them low, and hide them in the dust. He it is who *beholdeth all high things,* and when men deal proudly, he is above them. *He is a king over all the children of pride,* brutal or rational, and makes them either bend or break before him.

CHAPTER 42

2. *Thou canst.* Job here subscribes to God's unlimited power, knowledge, and dominion, to prove which was the scope of God's discourse out of the whirlwind. And his judgment being convinced of these, his conscience also was convinced of his own folly in speaking so irreverently concerning him.

5. *Seeth thee.* The knowledge which I had of your nature, perfection, and counsels was before now grounded chiefly upon the instructions of men. But now it is clear and certain, for it has

been immediately inspired into my mind by this your glorious apparition and revelation, and by the operation of your Holy Spirit; which makes these things as evident to me as if I saw them with my bodily eyes. When the mind is enlightened by the Spirit of God, our knowledge of divine things as far exceeds what we had before, as knowledge by ocular demonstration exceeds that by common fame.

7. *Ye have not.* This is not to be understood absolutely, but comparatively. Job was not so much to be blamed as they, because his opinion concerning the methods of God's providence and the indifference of its dispensations towards good and bad men was truer than theirs, which was that God did always reward good men and punish sinners in this life.

9. *Accepted Job.* And as Job prayed and offered sacrifice for those who had grieved and wounded his spirit, so Christ prayed and died for his persecutors, and "ever liveth to make intercession" for transgressors.

12. *Blessed.* Not only with spiritual, but also with temporal blessings. Just double to what they were (1:3). This is a remarkable instance of the extent of the divine providence to things that seem minute as this, the exact number of man's cattle, as also the harmony of providence and the reference of one event to another. For "known unto God are all his works from the beginning" to the end.

15. *So fair.* In the Old Testament we often find women praised for their beauty, but never in the New, because the beauty of holiness is brought to a much clearer light by the gospel.

psalms

PSALM 1

This psalm was put first as a preface to all the rest as a powerful persuasive to the serious study of the whole book and of the rest of the Holy Scripture, taken from that blessedness which attends upon the study and practice of it.

1. Many observe a gradation in this verse, the following clause still exceeding the former; for standing is more than walking, sitting more than standing, sinners in Scripture use are worse than the ungodly, and the scornful are the worst of sinners.

PSALM 2

There is nothing in this psalm which is not applicable to Christ, but some things are not applicable to David.

7. *My Son.* Which though it may in some sort be said to, or of, David; yet much more properly belongs to Christ, who is commonly known by this title both in the Old and New Testaments and to whom this title is expressly appropriated by the Holy Ghost, who is the best interpreter of his own words (Acts 13:33; Heb. 1:5).

9. *Them.* Those who will not quietly submit to you shall be crushed and destroyed by you. This was in part fulfilled when the Jews who persisted in unbelief were destroyed by the Roman power; and in the destruction of the pagan power when the Christian religion came to be established. But it will not be completely fulfilled until all opposing power and principality be put down.

PSALM 3

2. *Selah.* This word is nowhere used but in this poetical book and in the song of Habakkuk. Probably it was a musical note, directing the singer either to lift up his voice, to make a pause, or to lengthen the tune. But whatever it meant, it is generally placed at some remarkable passage, which gives occasion to think that it served also to quicken the attention of the singer and hearer.

PSALM 4

Title of the psalm. *Chief musician.* The director of the music of the temple.

4. *Upon your bed.* Calmly consider these things in the silent night when you are at leisure from distracting business. *Be still.* Compose your tumultuous minds.

7. *Thou hast.* Whatever you shall do with me for the future, I have at present unspeakable satisfaction in the testimonies of your love to my soul; more than worldly persons have in the time of a plentiful harvest.

PSALM 5

1. *Meditation.* My prayer accompanied with deep thoughts and fervent affections of soul.

3. *Morning.* Every morning. "When I awake, I am still with thee" (139:18). The first thing that I do is to pray to you.

PSALM 6

6. *My tears.* It well becomes the greatest spirits to be tender and to relent under the token of God's displeasure. David, who could face Goliath, himself melts into tears at the remembrance of sin and under the apprehension of divine wrath, and it is no diminution to his character.

8. *Hath heard.* By the working of God's grace upon his heart he knew his prayer was accepted. His tears had a voice in the ears of the God of mercy. Silent tears are not speechless ones. Our tears are cries to God.

PSALM 7

13. *Ordaineth.* Designs or fits for this very use. Of all sinners, persecutors are set up as the fairest marks of divine wrath. They set God at defiance, but cannot set themselves out of the reach of his judgments.

PSALM 8

1. *In.* Not only in Israel, but among all nations. Which shows that this psalm speaks of the Messiah and the times of the New Testament. *Heavens.* Where your throne of glory is established, where the blessed angels cele-brate your praises, where Christ sits at your right hand in glorious majesty, whence he pours down excellent gifts upon babes.

5. *For.* You have in Christ mercifully restored man to his primitive estate, wherein he was but one place removed below the angels; from which he was fallen by sin. *Crowned.* Man, fallen and lost man, who is actually restored to glory and dominion in Christ, his head and representative, who received this crown and dominion for man's good and in his stead; which he will in due time communicate to his members. And so the two expositions of this place concerning mankind and concerning Christ may be reconciled. For he speaks of that honorable estate conferred first upon Christ and then by his hands upon mankind. But the words more literally rendered are, "Thou madest him a little less than God." And hence some have inferred that man in his original state was the highest of all creatures.

PSALM 9

10. *Put their trust in thee.* The experience of your faithfulness to your people in all ages is a just ground for their confidence.

12. *For blood.* The bloodshed of his innocent and holy ones which, though he may not seem to regard for a season, yet he will certainly call the authors of it to a severe account.

16. *Higgaion.* This is either a musical term or a note of attention intimating that the matter deserves deep meditation or consideration.

PSALM 10

5. *Judgments.* Your threatenings denounced against, and punishments inflicted upon sinners. *Are far.* He does not regard or fear them; yes, he despises them, being confident that he can blow them away with a breath. This is a gesture of contempt both in Scripture and in other authors.

10. *Croucheth.* Like a lion (for he continues the same metaphor) which lies close upon the ground, partly that he may not be discovered, and partly that he may more suddenly and surely lay hold on his prey.

16. *The LORD is King.* To whom it belongs to protect his subjects. Therefore his people's case is never desperate, seeing he ever lives to help them.

PSALM 11

2. *For lo.* David, having directed his speech to his enemies, now turns it to God and pours out before him his complaints.

4. *Temple.* In heaven, which is mentioned as an evidence of his glorious majesty, of his sovereign power and dominion over all men and things, and of his accurate inspection into all men and their actions. *Throne.* Where he sits to examine all causes and to give righteous sentence according to every man's works. *Try.* He thoroughly discerns all men, their most inward and secret actions. And therefore he sees and will reward my innocence in spite of all the slanders of my enemies. And he sees all their secret designs and will expose and defeat them.

5. *Trieth.* He chastens even righteous persons, yet still he loves them and therefore will in due time deliver them. But as for the wicked, God hates them and will severely punish them.

PSALM 12

6. *Pure.* Without the least mixture of falsehood, and therefore shall infallibly be fulfilled.

7. *Thou shalt keep them.* Your words or promises. These you will observe and keep, now and *from this generation for ever.*

PSALM 13

6. *I will sing.* It is a common thing for David and other prophets to speak of future deliverances as if they were already come, so that they may signify both the infallible certainty of the thing and their firm assurance of it.

PSALM 14

7. *Oh that.* These words immediately concern the deliverance of Israel out of that sinful state in which they now were, which, having described, he concludes with a prayer to God to help them *out of Zion,* where the ark then was; but principally they design the spiritual redemption and salvation of all God's Israel by the Messiah.

PSALM 15

2. *Uprightly.* Loving and serving God and loving his neighbor, not in word only, but in truth; and this constantly. *Worketh.* Makes it his business to do justly, to give to every one his due, first to God and then to men. *Speaketh.* His words and professions to God and men agree with the thoughts and purposes of his heart.

PSALM 16

As David was both a member and an eminent type of Christ, he speaks of himself sometimes in the one and sometimes in the other capacity. And therefore having spoken of himself as a member of Christ in the former part of the psalm, he proceeds to consider himself as a type of Christ. Toward the close he speaks such things as though they might be accommodated to himself in a very imperfect sense, yet could not properly belong to any but to Christ, to whom therefore they are justly appropriated in the New Testament.

8. *I have set.* I have always presented him to my mind as my witness and judge, as my patron and protector. Until now, David seems to have spoken with respect to himself, but now he is transported by the spirit of prophecy and carried above himself to speak as a type of Christ, in whom this and the following verse were truly accomplished. Christ as man did always set his Father's will and glory before him. *Right hand.* To strengthen, protect, assist, and comfort me; as this assistance of God was necessary to Christ as man.

10. *Hell.* In the state of the dead. *Holy One.* Me your holy Son, whom you have sanctified and sent into the world. It is peculiar to Christ to be called "the Holy One of God."

11. *Life.* You will raise me from the grave and conduct me to the place and state of everlasting felicity. *Presence.* In that heavenly paradise, where you are gloriously present, where you do clearly and fully discover the light of your countenance; whereas in this life you hide your face. *Right hand.* Which he mentions as a place of the greatest honor, the place where the saints are placed at the last day and where Christ himself is said to sit (110:1). *Pleasures.* All our joys are empty and defective; but in heaven there is fullness of joy. Our pleasures here are transient and momentary; but those at God's right hand are *pleasures for evermore.* For they are the pleasures of immortal souls in the enjoyment of an eternal God.

PSALM 17

3. *Night.* When men's minds, being freed from the distraction of business and from the society of men, act more vigorously and freely, according to their several inclinations.

15. *I will.* I do not place my portion in earthly treasures, but in beholding God's face, in the enjoyment of God's presence and favor; which is enjoyed in part in this life, but not fully. *Satisfied.* The time is coming wherein I shall be abundantly satisfied with beholding your face. *Awake.* When I arise from the dead. *Likeness.* With the image of God stamped upon my glorified soul.

PSALM 18

2. *Horn.* It is a metaphor from those beasts whose strength lies in their horns.

10. *Upon a cherub.* Or, "upon the cherubim," upon the angels, who are also called God's chariots (68:17), on which he is said to sit and ride. All which is not to be understood grossly, but only to denote God's using the ministry of angels in raising such storms and tempests.

19. *Brought.* Out of my straits and difficulties into a state of freedom and comfort. So he ascribes all his mercies to God's good pleasure, as the first spring of them.

25. *Upright.* You give to everyone the same measure which he gives out to others. And therefore you will perform mercy and truth to those who are merciful and true to others.

49. *The heathen.* David is here transported beyond himself and speaks this in special relation to Christ, who was to be his seed, and of whom he was an eminent type, and by whom alone this was done. And therefore this is justly applied to him and to his calling of the Gentiles (Rom. 15:9).

PSALM 19

3. *Heard.* Or, "understood." There are many nations in the world which have several languages, so that one cannot converse with or be understood by another; but the heavens are such a universal teacher that they can speak to all people and can be clearly understood by all.

4. *Words.* Their magnificent structure, their exquisite order and most regular course, by which they declare their author no less than men discover their minds by their words.

7. *The law.* The doctrine delivered to his church, whether by Moses or by other prophets. Having discussed the glory of God shining in the visible heavens, he now proceeds to another demonstration of God's glory, which he compares with and prefers before the former. *Perfect.* Completely discovering both the nature and will of God and the whole duty of man, what he is to believe and practice, and whatever is necessary to his present and eternal happiness. Whereas the creation, although it did declare so much of God, has left all men without excuse, yet did not fully manifest the will of God, nor bring men to eternal salvation. *Converting.* From sin to God, from whom all men have naturally revolted.

8. *The eyes.* Of the mind, with a complete manifestation of God's will and man's duty. Both which the works of nature and all the writings of men discover but darkly and imperfectly.

12. *Cleanse.* Both by justification, through the blood of your Son, and by sanctification through your Holy Spirit. Though the first may seem to be principally intended because he speaks of his past sins. *Secret.* From the guilt of such sins as were secret; either from others, such as none knows but God and my own conscience; or from myself, such as I never observed or did not discern the evil of. Pardon my unknown sins of which I never repented particularly as I should have done.

13. *Presumptuous.* From known and evident sins such as are committed against knowledge, against the checks of conscience, and the motions of God's Spirit. *Dominion.* If I be at any time tempted to such sins, Lord, let them not prevail over me, and if I do fall into them, let me speedily rise again.

14. *Let.* Having prayed that God would keep him from sinful actions, he now prays that God would govern and sanctify his words and thoughts. And this was necessary to preserve him from presumptuous sins which have their first rise in the thoughts. *Redeemer.* This expression seems to be added emphatically and with special respect to Christ, to whom alone the Hebrew word *goel* can properly belong.

PSALM 20

6. *Now.* We are already sure of victory by the consideration of God's power and faithfulness and love to David and to his people. They speak as one person because they were unanimous in this prayer.

PSALM 21

Title of the psalm. *Of David.* The subject of this psalm is the same as the former, both being made for the people's use concerning the king. But the prayers there used are here turned into praises for the blessings received in answer to their prayers. And as David was an illustrious type of Christ, so in many of these expressions he looks beyond himself to Christ in whom they are properly and fully accomplished.

4. *For ever.* You gave him a long life and reign here, and after that did translate him to live with you for ever. But this was more eminently fulfilled in Christ, who asked of his Father life, or "to save him from death" (Heb. 5:7), though with submission to his will. But his Father, though he saw it necessary to take away his temporal life, yet instantly gave him another far more noble at his right hand, even the perfect possession of an everlasting life, both in his soul and body.

PSALM 22

It is confessed that David was a type of Christ and that many passages of the Psalms, though literally understood of David, yet had a further and mystical reference to Christ. But there are some other passages which were directly and immediately intended for, and are properly to be understood of, the Messiah. Though even in this there may be some respect and allusion to the state of the penman himself. And this seems to be the state of this psalm, which is understood of the Messiah by the Hebrew scholars themselves, and by Christ himself and by his apostles. And there are many passages in it which were literally accomplished in him and cannot be understood of any other.

7. This and the next verse are applied to Christ (Matt. 27:39, 43).

14. *Water.* My spirits are spent and gone like water, which once spilled can never be recovered. My very flesh is melted within me, and I am become as weak as water.

16. *Pierced.* These words cannot with any probability be applied to David, but were properly and literally verified in Christ.

18. *They part.* This also cannot be applied to David, but was literally fulfilled in Christ (Matt. 27:35; John 19:24).

22. *Congregation.* The same whom he called the congregation and the seed of Jacob and Israel. Which also does not so fitly agree to David, who never gives this title to any but such as were near akin to him, as it does to Jesus Christ, who extends this name to all his disciples (Matt. 12:48–49) and to whom this very text is applied (Heb. 2:11–12).

26. *Satisfied.* This is doubtless to be understood of those spiritual blessings such as the grace, peace, and comfort which all believing souls have in the sense of God's love, the pardon of their sins, and the influences of God's Spirit.

27. *The world.* All nations from one end of the world to the other. So this is an evident prophecy of the calling of the Gentiles, and a clear proof that this psalm immediately speaks of Christ, to whom alone this and many other passages of it belong.

29. *Fat.* Kings and princes, and the great men of the world. *Shall eat.* Shall feed upon the bread of life, Christ and all his benefits.

31. *Unto.* Unto succeeding generations. Whereby David gives us a key to understand this psalm and teaches us that he speaks not here of himself, but of things which were to be done in after-ages, even of the spreading of the gospel among the Gentiles in the time of the New Testament.

PSALM 23

2. *Lie down* To repose myself at noon, as the manner was in those hot countries. *Green.* Where there is both delight and plenty of provisions.

3. *For.* Not for any worth in me, but for the glory of his justice, faithfulness, and goodness.

4. *Thy rod and thy staff.* Two words

denoting the same thing, and both designating God's pastoral care over him.

5. *Oil.* With aromatic ointments, which were then great used at feasts; your comforts delight my soul. *Runneth over.* You have given me a plentiful portion, signified by the cup, given to the guests by the master of the feast.

PSALM 24

This psalm is generally thought to have been composed by David upon bringing the ark of God from the house of Obed–edom into the tabernacle which David had built for it (II Sam. 6). Wherein he has a further prospect to the temple which he earnestly desired and intended to build. Moreover, because the tabernacle, temple, and ark were types of Christ, of his church, and of heaven, David extended his thoughts to them also, or at least the Holy Ghost designed to comprehend them under these typical expressions.

7. *Lift up.* He speaks here of the gates and doors of the temple, which by faith and the spirit of prophecy he beheld as already built, whose doors he calls *everlasting,* not so much because they were made of strong and durable materials, as in opposition to those of the tabernacle which were removed from place to place. These gates he bids *lift up your heads,* or tops, by allusion to those gates which have a portcullis, which may be let down or taken up. And as the temple was a type of Christ, his church, and heaven, so this place may also contain a representation either of Christ's entrance into his church or into the hearts of his faithful people, who are here commanded to set open their hearts and souls for his reception. Or it could represent his ascension into heaven, where the saints or angels are poetically introduced as preparing the

way and opening the heavenly gates to receive their Lord and *King,* who is returning to his royal habitation with triumph and glory.

The King. The Messiah, the king of Israel, and of his church, called "the King," or "Lord of glory" (I Cor. 2:8; James 2:1); both for that glory which is inherent in him and that which is purchased by him for his members.

9. *Lift up.* The same verse is repeated again, to awaken the dullness of mankind who are so hardly brought to a serious preparation for such solemnities, and to signify the great importance of the matter contained under these expressions.

PSALM 25

10. *All the paths.* All the dealing of God with them; yes, even those that are afflictive are done in kindness and faithfulness to them.

14. *The secret.* His love and favor, which is called his "secret" (Job 29:4; Prov. 3:32) because it is known to none but him who enjoys it.

PSALM 26

3. *For.* I dare appeal to you, because you know I have a deep sense of your *lovingkindness,* by which I have been led to love and obey you.

12. *Standeth.* I stand upon a sure and solid foundation, being under the protection of God's promise and his almighty and watchful providence.

PSALM 27

1. *My light.* My counselor in all my difficulties, and my comforter and deliverer in all my distresses.

4. *Dwell.* Have opportunity of constant attendance upon God. *To behold.* That there I may delight myself in the contemplation of your amiable and glorious majesty and of your infinite wisdom, holiness, justice, truth, and mercy.

13. *The living.* David was thus earnestly desirous of this mercy in this life; not because he placed his portion in these things, but because the truth and glory of God were highly concerned in making good the promise of the kingdom to him.

PSALM 28

3. *Draw not.* Do not drag me, as you do these, to execution and destruction.

5. *They regard not.* The providential works of God towards his people.

7. *I am helped.* He speaks of it as past because God assured him by his Spirit that he had heard and accepted his prayers.

PSALM 29

It is possible David wrote this psalm during a storm of thunder, lightning, and rain; as that he wrote Psalm 8 in a moon-shining night, and Psalm 19 in a sun-shining morning.

2. *Give.* The honor which he deserves. Own him as the Almighty and the only true God.

9. *Glory.* Having showed the terrible effects of God's power in other places, he now shows the blessed privilege of God's people, who are praising God in his temple when the rest of the world are trembling under the tokens of his displeasure.

PSALM 30

5. *Cometh.* Speedily and in due season.

7. *Mountain.* My kingdom. Kingdoms are ususally called mountains in prophetical writings.

9. *Shall the dust.* Shall they who are dead celebrate your goodness in the land of the living? Or, shall my dust praise you?

11. *Girded me.* With joy, as with a garment, surrounding me on every side.

PSALM 31

4. *For thou.* You have delivered me formerly, and therefore I commit myself to you for the future.

5. *O LORD.* Who has showed yourself so, in making good your promise.

15. *My times.* All the affairs and events of my life are wholly in your power.

19. *Laid up.* His favor is not always manifested to them, but it is laid up for them in his treasure, whence it shall be drawn forth when they need it, and he sees it fit.

PSALM 32

Title of the psalm. *Maschil.* Or, an instructor. This psalm is fitly so called because it was composed for the information of the church in that most important doctrine, the way to true blessedness.

2. *Imputeth.* Whom God does not charge with the guilt of his sins, but graciously pardons and accepts him in Christ. *No guile.* Who freely confesses all his sins and turns from sin to God with all his heart.

8. *Mine eye.* So Christ did St. Peter when he turned and "looked upon him."

PSALM 33

4. *His works.* All his works of providence agree with his word and are the accomplishment of his promises or threatenings.

6. *By the word.* God made this admirable structure of the heavens and all its glorious stars, not with great pains and time, but with one single word.

10. *The LORD.* Thus he passes from the work of creation to the works of providence, and from the instances of his power in senseless and irrational creatures to his power in overruling the thoughts, wills, and actions of men, whether single or united.

18. *Behold, the eye.* Whoever therefore would have safety must expect it only from the watchful eye and almighty hand of God.

PSALM 34

8. *O taste.* Make trial of it by your own experience of it. *Good.* Merciful and gracious.

12. *Life.* A long and happy life, begun in this world and continued for ever in the next.

14. *Pursue it.* Do not only embrace it gladly when it is offered, but follow hard after it when it seems to flee away from you.

18. *Unto.* Those whose spirits are truly humbled under the hand of God and the sense of their sins, whose hearts are subdued and made obedient to God's will and submissive to his providence.

PSALM 35

16. *Mockers.* They made themselves buffoons and jesters, and accustomed themselves to mock and deride David, that thereby they might gain admittance to the tables of great men, which was all they sought.

17. *Darling.* My soul (Heb.: "my only one"). Which is now left alone and forsaken by my friends and hath none to trust in but God.

20. *Speak not peace.* They breathe out nothing but threatenings and war. They use not open violence, but subtle artifices against me and my followers, who desire nothing more than to live quietly and peaceably.

PSALM 36

1. *No fear.* When I consider the manifold transgressions of ungodly men, I conclude within myself that they have cast off all fear of the divine majesty.

2. *Flattereth.* He deceives himself with vain persuasions that God does not mind his sins or will not punish them.

7. *Lovingkindness.* Though all your attributes be excellent, yet above all, your mercy is most excellent, or precious and amiable.

9. *Thy light.* In the light of your glorious presence, which shall be fully manifested when we see you face to face. *See light.* Joy and comfort and happiness. The word "light" is elegantly repeated in another significance; in the former clause it is light discovering, here it is light discovered or enjoyed.

PSALM 37

5. *Commit.* All your cares and business and necessities commend to God by fervent prayer.

8. *Fret not.* Either against the sinner for his success, or against God. *Do evil.* If grief arise in you, take care that it does not transport you to sin.

11. *But.* Those who patiently bear God's afflicting hand and meekly pass by injuries. *Peace.* Partly of outward peace and prosperity, which God in his due time will give them, but principally of inward peace in the sense of God's favor and the assurance of endless happiness.

25. *Forsaken.* These temporal promises were more express to the Jews in the times of the Old Testament than to Christians.

PSALM 38

Title of the psalm. *To bring.* Either to God, that by this humble and mournful prayer he might prevail with God, to remember and pity him; or to himself, that by reviewing this psalm afterwards he might call to mind his former danger and misery, and God's wonderful mercy in delivering him; and that others also might remember what God had done to him.

7. *Disease.* The disease might be some burning fever, breaking forth outwardly in carbuncles or boils. It is true that this and the other expressions may be taken figuratively, but we should not forsake the literal sense of the words without necessity.

PSALM 39

6. *Vain shew.* In an imaginary rather than a real life. In the pursuit of vain imaginations in which there is nothing solid or satisfactory. Man and his life and all his happiness in the world are rather appearances and dreams than truths and realities. *Are disquieted.* Hebrew: "They make a noise, bustling, or tumult," with unwearied industry seeking for riches, and troubling and vexing both themselves and others in the pursuit of them.

12. *A stranger.* I am only in my journey or passage to my real home, which is in the other world.

PSALM 40

This psalm is a celebration of God's great goodness to him and all his people. In it there are some passages which cannot belong to Christ and some which do not properly belong to David or to that time and state of the church, but only to Christ and to the times of the New Testament.

4. *To lies.* To lying vanities such as worldly power, wisdom, and riches and all other earthly things or persons in which men are prone to trust; which are called lies because they promise more than they perform.

5. *Many.* This verse seems to be interposed as a wall of partition between that which David speaks in his own person and that which he speaks in the person of the Messiah in the following verses.

7. *Then said I.* These words literally and truly belong to Christ, and the sense is this: Seeing you require a better sacrifice than those of the law, lo, I offer myself to come and I will in due time come into the world. This phrase is explained in many places of Scripture and particularly Hebrews 10:5, where this place is expressly applied to Christ.

8. *I delight.* This is eminently true of Christ and is here observed as an act of heroic obedience, that he not only resolved to do but delighted in doing the will of God or what God had commanded, which was to die; and that a most shameful, painful, and cursed death. *My heart.* I do not only understand it, but receive it with heartiest love, delighting both to meditate on it and to yield obedience to it.

11. *Withhold not.* David, having been transported by the Spirit of God to the commemoration of the great mystery of the Messiah, now seems to be led back by the same Spirit to the consideration of his own case.

12. *Taken hold.* Men's sins are figuratively said to take hold of them, as an officer takes hold of a man whom he arrests.

PSALM 41

4. *Heal.* The soul is said to be healed when it is pardoned and purged.

9. *Yea.* These words were literally fulfilled in David, and yet the Holy Ghost looked further in them, even to Christ and Judas, in whom they received a fuller accomplishment.

13. *Amen.* Signifies a hearty assent and approbation and an earnest desire of the thing to which it is annexed. And as the Psalms are divided into five books, so each of them is closed with this word.

PSALM 42

1. *Panteth.* After the enjoyment of God in the sanctuary.

2. *Appear.* In the place of his special presence and public worship.

7. *Deep.* One affliction comes immediately after another as if it were called for by the former. A metaphor taken from violent and successive showers of rain; which frequently descend from heaven, as it were, *at the noise,* or call, of God's *waterspouts.*

PSALM 43

3. *Send out.* That is, actually discover them. *Truth.* Your favor, or the light of your countenance and the truth of your promises made to me; or the "true light," the illumination of your Spirit and the direction of your gracious providence whereby I may be led in the right way to your holy hill.

PSALM 44

17. *Yet.* Although we cannot excuse ourselves from many other sins, yet through your grace we have kept ourselves from apostasy and idolatry in spite of all examples and provocations.

25. *Our belly.* We are not only thrown down to the earth, but we lie there like carcasses.

PSALM 45

This psalm is an illustrious prophecy of the Messiah and points at him alone as a bridegroom espousing the church to himself and as a king ruling in it. And our Savior probably alludes to this where he compares the kingdom of heaven to a royal marriage. We have no reason to think it has any reference to Solomon's marriage with Pharaoh's daughter. It is meant purely of Christ and no other, and to him it is applied in the New Testament.

1. *Pen.* He was only the pen or instrument in uttering this song. It was the Spirit of God by whose hand this pen was guided.

2. *Fairer.* Than all other men. Which is most true of Christ; but not of Solomon, whom many have excelled in holiness and righteousness, which is the chief part of the beauty celebrated in this psalm.

4. The gospel is compared to a horse or chariot upon which Christ is said to ride when the gospel is preached and carried about from place to place.

5. *Arrows.* The same with the sword; this is no other than his word, which is sharp and powerful and pierces the hearts of men.

8. *Palaces.* The king is here supposed to reside in his ivory palaces, and his garments are so fragrant that they not only perfume the whole palace in which he is, but the sweet savor is perceived by those who pass by them, all which is poetically said with allusion to Solomon's glorious garments and palaces. The heavenly mansions may not unfitly be called ivory palaces, as elsewhere in the same figurative manner they are said to be adorned with gold and precious stones; from which mansions Christ came into the world, into which Christ went, and where he settled his abode after he went out of the world, and from where he poured all the fragrant gifts and graces of his Spirit. There is no necessity to strain every particular circumstance in such poetical descriptions, for some expressions may be used only as ornaments as they are in parables; and it may suffice to know that the excellencies of the king Christ are described by things in which earthly potentates place their glory.

9. As the queen is the church in general, so these honorable women are particular believers who are daily added to the church (Acts 2:47). And although the church is made up of particular believers, yet she is distinguished from them for the sake of the parable.

PSALM 46

2. *Though.* Though there should be nothing but confusion and desolations round about us; which are often expressed by such metaphors.

4. *A river.* This may design the gracious presence and blessing of the Lord, which is frequently described under the name of waters. *Make glad.* Shall not barely preserve it from danger, but give great occasion for rejoicing and thanksgiving.

10. *Be still.* Stir no more against my people. *God.* The only true and almighty God; your gods are but dumb and impotent idols.

PSALM 47

This psalm seems to have been composed upon the occasion of carrying the ark from the house of Obed–edom into the city of Zion (II Sam. 6). But as Zion was a type of the church and the ark a type of Christ, so it has a further reference even to Christ's ascension into heaven, and to the spreading of his kingdom in all parts of the world.

5. *God.* This is meant literally of the ark; but mystically of Christ's ascension into heaven, as may be gathered by comparing this with Ephesians 4:8, where the like words appear concerning the ark upon the same occasion.

8. *The throne.* Heaven is often called God's "throne," whence God is said to behold and to rule all nations; of which this general dominion of God he here speaks. And Christ sits at his Father's right hand for that purpose.

9. *The princes.* The Gentiles who were divided in their principles and interests and religions are now united and gathered together to Christ, laying their scepters at his feet and jointly owning his worship and service. And although he mentions their conversion only, yet the conversion of their people might reasonably be supposed.

PSALM 48

2. *The joy.* This is spoken prophetically, because the joyful doctrine of the gospel was to go from there to all nations.

8. *Establish.* God will defend her in all succeeding ages. And so God would have done if Jerusalem had not forsaken him and forfeited his protection.

PSALM 49

5. *Heels.* That is, supplanters. This character fitly suits David's enemies, who were not only malicious, but deceitful and treacherous.

14. *Sheep.* Which for a season are fed in sweet pastures, but at the owner's pleasure are led away to the slaughter. *Death.* The first death shall consume their bodies, and the second death shall devour their souls. *The upright.* Good men whom they abused at their pleasure. *Morning.* In the day of the general judgment and the resurrection of the dead.

15. *God.* Though no man can find out a ransom to redeem himself, yet God can and will redeem me. *The grave.* The grave shall not have power to retain me, but shall be forced to give me up into my Father's hands.

20. *The beasts.* Though he has the outward shape of a man, yet in truth he is a beast, a stupid and unreasonable creature.

PSALM 50

The design of this psalm is to reprove the common miscarriages of many professors of religion who satisfied their own consciences and fancied that they pleased God with their external and ceremonial performances, in spite of their neglect of piety, justice, and charity. And to instruct men concerning the nature of the true and acceptable worship of God.

Title of the psalm. *Asaph.* Who was not only the chief of the sacred singers, but also a prophet (II Chron. 25:1) and a composer of several psalms (II Chron. 29:30).

1. *Called.* All the inhabitants of the earth, from one end to the other, whom he here summons to be witnesses of his proceedings in this solemn judgment between him and his people, which is here poetically represented. For here is a tribunal erected, the judge coming to it, and the witnesses and delinquents summoned, and at last the sentence given.

5. *Those that have made a covenant with me* and have ratified that covenant by sacrifice. This seems to be added to acquaint them with the proper nature, use, and end of sacrifices, which were principally appointed to be signs and seals of the covenant made between God and his people; and consequently to convince them of their great mistake in trusting to their outward sacrifices when they neglected the very life and soul of them, which was the keeping of their covenant with God.

14. *Offer.* If you would know what sacrifices I prize and indispensably require, in the first place it is that of thankfulness, proportional to my great and numberless favors; which does not consist merely in verbal acknowledgments, but rather proceeds from a heart deeply affected with God's mercies and is accompanied with such a course of life as is well pleasing to God.

PSALM 51

4. *Thee only.* Which is not to be understood absolutely, because he had sinned against Bathsheba and Uriah, and many others; but comparatively. So the sense is, though I have sinned against my own conscience and against others, yet nothing is more grievous to me than that I have sinned against you.

5. *Behold.* Nor is this the only sin which I have reason to bewail before you; for this filthy stream leads me to a corrupt fountain. And upon a review of my heart, I find that this heinous crime was the proper fruit of my vile nature, which ever was and still is ready to commit ten thousand sins, as occasion offers.

6. *Truth.* Uprightness of heart; and this may be added as an aggravation of the sinfulness of original corruption because it is contrary to the holy nature and will of God, which requires rectitude of heart. And, as an aggravation of his actual sin, that it was committed against that knowledge which God had written in his heart.

8. *Joy.* By your Spirit seal the pardon

of my sins on my conscience, which will fill me with joy.

16. *Not sacrifice.* This is not to be understood absolutely with respect to David's crimes, which were not to be expiated by any sacrifice.

PSALM 52

1. *Continually.* God is continually doing good. You are continually doing mischief.

5. *Root.* Though you seem to have taken deep root, yet God shall pluck you up by the very roots and destroy you, both root and branch.

PSALM 53

5. *Scattered.* Has not only broken their bones, their strength, and force, but also dispersed them here and there so there is no hope of a restoration.

PSALM 54

3. *Strangers.* The Zephites,[1] whom, though Israelites, he calls "strangers" in regard of their barbarous and perfidious carriage.

5. *Thy truth.* Whereby you are engaged to fulfill your promises and threatenings.

PSALM 55

9. *Tongues.* Their speech, as you did at Babel (Gen. 11:1), their votes and opinions and counsels; which was eminently done among Absalom's followers (II Sam. 17). *City.* Jerusalem, which in Absalom's time was a sink of all sins.

15. *Them.* All such as pretend to religion and have manifestly apostasized both from the profession and practice of it.

18. *For.* For there were more with me than against me; even the holy angels whom God employed to defend and deliver me.

22. *Burden.* All your crosses, cares, and fears, lay them upon the Almighty by faith and prayer. He directs this speech to his own soul and to all good men in like circumstances.

PSALM 56

4. *Will praise.* I will praise the Lord for his word, for his promises of protection and deliverance made to his people. *Flesh.* Infirm and mortal men, called "flesh" by way of contempt (as Ps. 78:39; Isa. 31:3).

6. *They gather.* After they have severally employed their thoughts against me, they meet together to compare them and to put them in execution.

PSALM 57

4. *Lions.* Fierce and bloody men. *Set on fire.* From hell. Who are mere firebrands, breathing out wrath and threatenings and incensing Saul against me.

5. *Exalted.* Glorify your power, goodness, justice, and faithfulness by my deliverance.

PSALM 58

1. *O congregation.* The word seems to point at Saul's judges and counselors, who met together to consult what they should do against David. *Sons of men.* So he calls them to remind them that they were men and must give an account to God for all their hard speeches.

5. *Not hearken.* As they commonly

---

[1] (54:3) "Ziphim" in the title of the psalm. A clan or family affiliated with Caleb (I Chron. 2:42; 4:16) who settled in the hill country of Judah, where David hid from Saul (I Sam. 23:14–15).

say of the adders, such really are these men. They are deaf to all my counsels, to their own consciences, and to God's law.

7. *Melt away.* As waters arising from melted snow, which at first run with great force, but are suddenly gone.

PSALM 59

7. *Belch out.* Sharp and bitter words, abundantly and vehemently, as a fountain does waters.

11. *Scatter.* Let them wander from place to place, that they may carry the tokens of your justice and their own shame to all places.

PSALM 60

2. *Tremble.* A poetical expression signifying great changes among the people.

3. *To drink.* You have filled us with no less horror than men intoxicated with strong drink.

6. *Rejoice.* Therefore I will turn my prayers into praises for what God has already done.

PSALM 61

5. *Heritage.* You have granted me this singular mercy, to live in God's land, to enjoy his presence, and to worship in his tabernacle; which is the heritage that all who fear you prize and desire above all things.

6. *Prolong.* The years of my life and reign. Thus he speaks, because his kingdom was not like Saul's, but established to him and his heirs; and because Christ, his son and heir, should actually and in his own person possess the kingdom forever.

7. *Before God.* Living and ruling as in God's presence, serving God and worshipping him in his tabernacle.

PSALM 62

12. *Therefore.* God is almighty and therefore can easily destroy all his enemies. He is also merciful and therefore will pardon good men's failings. *Renderest.* And this as he is obliged to do by his holy nature, so is he able to do it, being omnipotent, and so is he willing to do it to the godly because he is merciful and gracious.

PSALM 63

1. *Flesh.* The desire of my soul is so vehement that my very body feels the effects of it.

2. *To see.* To enjoy. *Power.* The powerful and glorious effects of your gracious presence.

PSALM 64

6. *Iniquities.* They study diligently to find new ways of doing mischief. *Deep.* Cunning, both to contrive and conceal, and to execute their plots.

PSALM 65

4. *Satisfied.* With the blessings there conferred upon your people, the favor and fellowship of God, remission of sins, renovation of heart and life, joy and peace, and well-grounded assurance of eternal life.

5. *The confidence.* You are the stay and support of all mankind by your powerful and gracious providence.

8. The whole verse speaks of the natural works of God, the former clause of such as are extraordinary and terrible, the latter of such as are ordinary and delightful.

13. *Sing.* They are abundantly satisfied with your goodness and in their manner sing forth praise of their benefactor.

PSALM 66

10. *Proved us.* As it were in a burning furnace, and with a design to purge out our dross.

PSALM 67

6. *Then.* When the people of the earth shall be converted to God, God will cause it to yield them abundance of all sorts of fruits. Under which blessing, all other blessings both temporal and spiritual are comprehended.

PSALM 68

The occasion of the psalm seems to have been David's transporting of the ark to Zion, which was managed with great solemnity and devotion. For the first words are the very same which Moses appointed for just such occasions (Num. 10:35), and the following verses pursue the same matter. Thence he falls into a description of some of the glorious works of the God to whom this ark belonged.

But because David knew that both himself and the ark were types of Christ, and that the church of Israel were a type of the catholic church consisting of Jews and Gentiles, and that the legal administrations were types of those of the gospel. He therefore, by the spirit of prophecy, looked through the types to the great mysteries of Christ's resurrection and ascension and of the special privileges of the Christian church and of the conversion of the Gentiles, and intermixes passages which immediately belong to these things; although the words be so ordered that they carry a manifest allusion to the present actions and may be applied to them in a secondary sense.

13. *Gold.* Beautiful and glorious, like the feathers of a dove which, according to the variety of its postures and of the light shining upon it, look like silver or gold.

17. *Among them.* Here the psalmist seems to be transported by the prophetic spirit from the narration of those external successes to the prediction of more glorious things, even the coming of the Messiah; and of the transcendent privileges and blessings accruing to mankind thereby. *As in Sinai.* God is no less gloriously, though less terribly, present here than he was in Sinai when the great God, attended with thousands of his angels, solemnly appeared to deliver the law. Yes, here is a greater privilege than Sinai had, the Lord Jehovah descending from heaven into a human body, as appears by his ascending back again, which the next verse describes.

18. *Ascended.* This has a manifest reference to Christ and his ascension into heaven, in whom alone it is literally accomplished, and to whom therefore it is ascribed (Eph. 4:8). Although the expressions are borrowed from the ancient custom of princes, who, after some glorious achievements, used to go up into their royal cities in triumphant chariots, being attended by their captive enemies and afterward to distribute gifts to their soldiers and subjects, and sometimes to do some acts of clemency even to their rebels and enemies.

Captivity. Those whom you have taken captive; death and sin, and the devil, and all the enemies of Christ and of his people, whom Christ led in triumph, having "spoiled them," and making "a shew of them openly" (Col. 2:15). *Received.* According to your manhood you have received from God all the treasures of wisdom and knowledge and all those gifts and graces of the Holy Spirit which are necessary either to the perfection of your nature or to the good of your church and people.

21. *Hairy.* In ancient times many people used to wear long and shaggy hair that their looks might be more terrible to their enemies.

31. This prophecy, as also the next verse, evidently belongs to the times of the Messiah.

33. *His voice.* His gospel, published by Christ and his apostles, assisted by the Holy Spirit sent from heaven; which might well be called God's voice, and that *a mighty voice,* because it produced such great and wonderful effects.

PSALM 69

5. *My sins.* But, O lord, although I have been innocent to my enemies, I am guilty of many sins and follies against you.

6. *For my sake.* Because of my sad disappointments. for if they see me forsaken, they will be discouraged by this example.

9. *Upon me.* I have been affected with your reproaches, as with my own. This, though truly belonging to David, yet was also directed by the Spirit of God in him to represent the disposition and condition of Christ, in whom it was more fully accomplished, to whom therefore it is applied in the New Testament, the first part of it in John 2:17 and the latter in Romans 15:3.

21. *Gall.* Instead of giving me that comfort which my condition required, they added to my afflictions. *Vinegar.* These things were metaphorically fulfilled in David, but properly in Christ, the description of whose sufferings was principally intended here by the Holy Ghost.

23. *Eyes.* Not the eyes of their bodies, but of their minds. They who shut their eyes and will not see, so they shall be judicially blinded.

PSALM 70

This psalm is copied almost word for word from Psalm 11 and perhaps is for that reason entitled *A psalm . . . to bring to remembrance.* For it may sometimes be of use to pray over again the prayers we have formerly made to God on like occasions. David here prays that God would send help to him, shame to his enemies, and joy to his friends.

PSALM 71

16. *Make mention.* To support and comfort myself with the remembrance of it. *Righteousness.* Of your faithfulness in making good all your promises.

PSALM 72

Many passages of this psalm do not point to Solomon, nor to any other king but the Messiah. It must therefore be acknowledged that this is a mixed psalm, belonging to Solomon imperfectly, but to Christ clearly and fully. Many expressions being so ordered that the reader might be led by them to the contemplation of Christ and of his kingdom. Which was the more necessary for the support of God's true Israel, because the Spirit of God foresaw Solomon's dreadful apostasy and the great miscarriages and calamities of his successors and of the kingdom under their hands; and therefore was pleased to fortify their hearts with that glorious condition which they should certainly enjoy under the Messiah. It is probable David dictated this psalm a little before he died, when he gave orders to proclaim Solomon king.

6. *He shall come.* Christ did come down from heaven and brought or sent down from heaven his doctrine (which is often compared to rain) and the sweet and powerful influences of his Spirit.

8. *Dominion.* From one sea to another, or in all the parts of the habitable world. And this was accomplished in Christ, and in him only.

15. *Live.* Long and prosperous, as Solomon; yes, eternally as Christ. *Gold.* This was done to Solomon (I Kings 10:15) and to Christ (Matt. 2:11). But such expressions as these being used of Christ and his kingdom are commonly understood in a spiritual sense.

16. *An handful.* This intimates the small beginnings of his kingdom; and therefore does not refer to Solomon, whose kingdom was in a manner as large at the beginning of his reign as at the end; but it exactly refers to Christ.

20. *The prayers.* This psalm is the last which David composed, for this was written but a little before his death.

PSALM 73

13. *In vain.* Hence I was sometimes tempted to think that religion was a vain, unprofitable thing. True religion is here described by its two principal parts, the cleansing of the heart and of the hands.

23. *Nevertheless.* Although I gave you just cause to cast me off, yet you did continue your care and kindness to me.

PSALM 74

This psalm, which so particularly describes the destruction of Jerusalem, was probably written by a different Asaph, who lived at the time of the captivity.[2]

2. *Thine inheritance.* The tribe of Judah, which you have in a special manner chosen for your inheritance and for the birth of the Messiah. Nor is it strange that he mentions this tribe

particularly, because the calamity here remembered did principally befall this tribe and Benjamin, which was united with it.

17. *Set.* You have fixed the bounds of the habitable world in general and of all the countries and people upon earth. And as this clause shows God's power over all places, so the next displays his dominion over all times and seasons.

PSALM 75

3. *I bear.* I support it by maintaining religion and justice, by setting up good magistrates, and encouraging good ministers and good men, who are indeed the pillars of a nation.

5. *Lift not.* A metaphor from untamed oxen, which will not bow their heads to receive the yoke.

PSALM 76

8. *Thou.* Did execute judgment upon your enemies by an angel from heaven; which is said to be heard, either because it was accompanied with thunders and earthquakes, or because the fame of it was quickly spread abroad.

10. *Surely.* The furious attempts of your enemies shall cause your people and others to praise you for your admirable wisdom, power, and faithfulness.

PSALM 77

10. *I said.* These suspicions of God's faithfulness proceed from the weakness of my faith.

19. *Not known.* Because the water returned and covered them.

20. *Leddest.* First through the sea, and afterwards through the wilderness,

---

[2] (Ps. 74) See Psalm 50.

with singular care and tenderness as a shepherd does his sheep.

PSALM 78

2. *Dark sayings.* Not that the words are hard to understand, but that the things such as God's transcendent goodness, their unparalleled ingratitude, and their stupid ignorance and insensibleness under such excellent teachings of God's word and works are prodigious and hard to be believed.

18. *Tempted.* Desired a proof of God's power. *Lust.* Not for their necessary subsistence, but out of an inordinate and luxurious appetite.

49. *Evil angels.* Whom God employed in producing these plagues.

57. *Deceitful bow.* Which either breaks when it is drawn, or shoots awry and frustrates the archer's expectation.

PSALM 79

This psalm appears to have been written by the later Asaph upon the destruction of Jerusalem by the Chaldeans.

8. *Prevent.* Prevent our utter extirpation.

PSALM 80

This psalm was composed upon occasion of some calamity which befell the tribes of Israel after their division into two kingdoms and before the captivity of either of them. In which time all the evils mentioned herein did befall them, sometimes in one part, and sometimes in another.

3. *Before Ephraim.* Here is an allusion to the ancient situation of the tabernacle in the wilderness, where these tribes were placed on the west side of the tabernacle, in which the ark was, which consequently was before them.

16. *They.* Your people, signified by the vine. So now he passes from the metaphor to the thing designed by it.

17. *Right hand.* Benjamin signifies "the son of the right hand," a dearly beloved son, as Benjamin was to David. *Son of man.* The people of Israel, who are often spoken of as one person, as God's son and firstborn.

PSALM 81

5. *A language.* The Egyptian language, which at first was unknown to the Israelites (Gen. 42:23), and probably continued so for some considerable time because they were much separated both in place and conversation from the Egyptians.

7. *Secret place.* From the dark and cloudy pillar, whence I thundered against the Egyptians.

PSALM 82

1. *The gods.* Judges and magistrates are called gods because they have their commission from God and act as his deputies.

6. *All . . . children.* Representing my person and bearing both my name and authority.

PSALM 83

13. *A wheel.* Whereas they promise to themselves a sure possession, let them be like a wheel which is very unstable and soon removed.

14. *The mountains.* The woods upon the mountains which in those hot countries, when they have once taken fire, burn with irresistible violence.

PSALM 84

5. *Whose strength.* Who trusts in you as his only strength. *The ways.* Blessed are they whose hearts are set upon Zion and their journey is there.

6. *Baca.* A dry valley in the way to Jerusalem, here put for all places of like nature. *Make it a well.* They dig many little pits or wells in it for their relief. *The rain.* God recompenses their diligence with his blessing, sending rain with which they may be filled.

11. *Sun.* To enlighten and quicken, to direct and comfort his people. *Shield.* To save his people from all their enemies.

PSALM 85

9. *His salvation.* That complete salvation for which all the Israel of God wait, even the redemption by the Messiah. Of this, not only Christian but even Jewish writers understand this place and to which the following passages properly belong. And the psalmist might well say this salvation was nigh, because the seventy weeks determined by Daniel were begun. *Glory.* The glorious presence of God and the God of glory himself, even Christ, who is "the brightness of his [Father's] glory."

10. *Kissed.* That great work of redemption by Christ shall clearly manifest God's mercy in redeeming his people Israel and in the conversion of the Gentiles. It shall manifest his truth in fulfilling that great promise of sending his Son, his righteousness in punishing sin on his Son, and in conferring righteousness upon guilty and lost creatures. And it shall manifest his peace or reconciliation to sinners and that peace of conscience which attends upon it.

PSALM 86

2. *Holy.* Sincerely devoted to your service.

11. *Truth.* In the way of your precepts, which are true and right in all things. *My heart.* Knit my whole heart to yourself.

PSALM 87

2. *Zion.* That is, Zion itself, or Jerusalem, which was built upon and near Mount Zion. He said Zion rather than Jerusalem to intimate that he loved Jerusalem for Zion's sake, or for the temple which he chose for his peculiar dwelling place.

5. *Establish.* And this shall not be a transient, but a lasting work. Zion shall continue in its strength and fertility because the almighty God is her founder and protector.

7. *Singers.* There shall be great rejoicing and praising God, both with vocal and instrumental music, for this glorious work of the conversion of the Gentiles. He describes evangelical worship by legal phrases and customs, as the prophets frequently do.

PSALM 88

This is the most melancholy of the psalms; it is all lamentation and mourning and woe.

5. *Free.* Well-nigh discharged from the warfare of the present life and entered as a member into the society of the dead.

7. *Waves.* With your judgments, breaking in furiously upon me like the waves of the sea.

PSALM 89

This psalm manifestly treats the declining state of the house and kingdom of David in or about the Babylonian captivity.

4. *Build up.* I will perpetuate the kingdom to your posterity; which was promised upon condition and was literally accomplished in Christ.

27. *Firstborn.* As he calls me father (v. 26), so I will make him my son, yes, my firstborn; who had many privileges above other sons. This and the following passage in some sort agree to David, but are properly accomplished in Christ. *Higher.* This also was in some sort accomplished in David, but more fully in the Messiah.

29. *For ever.* To sit upon the throne for ever, as the next words explain it. This was accomplished only in Christ.

48. *What man.* All men at their best estate are mortal and miserable; kings and people must unavoidably die by the conditions of their natures; and therefore, Lord, do not increase our affliction.

52. *Blessed.* Let thine enemies reproach you and your promises concerning the sending of the Messiah; I will heartily bless and praise you for them and encourage myself with them.

PSALM 90

Title of the psalm. *A prayer of Moses.* Who, considering the terrible sentence of God concerning the cutting off of all that sinful generation in the wilderness, takes occasion to publish these meditations concerning man's mortality and misery.

1. *Dwelling place.* Although we and our fathers for some generations have had no fixed habitation, yet you have been instead a dwelling place to us by your watchful and gracious providence. And this intimates that all the following miseries were not to be imputed to God, but themselves.

3. *Sayest.* Did prounounce that sad sentence, *Return,* O men, to the dust out of which you were taken (Gen. 3:19).

4. *Past.* Indeed time seems long when it is to come, but when it is past, very short and contemptible.

12. *Teach us.* To consider the shortness of life and the certainty and speediness of death. *That.* That we may heartily devote ourselves to true wisdom.

17. *Let the beauty of the* LORD. His gracious influence and glorious presence. *Upon us.* Do not only work for us, but in us.

PSALM 91

3. *Pestilence.* From the pestilence which like a fowler's snare takes men suddenly and unexpectedly.

5. *By night.* When evil accidents are most terrible and least avoidable. *Arrow.* The pestilence or any such destructive calamity; such are frequently called God's "arrows." *By day.* You shall be kept from secret and open mischiefs.

13. *The lion.* Shall lie prostrate at your feet, and you shall securely put your feet upon his neck. *Dragon.* By which he understands all pernicious creatures, though never so strong, and all sorts of enemies.

14. *Because.* This and the two following verses are the words of God.

PSALM 92

13. *Planted.* Whom God by his gracious providence has fixed there. *The house.* In its courts; he means in the church of God, whereof all good men are living members.

14. *Old age.* Their last days shall be their best days, wherein they shall grow in grace and increase in blessedness.

PSALM 93

This and the six following psalms, according to the opinion of the Hebrew scholars, belong to the times of the Messiah.

1. *Moved.* He will overrule all the

confusions in the world so that they shall end in the erection of that kingdom of the Messiah, which can never be moved.

5. *Testimonies.* He seems here to speak of those precious promises concerning the erection of his kingdom in the world by the Messiah.

PSALM 94

11. *Thoughts.* Yes, he knoweth all things, even the most secret things as the thoughts of men; and in particular your thoughts, and much more your practices.

12. *Blessed.* Those afflictions which are accompanied with divine instructions are great and true blessings.

PSALM 95

The author of this psalm was David, as is affirmed in Hebrews 4:7. It has a special reference to the days of the Messiah; so it is understood by the apostle (Heb. 3:7; 4:3–9).

7. *Pasture.* Whom he feeds and keeps in his own pasture or in the land which he has appropriated to himself.

8. *Harden not.* By obstinate unbelief.

10. *Do err.* Their hearts are insincere and bent to backsliding.

PSALM 96

This psalm is a part of that which was delivered to Asaph and his brethren (I Chron. 16:7) on the occasion of bringing up the ark to the city of David.

1. *O sing.* Upon this new and great occasion, not the removal of the ark, but the coming of the Messiah.

9. *Beauty.* Clothed with all those gifts and graces which are necessary in God's worship.

13. *Before.* At the presence and approach of their Lord and Maker.

PSALM 97

Christ is the Alpha and Omega in this psalm.

7. *Gods.* All you whom the Gentiles have made the objects of their worship.

8. *Zion.* Your people dwelling in Zion, or Jerusalem, to whom Christ came. *Heard.* The fame of your judgments and the setting up of the kingdom of the Messiah.

PSALM 98

2. *Salvation.* The redemption of the world by the Messiah; which was hitherto reserved as a secret among the Jews, yes, was not thoroughly known by most Jews themselves. *Righteousness.* His faithfulness in accomplishing this great promise.

PSALM 99

4. *Judgment.* Though his dominion be absolute and his power irresistible, yet he manages it with righteousness.

6. *Moses.* Moses before the institution of the priesthood executed that office (Exod. 24:6). *That call.* Who used frequently and solemnly to intercede with God on behalf of the people.

8. *Forgavest.* The people for whom they prayed, so far as not to inflict that total destruction upon them which they deserved.

PSALM 100

An exhortation to praise God and to rejoice in him.

PSALM 101

This psalm was composed by David between the time of God's promising the kingdom to him and his actual possession of it.

1. *I will sing.* I will praise you, O Lord, for your mercy and justice, which you have so eminently revealed in the government of the world and of your people; and I will make it my care to imitate you herein.

PSALM 102

9. *Bread.* The sense is, dust and ashes are as familiar to me as the eating of my bread; I cover my head with them; I sit, yes, lie down in them, as mourners often did.

10. *Lifted me.* As a man lifts up a thing as high as he can, that he may cast it to the ground with greater force.

22. *When.* When the Gentiles shall gather themselves to the Jews and join with them in the worship of the true God.

23. *The way.* In the midst of the course of our lives. Some think the psalmist here speaks of the whole commonwealth as of one man, and of its continuance as of the life of one man.

24. *In the midst.* Before they come to a full possession of your promises and especially of that fundamental promise of the Messiah. *Thy years.* Though we die, yet you are the everlasting God.

PSALM 103

5. *The eagle's.* Which lives long in great strength and vigor.

14. *Knoweth.* The weakness and mortality of our natures and the frailty of our conditions, so that if he should let loose his hand upon us, we should be irrecoverably destroyed.

21. *His hosts.* A title often given to the angels in regard of their vast numbers, mighty power, unanimous concurrence, and exquisite order. *Ministers.* This Hebrew word is commonly used of the highest and most honorable sort of servants.

PSALM 104

David in the foregoing psalm praises God for his love to his people; in this, for his works of creation and providence.

5. *For ever.* As long as the world continues. God has fixed so strange a place for the earth that, being a heavy body, one would think it should fall every moment. And yet which way soever we would imagine it to stir, it must, contrary to the nature of such a body, fall upwards, and so can have no possible ruin but by tumbling into heaven.

19. *For seasons.* To distinguish the times, the seasons of many natural events, as of the ebbing and flowing of waters and other seasons for sacred and civil affairs, which were commonly regulated by the moon.

21. *Roar.* They roar when they come within sight of their prey. *Seek* Their roaring is a kind of natural prayer to God for relief.

30. *Spirit.* That quickening power of God by which he produces life in the creatures from time to time. For he speaks not here of the first creation, but of the continued production of living creatures.

31. *Rejoice.* Thus God advances the glory of his wisdom and power and goodness in upholding the works of his hands from generation to generation, and he takes pleasure in the preservation of his works as also in his reflection upon these works of his providence.

32. *He looketh.* This is a further illustration of God's powerful providence. As when he affords his favor to creatures, they live and thrive, so on the contrary, one angry look or touch of his upon the hills or earth makes them tremble and smoke, as Sinai did when God appeared in it.

35. *Praise ye the* LORD. Hebrew:

Hallelujah. This is the first time that this word occurs. It comes in here on the occasion of the destruction of the wicked. And the last time it occurs (Rev. 19) it is on a like occasion, the destruction of Babylon.

PSALM 105

In the former psalm we praise God for his common providence; in this, for his special favors to his church. The first eleven verses of it David delivered to Asaph (I Chron. 16:7) to be used in the daily service of the sanctuary.

15. *Anointed.* My prophets, Abraham, Isaac, and Jacob; who are called God's anointed because they were consecrated to be his peculiar people and to be kings and priests in their families. And they are called prophets because God familiarly conversed with them and revealed his will to them, and by them to others.

41. *River.* They flowed in channels which God provided for them, and followed the Israelites in their march.

PSALM 106

The foregoing psalm was a history of God's goodness to Israel; this is a history of their rebellions against him. Probably both were written by David at the same time, as we find the first verse and the two last verses in that psalm which he delivered to Asaph (I Chron. 16:35).

15. *Soul.* Into their bodies. So their inordinate desire of pampering their bodies was the occasion of destroying them.

23. *Breach.* God had made a wall about them; but they had made a breach in it by their sins, at which the Lord, who was now justly become their enemy, might enter to destroy them. This he certainly would have done if Moses by his prevailing intercession had not hindered him.

26. *Lifted up.* He swore. Of this dreadful and irrevocable oath of God, see Numbers 14.

37. *Devils.* They did not worship God as they pretended, but devils in their idols; for those spirits which were supposed by the heathen idolaters to inhabit in their images were not good spirits, but evil spirits, or devils.

45. *Repented.* Changed his course and dealing with them.

PSALM 107

The psalmist here observes God's providential care of the children of men in general and shows how he helps those who are in any distress in answer to their prayers.

6. *The* LORD. Hebrew: *Jehovah.* For the heathens had many of them some knowledge of the true God.

12. *Heart.* The pride and obstinacy of their hearts.

34. *For.* He does not inflict these judgments without cause, but for the punishment of sin in some, and the prevention of it in others.

PSALM 108

The first five verses of the psalm are taken out of Psalm 57, the rest out of Psalm 60.

1. *Glory.* With my tongue.

PSALM 109

7. *His prayers shall become sin.*[3] Because it is not from his heart.

---

[3] (109:7) KJV: "Let his prayer become sin." In this verse, verse 6, and succeeding verses, Wesley rejects the KJV's "let," which we interpret "allow." Instead he renders the meaning as "shall," relieving some matter of controversy.

17. *Delighted not.* In defining and promoting the welfare of others.

18. *Like water.* Water in the cavity of the belly, between the bowels, is almost certain death. *Like oil.* And oil soaking into any of the bones will soon utterly destroy it.

PSALM 110

That this psalm belongs to the Messiah is abundantly evident, both from the express testimony of the New Testament (Acts 2:34; I Cor. 15:25; Heb. 1:13; 10:13) and from the consent of the ancient Hebrew scholars. Of him it is directly and immediately to be understood. The Spirit of God wisely so ordered this matter that it might be a convincing testimony against the unbelieving Jews concerning the true Messiah, and concerning the nature and quality of his kingdom.

1. *The LORD.* God the father. *Said.* Decreed it from eternity, and in due time published this decree and actually executed it. This he did when he raised up Christ from the dead and brought him into his heavenly mansion. *Unto.* Unto his Son the Messiah, whom David designedly calls his Lord to admonish the whole church, that although he was his Son according to his human nature, yet he had a higher nature and was also his Lord as being God blessed for ever and consequently Lord of all things. The Hebrew word *Adon* is one of God's titles, signifying his power and authority over all things, and therefore is most fitly given to the Messiah, to whom God has delegated all his power (Matt. 28:18).

2. *The rod.* Your strong or powerful rod, and the rod is put for his scepter, or kingly power. But as the kingdom of Jesus Christ is not carnal, but spiritual, so this scepter is nothing else but his word.

3. *People.* Your subjects shall offer you as their king and Lord not oxen or sheep but themselves, their souls and bodies, as living sacrifices and as free-will offerings, giving up themselves to the Lord (II Cor. 8:5), to live with him and to die for him. *The dew.* That is, your offspring (the members of the Christian church) shall be more numerous than the drops of the morning dew.

7. *Drink.* He shall have a large portion of afflictions while he is in the way or course of his life, before he comes to that honor of sitting at his Father's right hand. Waters in Scripture frequently signify sufferings. To drink of them signifies to feel or bear them.

PSALM 111

This and several of the following psalms seem to have been written for the service of the church in their solemn feasts. It is composed alphabetically, each sentence beginning with a different letter of the Hebrew alphabet.

3. *Righteousness.* His justice or faithfulness in performing his word.

9. *Redemption.* The deliverance out of Egypt, which was a type of that higher redemption by Christ. *Reverend.* Terrible to his enemies, venerable in his people's eyes, and holy in all his dealings with all men.

PSALM 112

6. *Moved.* Though he may for a season be afflicted, yet he shall not be eternally destroyed.

9. *For ever.* What he gives is not lost, but indeed is the only part of his estate which will abide with him to all eternity.

10. *The desire.* Either of the misery of good men, or of his own constant prosperity.

PSALM 113

6. *Humbleth.* Who is so high that it is a wonderful condescension in him to take any notice of his heavenly host, and much more of sinful and miserable men upon earth.

PSALM 114

This and the four following psalms the Jews used to sing at the close of the Paschal supper. It is a solemn commemoration of God's delivering Israel, giving them the law, and water out of the rock.

4. *The mountains.* Horeb and Sinai, two tops of one mountain, and other neighboring mountains.

7. *Tremble.* The mountains did no more than what was fit at the appearance of the great God.

PSALM 115

13. *Both small.* Of whatever quality, high and low, rich and poor.

16. *The LORD's.* In a peculiar manner, where he dwells in that light and glory, to which no man can approach. *Given.* As the foregoing verse declares that God was the creator of heaven and earth, so this asserts that he is also their Lord and governor to dispose of all men and things as he pleases.

PSALM 116

13. *The cup.* The phrase is taken from the common practice of the Jews in thank offerings. The master of the feast took a cup of wine into his hand, solemnly blessed God, and then gave it to all the guests, who drank successively of it.

15. *Precious.* He sets a high price upon it; he will not readily grant it to those who greedily seek it. If any son of violence procure it, he will make him pay dearly for it; and when the saints suffer it for God's sake, it is a most acceptable sacrifice to God.

PSALM 117

This is an exhortation to all nations to praise God for his mercy and truth.

PSALM 118

The form of this psalm seems to be dramatic, and several parts of it are spoken in the name of several persons; as it is in the book of the Song of Solomon and in some parts of Ecclesiastes. David speaks in his own name from the beginning to verse 22; from then to verse 25 he speaks in the name of the people; and thence to verse 28 in the name of the priests; and then concludes in his own name.

20. *The righteous shall enter.* As David was a type of Christ and the temple of heaven, so this place has a further prospect than David and relates to Christ's ascending into heaven and opening the gates of that blessed temple, both for himself and for all believers.

22. *The builders.* The commonwealth of Israel and the church of God are here and elsewhere compared to a building, wherein, as the people are the stones, so the princes and rulers are the builders. *Head stone.* The chief stone in the whole building by which the several parts of the building are upheld and firmly united together. Thus David united all the tribes and families of Israel; and thus Christ united Jews and Gentiles. Therefore this place is justly expounded of Christ (Mark 12:10; Acts 4:11; Rom. 11:32; Eph. 2:20). And to him the words agree more properly than to David.

PSALM 119

Because this psalm was very large, and the matter of it of the greatest importance, the psalmist thought fit to divide it into twenty-two parts, according to the number of the Hebrew letters, so that he might both prevent tediousness and fix it in the memory. Each part consists of eight verses. All the verses of the first part begin with Aleph, all the verses of the second with Beth, and so on. It is observable that the word of God is here called by the names of "law," "statutes," "precepts" or "commandments," "judgments," "ordinances," "righteousness," "testimonies," "way," and "word." By which variety he designed to express the nature and perfection of God's word.

It is called his "word," as revealed by him to us; "his way," as prescribed by him for us to walk in; his "law," as binding us to obedience; his "statutes," as declaring his authority of giving us laws; his "precepts," as directing our duty; his "ordinances," as ordained by him; his "righteousness," as exactly agreeable to God's righteous nature and will; his "judgments," as proceeding from the great judge of the world, and being his judicial sentence to which all men must submit; and his "testimonies," as it contains the witnesses of God's will, and of man's duty. And there is but one of these 176 verses in which one or another of these titles is not found.

The general scope and design of this psalm is to magnify the law and make it honorable; to show the excellence and usefulness of divine revelation, and recommend it to us by the psalmist's own example; who speaks by experience of the benefits of it, for which he praises God and earnestly prays for the continuance of God's grace to direct and quicken him in his way.

11. *Hid.* I have laid it up in my mind like a choice treasure, to be ready upon all occasions to counsel, quicken, or caution me.

18. *Open.* Enlighten my mind by the light of your Holy Spirit, and dispel all ignorance and error. *Behold.* Those great and marvelous depths of divine wisdom and goodness, those profound mysteries of Christ and God's grace to mankind and of that everlasting state, which are not to be known but by divine illumination.

36. *Covetousness.* He mentions this in particular, because it is most opposite to God's testimonies and does most commonly hinder men from receiving his word and from profiting by it; and because it is most pernicious as being the root of all evil.

37. *Vanity.* The vain things of this present world, such as riches, honors, pleasures; from beholding them with desire or affection. *Quicken.* Make me lively, vigorous, and fervent in your service.

53. *Horror.* A mixed passion made up of abhorrence of their sins, and dread and sorrow at the consideration of the judgments of God coming upon them.

55. *Thy name.* Your holy nature and attributes, your blessed word, and your wonderful works. *In the night.* When darkness caused fear in others, I took pleasure in remembering you; when others gave themselves up to sleep, my thoughts and affections were working towards you.

80. *Sound.* That I may love and obey them sincerely, constantly, and universally.

96. *Perfection.* Of the greatest and most perfect enjoyments of this world. *Commandment.* Your word; one part of it being put for the whole. *Broad.* Or, large. Both for extent and for continuance; it is useful to all persons, it is of everlasting truth and efficacy, it will never deceive those who trust to it, as all worldly things will, but will make men happy both here and for ever.

100. *Because.* The practice of religion is the best way to understand it.

102. *Taught me.* By your blessed Spirit, illuminating my mind and working upon my heart.

129. *Wonderful.* In regard of the deep mysteries, the most excellent directions, and the exceeding great and precious promises of God contained in them.

136. *Rivers.* Plentiful tears, witness of my deep sorrow for God's dishonor and for the miseries which sinners bring upon themselves.

143. *Trouble.* Outward troubles and anguish of spirit.

175. *Judgments.* Your word or testimonies, which are the only ground of my hope in your help.

PSALM 120

4. *Arrows.* The wrath and vengeance of the mighty God, which in Scripture is often compared to arrows; and here to coals of juniper, which burn very fiercely and retain their heat for a long time.

5. *Mesech* and *Kedar* are two sorts of people often mentioned in Scripture and reckoned among the barbarous nations. But their names are here to be understood metaphorically. And so he explains himself in the next verse.

PSALM 121

1. *Hills.* To Zion and Moriah, which are called "the holy mountains."

5. *Shade.* To keep you from the burning heat of the sun.

6. *Smite.* With excessive heat. *Moon.* With that cold and moisture which come into the air by it. Intemperate

heats and colds are the springs of many diseases.

PSALM 122

This psalm seems to have been written for the use of the people when they came to Jerusalem at the three solemn feasts.

5. *Judgment.* The supreme courts of justice for ecclesiastical and civil affairs. *Thrones.* The royal throne allotted by God to David and to his posterity, and the inferior seats of justice under his authority.

PSALM 123

2. *Look.* For supply of their wants, and for help and defense against their oppressors. *Until.* Until he help and save us.

PSALM 124

5. *The proud.* Our enemies, compared to proud waters, for their great multitude and swelling rage.

PSALM 125

3. *Lest.* Lest they should be driven to indirect courses for relief.

5. *Lead them.* Unto sinful courses.

PSALM 126

This psalm was probably composed by Ezra at the return of the exiles from Babylon. Those who are returned are called upon to be thankful; those who remain there are prayed for and encouraged.

1. *Dream.* We were so surprised and astonished.

4. *Turn again.* As you have brought us home, bring also the rest of our brethren.

PSALM 127

1. *Build.* Assist and bless those who build it.

3. *Heritage.* Only from God's blessing, even as an inheritance is not the fruit of a man's own labor, but the gift of God.

4. *Youth.* These he prefers before other children because they live longest with their parents and to their comfort and support, whereas children born in old age seldom come to maturity before their parents' death.

5. *Speak.* They shall courageously plead their cause in courts of judicature, not fearing to be crushed by the might of their adversaries.

PSALM 128

3. *Olive plants.* Numerous, growing, and flourishing.

PSALM 129

4. *The cords.* With which the plow was drawn. By these cords he understands all their plots and endeavors.

8. *The blessing.* Which was a usual salutation given by passengers[4] to reapers; so the meaning is, it never continues until the harvest comes.

PSALM 130

4. *Forgiveness.* You are able and ready to forgive repenting sinners. *Feared.* Not with a slavish, but with a childlike fear. This mercy of yours is the foundation of all religion, without which men would desperately proceed in their impious courses.

7. *Israel.* Every true Israelite. *Plenteous.* Abundantly sufficient for all persons who accept upon God's terms.

PSALM 131

2. *Weaned.* Wholly depending upon God's providence, as the poor helpless infant relies upon its mother for support.

PSALM 132

Probably this psalm was written by Solomon to be sung at the dedication of the temple, of which he desires God would come and take possession (vv. 8–10). With these words he concluded his prayer (II Chron. 6:41–42).

5. *Until.* Until I have raised a house in which the ark may be put.

17. *A lamp.* A successor to continue forever in his family, as this phrase is expounded (I Kings 11:36; 15:4), and particularly one eminent and glorious light, namely, the Messiah.

PSALM 133

2. *Ointment.* It is no less grateful and refreshing than that oil which was poured forth upon Aaron's head at the time of his consecration to the priestly office.

3. *Zion.* It is as desirable as the dew which falls upon Mount Hermon, no, as desirable as that heavenly dew of God's ordinances and graces which he has commanded to fall upon the mountains of Zion and Moriah, and others which are round about Jerusalem.

PSALM 134

In this psalm the priests or Levites who watched all night in the temple exhort one another and pray for one another.

1. *Night.* Not only by day, but also by night, when their watch was more necessary.

---

[4](129:8) That is, "passersby."

3. *Thee*. You, whoever you are who faithfully perform the duty here commanded.

PSALM 135

6. *Seas*. In the visible seas and in the invisible depths, both of the earth and of the waters.

7. *Rain*. An eminent instance of his good providence.

PSALM 136

2. *The God of gods*. Who is infinitely superior to all that are called gods, whether angels or princes or idols.

25. *Food*. To all living creatures. For which God deserves great praises, which the psalmist teaches us to render to God for them, because those who are most concerned either cannot or do not perform this duty.

PSALM 137

Probably this psalm was written toward the end of the Babylonian captivity. Herein the captives complain of the scoffs of their enemies, yet remember Jerusalem and foresee the downfall of Babylon.

1. *Sat down*. The usual posture of mourners.

3. *A song*. Such songs as you used to sing in the temple of Zion.

8. *Happy*. As being God's instrument to vindicate his honor and execute his just judgments.

PSALM 138

5. *The ways*. His wonderful counsel and gracious providences.

8. *Perfect*. Will finish the great work of my deliverance. *Forsake not*. Or, do not give over the work of my salvation; which is thus far advanced, not by any human help, but by your power and providence.

PSALM 139

This psalm is, by many of the Jewish scholars, esteemed the most excellent in the whole book.

2. *Afar off*. You know what my thoughts will be in such and such circumstances long before I know it, yes, from all eternity.

3. *Compassest*. You discern every step I take. It is a metaphor from soldiers' besieging their enemies and setting watches 'round about them.

5. *Beset me*. With your all-seeing providence. *And laid*. You keep me, as it were, with a strong hand in your sight and under your power.

6. *I cannot* apprehend in what manner you do so perfectly know all things.

8. *Hell*. If I could hide myself in the lowest parts of the earth.

9. *The wings*. If I should flee from east to west. For the sea being the western border of Canaan is often put for the west in Scripture. And wings are poetically ascribed to the morning here, as they are elsewhere to the sun and to the winds.

10. *Hold me*. I could neither go thither without your conduct, nor subsist there without your powerful support.

11. *The night*. Shall be as clear to God as the light itself.

13. *Reins*. The most inward and hidden part of the body. *Covered*. With skin and flesh.

14. *For*. The infinite power and wisdom manifested in the curious structure of man's body fill me with wonder and astonishment, and with the dread of your majesty.

15. *In secret*. In the womb. *Wrought*. Hebrew: "embroidered." Exquisitely composed of bones and muscles and sinews and veins and arteries and other parts, all framed with such wonderful skill that even heathens, upon the contemplation of all the parts of man's body and how excellently they were framed both for beauty and use, have broken forth into admiration and adoration of the Creator. *Lowest parts*. In a place as secret and remote from human eyes as the lowest parts of the earth.

16. *Unperfect*. When I was first conceived. *Book*. In your counsel and providence, by which you did contrive and effect this great work, according to that model which you had appointed.

17. *Thoughts*. Your counsels on my behalf. You did not only form me at first, but ever since my conception and birth your thoughts have been employed for me.

18. *Count them*. Your wonderful counsels and works on my behalf come constantly into my mind.

22. *Perfect hatred*. See the difference between the Jewish and the Christian spirit!

PSALM 140

3. *Tongues*. Using words as sharp and piercing as the sting of a serpent.

10. *Coals*. Divine vengeance, which is compared to coals of fire.

13. *Dwell*. Shall constantly enjoy your gracious and powerful presence.

PSALM 141

4. *Heart*. Keep me not only from wicked speeches, but from all evil motions of my heart. *Dainties*. The pleasures or advantages which they gain by their wickedness.

7. *Our bones*. Our case is almost as hopeless as of those who are dead and whose bones are scattered in several places.

PSALM 142

3. *My path*. What paths I should choose whereby I might escape.

7. *Out of prison*. Set me at liberty. *Compass*. Shall flock to me from all parts, to rejoice and bless God with me and for me.

PSALM 143

3. *Soul*. My life; nothing less will satisfy him. *Dead*. I am in as hopeless a condition in the eye of man as those who have lain long in the grave.

PSALM 144

5. *Smoke*. As Sinai did at your glorious appearance (Exod. 19:18). This is a figurative and poetic description of God's coming to take vengeance upon his enemies.

8. *Falsehood*. Deceiving themselves, by being unable to do what they designed; and others, by not giving them that help which they promised.

12. *That*. This mercy I beg not only for my own sake, but for the sake of your people, that they may enjoy those blessings which you have promised them; and particularly, *that our sons*, who are the strength and hopes of a nation, may be like plants, flourishing and growing in height and strength, as plants do *in their youth;* for when they grow old, they wither and decay.

PSALM 145

14. *All*. All who look up to him for help.

15. *All*. Of all living creatures. *Wait*. Expect their supplies wholly from your bounty. Expectation is here figuratively ascribed to brute creatures.

PSALM 146

6. *For ever.* Both because he lives for ever to fulfill his promises, and because he is eternally faithful.

PSALM 147

4. *Calleth them.* He exactly knows them as we do those whom we can call by name.

9. *Ravens.* Which he mentions because they were most contemptible, especially to the Jews, to whom they were unclean; and because they are not only neglected by men, but also forsaken by their dams as soon as ever they can fly, and so are wholly left to the care of divine providence.

13. *Thy gates.* Your strength consists not in your walls, gates, and bars, but in his protection.

16. *Like wool.* Not only in color, shape, and softness, but also in use, keeping the fruits of the earth warm.

PSALM 148

6. *Stablished.* He has made them constant and incorruptible, not changeable, as the things of the lower world.

7. *Dragons.* Either serpents, which abide in the deep caverns of the earth; or whales and other sea-monsters, which dwell in the depths of the sea.

8. *Fulfilling his word.* Executing his commands, either for the comfort or punishment of the inhabitants of the earth.

14. *The horn.* In Scripture commonly denotes strength, victory, glory, and felicity.

PSALM 149

4. *The* LORD. He rejoices over them to do them good. *Beautify.* Make them amiable and honorable in the eyes of the world, who now hate and despise them.

7. *Vengeance.* For all their cruelties and injuries towards God's people. This was literally accomplished by David upon the Philistines, Ammonites, Syrians, and other neighboring nations.

PSALM 150

1. *Sanctuary.* In his temple. *The firmament.* In heaven; there let the blessed angels praise him.

6. *Every thing.* Every living creature in heaven and in earth.

PROVERBS

CHAPTER 1

2. *To know.* Written to help men to know thoroughly and practically. Both human wisdom to conduct our affairs in this life, and divine wisdom. *Instruction.* The instructions delivered either by God or men, in order to the attainment of wisdom.

3. *To receive.* Willingly to receive the counsels of others. Such as makes men wise and prudent and to teach just judgments or equity.

5. *Will hear.* Is willing to learn.

7. *The fear.* Reverence and obedience to God. *Beginning.* The foundation without which all other knowledge is vain. *Fools.* That is, wicked men are so far from attaining true wisdom that they despise it and all the means of getting it.

8. *My son.* He speaks to his scholars with paternal authority and affection.

17. *In vain.* The fowler who spreads his net in the sight of the bird loses his labor. But these are more foolish than the silly birds, and though they are not ignorant of the mischief which these evil courses will bring upon themselves, yet they will not take warning.

20. *Wisdom.* Having expressed the counsels of wicked men, he now declares the voice of wisdom. By wisdom he understands the wisdom of God revealed to men in his word. And this is said to cry with a loud voice, to intimate God's earnestness in inviting sinners to repentance.

22. *Scorners.* That scoff at religion and condemn the word and faithful ministers of God.

23. *My words.* By my Spirit I will cause you to understand my word.

24. *Called.* By my ministers, by my judgments, and by the motions of my Spirit and your own conscience.

29. *Knowledge.* The practical knowledge of God and of their duty.

CHAPTER 2

1. *Hide.* Lay them up in your heart with care, as men do their choicest treasures.

4. *Seekest her.* With unwearied diligence and earnest desire and patient expectation.

15. *Crooked.* Who swerve from the straight way of God's law, and have windings and turnings, to escape conviction.

17. *The covenant.* The marriage covenant; so called because God is the author of that mutual obligation. And because God is called to be the witness and judge of that solemn promise and covenant.

20. *That.* This depends on verse 11

and is mentioned as another happy fruit of wisdom.

CHAPTER 3

1. *My law.* The law of God, which might be called "his law," as the gospel is called "Paul's gospel" (II Tim. 2:8), because it was delivered by him.

3. *Mercy* denotes all benignity, charity, and readiness to do good to others. *Truth* or faithfulness respects all those duties which we owe to God or man, to which we have special obligation from the rules of justice. *Table.* In your mind and heart, in which all God's commands are to be received and engraved.

5. *Trust in the* LORD. Wholly rely upon God's promises and providences. *Lean not.* Under this one kind of carnal confidence he understands all other confidence in bodily strength, wealth, or friends.

13. *Findeth.* Which supposes his diligent searching for it.

18. *A tree.* A pledge of everlasting life. He alludes to the *tree of life,* and intimates that this is the only restorer of that life which we have lost by sin.

19. *By wisdom.* Either by Christ or by that divine perfection of wisdom, which is the fountain of wisdom in man.

32. *The righteous.* They are God's friends, to whom he imparts the favors and comforts to which other men are strangers.

CHAPTER 4

1. *A father.* Of me, who have paternal authority over you and affection for you.

4. *Said.* The following verses, at least as far as the tenth verse, are the words of David.

18. *But the path.* Just men daily grow in knowledge, grace, and consolation until all be perfected and swallowed up in glory.

25. *Right on.* Direct all your actions to a right end, and keep your mind fixed upon that way which leads to it, and neither look nor turn aside to the right hand or the left.

26. *Ponder.* Consider your actions before you do them, and see that they agree with the rule.

CHAPTER 5

9. *The cruel.* To the harlot; who, though she pretends love, yet in truth is one of the most cruel creatures in the world, wasting your estate and body without pity, and damning your soul forever.

14. *I am come in a moment into all evil.*[1] In how little a time am I now come into remediless misery!

15. *Drink.* Content yourself with those delights which God allows you in the sober use of the marriage bed.

19. *Satisfy thee.* At all convenient times; for that there may be excess in the marriage bed is manifest. *Ravished.* Love her fervently. It is a hyperbolical expression.

22. *Holden.* He is in perfect bondage to his lusts, and is neither able nor willing to set himself at liberty.

CHAPTER 6

3. *Make sure.* Or, prevail with thy friend; strive to win him by your incessant and earnest solicitations.

25. *Eyelids.* With her wanton glances.

31. *Restore.* He speaks not of that restitution which the law required, but of that which either the wronged per-

---

[1](5:14) KJV: "I was almost in all evil," the meaning of which is obscure both to his contemporaries and to us.

son might force the thief to make, or which the thief would willingly give rather than be exposed to public shame.

CHAPTER 7

3. *Bind them.* As a ring which is continually in a man's eye.

4. *And call.* Acquaint and delight yourself with her.

14. *Offerings.* I have paid my peace offerings which I had vowed. Whereby she signifies that she had plentiful provisions at her house for his entertainment. For the peace offerings were to be of the best flesh (Lev. 22:21), and a considerable part of these offerings fell to the offerer's share.

CHAPTER 8

1. *Wisdom.* It is a great question what this wisdom is. Some understand it of the divine wisdom; others of the second person in the Godhead. It cannot be denied that some passages best agree to the former, and others to the latter opinion. Possibly both may be joined together, and the chapter may be understood of Christ considered partly in his personal capacity, and partly in regard of his office, which was to impart the mind and will of God to mankind.

15. *By me.* They rule their kingdoms wisely and justly by my counsel and assistance. Their injustice is from themselves, but all the good they do they owe to my conduct.

21. *Substance.* Substantial happiness; opposed to all the worldly enjoyments, which are but mere shadows.

27. *I was there.* As co-worker with my Father.

31. *My delights were.* To uphold them by my power and providence, to reveal myself and my Father's will to them from age to age, to assume their nature, and to redeem and save them.

CHAPTER 9

3. *Maidens.* Her servants to invite the guests, ministers of the word whom he calls "maidens" for the sake of the parable. For wisdom, being compared to a great princess, was suited to be attended upon by maidens.

12. *For thyself.* You do not profit me, but yourself.

17. *Sweet.* From the difficulty of obtaining them; and because the very prohibition renders them more grateful to corrupt nature.

CHAPTER 10

6. *Violence.* Their own violence or injustice. This may be an allusion to the ancient custom of covering the mouths and faces of condemned malefactors.

14. *But.* Fools are more forward to lay out than to lay up, and for lack of knowledge speak much and foolishly, whereby they frequently bring destruction upon themselves.

18. *Lying lips.* With flattering words. He here condemns two opposite vices: secret hatred and manifest slander.

30. *The earth.* They shall not have so much as a quiet abode upon earth; much less shall they have a possession in heaven.

CHAPTER 11

22. *So is a fair woman which is without discretion.*

"Of beauty vain, of virtue void,
What art thou in the sight of God?
A slave to every base desire,
A creature wallowing in the mire.
Go, gaudy pageant of a day,
Thy folly, with thy face display:
Set all thy charms and graces out,
And shew—the Jewel in thy snout!"

29. *Wind.* Shall be as unable to keep what he gets as a man is to hold the wind in his hand.

CHAPTER 12

10. *Cruel*. There is cruelty mixed even with their most merciful actions.

12. *Desireth*. He approves those arts which wicked men use like nets to ensnare other men.

16. *Covereth*. The shame, or injury done to him, which he conceals and bears with patience.

17. *Deceit*. He who lies in his common talk will use falsehood and deceit in judgment.

19. *A moment*. Liars, though they may make a fair show for a season, yet are quickly convicted.

20. *Deceit*. They whose hearts devise mischief shall be deceived in their hopes and bring trouble upon themselves; but they who by good counsels labor to promote peace, shall reap the comfort of it themselves.

CHAPTER 13

7. *Maketh himself rich*. Some men who have little or nothing pretend to have great riches.

8. *Riches*. Riches enable a man to redeem his life when it is in greatest danger, and poverty preserves a man from many injuries.

9. *Rejoiceth*. Shines with a pleasant and constant brightness. Rejoicing is here ascribed to the light, as it is to the sun metaphorically (Ps. 19:5).

15. *Rough*. Offensive and hateful to God and men, as rough ways are to a traveler.

19. *Sweet*. Whatever men earnestly desire, the enjoyment of it is sweet to them; therefore sinners rejoice in the satisfaction of their sinful lusts and abhor all restraint of them.

CHAPTER 14

10. *Bitterness*. The inward griefs and joys of men's hearts are not known to any but a man's self.

13. *In laughter*. The outward signs of joy are often mixed with real sorrow.

17. *Dealeth foolishly*. His passion hurries him into foolish speeches and actions. *Wicked devices*. One who suppresses his passion, but meditates revenge.

24. *But*. As for rich fools, their folly is not cured, but made worse and more manifest by their riches.

30. *A sound heart*. Free from envy and inordinate passions. *Is the life*. Procures and maintains the health and vigor of the body.

31. *His Maker*. Whose image the poor man bears, by whose providence he is made poor, and who has declared himself to be their protector and their avenger.

CHAPTER 15

19. *An hedge*. As a way hedged up with thorns, troublesome, perplexed, and full of difficulties.

24. *The way*. The way a wise man takes to obtain life is to place his heart, treasure, and conversation on things above.

28. *The mouth*. Not the heart; for he rashly speaks what comes into his mouth, without the direction of his heart or conscience.

30. *Fat*. Not only cheers a man for the present, but gives him such stable comfort as revives his soul, and gives vigor to his body.

CHAPTER 16

1. *From the LORD*. Men can neither think nor speak wisely and well without divine assistance.

3. *Commit*. Refer all your actions and concerns to God as the end of them, and depend upon God's providence for success.

4. *The wicked*. Willful and impenitent

sinners. Men make themselves wicked, and God therefore makes them miserable.

17. *The highway.* The common road, in which they walk, though through frailty or temptation they slip into the bypath of sin.

CHAPTER 17

11. *Messenger.* Or, a cruel angel; the angel of death, the devil, or some bloody men employed by God to avenge his quarrel.

16. *No heart.* Neither discretion to discern the worth of wisdom, nor any sincere desire to get it.

17. *Is born.* Is sent into the world for this, that he might comfort and relieve his brother in adversity.

CHAPTER 18

4. *As a flowing brook.* That wisdom which is in his heart is continually pouring forth wise and good counsels.

20. *Satisfied.* Wise discourses tend to the satisfaction of the speaker, as well as to the good of the hearers.

21. *Death and life* are brought upon men by the good or bad use of their tongues.

CHAPTER 19

3. *Fretteth.* He ascribes his unhappiness not to his own sin, but to God and his providence.

10. *Delight.* To live in pleasure and outward glory does not become him nor suit him, because prosperity corrupts even wise men and makes fools mad.

25. *Simple.* Who sin through ignorance, being possibly drawn to it by the scorner's evil counsel or example.

CHAPTER 20

1. *Mocker.* Wine immoderately drunk makes men mockers.

11. *Is known.* The future disposition of a man may be probably conjectured from his childish manners.

13. *Open.* Shake off sloth and betake yourself to your employment with diligence and vigor.

18. *Established.* The way to bring our purposes to good effect is to manage them with serous consideration.

27. *The spirit.* The reasonable soul. *The candle* is a clear and glorious light set up in man for his information and direction. *Of the* LORD. So called because it comes from God in a more immediate manner than the body (Eccl. 12:7), and because it is in God's stead to observe and judge all our actions. *Searching all.* Discerning not only his outward actions, which are visible to others, but his most inward thoughts and affections.

30. *The belly.* Of the heart. Grievous wounds or stripes cleanse not only the outward man by keeping it from evil actions, but even the inward man, by expelling or subduing vile affections; which is a great and blessed benefit of afflictions.

CHAPTER 21

4. *The plowing.* Even their civil or natural actions which in themselves are lawful are made sinful as they are managed by ungodly men without any regard to the glory of God, which ought to be the end of all our actions.

11. *The wise.* The simple learn wisdom, both from the punishment of wicked men and from the prosperity of good men.

16. *Shall remain.* Shall, without repentance, be condemned to eternal death.

26. *Giveth.* By God's blessing upon his industry he procures enough not only for his own support, but for the relief of others.

CHAPTER 22

2. *The maker.* Not only as they are men, but as they are poor or rich, which difference comes from God's providence. They have one common creator, Lord, and judge, and the one cannot despise nor grudge at the other without reflecting upon God.

15. *Bound.* Is fixed and settled there, as being born with him and rooted in his very nature.

CHAPTER 23

2. *Put a knife.* Restrain your appetite, as if a man stood with a knife at your throat.

4. *Thine own wisdom.* From worldly wisdom, which persuades men to use all possible means to get riches.

7. *So is he.* You are not to judge him by his words, but by the constant temper of his mind.

23. *The truth.* The true and saving knowledge of God's will.

30. *Mixed wine.* Mixed either with water, or with other ingredients to make it strong and delicious.

31. *When it is red.* Which was the color of the best wines in that country. *Aright.* When it sparkles and seems to smile upon a man.

CHAPTER 24

5. *Is strong.* Is courageous and resolute, and able by wisdom to do greater things than others can accomplish by strength.

13. *Eat.* This is not a command, but a concession; and is only here expressed to illustrate the following verse. Honey in those parts was a usual food.

32. *Received.* I learned wisdom by his folly.

CHAPTER 25

1. *Men.* Certain persons appointed by Hezekiah for that work. Many of them are political precepts, and such as in a special manner concerned Hezekiah, and other princes, for the conduct of their house and kingdom. *Copied.* Out of the historical records which were then extant.

2. *The glory.* It is agreeable to the nature of God; it is a testimony of his infinite wisdom, and of his absolute power and sovereignty.

3. *The heart.* Though wise kings will search out other men, yet their inward thoughts and purposes are hardly discoverable.

6. *Stand not.* Do not affect frequent and familiar society with greater persons than yourself.

9. *Discover not.* Let not the heat of contention provoke you to divulge any of his secrets committed to your trust.

22. *For.* "In so doing," which words are expressed in Romans 12:20, where this text is quoted. You shall melt him into repentance and love.

CHAPTER 26

6. *Drinketh.* Drinking, in Scripture, frequently denotes the plentiful doing or receiving of anything.

9. *A thorn.* As a thorn is in a drunkard's hand, which he cannot manage cautiously, but employs to his own and others' hurt.

23. *Dross.* Such a tongue and heart are of no real worth, although sometimes they make a show of it, as dross does of silver.

CHAPTER 27

1. *Boast not.* Of any good thing which you purpose to do, or hope to receive tomorrow or hereafter. *Knowest not.* What may happen in the space of one day. The day is said to *bring forth* what God by his almighty power either causes or allows to be brought forth or done in it.

17. *Iron.* Iron tools are made sharp and fit for use by rubbing them against the file or some other iron.

19. *So.* So one man resembles another in the corruption of his nature.

20. *Hell . . . never full.* The grave devours all the bodies which are put into it and is always ready to receive and devour more.

CHAPTER 28

12. *Hidden.* Wise and good men, who only are worthy of the name of men, withdraw themselves into obscure places.

21. *For a piece of bread.* When a man has once accustomed himself to take bribes, a very small advantage will make him sell justice.

22. *Evil eye.* Is uncharitable to persons in need, and envious of those who get anything besides him.

26. *Wisely.* Distrusting his own judgment, and seeking the advice of others, and especially of God.

CHAPTER 29

15. *Left to himself.* Allowed to follow his own will without restraint and chastening.

18. *No vision.* No prophecy; no public preaching of God's word.

20. *Hasty.* Rash and heady in the management of his affairs.

21. *Delicately.* Allowing him too much freedom and familiarity.

CHAPTER 30

1. *The prophecy.* The prophetic instruction; for as the prophets were public preachers as well as foretellers of things to come, so their sermons, no less than their predictions, are commonly called their prophecies.

4. *Ascended.* To learn the mind of God who dwells there. *Descended.* To teach men below what he had learned above. No man can fully know and teach us these things unless he has been in heaven and sent down thence to the earth for that end.

9. *And deny thee.* By trusting to riches, which is a denial of God, and by unthankfulness for and abuse of his mercies.

15. *The horseleach.* An insatiable creature, sucking blood until it is ready to burst. *Two daughters.* The following things resemble the horseleach in its insatiableness; nothing being more ordinary than to call those persons or things the sons or daughters of those whose examples they imitate.

17. *The eye.* He who scorns or derides his parents, though it be with a look or gesture, and much more when he breaks out into opprobrious words and actions.

23. *Married.* For then she displays all those ill humors which before she concealed. *Is heir.* Which great and sudden change transports her beside herself and makes her insufferably proud and scornful.

CHAPTER 31

1. *Lemuel.* Of Solomon, by the general consent both of Jewish and Christian writers; this name signifies one from God, or belonging to God, and such a one was Solomon eminently, being given by God to David and Bathsheba as a pledge of his reconciliation to them after their repentance. Possibly his mother gave him this name, to remind him of his great obligations to God and of the justice of his devoting himself to God's service.

2. *My vows*. On whose behalf I have made many prayers and sacrifices and solemn vows to God; whom I have, as far as in me lay, devoted to the work and service and glory of God.

10. *A virtuous woman*. Here he lays down several qualifications of an excellent wife, which are delivered in alphabetical order, each verse beginning with a different letter of the Hebrew alphabet.

13. *Worketh*. She encourages them to work by her example; which was a common practice among princesses in those first ages. Not that it is the duty of kings and queens to use manual operations, but it is the duty of all persons, the greatest not excepted, to improve all their talents and particularly their time, which is one of the noblest of them, to the service of that God to whom they must give an account, and to the good of that community to which they are related.

18. *Her candle*. Which is not to be taken strictly, but only signifies her unwearied care and industry.

21. *Are clothed*. She has provided enough, not only for their necessity, but also for their delight and ornament.

23. *Known*. Observed and respected,

not only for his own worth, but for his wife's sake.

25. *Strength*. Strength of mind, magnanimity, courage, activity. *Rejoice*. She lives in constant tranquility of mind, from a just confidence in God's gracious providence.

26. *Openeth her mouth*. She is neither sullenly silent nor full of impertinent talk, but speaks discreetly and piously, as occasion offers. *In her tongue*. Her speeches are guided by wisdom and grace and not by inordinate passions. And this practice is called "a law" in "her tongue," because it is constant and customary and proceeds from an inward and powerful principle of true wisdom.

27. *Looketh well*. She diligently observes the management of her domestic business and the whole carriage of her children and servants.

30. *Favour is deceitful*. It gives a false representation of the person, being often a cover to a deformed soul; it does not give a man that satisfaction which at first he promised to himself from it; and it is soon lost, not only by death, but by many diseases and contingencies.

31. *Give her*. It is but just that she should enjoy those praises which her labors deserve. *Let her own works*. If men be silent, the lasting effects of her prudence and diligence will trumpet forth her praises.

ecclesiastes

CHAPTER 1

1. *The Preacher.* Who was not only a king, but also a teacher of God's people; who, having sinned grievously in the eyes of all the world, thought himself obliged to publish his repentance and to give public warning to all, to avoid those rocks upon which he had split.

2. This verse contains the general proposition which he intends particularly to demonstrate in the following book. *All.* All worldly things. *Is vanity.* Not in themselves, for they are God's creatures and therefore good in their kinds, but in reference to that happiness which men seek and expect to find in them. So they are unquestionably vain, because they are not what they seem to be and perform not what they promise, but instead of that are the occasions of innumerable cares, fears, sorrows, and mischiefs. No, they are not only vanity, but *vanity of vanities,* the vainest vanity, vanity in the highest degree. And this is redoubled because the thing is certain, beyond all possibility of dispute.

4. *Passeth.* Men continue but for one and that a short age, and then they leave all their possessions; and therefore they cannot be happy here, because happiness must needs be unchangeable

and eternal. Or else the certain knowledge of the approaching loss of all these things will rob a man of solid contentment in them.

9. *There is.* There is nothing in the world but a continued and tiresome repetition of the same thing. The nature and course of the beings and affairs of the world and the tempers of men are the same that they ever were and shall ever be. And therefore, because no man ever yet received satisfaction from worldly things, it is vain for any person hereafter to expect it.

15. *Crooked.* All our knowledge serves only to discover our miseries, but is utterly insufficient to remove them. It cannot rectify those disorders which are either in our own hearts and lives or in the men and things of the world.

CHAPTER 2

1. *I said.* Being disappointed of my hopes from knowledge, I resolved to try another course. *Go to.* O my soul! I will try whether I cannot make you happy by the enjoyment of sensual delights.

12. *I turned.* Being frustrated of my hopes in pleasure, I returned to a second consideration of my first choice to see whether there was not more satisfaction to be gotten from wisdom than I discovered at my first view.

13. *I saw.* I allowed thus much. Although wisdom is not sufficient to make men happy, yet it is of a far greater use than vain pleasures or any other follies.

CHAPTER 3

1. *A season.* A certain time appointed by God for its being and continuance, which no human wit or providence can alter. And by virtue of this appointment of God, all vicissitudes which happen in the world, whether comforts or calamities, come to pass. Which is here added to prove the principal proposition, that all things below are vain, and happiness is not to be found in them, because of their great uncertainty and mutability and transitoriness, and because they are so much out of the reach and power of men and wholly in the disposal of God.

Purpose. Not only natural, but even the voluntary actions of men are ordered and disposed by God. But it must be considered that he does not here speak of a time allowed by God wherein all the following things may lawfully be done, but only of a time fixed by God in which they are actually done.

11. Many events seem to be very irregular and unbecoming, as when wicked men prosper and good men are oppressed. But when men shall thoroughly understand God's works and the whole frame and texture of them, and see the end of them, they will say that all things were done wisely.

14. *Fear.* That by the consideration of his power in the disposal of all persons and things, men should learn to trust in him, to submit to him, to fear to offend him, and more carefully study to please him.

16. Solomon is still showing that every thing in this world without the fear of God is vanity. In these verses he shows that power, of which men are so ambitious, and life itself are worth nothing without it.

18. *Beasts.* That although God made them men, yet they have made themselves beasts by their brutish practices and that, considered only with respect to the present life, they are as vain and miserable creatures as the beasts themselves.

21. *Who knoweth?* True it is, there is a difference which is known by good men; but the majority of mankind never think of it. Their hearts are wholly set on present and sensible things and take no thought for the things of the future and invisible world.

CHAPTER 4

6. *Better.* These are the words of the sluggard making this apology for his idleness, that his little with ease is better than great riches got with much trouble.

13. *Better.* More happy. Now he proceeds to another vanity, that of honor and power.

CHAPTER 5

3. *A dream.* When men are oppressed with business in the day, they dream of it in the night.

7. *For.* There is a great deal of folly, as *in the multitude of dreams,* which for the most part are vain and insignificant, so also in *many words,* in making many vows whereby a man is exposed to many snares and temptations. *But.* Fear the wrath of God and therefore be sparing in making vows and just in performing them.

9. The wise man, after some interruption, returns to his former subject, the vanity of riches; whereof he mentions one evidence in this verse, that the poor laborer enjoys the fruits of the earth as well as the greatest monarch.

15. *To go.* Into the womb of the earth, the common mother of all mankind. *Take nothing.* This is another vanity. If his estate be neither lost nor kept to his hurt, yet when he dies he must leave it beyond him and cannot carry one handful of it into another world.

16. *The wind.* For riches, which are empty and unsatisfying, uncertain and transitory, which no man can hold or stay in its course; all which are the properties of the wind.

CHAPTER 6

7. *And yet.* Men are insatiable in their desires, and restless in their endeavors after more, and never say they have enough.

11. *Seeing.* This seems to be added as a conclusion from all the foregoing chapters; seeing not only man is a vain creature in himself, but there are also many other things which instead of diminishing do but increase this vanity, as wisdom, pleasure, power, wealth; seeing even the good things of this life bring so much toil, cares, and fears with them.

CHAPTER 7

7. *A gift.* A bribe given to *a wise man* deprives him of the use of his understanding. So this verse discovers two ways whereby a wise man may be made *mad:* by suffering oppression from others, or by receiving bribes to oppress others. And this also is an argument of the vanity of worldly wisdom that is so easily corrupted and lost.

11. *Good.* When wisdom and riches meet in one man, it is a happy conjunction.

12. *Life.* But herein knowledge or wisdom excels riches that whereas riches frequently expose men to destruction, true wisdom does often preserve a man from temporal and always from eternal ruin.

13. *For who.* No man can correct or alter any of God's works; and therefore all frettings at the injuries of men or calamities of time are not only sinful, but also vain and fruitless. This implies that there is a hand of God in all men's actions; either effecting them, if they be good, or permitting them, if they be bad, and ordering and overruling them whether they be good or bad.

14. *Be joyful.* Enjoy God's favors with thankfulness. *That.* No man might be able to foresee what shall befall him afterwards; and therefore might live in constant dependence upon God and neither despair in trouble nor be secure or presumptuous in prosperity.

29. *They.* Our first parents, and after them their posterity. *Sought out.* Were not contented with their present state, but studied new ways of making themselves more wise and happy than God had made them. We, their wretched children, are still prone to forsake the certain rule of God's word and the true way to happiness, and to seek new methods of attaining it.

CHAPTER 8

8. *Neither.* And although wicked men, who most fear death, use all possible means to free themselves from it, yet they shall not escape it. The most subtle wickedness cannot outwit death, or the most daring wickedness outbrave it.

17. *Find out.* No man, though ever so wise, is able fully and perfectly to understand these things. And therefore it is best for man not to perplex himself with endless inquiries, but quietly to submit to God's will and providence and to live in the fear of God and the comfortable enjoyment of his blessing.

CHAPTER 9

1. *Their works.* All events which befall them are governed by his providence and therefore, although we cannot fully understand the reasons of all, yet we may be assured they are done righteously. *No man.* No man can judge by their present outward condition whether God loves or hates them; for whom he loves, he chastens and permits those whom he hates to prosper in the world.

8. *White.* The Eastern people of the best sort used white garments, especially in times of rejoicing. *Ointment.* Which upon joyful occasions was poured upon men's heads.

CHAPTER 10

15. *Wearieth.* Fools discover their folly by their wearisome and fruitless endeavors after things which are too high for them.

16. *In the morning.* The fittest time for God's service, for the dispatch of weighty affairs, and for sitting in judgment.

CHAPTER 11

3. *Clouds.* Learn, O man, the practice of liberality from the very lifeless creatures, from the clouds. When they are filled with water, they do not hoard it up, but plentifully pour it forth for the refreshment of both the fruitful field and the barren wilderness. Therefore, let us just now bring forth the fruits of righteousness, because death will shortly cut us down and we shall then be determined to unchangeable happiness or misery, according as our works have been.

4. *He.* He who neglects the necessary works of sowing and reaping, because the weather is not exactly suitable to his desires, will lose his harvest.

10. *Sorrow.* Sensual and disorderly lusts, which he elegantly calls "sorrow," to intimate that although such practices at present gratify men's senses, yet they will shortly bring them to intolerable sorrows.

CHAPTER 12

1. *The evil days.* The time of old age, which is "evil"; burdensome in itself, and far more grievous when it is loaded with the sad remembrance of youthful follies, and with the dreadful prospect of approaching death and judgment. *No pleasure.* My life is now bitter and burdensome, which is frequently the condition of old age.

6. *The silver cord.* By the silver cord he seems to mean the marrow of the backbone, which comes from the brain and goes down to the lowest end of it. And this is aptly compared to a cord, both for its figure, which is long and round; and for its use, which is to draw and move the parts of the body. And to silver, both for its excellency and color, which is white and bright in a dead, much more in a living, body. This may properly be said to be loosed or dissolved, because it is relaxed or otherwise disabled for its proper service.

And by *the golden bowl* we may understand the membranes of the brain and especially that inmost membrane which insinuates itself into all the parts of it, following it in its various windings, keeping each parcel of it in its proper place and dividing one from another to prevent disorder. This is not unfitly called a bowl, because it is round and contains in it all the substance of the brain. And it is called a golden bowl, partly for its great preciousness; partly for its ductility, being drawn out into a great thinness or fineness; and partly for its color, which is somewhat yellow and comes nearer to that of gold than any other part of the body. And this, upon the approach of death, is commonly shriveled up and many times broken. As these clauses concern the brain, and the animal powers, so the two following respect the spring of the vital powers and of the blood, the great instrument whereof is the heart.

And so Solomon here describes the chief organs appointed for the production, distribution, and circulation of the blood. For though the circulation of the blood has been hid for many generations, yet it was well known to Solomon. According to this notion, *the fountain* is the right ventricle of the heart, which is now acknowledged to be the spring of life. And *the pitcher* is the veins which convey the blood from it to other parts, and especially that vein by which it is transmitted to the lungs and thence to the left ventricle, where it is better elaborated and then thrust out into the great artery called the aorta and by its branches dispersed into all the part of the body.

And *the cistern* is the left ventricle of the heart, and *the wheel* seems to be the great artery, which is fitly so called because it is the great instrument of this circulation. The pitcher may be said to *be broken at the fountain* when the veins do not return the blood to the heart, but allow it to stand still and cool, whence comes that coldness of the outward parts which is a near forerunner of death. And the wheel may be said to be *broken at the cistern* when the great arteries do not perform their office of conveying the blood into the left ventricle of the heart and of thrusting it out thence into the lesser arteries, whence comes that ceasing of the pulse which is a certain sign of approaching death.

13. *The conclusion.* The sum of all that has been said or written by wise men. *Fear God.* Which is put here for all the inward worship of God, reverence, love, and trust, and a devotedness of heart to serve and please him. *The whole.* It is his whole work and business, his whole perfection and happiness. It is the sum of what he need either know, or do, or enjoy.

14. *For.* All men must give an account to God of all their works, and this alone will enable them to do that with joy.

the song of solomon

CHAPTER 1

1. *The song.* The most excellent of all songs. And so this might well be called, whether you consider the author of it, who was a great prince and the wisest of all mortal men; or the subject of it, which is not Solomon but a greater than Solomon, even Christ and his marriage with the church. It is excellent also because of the matter of it, which is most lofty, containing in it the noblest of all the mysteries contained either in the Old or the New Testament. It is also most pious and emotional, breathing forth the hottest flames of love between Christ and his people, most sweet and comfortable, and useful to all who read it with serious and Christian eyes.

2. These are the words of the spouse wherein she breathes forth her passionate love to the bridegroom, whom she does not name, because it was needless as being so well known to the persons to whom she speaks and being the only person who was continually in her thoughts. By *kisses,* the usual tokens of love and good will, she means the communications of his love and favor, his graces and comforts breathed into her from the spirit of Christ.

3. *Ointments.* Because of those excellent gifts and graces of God's Spirit wherewith you are replenished.

4. *Draw me.* By your grace and Holy Spirit.

6. *Mother's children.* False brethren, who pretend that the church is their mother when their actions demonstrate that God, the husband of the church, is not their father. They are hypocritical professors who are, and ever were, the keenest enemies. They were false teachers and their followers, who by their corrupt doctrines, divisions, and contentions bring great mischief to the church.

7. *The flocks.* The assemblies of corrupt teachers and worshippers. These he calls Christ's companions, because they profess the name of Christ and their conjunction with him in God's worship.

10. *Chains.* Whereby, as well as by the *rows of jewels,* he may seem to mean all those persons and things with which the church is made beautiful in the eyes of God and of men, such as excellent ministers, saints, righteous laws, holy ordinances, and the gifts and graces of God's Spirit.

15. *Behold.* This is the speech of Christ. The words are doubled to manifest his fervent affection for her.

16. *Behold.* The church here again speaks and retorts Christ's words; you and you only are fair indeed. *Bed.* This seems to denote the place where the church enjoys sweet fellowship with Christ, by his Spirit accompanying his ordinances.

CHAPTER 2

4. *Banqueting house.* The places in which believers receive the graces and blessings of Christ. *Love.* The love of Christ crucified, which, like a *banner,* is displayed in the gospel.

8. *The voice.* Christ's voice, the word of grace revealed outwardly in the gospel, and inwardly by the Spirit of God.

9. *At the windows.* This phrase and that *through the lattice* intimate that the church does indeed see Christ, but as "through a glass, darkly," as it is said even of gospel revelations (I Cor. 13:12), which was much more true of legal administrations.

11. *Lo, the winter.* Spiritual troubles arising from a deep sense of the guilt of sin, the wrath of God, the curse of the law; all which made them afraid to come unto God. But, says Christ, I have removed these impediments, God is reconciled. Therefore cast off all discouragements and excuses and come to me.

17. *Until the day break.* Until the morning of that blessed day of the general resurrection, when all the shadows, not only of ignorance, sin, and calamity, but even of outward administrations shall cease.

CHAPTER 3

1. *I sought.* I sought Christ's gracious and powerful presence. *Found him not.* For he had withdrawn the manifestations of his love from me, either because I had not sought him diligently, or because I had abused his favor.

2. *City.* The city of God, the church in which Christ resides. *Broad ways.* Not finding him in private prayer and meditation, I sought him in the places of public assemblies and ordinances.

3. *The watchmen.* The ministers of Christ and rulers of the church.

4. *Mother's house.* As the spouse here signifies particular believers, so her mother is the universal church, or the true Jerusalem, which has its rise from "above, . . . which is the mother of us all" (Gal. 4:26), in which Christ and believers are united and have sweet communion together in holy ordinances, into which believers are said to bring Christ by faith and prayer.

7. *Bed.* The bed seems to denote the church, which is comely through the beauty of Christ and safe by his protection; in which Christ is glorified, and believers enjoy sweet fellowship with him. *Threescore.* Very many, the certain number being put for an uncertain. He alludes to Solomon's guard, whereby he designs all those creatures, whether angels, princes, ministers, or others, whose ministry God uses for the protection of his church.

9. *A chariot.* By this he seems to understand the word of Christ dispensed by his ministers, whereby Christ rides triumphantly in the world and believers are carried into heavenly glory.

11. *In the day.* When the church is married to him, which is done when the covenant is confirmed between them or when persons are converted to Christ; and more completely when they are received by Christ into his immediate fellowship in the kingdom of glory.

CHAPTER 4

1. *Fair.* Being clothed with my righteousness, and adorned with all the graces of my spirit. *Doves' eyes.* Whereas the beauty of the spouse is here described in her several parts, we need not labor much about the application of each particular to some distinct grace of the church, this being the chief design of the description to show that completeness and absolute perfection which the church has in part received and shall more fully receive in the future life.

4. *Thy neck.* This may represent the grace of faith by which we are united to Christ, as the body is to the head by the neck, by which Christians receive their spiritual food and consequently their strength and ability for action.

11. *Thy lips.* Your speeches, both to me in prayer and praises and to men for their edification, are highly acceptable to me.

15. *Living waters.* The church conveys those waters of life which she receives from Christ to particular believers.

16. *North wind.* These winds may signify the several dispensations of God's Spirit.

CHAPTER 5

1. *O friends.* Believers are here encouraged with freedom and cheerfulness to eat and drink their spiritual food.

2. *Knocketh.* By his word, providence, and Spirit, at the door of my heart. *Open.* Inviting me to let him into my soul.

7. *Watchmen.* The governors of the church, who, though by their place they are obliged to comfort the faithful, do frequently discourage them.

11. We need not aim at a distinct application of this and the following particulars unto some special excellence of Christ, because such things are mere conjectures; and the only design of this description is to set forth the beauty of Christ under the notion of a most amiable person in whom there is no

defect or blemish from the crown of his head to the sole of his feet.

CHAPTER 6

2. The garden may signify the church catholic, and the gardens, as it follows, as also the beds, the particular assemblies of the faithful in which Christ affords his presence. *Lilies.* Which may denote either particular believers whom Christ gathers to himself in his church, or the prayers and praises of his people in the public congregations.

4. *Thou.* These are the words of Christ, who had now again manifested himself to his church.

13. *Return.* Christ recalls his spouse who, as when Christ was gone, she pursued after him, so now when Christ was coming to her she was ready to wander from him. *Return.* This word is repeated four times to signify both Christ's passionate love to her and her backwardness.

CHAPTER 7

10. *I am.* This and the following verses contain the words of the bride in answer to the bridegroom's endearing expressions delivered in the foregoing verses.

12. *Early.* The church, having lost her beloved by her former laziness, now doubles her diligence.

CHAPTER 8

1. *O that.* The church here expresses her desire of a stricter union and closer communion with Christ.

5. *Who.* This and the next clause are the words of the bridegroom.

6. *Set me.* These are undoubtedly the words of the bride.

7. *Many waters.* My love to you cannot be taken off, either by terrors and afflictions which are commonly signified in Scripture by waters and floods, or by temptations and allurements. Therefore, give me yourself, without whom, and in comparison of whom, I despise all other persons and things.

8. *We.* Still the words of the bride.

9. *If.* This seems to be the answer of Christ to the foregoing question of the Jewish church. Christ engages himself to provide for her as suits best with her condition. If the Gentiles, when they are converted, shall be like a wall, strong and firm in faith; we—my Father and I and the Holy Ghost, as the principal builders, and my ministers as workers with and under us—*will build upon her a palace of silver,* will add more strength and beauty to her, will enlarge and adorn her; *and if she be as a door,* which is weaker than a wall; if she be weak in faith, yet we will not therefore reject her, but *we will inclose* or (as many others render the word) "strengthen" or *inclose her with boards of cedar,* which are not only beautiful, but also strong and durable.

10. *I am.* These seem to be the words of the Jewish church.

12. Possibly we may ascribe the first clause to Christ and the latter to the spouse. *Mine.* This repetition is very emphatic to show that Christ had a more eminent title to his vineyard, the church, than Solomon had to his vineyard, because it was purchased not by his money but by his blood. *Thou.* These words are the church's return to Christ, who is here called "Solomon," as he was in chapter 3, verses 9 and 11, as elsewhere he is called "David."

Do you, O Christ, keep your own vineyard, which Solomon did not? Then surely it is right that you should receive as large a revenue from your vineyard as he did from his.

13. *Thou.* Christ speaks here to his spouse.

14. *Make haste.* Seeing we must part for a time, make haste, O my beloved bridegroom, and speedily finish the work which you have to do in the world, that you may take me to yourself that I may live in your everlasting embraces.

Isaiah

CHAPTER 1

1. *Vision.* As prophets were called seers (I Sam. 9:9), so prophecies are called visions, because they were as clearly and certainly represented to the prophet's minds as bodily objects are to men's eyes.

2. *Hear.* He directs his speech to those senseless creatures, that he might awaken the Israelites, whom he hereby proclaims to be so dull and stupid that they were past hearing, and therefore calls on the whole creation of God to bear witness against them.

11. *Unto me.* Who am a spirit, and therefore cannot be satisfied with such carnal oblations, but expect to have your hearts and lives as well as your bodies and sacrifices presented unto me.

CHAPTER 2

2. *In the last days.* In the times of the Messiah. For Christ's institutions were to continue to the end of the world. *The mountain.* The temple of the Lord which is upon Mount Moriah; which yet is not to be understood literally of that material temple, but mystically of the church of God.

3. *The law.* The new law, the doctrine of the gospel, which is frequently called a law because it has the nature and power of a law, obliging us no less to the belief and practice of it than the old law did.

4. *He.* Christ shall set up his authority among all nations, not only giving laws to them, but doing what no other can do, convincing their consciences, changing their hearts, and ordering their lives.

CHAPTER 3

20. *Tablets.* He seems to mean boxes of perfumes.

21. *Nose jewels.* Which were fastened to the head and hung down upon the forehead to the beginning of the nose.

26. *Gates.* The gates of Zion or Jerusalem which, by a figure, are said to lament, to imply the great desolation of the place; that there would be no people to go out and come in by the gates, as they used to do.

CHAPTER 4

2. *The earth.* The land, which for the sins of the people was made barren, upon their return to Christ shall recover its fertility. Under this one mercy he includes all temporal blessings, together with spiritual and eternal.

4. *Burning.* This is opposed to the

former legal way of purification, which was by water. The Holy Spirit of old accompanies the preaching of the gospel and did this work in part and will do it fully. This Spirit may well be called *the spirit of judgment,* because it executes judgment in the church and in the consciences of men, separating the precious from the vile, convincing men of sin, righteousness, and judgment. And the same Spirit may be fitly called *the spirit of burning,* because he burns up and consumes the dross which is in the church and in the hearts of men, and inflames the souls of believers with love to God and zeal for his glory.

CHAPTER 5

6. The meaning is, I will remove my ministers who used great care and diligence to make you fruitful.

18. *That draw.* That are not only drawn to sin by the allurements of the world, but are active and illustrious in drawing sin to themselves.

20. *Unto them.* That take away the difference between good and evil; that justify wicked men and things, and condemn piety or righteous persons.

24. *Rottenness.* They shall be like a tree which not only withers in its branches, but dies and rots at the roots; therefore is past recovery.

30. *The heavens.* When they look up to the heavens, as men in distress usually do, they see no light there.

CHAPTER 6

1. *His train.* His royal and judicial robe; for he is represented as a judge.

3. *Holy.* This is repeated thrice to intimate the Trinity of persons united in the divine essence.

5. *I am.* I am a great sinner, as in many other ways so particularly by my lips. I am an unclean branch of an unclean tree; besides my own uncleanness, I have by both my omissions and commissions involved myself in the guilt of their sins.

8. The change of the number, *I* to *us,* is very remarkable; and both being meant of one and the same Lord do sufficiently intimate a plurality of elders in the Godhead.

9. The sense is, because you have so long heard my words and seen my works, to no purpose, and have hardened your hearts and will not learn nor reform, I will punish you in your own kind; your sin shall be your punishment. I will still continue my word and works to you, but will withdraw my Spirit so that you shall be as unable, as now you are unwilling, to understand.

10. *Fat.* Stupid and senseless. This making their hearts fat is ascribed here to the prophet, as it is ascribed to God in the repetition of this prophecy (John 12:40), because God inflicted this judgment upon them by the ministry of the prophet; partly by way of prediction, foretelling that this would be the effect of his preaching; and partly by withdrawing the light and help of his Spirit.

CHAPTER 7

1. *Ahaz.* A most wicked king; yet no prophecies are more comforting than those which were delivered in his time. God ordered it for the encouragement of the faithful who lived under his impious reign.

14. *Therefore.* Because you despise me and the sign which I now offer to you, God of his own free grace will send you a more honorable messenger and give you a nobler sign. *A sign.* Of your deliverance. But how was this birth, which was not to happen till many ages after, a sign of their deliverance from present danger? This promised birth supposed the preservation of that city and nation and tribe in and of which the Messiah was to be born; and therefore there was no cause to fear that ruin which their enemies now threatened.

Immanuel. "God with us"; God dwelling among us, in our nature (John 1:14). God and man meeting in one person, being a mediator between God and men. For the design of these words is not so much to relate the name by which Christ should commonly be called, as to describe his nature and office.

16. *This child.* Shear–jashub, whom in all probability the prophet pointed at, and who was brought hither by God's special command (v. 3) for this very use.

CHAPTER 8

17. *Wait.* I will cast my care upon him and expect the accomplishment of his promise, in sending the Messiah and in conferring upon me and all believing Israelites all his mercies and blessings.

18. *Behold.* These words are literally spoken by Isaiah concerning himself, but mystically concerning Christ; and therefore they are fitly applied to Christ (Heb. 2:13).

CHAPTER 9

6. *For.* Having spoken of the glorious light, joy, and victory of God's people, he now proceeds to show the ground of it. *Us.* Unto us Jews, of whom Christ was born, and to whom he was primarily sent. *Child.* The Messiah, by the consent of interpreters, not only Christian but Jewish.

His name. This is not to be taken for a description of his name, but of his glorious nature and qualities. *Wonderful Counsellor.*[1] And so Christ is, because he has been the counselor of his church in all ages, and the author and giver of all those excellent counsels delivered not only by the apostles, but also by the prophets, and has gathered and enlarged and preserved his church by admirable counsels and methods of his providence; and, in a word, has in him "all the treasures of wisdom and knowledge" (Col. 2:3). *Mighty God.* This title can agree to no man but Christ, who was God as well as man, to whom the title of "God" or "Jehovah" is given, both in the Old and New Testaments. And it is a true observation that this Hebrew word *El* is never used in the singular number of any creature, but only of the almighty God. *The everlasting Father.* The father of eternity. Who, though as man he was then unborn, yet was and is from everlasting to everlasting.

CHAPTER 10

27. *The anointing.* Possibly this may be understood of David, who is often mentioned in the Scripture by the name of God's anointed; and for whose sake God gave many deliverances to the succeeding kings and ages, as it is expressly affirmed (I Kings 11:32, 34). God declares that he would give this very deliverance from the Assyrian, "for David's sake" (II Kings 19:34; 20:6). But the Messiah is principally intended, of whom David was but a type and who was in a particular manner anointed above his fellows, as is said in Psalm 45:7. For he is the foundation of all the promises (I Cor. 1:20) and of all

---

[1](9:6) KJV: "Wonderful, Counsellor."

the deliverances and mercies granted to God's people in all ages.

CHAPTER 11

1. *Of Jesse.* He does not say of David, but of Jesse, who was a private and lowly person, to intimate that at the time of Christ's birth the royal family should be reduced to its primitive obscurity.

4. *Rod.* With his word, which is his scepter, and "the rod of [his] strength" (Ps. 110:2), which is "sharper than any . . . sword" (Heb. 4:12), by the preaching whereof he subdued the world to himself and will destroy his enemies (II Thess. 2:8). This he adds further to declare the nature of Christ's kingdom, that it is not of this world.

6. *The wolf.* Men of fierce and cruel dispositions shall be so transformed by the grace of Christ that they shall become gentle and tractable.

10. *Glorious.* Shall be filled with greater glory than the Jewish tabernacle and temple were; only this glory shall be spiritual, consisting in the plentiful effusions of the gifts and graces of the Holy Spirit.

CHAPTER 12

3. *With joy.* Your thirsty souls shall be filled with divine graces and comforts, which you may draw from God in the use of gospel ordinances.

CHAPTER 13

3. *Sanctified ones.* The Medes and Persians, so called because they were set apart by God for his holy work of executing his just vengeance.

13. *Therefore.* A poetical and prophetic description of great horrors and confusions, as if heaven and earth were about to meet together.

CHAPTER 14

2. *Rule.* Which they literally did after their return into their own land. But this was more eminently verified in a spiritual sense in the days of the gospel.

12. *Fallen.* From the height of your glory. *Lucifer.* Which properly is a bright star that ushers in the morning, but is here metaphorically taken for the mighty king of Babylon. *Son.* The title of "son" is given in Scripture not only to a person or thing begotten or produced by another, but also to any thing which is related to it; in which sense we read of "the son of a night" (Jonah 4:10), "the son of perdition" (John 17:12), and, which is more agreeable to the present case, "Arcturus with his sons" (Job 38:32).

29. *Of him.* Most understand this of Uzziah, who did then much mischief (II Chron. 26:6). But he was dead thirty-two years before this time, and therefore their joy for his death was long since past. Others understand it of Ahaz; but he was so far from smiting them that he was smitten by them. We may understand this of the royal race of Judah, who had been a terrible scourge to them, whose rod might be said to be broken because that scepter was come into the hands of slothful princes.

CHAPTER 15

3. *On the tops.* Which were made flat, to which men used to go up to cry to God in heaven, or to men for help.

5. *Of destruction.* Such a cry as men send forth when they are just falling into the pit of destruction.

CHAPTER 16

1. *Send.* The prophet continues his prophecy against Moab and gives them counsel what to do to prevent, if possible, the desolation.

5. *In mercy.* By my mercy. I am now punishing their sins, yet I will deliver them for my own mercy's sake.

6. *We.* The prophet, having spoken to the Moabites, now turns his speech to God's people. The sense is, I do not expect that my counsels will have any good effect upon Moab; they will still carry themselves insolently and outrageously.

CHAPTER 17

7. *Look.* They shall sincerely respect, trust, and worship God, and God only.

9. And this was a fit example, to awaken the Israelites to a serious belief of this threatening, because God had inflicted the same judgment upon the Canaanites for the same sins of which they were guilty.

12. *Woe.* This is a new prophecy, added for the comfort of God's people.

CHAPTER 18

1. *Wings.* The title of wings is given, in Scripture, to many things which have some kind of resemblance to wings, as to the battlements of a house or temple, to an army, and to the sails of a ship, as this word is here commonly understood. And *shadowing with wings* is nothing else but overspread or filled with them. Which title may be given either to Ethiopia or Egypt, in regard of the great numbers either of their armies, or of their ships or vessels sailing upon the sea or rivers.

2. *Peeled.* Having their hair plucked off. This is metaphorically used in the Scripture for some great calamity whereby men are stripped of all their comforts. And this title may be given to them prophetically to signify their approaching destruction.

4. *Rest.* I will not stir myself to help this people. God is said in Scripture to

rest, or sit still, when he does not work on the behalf of a person or people.

CHAPTER 19

7. *Paper reeds.* These by a needle or other fit instrument were divided into thin and broad leaves, which being dried and fitted were used at that time for writing; and consequently was a very good commodity.

14. *Staggereth.* When he is so drunk that he reels to and fro and vomits up his drink.

18. *Swear.* This implies the dedication and yielding up of a person or thing to the Lord, by a solemn vow or covenant.

19. *An altar.* The altar is put for the worship of God, as it is in many places in both the Old and New Testaments. And nothing is more common in the prophets than to speak of gospel-worship in the phrases of the law.

23. *Assyria.* They who were implacable enemies one to another, and both to the church of God, shall now be reconciled and united together in the service of God and love to his church.

CHAPTER 20

2. *Sackcloth.* Which he wore in token of his grief for the calamities that were already come upon Israel and were coming upon Judah.

6. *Such.* So vain is our hope placed upon such a people as are unable to deliver themselves.

CHAPTER 21

2. *The sighing.* The sighing and groaning of God's people and other nations under the oppression of that cruel empire.

5. *Shield.* Prepare yourselves and your arms for the approaching battle.

The shield is put for all their weapons of offense and defense. They used to anoint their shields with oil to preserve and polish them and to make them slippery.

12. *Night.* The night is past without any mischief, and the light of the morning is approaching; but though the morning is coming, it will be gone and the night will return, and your fears with it.

CHAPTER 22

16. *An habitation.* He erected a stately house to live in and a stately sepulcher to receive him when he died. And these two are fitly joined together because their sepulchers were commonly built in or near their houses.

22. *The key.* The government, the power of opening and shutting, of letting men into it or putting them out of it, whereof a key is a fit emblem. *Shoulder.* He mentions the shoulder rather than the hand, in which keys are commonly carried, from some ceremony then in use of carrying a key upon the shoulder of the officer of state.

CHAPTER 23

1. *Of Tyre.* Tyre was, according to this prophecy, destroyed; first by Nebuchadnezzar and afterwards by Alexander the Great. And though this prophecy seemed directly to respect the former destruction, yet it seems to have some reference to the latter also. Only it is intimated that after seventy years, Tyre should recover her former power and glory before her second and final destruction.

16. *Thou harlot.* So he calls Tyre, because she enticed the merchants to deal with her by various artifices and even by dishonest practices, and be-

cause of the great and general uncleanness which was committed in it.

18. *Shall be.* For the support and encouragement of the ministers of holy things, who shall teach the good knowledge of the Lord. Although this does not exclude, but rather implies their liberality in contributing to the necessities of all Christians.

CHAPTER 24

7. *Mourneth.* Because there are none to drink it. Grief is ascribed to senseless creatures by a figure usual in all authors.

11. *A crying.* Such was their gross sensuality and sottishness that, instead of crying for their sins, they did only howl for their corn and wine and oil (Hos. 7:14).

22. *After.* After the apostate Jews shall have been shut up in unbelief and in great tribulations for many ages together, they shall be convinced of their sin in crucifying the Messiah and brought home to God and Christ by true repentance.

23. *The sun.* All earthly powers and glories shall be obscured with the far greater splendor of Christ, the King of Kings, at whose feet even the kings of the earth shall fall down and worship. *The LORD.* The Messiah, who, though man, yet is also God and the Lord of Hosts. *Shall reign.* Shall come in the flesh and set up his kingdom, first in Jerusalem and afterward in all other nations. *Before.* Before his ministers, who are in some sort the courtiers of the King of Glory. But the ancient are here designated for the whole church, in whose name and for whose service they act.

CHAPTER 25

1. *O LORD.* The prophet, reflecting upon those great and glorious prophecies which he had delivered, interrupts the course of his prophecies and breaks forth into a solemn celebration of God's wonderful works.

8. *He.* Christ will by his death destroy the power of death, take away the sting of the first death, and prevent the second.

9. *Our God.* Our Messiah, long since promised, and for whom we have waited long, is come into the world bringing salvation with him.

11. *He.* The Lord, whose power they shall be no more able to resist, than the waters can resist a man who swims.

CHAPTER 26

9. *For.* And good reason it is that we should thus desire and seek you in the way of your judgments, because this is the very design of your judgments, that men should thereby be awakened to learn and return to their duty; and this is a common effect, that those who have been careless in prosperity are made wiser and better by afflictions.

10. *Will not behold.* Though God gives such plain discoveries of his majesty and glory, not only in his word but also in works, and especially in this glorious work of his patience and mercy to wicked men, yet they will not acknowledge it.

19. *Thy.* The prophet here turns his speech to God's people and gives them a cordial[2] in their distress.

CHAPTER 27

1. *Leviathan.* By this leviathan, serpent, or dragon (for all signify the same thing) he understands some powerful enemy or enemies of God and of his church or people, which may well be called by these names; partly for their great might, and partly for the great terror and destruction which they cause upon the earth.

6. *Fruit.* Their posterity shall seek habitations in other countries and replenish them with people. But this seems to be understood of the spiritual seed of Jacob.

13. *Trumpet.* God shall summon them altogether by sound of trumpet, by an eminent call of his providence. He alludes to the custom of calling the Israelites together with trumpets.

CHAPTER 28

9. *Them.* Who is there among this people who are willing to be taught the knowledge of God? A minister may as soon teach an infant as these men.

13. *Here a little.* As this method has been used and was altogether necessary for them; so it still is, and for the future shall be. As they were children in understanding, they shall still continue to be such; they shall be ever learning and never come to the knowledge of the truth.

16. *In Zion.* In my church. *A foundation.* Upon which I will build my church. *A stone.* The Messiah. *Tried.* Which I have tried and approved as every way sufficient.

17. *Plummet.* The line and plummet, or the plumb line, was not only used in erecting buildings, but also in pulling them down, those parts of the building being thus marked out which were to be demolished.

24. *Doth.* The plowman does not spend all his time in plowing the ground; but he has several times for several works. And so God has his times and seasons for several works,

---

[2](26:19) An invigorating or exhilarating stimulant.

and his providence is various at several times and towards several people.

29. The husbandman manages his affairs with common discretion; but God governs the world and his church with wonderful wisdom. He is great and marvelous, both in the contrivance of things and in the execution of them.

CHAPTER 29

9. *Stagger.* With giddiness or stupidity, which makes them like drunken men insensible of their danger.

19. *The poor.* Lowly and despicable people, shy as the Gentiles were in the opinion of the Jews, and such as the greatest part of the first Christians were.

22. *Jacob.* The Israelites or posterity of Jacob, who had great cause to be ashamed for their continued infidelity, shall at last be brought back to the God of their fathers and to their Messiah.

CHAPTER 30

19. *Shall dwell.* After a set time they shall return to Jerusalem and have a fixed abode. This was in part accomplished upon their return from Babylon; but more fully in the times of the gospel, when many of them were, and the whole body of them shall be brought into Christ's church.

29. *The night.* He seems to have a particular respect to the solemnity of the Passover, in which they spent some considerable part of the night in rejoicing and singing psalms before the Lord.

33. *Tophet.* This was a place near Jerusalem in which the idolatrous Israelites used to offer up their children to Molech. It may refer to any place of torment; and particularly it is put for hell.

CHAPTER 31

5. *As birds.* Which come from above and so cannot be kept off; which fly swiftly and engage resolutely when their young ones are in danger.

CHAPTER 32

1. *Behold.* This seems to be a distinct prophecy from the former and delivered before that which is related in the former chapters. The prophecies are not always set down in the order in which the prophets delivered them. The foregoing prophecy was delivered not in the time of Ahaz, for he sent to the Assyrian, not the Egyptian for help. It was Hezekiah who "rebelled against the king of Assyria" and was too prone to trust upon the staff of Egypt. But this seems to have been delivered in the time of Ahaz. *A king.* Hezekiah, a type of Christ, and Christ typified by him.

2. *Shadow.* In a dry and scorched country, which is called *weary* because it makes travelers weary; as death is called "pale" in other authors because it makes men's faces pale.

4. *Tongue.* That used to speak of the things of God darkly and doubtfully; which, though it was in part fulfilled in Hezekiah, yet was truly and fully accomplished only by Christ, who wrought this wonderful change in an innumerable company of Jews and Gentiles.

15. Until the time come in which God will pour—or, as the Hebrew word properly signifies, reveal—evidently and plentifully pour out his Spirit from heaven upon his people, which was fully accomplished in the days of the Messiah.

19. *The city.* Jerusalem, which though now it was the seat of God's worship and people, yet he foresaw would be the great enemy of the Messiah.

CHAPTER 33

2. *Every morning.* When we offer the morning sacrifice and call upon you. Which is not meant exclusively, as if he did not desire God's help at other times; but comprehensively, the morning put for the whole day. The sense is, "Help us speedily and continually."

17. *The king.* First Hezekiah and then Christ, triumphing over all enemies and ruling his own people with righteousness.

21. *Rivers.* Though we have nothing but a small and contemptible brook to defend us, yet God will be as sure a defense to us as if we were surrounded with great rivers.

24. *Forgiven.* They shall not only receive from me a glorious temporal deliverance; but, which is infinitely better, the pardon of all their sins and all those spiritual and everlasting blessings which attend upon that mercy.

CHAPTER 34

4. *Dissolved.* The sun, moon, and stars. So great shall be the confusion and consternation of mankind as if all the frame of the creation were broken into pieces. It is usual for prophetic writers in both the Old and New Testaments to represent great and general calamities in such words and phrases as properly agree to the day of judgment; as on the contrary, the glorious deliverances of God's people in such expressions as properly agree to the resurrection from the dead.

7. *The unicorns.* It is confessed, this was a beast of great strength and fierceness; and it is used in this place to signify their princes and potentates, who shall be humbled and cast down.

16. *His.* My Spirit (such sudden changes of persons being frequent here) has brought all these creatures together, as he formerly brought the creatures to Adam and to Noah by an instinct which he put into them.

CHAPTER 35

1. *The solitary place.* Emmanuel's land, or the seat of God's church and people, which formerly was despised like a wilderness and which the rage of their enemies had brought to desolation, shall flourish exceedingly.

3. *Strengthen.* You ministers of God, comfort and encourage God's people who are now ready to faint.

8. *Fools.* The way shall be so plain and strait that even the most foolish travelers cannot easily mistake it.

CHAPTER 36

The history related here and in the three following chapters is almost in the same words contained in II Kings 18, 19, and 20. It is inserted here to explain and confirm some of the foregoing predictions. It may seem to have first been written by this prophet and from him taken into the book of Kings to complete that history.

CHAPTER 37

Hezekiah mourns and sends to Isaiah to pray for them (vv. 1–5). Sennacherib, called away against the king of Ethiopia, sends a blasphemous letter to Hezekiah (vv. 8–13). His prayer (vv. 14–20). Isaiah's prophecy (vv. 21–35). An angel slays the Assyrians (v. 36). Sennacherib is slain at Nineveh by his own sons (vv. 37–38).

CHAPTER 38

13. *I reckoned.* When I could not rest all the night even until morning, my thoughts were presaging that God would instantly break me to pieces, and the like thoughts followed me from morning until evening.

18. *Praise.* The dead are not capable of glorifying your name among men upon earth. They cannot expect nor receive the accomplishment of your promised goodness in the land of the living.

CHAPTER 39

The king of Babylon sends ambassadors with letters and a present to Hezekiah, who shows them his treasures (vv. 1–2). Isaiah foretells the Babylonian captivity (vv. 4–7). His resignation (v. 8).

CHAPTER 40

3. *Wilderness.* This immediately relates to the deliverance of the Jews out of Babylon, and smoothing their passage from there to Judea, which lay through a great wilderness. But principally to their redemption by the Messiah, whose coming was ushered in by the cry of John the Baptist in the wilderness. *Prepare ye the way.* The meaning is, God shall by his Spirit so dispose men's hearts, and by this providence so order the affairs of the world, as to make way for the accomplishment of his promise. This was eminently fulfilled when Christ, who was and is God blessed for ever, came into the world in a visible manner.

5–6. *Cry.* God speaks unto his ministers. *All flesh.* The prophet, having foretold glorious things, confirms the certainty of them by representing the vast difference between the nature, word, and work of men and of God. All that men are or have, yes, their highest accomplishments, are but like the grass of the field, weak and vanishing, soon snipped and brought to nothing. But God's word is like himself, immutable and irresistible. And therefore, as *the mouth of the Lord,* and not of man, *hath spoken* these things, so doubt not but they shall be fulfilled.

22. *Sitteth.* Far above this round earth, even in the highest heavens; from where he looks down upon the earth, where men appear to him like grasshoppers. As here we have *the circle of the earth,* so elsewhere we read of "the circuit of heaven" (Job 22:14) and of "a compass upon the face of the depth," or sea (Prov. 8:27), because the form of the heaven, earth, and sea is circular.

CHAPTER 41

2. *The righteous man.* Cyrus. He was raised up by God in an eminent manner. And although these things were yet to come, yet the prophet speaks of them as if they were already past. And by this instance he pleads his cause against the Gentiles, because this was an evident proof of God's almighty power and of the vanity of idols, which eminently appeared in the destruction of the Babylonians, who were a people devoted to their idols.

23. *Do good.* Protect your worshippers who I intend to destroy, and destroy my people whom I intend to save.

29. *Wind.* Empty and unsatisfying things. *Confusion.* Confused and useless things, like that rude heap in the beginning of God's creation, of which this very word is used (Gen. 1:2).

CHAPTER 42

1. *Behold.* The prophet, having given one eminent instance of God's certain foreknowledge in the deliverance of the Jews by Cyrus, now adds another more eminent example of it by foretelling the coming of the Messiah. This place therefore is expressly interpreted of Christ (Matt. 12:18). And to him and to him only all the particulars which follow truly and evidently belong.

3. *Break.* Christ will not deal rigorously with those who come to him, but he will use all gentleness, cherishing the smallest beginnings of grace, comforting and healing wounded consciences. *Quench.* That wick of a candle which is almost extinct, he will not quench but revive and kindle it again.

10. *Sing.* Upon this new and great occasion, the salvation of the world by Christ. *Ye.* You who go by sea carry these glad tidings from Judea, where Christ was born, lived, died, and published the gospel unto the remotest parts of the earth.

16. I will direct them in the right way. I will enlighten their dark minds and rectify their perverse wills and affections until I have brought them to the end of their journey.

21. *Well pleased.* Although God might justly destroy you suddenly, yet he will patiently wait for your repentance, that he may be gracious; and that not for your sake, but for the glory of his own faithfulness in fulfilling that covenant which he made with your pious progenitors.

CHAPTER 43

10. *My servant.* Cyrus, who is an eminent instance and proof of God's foreknowledge. Or, the Messiah, who is the most eminent witness in this cause.

18. *Remember ye not.* Though your former deliverance out of Egypt was glorious, yet in comparison with that inestimable mercy of sending the Messiah, all your former deliverances are scarce worthy of your remembrance and consideration.

19. *Now.* The Scripture often speaks of things at a great distance of time as if they were now at hand, to make us sensible of the inconsiderableness of time and all temporal things in comparison with God and eternal things; upon which account it is said, that "one day is with the Lord as a thousand years, and a thousand years as one day."

CHAPTER 44

20. *Deceived heart.* A mind corrupted and deceived by deep prejudice, gross error, and especially by his own lusts.

23. *Sing.* By such invitations to the senseless creatures, he signifies the transcendent greatness of this mercy, sufficient to make even the stones, if it were possible, break forth into God's praises.

28. *Cyrus.* Whom God here mentions by his proper name two hundred years before he was born, that this might be an undeniable evidence of the exactness of God's foreknowledge and a convincing argument to conclude this dispute between God and idols.

CHAPTER 45

14. *Thee.* Jerusalem shall not only be rebuilt, but the wealth and glory of other countries shall be brought to it again. This was in part verified in Jerusalem. But it was much more fully accomplished in the church of the gospel in the accession of the Gentiles to that church, which began in Jerusalem and from there spread itself into all the parts of the world.

24. *In the LORD.* By or from God alone, or the Messiah, who is the true Jehovah as well as man.

CHAPTER 46

3. *Carried.* Whom I have nourished ever since you were a people and came out of Egypt, and that as tenderly as parents bring up their own children.

10. *Declaring.* Foretelling from the beginning of the world events which should happen in succeeding ages, even to the end of the world.

CHAPTER 47

10. *Trusted.* Confidently expecting to preserve yourself by these and other wicked arts.

13. *Wearied.* You have spent your time and strength in going from one to another, and all to no purpose.

CHAPTER 48

9. *For my name's sake.* I will spare you and deliver you out of captivity, not for your sake, but merely for my own sake and for the vindication of my own name, that I may be praised for my power, faithfulness, and goodness.

16. *Me.* The prophet Isaiah, who was a type of Christ; and so this may have a respect to him also.

CHAPTER 49

1. *Listen.* God turns his speech to the Gentiles and invites them to hearken to those counsels and doctrines which the Jews would reject. *Me.* Unto Christ. Isaiah speaks these words in the name of Christ.

2. *A sharp sword.* As he made me the great teacher of his church, so he made my word "quick, and powerful, and sharper than any two-edged sword."

3. *O Israel.* As the name of David is sometimes given to his successors, so here the name of Israel may not unfitly be given to Christ, not only because he descended from his loins, but also because he was the true and the great Israel, who in a more eminent manner prevailed with God, as that name signifies, of whom Jacob, who was first called Israel, was but a type.

7. *His Holy One.* The Holy One of Israel. *To him.* To Christ, to whom in the days of his flesh this description fully agrees. For men, both Jews and Gentiles among whom he lived, did despise him from their hearts. And *the nation,* of which he was a member, abhorred both his person and his doctrine. And he was so far from being a temporal monarch that he came in the form of a servant and was a *servant of rulers,* professing subjection and paying tribute unto Caesar.

8. *The LORD.* God the Father unto Christ. *To establish.* To establish truth and righteousness upon earth and subdue those lusts and passions which are the great disturbers of human society. *Desolate heritages.* That desolate places may be repaired and repossessed. That Christ may possess the heathen, who were in a spiritual sense in a most desolate condition.

9. *Prisoners.* To the Gentiles, who are fast bound by the cords of their sins and taken captive by the devil at his will.

12. He speaks here, and in many other places, of the conversion of the Gentiles, with allusion to that work of gathering and bringing back the Jews from all parts where they were dispersed.

24. *Shall the prey.* Here is a double impediment to their deliverance: the power of the enemy who kept them in bondage, and the justice of God which pleads against their deliverance.

CHAPTER 50

4. *Given me.* This and the following passages may be in some sort understood of the prophet Isaiah. But they are far more evidently and eminently verified in Christ and indeed seem to be meant directly of him. *To hear.* He by his divine power assists me to the practice of all his commands and my duties, with all attention and diligence.

10. *The voice.* Of Christ, who is called God's servant by way of eminence, and to intimate that, though he was God, yet he would take "upon him the form of a servant."

CHAPTER 51

5. *My righteousness.* My salvation, the redemption of all my people, Jews and Gentiles, which is the effect of his righteousness, his justice, faithfulness, or mercy.

11. *Therefore.* This verse contains an answer to the prophet's prayer. I did these great things, and I will do the like again.

16. *I have.* These words are spoken by God to his church and people, to whom he speaks both in the foregoing and following verses. For God's word is frequently said to be put into the mouths, not only of the prophets, but of the people also. *Covered.* Have protected you by my almighty power, that I may bring you to that perfect and blessed estate which is reserved for the days of the Messiah, which in Scripture phrase is called a making of "new heavens and a new earth" (65:17).

CHAPTER 52

3. *Sold yourselves.* By your sins, without any valuable consideration paid by them either to you, or to your Lord and owner.

7. *Reigneth.* In the days of the Messiah, God did reveal and exercise his dominion over the world far more eminently than ever he had done from the beginning of the world until that time.

8. *Eye.* Distinctly and familiarly, their eyes beholding the eyes of this King of Glory. They shall be eye- and ear-witnesses of the words and works of Christ, and therefore their testimony shall be more certain and valuable.

13. *Behold.* This is the beginning of a new prophecy, which is continued from here to the end of the next chapter. *My servant.* That it is Christ who is here spoken of is so evident that some later Hebrew doctors understand it directly of him, and that many Jews have been convinced and converted to the Christian faith by the evidence of this prophecy.

14. *His form.* Christ, in respect of his birth, breeding, and manner of life, was most obscure and contemptible. His countenance was so marred with frequent watchings, fastings, and troubles that he was thought to be near fifty years old when he was but about thirty (John 8:57), and was further spoiled with buffetings and crowning with thorns and other cruel and despiteful usages.

15. *So.* His exaltation shall be answerable to his humiliation.

CHAPTER 53

1. *Arm.* The Messiah, called the arm or power of God, because the almighty power of God was seated in him.

2. *As a root.* And the reason why the Jews will generally reject their Messiah is because he shall not come into the world with secular pomp, but *he shall grow up,* (or spring up, out of the ground) *before him, as a tender plant* (small and inconsiderable) *and as a root* (or branch) grows out of a dry, barren ground. *No form.* His bodily presence shall be lowly and contemptible. *No beauty.* This the prophet speaks in the person of the unbelieving Jews.

5. *Wounded.* Which word comprehends all his pains and punishments. *For our iniquities.* For the guilt of their sins, which he had voluntarily taken upon himself; and for the expiation of their sins, which was hereby purchased. *The chastisement.* Those punishments by which our peace, our reconciliation to God, was to be purchased were laid upon him by God's justice with his own consent. *Healed.* By his sufferings we are saved from our sins.

6. *Have turned.* In general, to the way of sin, which may well be called a man's own way, because sin is natural to us, inherent in us, born with us; and in particular, to those several paths which several men choose, according to their different opinions and circumstances. *The iniquity.* Not properly, for he knew no sin; but the punishment of iniquity, as that word is frequently used. That which was due for all the sins of all mankind, which must needs be so heavy a load that, if he had not been God as well as man, he must have sunk under the burden.

8. *His generation.* His posterity. For his death shall not be unfruitful. When he is raised from the dead he shall have a spiritual seed, a numberless multitude of those who shall believe in him.

9. *With the wicked.* This was a further degree of humiliation. He said, *he made his grave,* because this was Christ's own act and he willingly yielded up himself to death and burial. And that which follows, *with the wicked,* does not denote the sameness of place, as if he should be buried in the same grave with other malefactors, but the sameness of condition.

10. *He.* God was the principal cause of all his sufferings, though men's sins were the deserving cause. *When.* When you, O God, shall have made your Son a sacrifice by giving him up to death for the atonement of men's sins. *The pleasure.* God's gracious decree for the salvation of mankind shall be effectually carried on by his ministry and mediation.

11. *Justify.* Acquit them from the guilt of their sins and all the dreadful consequences thereof. And Christ is said to justify sinners meritoriously because he purchases and procures it for us. *For.* For he shall satisfy the justice of God by bearing the punishment due to their sins.

12. *Transgressors.* He prayed upon earth for all sinners, and particularly for those who crucified him. And in heaven he still intercedes for them by a legal demand of those good things which he purchased; by the sacrifice of himself, which, though past, he continually represents to his Father as if it were present.

CHAPTER 54

1. *Sing.* The prophet having largely discussed the sufferings of Christ and the blessed fruits thereof, and here foreseeing that glorious state of the church, he breaks forth into this song of triumph. And as the foregoing chapter literally speaks of Christ, so does this of the church of Christ.

3. *Thy seed.* Your spiritual seed, the church of the New Testament, which is accounted Abraham's seed, or children.

10. *The covenant.* That covenant whereby I have made peace and friendship with you, and have promised to you all manner of happiness. God will not cast off his Christian church as he cast off the church of the Jews. The New Covenant is established upon better and surer promises than the Old.

13. *The peace.* (1) Inward peace arising from the clear revelations of God's love and reconciliation to us, and wrought by the Spirit of adoption, which is more abundantly given to believers under the gospel than under the law. (2) Outward peace, safety, and happiness.

CHAPTER 55

1. *Thirsteth.* For the grace of God and the blessings of the gospel. This thirst implies a vehement, active, and restless desire after it. *Wine and milk.* All gospel blessings; in particular that peace and joy in the Holy Ghost which are better than wine, and that love of God which nourishes the soul as milk does the body.

6. *Seek.* Labor to get the knowledge of God's will, and to obtain his grace and favor. *While.* In this day of grace, while he offers mercy and reconciliation. *Near.* Ready and desirous to receive you to mercy.

8. *For.* If any man injure you, especially if he does it greatly and frequently, you are slow and backward to forgive him. But I am ready to forgive all penitents no matter how many, great, and numberless their sins be.

13. *An everlasting sign.* For a monument of God's infinite power, faithfulness, and love to his people to all succeeding generations.

CHAPTER 56

3. *The stranger.* The stranger, the Gentile, who by birth is a stranger to God, that has turned from dumb idols to the living God. *Eunuch.* Who is here joined with the stranger, because he was forbidden to "enter into the congregation of the LORD" (Deut. 23:1). Under these two instances he understands all those who, either by birth or by any ceremonial pollution, were excluded from church privileges, and so he throws open the door to all true believers.

9. *Come.* This is a prediction of Israel's destruction by their cruel enemies. The prophet, having largely discussed the Messiah and his kingdom and having encouraged the Gentiles with God's gracious promises made to them, now proceeds to terrify the unbelieving Jews and to show that as the Gentiles would believe and be saved, so they would reject their Messiah and be destroyed.

CHAPTER 57

2. *Beds.* In their graves, which are not unfitly called their beds, as their death is commonly called "sleep" in Scripture.

6. *Offered.* For the devil is God's ape, and idolaters used the same rites and offerings in the worship of idols which God had prescribed in his own.

7. *Thy bed.* Your altar, in which you did commit spiritual whoredom with idols.

19. *Peace.* That peace which is not wrought by men's hands, but only by God's lips or word. The doubling of the word signifies the certainty and abundance of this peace. *Far off.* To the Gentiles who are far from God, as well as to the Jews, who are called "a people near unto him" (Ps. 148:14).

20. *Cast up.* Their minds are restless, being perpetually hurried with their own lusts and passions, and with guilt and the dread of the divine vengeance.

CHAPTER 58

2. *Yet.* They cover all their wickedness with a profession of religion. *Delight.* There are many men who take some pleasure in knowing God's will and word and yet do not conform their lives to it.

4. *Behold.* Your fasting days, wherein you ought in a special manner to implore the mercy of God and to show compassion to men you employ, in injuring or quarreling with your brethren, your servants or debtors, or in contriving mischief against them.

7. *Thine own flesh.* Some confine this

to our own kindred; but we can look on no man but there we contemplate our *own flesh,* and therefore it is barbarous not only to tear, but not to love and encourage him. Therefore feed him as you would feed yourself or be fed; shelter him as you would shelter yourself or be sheltered; clothe him as you would clothe yourself or be clothed; if in any of these respects you were in his circumstances.

11. *Garden.* If you relieve the poor, you shall never be poor, but as a well-watered garden, always flourishing.

14. *In the* LORD. In his goodness and faithfulness to you, and in the assurance of his love and favor.

CHAPTER 59

13. *From the heart.* And when they dealt with men in ways of fraud, it was *from the heart,* but when they spoke with God it was but from the lip.

17. *Zeal.* For his own honor and for his own people. The sum of all these expressions is to describe both the cause and effect together. The cause was righteousness and zeal in God; the effect was salvation to his people and vengeance on his enemies.

20. *The Redeemer.* Christ, of whom the apostle writes (Rom. 11:26), the prophets having usually concluded their promises of temporal deliverance with the promises of spiritual, especially such of which the temporal were evident types.

21. *Of thy seed.* A promise of the perpetual presence of his word and Spirit with the prophets, apostles, and teachers of the church to all ages.

CHAPTER 60

6. *The multitude.* The treasure that is brought upon camels. By these and such like figurative expressions in several verses of this chapter is implied the coming in of all nations to Christ, and therefore they are brought in as presenting the chief commodities of their respective countries.

13. Kings and great ones, the glory of the world, and also persons of a lower rank shall be the materials and members of Christ's church.

18. *Thy gates.* Within and upon your gates and walls you shall sing praises. And this will be fulfilled during the thousand years wherein Christ shall reign upon earth.

19. *The sun.* These shall not be esteemed in comparison of the spiritual light of the church, but here laid down for the churches' comfort as the former was for her safety, so that God will not only be a shield, but a sun. *The* LORD. Christ shall scatter all darkness and ignorance, and this light shall not wax and wane and suffer eclipses and settings as the sun and moon do, but shall be constant without shadow of change.

CHAPTER 61

1. *Upon me.* Though the prophet may speak of himself, yet it is principally to be understood of Christ. *Anointed.* Set me apart, both capacitating him with gifts and commissioning him with authority; and yet more as it is applied to Christ, a power to make all effectual, for whence he has also the name of "Messiah" among the Hebrews and of "Christ" among the Greeks. No, Christ alone among the prophets has obtained this name (Ps. 45:7). The prophet describes first who Christ is, and then what are his offices. *Liberty.* This applies to Christ's kingly office, whereby he proclaims liberty from the dominion of sin and from the fear of hell.

3. *Trees.* That they shall be firm, solid, and well rooted, being by faith engrafted into Christ, and bring forth fruit suitable to the soil wherein they are planted.

8. *Love judgment.* I will do them right, for I love justice in myself and in them who practice it. *Everlasting covenant.* Though you have broken covenant with me, yet I will renew the ancient covenant which I made with our fathers, confirmed with the blood of Christ, and it shall be everlasting, never to be abrogated.

9. *Shall be.* That is, eminently a promise of the increase of the church. Such shall be their prosperity and multiplying that they shall be known abroad by their great increase. Or else, the meaning is, the church shall have a seed of the Gentiles; whereas the church has been confined to one corner of the world, now it shall remain in one nation alone no more, but shall fill all the nations of the earth.

CHAPTER 62

1. *My peace.* These seem to be the words of the prophet strongly resolving, in spite of all difficulties, to solicit God for the church's happiness, and to constantly encourage the belief of it by his preaching, though it were long before it came, for Isaiah lived near two hundred years before this was accomplished.

CHAPTER 63

1. *Righteousness.* Here Christ gives an answer, wherein he both asserts his fidelity that he will faithfully perform what he has promised and that he will truly execute justice. *Mighty.* I have power to accomplish salvation.

7. *Mention.* Here begins a new matter, which contains the prophet's prayer to the end of chapter 64, wherein he begins by mentioning the great kindnesses that God had showed the Jews, and that emphatically, setting them forth with the greatest advantages.

9. *The angel.* The same who conducted them through the wilderness; the Lord Jesus Christ, who appeared to Moses in the bush.

15. *Look.* Now the prophet begins to expostulate with God, and to argue both from the goodness of his nature and from the greatness of his works.

CHAPTER 64

1. *Flow down.* That all impediments might be removed out of the way. This is possibly an allusion to God's coming down upon Mount Sinai in those terrible flames of fire.

2. *Fire.* Come with such zeal for your people that the solid mountains may be no more before your breath than metal that runs, or water that boils, by the force of a vehement fire.

6. *Unclean.* Formerly there were some who feared you; but now we are all as one polluted mass, nothing of good left in us by reason of a universal degeneracy. *And all.* The very best of us all are no better than the uncleanest things. *Taken.* Carried away to Babylon, as leaves hurried away by a boisterous wind.

8. *Our father.* In spite of all this, you are our Father both by creation and by adoption; therefore, pity us your children.

9. *Pleasant things.* The palace of the king, and the houses of the nobles, and other places of state and magnificence.

CHAPTER 65

1. *I am.* This, in the primary sense of this text, is a prophecy of the "conversion of the Gentiles" upon the rejection of the Jews; for their contempt and crucifying of Christ cannot be doubted by any who will not arrogate to themselves a greater ability to interpret the prophecies of the Old Testament than Paul had, who expressly so interprets it and applies it (Rom. 10:20), which shows the vanity of the Jews in their other interpretations of it.

2. *I have spread.* Applied to the Jews (Rom. 10:21). I have used all means to reduce them, I have stretched out the hands of a passionate orator to persuade them, of a liberal benefactor to load them with my benefits. This I have done continually in the whole course of my providence with them.

24. *Before they call.* God promised (58:9) to answer them when they called. Here he promises to answer the words as soon as they should be formed in their hearts, before they could get them out of their lips.

CHAPTER 66

2. *Look.* Yet God will look with a favorable eye to him who has a *poor and . . . contrite spirit,* whose heart is subdued to the will of God, and who is poor and low in his own eyes.

7. *Before.* The whole verse is expressive of a great and sudden salvation which God would work for his church, like the delivery of a woman and that of a *man child,* before her travail and without *pain.* Doubtless it refers to the coming of Christ and the sudden propagation of the gospel.

16. *Plead.* God at first pleads with sinners by words, but if he cannot so prevail he will plead with them in a way by which he will overcome; by fire, pestilence, and blood.

17. *The abomination.* All those beasts forbidden the Jews for meat. God will not only destroy gross idolaters, but all those who make no conscience of yielding obedience to the law of God in such things as seemed to them of a minute nature and such as they easily might have obeyed.

19. *A sign.* By this may be understood Christ (Luke 2:34), or the "ministry of the word" attended with miracles; these were set up among the Jews first, then among the Gentiles.

22. *The new heavens.* The new state of the church to be raised up under the Messiah.

23. *And.* In the gospel-church there shall be as constant and settled a course of worship (though of another nature) as ever was in the Jewish church. Christians are not bound to keep the Jewish sabbaths or new moons. But New Testament worship is expressed by Old Testament phrases. The Jews were only obliged to appear three times in a year at Jerusalem, but (says the prophet) the gospel-church shall worship God *from one sabbath to another.*

JEREMIAH

CHAPTER 1

5. *I sanctified.* I ordained you for this public service. He speaks thus to Jeremiah, not to the other prophets, because he stood in need of greater encouragement than they, both in respect of the tenderness of his years and of the difficulties which he was to encounter.

9. *Then.* God, having excited the prophet by command and promise, now in a vision confirms him, either by the hand of an angel or by himself in some visible shape.

11. *Came unto me.* This and the boiling caldron (v. 13) are thought to be at the same time and in the same vision, when he was first appointed to the work. *Almond tree.* This is a tree that blossoms early, and speedily, and so it may point at either God's readiness to smite (v. 12) or Israel's ripeness to be smitten; this rod being like a portentous comet, showing to Jeremiah the miseries that were at hand.

CHAPTER 2

3. *Evil.* Evil was inflicted on them from the Lord, as upon the Egyptians, Amalekites, Midianites, and Canaanites.

6. *Neither.* They never concerned themselves about what God had done for them, which should have engaged them to cleave to him.

12. *Be ye very desolate.* Lose your brightness, as the sun seemed to do when Christ suffered.

22. *Marked.* Your filthiness is so foul that it leaves a brand behind which cannot be hid or washed out, but will abide (17:1).

31. *A land of darkness.* As it were a land uninhabitable because of the total lack of light. Have I been a God of no use or comfort to them, that they thus leave me? Have they had nothing from me but misery and affliction?

CHAPTER 3

16. *Multiplied.* After the growth of the church under the Messiah. *The ark.* That whole worship with all the rites and ceremonies belonging to it shall cease, Christ being come, who was the substance of what the ark and all other rites shadowed.

23. *The hills.* From idols, which were worshipped upon hills. *Mountains.* The multitude of sacrifices, which they offer in the mountains.

25. *Lie down.* An expression to set forth the greatness of their repentance and sorrow in great perplexity. Not knowing what to do, they throw themselves down upon their couch or bed.

CHAPTER 4

3. *For.* The Lord turns now his speech from Israel to Judah. *Break up.* Prepare your hearts by making them soft, tender, and pliable, fit to embrace my word. A metaphor taken from plowmen.

11. *A dry wind.* A drying wind, such as shall blast and scorch where it comes, without any rain or moisture. It points at the stormy and furious irruption of the Babylonian army. *In the wilderness.* Where there is no stop in the way to break its fury. *Not.* Not such a gentle wind, as is made choice of to separate the chaff from the wheat; but so boisterous and violent that it shall sweep away and lay waste all together.

24. *Trembled.* He proceeds in his figurative expressions. Behold how the very mountains of Judea do tremble! *Moved.* As easily as dust or feathers in a whirlwind.

31. *Spreadeth her hands.* According to the use of persons in great anguish, clapping or wringing their hands together.

CHAPTER 5

1. *Run.* God gives leave to all the earth to look into the state of Jerusalem, by which he vindicates himself in the face of the whole world from all severity towards his people, whatever he brings upon them. *A man.* It seems worse than Sodom and Gomorrah, for God condescends to pardon Jerusalem if there be but one righteous man found in it; there he came no lower than ten. A man might walk the streets of Jerusalem long enough before he could meet with any one truly religious.

21. *And hear not.* They are willfully blind and obstinately deaf. They will neither see nor hear the word, will, or works of God, of which he gives two instances in the two following verses.

24. *Reserveth.* He gives seasonable harvests according to his appointment. God would let them know what a foolish, as well as wicked, thing it is to set themselves against that God who keeps the whole order of nature at his own disposal, which he can order as he sees men behave towards him.

CHAPTER 6

1. *Benjamin.* Judah; when the ten tribes fell off, the tribe of Benjamin adhered to Judah and was incorporated into them. If it be asked why the prophet rather speaks to Benjamin than to Judah, the reason probably may be because he, being of Anathoth, was of that tribe and therefore mentions them as his own countrymen.

10. *Their ear.* An uncircumcised ear signifies the rejecting of instruction; an uncircumcised heart, an obstinate and rebellious will.

11. *I am full.* I am, as it were, filled with the fire of God's wrath, of which I am forced to discharge myself.

16. *Stand.* He now turns his speech to the people and gives them counsel by a metaphor taken from travelers, that, being in doubt of their way, stand still and consider whether the direction they have received from some false guide be right or not.

27. *I have set thee.* Here God speaks by way of encouragement to the prophet and tells him he had made him a fortified tower, that he might be safe in spite of all the attempts against him. *And try.* As refiners do metals. Hereby he is encouraged to reprove them more freely; God will give him prudence to see what is amiss and undauntedness to oppose it.

CHAPTER 7

9. *Will ye steal.* Can you think that it can be grateful to me or advantageous to yourselves to frequent my house and yet retain these odious sins?

10. *Delivered.* After they had appeared before God with their sacrifices, they thought they were privileged to return to all those wickednesses.

25. *Since the day.* The church of God has never lacked teachers raised up and sent by God.

31. *Tophet.* It comes from *toph,* a drum, because they beat drums to drown the children's screeches when they burnt them in sacrifice upon the altars, called here the *high places,* to Molech.

CHAPTER 8

5. *Deceit.* Their false prophets, encouraging themselves in their wickedness and pleasing themselves, that their miseries should not come upon them.

21. *Am I hurt.* The prophet here shows how deeply he is affected with the people's misery. *Black.* I am as those who are clad in deep mourning.

CHAPTER 9

10. *Wailing.* The prophet, having taken up a lamentation for the slaughter of the people, now resumes it for the desolation of the whole land.

17. *Women.* Who were hired to tear their hair, beat their breasts, and assume other mourning postures; a foolish custom which has prevailed in most ages and countries.

24. *Knoweth.* Whether we make any curious distinction between understanding God, as if that be more speculative, whereby we rightly apprehend his nature; and knowing God, as if that be more practical, as directing the conversation, we need not here enquire. Yet certainly both center in this, that we so know and understand

God as to trust in him and depend on him alone in all conditions.

CHAPTER 10

10. *Living.* These are all but dead stocks and stones; Jehovah is the only living God, having life in himself and giving life to all things else. *An everlasting king.* Time devours them all, but the true God is everlasting.

23. *It is not.* Lord, we know it is not in our power to divert these judgments that are coming upon us, but you can moderate and limit them as you please.

24. *Correct me.* Seeing you will punish us, let it be a correction only, not a destruction. Let it be in measure; in the midst of judgment, remember mercy.

CHAPTER 11

11. *I will not hearken.* God will not hear them crying to him in their adversity who refuse to hear him speaking to them in their prosperity.

15. *The holy flesh.* Flesh of their sacrifices, being set before idols as well as before God, became polluted and was an abomination to the Lord.

19. *Let us destroy.* We have no other mention of this conspiracy, but it is plain, both from this verse and what follows, that the men of Anathoth (which was Jeremiah's own town) were offended at his prophesying and had conspired to kill him.

CHAPTER 12

1. *Wherefore.* I know your ways are just and righteous, but they are dark. I cannot understand why you do this.

13. *Shall not profit.* All the works of their hands, all their counsels and deliberations should be of no profit unto them. *Because.* The fierce anger of God shall be so revealed that the returns of their labors or estates, the profits of their trades, shall be so small that they shall be ashamed of them.

16. *If.* If they will leave their idolatries and learn to worship me and *swear by my name, The LORD liveth,* that is, pay that homage which they owe the divine being to me, the living and true God. *Then.* They shall have a portion among my people. This was eminently fulfilled in the conversion of the Gentiles.

CHAPTER 13

13. *Behold.* This speaks of a wine of astonishment and confusion (Ps. 60:3). With that wine, says God (v. 12), I will fill all orders of persons, *kings, . . . priests, and . . . prophets, and all the inhabitants of Jerusalem.*

16. *Give glory.* Glorify God by a humble confession of your sins, by submitting yourselves to God, and by humbling yourselves under his word and under his mighty hand, before God brings upon you his great and heavy judgments.

CHAPTER 14

6. *The wild asses.* The wild asses, lacking water, got upon high places, where was the coolest air, and sucked in the wind. This, it is said, they did like dragons, of whom Aristotle and Pliny report that they ordinarily stand upon high places sucking in the cool air.

7. *Do thou it.* Do what we stand in need of; give us rain, though not for our sake, we deserve no such kindness from you, yet for your name's sake. Do it for your promise, or for your honor and glory.

10. *Thus.* Here begins the answer to the prophet's complaint and prayer in the first nine verses. The substance is that for their manifold sins he was resolved to punish them.

22. *Art not.* Lord, are not you he alone who is able to do it? The Scripture constantly gives God the honor of giving rain.

CHAPTER 15

8. *Their widows.* The prophet still speaks of things to come as if present. In Jehoiakim's time we read of no such plenty of widows; they were multiplied when the city was besieged and taken in Zedekiah's time, to a great number, hyperbolically compared to the sands of the sea.

17. *I sat not.* God had all along filled his mouth with such dreadful messages that his whole prophetical life had been to him a time of mourning and solitude, a time when he sat alone mourning and weeping in secret for the wrath of God revealed to him against his people.

18. *Why.* Jeremiah, though a great prophet, was (as Elijah) a man subject to like passions with other men.

19. *If thou.* These are God's words to the prophet, rebuking his distrust in God and promising him that if he did return from his distrust in God's providence, he would restore him to the former favor he had with him, and he should be his prophet to reveal his mind to the people. And if he would separate the precious truths of God from the vile conceits of men, then God would continue him as his prophet to speak in his name to the people.

CHAPTER 16

6. *Nor cut.* Cutting themselves and cutting off their hair were pagan customs which God forbade his own people to do, yet it seemed they practiced them. But God says, Men shall die so fast that they shall have no leisure to cut themselves.

21. *And.* They shall know that my name is Jehovah; that I am not such a one as their idols, but one who has my being from myself and gives life and being to all other things, and has all might and power in my hand and can do whatever I please.

CHAPTER 17

9. *The heart.* There is nothing so false and deceitful as the heart of man. It is deceitful in the apprehension of things, in the hopes and promises which it nourishes, in the assurances that it gives us. It is unsearchable by others, deceitful with reference to ourselves, and abominably wicked so that neither can a man know his own heart nor can any other know that of his neighbor's.

CHAPTER 18

6. *Cannot I do.* That God has an absolute sovereign power to do what he pleases with the work of his hands. But he acts as a just judge, rendering to every man according to his works.

21. *Therefore.* But is it lawful for God's servants to pray for evil against their enemies? It is not lawful for Christians. It is doubtless our duty to pray for the conversion, forgiveness, and eternal salvation of our worst enemies.

CHAPTER 19

5. *To burn.* This and the following verse contain another great sin of this people, with the punishment which God proportions to it. The sin in general was idolatry; but a most barbarous species of it, mentioned also in 7:31 and 32:35, is that they made their sons and their daughters pass through the fire to Molech. "Baal" and "Molech" signify the same thing; Baal sig-

nifies a lord, Molech a king. Both seem common names to all idols.

14. *Then.* Jeremiah had now dispatched the errand upon which God had sent him to Tophet; coming back by God's direction, he stands in the court which was common to all people, where the most might hear.

CHAPTER 20

7. *Hast prevailed.* Jeremiah at first excused himself to God (1:6), but the Lord prevailed against him, replying, "Say not, I am a child: for thou shalt go to all that I shall send thee, and whatsoever I command thee thou shalt speak" (1:7). This is all that is here meant, namely God's overruling him, contrary to his own inclinations.

11. *But.* The prophet, recovering from his fit of passion, encourages himself in his God, whom he calls the *mighty terrible one,* so declaring his faith in the power of God as one able to save him, and in the promise and good will of God toward him; therefore he says, *The LORD is with me.* Such was the promise of God to this prophet when he first undertook the prophetical office (1:8). Be not afraid of their faces, for "I am with thee to deliver thee, saith the LORD." From this he concludes that though he had many who pursued after his life, yet they should stumble in their ways of violence and should not prevail.

CHAPTER 21

2. *Inquire.* Zedekiah, as he was none of the best, so he was none of the worst of the kings of Judah. Having some reverence of God, he sends the prophet to inquire *of the LORD.*

9. *His life.* This is a proverbial expression signifying a man's possession of his life as a prey, or booty received from the enemy.

CHAPTER 22

10. *Weep ye not.* For Josiah, your dead prince. Josiah is happy, you need not trouble yourselves for him; but weep for Jehoahaz, who is to go into captivity.

16. *Was not this.* They only truly know God who obey him; men vainly pretend to piety who are defective in justice and charity.

CHAPTER 23

5. *Behold.* Even the Jewish scholars, as well as the Christian interpreters, understand this as a prophecy of the Messiah, who is called the branch (Isa. 4:2; 53:2). And here he is called the *righteous Branch,* not only because he was righteous, but because he makes his people righteous.

6. *Judah.* During the reign and kingdom of the Messiah, the people of God, typified by Judah and Israel, shall be saved with a spiritual salvation and God will be a special protection to them. *And this.* The name wherewith the branch shall be called shall be THE LORD OUR RIGHTEOUSNESS. This place is an eminent proof of the Godhead of Christ. He is here called "Jehovah," and what is proper to God alone, namely to justify, is here applied to Christ. He "who knew no sin" was made sin (that is, a sacrifice for sin) for us, "that we might be made the righteousness of God in him."

8. *They shall dwell.* Possibly part of this prophecy remains yet to be accomplished, for the Jews are not yet come to dwell in their own land.

20. *Ye shall consider.* And though you will not now believe it, yet hereafter, when it shall be too late, you shall consider it perfectly.

36. *For.* These false and irreverent speeches, which are in every man's mouth, shall be burdensome to them, shall bring down vengeance upon them.

CHAPTER 24

5. *Acknowledge.* I will acknowledge them for their good. I will show them favor, being of the number of those who were not leaders to sin, but led away by the ill example of others, and who, being carried away, grew sensible of their sins and so accepted the punishment of their iniquities.

CHAPTER 25

9. *Nebuchadrezzar.* In this work shall be my servant; though you will not be my servants in obeying my commands.

10. *Moreover.* No, I will not only deprive you of your mirth, but of those things that are necessary for you, as necessary as bread and light. The millstone shall not move, you shall not have the light so much as of a candle.

34. *A pleasant vessel.* Like a crystal glass, or some delicate vessel, which breaks in pieces and cannot again be set together.

CHAPTER 26

18. *Micah.* This was that Micah whose prophecies are part of holy writ, as appears in Micah 1:1 and 3:12, where are the very words of the prophecy here mentioned. The substance of the prophecy was the same as this, that Zion should be plowed up and the place where the temple stood should become so desolate that trees should grow there, as in a forest.

20. *And there was.* This is a story which we have recorded in no other part of Scripture. They are probably the words of some others who were enemies to Jeremiah.

CHAPTER 27

2. *Thus saith.* God commands the prophet to procure some yokes with bonds to make them more fast. And to put one of them upon his own neck, that therein he might be a type both to his own people and to the people afterward mentioned, that they should be in bondage to the king of Babylon.

CHAPTER 28

17. *Died.* Within two months after Jeremiah had thus prophesied; so dangerous a thing it is for ministers to teach people contrary to the revealed will of God.

CHAPTER 29

11. *To give.* This deliverance will not depend upon your merits, but upon my own mercy, kind thoughts, and the purposes I have for the seed of Abraham my servant. I am resolved in my own thoughts what to do, I intend not the blotting out of the name of Israel from the earth, but to give such an end to their trouble as they expect and desire.

CHAPTER 30

9. *But.* Either this must be understood of the kingdom of Christ, under which the Jews who received him were made spiritually free; or there is a time yet to come when this ancient people of God shall be restored to a further civil liberty than they have enjoyed ever since the captivity of Babylon.

11. *Unpunished.* But yet God will not let his own people go unpunished, that by it they may be reclaimed and the world may take notice that God is of purer eyes than that he can, in any persons, behold iniquity.

CHAPTER 31

6. *Arise.* This was fulfilled under the gospel, for both Galilee and Samaria received the gospel.

11. *Hath redeemed.* God will as certainly do it as if he had already done it. In their deliverance as well from Babylon as Egypt, they were types of the deliverance of God's people by Christ. As well as in their entering into Canaan, they were types of the saints entering into heaven.

12. *Not sorrow.* In that manner they have been. But under these expressions is also promised the spiritual joy which the true Israel of God will have under the gospel and the eternal joy they shall have in heaven.

22. *A woman.* This seems to be a promise of the Jewish church in its time, and of the gospel-church, prevailing over all its enemies. Though, considering the fewness of the church's members compared with the multitude of its enemies and their power, it seemed as strange a thing as for a woman to prevail against a strong and mighty man.

33. *With.* That is, with those who are Jews inwardly. *And write it.* The prophet's design is here to express the difference between the law and the gospel. The first shows duty, the latter brings the grace of regeneration by which the heart is changed and enabled for duty. All who came to salvation under the time of the law were saved by this new covenant. But this was not evidently exhibited. Neither was the regenerating grace of God so common under the time of the law as it has been under the gospel.

34. *I will forgive.* God makes the root of all this grace to be the free pardon and the remission of their sins.

CHAPTER 32

24. *The mounts.* Rather, engines of war, with which those nations used to batter walls or to shoot great stones into places besieged.

40. *I will make.* This promise manifestly relates to those Jews who should receive the Lord Jesus Christ; unless it is to be understood of a national conversion of the Jews not yet effected.

CHAPTER 33

16. *Saved.* It is the opinion of some that a spiritual salvation and security is promised under these expressions, but by the most and best interpreters, a temporal salvation. This was typical of that spiritual and eternal salvation which is promised to the true Israel of God; as their rest in Canaan typified that rest which remains for the people of God. *The LORD our righteousness.* There is no such name anywhere given, either to the Jewish or Christian church, as "the LORD our righteousness" but that the full import of that name is spoken of Christ (Isa. 45:23), which text is applied to Christ (Rom. 14:11; Phil. 2:10).

17. *David.* That is, apparently a promise relating to Christ, for David's line would have failed long since had it not been continued in Christ, whose kingdom is and shall be an everlasting kingdom.

18. *A man.* That is, a ministry to abide in the church to the end of the world, nor is it unusual for God in the Old Testament to express promises to be fulfilled under the gospel by expressions proper to the Old Testament.

22. *Of David.* Christ is himself called David, whose seed and whose Levites are multiplied in the multiplying of Christians and of faithful ministers under the gospel, which are the things here promised.

24. *The two families.* The families of David and Aaron.

CHAPTER 34

5. *Ah lord!* The Jews in their chronology give us the form of the lamentation thus: "Alas! Zedekiah is dead, who drank the dregs of all ages"; that is, who was punished for the sins of all former ages.

18. *Cut the calf.* It seems these Jews, in their making of the solemn covenant with God about releasing their servants, used this rite. They caused a calf, or heifer, to be cut in pieces and laid the parts in the temple, the right over against one another. Then they received this covenant and passed between the parts of the heifer so cut, silently agreeing that God should cut them in pieces like that beast if they did not make their words good.[1]

CHAPTER 35

1. *The word.* This is another evidence that the prophecies of this book are not left us in that order wherein they were delivered. For those which we had in the two or three foregoing chapters, being the time of Zedekiah, must be ten or eleven years after this.

7. *That ye may live.* Jonadab cautions his sons by a thrifty, sober, laborious life, to which they had been bred, in keeping flocks, to avoid any thing which might expose them to the envy or hatred of the people among whom they were come to sojourn.

---

[1] (34:18) See Genesis 15:9–11, 17. The Hebrew word usually used for making a covenant literally means "to cut."

CHAPTER 36

2. *All the words.* All the revelations he had from God for twenty-two years last past. God would have them recorded that there might be a memorial of them, that so the truth of them might appear when God should bring them to pass; the time of which now drew near.

6. *Upon the fasting day.* It was undoubtedly, because of the concourse of people which the prophet knew would that day be in the temple, that he chose that day, when some would be present from all parts of Judah.

10. *Then read.* Most likely out of some window or balcony, the people being below and hearing it.

18. *He pronounced.* This could not but add to the princes' fear. They must conceive that without a special influence of God, it had been impossible that Jeremiah should have called to mind all that he had spoken at several times in so many years.

CHAPTER 37

10. *And burn this city.* When God is resolved upon an effect, the instruments are little to be regarded. It is not the arm of flesh, but the power of God which is to be considered.

16. *The dungeon.* The Hebrew words signify some pit or deep hole where were some cells or apartments in which they kept those whom they judged great malefactors.

CHAPTER 38

22. *The women.* You who are afraid of the insultings of men shall fall under the insultings of the women. *And they* have forsaken you, every one shifting for himself.

CHAPTER 39

12. *Take him.* It is improbable that Nebuchadnezzar had been informed, since Jeremiah had constantly told the king that the Chaldeans should take the city. He steadily persuaded both the king and princes to surrender it to them.

15. *Now the word.* These four verses (vv. 15–18) mention a matter that happened before the things mentioned in the foregoing verses.

CHAPTER 40

1. *Babylon.* Jeremiah was by mistake, and expressly contrary to the king's orders, carried among the other prisoners. Probably the captain of the guard at that place called over his prisoners and among them found the prophet, contrary to his expectation.

CHAPTER 41

1. *Ishmael.* The same Ishmael who came to Gedaliah (vv. 8–9), to whom he swore protection. Only here we are told he was of the royal blood, which might both raise his spirits as having a more legal pretense to the government and render him a fitter instrument for Baalis, the king or queen of the Ammonites, to make use of.

8. *He forbare.* His covetousness prevailed over his cruelty.

CHAPTER 42

10. *I repent.* I am satisfied with the punishment your nation has undergone and, as to the remainder, will change the course of my providence.

CHAPTER 43

6. *Good, or . . . evil.* Whether grateful or ungrateful unto us.

12. *Carry them.* He shall carry away both the idols and the inhabitants of Egypt captives. *With the land.* With the spoils of the land of Egypt he shall clothe his army.

CHAPTER 44

14. *For none.* Only such shall escape as have been forced into Egypt against their wills; and as did not fall in with the idolatry of the Egyptians.

15. *All the men.* It should seem those who did it were mostly women, and that they did it with some privacy so that their husbands did not know of it.

CHAPTER 45

3. *I find no rest.* Upon Baruch's reading the prophecies, both he and Jeremiah were advised to hide themselves. This probably disturbed Baruch and made him lament his condition.

CHAPTER 46

1. *The word.* This verse contains the title of all the ensuing discourses; for though there be some verses in these chapters that relate to the Jews, yet they are all concerning their restoration. The prophecies of judgments from the beginning of this chapter to the fifty-second are all against foreign nations, which are called Gentiles.

6. *Let not the swift.* It is in vain for the swift to flee away. The mighty men shall not escape, but they shall stumble and fall at Carchemish.

10. *Made drunk.* These phrases only metaphorically signify the great slaughter God would make that day among the Egyptians.

12. *Stumbled.* Stumbling one upon another, so that both those who went before and those who followed after should fall together.

22. *A serpent.* Egypt is now like a heifer that makes a great bellowing; but the time shall come when she shall make a lesser noise like the hissing of a serpent.

CHAPTER 47

6. *O thou sword.* Perhaps they are the words of the prophet, lamenting the havoc which the Lord made among the Philistines by the Chaldeans.

7. *How.* God lets the prophet know that he had given this sword its commission and therefore it could not stop until Ashkelon and the people on the seashore were destroyed by it.

CHAPTER 48

26. *Drunken.* Fill him with the intoxicating wine of God's vengeance.

30. *I know.* He shall never execute what he thinks to do. *But.* His boastings and his lies shall never effect his designs.

47. *Bring again.* It seems this is to be understood of a spiritual reduction of them by calling them into the kingdom of the Messiah.

CHAPTER 49

6. *I will bring.* Probably this refers to the conversion of the Ammonites as well as other heathens to Christ.

12. *They.* The Jews, who in comparison with others did not deserve to drink of the cup, yet have drunk of it; and can you think to escape? When an Israelite has not escaped the justice of God, an Edomite must not expect it.

30. *Flee.* These seem to be the prophet's words.

39. *But.* We had the like promise as to Moab (48:47) and as to Ammon (v. 6). The same *latter days* signify either after many days or in the time of the Messiah. In the former sense it may refer to Cyrus, who conquered Persia. In the latter sense it refers to the spiritual liberty which some of these poor heathens were brought into by the gospel. We read in Acts 2:9 that some of the Elamites were at Jerusalem at Pentecost and were among those who were converted to Christ.

CHAPTER 50

7. *Habitation.* Some think this is a name here given to God, who indeed is the habitation of justice; but whether the Chaldeans would call him so may be a question. Others therefore think the preposition *in* is understood, making this the aggravation of the Jews' sins, that they were committed in a land which ought to have been a habitation of justice.

12. *Mother.* Your country shall be ashamed of you who are not able to defend her.

CHAPTER 51

10. *Come.* These words are spoken in the person of the Jews, owning the destruction of Babylon to be the mighty work of God and an act of justice, avenging the wrongs of his people.

23. *Break in pieces.* The sense of these three verses is the same; that God had made use and was still making use of the Babylonians to destroy many nations, to spoil much people, wasting their goods, routing their armies, killing all sorts of their inhabitants.

48. *Then.* All the creatures in heaven and earth shall rejoice at the vengeance which God shall take upon Babylon.

57. *Drunk.* A plain allusion to the posture the king of Babylon and the thousand of his lords were in, when their city was taken while they were drinking wine in the bowls that were brought from the temple at Jerusalem.

58. *Weary.* Though the people should labor to quench this fire or to rebuild this city, yet it would be all lost labor.

64. *The words.* The prophetic words of Jeremiah; for the matter of the next chapter is historical and the Book of Lamentations is not prophetic.

CHAPTER 52

1. *Zedekiah.* It is generally thought that this chapter was not penned by Jeremiah, who, it is not probable, would have so largely repeated what he had related before. Nor could he historically relate what happened after his time, as some things did which are mentioned toward the end of the chapter. Probably it was penned by some of those in Babylon and put in here as a preface to the Book of Lamentations.

34. *All the days of his life.* Here ends the history of the kingdom of Judah. I shall only observe the severe judgment of God upon this people, whose kingdom was made up of the two tribes of Judah and Benjamin and half the tribe of Manasseh. In the numbering of the persons belonging to these two tribes in Numbers 1 (counting half of the number of the tribe of Manasseh), we find 126,100. In Numbers 26 we find of them 148,450. Here, in verse 30, we find no more of them carried into captivity than 4,600. From this we may judge what a multitude of them were slain by the sword, by the famine and pestilence! "It is a fearful thing to fall into the hands of the living God," to mock his messengers, and despise his words, and misuse his prophets, until there be no remedy (II Chron. 36:16).

lamentations

CHAPTER 1

1. *Widow.* She who had a king, or rather a God, who was a husband to her now was forsaken of God, and her king taken from her.

11. *Bread.* Even in a land that ordinarily flowed with milk and honey, they were at a loss for bread to eat.

14. *Is bound.* Put upon my neck on account of my transgressions. *Are wreathed.* My punishments are twisted as cords; I have a complication of judgments upon me: sword, famine, pestilence, captivity.

CHAPTER 2

3. *Round about.* God consumed them, not in this or that part, but round about, as a fire seizing a house at once on all sides.

9. *The law* is no more read, opened, or observed. *Her prophets.* They had but very few prophets, from this time to the time of the gospel, and very few of those at this time alive had any revelation from God.

13. *Who.* There was no people whose condition was in any degree parallel to the misery of the Jews. Nor was there any cure for them; their breach was like a sea breach, where the waters come in with such a torrent that there is no making any defense against them.

22. *My terrors.* As my people were prone to be called together from all parts in a solemn day, so now my terrible enemies, or terrible things, are by thee called together.

CHAPTER 3

9. *Enclosed.* He has defeated all my methods and counsels for security, by insuperable difficulties, like walls of hewed stone. *Crooked.* No, God not only defeated their counsels, but made them fatal and pernicious to them.

19. *The wormwood and the gall* are often made use of to signify great affliction.

21. *This.* Which follows, concerning the nature of God and his good providences.

24. *Bear.* Quietly and patiently bear what afflictions God will please to lay upon us. And if God tame us when young, by his word or by his rod, it is an unspeakable advantage.

33. *Willingly.* Not from his own mere motion without a cause given him from the persons afflicted. Hence judgment is called God's "strange work."

37. *Who.* Nothing comes to pass in the world but by the disposal of divine providence. This seems to be spoken in the name of the people of God, arguing themselves into a quiet submission to their afflictions from the consideration of the hand of God in them.

38. *Evil.* Does not evil or trouble come out of God's mouth from his direction and providence, as well as good?

CHAPTER 4

6. *Of Sodom.* Their punishment was greater because it was more lingering and gradual, whereas Sodom was overthrown in a moment, and that by no human hands, causing her a continued torment.

13. *Priests.* The ecclesiastical men were a great cause of the first and last destruction of Jerusalem. And so they are of most other places that come to ruin, through their neglect of their duty, or encouraging others in their wicked courses.

14. *They.* The prophets and priests wandered up and down the streets polluting themselves with blood, either the blood of the children which they slew, or the just men mentioned in verse 13; the slaughter of whom they either encouraged or at least did not discourage. One could not touch a prophet or priest without becoming legally polluted, and there were so many of them that men could not walk in the streets without touching some of them.

CHAPTER 5

3. *We.* We are all of us without a king (our common father), we are deprived of your fatherly protection, and many young children among us are left without an earthly parent.

6. *We.* The ten tribes were all carried captives into Assyria, and many of the kingdom of Judah fled into Egypt. "Giving the hand" may signify laboring for them, or yielding up themselves to their power.

19. *Thy throne.* Although for our sins you allowed our throne to be cast down, yet you are the same; your power is not diminished, nor your goodness abated.

ezekiel

CHAPTER 1

2. *Jehoiachin.* Who is also called Jeconiah, or Coniah. It may be of use to keep an account when and where God has manifested himself to us in a peculiar manner. Remember, O my soul, what you did receive at such a time, at such a place. Tell others what God did for you.

3. *The hand.* He felt the power of God opening his eyes to see the visions, opening his ear to hear the voice and his heart to receive both. When *the hand of the* LORD goes along with his word, then it becomes effectual.

5. *The likeness.* Such a representation of the holy angels as God saw fit to make use of *came out . . . of the midst of the fire.* For angels derive their being and power from God; their glory is a ray of his.

14. *Ran.* They ran into the lower world to do what was to be done there. And when they had done, *returned as . . . a flash of lightning,* to the upper world to the vision of God. Thus we should be in the affairs of this world. Though we run into them, we must not repose in them, but our souls must presently return like lightning to God, who is their rest and center.

15. *Four faces.* By this it appears that each wheel had its four faces. While he was contemplating the glory of the former vision, this other was presented to him. The dispensations of providence are compared to the wheels of a machine, which all contribute to the regular motion of it. Providence orders, changes. Sometimes one spoke of the wheel is uppermost, sometimes another. But the motion of the wheel on its own axle is still regular and steady. And the wheel is said to be *by the living creatures,* who attend to direct its motion. For all the inferior creatures are, move, and act as the Creator, by the ministration of angels, directs and influences them. Visible effects are managed and governed by invisible causes.

18. *Them four.* Every one of the four wheels. How fitly do the wheels, their motion, their height, and eyes signify the height, unsearchableness, wisdom, and vigilance of the divine providence.

20. *The spirit.* The Spirit of God. These angels in their ministry punctually observed both his impulse and conduct. *Their spirit.* The wheels concurred with the spirit of the living creatures so that there was a hearty accord between those superior and inferior causes. *For.* An undiscerned yet divine, mighty, wise, and ever-living power, spirit, and being actuated all and governed all.

21. *For.* The same wisdom, power, and holiness of God, the same will and counsel of his that guides and governs the angels, does by them order and dispose all the motions of the creatures in this lower world.

26. *A man.* Christ, God-man, who here appears as king and judge.

27. *Amber.* In this color Christ appears against the rebellious Jews. He who would have visited them clothed with the garments of salvation now puts on the garments of vengeance, expressed by such metaphors.

28. *The bow.* A like appearance of Christ in a surrounding brightness, as in Revelations 4:3. Mercy and truth, both according to covenant, are about the throne of Christ.

CHAPTER 2

1. *And.* He who sat upon the throne, Jesus Christ. *Son of man.* A phrase which is used at least ninety-five times in this prophecy to keep him humble who had such great revelations.

CHAPTER 3

3. *Honey.* It was sweet to receive things by revelation from God and so to converse with God. And usually the first part of the ministerial work is pleasant.

8. *I have.* I have given you constancy and manly carriage. The more impudent wicked people are in their opposition to religion, the more openly and resolutely should God's people appear in the practice and defense of it.

12. *A voice.* An articulate sound of many angels, attended with the rushing of the wheels, added to the noise of their wings.

13. *Rushing.* The wheels of providence moved over against the angels, and in concert with them.

23. *As the glory.* We are not now to expect such visions. But we have a blessing not inferior if we by faith *behold the glory of the LORD,* so as to be "changed into the same image." And "this honour have all his saints."

CHAPTER 4

6. *Forty days.* Probably from Josiah's renewing the covenant until the destruction of the temple, during which time God deferred to punish, expecting whether they would keep their covenant or retain their idolatries, which latter they did, which amount to just forty years.

17. *May want.* So because they served not God with cheerfulness in "the abundance of all things," he made them serve their enemies "in want of all things."

CHAPTER 5

17. *Pestilence and blood.* Your land shall be the common road for pestilence and blood. Though this prophecy was to be accomplished presently in the destruction of Jerusalem by the Chaldeans, yet it may well be supposed to look forward to the final destruction of it by the Romans, when God made a full end of the Jewish nation and "caused [his] fury to rest upon them."

CHAPTER 6

9. *Whorish heart.* Idolatrous hearts depart from God, as an adulterous wife departs from her husband. *Loathe.* With a mixture of grief towards God, of indignation against themselves, and abhorrence of the offense.

11. *Smite.* To show your wonder, indignation, sorrow, and pity for their sins and sufferings.

CHAPTER 7

5–6. *An evil.* An evil and sore affliction, a singular, uncommon one. *An end.* When the end is come upon the wicked world, then *an only evil* comes upon it. The sorest of temporal judgments have their allays; but the torments of the damned are *an evil, an only evil.*

12. *Mourn.* Men usually part with their estates grieving that they must transmit their right to others. But let them now think how little a while they could have kept them, and how little time they shall keep them who have bought them.

19. *Stumblingblock.* This silver and gold they coveted immeasurably and abused to pride, luxury, idolatry, and oppression. This that they stumbled at and fell into sin, now they stumble at and fall into the deepest misery.

27. *Troubled.* Hang down and melt away. What can men contrive or do for themselves when God is departed from them? All must be in tears, all in trouble, when God comes to *judge them according to their deserts,* and so make them know that he is the Lord, to whom vengeance belongs.

CHAPTER 8

2. *A likeness.* Of a man, the man whom he had seen upon the throne. *Fire.* This fire might denote the wrath of God against Jerusalem.

3. *And.* This and all the passages to the end of the 26th verse were done in vision only.

16. *The sun.* In imitation of the Persians, Egyptians, and other eastern idolaters; these Jews turn their back on God, who created the sun, and worship the creature in contempt of the Creator.

18. *Will I not hear.* The time was, when God was ready to have heard even before they cried. But now they cry aloud and yet cry in vain. It is the upright heart which God regards, and not the loud voice.

CHAPTER 9

1. *He.* The man whom he had seen upon the throne. *Them.* Those whom God has appointed to destroy the city; perhaps angels.

2. *And.* As soon as the command was given, the ministers of God's displeasure appear. *Men.* In appearance and vision they were men, and the prophet calls them as he saw them.

CHAPTER 10

3. *The man.* Christ, the Lord of angels, who now attend his coming and commands. *The cloud.* As the sign of God's presence.

4. *The glory.* The visible token of the presence of the God of glory.

10. *They.* The wheels. This intimates the references of providence to each other and their dependence on each other. And it intimates the joint tendency of all to one common end, while their motions appear to us intricate and perplexed, yes, seemingly contrary.

12. *And.* Now he describes both the cherubim and wheels as full of wisdom and as governed by an excellent wisdom. *The wheels.* Which the four cherubim had to move, govern, and direct.

17. *For.* There is a perfect harmony between second causes in their dependence on, and subjection to, the one infinite, wise, good, holy, and just God. The Spirit of God directs all the creatures, upper and lower, so that they shall serve the divine purpose. Events are not determined by the wheel of fortune, which is blind, but by the wheels of providence, which are full of eyes.

CHAPTER 11

15. *Get you far.* You are gone far from the Lord; as much as the heathens accused the Christians of atheism.

19. *One heart.* Cyrus shall give them leave, and I will give them a heart to return. And on their way shall there be great unity. And when they come to Jerusalem, they shall own me and my laws and with one consent build Jerusalem and the temple and restore true religion. *Stony.* That hard, inflexible, undutiful, incorrigible disposition.

CHAPTER 12

11. We cannot say concerning our dwelling place that it is our resting place. For how far we may be tossed from it before we die we cannot foresee.

16. *They.* The Chaldeans. See how God brings good out of evil! The dispersion of sinners who had done God much dishonor and disservice in their own country proves the dispersion of penitents who shall do him much honor and service in other countries!

25. *I will speak.* There has been and shall be a succession of God's ministers by whom he will speak to the end of the world. Even in the worst times, God "left not himself without witness," but raised up men who spoke for him and who spoke from him.

CHAPTER 13

3. *Foolish prophets.* Foolish prophets are not of God's sending. For whom he sends, he either sends fit or makes fit. Where he gives warrant, he gives wisdom.

10. *Peace.* They told sinners that no harm would happen to them. And those are the most dangerous seducers who suggest to sinners that which tends to lessen their dread of sin or their fear of God. These are compared to men who build a slight tottering wall, which others daub with untempered mortar; sorry stuff that will not bind, nor hold the bricks together—doctrines not grounded on the word of God.

14. *Ye shall know.* Those who deceived others will in the end be found to have deceived themselves. And no doom will be more fearful than that of unfaithful ministers.

CHAPTER 14

5. *Through their idols.* It is always through some idol or other that the hearts of men *are all estranged* from God. Some creature has gained that place in the heart which belongs to none but God.

14. *Noah.* Who, it is probable, prevailed with God to spare the world for some years and saved his near relations when the flood came. *Daniel.* Who prevailed for the life of the wise men of Chaldea. *Job.* Who daily offered sacrifice for his children, and at last reconciled God to those who had offended.

23. *Comfort you.* That is, you will be comforted when you compare their case with your own; when they tell you how righteous God was in bringing these judgments upon them. This will reconcile you to the justice of God in thus punishing his own people, and to the goodness of God, who now appeared to have had kind intentions in all.

CHAPTER 15

2. *The vine tree.* Israel is here compared to a vine, which, when fruitless, is utterly unprofitable. This the prophet reminds them of to humble them and awaken them to fruitfulness. *A branch.* One branch of a tree in the forest is of more use than the whole vine tree is, except for its fruit.

CHAPTER 16

5. This is an apt illustration of the natural state of all the children of men. In the day that we were born, we were shaped in iniquity, our understanding darkened, our minds alienated from the life of God; we were all polluted with sin, which rendered us loathsome in the eyes of God.

30. *An imperious whorish woman.* A woman who knows no superior, nor will be neither guided nor governed.

31. *Not been as an harlot.* Common harlots make gain of their looseness and live by that gain. You do worse: you lavish out your credit, wealth, and all to maintain your adulterers.

34. *Contrary.* Here we may see what the nature of men is when God leaves them to themselves; yes, though they have the greatest advantage to be better and to do better.

60. *Nevertheless.* The Lord, having denounced a perpetual punishment to the impenitent body of the Jewish nation, does now promise to the remnant that they shall be remembered and obtain covenanted mercy. *An everlasting covenant.* Of long continuance as to their condition in the land of Canaan, and in what is spiritual it shall be absolutely everlasting.

61. *Receive.* Admit into church communion the Gentiles, now strangers but then sisters. *For daughters.* As daughters hearken to and obey, so shall the Gentiles brought into the church hearken to the word of God which sounded out from Jerusalem. *But not.* Not by that old covenant which was violated, not by external ceremonies which were a great part of the first covenant, but by

that covenant which writes the law in the heart and puts the fear of God into the inward parts.

63. The more we feel of God's love, the more ashamed we are that ever we offended him. And the more our shame for sin is increased, the more will our comfort in God be increased also.

CHAPTER 17

3. *A great eagle.* Nebuchadnezzar, king of Babylon, is compared to a great eagle, the king of birds—swift, strong, rapacious.

9. *Without great power.* The king of Babylon shall do this easily when it is God who sends him. For God needs not great power and many people to effect his purposes. He can without any difficulty overturn a sinful king and kingdom and make no more of it than we do of rooting up a tree that cumbers the ground.

22. *The highest branch.* Of the royal seed; of the highest branch that is heir to the throne; namely, the Messiah.

CHAPTER 18

20. *Shall not bear.* This is a most unquestionable truth; and though perhaps it may seem otherwise in some cases, yet could we see perfectly the connection between persons and persons; could we see the connection of sins and sins, and how easily, secretly, and undiscerned men become guilty of the same sins, we should see father and son, though perhaps one of them might not do the evil, both guilty, and neither punished for the sin farther than it was his own. Nor do the Scriptures (Exod. 20:5; Deut. 28:18) doom persons to punishment for sins from which they are wholly free; but if children shall follow their fathers in sin, then if they die for those sins, it is because they are their own, not as they are their fathers'.

CHAPTER 19

1. *For the princes.* Jehoahaz, Jehoiachim, Jehoiachin, and Zedekiah.

2. *What.* What resemblance shall I use to set out the nature, deportment, and state of the other of these princes? *Thy.* Only one of whom was upon the throne at once, and therefore the prophet speaks to one at a time. *Mother.* The land of Judea and Jerusalem the chief city of it, the royal family of David. *Lioness.* Though chosen of God to execute justice, yet they soon degenerated into the fierce and ravening nature of the lioness.

13. *In the wilderness.* Though Babylon was in a very fruitful place, yet the cruelty of the Babylonians made it to the Jews as terrible as a wilderness.

CHAPTER 20

5. *When I chose.* When I showed that I had chosen them. The history of the rebellions of the children of Israel begins as early as their beginning. So does the history of man's apostasy from his Maker. No sooner have we read the story of his creation but we meet with that of his rebellion. So, we see here, it was with Israel, a people designed to represent the body of mankind, both in their dealings with God and in God's dealings with them.

22. *I withdrew.* God seems to take the posture of one who was just going to smite, yet draws back that he might spare.

29. *What.* What do you mean, you that go to the high place? What do you find so inviting there that you will leave God's altar, where he requires your attendance, to frequent such places where he has forbidden you to worship?

40. *Of the height.* Zion, though lower than many other hills, yet was above them all for God's peculiar preference.

46. *Drop thy word.* Let your word distill; begin with softer words before you shower down with the vehemence of a storm.

CHAPTER 21

10. *Of my son.* To whom God says, "Thou shalt break them with a rod of iron" (Ps. 2:9). This sword is that "rod of iron" which *despiseth every tree*[1] and will cut it down.

21. *He consulted.* Perhaps by a divine permission, the devil gave them answers from those images.

27. *Shall be no more.* Never recover its former glory until the scepter be quite taken away from Judah and way be made for the Messiah. He has an incontestable right to the dominion both in the church and in the world. And in due time he shall have the possession of it, all adverse power being overturned.

31. *I will blow.* As those who melt down metals blow upon the metal in the fire, that the fire may burn the fiercer.

CHAPTER 22

8. *Mine holy things.* All my institutions, temple, sacrifices, feasts.

18. *The furnace.* The afflictions I have laid upon them have not bettered them. *The dross.* While they loved mercy, did justly, and walked humbly with their God they were as silver; now they are but dross.

---

[1] (21:10) Cf. KJV: "contemneth." Wesley's rendering of this part of the verse reads, "It is the rod of my son, it despiseth every tree."

CHAPTER 23

24. *According.* To their will, power, wrath, and custom against rebels; for these are their rules of judgment.

29. *Take away.* Deprive you of the comfortable use of all your labor which they will exact of you in captivity.

34. *Thou.* Shall stagger with sorrows that shall intoxicate and astonish.

35. *Bear thou.* The guilt, I will impute it; the punishment, I will not pardon it.

CHAPTER 24

4. *Fill it.* With those pieces that are biggest, fullest of marrow, and which are divided according to the bones. These are the principal members of the state: the king, princes, priests, magistrates, and the most wealthy citizens.

16. *With a stroke.* A sudden stroke by my own immediate hand. We know not how soon the desire of our eyes may be removed from us. Death is a stroke which the most pious, the most useful, the most amiable are not exempted from.

23. *Pine away.* You shall languish with secret sorrow when you shall not dare to show it openly.

25. *The joy.* All their public and private joys and hopes shall be destroyed in the destruction of the kingdom and their children.

CHAPTER 25

7. *Know.* Thus God will bring those who were strangers to him into an acquaintance with him, and it will be a blessed effect of their calamities. How much better is it to be poor and know God than to be rich and ignorant of him?

16. *The remnant.* Who had escaped the sword of Samuel, David, Hezekiah, and Psammetichus, king of Egypt.

CHAPTER 26

4. *Scrape.* I will leave you nothing. You shall be scraped and swept that not so much as dust shall remain in you.

12. *Shall lay.* It had been a quicker way to have burned all. But the greedy soldier might dream of treasures hid in walls or under the timber and therefore take the pains to pull all down and throw it into the sea.

CHAPTER 27

2. *A lamentation.* We ought to mourn for the miseries of other nations as well as of our own, out of an affection for mankind in general; yes, though they have brought their miseries upon themselves.

29. *Shall come down.* In the allegory of a miserable shipwreck, the prophet sets forth the fall of Tyre. And in this verse he represents them all shifting out of the sinking ship in great confusion.

34. *By the seas.* The Babylonians, that like seas shall swell, roar, and break in upon you.

CHAPTER 28

14. *Cherub.* For your wisdom, power, and excellence, like a cherub, or angel. For the sacredness of your person and office as the anointed of God. For the exercise of your power as a shield, as a protector of the weak.

15. *Thou wast perfect.* Is not this an irony?

22. *I will be glorified.* When my judgments make my justice, power, and truth appear, both you and others shall confess my glory. *Sanctified.* Owned as holy, reverenced as just, obeyed as sovereign.

24. This never had a full accomplishment yet. But it will, for the Scripture cannot be broken.

CHAPTER 29

18. *Caused.* The army and commanders were weary of the siege, but the immovable resolution of the king kept them on. *A great service.* It was great service both for hardness of work, heaviness of burdens, and length of siege. *Made bald.* Through age or sicknesses, or continued wearing of helmets.

19. *The wages.* God will be behindhand with none who do any service for him. One way or other he will recompense them. None shall kindle a fire at his altar for nought.

CHAPTER 30

8. *Destroyed.* The fire that consumes nations is of God's kindling. And when he sets fire to a kingdom, all they that go about to quench the fire shall be consumed by it.

21. *The sword.* None can heal the wounds that God gives but himself. They whom he disables cannot again *hold the sword.*

CHAPTER 31

15. *Fainted.* Probably there were portentous signs in the sea and great waters, and the rivers, and among the trees.

17. *Hell.* Perished with him and went to those whom God had slain for their pride and wickedness.

CHAPTER 32

10. *Shall tremble.* Be greatly afraid lest Nebuchadnezzar, who is God's sword, should smite them.

14. *Like oil.* A figurative expression, signifying there shall be such a universal sadness and heaviness upon the whole nation that the very rivers which used to flow briskly shall grow deep and slow and heavy.

21. *Hell.* That is, the grave, where they lie without strength as dead mortals, though while they lived they bore themselves as gods.

27. *Laid their swords.* In their graves, as if they could sleep the sweeter there when they laid their heads on such a pillow.

32. *My terror.* These tyrants were a terror to the world by their cruelty; and God has made them a terror by his just punishments. And so, says God, will I do with Pharaoh. Come and see the calamitous state of human life! See what a dying world this is! The strong die, the mighty die; *Pharaoh and all his multitude.* But here is likewise an allusion to the final and everlasting death of impenitent sinners. Those who are uncircumcised in heart are *slain with the sword* of divine justice. Their iniquity is upon them, and they will "bear their shame" for ever.

CHAPTER 33

10. *Our sins.* The unpardoned guilt and the unsupportable punishment of our sins in the wasting of our country, burning our city, abolishing the public worship of God. We shall pine away, for it is too late to hope.

22. *Opened my mouth.* Not that the prophet was utterly dumb before, for he had prophesied against many nations, only he was forbidden to say anything of the Jews. But now the Spirit moved him to speak and continued his motion until the messenger came, and ever after.

CHAPTER 34

3. *Ye kill.* You contrive methods to take first the life and next the estate of the well-fed, the rich and wealthy.

23. *One shepherd.* Christ, the great, good, chief, only shepherd, who laid down his life for his sheep. *My servant David.* The seed of David, the beloved one, who was typified by David and is in other places called by his name (Jer. 30:9; 37:24; Isa. 37:35; Hos. 3:5).

24. *My servant.* Jesus Christ was in this great work his father's servant (Isa. 42:1).

29. *A plant.* The Messiah.

CHAPTER 35

6. *Hast not hated.* You have loved rather than hated bloodshed. Therefore, vengeance follows you.

CHAPTER 36

23. *I will sanctify my great name.* They gave the heathen occasion to think meanly of me, but I will show I am as great as good. When God performs what he has sworn by his holiness, then he sanctifies his name.

26. *A new heart.* A new frame of soul, a mind changed from sinful to holy, from carnal to spiritual. A heart in which the law of God is written (Jer. 31:33). A sanctified heart in which the almighty grace of God is victorious and turns it from all sin to God. *A new spirit.* A new, holy frame in the spirit of man, which is given to him, not wrought by his own power.

27. *My spirit.* The Holy Spirit of God, who is given to and dwells in all true believers. *And cause you.* Sweetly, powerfully, yet without compulsion. For our spirits, framed by God's Spirit to a disposition suitable to his holiness, readily concurs. *Ye shall keep.* Be willing and able to keep the judgments and to walk in the statutes of God, which is to live in all holiness.

29. *From all your uncleannesses.* Salvation from all uncleannesses includes justification, entire sanctification, and meetness for glory.

38. *As the holy flock.* Flocks designed to holy uses. *In her solemn feasts.* These flocks were for quality, the best of all; and for numbers, very great on the solemn feasts. Thus shall men multiply and fill the cities of replanted Judea. And the increase of the numbers of men is then honorable when they are all dedicated to God as a *holy flock,* to be presented to him for "living sacrifices." Crowds are a lovely sight in God's temple.

CHAPTER 37

1. *And set me down.* So it seemed to me in the vision. Which is a lively representation of a threefold resurrection: (1) Of the resurrection of souls from the death of sin to the life of righteousness; (2) The resurrection of the church from an afflicted state to liberty and peace; (3) The resurrection of the body at the great day, especially the bodies of believers to life eternal.

7. *A noise.* A rattling of the bones in their motion. *A shaking.* A trembling or commotion among the bones, enough to manifest a divine presence working among them. *Came together.* Glided nearer and nearer until each bone met the bone to which it was to be joined. Of all the bones of all those numerous slain, not one was missing, not one missed its way, not one missed its place, but each knew and found its fellow. Thus in the resurrection of the dead, the scattered atoms shall be ranged in their proper place and order and every bone come to his bone, by the same wisdom and power by which they were first formed in the womb of her who is with child.

22. *One nation.* They were one in David's time, who was a type of the Messiah, and continued so to the end of Solomon's time, whose name includes peace. So when the Beloved, the Peacemaker, the Messiah, shall be king, they shall be one again. *And one king.* The Messiah.

25. *For ever.* Until Christ's coming to judgment, the Jews converted to Christ shall inherit Canaan.

27. *My tabernacle.* The tabernacle wherein I will show my presence among them. Their fathers had a tabernacle, but the Messiah shall bring with him a better, a spiritual, an heavenly. *Shall be my people.* By my grace I will make them holy, as the people of a holy God. And I will make them happy, as the people of the ever blessed God.

CHAPTER 38

2. *Gog.* This cannot be one single person or prince, though perhaps it points out someone by whom the troubles foretold were begun. Some believe the time is still to come wherein this prophecy is to be fulfilled, and that it must intend those enemies of God's church, descended from the Scythians and now masters of Iberia, Armenia, Cappadocia, or in confederacy with the Tartars and those northern heathens. But others think, all the enemies of Israel in all quarters, both open and secret, are here intended and that the Antichristian forces and combination are what the prophet foretells.

7. *Be thou prepared.* God and the church deride this mighty preparation.

8. *After many days.* In the latter days of the Messiah's kingdom among men.

13. *The young lions.* Young men thirsty of blood, but more of spoil, resolved to join if they may rob and spoil for themselves.

16. *Shall be sanctified.* Confessed to be a great God over all, a gracious and faithful God to his people, and a dreadful enemy and avenger against the

wicked. *Before.* In the sight of all the heathen that are with *Gog,* and much more in the sight of God's own people.

23. *Magnify.* Undeniably prove that I am the mighty, just, faithful, wise, holy, and merciful God. *Sanctify.* Declare I am holy and true to my word.

CHAPTER 39

9. *Shall burn.* It may be wondered that they burned these weapons which might be of use to them for defense. But it was done in testimony that God was their defense, on whom only they relied. *With fire.* In such a country where the need of fire is much less than with us it will not seem incredible that the warlike utensils of so numerous an army might be enough to furnish them with fuel for many years.

11. *Graves.* Gog came to take possession; and so he shall, but not as he purposed and hoped. He shall possess his house of darkness in that land which he invaded.

17. *I do sacrifice.* The punishment of these God calls a sacrifice, which he offers to his own justice. *Upon the mountains.* Where more thousands are offered at once than ever were at any time offered; it is a sacrifice so *great* that none ever was or will be like it.

CHAPTER 40

1. *Of our captivity.* Of those who were carried away into captivity with Jeconiah eleven years before Jerusalem was burned. And this falls in with the three thousand three hundred and seventy-fourth year of the world, about five hundred and seventy-four years before Christ's incarnation.

3. *A man.* The same no doubt who appeared to the prophet (1:26), whose name is the branch and who builds the temple (Zech. 6:12–13), and whose color was like burnished brass (Rev. 1:15), which speaks of glory and strength.

5. *The man's hand.* Christ has and keeps the reed in his own hand as the only fit person to take the measurements of all.

15. *And.* This verse seems to sum up all the dimensions; this gate, its porch, and thickness of its walls, and so sum the cubits, six in the thickness of the outer wall, eighteen in the three chambers, twenty in the spaces between the chambers, and six in the thickness in the inner wall of the porch.

19. Many courts are here spoken of, which may cause us to consider the diversity of gifts, graces, and offices in the church; as also of the several degrees of glory in the courts and mansions of heaven.

CHAPTER 41

1. *The breadth.* These walls in their thickness took up as much space as the whole breadth of Moses' tabernacle (Exod. 26:22).

18. *Cherubim.* Generally taken for the portrait of angels, or young men with wings. Yet the description of them is very different in different places; in Ezekiel's vision (Ezek. 1), Isaiah's vision (Isa. 6), John's vision (Rev. 4), and in Solomon's temple.

CHAPTER 42

20. *Five hundred broad.* Each reed was above three yards and a half, so that it was about eight miles round. Thus large were the suburbs of this mystical temple, signifying the great extent of the church in gospel times. It is in part fulfilled already by the accession of the Gentiles to the church; and will be thoroughly accomplished when "the fulness of the Gentiles be come in" and "all Israel shall be saved."

CHAPTER 43

2. *And his voice.* Though by the voice of God thunder is sometimes meant, yet here it was an articulate voice.

4. *Came.* The sins of Israel caused the glory of the Lord to go out of his house; now the repentance of Israel is blessed with the return of this glory.

6. *The man.* Christ. *Stood.* To encourage and strengthen him.

7. *He.* The glorious God of Israel. *My throne.* The throne of his grace is in his temple; in the dispensations of grace God manifests himself as a king. *My feet.* Speaking after the manner of men and expressing his abode and rest in his temple as the type, in his church as the antitype.

12. *The law.* This is the first comprehensive rule: holiness becomes God's house. And this relative holiness referred to personal and real holiness.

27. *I will accept you.* Those who give themselves to God shall be accepted of God, their persons first and then their performances, through the mediator.

CHAPTER 44

4. *He.* Christ in the appearance of a man.

16. *To minister.* To offer sacrifice at the altar and incense in the house. God will put marks of honor upon those who are faithful to him in trying times and will employ those in his service who have kept close to it when others drew back.

21. *Drink wine.* Or any other strong liquor when they go either to trim the lamps, or set the shewbread in order, or to offer incense in the temple, or when they go to the altar to offer a sacrifice.

CHAPTER 45

25. *In the feast of the seven days.* Hence we also may learn the necessity

of frequently repeating the same religious exercises. Indeed, the sacrifice of
atonement was offered once for all; but
the sacrifice of acknowledgment, that of
a broken heart and that of a thankful
heart, must be offered every day. And
these spiritual sacrifices are always acceptable to God through Christ Jesus.

CHAPTER 46

3. *In the sabbaths.* Both weekly and
other holy days, which are called "sabbaths."

9. *Go forth over against it.* Perhaps
only to prevent all justling and confusion.

17. *His inheritance.* Whatever lands
of the prince are given to servants shall
at the year of Jubilee revert to the sons
of the prince.

CHAPTER 47

8. *The sea.* The Dead Sea, or "Lake of
Sodom." *Shall be healed.* The waters of
the sea shall be healed, made wholesome. So where the grace of God from
his temple and altar flows, it heals the
corrupt nature of man and renders
barren terrible deserts as a land of
waters and gardens.

9. *For they.* The poisonous waters of
the Dead Sea shall be made wholesome
for fish. *Shall live.* Thrive and multiply
in the virtue of the healing streams.
Thus is the fruitfulness of the grace of
God in the church set forth.

23. *His inheritance.* This certainly

looks at gospel times, when the wall of
partition between the Jew and Gentile
was taken down and both put on a level
before God, both made one in Christ
Jesus.

CHAPTER 48

35. *From that day.* From the day of
the Lord's restoring this people and
rebuilding their city, and their thankful,
holy, and pure worshipping of God
there, from that day it shall be said of
Jerusalem. *The LORD is there.* The Lord
who, as his name alone is Jehovah, so is
the only true God, faithful to his
promise, rich in mercy, glorious in
majesty, righteous in his judgments,
wise and holy in his government,
whose presence makes us happy, whose
withdrawing from us leaves us to misery. This God will by his favor and
presence bring the confluence of all
good to persons, families, and cities.
This God will be there to dwell, govern, defend, prosper, and crown.

Such is to be the case of earthly
Jerusalem, such shall be for ever the
case of the heavenly Jerusalem. Such is
the case of every true believer, who
may, where ever he is in his way of
duty, still write "Jehovah–Shammah,"
My God is here. And it is best to be
where he is until he brings us within
the gates of the glorious city, where
inconceivable light and love from the
immediate presence of God give every
one an eternal demonstration that God
is here. To him be glory for ever.

ᴅᴀɴɪᴇʟ

CHAPTER 1

2. *With part of the vessels.* In this expedition Nebuchadnezzar carried off some captives, among whom were Daniel and his friends.

8. *But Daniel purposed.* There may be several weighty reasons assigned why Daniel did this. (1) Because many of those meats provided for the king's table were forbidden by the Jewish law. (2) Daniel knew these delicacies would too much gratify the flesh. (3) He did not dare to eat and drink things consecrated to idols. (4) He was sensible as to how unsuitable delicate fare would be to the afflicted state of God's people. Therefore he was herein a rare pattern of avoiding all the occasions of evil.

15. *Fairer and fatter.* The blessing of God upon homely fare affords often more health and strength than more costly fare to them who eat the fat and drink the sweet.

CHAPTER 2

3. *To know.* He remembered the fact in general, but could not repeat it perfectly. Yet it had left such an impression on him as to put him in great perplexity. The Lord has ways to affright the greatest men in the world in the midst of their security.

13. *Daniel and his fellows.* Daniel and his fellows were not called because of their youth, which the Chaldeans despised. Several things are to be observed. (1) The magicians confessed that knowledge and revelation must come from God and therefore what Daniel did was not by any human strength. (2) That the Lord held the governor's hands so that he did not slay Daniel presently with the first. (3) That Daniel by his prudence and piety saved all the magicians' lives.

21. *He changeth.* God can make the sun go back or stand still, as in Ahaz's and Joshua's time. It is the great part of God's power and prerogative to change times. Daniel here attributes that to God which heathens attributed to nature or chance. God only, who made all by his power, does rule and overrule all by his providence.

28. *What shall be.* Observe the prophet's wisdom, that he does not fall abruptly upon the dream, but first prepares this lofty king for it and by degrees labors to win him to the knowledge of the true God.

36. *And we.* By this word, *we*, appears Daniel's piety and modesty, for he declares by it that he and his companions had begged this skill from God, and therefore he did not arrogate it to himself.

40. *Fourth kingdom.* This is the kingdom of the Romans and was to last not only to Christ's first coming but, under Antichrist, to his second coming.

44. *In the days of these kings.* While the iron kingdom stood, for Christ was born in the reign of Augustus Caesar. And this kingdom is not bounded by any limits, as worldly empires are, but is truly universal. And it shall be for ever, never destroyed or given to others as the rest were.

45. *And the gold.* This denotes the small beginning of Christ's visible kingdom and the different rise of Christ from all other; and his conception by the Holy Ghost, without father and mother, respectively as to his two natures. This stone, falling from the mountain, broke the image in pieces; for Christ is a stone that grinds to powder those it falls on. And he is a growing stone even to a mountain and therefore will fill the earth.

CHAPTER 3

1. *Made an image.* Perhaps he did this that he might seem no ways inclined to the Jews or their religion, whereof the Chaldeans might be jealous, seeing he had owned their God to be greatest and had preferred Daniel and his friends to great honors.

16. *We are not careful.* Hebrew: "We care not." There is no need of any answer in this case, for it is in vain for us to debate the matter. The king is resolved to have his will of us, and we are resolved on the contrary.

18. *But if not.* It was therefore all one to them which way God would honor himself. They were resolved to suffer rather than sin and leave the cause to God. Indeed, if God be for us, we need not fear what man can do unto us. Let him do his worst. God will deliver us either from death or in death.

20. *To bind.* What, did he think these three men would have resisted? Or that their God would defend them from his power, or that if he had, his mighty men could have prevailed? None of this was the case, for God purposed to show his power when the king did his worst, and in the thing wherein he dealt proudly, to be above him.

23. *Fell down.* All this is expressed with emphasis to make the power of God more glorious in their preservation. For that flame that slew the executioners might much more easily have killed them, even before they fell down.

25. *No hurt.* See how the God of nature can, when he pleases, control the powers of nature! *The Son of God.* Probably he had heard Daniel speak of him. Jesus Christ, the Angel of the covenant, did sometimes appear before his incarnation. Those who suffer for Christ have his gracious presence with them in their sufferings, even in the fiery furnace, even in the valley of the shadow of death, and therefore need fear no evil.

26. *And spake.* With a milder tone than before, God having abated the fire of his fury. Now he could at once acknowledge the true God to be the most high above all gods, and the three worthies to be his faithful servants.

CHAPTER 4

2–3. *How great are his signs.* Nothing less than a real change of heart could cause such a confession as this! Nebuchadnezzar was now old, had reigned more than forty years and seen as much of the world as most men ever did. And yet never until now did he admire surprising events as *the signs and wonders* [of] *the high God!*

17. *The most High ruleth.* Nebuchadnezzar and his flatterers conceited he was a god in earth unaccountable to any. But the great God will make all men know he rules all in earth too, and sets up at his pleasure whom he will and plucks them down again.

25. *They shall drive thee.* This was such a thundering peal that it was wonderful the king could endure to hear it without fury boiling in his heart, yet the Lord withheld him.

28. *The king Nebuchadnezzar.* With how admirable propriety is the person changed here! These six verses speak in the third person. But in the thirty-fourth verse Nebuchadnezzar, having recovered his reason, speaks in the first person again.

35. *As nothing.* A due consideration of God's infinite greatness makes the creature appear as nothing; creatures are nothing to help, nothing to hurt, nothing in duration, nothing solid and substantial, nothing without dependence, influence, and support from God. *His will.* Being the Lord of hosts and the only absolute and universal monarch of the world.

37. *Now I Nebuchadnezzar praise.* Thus can the Lord make the stoutest hearts to stoop and do him homage. This doxology proceeds from his heart. *Are truth.* God is truth essentially. He is the rule and standard of truth, his words are truth, his ways are truth, and they are judgment. He is wise and has dealt justly with me for my pride, and in very faithfulness has afflicted me, and in very tenderness has restored me. I do, and ever shall adore him for it. *Able to abase.* As he has declared upon me, in stupendous changes, which I proclaim to all the world. He had a just controversy with me, and I have no ground to quarrel with him but to give him glory by this confession. What authority had any one to say that this man "was no convert"? We can no more doubt his salvation than Solomon's.

CHAPTER 5

6. *His knees smote.* So soon can the terrors of God shake the loftiest cedars, the tyrants of the earth.

10. *The queen . . . came.* The women in those courts had an apartment by themselves; and this, being the queen-mother and aged, did not mingle with the king's wives and concubines. Yet she broke the rule in coming in now upon this solemn occasion.

25. MENE, MENE. "It is numbered, it is numbered." The words are doubled for the greater confirmation. It relates to the number of the seventy years for the overthrow of the Babylonian empire.

27. *Art found wanting.* There is no weight nor worth in you. You have made light of God and the Lord makes light of you.

CHAPTER 6

10. *Toward Jerusalem.* The temple was the place where the Lord placed his name and promised to appear and accept his people, all being a type of Christ, through whom alone sinners are accepted.

20. *Able to deliver.* What he doubted of we are sure of, that the servants of the living God have a master who is able to deliver them and bear them out in his service.

22. *His angel.* The same that was with the three children in the fiery furnace, whose presence made even the lion's den a stronghold, his palace, his paradise. See the power of God over the fiercest creatures! See the care God takes of his faithful servants, especially when they are called to suffer for him! See how ready the angels are to minister to the heirs of salvation!

CHAPTER 7

1. *Then he wrote.* These visions were recorded for the benefit of the church, to rectify their mistake. For they thought all things would succeed prosperously after they returned out of their captivity.

3. *Four great beasts.* That is, four great monarchies, great in comparison of particular kingdoms; beasts for their tyrannical oppressions.

4. *The first.* This was the Chaldean, or Assyrian; whose seat was first at Babylon, afterwards at Nineveh, and then at Babylon again.

5. *Another beast.* The Medes and Persians, a fierce, ravenous creature.

6. *Like a leopard.* This leopard was the Grecian monarchy. A leopard is less than a lion, so was this monarchy at first, but yet dared fight with a lion; so did Alexander encounter Darius with an inferior force. *Four heads.* He was succeeded by four of his chief commanders, who divided that empire into four parts.

7. *A fourth beast.* The Roman empire.

13. *The Son of man.* That is, the Messiah. He came *with the clouds of heaven,* gloriously, swiftly, and terribly. *And came.* This relates to his ascension, at which time he received his royal investiture for the protection of his church and curbing of their enemies.

18. *But the saints.* Jesus Christ being their king, they shall reign with him and possess the kingdom for ever.

24. *And another.* This seems to mean the Roman Antichrist.

25. *Until a time and times.* The numbers of Daniel and John seem to agree. Daniel was certainly prophetic in these things, and his prophecy reaches to the end of times, even of Antichrist's reign.

CHAPTER 8

10. *The host of heaven.* The church of God militant, who worship the God of heaven, who are citizens of heaven, whose names are written in heaven. And among these, the priests and champions, who were as stars shining above the rest, these he profaned and slew cruelly.

15. *The appearance of a man.* Probably Gabriel.

16. *A man's voice.* Of him before mentioned, namely, Christ.

17. *He came near.* That he might speak more familiarly to him, yet Daniel could not bear the glory of it. How much less can we bear the glory of God, and how graciously has the Lord dealt with us, to teach us by men and not by angels? *O son of man.* He calls him "son of man" to make him remember his frailty and so not to be lifted up with this great condescension of heaven. *At the time.* God's appointed time, in the latter day, but not now in your lifetime.

CHAPTER 9

1. *In the first year of Darius.* That is, immediately after the overthrow of the kingdom of Babylon, which was the year of the Jews' deliverance from captivity. *Of the Medes.* This Darius was not Darius the Persian under whom the temple was built, as some have asserted to invalidate the credibility of this book; but Darius the Mede, who lived in the time of Daniel.

17. *For the Lord's sake.* For the sake of the Messiah, to whom the title "Lord" is frequently given in the Old Testament.

21. *About the time.* The time of the evening sacrifice was a solemn and set time of devotion. This was peculiarly a type of that great sacrifice which Christ was to offer. And it was in virtue of that sacrifice that Daniel's prayer was accepted when he prayed "for the Lord's sake."

24. *Seventy weeks.* These weeks are weeks of days and these days are so many years. *To bring in everlasting righteousness.* To bring in justification by the free grace of God in Christ and sanctification by his Spirit. This is called "everlasting," because Christ is eternal and so are the acceptance and holiness purchased for us. Christ brings this in: (1) By his merit. (2) By his gospel declaring it. (3) by faith applying and sealing it by the Holy Ghost. *Seal up.* To abrogate the former dispensation of the law and to ratify the gospel covenant. *To anoint.* This alludes to his names "Messiah" and "Christ," both which signify "anointed." Christ was anointed at his first conception and personal union (Luke 1:35). He was anointed in his baptism (Matt. 3:17) to his three offices by the Holy Ghost: (1) King (Matt. 2:2). (2) Prophet (Isa. 61:1). (3) Priest (Ps. 110:4).

27. *He shall confirm.* Christ confirmed the new covenant: (1) By the testimony of angels, of John the Baptist, of the wise men, of the saints then living, of Moses and Elijah. (2) By his preaching. (3) By signs and wonders. (4) By his holy life. (5) By his resurrection and ascension. (6) By his death and blood-shedding. *Shall cause the sacrifice . . . to cease.* All the Jewish rites and levitical worship. By his death he abrogated and put an end to this laborious service for ever.

CHAPTER 10

2. *Was mourning.* Because he foresaw the many calamities that would befall the Jews for their sins, especially for destroying the Messiah and rejecting his gospel.

5. *A certain man.* Very probably Christ, who appeared to Daniel in royal and priestly robes and in so great brightness and majesty.

12. *He.* Not Christ, but Gabriel. *Michael.* Michael here is commonly thought to mean Christ.

16. *One like the . . . sons of men.* This likewise seems to have been Gabriel.

21. *Michael.* Christ alone is the protector of his church when all the princes of the earth desert or oppose it.

CHAPTER 11

12. *His heart shall be lifted up.* He might have recovered all, but he grew proud of his victory and returned again to his luxury.

21. *A vile person.* Antiochus, called "Epiphanes" by his flatterers, but the people of God accounted him infamous, base, and treacherous.

26. *Yea.* His most familiar friends and confidants; for he shall be overthrown with a great slaughter, as when the Nile overflows the country.

36. *The king.* Antiochus was an eminent type of antichrist, to whom many things that follow may be applied by way of accommodation, although they principally refer to Antiochus and had their primary accomplishment in him.

45. *None shall help him.* God shall cut him off in the midst of his days. And when God destroys, who can help?

CHAPTER 12

1. *For the children.* The meaning seems to be, as after the death of Antiochus the Jews had some deliverance, so there will be yet a greater deliverance to the people of God when Michael your prince, the Messiah, shall appear for your salvation. *A time of trouble.* At the siege of Jerusalem, before the final judgment. The phrase *at that time* probably includes all the time of Christ from his first to his last coming.

4. *Seal the book.* The book was commanded to be sealed because it would be long before the words would be fulfilled, whereas those that were shortly to be fulfilled were forbidden to be sealed.

6. *To the man.* To Christ, who seemed to stand in the air above the waters or upon them.

7. *He held up his right hand.* He held up both hands to heaven, for the more sure and solemn confirmation of it; and to denote the unchangeableness of God's decrees, both for good to the church and for evil to her enemies.

9. *And sealed.* They shall not be clearly understood until the event makes them good.

10. *And tried.* The afflictions of the church are to prepare them for the bridegroom by taking away their filth, as gold and silver are tried and refined.

13. *But go thou.* I have revealed to you these things that you and your people might be prepared for sufferings and yet not without hope of a glorious deliverance. *Shalt rest.* In which hope you shall die and rest from trouble until the resurrection of the just. It ought to be the great concern of every one of us to secure a happy lot in the *end of the days,* and then we may well be content with our present lot, welcoming the will of God.

hosea

CHAPTER 1

2. *Go take.* This was probably done in vision and was to be told to the people as other visions were. It was parabolically proposed to them and might have been sufficient to convince the Jew if they had considered it as David considered Nathan's parable.

11. *Then.* This verse has both an historical and a spiritual sense; the one referring to the return out of Babylon, the other to a more glorious deliverance from a more miserable captivity. *Of Jezreel.* Israel is here called Jezreel, "the seed of God." This seed is now sown in the earth and buried under the clods; but great shall be its day when the harvest comes. Great was the day of the church when there were daily added to it "such as should be saved."

CHAPTER 2

5. *That give me.* Whereas every mercy she enjoyed was God's gift, a fruit of his covenant, love and faithfulness towards her; yet she denies all his kindness and ascribes to her idols the bread she ate, the water she drank, and the clothes she wore.

18. *Safely.* This was in some measure made good to the Jews returning out of captivity. But the full accomplishment will be to the church of Christ.

21. *In that day.* In the day of gospel-grace. *I will hear.* God the first and universal cause will influence the heavens, he will command their dew and showers. When the earth is dry it does, as it were, cry to heaven for refreshing showers. When the seed is sown, they cry to the earth for its kindly influences that they may spring up and yield fruit for Jezreel. They can call and cry, but never will be satisfied if God does not hear them and command his blessing, which he promises to his people on renewing covenant with them. Now their repentance shall be blessed with plenty, and God will set the frame of heaven and earth in due order to effect this. There shall be a harmony between all the subordinate causes moved by God, the first great cause, which expected events and fruits shall be produced for their good and comfort.

CHAPTER 3

4. *For.* Now the parable is unfolded; it shall be with Israel as with such a woman, they and she were guilty of adultery, both punished long, both made slaves, kept hardly and valued meanly, yet in mercy at last pardoned and reaccepted, though after a long time of probation.

5. *And David.* The Messiah, who is the son of David. *And his goodness.* That is, the good and gracious God. God in Christ and with Christ shall be worshipped. *The latter days.* In the days of the Messiah, in gospel-times.

CHAPTER 4

16. *As a backsliding heifer.* Which, when it is grown lusty and wanton, will neither endure the yoke nor be confined in her allowed pastures.

19. *The wind hath bound.* The whirlwind of wrath from God has seized this old adulteress and carried some of her children away already.

CHAPTER 5

6. *To seek the* LORD. The Jewish doctors tell us that, under Hosea, Israel had liberty of bringing their sacrifices to Jerusalem.

12. *A moth.* Moths leisurely eat up our clothes. So God was then and had been, from Jeroboam's death, weakening the ten tribes.

CHAPTER 6

3. *Know.* What worship he requires. And the knowledge of God shall be to us a spring of all holy, righteous, sober conversation. *Follow on.* By a diligent attendance to the word and works of God we shall know experimentally[1] how holy, how good, how faithful God is. *His going forth.* Before his people; his gracious, faithful, holy, just, and wise providence for his people's good and comfort. *As the morning.* As sure, beautiful, grateful, and clear as the morning, which dispels the darkness and proclaims its own approach. *As the rain.* Which revives the earth, makes it fruitful, beautifies it, and gives a new face to all.

6. *The knowledge of God.* The affectionate knowledge of God, which fills the mind with reverence of his majesty, fear of his goodness, love of his holiness, trust in his promise, and submission to his will.

CHAPTER 7

3. *They.* The courtiers in particular make it their work to invent pleasing wickedness and to acquaint the king with it.

6. *Like an oven.* Hot with ambition, revenge, or covetousness. *Lie in wait.* Against the life or estate of some of their subjects. As the baker, having kindled a fire in his oven, goes to bed and sleeps all night and in the morning finds his oven well heated and ready for his purpose, so these when they have laid some wicked plot, though they may seem to sleep for a while, yet the fire is glowing within and flames out as soon as ever there is opportunity for it.

16. *A deceitful bow.* Though they seem bent for and aiming at the mark, yet like weak bows they carried not the arrow home, and like a false bow they never carried it straight toward the mark.

CHAPTER 8

2. *Shall cry.* But not sincerely.

7. *Sown the wind.* A proverbial speech to denote lost labor. *Whirlwind.* A tempest which destroys all that is in its way; an emblem of the wrath of God. *No stalk.* All your dependance on idols and foreign assistance will be as seed that bear neither stalk nor bud.

---

[1] (6:3) That is, "experientially."

CHAPTER 9

4. *Offer wine offerings.* These were appointed to be offered with the morning and evening sacrifice, the sacrifice representing Christ and pardon by him; the wine offering, the spirit of grace. The sacrifice repeated daily continued their peace and pardon.

7. *The prophet.* The false prophet. *The spiritual man.* That pretends to be full of the spirit of prophecy. *The great hatred.* Which God had against your sins.

10. *I found Israel.* The Lord speaks of himself in the person of a traveler who unexpectedly in the wilderness finds a vine loaded with grapes; such love did God bear to Israel. *As the firstripe.* As the earliest ripe fruit of the fig tree, which is most valued and desired.

12. *When I depart.* To complete their misery, I will depart from them. It is sad to lose our children, but sadder to lose our God.

CHAPTER 10

1. *The goodness.* Imagining that the goodness of their land was a blessing from their idols.

8. *They shall say.* When this shall be brought to pass, the idolatrous Israelites shall be in such perplexity that they shall wish the mountains and hills might fall on them.

12. *Fallow ground.* Your hearts are as ground overrun with weeds, which need to be plowed and broken up that good seed may be sowed in them.

CHAPTER 11

1. *Out of Egypt.* But Israel, the first adopted son, was a type of Christ, the firstborn. And the history of Israel's coming out was a type of Christ's future coming out of Egypt.

8. *My repentings.* Not that God is ever fluctuating or unresolved; but these are expressions after the manner of men to show what severity Israel had deserved and yet how divine grace would be glorified in sparing them.

10. *Like a lion.* Christ is called "the Lion of the tribe of Judah"; and when he cried with a loud voice, it was *as when a lion roared.* The voice of the gospel was heard far, as the roaring of a lion, and it was "a mighty voice."

CHAPTER 12

1. *Feedeth on wind.* It is a proverbial speech denoting his supporting himself with hopes, as unfit to sustain him as the wind is to feed us.

4. *The angel.* Called "God" (v. 3) and "Jehovah, Lord of Hosts" (v. 5). He was no created angel, but the Messiah; eternal God by nature and essence, an angel by office and voluntary undertaking.

6. *Wait on thy God.* In public worship and private duties serve and trust God alone. Let not idols have either sacrifice, prayer, praise, or trust from you. And let your hope and worship be for ever continued.

CHAPTER 13

12. *Is bound up.* As sins unpardoned; for to loose sins is to forgive, and to bind sins is to charge them upon the sinner (Matt. 16:19).

14. *Ransom.* By power and purchase, by the blood of the lamb of God, and by the power of his Godhead. *Them.* That repent and believe. *From the . . . grave.* He conquered the grave and will at the great day of the resurrection open those prison-doors and bring us out in glory. *From death.* From the curse of the first death and from the second death, which shall have no power over us. *Repentance shall be hid.* I will never, as a man who repents, change my word and purpose, says the Lord. What a glorious promise is this which is interposed in the midst of all these judgments!

CHAPTER 14

5. *As Lebanon.* As the cedars in Lebanon, so shall the true Israel, converted backsliders, be blessed of God; so flourishing and happy shall the church be under Christ.

8. *A green fir tree.* As a weary traveler finds rest and safety under a thick tree, so there is safety and refreshment under the protection of the Lord.

9. *The ways.* The ways which he would have us walk in towards him—his law, his ordinances, his whole doctrine—are all righteous and equal. And the ways wherein God walks towards us, in afflicting or comforting all, are righteous and equal. *Shall walk in them.* Will approve them all, justifying the righteousness of God's displeasure and confessing that he remembers mercy in the midst of judgment. And justifying the righteousness of his precepts by endeavoring to observe them. *The transgressors.* Willful, obstinate sinners, stumble and are offended at his commands, but more at his judgments; they cast off the one and vainly hope to shift off the other until at last they fall under the weight of their own sins and God's wrath.

JOEL

CHAPTER 1

1. *Came to Joel.* Probably in the latter end of Jeroboam the second's reign over Israel, and in the days of Uzziah over Judah.

6. *A nation.* An innumerable multitude of locusts and caterpillars, called a nation here, as Solomon calls the conies and the ant (Prov. 30:25–26), and perhaps a prognostic of a very numerous and mighty nation, that before long will invade Judah. *Strong.* Mighty in power and undaunted in courage, if you refer to it the Assyrians or Babylonians; if to those vermin, they are, though each weak by itself, yet in those multitudes strong and irresistible. *A great lion.* Such waste as lions make, these the locusts do, and the Assyrians will make.

15. *The day of the Lord.* A day of greater trouble than yet they felt, the troubles which God will heap upon them. *Shall it come.* Unless fasting, prayers, and amendment prevent.

20. *Cry.* They utter their complaints and their sad tones, they have a voice to cry as well as an eye to look to God.

CHAPTER 2

2. *A day of darkness.* A time of exceeding great troubles and calamities.

And this passage may well allude to the day of judgment and the calamities which precede that day.

14. *He will return.* God does not move from one place to another; but when he withholds his blessings, he is said to withdraw himself. And so when he gives out his blessing, he is said to return.

16. *The children.* Though they understand little what is done, yet their cries ascend and God with pity looks on their tears.

20. *His stink.* The stench of these locusts destroying and lying putrefied on the face of the earth, or the corpses of the Assyrians slain and unburied.

28. *Shall prophesy.* This was in part fulfilled according to the letter in the first days of the gospel; but the promise means further that by pouring out of the Spirit on your sons and your daughters, they shall have as full a knowledge of the mysteries of God's law as prophets before had. *Shall dream dreams.* This also was literally fulfilled in the apostles' days. But it may mean further that the knowledge of God and his will shall abound among all ranks, sexes, and ages in the Messiah's days, and not only equal but surpass all that formerly was by prophecy, dreams, or visions.

30. *Wonders.* They who read what historians report of those times will see this fulfilled to the very letter.

32. *Whosoever shall call.* Who hearing the gospel repents and believes in Christ. *Shall be delivered.* Either from those outward afflictions or, which is infinitely better, from eternal miseries which will swallow up the unbelieving world; "and it will aggravate the ruin of those who perish, that they might have been saved on such easy terms." Is it then easy for a non-elect to repent and believe? May he not as easily pull the sun out of the firmament? *In mount Zion.* In the true church, typified by Zion. *Jerusalem.* In mystical Jerusalem, the church and the city of the Messiah.

CHAPTER 3

1. *And Jerusalem.* For beside what refers to the two tribes restored by Cyrus, the bringing back from the captivity of the whole Israel of God by Christ is to be considered all along through this chapter.

2. *All nations.* In the type it is all those nations that have oppressed Judah; in the antitype, all nations that have been enemies to Christ and the church.

13. *The press.* As the grapes in the press are trod, so the enemies of God's people are to be trodden in the wine-press of God's displeasure. *Overflow.* The blood of slaughtered men runs as wine pressed out in greater abundance than the vats can hold. *Is great.* The violence and all manner of sins of these kingdoms is grown exceeding great.

17. *Dwelling.* Very graciously present with you and ever watching over you and delighting to save you. *Then.* After her enemies are destroyed and the remnant is saved and the Messiah is come; for to him and his days these things ultimately refer. *Jerusalem.* The church of Christ.

18. *A fountain.* The prophet alludes to those waters which were conveyed from some spring through conduit pipes towards the altar. This no doubt is a shadow of the purifying blood of Christ and his sanctifying Spirit and word. And in that it is said to come from *the house of the* LORD, it intimates that this saving grace shall be first preached from Jerusalem and by the church, which is the house of God, shall be published to others.

20. *Judah.* The redeemed of the Lord, his church.

21. *For I will cleanse.* Purge away both by the spirit of sanctification and by free pardon in the blood of the redeemer.

amos

CHAPTER 1

1. *Israel.* The kingdom of the ten tribes.

2. *Jerusalem.* The city God had chosen where he dwelt, the seat of God's instituted worship and the royal seat of the kingdom as God had settled it, from which in both respects the ten tribes had revolted. *Shall wither.* So the whole kingdom of the ten tribes, though as fruitful as *Carmel,* should be made horrid and desolate as a wilderness.

3. *For three.* This certain number is put for an uncertain: three, that is, many. *Of Damascus.* Here Damascus is put for the whole kingdom of Syria.

CHAPTER 2

1. *The bones.* Or ashes, reduced them by fire into fine dust and used these ashes instead of lime to plaster the walls and roofs of his palace, and this in hatred and contempt of the king of Edom.

4. *To err.* Their idolatry blinded them, partly from the natural tendency of this sin and partly from the just judgment of God.

6. *Shoes.* The smallest bribe, expressed here proverbially.

CHAPTER 3

3. *Agreed.* Can you have God's presence while you walk so contrary to him?

6. *Done it?* Either immediately by his own hand or by the hands of those he employs. Whoever the instruments, God is the principal agent. "Out of the mouth of the most High proceedeth not evil and good?"

7. *Will do nothing.* Usually the Lord does no great thing for or against his people without giving warning of it before it comes.

12. *As the shepherd.* As the shepherd does hardly[1] rescue a small part of a sheep or lamb from the lion, so a small part of the children of Israel shall escape when Samaria is taken.

CHAPTER 4

6. *Cleanness of teeth.* This is a description of famine.

13. *Declareth.* Knows the thoughts of all men. *The God of hosts.* Whose sovereign power all creatures obey, and

---

[1] (3:12) That is, with difficulty.

who acts for or against us as he wills. Let us humble ourselves before this God and give all diligence to make him our God. For happy are the people whose God he is and who have all this power engaged for them.

CHAPTER 5

15. *Love.* Commend, encourage, defend. Let your heart be towards good things and good men.

16. *Therefore.* The prophet, foreseeing their obstinacy, proceeds to denounce judgment against them. *The husbandman.* This sort of men are little used to such ceremonies as mourning, but now such also shall be called upon; leave your toil, betake yourselves to public mourning.

17. *Vineyards.* In these places were usually the greatest joy.

18. *That desire.* Scoffingly, not believing any such day would come.

23. *Thy songs.* Used in their sacrifices and solemn feasts. Herein they imitated the temple worship, but all was unpleasing to the Lord. *Will not hear.* Not with delight and acceptance.

CHAPTER 6

1. *At ease.* That neither fear nor believe the threatened judgments of God. *Samaria.* Woe to them also who rely upon the strength, wealth, and policy of the kingdom of Samaria or *Israel.*

2. *Pass ye.* Run over the history of that great and ancient city. *Hamath.* Head of the Syrian kingdom, lately overthrown by Tiglath-Pilneser, and fresh instance of God's just indignation against secure sinners.

10. *For.* It is too late to seek God, who is executing his immutable decree.

11. *For behold.* It seems to be the continued speech of him who took care

of the dead (v. 10). God has sent out war, famine, and pestilence.

12. *Shall horses.* If prophets exhort or advise, it does no more good than if you would run your horses upon the precipices of rocks.

CHAPTER 7

1. *Thus.* This is the first of five prophetic representations of what was coming upon this people. *The latter growth.* The shooting up of the first growth being too luxuriant, they often eat it down with cattle; but if the second growth were eaten up, it marred the whole harvest. *Mowed.* It is supposed the first mowing of the corn in the blade was for the king's use; and after this the second springing grew up to the harvest.

14. *No prophet.* Not originally, or by study, or by any human designation. *An herdman.* By breeding and occupation, I was and still am a herdsman.

CHAPTER 8

6. *That we may buy.* They would have more new moons and sabbaths that they might go to market to buy the poor. And when these poor owed but for a very little commodity, as suppose a pair of shoes, these merciless men would take advantage of them and make them sell themselves to pay the debt.

9. *Darken.* Bring a thick cloud of troubles and afflictions. *In the clear day.* When they think all is safe, sure, and well settled.

12. *Shall wander.* Search all places for a prophet or preacher, from the midland sea to the Dead Sea, they shall search all corners for a prophet.

CHAPTER 9

1. *The altar.* Of burnt offering before the temple at Jerusalem. This altar and temple Israel had forsaken and set up others against it; and here God in his jealousy appears prepared to take vengeance. Possibly it may intimate his future departure from Judah too. There Ezekiel (Ezek. 9:2) saw the slaughter-men stand.

7. *Have not I brought.* And whereas you boast of my kindness to you in bringing you out of Egypt, and thereupon conclude that God cannot leave you whom he has so redeemed, you argue amiss, for this aggravates your sin.

9. *The least grain.* Though tumbled and tossed with the great violence, yet the smallest good grain shall not be lost or destroyed.

13. *Behold the days come.* Here is another promise, literally of abundant plenty to the returned captives, and mystically of abundant grace poured forth in gospel days. If any object that it never was so, I answer, the sins of the returned captives prevented these blessings, which are promised under a tacit condition.

15. *Pulled up.* On condition that they seek the Lord. This was on God's part with admirable constancy performed through six hundred years, perhaps the longest time of freedom from captivity they ever knew.

OBADIAH

CHAPTER 1

1. *Obadiah.* His name speaks a servant or a worshipper of the Lord, but who he was we know not. *A rumour.* Not an uncertain report, but it comes from God. *Is sent.* By the Lord first and next by Nebuchadnezzar, who executed on Edom what is here foretold.

3. *The pride.* The Edomites were, as most mountaineers are, a rough, hardy, and daring people. And proud above measure.

4. *Bring thee down.* God who is in the heavens would throw you down. When men could not marshal armies against you, stars should fight in their courses against you. Nothing can stand which God will cast down (Jer. 49:16–17).

17. *Zion.* Literally this refers to the Jews; typically, to the gospel-church. *Deliverance.* A remnant that shall be delivered by Cyrus, a type of Israel's redemption by Christ. *Holiness.* The temple, the city, the people returned from captivity shall be holy to the Lord.

19. *They.* The Jews who live in the south parts of Canaan, next to Idumea, shall after their return and victories over Edom possess his country. *Of the plain.* The Jews who dwell in the plain country shall enlarge their borders, possess the Philistines country, together with their ancient inheritance. The former was fully accomplished by Hyrcanus. And if this were the time of fulfilling the one, doubtless it was the time of fulfilling the other also. And all the land which the ten tribes possessed shall again be possessed by the Jews. *Gilead.* Here is promised a larger possession than ever they had before the captivity; and it does no doubt point out the enlargement of the church of Christ in the times of the gospel.

21. *Saviours.* Deliverers, literally the leaders of those captive troops who shall come up from Babylon, such as Zerubbabel, Ezra, and Nehemiah; mystically, Christ and his apostles and other preachers of the gospel. *The LORD's.* Jehovah shall be honored, obeyed, and worshipped by all.

Jonah

CHAPTER 1

3. *From the presence.* From the place where God usually had showed himself present, by revealing his word and will to his prophets. Perhaps he might think God would not put him upon this work when he was in a strange country.

16. *Feared the Lord.* Perhaps as Jonah's casting overboard was a type of Christ's death, so the effect it had upon the mariners might be a type of the conversion of the heathen from idols unto God.

17. *A great fish.* God has the command of all his creatures and can make any of them serve his designs of mercy to his people.

CHAPTER 2

2. *Affliction.* Straits with which he was encompassed, his body and mind being both shut up, the one by the monstrous dungeon of the fish's belly and the other by the terrors of the Almighty. *Heardest my voice.* Of which undoubtedly God gave him an assurance in his own soul.

6. *I went down.* The fish carried him down as deep in the sea as are the bottoms of the mountains.

9. *Vowed.* Which probably was to go to Nineveh and preach what God commanded him.

10. *Spake.* Though fishes understand not as man, yet they have ears to hear their Creator.

CHAPTER 3

3. *Exceeding great.* The greatest city of the known world at that day; it was then in its flourishing state greater than Babylon, whose compass was 385 furlongs, but Nineveh was in compass 480.[1] *Of three days' journey.* To walk around the walls, allowing twenty miles to each day's journey.

4. *Shall be overthrown.* The threat is express. But there was a reserve with God on condition of repentance.

CHAPTER 4

8. *Better . . . to die.* But Jonah must be wiser and humbler and more merciful too, before he dies. Before God is done with him, he will teach him to value his own life more and to be more tender of the life of others.

9. *I do well to be angry.* What a speech! Verily "the law made nothing perfect"!

---

[1] (3:3) Furlong = 202.5 yards or an eighth of a Roman mile.

11. *I.* The God of infinite compassion and goodness. *That great city.* Would you have me less merciful to such a goodly city than you are to a weed? *Much cattle.* Besides men, women, and children who are in Nineveh there are many other of my creatures that are not sinful, and my tender mercies are and shall be over all my works. If you would be their butcher, yet I will be their God. Go, Jonah, rest yourself content and be thankful. That goodness which spared Nineveh has spared you in this your inexcusable frowardness. I will be to repenting Nineveh what I am to you, a God gracious and merciful, slow to anger, and of great kindness, and I will turn from the evil which you and they deserve.

micah

CHAPTER 1

1. *Hezekiah.* The best son, of the worst father. How long Micah prophesied during his reign, we can but conjecture, possibly until the fourteenth year of Hezekiah.

2. *O earth.* This seems to be an appeal to the senseless creatures, or a summons to bring in evidences for God against those kingdoms.

8. *Dragons.* Or rather, jackals, which haunt desolate places and make a great and hideous noise by night.

CHAPTER 2

4. *Portion.* Their wealth, plenty, freedom, joy, and honor into poverty, famine, servitude, grief, and dishonor. *How.* How dreadfully has God dealt with Israel, removing their persons into captivity and transferring their possession to their enemies. *Turning away.* Turning away from us in displeasure. God has divided our fields among others.

10. *Your rest.* Though it was given this people for a rest under God's wing, yet it was on condition of continued obedience.

12. *The multitude of men.* This was fulfilled in part when the Jews returned out of Babylon, but more fully when Christ by his gospel gathered together in one all the children of God that were scattered abroad.

CHAPTER 3

6. *And the sun.* The hand of God shall be against them making their sorrows the more dreadful, like darkness by the sun going down at noon.

10. *They.* The heads and great ones enlarge, beautify, and fortify the house in Zion, particularly the temple and the royal palace. *Blood.* With wealth, which they made themselves masters of by violence, taking away the life of the owners.

12. *For your sake.* Because of your sins. *The mountain.* The mountain on which the temple stood. This is that passage which is quoted in Jeremiah 26:18, which Hezekiah and his princes took well; they repented, and so the execution of it did not come in their days.

CHAPTER 4

1. *In the last days.* Or, in the latter days at the expiring of the seventy years' captivity, nearly two hundred years from Micah's time, a type of the days of the Messiah's kingdom. *The mountain.* The mountain on which the temple stood, a type of Christ and the gospel church. *Established.* Literally fulfilled when the second temple was built by the Jews; spiritually, when Christ established his church by the preaching of the gospel.

2. *Many nations.* This was in part fulfilled when so many proselyted servants of several nations, out of love for their Jewish masters and more for the God of the Jews, came up with them from Jerusalem. *Come.* So the Jews, released from captivity, encouraged each other; which was a fulfilling of this prophecy in part. The conversion of the multitude of the Gentiles to Christ was a more eminent fulfilling of it. *From Jerusalem.* In Jerusalem is declared the only way of worshipping God, and from thence the only law of right worship shall go forth when the Messiah is come.

3. *He.* The Messiah shall act as a judge and king. *Rebuke.* So Christ commissioned his apostles to teach all nations.

4. *They.* The redeemed of the Lord, redeemed from Babylonian captivity, the type of a greater redemption by Jesus Christ. *Shall sit.* That is, they shall enjoy peace, security, and plenty. This was more fully made good in the gospel days.

6. *Her.* Captive Judah, driven out of their own land. And Christ will much more gather to his fold those who were captive to Satan.

7. *A remnant.* Which as they are preserved for a seed, so they take root and increase and continue to the coming of the Messiah.

8. *The first dominion.* The former dominion; the government (after seventy years captivity) shall return to the former royal family and continue in it until Shiloh come. This in the type was fulfilled, under Zerubbabel and his successors; but the whole antitype concerns the Messiah's kingdom.

9. *Thy counsellor.* Have you none among your wise counselors left? Yet the Wonderful Counsellor is with you. Messiah, the wisdom of his Father, has the conduct of your sufferings, deliverance, and reestablishment.

10. *Shall redeem.* The Hebrew word points out a redemption by the next kinsman and so reminds us of the Messiah, the great redeemer of the church.

12. The husbandman gathers the sheaves onto the floor to thresh them; so God in due time will bring his enemies together that they may be bruised, broken, and destroyed.

13. *Brass.* By this figurative speech is the strength of Zion expressed, treading underfoot and breaking the power of her enemies in pieces.

CHAPTER 5

2. *Thou be little.* If you are the least in other respects, in this you are honored above them all. *Goings forth.* Whose generation, as he is the Son of God, equal with his Father, is eternal.

4. *He.* The ruler, the Messiah, shall stand. This posture speaks the readiness, cheerfulness, and stability of the Christ, his government, and kingdom. *Of the name.* By commission from the Father, in whose name Christ came, preached, wrought miracles, and instituted his gospel church. *They.* His church, made up of converted Jews and Gentiles, shall continue; the gates of hell shall not prevail against them. *For.* The church is so redeemed and established that Christ the Messiah might be glorified throughout the world.

5. *This man.* The Messiah.

6. *The entrances.* The fortified frontiers. In this manner shall he, the Messiah, deliver the Jews, his people. *The Assyrian.* The type of all other enemies to the people of God.

7. *As the showers.* God shall bless them by his immediate hand as he alone, without the help of man, gives dew and showers. As this was fulfilled in the type before the gospel was preached to all nations, so it has been, now is, and ever shall be fulfilled in ages to come. God's remnant shall be a blessing to the places they live in.

15. *Have not heard.* In an unprecedented manner. God will give his Son either the hearts or necks of his enemies and make them either his friends or his footstool.

CHAPTER 6

8. *He.* God has already told you in his word with what you ought to come before him. *To do justly.* To render to every one their due; superiors, equals, inferiors, to be equal to all and oppress none in body, goods, or name. *To love mercy.* To be kind, merciful, and compassionate to all, not using severity towards any. *Walk humbly with thy God.* Keep up a constant fellowship with God by humble, holy faith.

CHAPTER 7

7. *Therefore.* Since all sorts of men are so perfidious. *Look.* As one set in a watchtower looks round about and diligently observes all that stirs, so will the prophet; and so did they who in Israel and Judah feared the Lord.

8. *Rejoice not.* The prophet impersonates the church. Let it be no matter of glorying to you that the day of calamity has overtaken me. *In darkness.* When affliction, war, famine, and captivity cover me. *A light* shall support, comfort, and deliver me.

14. *Feed thy people.* So Christ directs his officers. *With thy rod.* An allusion to the custom of shepherds, who guided their sheep by a pastoral staff.

17. *Shall lick the dust.* In the most submissive, servile manner, testify their subjection.

nahum

CHAPTER 1

1. *The burden.* When the prophets were sent to denounce judgments against a nation or city, the word was usually called "the burden" of that nation or city. *The vision.* As prophets were of old called seers (I Sam. 9:9), so their prophesies were called visions. *Nahum.* His name speaks of a comforter, but it is God's people to whom he gives notice of the destruction of their oppressors.

3. *The dust of his feet.* Though he be surrounded with darkness, yet as an army afar off is discovered by the dust that their feet raise, so will God appear with great power marching against his enemies.

10. *As thorns.* They shall be like thorns easily burnt, and like thorns folded together, which burn together and help to destroy each other. *As drunkards.* As men drunken and unable to help themselves, so the Assyrians, drunk with pleasure and pride, shall be surprised and easily overthrown.

CHAPTER 2

2. *For.* Israel and Jacob were more to God, yet he punished them; much more will he punish Nineveh.

4. *Like torches.* What with sparkling fire caused by their horses and chariots, what with the glittering of the polished irons about them, and what with the light of flaming torches carried in them. *Like the lightnings.* Both for speed, irresistibleness, and terror.

7. *The voice of doves.* Sighing out their complaints. *Upon their breasts.* Instead of musical instruments on which they used to play, now they only strike their breasts.

8. *Like a pool.* Very populous, like a pool which has been long breeding fish and is full of them.

13. *Thy messengers.* Ambassadors or muster-masters.[1] Probably this refers to Rabshakeh, who had blasphemed the living God. Those are not worthy to be heard again who have once spoken reproachfully against God.

CHAPTER 3

4. *Whoredoms.* The idolatries which were multiplied by the many people that served the Assyrian idols. And whoredom literally understood did undoubtedly abound, where wealth, luxury, ease, and long continuance of these were to be found. *Wellfavoured.* Glori-

---

[1] (2:13) Perhaps meaning those who assemble a group for service, as in mustering soldiers.

ous in their state and government and in the splendor of their idols, temples, and sacrifices. *Of witchcrafts.* Bewitching policies; or it may be taken for witchcrafts or necromancers, which abounded among the Assyrians. *And families.* This may intimate the seducing of some particular and eminent families to an hereditary service of the Assyrian idols or to witchcrafts, in which the devil imitated God's institution in taking a family to his service.

11. *Thou also.* You shall drink deep of the bitter cup of God's displeasure.

16. *The cankerworm spoileth.* So these are like the cankerworms which spoil wherever they come and, when no more is to be gotten, flee away.

17. *The sun ariseth.* When trouble, war, and danger, like the parching sun, scald them.

18. *Thy shepherds.* Your rulers and counselors. *Slumber.* Are remiss, heartless, or dead.

19. *Shall clap the hands.* Insulting and rejoicing. *Thy wickedness.* Your tyranny, pride, oppression and cruelty; treading down and trampling upon them.

habakkuk

CHAPTER 1

1. *The burden.* The prophet seems to speak of these grievous things as a burden which he himself groaned under.

4. *The law.* The whole law, moral, ceremonial, and judicial.

8. *The evening wolves.* Which with fasting in the day came out in the evening fierce and ravenous.

9. *Their faces.* Their very countenances shall be as blasting as the east wind.

14. *And makest.* Not infusing cruel appetites, but permitting them to act according to such appetite which was already in them.

CHAPTER 2

2. *Upon tables.* What was of public concern, and therefore to be published, was anciently written or engraved upon tables, smooth stones, or wood and then hung up in a public place to be read. *May run.* That none may need to stop, but every one may plainly and clearly discern what is written.

4. *Which is lifted up.* That proudly contests with the justice and wisdom of the divine providence and provides for his own safety by his own wit. *The just.* The humble and upright one, who adores the depth of divine providence and is persuaded of the truth of divine promises. *Shall live.* Supports himself by a firm expectation of the deliverance of Zion.

16. *Shall be turned.* They turned the cup of pleasure about; God will carry the cup of indignation about also and make them drink deep of it. *Shameful spewing.* You shall be as much loathed as a shameful drunkard is in his vomit.

17. *The spoil of beasts.* Such spoil as by hunters is made among wild beasts when they endeavor to destroy the whole kind.

20. *The* LORD. He is Jehovah, the fountain of being, life, power, and salvation to his people. *Keep silence.* Fear, submit, and depend on him. Let his enemies be silent. Reverence, hope, pray, and wait for him who will arise and have mercy on them; who will make it to be well with the righteous and ill with the wicked; who will fully and satisfactorily solve the doubts and unfold the riddles of his providence.

CHAPTER 3

4. *As the light.* Pure, clear as the sun, but much more dazzling. *His hand.* The face of Moses shone; the face, yes, the hands of our God shine with glorious light.

6. *He stood.* Gave his presence with Joshua, as one who stood by while the work was done. *The earth.* The promised land. He beheld. Looked with a frowning countenance. *Drove asunder.* Cast them out. His eye did this, for he looked on them and did this. *His ways.* The wisdom, goodness, justice, holiness, and power which God shows in governing his people.

13. *With thine anointed.* Under the conduct of your anointed, Joshua, the type of the Messiah.

16. *When I heard.* What dreadful desolations God threatened against Israel. *My heart*[1] *trembled.* Another effect of surprising fears and astonishment. *Rottenness.* A decay of all my strength. *That I might rest.* These fears made me take myself to God that I might rest in him. *He.* The king of Babylon. *The people.* The Jews.

---

[1] (3:16) KJV: "belly."

zephaniah

CHAPTER 1

1. *Zephaniah.* He is thought to have been the great grandson of king Hezekiah.

7. *His guests.* Summoned the beasts of the field and the fowls of the air to eat the flesh and drink the blood.

12. *I will search.* God speaks after the manner of men, searching dark places with candles. He will fully discover and punish. *Their lees.* In allusion to liquors which, not being poured out from vessel to vessel to refine them, grow thick and foul.

18. *In the land.* Therefore let not sinners be laid asleep by the patience of God; for when the measure of their iniquity is full, his justice will both overtake and overcome them, will make quick and thorough work.

CHAPTER 2

3. *Seek.* Fear, worship, depend on him alone. *Hid.* Under the wing of divine providence.

5. *Cherethites.* Or destroyers; men who were stout, fierce, and terrible to their neighbors.

CHAPTER 3

5. *In the midst thereof.* Observing all. *Not do iniquity.* He will judge them righteously. *Every morning.* Daily he discovers his displeasure against the wicked. *Faileth not.* Lets no season slip to convince them by public and visible punishments. *The unjust.* But the wicked Jews proceed without shame and without fear.

9. *A pure language.* I will give them a pure way of worshipping me, the issue of a pure heart.

10. *My dispersed.* The praying remnant of the scattered Jews shall return to their own land and bring themselves an offering unto the Lord.

20. *A praise.* So the universal church of the firstborn will be in the great day. And then the Israel of God will be made a name and a praise to all eternity.

haggai

CHAPTER 1

1. *Joshua*. A type of the great deliverer. One Joshua leads them into Canaan, another restores the temple.

6. *Are not filled*. Your water quenches not your thirst, your wine does not revive your spirit.

11. *Upon men*. The very blood and constitutions of men were changed, and many diseases afflicted them.

14. *The LORD of hosts*. By which name he delights to be known among the returned captives; and it was a name best suited to their present state, compassed on all hands with enemies.

CHAPTER 2

6. *A little while*. Though about five hundred years, yet this was but a little time compared with that between the promise to Adam and Christ's coming. *I will shake*. Whether it be metaphorical or literal, it was verified at the time of Christ's coming into the world. After the return of the captivity, by the commotions among the Grecians, Persians, and Romans which began soon after this time, this was metaphorically fulfilled. And it was literally fulfilled by prodigies and earthquakes at the birth, death, and resurrection of Christ.

7. *The desire*. Christ, the most desirable to all nations, and who was desired by all who knew their own misery and his sufficiency to save them; who was to be the light of the Gentiles as well as the glory of his people Israel. *With glory*. The first temple had a glory in its magnificent structure, rich ornaments, and costly sacrifices; but this was a worldly glory. That which is here promised is a heavenly glory from the presence of Christ in it. He who was the brightness of the Father's glory, who is the glory of the church, appeared in this second temple.

9. *In this place*. In my house, a type of Christ. *Peace*. A spiritual, internal, and heavenly peace.

23. *My servant*. A type of him who was God's most beloved servant. *As a signet*. Which is very highly valued and carefully kept. So shall the antitypical Zerubbabel, the Messiah, be advanced, loved, and inviolably preserved king and supreme over his church. He is indeed the signet on God's right hand. For all power is given to him and derived from him. In him the great charter of the gospel is signed and sanctified, and it is in him that all the promises of God are yea and amen.

ZECHARIAH

CHAPTER 1

8. *A man.* Christ Jesus in the shape of a man.

9. *O my lord.* This was Christ, the Lord of Hosts. *The angel.* Christ, the Angel of the covenant.

10. *These.* Horsemen are angels who are ministers of the divine providence in the government of the world.

21. *He.* Christ. *But these.* These carpenters are emblems of the those instruments God will employ in breaking those destroyers.

CHAPTER 2

3. *The angel.* Christ, who had so long talked with Zechariah.

10. *I will dwell.* This was fulfilled in part to the Jews, but more fully to the gospel church.

11. *In that day.* When Christ shall come in the flesh and take down the partition wall. *Sent me.* The Messiah.

CHAPTER 3

2. *The Lord.* Christ, as a mediator, rather chooses to rebuke him in his Father's name than in his own.

4. *I have caused.* What angels could not take away, Christ did. He removed the filth of sin, the guilt and stain of it.

9. *Upon one stone.* On that stone are seven eyes, probably so placed that they may look many ways. So it was a more exact emblem of Christ and of his perfect knowledge and wisdom.

CHAPTER 4

3. *Two olive trees by it.* All which is an emblem of the church, made of pure gold; to be a light in the world; to shine as lamps that continually burn, maintained with pure oil, distilled from the olive trees, not pressed out by man but continually, abundantly, and freely flowing from God.

10. *For who hath despised.* In the work of God, the day of small things is not to be despised. God often chooses weak instruments to bring about mighty things. And though the beginnings be small, he can make the latter end greatly to increase.

14. *The two anointed ones.* Christ and the Holy Spirit. The Son was to be sent by the Father, and so was the Holy Ghost. They stand by him, ready to go.

CHAPTER 5

7. *And, behold.* Here is another part of this vision. *A woman.* The third in the vision. Perhaps this vision was purposely obscure, lest a plain denunciation of the second overthrow of the state and temple might discourage them from going forward in the present restoration of them.

8. *This.* This woman represents the wickedness of the Jews.

9. *Their wings.* They had wings like the wings of storks, large and strong, and flew before the wind with great swiftness. The judgments came thus flying and so bore away with them those who were incorrigible.

CHAPTER 6

1. *Four chariots.* Angels who are sometimes characterized as chariots of God. These as employed in the affairs of church and empire act their part in the revolution and changes of things until the gospel be preached by the Messiah and the apostles. *Of brass.* These denote the immovable decrees of God, his steady execution of his counsels, and the insuperable restraints upon all empires and countries which God keeps within the barriers of such impregnable mountains.

8. *Cried he.* Christ spoke aloud and called to him.

12. *Unto him.* Joshua, but in the hearing of others. *Whose name is The* BRANCH. Whom you know by the name of "the Branch," who was called so long since. You, O Joshua, are the portrait, he is the Branch itself. *He shall build.* He it is, though unseen, who stands by you, who builds the material temple, far inferior to the spiritual temple which Christ will build, preserve, and dwell in for ever.

13. *The counsel of peace.* The peace made for God's people shall rest upon these two, the kingly and priestly office of Christ; by his priestly office he shall make their peace with God, by his kingly office he shall deliver them from their spiritual enemies.

15. *And this.* The literal part shall come to pass in your day if you will obey the voice of the Lord. The mystical part shall come to pass also, and if you will believe and obey, the Gentiles shall come in and be your brethren and help to build the temple, the spiritual temple. But if you rebel and obey not, you shall be cast out and the Gentiles be taken in, to be God's people.

CHAPTER 7

7. *Prophets.* Who have called for repentance and sincere love to God and man, and showed how light formal services are. *Prosperity.* Did such observances preserve Jerusalem in its prosperity? Were they sufficient to save the men who inhabited the south of the plain? Did they do no good when things were all safe and well? And do you imagine they can profit you now that all is in ruins?

CHAPTER 8

2. *Jealousy.* With great care that she should not, as formerly, sin against my love and her own welfare; and with a great desire to do her good and to rescue her from her enemies.

3. *Shall be called a city of truth.* Her citizens shall love the truth and speak it, shall worship me in truth of heart as well as in the true manner prescribed to them.

8. *In truth and in righteousness.* This signifies both God's part and their part; on God's part truth, on theirs righteousness, obedience to God's righteous law.

19. *Thus saith the* LORD. This verse is the final decision of the case; provided they do these things required (vv. 16–17), then shall the fasting cease and turn into joyful feasts.

22. *In Jerusalem.* Literally understood, you have the first fruits of them mentioned (Acts 2:10–12). Mystically, Jerusalem is the church of Christ.

23. *That God.* The true God, the only true God, whom to know is life eternal.

CHAPTER 9

9. *Thy King.* The Messiah. *He is just.* The righteous one, who comes to fulfill all righteousness. *Having salvation.* To bestow on all who believe in him.

10. *I will cut off.* When the Messiah comes and sets up his kingdom, he will need no external force. Neither chariot, bow, nor sword brought salvation to him, neither shall they be mentioned in the day of his conquest.

11. *As for thee.* O Jerusalem; these words are Christ's words to her. *By the blood.* By my blood, in which your covenant is confirmed; it is God's covenant as made by him, it is Zion's covenant as made for her, it is Christ's also as made in him.

12. *Turn you.* The prophet exhorts the Jews to hasten to Christ, who is the salvation and high tower of the church.

15. *Make a noise.* Celebrate with shouts of triumph, as men do whose hearts are glad with success and cheered with wine.

17. *His goodness.* Infinite goodness is the fountain of all the good done for this people. *His beauty.* How wonderful the beauty of divine providence in Israel's deliverance and salvation.

CHAPTER 10

11. *And he shall pass through.* The whole verse is an allusion to what God had done in the two famous deliverances of his people, bringing them out of Egypt through the Red Sea and through Jordan, and destroying the Egyptians, and delivering them out of

Assyrian bondage, and in order thereto, destroying that kingdom.

CHAPTER 11

1. *Open thy doors.* That destruction of the Jewish church and nation is here foretold in dark and figurative expressions which our Lord, when the time was at hand, prophesied of very plainly.

4. *My God.* God the Father speaks to Christ.

9. *The flesh.* Either live to be besieged until hunger makes the living eat the dead, or by seditions and bloody quarrels destroy each other.

10. *That I might break.* Declare it null. Christ calls it his covenant, for he was the mediator of it.

12. *And I said.* Upon parting Christ seems, after the manner of men, to remind them of his pains for them and his desire for them to reckon with him. *Thirty pieces.* The value of the life of a slave (Exod. 21:32). This was fulfilled when they paid Judas Iscariot so much to betray Christ.

13. *The LORD.* God the Father. *A goodly price.* God upbraids the shepherds of his people, who prized the great Shepherd no higher.

14. *I cut asunder.* Christ did it really, the prophet did it in the type.

16. *Tear their claws.* Tear off their skin unto the very nails. In brief, a sluggish, negligent, covetous, riotous, oppressive, and cruel government is shadowed out by a foolish shepherd.

17. *Dried up.* They who have gifts which qualify them to do good, if they do it not, they will be taken away. They who should have been workmen, but were slothful and would do nothing, will justly have their arm dried up. And they who should have been watchmen, but were drowsy, will justly have their eyes blinded.

CHAPTER 12

2. *In the siege.* Now when all this is in readiness, and with no visible means of escape, then will God make them drink the wine of astonishment.

3. *In that day.* The day of the full accomplishment of this prophecy is a day known to the Lord.

8. *As the angel.* No, like the angel of the Lord, like Christ, who is captain of our salvation.

10. *I will pour.* This was fulfilled on Christ's exaltation when he sent the Comforter to his disciples. It is daily performed to the children of God and will be continually until we are bought to be with Christ for ever.

Pierced. Every one of us by our sins pierced him, and many of the Jews literally. *Mourn.* They shall literally lament the crucifying of the Lord Jesus.

11. *In that day.* When the Jews shall mourn for their sins and for that great sin, crucifying the Lord of glory.

13. *The house of Levi.* The sacerdotal tribe was the most bitter persecutor of Christ. They hired the traitor, they sought witness, the high priest condemned him to die. For all of this they shall one day reckon with God. Above other tribes they are particularly named as chief mourners for their cruelty to Christ.

CHAPTER 13

1. *A fountain.* The blood of Christ. *Opened.* The spouse is to Christ a fountain sealed, but Christ is to sinners a fountain opened.

7. *O sword.* Afflictions, persecutions, and the cross. *My shepherd.* Who is my faithful shepherd and will lay down his life for my sheep. *My fellow.* This speaks of Christ, a man with us and God with his Father, God-man in one person.

CHAPTER 14

1. *The day* of vengeance (Joel 2:1–2) comes or will soon overtake you, O sinful, unthankful, bloody Jews!

5. *The LORD my God.* As if it were said, though it will, O Lord, put us into fear. Yet without such wonderful works we shall not see your salvation; therefore, O Lord my God, come and bring your holy ones with you.

8. *Living waters.* The quickening, saving truths of the gospel with all its ordinances in purity.

10. *As a plain.* All high, uneven places, all rocky and barren grounds, shall be changed into fruitful vineyards. So the church of Christ shall be fruitful, humble, and lovely.

20. *HOLINESS UNTO THE LORD.* Their persons shall bear the dedicating inscription of holiness to the Lord and by their study of holiness they shall make good their motto.

21. *That sacrifice.* So the prophet expresses all religious affections, practice, and worship which shall be as pleasing to God as were the sacrifices of his people offered up with divine warrant and approbation.

malachi

CHAPTER 1

2–3. *Yet I loved Jacob.* I preferred him to the birthright, and this of free love. I loved his person and his posterity. *I hated.* I loved not Esau's posterity as I loved Jacob's. *His heritage.* Mount Seir with the neighboring mountains. *Waste.* By Nebuchadnezzar's arms five years after the sacking of Jerusalem; and whereas Jacob's captivity returned and their cities were rebuilt, Esau's never were.

11. *Incense.* A law term for a gospel duty, and under this type are contained the prayers and praises, no, the whole gospel-worship. *A pure offering.* Both sincere in opposition to hypocrisy, and holy in opposition to impurity, superstition and idolatry.

CHAPTER 2

3. *Of your solemn feasts.* Your most solemn days and feasts shall be as loathsome to me as dung, and shall make you who offer them as unclean and loathsome as if I had thrown the dung of those sacrifices into your faces.

9. *Have been partial.* You have perverted the law to please great men or to serve some unworthy design. When we inquire into "the reasons of the contempt of the clergy," ought we to forget this?

10. *Created us.* The prophet speaks of that great and gracious work of God, creating them to be a chosen people. And so we Christians are created in Christ Jesus.

16. *Putting away.* Divorce, such as these petulant Jews used to make way for some new wives, which God hates as much as putting away.

CHAPTER 3

1. *I.* The Messiah. *My messenger.* John the Baptist. *The Lord.* The Messiah. *Whom ye seek.* Whom you who truly fear God long and wait for. *Suddenly come.* After the coming of his forerunner. *The messenger.* The Angel of the covenant, the Messiah, in whose blood the covenant between God and man was confirmed.

2. *The day.* This day was from his preaching until the utter destruction of Jerusalem, about seventy years after the birth of Christ.

3. *Sons of Levi.* Either the Jewish Levites, or all Christians, who are made priests unto God.

4. *The offering.* The services and duties of the whole Christian church.

5. *To you.* O Jews, not those very persons Malachi preached to, but those who were living when the Messiah came.

6. *Change not.* I have an unchangeable hatred to sin. And my longsuffering also changes not; therefore you are not consumed in your sins.

10. *Bring ye.* Make a punctual and full payment of all tithes; about this did Nehemiah contend with the rulers and made them comply, and then all Judah obeyed and did the like (Neh. 13:10–13). *Prove me.* Make the experiment. *The windows of heaven.* A kind of proverbial speech to express great abundance. *A blessing.* First of rain to water the earth, next a blessing of corn, wine, and oil, and all other products of the earth.

11. *The devourer.* All kind of devourers, the locusts, the cankerworm, and the caterpillar; which though they are in incredible multitudes, yet a rebuke from God will check them all at once, as if they were but one.

12. *A delightsome land.* The revival of religion in a land will make it delightful, both to God and to all good men.

CHAPTER 4

1. *As an oven.* The refiner's fire (3:2) is now represented as a fire burning more dreadfully, as it did indeed when Jerusalem and the temple were on fire, when the fire raged everywhere, but most fiercely where the arched roofs make it double itself and infold flames with flames. And this may well be an emblem of the day of judgment.

2. *The Sun of righteousness.* Christ, who is fitly compared to the sun, being the fountain of light and vital heat to his church. *With healing.* His beams shall bring health and strength with delight and joy, safety and security.

3. *Tread down the wicked.* When deliverers by faith overcome the world, when they suppress their corrupt appetites and passions, and when the God of peace bruises Satan under their feet, then they indeed *tread down the wicked.*

5. *Behold, I will send.* Though the spirit of prophecy will cease for four hundred years, yet at the expiring of those years you shall have one sent as great as Elijah. *Elijah.* Namely, John the Baptist, who came in the spirit and power of Elijah (Luke 1:17) and therefore bears his name. *Before.* That is, immediately before, so he was born six months before Christ and began his preaching a few years before Christ began to exercise his public office. *The great and dreadful day of the LORD.* This literally refers to the times of vengeance upon the Jews from the death of Christ to the final desolation of the city and temple, and by accommodation, to the end of the world.

6. *With a curse.* Which ends in utter destruction; leaving Jerusalem a desolate heap and a perpetual monument of God's displeasure. Some observe that the last word of the Old Testament is a curse; whereas the New Testament ends with a blessing, yes, the choicest of blessings, "The grace of our Lord Jesus Christ be with you all. Amen."

the new testament

preface to the new testament

For many years I have had a desire of setting down and laying together what has occurred to my mind, either in reading, thinking, or conversation, which might assist serious persons, who have not the advantage of learning, in understanding the New Testament. But I have been continually deterred from attempting anything of this kind by a deep sense of my own inability; of my want, not only of learning for such a work, but much more of experience and wisdom. This has often occasioned my laying aside the thought. And when, by much importunity, I have been prevailed upon to resume it, still I determined to delay it as long as possible that (if it should please God) I might finish my work and my life together.

But having lately had a loud call from God to arise and go hence, I am convinced that, if I attempt anything of this kind at all, I must not delay any longer. My day is far spent, and even in a natural way the shadows of the evening come on apace; and I am rather induced to do what little I can in this way because I can do nothing else, being prevented by my present weakness from either traveling or preaching. But blessed be God, I can still read and write and think. Oh, that it may be to his glory!

It will be easily discerned, even from what I have said already, and much more from the notes themselves, that they were not principally designed for men of learning, who are provided with many other helps; and much less for men of long and deep experience in the ways and word of God. I desire to sit at their feet and to learn of them. But I write chiefly for plain, unlettered men, who understand only their mother tongue and yet reverence and love the word of God and have a desire to save their souls.

I have endeavored to make the notes as short as possible, that the comment may not obscure or swallow up the text; and as plain as possible, in pursuance of my main design, to assist the unlearned reader. For this reason I have studiously avoided, not only all curious and critical inquiries and all use of the learned languages, but all such methods of reasoning and modes of expression as people in common are unacquainted with. For the same reason as I rather endeavor to obviate than to propose and answer objection, so I purposely decline going deep into many difficulties, lest I should leave the ordinary reader behind me.

I once designed to write down barely what occurred to my own mind, consulting none but the inspired writers. But no sooner was I acquainted with that great light of the Christian world (lately gone to his reward) Bengelius, than I entirely changed my design, being thoroughly convinced it might be of more service to the cause of religion were I barely to translate his *Gnomon Novi Testamenti* than to write many volumes upon it. Many of his excellent notes I have therefore translated; many more I have abridged, omitting that part which was purely critical and giving the substance of the rest.

I am likewise indebted for some useful observations to Dr. Heylyn's *Theological Lectures;* and for many more to Dr. Guyse, and to the *Family Expositor* of the late pious and learned Dr. Doddridge. It was a doubt with me for some time whether I should not subjoin to every note I received from them the name of the author from whom it was taken, especially considering I had transcribed some, and abridged many more, almost in the words of the author. But upon further consideration I resolved to name none, that nothing might divert the mind of the reader from keeping close to the point in view and receiving what was spoken only according to its own intrinsic value.

I cannot flatter myself so far (to use the words of one of the above-named writers) as to imagine that I have fallen into no mistakes in a work of so great difficulty. But my own conscience acquits me of having designedly misrepresented any single passage of Scripture, or of having written one line with a purpose of inflaming the hearts of Christians against each other. God forbid that I should make the words of the most gentle and benevolent Jesus a vehicle to convey such poison! Would to God that all the party names and unscriptural phrases and forms which have divided the Christian world were forgot, and that we might all agree to sit down together as humble, loving disciples at the feet of our common Master, to hear his word, to imbibe his Spirit, and to transcribe his life in our own!

Concerning the Scriptures in general, it may be observed that the word of the living God which directed the first patriarchs also was, in the time of Moses, committed to writing. To this were added, in several succeeding generations, the inspired writings of the other prophets. Afterwards, what the Son of God preached and the Holy Ghost spake by the apostles, the apostles and evangelists wrote. This is what we now style the Holy Scripture: This is that "word of God which remaineth for ever";

of which, though "heaven and earth pass away, one jot or tittle shall not pass away." The Scripture, therefore, of the Old and New Testament is a most solid and precious system of divine truth. Every part is worthy of God and all together are one entire body, wherein is no defect, no excess. It is the fountain of heavenly wisdom, which they who are able to taste prefer to all writings of men, however wise or learned or holy.

An exact knowledge of the truth was accompanied in the inspired writers with an exactly regular series of arguments, a precise expression of their meaning, and a genuine vigor of suitable affections. The divisions of the New Testament into chapters was made in the Dark Ages, and very incorrectly, often separating things that are closely joined, and joining those that are entirely distinct from each other.

In the language of the sacred writings we may observe the utmost depth together with the utmost ease. All the elegancies of human composures sink into nothing before it; God speaks, not as man, but as GOD. His thoughts are very deep, and thence his words are of inexhaustible virtue. And the language of his messengers also is exact in the highest degree; for the words which were given them accurately answered the impression made upon their minds; and hence Luther says, "Divinity is nothing but a grammar of the language of the Holy Ghost." To understand this thoroughly, we should observe the emphasis which lies on every word—the holy affections expressed thereby, and the tempers shown by every writer. But how little are these—the latter especially—regarded, though they are wonderfully diffused through the whole New Testament, and are in truth a continued commendation of him who acts or speaks or writes.

The New Testament is all those sacred writings in which the new testament, or covenant, is described. The former part of this contains the writings of the evangelists and apostles; the latter, the Revelation of Jesus Christ. In the former is, first, the history of Jesus Christ from his coming in the flesh to his ascension into heaven; then, the institution and history of the Christian church from the time of his ascension. The Revelation delivers what is to be with regard to Christ, the church, and the universe, until the consummation of all things.

BRISTOL HOT-WELLS
January 4, 1754

the gospel of matthew

CHAPTER 1

1. *The book of the generation of Jesus Christ.* That is, the account of his birth and genealogy. It may also signify the history of a person. If there were any difficulties in this genealogy, or that given by Luke, which could not easily be removed, they would rather affect the Jewish tables than the credit of the Evangelists; for they act only as historians, setting down these genealogies as they stood in those public records. They unquestionably prove that Jesus was of the family from which the promised Seed was to come.

16. *Jesus, who is called Christ.* The word "Christ" in Greek and "Messiah" in Hebrew signify "Anointed" and imply the prophetic, priestly, and royal character of the Messiah. Among the Jews, anointing was the ceremony whereby prophets, priests, and kings were initiated into their offices. And if we look into ourselves, we shall find a need of Christ in all these respects. We are by nature at a distance from God, alienated from him, and incapable of free access to him. Hence we want a mediator, an intercessor—in a word, a Christ in his priestly office; this regards our state with respect to God.

And with respect to ourselves we find a total darkness, blindness, and ignorance of God and the things of God. Here we want Christ in his prophetic office, to enlighten our minds and teach us the whole will of God. We find also within us a strange misrule of appetites and passions. For these we want Christ in his kingly office, to reign in our hearts and subdue all things to himself.

17. *So all the generations.* When we survey such a series of generations, it is natural and obvious to reflect, "How like the leaves of a tree one passeth away, and another cometh!" Yet "the earth still abideth," and with it the goodness of the Lord, which continues from generation to generation, the common hope of parents and children.

23. *They shall call his name Emmanuel.* "To be called" means, according to the Hebrew manner of speaking, that the person spoken of shall really and effectually become what he is called and actually fulfill that title. Thus, "unto us a child is born: . . . and his name shall be called Wonderful, Counsellor, the mighty God, . . . the Prince of Peace"; that is, he shall be all these, though not so much nominally as really, and in effect. And thus was he called "Emmanuel"; which was no common name of Christ, but points out his nature and office. As he is God incarnate and dwells by his Spirit in the hearts of his people.

CHAPTER 2

1. *Wise men.* The firstfruits of the Gentiles. Probably they were Gentile philosophers who, through divine assistance, had improved their knowledge of nature as a means of leading them to the nature of the one, true God. Nor is it unreasonable to suppose that God had favored them with some extraordinary revelations of himself, as he did Melchizedek, Job, and several others who were not of the family of Abraham; to which he never intended absolutely to confine his favors. The title given them in the original language was anciently given to all philosophers or men of learning, those particularly who were curious in examining the works of nature and observing the motions of the heavenly bodies.

6. *Thou . . . art not the least among the princes of Juda.* When this and several other quotations are compared with the Old Testament original, it plainly appears that the apostles did not always think it necessary exactly to transcribe the passages they cited; but contented themselves with giving the general sense, though with some diversity of language. The words of Micah, which we render "though thou be little," may be rendered "Art thou little?" And then the difference which seems to be here between the Prophet and the Evangelist vanishes away.

11. *Gold, and frankincense, and myrrh.* Probably these were the best things their country afforded, and the presents ordinarily made to great persons. This was a most seasonable providential assistance for a long and expensive journey into Egypt, a country where they were entirely strangers and were to stay for a considerable time.

17. *Then was fulfilled.* A passage of Scripture, whether prophetic, historical, or poetical, is in the language of the New Testament fulfilled when an event happens to which it may with great propriety be accommodated.

18. *Rachel weeping for her children.* The Benjamites, who inhabited Ramah, sprung from her. She was buried near this place and is here beautifully represented risen, as it were, out of her grave and bewailing her lost children.

CHAPTER 3

2. *The kingdom of heaven* and "the kingdom of God" are but two phrases for the same thing. They mean, not merely a future happy state in heaven, but a state to be enjoyed on earth; the proper disposition for the glory of heaven rather than the possession of it.

Is at hand. As if he had said, God is about to erect that kingdom, spoken of by Daniel (2:44; 7:13–14), the kingdom of the God of heaven. It properly signifies here the gospel dispensation, in which subjects were to be gathered to God by his Son, and a society formed which was to subsist first on earth and afterwards with God in glory. In some passages of Scripture the phrase more particularly denotes the state of it on earth; in others it signifies only the state of glory; but it generally includes both. The Jews understood it of a temporal kingdom, the seat of which they supposed would be Jerusalem; and the expected sovereign of this kingdom they learned from Daniel to call "the Son of Man."

Both John the Baptist and Christ took up that phrase, *the kingdom of heaven,* as they found it and gradually taught the Jews, though greatly unwilling to learn, to understand it right. The very demand of repentance, as previous to it, showed it was a spiritual kingdom, and that no wicked man—how politic, brave, or learned—could possibly be a subject of it.

4. *John had his raiment of camel's hair.* Coarse and rough, suiting his character and his doctrine.

6. *Confessing their sins.* Of their own accord, freely and openly. Such prodigious numbers could hardly be baptized by immersing their whole bodies under water; nor can we think they were provided with a change of raiment for it, which was scarcely practicable for such vast multitudes. And yet they could not be immersed naked with modesty, nor in their wearing apparel with safety. It seems therefore that they stood in ranks on the edge of the river and that John, passing along before them, cast water on their heads or faces; by which means he might baptize many thousands in a day.

8. Repentance is of two sorts: that which is termed "legal," and that which is styled "evangelical" repentance. The former, which is the same that is spoken of here, is a thorough conviction of sin. The latter is a change of heart (and consequently of life) from all sin to all holiness.

11. *He shall baptize you with the Holy Ghost, and with fire.* He shall fill you with the Holy Ghost, inflaming your hearts with that fire of love which many waters cannot quench. And this was done, even with a visible appearance as of fire, on the Day of Pentecost.

15. *It becometh us to fulfil all righteousness.* It becomes every messenger of God to observe all his righteous ordinances. But the particular meaning of our Lord seems to be that it becometh us to do this (me to receive baptism, you to administer it) in order to fulfill—that is, that I may fully perform—every part of the righteous law of God and the commission he has given me."

16. *And Jesus, when he was baptized.* Let our Lord's submitting to baptism teach us a holy exactness in the observance of those institutions which owe their obligation merely to a divine command. Jesus had no sin to wash away, yet he was baptized. And God owned his ordinance so as to make it the season of pouring forth the Holy Spirit upon him. And where can we expect this sacred effusion, but in a humble attendance on divine appointments?

17. *And lo a voice.* We have here a glorious manifestation of the ever blessed Trinity: the Father speaking from heaven, the Son spoken to, and the Holy Ghost descending upon him. *In whom I am well pleased.* What an encomium is this! How poor to this are all other kinds of praise! To be the pleasure, the delight of God, this is praise indeed! This is true glory; this is the highest, the brightest light that virtue can appear in.

CHAPTER 4

1. *Then.* After this glorious evidence of his Father's love, Jesus was completely armed for combat. Thus, after the clearest light and the strongest consolation, let us expect the sharpest temptations.

3. *Came to him* in a visible form, probably in a human shape, as one who desired to inquire farther into the evidences of his being the Messiah.

11. *Angels came and ministered unto him.* Both to supply him with food and to congratulate his victory.

17. *Repent: for the kingdom of heaven is at hand.* Although it is the peculiar business of Christ to establish the kingdom of heaven in the hearts of men, yet he begins his preaching in the same words with John the Baptist; because the repentance which John taught still was, and ever will be, the necessary preparation for that inward kingdom. But that phrase is not only used with regard to individuals, in whom it is to be established, but also with regard to the Christian church, the whole body of believers.

23. *The gospel of the kingdom.* The gospel—that is, the joyous message— is the proper name of our religion, as will be amply verified in all who earnestly and perseveringly embrace it.

CHAPTER 5

2. *Taught.* To bless men, to make men happy, was the great business for which our Lord came into the world. And accordingly he here pronounces eight blessings together, annexing them to so many steps in Christianity. Knowing that happiness is our common aim, and that an innate instinct continually urges us to the pursuit of it, he in the kindest manner applies to that instinct and directs it to its proper object. Though all men desire, yet few attain happiness, because they seek it where it is not to be found.

3. *The poor in spirit.* They who are unfeignedly penitent; they who are truly convinced of sin; who see and feel the state they are in by nature, being deeply sensible of their sinfulness, guiltiness, helplessness. *For theirs is the kingdom of heaven.* The present, inward kingdom—righteousness and peace and joy in the Holy Ghost; as well as the eternal kingdom, if they endure to the end.

4. *They that mourn.* Either for their own sins, or for other men's, and are steadily and habitually serious.

5. *Happy[1] are the meek.* They that hold all their passions and affections evenly balanced. *They shall inherit the earth.* They shall have all things really necessary for life and godliness. They

shall enjoy whatever portion God has given them here, and shall hereafter possess the new earth, wherein dwells righteousness.

7. *They shall obtain mercy.* Whatever mercy therefore we desire from God, the same let us show to our brethren. He will repay us a thousandfold the love we bear to any for his sake.

8. *The pure in heart.* The sanctified; they who love God with all their hearts. *They shall see God.* In all things here; hereafter in glory.

9–10. *They shall be called the children of God.* Shall be acknowledged such by God and men. One would imagine a person of this amiable temper and behavior would be the darling of mankind. But our Lord well knew it would not be so as long as Satan was the prince of this world. He therefore warns them before of the treatment all were to expect who were determined to tread in his steps, by immediately adjoining, *Happy are they which are persecuted for righteousness' sake.*

Through this whole discourse we cannot but observe the most exact method which can possibly be conceived. Every paragraph, every sentence, is closely connected both with that which precedes and that which follows it. And is not this the pattern for every Christian preacher? If any then are able to follow it without any premeditation, well; if not, let them not dare to preach without it. No rhapsody, no incoherency, whether the things spoken be true or false, comes of the Spirit of Christ.

12. *Your reward.* Even over and above the happiness that naturally and directly results from holiness.

13. *Ye are the salt of the earth.* Not the apostles, not ministers only, but all

---

[1](5:5) KJV: "Blessed." See also verse 9.

ye who are thus holy are to season others.

14. *Ye are the light of the world.* If ye are thus holy, you can no more be hid than the sun in the firmament; no more than *a city* on a mountain—probably pointing to that on the brow of the opposite hill.

22. *That whosoever is angry with his brother.* Christ teaches that we ought not for any cause to be so angry as to call any man *Raca,* or *Fool.* We ought not for any cause to be angry at the person of the sinner, but at his sin only. Happy world, were this plain and necessary distinction thoroughly understood, remembered, practiced! *Raca* means a silly man, a trifler.

Hell fire. In the valley of Hinnom (from where the word in the original was taken) the children were used to be burned alive to Moloch. It was afterwards made a receptacle for the filth of the city, where continual fires were kept to consume it. And it is probable, if any criminals were burned alive, it was in this accursed and horrible place. Therefore both as to its former and latter state, it was a fit emblem of hell. It must here signify a degree of future punishment as much more dreadful than those incurred in the two former cases, as burning alive is more dreadful than either strangling or stoning.

29–30. If a person as dear as a right eye, or as useful as a right hand, causes you thus to offend, though but in heart.

Perhaps here may be an instance of a kind of transposition which is frequently found in the sacred writings: so that the twenty-ninth verse may refer to verses 27–28, and the thirtieth to verses 21–22. As if he had said, "Part with anything, however dear to you or otherwise useful, if you cannot avoid sin while you keep it. Even cut off your right hand if you are of so passionate a temper that you cannot otherwise be restrained from hurting your brother. Pull out your eyes if you can no otherwise be restrained from lusting after women."

33. Our Lord here refers to the promise made to the "pure in heart," of seeing God in all things; and points out a false doctrine of the scribes, which arose from their not thus seeing God. What he forbids is the swearing at all (1) By any creature, (2) In our ordinary conversation; both of which the scribes and Pharisees taught to be perfectly innocent.

40–41. Where the damage is not great, choose rather to suffer it— though possibly it may on that account be repeated—than to demand "an eye for an eye," to enter into a rigorous prosecution of the offender. The meaning of the whole passage seems to be, rather than return evil for evil, when the wrong is purely personal, submit to one bodily wrong after another; give up one part of your goods after another; submit to one instance of compulsion after another. That the words are not literally to be understood appears from the behavior of our Lord himself (John 18:22–23).

42. *Give to him that asketh thee.* Give and lend to any so far (but no farther, for God never contradicts himself) as is consistent with your engagements to your creditors, your family, and the household of faith.

44. *Bless them that curse you.* Speak all the good you can to and of them who speak all evil to and of you. Repay love in thought, word, and deed to those who hate you, and show it both in word and deed.

47. *And if ye salute your brethren only.* Would to God this had been more attended to among the unhappy divisions and subdivisions into which his church has been crumbled; and that we might at least advance so far as cordially to embrace our brethren in Christ, of whatever party or denomination they are.

48. *Therefore ye shall be perfect, even as your Father which is in heaven is perfect.* So the original[2] runs, referring to all that holiness which is described in the foregoing verses, which our Lord in the beginning of the chapter recommends as happiness, and in the close of it as perfection.

CHAPTER 6

6. *Enter into thy closet.* That is, do it with as much secrecy as you can.

7. *Use not vain repetitions.* We should be extremely careful in all our prayers to mean what we say; and to say only what we mean from the bottom of our hearts. The vain and heathenish repetitions which we are here warned against are most dangerous, and yet very common; which is a principal cause why so many who still profess religion are a disgrace to it. Indeed, all the words in the world are not equivalent to one holy desire. And the very best prayers are but "vain repetitions" if they are not the language of the heart.

9. *Therefore pray ye.* He who best knew what we ought to pray for and how we ought to pray—what matter of desire, what manner of address would most please himself, would best become us—has here dictated to us a most perfect and universal form of prayer, comprehending all our real needs, expressing all our lawful desires; a complete directory and full exercise of all our devotions.

10. *Thy kingdom come.* May your kingdom of grace come quickly, and swallow up all the kingdoms of the earth! May all mankind, receiving you, O Christ, for their King, truly believing in your name, be filled with righteousness and peace and joy, with holiness and happiness, until they are removed hence into your kingdom of glory, to reign with you for ever and ever.

Thy will be done in earth, as it is in heaven. May all the inhabitants of the earth do your will as willingly as the holy angels! May these do it continually even as they, without any interruption of their willing service; yes, and perfectly as they! May you, O Spirit of grace, through the blood of the everlasting covenant, make them perfect in every good work to do your will, and work in them all that is pleasing in your sight!

13. *And lead us not into temptation, but deliver us from evil.* Whenever we are tempted, O you who helps our infirmities, permit us not to "enter into temptation"; to be overcome or suffer loss thereby; but make a way for us to escape so that we may be more than conquerors, through your love, over sin and all the consequences of it. Now, the principal desire of a Christian's heart being the glory of God (vv. 9–10), and all he wants for himself or his brethren being the "daily bread" of soul and body (or the support of life, animal and spiritual), pardon of sin, and deliverance from the power of it and of the devil (vv. 11–13), there is nothing besides that a Christian can wish for. Therefore this prayer comprehends all his desires. Eternal life is the certain consequence, or rather completion, of holiness.

16. *When ye fast.* Our Lord does not enjoin either fasting, alms deeds, or prayer; all these being duties which were before fully established in the church of God.

---

[2] (5:48) Wesley departs from the imperative mood given in the KJV, which renders this: "Be ye therefore perfect, . . ."

22. *The light of the body is the eye.* And what the eye is to the body, the intention is to the soul. We may observe with what exact propriety our Lord places purity of intention between worldly desires and worldly cares, either of which directly tend to destroy it. *If thine eye be single,* singly fixed on God and heaven, your whole soul will be full of holiness and happiness.

31. *Therefore take no thought.* How kind are these precepts, the substance of which is only this, Do yourself no harm! Let us not be so ungrateful to him, nor so injurious to ourselves, as to harass and oppress our minds with that burden of anxiety which he has so graciously taken off. Every verse speaks at once to the understanding and to the heart. We will not, therefore, indulge these unnecessary, these useless, these mischievous cares. We will not borrow the anxieties and distresses of the morrow to aggravate those of the present day. Rather, we will cheerfully repose ourselves on that heavenly Father, who knows we have need of these things; who has given us the life which is more than meat, and the body which is more than raiment. And thus instructed in the philosophy of our heavenly Master, we will learn a lesson of faith and cheerfulness from every bird of the air and every flower of the field.

33. *Seek.* And indeed, whoever seeks this first will soon come to seek this only.

CHAPTER 7

Our Lord now proceeds to warn us against the chief hindrances of holiness. And how wisely does he begin with judging, wherein all young converts are so apt to spend that zeal which is given them for better purposes.

1. *Judge not.* Without full, clear, certain knowledge, without absolute necessity, without tender love.

6. *Give not.* That is, talk not of the "deep things of God" to those whom you know to be wallowing in sin. Neither declare the great things God has done for your soul to the profane, furious, persecuting wretches. Talk not of perfection, for instance, to the former; nor of your own experience to the latter. But our Lord does in no wise forbid us to reprove, as occasion is, both the one and the other.

8. *For every one that asketh receiveth.* Provided he asks rightly, asking for what is agreeable to God's will.

13. *The strait gate.* The holiness described in the previous chapters.

16. *Ye shall know them by their fruits.* A short, plain, easy rule, whereby to know true from false prophets; and one that may be applied by people of the most ordinary capacity, who are not accustomed to deep reasoning. True prophets convert sinners to God, or at least confirm and strengthen those that are converted. False prophets do not.

18. *A good tree cannot bring forth evil fruit, neither can a corrupt tree bring forth good fruit.* The goodness or badness here mentioned respects the doctrine rather than the personal character. A bad man, preaching the good doctrine here delivered, is sometimes an instrument of converting sinners to God. Yet I do not suggest that all are true prophets who speak the truth and thereby convert sinners; I only affirm that none are such who do not.

22. *Have we not prophesied.* We have declared the mysteries of your kingdom; wrote books; preached excellent sermons. *In thy name done many wonderful works?* So that even the working of miracles is no proof that a man has saving faith.

23. *I never knew you.* There never was a time that I approved of you; so that as many souls as they had saved, they were themselves never saved from their sins. Lord, is it my case?

CHAPTER 8

4. *See thou tell no man.* Perhaps our Lord only meant here: not until you have shown yourself to the priest, who was appointed to to inquire into the case of leprosy. But many others he commanded absolutely to tell none of the miracles he had wrought upon them. And this he seems to have done, chiefly for one or more of these reasons: (1) To prevent the multitude from thronging him, in the manner related in Mark 1:45. (2) To fulfill the prophecy (Isa. 42:2) that he would not be vain or ostentatious; this reason Matthew assigns (12:17, etc.). (3) To avoid being taken by force and made a king (John 6:15). And (4) That he might not enrage the chief priests, scribes, and Pharisees, who were the most bitter against him, any more than was unavoidable (Matt. 16:20–21).

5. *There came unto him a centurion.* Probably he came a little way towards him and then went back. He thought himself not worthy to come in person, and therefore spoke the words that follow by his messengers. As it is not unusual in all languages, so in the Hebrew it is peculiarly frequent, to ascribe to a person himself the thing which is done, and the words which are spoken by his order. And accordingly, Matthew relates as said by the centurion himself what others said by order from him. An instance of the same kind we have in the case of Zebedee's children. From Matthew 20:20 we learn it was their mother that spoke those words which (Mark 10:35, 37) themselves are said to speak; because she was only their mouth.

17. *That it might be fulfilled which was spoken by Esaias the prophet.* He spoke it in a more exalted sense. The Evangelist only alludes to those words as being capable of this lower meaning also.

Such instances are frequent in the sacred writings and are elegancies rather than imperfections. He fulfilled these words in the highest sense by bearing "our sins in his own body on the tree"; in a lower sense by sympathizing with us in our sorrows, and healing us of the diseases which were the fruit of sin.

22. *But Jesus said.* When God calls, leave the business of the world to them who are dead to God.

24. *The ship was covered.* So man's extremity is God's opportunity.

26. *Why are ye fearful?* First he composed their spirits, and then the sea.

28. *There met him two possessed with devils.* Mark and Luke mention only one, who was probably the fiercer of the two, and the person who spoke to our Lord first. But this is in no way inconsistent with the account which Matthew gives.

30. *There was . . . an herd of many swine.* Which it was not lawful for the Jews to keep. Therefore our Lord both justly and mercifully permitted them to be destroyed.

34. *They besought him that he would depart out of their coasts.* They loved their swine so much better than their souls! How many are of the same mind!

CHAPTER 9

17. *Put new wine into new bottles.* Give harsh doctrines to such as have strength to receive them.

24. *For the maid is not dead.* Her life is not at any end. But sleepeth. This is only a temporary suspension of sense and motion, which should rather be termed sleep than death.

25. *The maid arose.* Christ raised three dead persons to life—this child, the widow's son, and Lazarus; one newly departed, another on the bier, the third smelling in the grave—to show us that no degree of death is so desperate as to be past his help.

36. *As sheep having no shepherd.* They had scribes in every city. But they had none who cared for their souls; and none that were able, if they had been willing, to have "wrought any deliverance." They had no pastors after God's own heart.

38. *That he will send forth.* For it is an employ not pleasing to flesh and blood; so full of reproach, labor, danger, temptation of every kind, that nature may well be averse to it. Those who never felt this never yet knew what it is to be laborers in Christ's harvest. He sends them forth when he calls them by his Spirit, furnishes them with grace and gifts for the work, and makes a way for them to be employed therein.

CHAPTER 10

5. *These twelve Jesus sent forth.* Herein exercising his supreme authority as God over all. None but God can give men authority to preach his word.

27. *What ye hear in the ear.* Two customs of the Jews seem to be alluded to here: their doctors, or teachers, used to whisper in the ear of their disciples what they were to pronounce aloud to others; as their houses were low and flat-roofed, they sometimes preached to the people thence.

28. *Fear him which is able to destroy both soul and body in hell.* It is remarkable that our Lord commands those who love God still to fear the devil, even on this account, under this notion.

29–30. The particular providence of God is another reason for your not fearing man. For this extends to the very smallest things. And if he has such care over the most inconsiderable creatures, how much more will he take care

of you (provided you "confess him before men," before powerful enemies of the truth), and that not only in this life, but in the other also.

37. *He that loveth father or mother more than me.* He that is not ready to give up all these, when they stand in competition with his duty.

42. *One of these little ones.* The very least Christian.

CHAPTER 11

13. *Prophesied until John.* In John the old dispensation expired and the new began.

18. *John came neither eating nor drinking.* In a rigorous, austere way, like Elijah. *He hath a devil.* Is melancholy, from the influence of an evil spirit.

19. *The Son of man came eating and drinking.* Conversing in a free, familiar way.

28. *Ye that labour.* Seeking rest in God. *And are heavy laden.* With the guilt and power of sin. *And I will give you rest.* I alone (for none else can) will freely give you (what you cannot purchase) rest from the guilt of sin by justification, and from the power of sin by sanctification.

29. *Take my yoke upon you.* Believe in me; receive me as your prophet, priest, and king. *For I am meek and lowly in heart.* Meek towards all men, lowly towards God. *And ye shall find rest.* Whoever therefore does not find rest of soul is not meek and lowly. The fault is not in the yoke of Christ, but in you who have not taken it upon you. Nor is it possible for any one to be discontented but through lack of meekness or lowliness.

30. *For my yoke is easy.* Or rather, gracious, sweet, benign, delightful. *And my burden.* Contrary to those of men, is ease, liberty, and honor.

CHAPTER 12

8. *Is Lord even of the sabbath.* This certainly implies that the Sabbath was an institution of great and distinguished importance. It may perhaps also refer to that signal act of authority which Christ afterwards exerted over it, in changing it from the seventh to the first day of the week. If we suppose there is a transposition of the seventh and eighth verses, then the eighth verse is a proof of the sixth.

19. *He shall not strive, nor cry; neither shall any man hear his voice in the streets.* That is, he shall not be contentious, noisy, or ostentatious; but gentle, quiet, and lowly. We may observe that each word rises above the other, expressing a still higher degree of humility and gentleness.

20. *A bruised reed.* A convinced sinner, one that is bruised with the weight of sin. *Smoking flax.* One that has the least good desire, the faintest spark of grace.

22. *A demoniac,[3] blind and dumb.* Many undoubtedly supposed these defects to be merely natural. But the Spirit of God saw otherwise and gives the true account both of the disorder and the cure. How many other disorders, seemingly natural, may even now be owing to the same cause.

30. *He that is not with me is against me.* There are no neutrals in this war. Every one must be either with Christ or against him, either a loyal subject or a rebel. And there are none upon earth who neither promote nor obstruct his kingdom. For he that does not gather souls to God scatters them from him.

31. *The blasphemy against the Holy Ghost.* How much stir has been made about this! How many sermons, yea,

volumes, have been written concerning it! And yet there is nothing plainer in all the Bible. It is neither more nor less than ascribing those miracles to the power of the devil which Christ wrought by the power of the Holy Ghost.

37. *For by thy words* (as well as your tempers and works). Your words as well as actions shall be produced in evidence for or against you, to prove whether you were a true believer or not. And according to that evidence you will either be acquitted or condemned in the great day.

39. *An evil and adulterous generation.* Whose heart wanders from God, though they profess him to be their husband. Such adulterers are all those who love the world and all who seek the friendship of it. *The sign of the prophet Jonas.* Who was herein a type of Christ.

44. *Whence I came out.* He speaks as if he had come out of his own accord: see his pride! *He findeth it empty.* Of God, of Christ, of his Spirit. *Swept.* From love, lowliness, meekness, and all the fruits of the Spirit. *And garnished.* With levity and security, so that there is nothing to keep him out and much to invite him in.

45. *Seven other spirits.* That is, a great many; a certain number being put for an uncertain. *More wicked than himself.* Whence it appears that there are degrees of wickedness among the devils themselves. *So shall it be.* Yes, and to apostates in all ages.

49–50. See the highest severity and the highest goodness! Severity to his natural relations, goodness to his spiritual. He disclaims the former, who opposed the will of his heavenly Father, and owns the latter, who obeyed it.

---

[3] (12:22) KJV: "one possessed with a devil."

CHAPTER 13

3. *In parables.* The word here is taken in its proper sense, for apt similes or comparisons. This way of speaking, extremely common in the eastern countries, drew and fixed the attention of many and occasioned the truth delivered to sink the deeper into humble and serious hearers. At the same time, by an awful mixture of justice and mercy, it hid them from the proud and careless.

In this chapter our Lord delivers seven parables, directing the four former as being of general concern to all the people, the three latter to his disciples.

Behold, a sower. How exquisitely proper is this parable to be an introduction to all the rest! In this our Lord answers a very obvious and very important question. The same sower, Christ, and the same preachers sent by him always sow the same seed. Why has it not always the same effect?

4. *And when he sowed, some seeds fell by the way side, and the fowls came and devoured them.* It is observable that our Lord points out the grand hindrances of our bearing fruit in the same order as they occur. A vast majority of those who hear the word of God receive the seed as by the highway side. Of those who do not lose it by the birds, yet many receive it as on stony places. Many of them who receive it in a better soil yet suffer the thorns to grow up and choke it; so that few even of these endure to the end and bear fruit unto perfection. Yet in all these cases it is not the will of God that hinders, but their own voluntary perverseness.

14. *Hearing ye shall hear, and shall not understand.* That is, you will surely hear; all possible means will be given

you. Yet they will profit you nothing, because your heart is sensual, stupid, and insensible. Your spiritual senses are shut up. Yes, you have closed your eyes against the light, as being unwilling to understand the things of God; and afraid, not desirous, that he should heal you.

22. *The deceitfulness of riches.* Deceitful indeed! For they smile, and betray; kiss, and smite into hell. They put out the eyes, harden the heart, steal away all the life of God; fill the soul with pride, anger, love of the world; make men enemies to the whole cross of Christ; and all the while are eagerly desired and vehemently pursued, even by those who believe there is a God!

24. *The kingdom of heaven* (as has been observed before) sometimes signifies eternal glory; sometimes the way to it, inward religion; sometimes, as here, the gospel dispensation. So in this place it means Christ preaching the gospel, "who is like a man sowing good seed."

28. *He said unto them, An enemy hath done this.* A plain answer to the great question concerning the origin of evil. God made men, as he did angels, intelligent creatures and consequently free either to choose good or evil. But he implanted no evil in the human soul. "An enemy," with man's concurrence, "hath done this."

Darnel[4] in the church, is properly "outside Christians," such as have the form of godliness without the power. Open sinners, such as have neither the form nor the power, are not so properly darnel as thistles and brambles; these ought to be rooted up without delay and not allowed into the Christian community. Whereas should fallible men attempt to *gather* up the

---

[4] (13:28) KJV: "tares."

darnel, they would often "root up also the wheat with them."

31. *Another parable.* The former parables relate chiefly to unfruitful hearers; these that follow, to those who bear good fruit. *The kingdom of heaven.* Both the gospel dispensation and the inward kingdom.

33. *Till the whole was leavened.* Thus will the gospel leaven the world and grace the Christian.

45. *The kingdom of heaven.* That is, one who earnestly seeks for it. In the forty-seventh verse it means the gospel preached, which is like a net gathering of every kind. Just so the gospel, wherever it is preached, gathers at first both good and bad, who are for a season full of approbation and warm with good desires. But Christian discipline and strong, close exhortation begin that separation in this world which shall be accomplished by the angels of God in the world to come.

55. *The carpenter's son.* The Greek word means one that works either in wood, iron, or stone. *His brethren.* Or kinsmen. They were the sons of Mary, sister to the Virgin, and wife of Cleophas or Alpheus.

58. *He did not many mighty works there because of their unbelief.* And the reason why many mighty works are not wrought now is not that faith is everywhere planted, but that unbelief everywhere prevails.

CHAPTER 14

10–11. *And he sent, and beheaded John in the prison. And his head was . . . given to the damsel.* How mysterious is the providence which left the life of so holy a man in such infamous hands! Which permitted it to be sacrificed to the malice of an abandoned harlot, the petulance of a vain girl, and the rashness of a foolish, perhaps drunken,

prince, who made a prophet's head the reward of a dance! But we are sure the Almighty will repay his servants in another world for whatever they suffer in this.

28. *If it be thou.* It is the same as "Since it is you." The particle "if" frequently bears this meaning, both in ours and in all languages. So it means in John 13:14, 17. Peter was in no doubt, or he would not have quitted the ship.

30. *He was afraid.* Though he had been used to the sea and was a skillful swimmer. But so it frequently is. When grace begins to act, the natural courage and strength are withdrawn.

CHAPTER 15

13. *Every plant.* That is, every doctrine.

16. *Are ye also yet without understanding?* How fair and candid are the sacred historians, never concealing or excusing their own blemishes!

23. *Not a word.* He sometimes tries our faith in like manner.

24. *I am not sent.* Not primarily; not yet.

CHAPTER 16

4. *A wicked and adulterous generation.* You would seek no further sign, did not your wickedness, your love of the world, which is spiritual adultery, blind your understanding.

6. *Beware of the leaven of the Pharisees.* That is, of their false doctrine. This is elegantly so called; for it spreads in the soul or the church as leaven does in meal.

18. *Upon this rock.* Alluding to Peter's name, which signifies a rock; namely, the faith which thou hast now professed. *I will build my church.* But perhaps when our Lord uttered these words, he pointed to himself, in like manner as when he said, "Destroy this temple" (John 2:19), meaning the temple of his body. And it is certain that as he is spoken of in Scripture as the only foundation of the church, so this is that which the Apostles and Evangelists laid in their preaching. It is in respect of laying this that the names of the twelve apostles (not of Peter only) were equally inscribed on the twelve foundations of the city of God (Rev. 21:14). *Shall not prevail against it.* Not against the church universal so as to destroy it. And they never did. There has been a small remnant in all ages.

19. *I will give unto thee the keys of the kingdom of heaven.* Indeed, not to him alone (for they were equally given to all the apostles at the same time, John 20:21–23), but to him were first given the keys both of doctrine and discipline. He first, after our Lord's resurrection, exercised the apostleship (Acts 1:15); he first by preaching opened the kingdom of heaven both to the Jews (Acts 2) and to the Gentiles (Acts 10).

Under the terms of "binding" and "loosing" are contained all those acts of discipline which Peter and his brethren performed as apostles. And undoubtedly, what they thus performed on earth God confirmed in heaven.

21. *From that time forth began Jesus.* Perhaps this expression *began* always implies his entering on a set and solemn discourse. Heretofore he had mainly taught them only one point—that he was the Christ. From this time he taught them another—that Christ must through sufferings and death enter into his glory.

23. *Get thee behind me.* Out of my sight. It is not improbable Peter stepped before him to stop him. *Satan.* Our Lord is not recorded to have given so sharp a reproof to any other of his apostles on any occasion. He saw it was

needful for the pride of Peter's heart, puffed up with the commendation lately given him. Perhaps the term "Satan" may not merely mean "You are my enemy, while you think yourself most my friend." but also, "You are acting the very part of Satan, both by endeavoring to hinder the redemption of mankind and by giving me the most deadly advice that can ever spring from the pit of hell."

Thou savourest not. Does not relish or desire. We may learn from hence: (1) That whoever says to us in such a case, "Favor yourself," is acting the part of the devil. (2) That the proper answer to such an adviser is, "Get behind me." (3) That otherwise he will be "an offense" to us, an occasion of our stumbling, if not falling. (4) That this advice always proceeds from not relishing the things of God, but the things of men. So far is this advice, "Favor yourself," from being fit for a Christian either to give or take, that, if any man will come after Christ, his very first step is to deny or renounce himself; in the room of his own will to substitute the will of God as his one principle of action.

24. *Let him deny himself, and take up his cross.* Should we not consider all crosses, all things grievous to flesh and blood, as what they really are: as opportunities of embracing God's will at the expense of our own? And consequently, as so many steps by which we may advance toward perfection? We should make a swift progress in the spiritual life, if we were faithful in this practice. Crosses are so frequent that whoever makes advantage of them will soon be a great gainer. Great crosses are occasions of great improvement; and the little ones which come daily, and even hourly, make up in number what they lack in weight. We may, in these daily and hourly crosses, make effectual oblations of our will to God; which oblations, so frequently repeated, will soon mount to a great sum.

Let us remember, then (what can never be sufficiently inculcated), that God is the Author of all events, that none is so small or inconsiderable as to escape his notice and direction. Every event, therefore, declares to us the will of God; to which thus declared, we should heartily submit. We should renounce our own to embrace it; we should approve and choose what his choice warrants as best for us. Herein should we exercise ourselves continually; this should be our practice all the day long. We should in humility accept the little crosses that are dispensed to us as those that best suit our weakness. Let us bear these little things, at least for God's sake, and prefer his will to our own in matters of so small importance.

28. And, as an emblem of this, there are some here who shall live to see the Messiah coming to set up his mediatorial kingdom with great power and glory, by the increase of his church, the destruction of the temple, city, and polity of the Jews.

CHAPTER 17

2. *And was transfigured.* Or, transformed. The indwelling deity darted out its rays through the veil of his flesh, and that with such transcendent splendor that he no longer bore the form of a servant. His face shone with divine majesty, like the sun in its strength; and all his body was so irradiated by it that his clothes could not conceal its glory, but became white and glittering as the very light with which he covered himself as with a garment.

20. *If ye have faith as a grain of mustard seed.* That is, the least measure of it; but it is certain, the faith which is here spoken of does not always imply saving faith. Many have it who thereby cast out devils and yet will at last have their portion with them. It is only a supernatural persuasion given a man that God will work thus by him at that hour. Now, "though I have all" this "faith, so as to remove mountains," yet if I have not the "faith which worketh by love," I am nothing.

"To remove mountains" was a proverbial phrase among the Jews and is still retained in their writings to express a thing which is very difficult and to appearance impossible.

24. *When they were come to Capernaum.* Where our Lord now dwelt. This was the reason why they stayed until he came there to ask him for for the tribute.

27. How illustrious a degree of knowledge and power did our Lord here discover! Knowledge penetrating into this animal, though beneath the waters; and power, in directing this very fish to Peter's hook, though he himself was at a distance. How must this have encouraged both Peter and his brethren in a firm dependence on divine providence!

CHAPTER 18

3. *Except ye be converted.* The first step towards entering into the kingdom of grace is to become as little children: lowly in heart, knowing yourselves utterly ignorant and helpless, and hanging wholly on your Father who is in heaven for a supply of all your needs.

8–9. *If thy hand or thy foot offend thee.* If the most dear enjoyment, the most beloved and useful person, turn you out of or hinder you in the way. Is not this a hard saying? Yes, if you take counsel with flesh and blood.

10. *Take heed that ye despise not one of these little ones.* As if they were beneath your notice. Be careful to receive and not to offend the very weakest believer in Christ. For as inconsiderable as some of these may appear to you, the very angels of God have a peculiar charge over them.

15–17. How can we avoid giving offense to some or being offended at others; especially, suppose they are quite in the wrong; suppose they commit a known sin? Our Lord here teaches us how. He lays down a sure method of avoiding all offenses. Whoever closely observes this threefold rule will seldom offend others and never be offended himself.

18. *Whatsoever ye shall bind on earth.* By excommunication, pronounced in the spirit and power of Christ. *Whatsoever ye shall loose.* By absolution from that sentence. In the primitive church absolution meant no more than a discharge from church censure.

20. *There am I in the midst of them.* By my Spirit, to quicken their prayers, guide their counsels, and answer their petitions.

23–35. How observable is this whole account, as well as the great inference our Lord draws from it. (1) The debtor was freely and fully forgiven. (2) He willfully and grievously offended. (3) His pardon was retracted, the whole debt required, and the offender delivered to the tormentors for ever. And shall we still say, "But when we are once freely and fully forgiven, our pardon can never be retracted"? Verily, verily I say unto you, *So likewise shall my heavenly Father do also unto you, if ye from your hearts forgive not every one his brother their trespasses.*

CHAPTER 19

11. *But he said unto them.* This is not universally true; it does not hold with regard to all men, but with regard to

those only "to whom is given" this excellent gift of God. Now, this is given to three sorts of persons: to some by a natural constitution, without their choice; to others, by violence against their choice; and to others, by grace with their choice, who steadily withstand their natural inclinations that they may "wait upon God without distraction."

21. *If thou wilt be perfect.* That is, to be a real Christian. *Sell that thou hast.* He who reads the heart saw his bosom-sin was love of the world, and knew he could not be saved from this but by literally renouncing it. To him therefore he gave this particular direction, which he never designed for a general rule. For him this was necessary to salvation; to us it is not so. To sell all was an absolute duty to him; to many of us it would be an absolute sin.

26. *Jesus beheld them.* To compose their hurried spirits. Oh, what a speaking look was there! *Said unto them.* With the utmost sweetness. *With men this is impossible.* It is observable he does not retract what he had said. No, nor soften it in the least degree. But rather strengthens it by representing the salvation of a rich man as the utmost effort of omnipotence.

CHAPTER 20

15. *Is it not lawful for me to do what I will with mine own?* Yes, doubtless; to give either to Jew or Gentile a reward infinitely greater than he deserves. But can it be inferred from this that it is lawful or possible for the merciful Father of spirits to

"Consign an unborn soul to hell?
Or damn him from his mother's womb?"

16. *So the last shall be first, and the first last.* Not only with regard to the Jews and Gentiles, but in a thousand other instances. *For many be called.* All who hear the gospel. *But few chosen.* Only those who obey it.

23. *But to sit on my right hand.* Christ applies to the glories of heaven what his disciples were so stupid as to understand of the glories of earth. But he does not deny that this is his to give. It is his to give in the strictest propriety, both as God and as the Son of Man. He only asserts that he give it to none but those for whom it is originally prepared; namely, those who endure to the end in the "faith that worketh by love."

30. *Behold, two blind men . . . cried out.* Mark and Luke mention only one of them—blind Bartimaeus. He was far the more eminent of the two, and as it seems, spoke for both.

31. *The multitude rebuked them, because they should hold their peace.* And so they will all who begin to cry after the Son of David; but let those who feel their need of him cry the more, otherwise they will come short of a cure.

CHAPTER 21

9. *The multitudes . . . cried, saying.* Our Lord restrained all public tokens of honor from the people until now, lest the envy of his enemies should interrupt his preaching before the time. But this reason now ceasing, he allowed their acclamations that they might be a public testimony against their wickedness who in four or five days after cried out, "Crucify him! Crucify him!" The expressions recorded by the other Evangelists are somewhat different from these; but all of them were undoubtedly used by some or others of the multitude.

12. *Jesus . . . cast out all them that sold and bought.* He cast them out three years before (John 2:14), bidding them "not make" that "house an house of merchandise." Upon the repetition of the offense, he uses sharper words.

21. *Jesus answered and said, . . . If ye have faith.* Whence we may learn that one great end of our Lord in this miracle was to confirm and increase their faith; another was to warn them against unfruitfulness.

30. *He answered, . . . I go, sir: and went not.* Just so did the scribes and Pharisees. They professed the greatest readiness and zeal in the service of God; but it was bare profession, contradicted by all their actions.

44. *Whosoever shall fall on this stone shall be broken.* Stumbles at Christ, shall even then receive much hurt. He is said to fall on this stone who hears the gospel and does not believe. *But on whomsoever it shall fall.* In vengeance it will utterly destroy him. It will fall on every unbeliever when Christ comes in the clouds of heaven.

CHAPTER 22

5. *One to his farm, another to his merchandise.* One must mind what he has; another, gain what he wants. How many perish by misusing lawful things!

12. *A wedding garment.* The righteousness of Christ, first imputed, then implanted. It may easily be observed, this has no relation to the Lord's Supper, but to God's proceeding at the last day.

14. *Many are called, but few are chosen.* Many hear; few believe. Many are members of the visible church, but few of the invisible.

32. *I am the God of Abraham.* The argument runs thus: God is not the God of the dead, but of the living. That expression "thy God" implies both benefit from God to man, and duty from man to God. But he is the God of Abraham, Isaac, and Jacob; therefore Abraham, Isaac, and Jacob are not dead, but living. Therefore the soul does not die with the body. So indeed the Sadducees supposed, and it was on this ground that they denied the resurrection.

CHAPTER 23

3–30. From the third to the thirtieth verses is exposed everything that commonly passes in the world for religion, whereby the pretenders to it keep both themselves and others from entering into the kingdom of God; from attaining or even seeking after those tempers in which alone true Christianity consists.

As: (1) Punctuality in attending on public and private prayer (vv. 4–14). (2) Zeal to make proselytes to our opinion or communion, though they have less of the spirit of religion than before (v. 15). (3) A superstitious reverence for consecrated places or things without any for him to whom they are consecrated (vv. 16–22). (4) A scrupulous exactness in little observances, though with the neglect of justice, mercy, and faith (vv. 23–24). (5) A nice cautiousness to cleanse the outward behavior without any regard to inward purity (vv. 25–26). (6) A specious face of virtue and piety covering the deepest hypocrisy and villainy (vv. 27–28). (7) A professed veneration for all good men except those among whom they live.

8–10. The Jewish rabbis were also called "Father" and "Master" by their several disciples, whom they required (1) To believe implicitly what they affirmed without asking further reason. (2) To obey implicitly what they enjoined without seeking further authority. Our Lord therefore, by forbidding us either to give or receive the title of Rabbi, Master, or Father, forbids us either to receive any such reverence or to pay any such to any but God.

12. *Whosoever shall exalt himself shall be abased; and he that shall humble himself shall be exalted.* No one sentence of our Lord's is so often repeated as this. It occurs, with scarce any variation, at least ten times in the Evangelists.

13. *Woe unto you.* Our Lord pronounced eight blessings on the mount. He pronounces eight woes here; not as imprecations, but solemn, compassionate declarations of the misery which these stubborn sinners were bringing upon themselves.

CHAPTER 24

3. *When shall these thing be? And what shall be the sign of thy coming, and of the end of the world?* The disciples inquire confusedly concerning (1) The time of the destruction of the temple. (2) The signs of Christ's coming, and of the end of the world; as if they imagined these two were the same thing.

Our Lord answers distinctly concerning (1) The destruction of the temple and city, with the signs preceding (vv. 4ff., 15ff.). (2) His own coming and the end of the world, with the signs thereof (vv. 29–31). (3) The time of destruction of the temple (vv. 32ff.). (4) The time of the end of the world (v. 36).

4. *Take heed that no man deceive you.* The caution is more particularly designed for the succeeding Christians, whom the apostles then represented. The first sign of his coming is the rise of false prophets. But it is highly probable many of these things refer to more important events, which are yet to come.

14. *This gospel . . . shall be preached in all the world.* Not universally; this is not done yet. But in general, through the several parts of the world, and not only in Judea. And this was done by Paul and the other apostles before Jerusalem was destroyed. *And then shall the end come.* Of the city and temple.

Josephus's *History of the Jewish War* is the best commentary on this chapter. It is a wonderful instance of God's providence that he, an eyewitness and one who lived and died a Jew, should, especially in so extraordinary a manner, be preserved to transmit to us a collection of important facts which so exactly illustrate this glorious prophecy in almost every circumstance.

22. *And except those days should be shortened.* By the taking of Jerusalem sooner than expected. *No flesh be saved.* The whole nation would be destroyed. *But for the elect's sake.* That is, for the sake of the Christians.

29. *Immediately after the tribulation of those days.* Here our Lord begins to speak of his last coming. But he speaks not so much in the language of man as of God, with whom a thousand years are as one day, one moment. Many of the primitive Christians, not observing this, thought he would come "immediately," in the common sense of the word; a mistake which Paul labors to remove in his Second Epistle to the Thessalonians.

30. *Then shall appear the sign of the Son of man in heaven.* It seems, a little before he himself descends. The sun, moon, and stars being extinguished (probably not those of our system only), the sign of the Son of Man (perhaps the cross) will appear in the glory of the Lord.

34. *This generation* of men now living *shall not pass, till all these things be fulfilled.* The expression implies that a great part of that generation would be passed away, but not the whole. Just so it was; for the city and temple were destroyed thirty-nine or forty years after.

51. *And shall . . . appoint him his*

portion with the hypocrites. If ministers are the persons here primarily intended, there is a peculiar propriety in the expression. For no hypocrisy can be baser than to call ourselves ministers of Christ while we are slaves of avarice, ambition, or sensuality. Wherever such are found, may God reform them by his grace, or disarm them of that power and influence which they continually abuse to his dishonor and to their own aggravated damnation.

CHAPTER 25

3. *They that were foolish . . . took no oil with them.* No more than kept them burning just for the present; none to supply their future needs, to recruit their lamps' decay. The lamp is faith. A lamp and oil with it is faith working by love.

4. *The wise took oil in their vessels.* Love in their hearts. And they daily sought a fresh supply of spiritual strength until their faith was made perfect.

9. *The wise answered.* Beginning the sentence with a beautiful abruptness, such as showed their surprise at the state of these poor wretches, who had so long deceived them as well as their own souls. *Lest there be not enough.* It is sure there is not, for no man has more than holiness enough for himself. *Go ye rather to them that sell.* Without money and without price; that is, to God, to Christ. *And buy.* If you can. O no! The time is past and returns no more!

24. *I knew thee that thou art an hard man.* No. You know him not. He never knew God who thinks him a hard master. *Reaping where thou hast not sown.* That is, requiring more of us than you give us power to perform. So does every obstinate sinner in one kind or another lay the blame of his own sins on God.

30. *Cast ye the unprofitable servant into outer darkness.* For what? What had he done? It is true he had not done good. But neither is he charged with doing any harm. Why, for this reason, for merely doing no harm, is he consigned to outer darkness? He is pronounced wicked, because he was a slothful, unprofitable servant. So mere harmlessness, on which many build their hope of salvation, was the cause of his damnation.

31. *When the Son of man shall come in his glory, and all the holy angels with him.* With what majesty and grandeur does our Lord here speak of himself! He gives us one of the noblest instances of the true sublime. Indeed, not many descriptions in the Scriptures themselves seem to equal this. Methinks we can hardly read it without imagining ourselves before the awful tribunal it describes.

36. *In prison.* Prisoners need to be visited above all others, as they are commonly solitary and forsaken by the rest of the world.

41. *Depart . . . into everlasting fire, prepared for the devil and his angels.* Not originally for you; you are intruders into everlasting fire.

46. *And these shall go away into everlasting punishment: but the righteous into life eternal.* Either the punishment is strictly eternal or the reward is not, the very same expression being applied to the former as to the latter. The Judge will speak first to the righteous in the audience of the wicked. The wicked shall then go away into everlasting fire in the view of the righteous. Thus the damned shall see nothing of the everlasting life; but the just will see the punishment of the ungodly. It is not only particularly observable here that the punishment lasts as long as the reward, but that this punishment is so far from ceasing at the end of the world that it does not begin till then.

CHAPTER 26

11. *Ye have the poor always with you.* Such is the wise and gracious providence of God that we may have always opportunities of relieving their needs and so laying up for ourselves treasures in heaven.

24. *It had been good for that man if he had not been born.* May not the same be said of every man that finally perishes? But who can reconcile this, if it were true of Judas alone, with the doctrine of universal salvation?

37. *Began to be sorrowful and in deep anguish.*[5] Probably from feeling the arrows of the Almighty sticking fast in his soul, while God "laid on him the iniquities of us all." Who can tell what painful and dreadful sensations were then impressed on him by the immediate hand of God? The former word in the original properly signifies "to be penetrated with the most exquisite sorrow"; the latter, "to be quite depressed and almost overwhelmed with the load."

41. *The spirit.* Your spirit; you yourselves. The flesh. Your nature. How gentle a rebuke was this, and how kind an apology, especially at a time when our Lord's own mind was so weighed down with sorrow!

50. The heroic behavior of the blessed Jesus, in the whole period of his sufferings, will be observed by every attentive eye and felt by every pious heart; although the sacred historians, according to their usual but wonderful simplicity, make no elaborations upon

---

[5] (26:37) KJV: "sorrowful and very heavy."

it. With what composure does he go forth to meet the traitor, with what calmness receive that malignant kiss! With what dignity does he deliver himself into the hands of his enemies, yet plainly showing his superiority over them and even then "leading," as it were, "captivity captive"!

58. *But Peter followed him afar off.* Variously agitated by conflicting passions: love constrained him to follow his Master; fear made him follow afar off.

64. *And coming in the clouds of heaven.* As he is represented by Daniel (7:13–14). Our Lord looked very unlike that person now; but nothing could be more awful, more majestic, and more becoming than such an admonition in such circumstances.

73. *Surely thou also art one of them; for thy speech bewrayeth thee.* Malchus might have brought a stronger proof than this; but such is the overruling providence of God that the world, in the height of their zeal, commonly catch hold of the very weakest of all arguments against the children of God.

74. *Then began he to curse and to swear.* Having now quite lost the reins, the government of himself.

CHAPTER 27

9. *What was spoken by the prophet.*[6] The word "Jeremy," which was added to the text in later copies and thence received into many translations, is evidently a mistake; for he who spoke what Matthew here cites, or rather paraphrases, was not Jeremiah, but Zechariah.

22. *They all say unto him, Let him be crucified.* The punishment which Barabbas had deserved; and this probably made them think of it. But in their malice they forgot how dangerous a precedent they furnished the Roman governor. And indeed, within the compass of a few years it turned dreadfully upon themselves.

25. *His blood be on us, and on our children.* As this imprecation was dreadfully answered in the ruin so quickly brought on the Jewish nation, and the calamities which have ever since pursued that wretched people, so it was peculiarly fulfilled by Titus, the Roman general, on the Jews whom he took during the siege of Jerusalem. So many, after having been scourged in a terrible manner, were crucified all round the city, that in a while there was not room near the walls for the crosses to stand by each other. Probably this befell some of those who now joined in this cry, as it certainly did many of their children, the very finger of God thus pointing out their crime in crucifying his Son.

45. *There was darkness over all the land.* Insomuch that even a heathen philosopher, seeing it and knowing it could not be a natural eclipse, because it was the time of the full moon and continued three hours, cried out, "Either the God of nature suffers, or the frame of the world is dissolved." By this darkness God testified his abhorrence of the wickedness which was then committing. It likewise intimated of Christ's sore conflicts with the divine justice and with all the powers of darkness.

46. *About the ninth hour Jesus cried with a loud voice.* Our Lord's great agony probably continued these three whole hours, at the conclusion of which he thus cried out, while he suffered from God himself what was unutterable. *My God, my God, why hast*

---

[6](27:9) KJV: "that which was spoken by Jeremy the prophet."

thou forsaken me? Our Lord hereby at once expresses his trust in God and a most distressing sense of his letting loose the powers of darkness upon him, withdrawing the comfortable discoveries of his presence, and filling his soul with a terrible sense of the wrath due to the sins which he was bearing.

50. *When he had cried again with a loud voice.* To show that his life was still whole in him. *Yielded up the ghost.* He died by a voluntary act of his own and in a way peculiar to himself. He alone, of all men that ever were, could have continued alive, even in the greatest tortures, as long as he pleased or have retired from the body whenever he had thought fit. And how does it illustrate that love which he manifested in his death inasmuch as he did not use that power to quit his body as soon as it was fastened to the cross, leaving only an insensible corpse to the cruelty of his murderers; but continued his abode in it, with a steady resolution, as long as it was proper. He then retired from it, with a majesty and dignity not known or to be known in any other death; dying, if one may so express it, like the Prince of Life.

52–53. Some of the tombs were scattered and laid open by the earthquake; and while they continued unclosed (and must have stood open all the Sabbath, seeing the law would not allow any attempt to close them), *many bodies of the saints which slept arose.* Perhaps Simeon, Zacharias, John the Baptist, and others who had believed in

Christ and were known to many in Jerusalem. *And appeared unto many.* God hereby signifying that Christ had conquered death and would raise all his saints in due season.

CHAPTER 28

2. *The angel of the Lord . . . rolled back the stone, . . . and sat upon it.* Luke and John speak of two angels that appeared; but it seems as if only one of them had appeared sitting on the stone outside the sepulcher; and then, going into it, was seen with another angel, sitting one where the head, the other where the feet of the body had been.

6. *Come, see the place where the Lord lay.* Probably, in speaking he rose up and, going before the women into the sepulcher, said, "Come, see the place." This clearly reconciles what John relates (20:12), this being one of the two angels there mentioned.

19. *Disciple all nations.*[7] Make them my disciples. This includes the whole design of Christ's commission. Baptizing and teaching are the two great branches of that general design. And these were to be determined by the circumstances of things; which made it necessary, in baptizing adult Jews or heathens, to teach them before they were baptized. And in discipling their children, to baptize them before they were taught; as the Jewish children, in all ages, were first circumcised and afterwards taught to do all God had commanded them.

---

[7] (28:19) KJV: "teach all nations."

the gospel of mark

CHAPTER 1

4. *Preach the baptism of repentance.* That is, preaching repentance and baptizing as a sign and means of it.

12. *And immediately the Spirit driveth him into the wilderness.* So, in all the children of God, extraordinary manifestations of his favor are likely to be followed by extraordinary temptations.

13. *Was with the wild beasts.* Though they had no power over him. Mark not only gives a compendium of Matthew's Gospel, but likewise several valuable particulars which the other Evangelists have omitted.

18. *Straightway they forsook their nets, and followed him.* From this time they forsook their employ and constantly attended him. Happy are they who follow Christ at the first call!

26. *A loud noise.*[1] For he was forbidden to speak. Christ would not allow these evil spirits to speak in opposition nor yet in favor of him. He needed not their testimony nor would encourage it, lest any should infer that he acted in concert with them.

33. *And all the city was gathered together at the door.* O what a fair prospect was here! Who could then have imagined that all these blossoms would die away without fruit?

44. *See thou say nothing to any man.* But our blessed Lord gives no such charge to us. If he has made us clean from our leprosy of sin, we are not commanded to conceal it. On the contrary, it is our duty to publish it abroad, both for the honor of our benefactor and so that others who are sick of sin may be encouraged to ask and hope for the same benefit.

CHAPTER 2

6. *But there were certain of the scribes.* See whence the first offense comes! As yet not one of the plain unlettered people were offended. They all rejoiced in the light until these men of learning came to put darkness for light and light for darkness. Woe to all such blind guides! Good had it been for these if they had never been born. O God, let me never offend one of thy simple ones! Sooner let my tongue cleave to the roof of my mouth!

15. *Many publicans and sinners.* Some of them doubtless invited by Matthew, moved with compassion for his old companions in sin. But the next words,

---

[1](1:26) KJV: "a loud voice."

for there were many, and they followed him, seem to imply that the greater part, encouraged by his gracious words and the tenderness of his behavior, and impatient to hear more, stayed for no invitation, but pressed in after him and kept as close to him as they could.

27. *The sabbath was made for man.* And therefore must give way to man's necessity.

28. *Therefore the Son of man is Lord also of the sabbath.* Being the supreme Lawgiver, he has power to dispense with his own laws, and with this in particular.

CHAPTER 3

2. *They watched him, . . . that they might accuse him.* Pride, anger, and shame, after being so often put to silence, began now to ripen into malice.

5. *Had looked round about on them with anger, being grieved.* Angry at the sin, grieved at the sinner—the true standard of Christian anger. But who can separate anger at sin from anger at the sinner? None but a true believer in Christ.

12. *He straitly charged them that they should not make him known.* It was not the time; nor were they fit preachers.

13. *Calleth unto him whom he would.* With regard to the eternal states of men, God always acts as just and merciful. But with regard to numberless other things, he seems to us to act as mere Sovereign.

22. *The scribes which came down from Jerusalem.* Purposely, on the devil's errand; and not without success. For the common people now began to drink in the poison from these learned, good, honorable men! *And by the prince of the devils casteth he out devils.* How easily may a man of learning elude the strongest proof of a work of God! How readily can he account for every inci-

dent without ever taking God into the question!

34. *He looked round about on them which sat about him.* With the utmost sweetness. *And said, Behold my mother and my brethren!* In this preference of his true disciples, even to the Virgin Mary, considered merely as his mother after the flesh, he not only shows his high and tender affection for them, but seems designedly to guard against those excessive and idolatrous honors which he foresaw would in after ages be paid to her.

CHAPTER 4

12. *That seeing they may see, and not perceive.* They would not see before; now they could not, God having given them up to the blindness which they had chosen.

19. *The lusts of other things . . . choke the word.* A deep and important truth! The desire of anything, otherwise than as it leads to happiness in God, directly tends to barrenness of soul. *Entering in.* Where they were not before. Let him, therefore, who has received and retained the word see that no other desire then enter in, such as perhaps till then he never knew. *It becometh unfruitful.* After the fruit had grown almost to perfection.

24. *Take heed what ye hear.* That is, attend to what you hear, that it may have its due influence upon you. *With what measure ye mete.* That is, according to the improvement you make of what you have heard, still further assistance shall be given.

26–28. *So is the kingdom of God.* The inward kingdom is like seed which a man casts *into the ground.* This a preacher of the gospel casts into the heart. *And rise night and day.* That is, he has it continually in his thoughts. Meantime it will *spring and grow up, he* *knoweth not how.* Even he that sowed it cannot explain how it grows. For as the earth by a curious kind of mechanism, which the great philosophers cannot comprehend, brings forth *first the blade, then the ear, after that the full corn in the ear;* so the soul in an inexplicable manner brings forth first weak graces, then stronger, then full holiness. And all this of itself, like a machine whose spring of motion is within itself. Yet observe the amazing exactness of the comparison: the earth brings forth no corn, as the soul no holiness, without both the care and toil of man and the benign influence of heaven.

33. *Spake he the word unto them, as they were able to hear it.* Adapting it to the capacity of his hearers, and speaking as plain as he could without offending them. A rule never to be forgotten by those who instruct others.

39. *Peace.* Cease your tossing. *Be still.* Cease your roaring. Literally, "Be you gagged."

CHAPTER 5

2. *There met him a man . . . with an unclean spirit.* Matthew mentions two. Probably this one, so particularly spoken of here, was the most remarkably fierce and ungovernable.

37. *John the brother of James.* When Mark wrote, not long after our Lord's ascension, the memory of James, lately beheaded, was so fresh that his name was more known than that of John himself.

43. *He charged them straitly that no man should know it.* That he might avoid every appearance of vain-glory, might prevent too great a concourse of people, and might not further enrage the scribes and Pharisees against him; the time for his death and for the full manifestation of his glory being not yet come. *Commanded that something should*

be given her to eat. So that when either natural or spiritual life is restored, even by immediate miracle, all proper means are to be used in order to preserve it.

CHAPTER 6

5. *He could there do no mighty work.* Not consistently with his wisdom and goodness, it being inconsistent with his wisdom to work miracles there, where it could not promote his great end; and inconsistent with his goodness, seeing he well knew his countrymen would reject whatever evidence could be given them. And therefore to have given them more evidence would only have increased their damnation.

6. *He marvelled.* As a man. As he was God, nothing was strange to him.

13. *They . . . anointed with oil many that were sick.* Which James gives as a general direction (5:14–15), adding those peremptory words, "And the Lord shall heal him." He shall be restored to health, not by the natural efficacy of the oil, but by the supernatural blessing of God. And it seems this was the great standing means of healing desperate diseases in the Christian church, long before extreme unction was used or heard of, which bears scarce any resemblance to it. The former being used only as a means of health; the latter, only when life is despaired of.

52. *Their heart was hardened.* And yet they were not reprobates. It means only that they were slow and dull of comprehension.

CHAPTER 7

4. *Washing of cups, and pots, brasen vessels, and of tables.* The Greek word "baptism" means indifferently either washing or sprinkling. The cups, pots, and vessels were washed; the couches sprinkled.

15. *There is nothing from without a man, that entering into him can defile him.* Though it is very true a man may bring guilt, which is moral defilement, upon himself by eating what hurts his health or by excess either in meat or drink. Yet even here the pollution arises from the wickedness of the heart and is just proportionable to it. And this is all that our Lord asserts.

22. *Wickedness.* The word means ill nature, cruelty, inhumanity, and all malevolent affections. *Foolishness.* That is, directly contrary to sober thought and discourse; all kind of wild imaginations and extravagant passions.

33. *Put his fingers into his ears.* Perhaps intending to teach us that we are not to prescribe to him, as they who brought this man attempted do to, but to expect his blessing by whatever means he pleases. Even though there should be no proportion or resemblance between the means used and the benefit to be conveyed.

34. *Ephphatha.* This was a word of sovereign authority, not an address to God for power to heal. Such an address was needless, for Christ had a perpetual fund of power residing in himself to work all miracles whenever he pleased, even to the raising of the dead (John 5:21, 26).

CHAPTER 8

8. *So they did eat.* This miracle was intended to demonstrate that Christ was the true bread which comes down from heaven. For he who was almighty to create bread without means to support natural life could not lack power to create bread without means to support spiritual life. And this heavenly bread we stand so much in need of every moment that we ought to be always praying, "Lord, evermore give us this bread."

17–18. Our Lord here affirms of all the apostles (for the question is equivalent to an affirmation) that their hearts were *hardened;* that *having eyes,* they saw not; *having ears,* they heard not; that they did not *perceive,* neither *understand:* the very same expressions that occur in the thirteenth chapter of Matthew. And yet it is certain they were not judicially hardened. Therefore all these strong expressions do not necessarily import anything more than the present lack of spiritual understanding.

34. *Let him deny himself.* His own will, in all things, small and great, however pleasing, and that continually. *And take up his cross.* Embrace the will of God, however painful, daily, hourly, continually. Thus only can he *follow me* in holiness to glory.

38. *Whosoever therefore shall be ashamed of me and of my words.* That is, of avowing whatever I have said, particularly of self-denial and the daily cross, both by word and action.

CHAPTER 9

1. *Till they have seen the kingdom of God come with power.* So it began to do at the Day of Pentecost, when three thousand were converted to God at once.

4. *Elias.* Whom they expected. *Moses.* Whom they did not.

7. *There was a* bright, luminous *cloud that overshadowed them.* This seems to have been such a cloud of glory as accompanied Israel in the wilderness, which, as the Jewish writers observe, departed at the death of Moses. But it now appeared again in honor of our Lord as the Great Prophet of the church, who was prefigured by Moses. *Hear him.* Even preferably to Moses and Elijah.

15. *All the people, when they beheld him, were greatly amazed.* At his coming so suddenly, so seasonably, so unexpectedly. Perhaps also at some unusual rays of majesty and glory which yet remained on his countenance.

20. *When he saw him.* When the child saw Christ; when his deliverance was at hand. *Straightway the spirit tare him.* Made his last, grand effort to destroy him. Is it not generally so, before Satan is cast out of a soul of which he has long had possession?

23. *If thou canst believe.* As if he had said, the thing does not turn on my power, but on your faith. I can do all things; can you believe?

24. *Help thou mine unbelief.* Although my faith be so small that it might rather be termed unbelief, yet help me.

25. *Thou dumb and deaf spirit.* So termed because he made the child so. When Jesus spoke, the devil heard, though the child could not.

32. *Understood not that saying.* They did not understand how to reconcile the death of Christ (nor consequently his resurrection, which supposed his death) with their notions of his temporal kingdom.

34. *Who should be the greatest.* Prime minister in his kingdom.

35. *The same shall be last of all.* Let him abase himself the most.

37. *One of such children.* Either in years or in heart.

38. *Master, we saw one casting out devils in thy name.* Probably this was one of John the Baptist's disciples who believed in Jesus, though he did not yet associate with our Lord's disciples. *And we forbad him, because he followeth not us.* How often is the same temper found in us! How readily do we also "lust to envy"! But how does that spirit become a disciple, much more a minister, of the benevolent Jesus? Paul had learned a better temper when he rejoiced that Christ was preached even by those who

were his personal enemies. But to confine religion to them that follow us is a narrowness of spirit which we should avoid and abhor.

39. *Jesus said.* Christ here gives us a lovely example of candor and moderation. He was willing to put the best construction on doubtful cases and to treat as friends those who were not avowed enemies. Perhaps in this instance it was a means of conquering the remainder of prejudice, and perfecting what was lacking in the faith and obedience of these persons. *Forbid him not.* Neither directly nor indirectly discourage or hinder any man who brings sinners from the power of Satan to God, "because he followeth not us" in opinions, modes of worship, or anything else which does not affect the essence of religion.

40. *For he that is not against us is on our part.* Our Lord had formerly said, "He that is not with me is against me," thereby admonishing his hearers that the war between him and Satan admitted of no neutrality; and that those who were indifferent to him now would finally be treated as enemies. But here, in another view, he uses a very different proverb, directing his followers to judge men's characters in the most candid manner, and charitably to hope that those who did not oppose his cause wished well to it. Upon the whole, we are to be rigorous in judging ourselves and candid in judging each other.

43. *And if thy hand offend thee.* The discourse passes from the case of offending to that of being offended. If one who is as useful or dear to you as a hand or eye hinder or slacken you in the ways of God, renounce all conversation with him. This primarily relates to persons; secondarily, to things.

44. *Where their worm.* That gnaws the soul (pride, self-will, desire, malice, envy, shame, sorrow, despair) dieth not. No more than the soul itself. *And the fire* (either material or infinitely worse) that torments the body *is not quenched* for ever.

49. *Every one.* Who does not cut off the offending member, and conse-quently is cast into hell *shall be,* as it were, *salted with fire.* Preserved, not consumed, thereby. Whereas every acceptable *sacrifice shall be salted* with another kind of salt—that of divine grace, which purifies the soul (though frequently with pain) and preserves it from corruption.

50. Such *salt is good* indeed; highly beneficial to the world, in respect of which I have termed you "the salt of the earth." *But if the salt,* which should season others, have lost its own *saltness, wherewith will ye season it?* Beware of this: See that you retain your savor. And as a proof of it, *have peace one with another.*

More largely this obscure text might be paraphrased thus: As every burnt offering was salted with salt in order to its being cast into the fire of the altar, so every one who will not part with his hand or eye shall become a sacrifice to divine justice and be cast into hell fire; which will not consume, but preserve him from a cessation of being. On the other hand, every one who, denying himself and taking up his cross, offers up himself as a living sacrifice to God shall be seasoned with grace; which, like salt, will make him savory and preserve him from destruction for ever.

As salt is good for preserving meats and making them savory, so it is good that you be seasoned with grace, for the purifying of your hearts and lives and for spreading the savor of my knowledge, both in your own souls and wherever you go. But as salt, if it loses its saltness, is fit for nothing, so you, if you lose your faith and love, are fit for

nothing but to be utterly destroyed. See, therefore, that grace abide in you and that you no more contend who shall be greatest.

CHAPTER 10

6. *From the beginning of the creation.* Therefore Moses in the first of Genesis gives us an account of things from the beginning of the creation. Does it not clearly follow that there was no creation previous to that which Moses describes? *God made them male and female.* Therefore Adam did not at first contain both sexes in himself. God made Adam, when first created, male only; and Eve female only. And this man and woman he joined together in a state of innocence as husband and wife.

14. *Of such is the kingdom of God.* The members of the kingdom which I am come to set up in the world are such as these, as well as grown persons of a childlike temper.

15. *Whosoever shall not receive the kingdom of God as a little child.* As totally disclaiming all worthiness and fitness as if he were but a week old.

21. *Jesus beholding him.* And looking into his heart. *Loved him.* Doubtless for the dawnings of good which he saw in him. *And said unto him.* Out of tender love. *One thing thou lackest.* The love of God, without which all religion is a dead carcass. In order to obtain this, throw away what is to you the grand hindrance of it. Give up your great idol, riches.

30. *He shall receive an hundredfold, . . . houses.* Not in the same kind; for it will generally be *with persecutions.* But in value; a hundredfold more happiness than any or all of these did or could afford. But let it be observed, none is entitled to this happiness but he that will accept of it with persecutions.

32. *They were in the way going up to*

Jerusalem; and Jesus went before them: and they were amazed. At his courage and intrepidity, considering the treatment which he had himself told them he should meet with there. *And as they followed, they were afraid.* Both for him and for themselves. Nevertheless, he judged it best to prepare them by telling them more particularly what was to ensue.

38. *Ye know not what ye ask.* You know not that you are asking for sufferings, which pave the way to glory. *The cup,* of inward sufferings; *the baptism,* of outward. Our Lord was filled with sufferings within, and covered with them without.

40. *It shall be given to them for whom it is prepared.* To those "who by patient continuance in well-doing seek for glory and honor and immortality." For these only eternal life is prepared. To these only he will give it in that day, and to every man his own reward according to his own labor.

CHAPTER 11

16. *Would not suffer that any man should carry any vessel through the temple.* So strong notions had our Lord of even relative holiness; and of the regard due to those places, as well as times, that are peculiarly dedicated to God.

22. *Have faith in God.* And who could find fault if the Creator and Proprietor of all things were to destroy, by a single word of his mouth, a thousand of his inanimate creatures, were it only to imprint this important lesson more deeply on one immortal spirit?

CHAPTER 12

12. *But feared the people.* How wonderful is the providence of God, using all things for the good of his children!

Generally the multitude is restrained from tearing them in pieces only by the fear of their rulers. And here the rulers themselves are restrained through fear of the multitude!

27. *He is not the God of the dead, but the God of the living.* That is, if the argument be proposed at length: Since the character of his being the God of any persons plainly intimates a relation to them, not as dead, but as living; and since he cannot be said to be at present their God at all if they are utterly dead; nor to be the God of human persons, such as Abraham, Isaac, and Jacob, consisting of souls and bodies, if their bodies were to abide in everlasting death; so there must be a future state of blessedness, and a resurrection of the body to share with the soul in it.

28. *Which is the first commandment.* The principal and most necessary to be observed.

29. *The Lord our God is one Lord.* This is the foundation of the first commandment, yes, of all the commandments. The Lord our God, the Lord, the God of all men, is one God essentially, though three persons. From this unity of God it follows that we owe all our love to him alone.

30. *With all thy strength.* That is, the whole strength and capacity of your understanding, will, and affections.

31. *The second is like.* Of a like comprehensive nature; comprising our whole duty to our fellow creatures as the other does our whole duty to God.

33–34. *To love him with all the heart.* To love and serve him with all the united powers of the soul in their utmost vigor. *And to love his neighbour as himself.* To maintain the same equitable and charitable temper and behavior towards all men, as we in like circumstances would wish for from them towards ourselves, is a more necessary and important duty than offering the most noble and costly sacrifices.

He said unto him, Thou art not far from the kingdom of God. Reader, are not you? Then go on, be a real Christian. Else it had been better for you to have been afar off.

38. *Beware of the scribes.* There was an absolute necessity for these repeated cautions. For, considering their inveterate prejudices against Christ, it could never be supposed that the common people would receive the gospel until these incorrigible blasphemers of it were brought to just disgrace.

Yet he delayed speaking in this manner until a little before his passion, as knowing what effect it would quickly produce. Nor is this any precedent for us; we are not invested with the same authority.

43. *I say unto you, That this poor widow hath cast more in, than all they.* See what judgment is cast on the most specious outward actions by the Judge of all! And how acceptable to him is the smallest which springs from self-denying love!

CHAPTER 13

4. Two questions are here asked: the one, concerning the destruction of Jerusalem; the other, concerning the end of the world.

11. *The Holy Ghost* will help you. But do not depend on any other help, for all the nearest ties will be broken.

20. *The elect.* The Christians. *Whom he hath chosen.* That is, whom he has taken out of, or separated from, the world, "through sanctification of the Spirit, and belief of the truth."

30. *All these things.* Relating to the temple and the city.

32. *Neither the Son.* Not as man. As man he was no more omniscient than omnipresent; but as God he knows all the circumstances of it.

CHAPTER 14

10. *Judas . . . went unto the chief priests.* Immediately after this reproof, having anger now added to his covetousness.

13. *Go ye into the city, and there shall meet you a man.* It was highly seasonable for our Lord to give them this additional proof both of his knowing all things and of his influence over the minds of men.

15. *Furnished.* The word properly means "spread with carpets."

24. *This is my blood of the new testament.* That is, this I appoint to be a perpetual sign and memorial of my blood, as shed for establishing the new covenant; that all who shall believe in me may receive all its gracious promises.

33. *Sore amazed.* The original word imports the most shocking amazement mingled with grief; and that word in the next verse which we render "sorrowful" intimates that he was surrounded with sorrow on every side, breaking in upon him with such violence as was ready to separate his soul from his body.

44. *Whomsoever I shall kiss.* Probably our Lord in great condescension had used to permit (according to the Jewish custom) his disciples to do this after they had been some time absent.

51. *A certain young man.* It does not appear that he was one of Christ's disciples. Probably hearing an unusual noise, he started up out of his bed, not far from the garden, and ran out with only the sheet about him to see what was the matter. *And the young men laid hold on him.* Who was only suspected to be Christ's disciple; but could not touch them who really were so.

55. *All the council sought for witness . . . ; and found none.* What an amazing proof of the overruling providence of

God, considering both their authority and the rewards they could offer, that no two consistent witnesses could be procured to charge him with any gross crime!

58. *We heard him say.* It is observable that the words which they thus misrepresented were spoken by Christ at least three years before (John 2:19). Their going back so far to find matter for the charge was a glorious, though silent, attestation of the unexceptionable manner wherein he had behaved through the whole course of his public ministry.

CHAPTER 15

9. *Will ye that I release unto you the King of the Jews?* Which does this wretched man lack most—justice, courage, or common sense? The poor coward sacrifices justice to popular clamor and enrages those whom he seeks to appease by so unseasonably repeating that title, *the King of the Jews,* which he could not but know was so highly offensive to them.

17. *Purple.* As royal robes were usually purple and scarlet, Mark and John term this a purple robe, Matthew a scarlet one. The Tyrian purple is said not to have been very different from scarlet.

34. *My God, my God, why hast thou forsaken me?* Thereby claiming God as his God; and yet lamenting his Father's withdrawing the tokens of his love and treating him as an enemy while he bore our sins.

43. *Honourable.* A man of character and reputation. *Counsellor.* A member of the Sanhedrin. *Which also waited for the kingdom of God.* Who expected to see it set up on earth.

CHAPTER 16

2. *At the rising of the sun.* They set out "while it was yet dark" and came within sight of the sepulcher for the first time just as it grew light enough to discern that the stone was rolled away (Matt. 28:1; Luke 24:1; John 20:1). But by the time Mary had called Peter and John and they had viewed the sepulcher, the sun was rising.

7. *Peter.* Though he so often denied his Lord. What amazing goodness was this!

15. *Go ye into all the world, and preach the gospel to every creature.* Our Lord speaks without any limitation or restriction. If, therefore, every creature in every age has not heard it, either those who should have preached or those who should have heard it, or both, make void the counsel of God.

17. *Shall follow.* The word and faith must go before. *In my name.* By my authority committed to them. Raising the dead is not mentioned. So our Lord performed even more than he promised.

18. *If they drink any deadly thing.* But not by their own choice. God never calls us to try any such experiments.

20. *Preached every where.* At the time Mark wrote, the apostles had already gone into all the known world (Rom. 10:18). And each of them was there known where he preached. The name of Christ only was known throughout the world.

the Gospel of luke

CHAPTER 1

6. *Walking in all* the moral and ceremonial ordinances *blameless.* How admirable a character! May our behavior be thus unblamable, and our obedience thus sincere and universal!

12. *Zacharias . . . was troubled.* Although he was accustomed to conversing with God, yet we see he was thrown into a great consternation at the appearance of his angelic messenger, nature not being able to sustain the sight. Is it not then an instance of the goodness as well as the wisdom of God that the services which these heavenly spirits render us are generally invisible?

13. *Thy prayer is heard.* Let us observe with pleasure that the prayers of pious worshippers come up with acceptance before God; to whom no costly perfume is so sweet as the fragrance of an upright heart. An answer of peace was here returned, when the case seemed to be most helpless. Let us wait patiently for the Lord and leave to his own wisdom the time and manner wherein he will appear for us.

19. *I am Gabriel, that stand in the presence of God.* Seven angels thus stand before God (Rev. 8:2) who seem the highest of all. There seems to be a remarkable gradation in the words, enhancing the guilt of Zacharias' unbelief. As if he had said, "I am Gabriel, a holy angel of God"; yes, one of the highest order. Not only so, but am now peculiarly sent from God; and that with a message to you in particular. Nay, and to show you glad tidings, such as ought to be received with the greatest joy and readiness.

28. *Hail, thou that art highly favoured, the Lord is with thee: blessed art thou among women.* "Hail" is the salutation used by our Lord to the women after his resurrection. "Thou art highly favoured," or "hast found favour with God" (v. 30), is no more than was said of Noah, Moses, and David. "The Lord is with thee" was said to Gideon (Judg. 6:12); and "Blessed shall she be above women," of Jael (Judg. 5:24). This salutation gives no room for any pretense of paying adoration to the Virgin, as having no appearance of a prayer or of worship offered to her.

35. *The Holy Ghost shall come upon thee, and the power of the Highest shall overshadow thee.* The power of God was put forth by the Holy Ghost as the immediate divine agent in this work; and so he exerted the power of the Highest as his own power who, together with the Father and the Son, is the Most High God. *Therefore also.* Not only as he is God from eternity, but on this account likewise, he *shall be called the Son of God.*

38. *And Mary said, Behold the handmaid of the Lord.* It is not improbable that this time of the Virgin's humble faith, consent, and expectation might be the very time of her conceiving.

47—48. *My spirit hath rejoiced in God my Saviour.* She seems to turn her thoughts here to Christ himself, who was to be born of her, as the angel had told her, "He should be the Son of the Highest, whose name should be Jesus, the Savior." And she rejoiced in hope of salvation through faith in him, which is a blessing common to all true believers, more than in being his mother after the flesh, which was an honor peculiar to her. And certainly she had the same reason to rejoice in God her Savior that we have. Because he had *regarded the low estate of his handmaiden.* In like manner has he regarded our low estate; and vouchsafed to come and save her and us when we were reduced to the lowest estate of sin and misery.

55. *To his seed.* His spiritual seed; all true believers.

74. *Might serve him without fear.* Without any slavish fear. Here is the substance of the great promise, that we shall be always holy, always happy; that being delivered from Satan and sin, from every uneasy and unholy temper, we shall joyfully love and serve God in every thought, word, and work.

77. *To give knowledge of salvation . . . by the remission of their sins.* The knowledge of the remission of our sins being the grand instrument of present and eternal salvation (Heb. 8:11–12). But the immediate sense of the words seems to be to preach to them the gospel doctrine of salvation by the remission of their sins.

CHAPTER 2

14. *Glory to God in the highest, and on earth peace, good will toward men.* The shouts of the multitude are generally broken into short sentences. This rejoicing acclamation strongly represents the piety and benevolence of these heavenly spirits; as if they had said, "Glory be to God in the highest heavens; let all the angelic legions resound his praises. For with the Redeemer's birth, peace and all kinds of happiness have come down to dwell on earth; yes, the overflowings of divine goodwill and favor are now exercised toward men."

38. *To all them that looked for redemption.* The scepter now appeared to be departing from Judah, though it was not actually gone; Daniel's weeks were plainly near their period; and the revival of the spirit of prophecy, together with the memorable occurrences relating to the birth of John the Baptist and of Jesus, could not but encourage and quicken the expectation of pious persons at this time.

Let the example of these aged saints animate those whose hoary heads, like theirs, are "a crown of glory," being "found in the way of righteousness." Let those venerable lips, so soon to be silent in the grave, be now employed in the praises of their Redeemer. Let them labor to leave those behind to whom Christ will be as precious as he has been to them; and who will be waiting for God's salvation when they are gone to enjoy it.

40. *And the child grew.* In bodily strength and stature. *And waxed strong in spirit.* The powers of his human mind daily improved. *Filled with wisdom.* By the light of the indwelling Spirit, which gradually opened itself in his soul. And the grace of God was upon him. That is, the peculiar favor of God rested upon him even as man.

43. *The child Jesus.* Luke describes in order Jesus "the fruit of the womb" (1:42); "an infant" (2:12); "a little

child" (2:40); "a child" here; and afterwards "a man." So our Lord passed
through and sanctified every stage of
human life. Old age only did not
become him.

49. *How is it that ye sought me?* He
does not blame them for losing him,
but for thinking it needful to seek him.
He intimates that he could not be lost
nor found anywhere but doing the will
of a higher Parent.

52. *Jesus increased in wisdom.* As to
his human nature. *And in favour with
God.* In proportion to that increase. It
plainly follows that though a man were
pure, even as Christ was pure, still he
would have room to increase in holiness and, in consequence, to increase in
the favor as well as in the love of God.¹

CHAPTER 3

8. *Not to say within yourselves, We
have Abraham to our father.* That is,
trust not in your being members of the
visible church nor in any external privileges whatsoever; for God now requires
a change of heart, and that without
delay.

11. *He answereth.* It is not properly
John, but the Holy Ghost who teaches
us in the following answers how to
come ourselves and how to instruct
other penitent sinners to come to
Christ, that he may give them rest. The
sum of all is, "Cease to do evil, learn to
do well." These are the "fruits worthy
of repentance" (v. 8).

21. *Jesus . . . praying, the heaven was
opened.* It is observable that the three
voices from heaven (see Luke 9:29, 35;
John 12:28) by which the Father bore
witness to Christ were pronounced
either while he was praying, or quickly
after it.

23. *And Jesus himself began to be.*
John's beginning was computed by the
years of princes; our Savior's, by the
years of his own life, as a more august
era. *About thirty years of age.* He did not
now enter upon his thirtieth year, as
the common translation would induce
one to think, but he now entered on his
public ministry, being of such an age as
the Mosaic law required. Our great
master attained not, as it seems, to the
conclusion of his thirty-fourth year. Yet
what glorious achievements did he
accomplish within those narrow limits
of time! Happy that servant who with
any proportional zeal dispatches the
great business of life; and so much the
more happy, if his sun go down at
noon! For the space that is taken from
the labors of time shall be added to the
rewards of eternity.

38. *Adam, which was the son of God.*
That is, whatever the sons of Adam
receive from their human parents,
Adam received immediately from God,
except sin and misery.

CHAPTER 4

6. *To whomsoever I will give it.* Not so,
Satan. It is God, not you, that puts
down one and sets up another; although sometimes Satan, by God's
permission, may occasion great revolu-
tions in the world.

14. *Jesus returned in the power of the
Spirit.* Being more abundantly strengthened after his conflict.

15. *Glorified of all.* So God usually
gives strong cordials¹ after strong
temptations. But neither their approbation continued long, nor the outward
calm which he now enjoyed.

18. *He hath anointed me.* With the
Spirit. He has, by the power of his

---

¹(4:15) An invigorating or exhilarating stimulant.

Spirit which dwells in me, set me apart for these offices. *To preach the gospel to the poor.* Literally and spiritually.

How is the doctrine of the ever-blessed Trinity interwoven even in those Scriptures where one would least expect it! How clear a declaration of the great Three-One is in those very words, *The Spirit of the Lord is upon me.*

22. *The gracious words which proceeded out of his mouth.* A person of spiritual discernment may find in all the discourses of Christ a peculiar sweetness, gravity, and becomingness such as is not to be found in the same degree, not even in those of the apostles.

23. *Ye will surely say.* That is, your approbation now outweighs your prejudices. But it will not be for long. You will soon ask why my love does not begin at home? Why I do not work miracles here, rather than at Capernaum? It is because of your unbelief. Nor is it any new thing for me to be despised in my own country. So were both Elijah and Elisha, and thereby driven to work miracles among heathens rather than in Israel.

24. *No prophet is accepted in his own country.* That is, in his own neighborhood. It generally holds that a teacher sent from God is not so acceptable to his neighbors as he is to strangers. The meekness of his family or lowness of his circumstances bring his office into contempt. Nor can they accept that he who was formerly equal with or below themselves would now bear a superior character.

28. *And all they in the synagogue . . . were filled with wrath.* Perceiving the purport of his discourse; namely, that the blessing which they despised would be offered to and accepted by the Gentiles. So changeable are the hearts of wicked men! So little are their starts of love to be depended on! So unable are they to bear the close application

even of a discourse which they most admire!

30. *Passing through the midst of them.* Perhaps invisibly. Or perhaps they were overawed so that, though they saw, they could not touch him.

34. *What have we to do with thee?* Your present business is with men, not with devils. *I know thee who thou art.* But surely he did not know a little before that he was "God over all, blessed for ever," or he would not have dared to tell him, "All this power is delivered to me, and I give it to whomever I will." *The Holy One of God.* Either this confession was extorted from him by terror (for the "devils believe and tremble"), or he made it with a design to cast suspicion on the character of Christ. Possibly it was from this that the Pharisees took occasion to say, "He casteth out devils by the prince of the devils."

CHAPTER 5

11. *They forsook all, and followed him.* They had followed him before (John 1:43), but not so as to forsake all. Until now they worked at their ordinary calling.

17. *Sitting by.* As being more honorable than the bulk of the congregation, who stood. *And the power of the Lord was present to heal them.* To heal the sickness of their souls as well as all bodily diseases.

36. *He spake also a parable unto them.* Taken from clothes and wine; therefore peculiarly proper at a feast.

39. *No man also having drunk old wine.* And besides, men are not likely to be immediately free from old prejudices.

CHAPTER 6

2. *Why do ye?* Matthew and Mark represent the Pharisees as proposing the question to our Lord himself. It was afterwards, probably, that they proposed it to his disciples.

9. *To save life, or to destroy it?* He just then, probably, saw the design to kill him rising in their hearts.

20. In the following verses our Lord, in the audience of his newly chosen disciples and of the multitude, repeats, standing on the plain, many remarkable passages of the sermon he had before delivered sitting on the mount.

He here again pronounces the poor and the hungry, the mourners and the persecuted, happy; and represents as miserable those who are rich and full and joyous and applauded; because generally, prosperity is a sweet poison and affliction a healing, though bitter, medicine. Let the thought reconcile us to adversity and awaken our caution when the world smiles upon us; when a plentiful table is spread before us and our cup is running over; when our spirits are high and we hear (what nature loves) our own praise from men. *Happy*[2] *are ye poor.* The word seems here to be taken literally: you who have left all for me.

24. *Miserable are you that are rich!*[3] If you have received or sought your consolation or happiness therein.

26. *Woe unto you, when all men shall speak well of you!* But who will believe this?

30. *Give to every man.* Friend or enemy, what you can spare and he really needs. *And of him that taketh away thy goods.* By borrowing, if he be insolvent, *ask them not again.*

32. It is greatly observable, our Lord has so little regard for one of the highest instances of natural virtue, namely, the returning love for love, that he does not account it even to deserve

thanks. *For sinners also,* says he, do the same thing; men who do not regard God at all. Therefore he may do this who has not taken one step in Christianity.

38. *With the same measure that ye mete withal it shall be measured to you again.* Amazing goodness! So we are permitted even to carve for ourselves! We ourselves are, as it were, to tell God how much mercy he shall show us! And can we be content with less than the very largest measure? Give, then, to man what you desire to receive from God.

39. *He spake a parable.* Our Lord sometimes used parables when he knew plain and open declarations would too much inflame the passions of his hearers. It is for this reason that he uses this parable. *Can the blind lead the blind?* Can the scribes teach this way which they know not themselves? Will not they and their scholars perish together? Can they make their disciples any better than themselves? But as for those who will be my disciples, "they shall be all taught of God," who will enable them to "come to the measure of the stature of the fullness of" their Master. Be not like their disciples, censuring others and not amending yourselves.

CHAPTER 7

22. *To the poor the gospel is preached.* Which is the greatest mercy and the greatest miracle of all.

24. *When the messengers of John were departed.* He did not speak the following things in the hearing of John's disciples, lest he should seem to flatter John or to compliment him into an adherence to his former testimony. To avoid all suspicion of this kind, he

---

[2](6:20) KJV: "Blessed."
[3](6:24) KJV: "Woe unto you that are rich!"

deferred his commendation of him till the messengers were gone. Then he delivered it to the people to prevent all imaginations, as if John were wavering in his judgment and had sent the two disciples for his own rather than their satisfaction.

32. *They are like unto children sitting in the marketplace.* So froward and perverse that no contrivance can be found to please them. It is plain, our Lord means that they were like the children complained of, not like those that made the complaint.

35. *But wisdom is justified of all her children.* The children of wisdom are those who are truly wise—wise unto salvation. The wisdom of God in all these dispensations, in all these various methods of calling sinners to repentance, is owned and heartily approved by all these.

36. *And one of the Pharisees desired him that he would eat with him.* Let the candor with which our Lord accepted this invitation, and his gentleness and prudence at this ensnaring entertainment, teach us to mingle the wisdom of the serpent with the innocence and sweetness of the dove. Let us neither absolutely refuse all favors, nor resent all neglects, from those whose friendship is at best very doubtful and their intimacy by no means safe.

40. *And Jesus answering said unto him, Simon, I have somewhat to say unto thee.* So tender and courteous an address does our Lord use even to a proud, censorious Pharisee!

42. *Which of them will love him most?* Neither of them will love him at all before he has forgiven them. An insolvent debtor, until he is forgiven, does not love, but flees his creditor.

47. *Her sins, which are many, are forgiven; for she loved much.* The fruit of her having had much forgiven. It should be carefully observed here that

her love is mentioned as the effect and evidence, not the cause, of her pardon. She knew that much had been forgiven her; and therefore she loved much.

50. *Thy faith hath saved thee.* Not thy love. Love is salvation.

CHAPTER 8

17. *For nothing is secret.* Strive not to conceal it at all; for you can conceal nothing long.

18. The word *seemeth,* wherever it occurs, does not weaken, but greatly strengthens the sense.

29. *For oftentimes it had caught him.* Therefore our compassionate Savior made the more haste to cast him out.

52. *She is not dead, but sleepeth.* Her soul is not separated finally from the body; and this short separation is rather to be called sleep than death.

CHAPTER 9

23. *Let him deny himself, and take up his cross.* The necessity of this duty has been shown in many places. The extent of it is specified here *daily.* Therefore that day is lost wherein no cross is taken up.

32. *They saw his glory.* The very same expression in which it is described by John (1:14) and by Peter (II Peter 1:16).

44. *Let these sayings sink down into your ears.* That is, consider them deeply. In joy remember the cross. So wisely does our Lord balance praise with sufferings.

46. *And there arose a reasoning among them.* This kind of reasoning always arose at the most improper times that could be imagined.

55. *Ye know not what manner of spirit.* It is not a spirit of wrath and vengeance, but of peace and gentleness and love.

CHAPTER 10

2. *Pray ye therefore the Lord of the harvest, that he would send forth labourers.* For God alone can do this; he alone can qualify and commission men for this work.

4. *Salute no man by the way.* The salutations usual among the Jews took up much time. But these had so much work to do in so short a space that they had not a moment to spare.

18. *I beheld Satan.* That is, when you went forth, I saw the kingdom of Satan, which was highly exalted, swiftly and suddenly cast down.

20. *Rejoice not* so much *that the spirits are subject unto you* as that *your names are written in heaven.* Reader, so is yours, if you are a true believer. God grant it may never be blotted out!

21. *Lord of heaven and earth.* In both of which thy kingdom stands and that of Satan is destroyed. *That thou hast hid these things.* He rejoiced not in the destruction of the wise and prudent, but in the display of the riches of God's grace to others, in such a manner as reserves to him the entire glory of our salvation and hides pride from man.

27. *Thou shalt love the Lord thy God.* That is, you shall unite all the faculties of your soul to render him the most intelligent and sincere, the most affectionate and resolute service. We may safely rest in this general sense of these important words if we are not able to fix the particular meaning of every single word. If we desire to do this, perhaps *the heart,* which is a general expression, may be explained by the three following. *With all thy soul,* with the warmest affection; *with all thy strength,* the most vigorous efforts of your will; and *with all thy mind,* or understanding; in the most wise and reasonable manner you can, your understanding guiding your will and affections.

28. *Thou hast answered right: this do, and thou shalt live.* Here is no irony, but a deep and weighty truth. He, and he alone, shall live for ever who thus loves God and his neighbor in the present life.

31. The common translation is *by chance,* which is full of gross improprieties. For if we speak strictly, there is no such thing in the universe as either chance or fortune. *There came down a certain priest that way: and . . . passed by on the other side.* And both he and the Levite, no doubt, could find an excuse for passing over on the other side and might perhaps gravely thank God for their own deliverance while they left their brother bleeding to death. Is it not an emblem of many living characters, perhaps of some who bear the sacred office? O house of Levi and of Aaron, is not the day coming when the virtues of heathens and Samaritans will rise up in the judgment against you?

33. *But a certain Samaritan . . . came where he was.* It was admirably well judged to represent the distress on the side of the Jew and the mercy on that of the Samaritan. For the case being thus proposed, self-interest would make the very scribe sensible how amiable such a conduct was and would lay him open to our Lord's inference. Had it been put the other way, prejudice might more easily have interposed before the heart could have been affected.

34. *Pouring in oil and wine.* Which, when well beaten together, are one of the best balsams that can be applied to a fresh wound.

37. *And he said, He that shewed mercy on him.* He could not for shame say otherwise, though he thereby condemned himself and overthrew his own false notion of the neighbor to whom our love is due. *Go, and do thou likewise.* Let us go and do likewise, regarding every man as our neighbor who needs our assistance. Let us renounce that bigotry and party zeal which would contract our hearts into an insensibility for all the human race except for a small number whose sentiments and practices are so much our own that our love to them is but self-love reflected. With an honest openness of mind, let us always remember the kindred between man and man; and cultivate that happy instinct whereby, in the original constitution of our nature, God has strongly bound us to each other.

40. *Martha was cumbered.* The Greek word properly signifies "to be drawn different ways at the same time" and admirably expresses the situation of a mind surrounded (as Martha's then was) with so many objects of care that it hardly knows which to attend to first.

41. *Martha, Martha.* There is a peculiar spirit and tenderness in the repetition of the word. *Thou art careful* inwardly and hurried outwardly.

42. *Mary hath chosen that good part.* To save her soul. Reader, have you?

CHAPTER 11

1. *Lord, teach us to pray, as John also taught his disciples.* The Jewish masters used to give their followers some short form of prayer as a peculiar badge of their relation to them. This it is probable John the Baptist had done. And in this sense it seems to be that the disciples now asked Jesus to teach them to pray. Accordingly he here repeats that form which he had before given them in the Sermon on the Mount, and likewise enlarges on the same heading, though still speaking the same things in substance. And this prayer, uttered from the heart and in its true and full meaning, is indeed the badge of a real Christian; for is not he such whose first and most ardent desire is the glory of God and the happiness of man by the coming of his kingdom? And who asks for no more of this world than his daily bread, longing meantime for the bread that came down from heaven; whose only desires for himself are forgiveness of sins (as he heartily forgives others) and sanctification?

2. *When ye pray, say.* And what he said to them is undoubtedly said to us also. We are therefore here directed not only to imitate this in all our prayers, but to use this very form of prayer.

4. *Forgive us our sins; for we also forgive.* Not once, but continually. This does not denote the meritorious cause of our pardon, but the removal of that hindrance which otherwise would render it impossible.

5. *At midnight.* The most unseasonable time. But no time is unseasonable with God, either for hearing or answering prayer.

13. *How much more shall your heavenly Father.* How beautiful is the gradation—a friend, a father, God! *Give the Holy Spirit.* The best of gifts, and that which includes every good gift.

26. *The last state of that man is worse than the first.* Whoever reads the sad account Josephus gives of the temper and conduct of the Jews after the ascension of Christ and before their final destruction by the Romans must acknowledge that no emblem could have been more proper to describe them. Their characters were the vilest that can be conceived, and they pressed on to their own ruin as if they had been possessed by legions of devils and wrought up to the last degree of madness. But this also is fulfilled in all who totally and finally apostatize from true faith.

27. *Blessed is the womb that bare thee, and the paps which thou hast sucked.* How natural was the thought for a woman! And how gently does our Lord reprove her!

28. *Yea rather, blessed are they that hear the word of God, and keep it.* For if even she that bare him had not done this, she would have forfeited all her blessedness.

29. *They seek.* The original word implies "seeking more," or over and above what one has already.

32. *They repented at the preaching of Jonas.* But it was only for a season. Afterwards they relapsed into wickedness until, after about forty years, they were destroyed. It is remarkable that in this also the comparison held. God reprieved the Jews for about forty years; but they still advanced in wickedness until, having filled up their measure, they were destroyed with an utter destruction.

33. The meaning is "God gives you this gospel light that you may repent." Let your eye be singly fixed on him, aim only at pleasing God. And while you do this, your whole soul will be full of wisdom, holiness, and happiness.

34. *When thine eye is evil.* When you aim at anything else, you will be full of folly, sin, and misery.

36. *If thy whole body therefore be full of light.* If you are filled with holy wisdom. *Having no part dark.* Giving way to no sin or folly. Then that heavenly principle will, like the clear flame of a lamp in a room that was dark before, shed its light into all thy powers and faculties.

41. *Give what is in them.* The vessels which you clean. *In alms; and, behold, all things are clean unto you.*[4] As if he had said, by acts directly contrary to wickedness show that your hearts are cleansed and these outward washings are needless.

44. *For ye are.* Probably in speaking

this our Lord fixed his eyes on the scribes. *As graves which appear not.* Being overgrown with grass so that men *are not aware,* until they stumble upon them and either hurt themselves or at least are defiled by touching them. On another occasion Christ compared them to "whited sepulchres," fair without, but foul within (Matt. 23:27).

48. *They indeed killed them, and ye build their sepulchres.* Just like them, pretending great reverence for the ancient prophets, while you destroy those whom God sends to yourselves. You therefore *bear witness* by this deep hypocrisy that you are of the very same spirit with them.

49. *I will send them prophets.* Chiefly under the Old Testament. *And apostles.* Under the New.

51. And so it was, within forty years, in a most astonishing manner, by the dreadful destruction of the temple, the city, and the whole nation.

52. *Ye have taken away the key of knowledge.* You have obscured and destroyed the true knowledge of the Messiah, which is the key of both the present and the future kingdom of heaven; the kingdom of grace and of glory. *Ye entered not in.* Into the present kingdom of heaven.

CHAPTER 12

4. *And I say unto you, . . . Be not afraid.* Let not the fear of man make you act the hypocrite or conceal anything which I have commissioned you to publish.

5. *Fear him, which . . . hath power to cast into hell.* Even to his peculiar "friends" Christ gives this direction. Therefore the fearing of God as having

---

[4] (11:41) Thus the translation Wesley uses renders this verse: "But give what is in them in alms; and, behold, all things are clean to you." KJV: "But rather give alms of such things as ye have; and, behold, all things are clean unto you."

power to cast into hell is to be pressed even on true believers.

10. *And whosoever.* As if he had said, "Yet the denying me in some degree may, upon true repentance, be forgiven; but if it rise so high as that of the blasphemy against the Holy Ghost, it shall never be forgiven, neither is there place for repentance."

14. *Who made me a judge.* In worldly things. His kingdom is not of this world.

17. *What shall I do.* The very language of want. Do? Why, lay up treasure in heaven.

20. *Thou fool.* To think of satisfying your soul with earthly goods! To depend on living many years! Yes, one day! The messengers of death, commissioned by God, require *thy soul* of thee!

21. *Rich toward God.* Namely, in faith and love and good works.

32. *It is your Father's good pleasure to give you the kingdom.* How much more, food and raiment? And since you have such an inheritance, regard not your earthly possessions.

33. *Sell that ye have.* This is a direction not given to all the multitude (much less is it a standing rule for all Christians), neither to the apostles; for they had nothing to sell, having left all before. But this applies to his other disciples (v. 22; Acts 1:15). Especially to the seventy, that they might be free from all worldly entanglements.

37. *Will come and serve them.* The meaning is, he will show them his love in the most condescending and tender manner.

42. *Who then is that faithful and wise steward.* Our Lord's answer manifestly implies that he had spoken this parable primarily (though not wholly) to the ministers of his word.

43. *Blessed is that servant.* God himself pronounces him wise, faithful, and happy. Yet we see he might fall from all and perish for ever.

46. *The lord . . . will appoint him his portion.* His everlasting portion. *With the unfaithful.*[5] As faithful as he was once, God himself being the Judge!

49. *I am come to send fire.* To spread the fire of heavenly love over all the earth.

50. *But I have a baptism to be baptized with.* I must suffer first, before I can set up my kingdom. And how I long to fight my way through it all!

58. *When thou goest.* As if he had said, "And you have not a moment to lose." For the executioners of God's vengeance are at hand; and when he has once delivered you over to them, you are undone for ever.

CHAPTER 13

3. *Ye shall all likewise perish.* All you of Galilee and of Jerusalem shall perish in the very same manner. So the Greek word implies. And so they did. There was a remarkable resemblance between the fate of these Galileans and of the main body of the Jewish nation, the flower of which was slain at Jerusalem by the Roman sword while they were assembled at one of their great festivals. And many thousands of them perished in the temple itself and were literally buried under its ruins.

6. *A certain man had a fig tree.* Either we may understand God the Father by him that had the vineyard, and Christ by him that kept it; or Christ himself is he that has it, and his ministers they that keep it.

7. *Three years.* Christ was then in the third year of his ministry. But it may

---

[5] (12:46) KJV: "with the unbelievers."

mean only several years; a certain number being put for an uncertain.

11. *Bowed together, and could in no wise lift up herself.* The evil spirit which possessed her afflicted her in this manner. To many, doubtless, it appeared a natural distemper. Would not a modern physician have termed it a nervous case?

15. *Thou hypocrite.* For the real motive of his speaking was envy and not, as he pretended, pure zeal for the glory of God.

24. *Strive to enter in.* Agonize. Strive as in an agony. So the word signifies. Otherwise, none shall enter in. Merely seeking will not avail.

25. And even agonizing will not avail after the door is shut. Agonize therefore by faith, prayer, holiness, patience. *And ye begin to stand without.* Until then they had not thought of it. O how new will that sense of their misery be! How late, how lasting! *I know you not whence ye are.* That is, I approve not of your ways.

30. *There are last.* Many of the Gentiles, who were latest called, shall be most highly rewarded; and many of the Jews, who were first called, shall have no reward at all.

32. *And he said unto them, Go ye, and tell that fox.* With great propriety so called for his subtlety and cowardice. The meaning of our Lord's answer is, "Notwithstanding all that he can do, I shall, for the short time I have left, do the works of him that sent me. When that time is fulfilled, I shall be offered up. Yet not here, but in the bloody city." *Behold, I cast out devils.* With what majesty does he speak to his enemies! With what tenderness to his friends! *The third day I shall be perfected.* On the third day he left Galilee and set out for Jerusalem, to die there.

But let us carefully distinguish between those things wherein Christ is our pattern and those things which were peculiar to his office. His extraordinary office justified him in using that severity of language when speaking of wicked princes and corrupt teachers, to which we have no call; and by which we should only bring scandal on religion, and ruin on ourselves, while we irritated rather than convinced or reformed those whom we so indecently rebuked.

35. *Your house is left unto you desolate.* Is now irrevocably consigned to desolation and destruction. *And verily I say unto you,* after a very short space, *Ye shall not see me, until the time come* when, taught by your calamities, you shall be ready and disposed to say, *Blessed is he that cometh in the name of the Lord.* It does not imply that they should then see Jesus at all; but only that they would earnestly wish for the Messiah, and in their extremity be ready to entertain any who should assume that character.

CHAPTER 14

2. *There was a certain man before him.* It does not appear that he had come with any insidious design. Probably he came hoping for a cure; or perhaps was one of the family.

3. *And Jesus answering spake.* Answering the thoughts which he saw rising in their hearts.

12. *Call not thy friends.* That is, I do not bid you to call thy friends or thy neighbors. Our Savior leaves these offices of humanity and courtesy as they were and teaches a higher duty. But is it not implied herein that we should be sparing in entertaining those that need it not, in order to assist those that do need with all that is saved from those needless entertainments?

18–20. *They all with one consent began to make excuse.* One of them pleads only his own will, *I go;* another, a pretended necessity, *I must needs go;* the third, impossibility, *I cannot come.* All of them lack the holy hatred mentioned in verse 26. All of them perish by things in themselves lawful. *I must needs go.* The most urgent worldly affairs frequently fall out just at the time when God makes the freest offers of salvation.

21. *Came, and shewed his lord these things.* So ministers ought to lay before the Lord in prayer the obedience or disobedience of their hearers.

23. *Compel them to come in.* With all the violence of love and the force of God's Word. Such compulsion, and such only, in matters of religion was used by Christ and his apostles.

28. *For which of you, intending to build a tower.* That is, Whoever of you intends to follow me, let him first seriously weigh these things.

31. *Another king.* Does this mean the prince of this world? Certainly he has greater numbers on his side. How numerous are his children and servants!

33. *Whosoever he be of you that forsaketh not all that he hath.* (1) By withdrawing his affections from all the creatures. (2) By enjoying them only in and for God, only in such a measure and manner as leads to him. (3) By hating them all, in the sense above mentioned. *Cannot be my disciple.* But will surely desist from building that tower; neither can he persevere in fighting the good fight of faith.

34. *Salt.* Every Christian; but more eminently every minister.

CHAPTER 15

3. *He spake.* Three parables of the same import. The sheep, the piece of silver, and the lost son all declare, contrary to the Pharisees and scribes, in what manner God receives sinners.

4. *And go after.* In recovering a lost soul, God, as it were, labors. May we not learn that to let them alone who are in sin is both unchristian and inhuman?

7. *Joy shall be.* Solemn and festal joy, *in heaven.* First in our blessed Lord himself, and then among the angels and spirits of just men, perhaps informed by God himself or by the angels who ministered to them. *Over one sinner.* One gross, open, notorious sinner. *That repenteth.* That is thoroughly changed in heart and life. *Ninety and nine just persons.* Comparatively just, outwardly blameless. *Which need no* [such] *repentance.* For they need not, cannot repent of the sins which they never committed.

The sum is, as a father peculiarly rejoices when an extravagant child, supposed to be utterly lost, comes to a thorough sense of his duty; or as any other person who has recovered what he had given up for gone, has a more sensible satisfaction in it than in several other things equally valuable, but not in such danger; so do the angels in heaven peculiarly rejoice in the conversion of the most abandoned sinners. Yea, and God himself so readily forgives and receives them that he may be represented as having part in the joy.

12. *Give me the portion of goods that falleth to me.* See the root of all sin—a desire of disposing of ourselves; of independency on God!

13. *Took his journey into a far country.* Far from God. God was not in all his thoughts. *And there wasted his substance.* All the grace he had received.

14. *He began to be in want.* All his worldly pleasures failing, he grew conscious of his lack of real good.

15. *And joined himself to a citizen of that country.* Either the devil or one of his children, the genuine citizens of that country which is far from God. *He sent him . . . to feed swine.* He employed him in the base drudgery of sin.

16. *He would fain have filled his belly with the husks.* He would fain have satisfied himself with worldly comforts. Vain, fruitless endeavor!

17. *And when he came to himself.* For until then he was beside himself, as all men are, as long as they are without God in the world.

18. *I will arise and go to my father.* How accurately are the first steps of true repentance here pointed out!

20. *And he arose, and came to his father.* The moment he had resolved, he began to execute his resolution. *When he was yet a great way off, his father saw him.* Returning, starved, naked.

22. *But the father said.* Interrupting him, before he had finished what he intended to say. So does God frequently cut an earnest confession short by a display of his pardoning love.

23. *Let us eat, and be merry.* Both here and wherever else this word occurs, whether in the Old or New Testament, it implies nothing of levity, but a solid, serious, religious, heartfelt joy. Indeed, this was the ordinary meaning of the word two hundred years ago, when our translation was made.

25. *His elder son* seems to represent the Pharisees and scribes, mentioned in verse 2.

28. *He was angry, and would not go in.* How natural to us is this kind of resentment!

29. *Yet thou never gavest me a kid, that I might make merry with my friends.* Perhaps God does not usually give much joy to those who never felt the sorrows of repentance.

31. *Thou art ever with me, and all that I have is thine.* This suggests a strong reason against murmuring at the indulgence shown to the greatest of sinners. As the father's receiving the younger son did not cause him to disinherit the elder, so God's receiving notorious sinners will be no loss to those who have always served him. Neither will he raise these to a state of glory equal to that of those who have always served him if they have, on the whole, made a greater progress in inward as well as outward holiness.

32. *This thy brother was dead, and is alive.* A thousand of these delicate touches in the inspired writings escape an inattentive reader. In the thirtieth verse the elder son had unkindly and indecently said, "This thy son." The father in his reply mildly reproves him and tenderly says, *This thy brother.* Amazing intimation, that the best of men ought to account the worst sinners their brethren still; and should especially remember this relation when they show any inclination to return.

Our Lord in this whole parable shows not only that the Jews had no cause to murmur at the reception of the Gentiles (a point which did not at that time so directly fall under consideration), but that if the Pharisees were indeed as good as they fancied themselves to be, still they had no reason to murmur at the kind treatment of any sincere penitent. Thus does he condemn them on their own principles and so leaves them without excuse.

We have in this parable a lively emblem of the condition and behavior of sinners in their natural state. Thus, when enriched by the bounty of the great common Father, do they ungratefully run from him (v. 12). Sensual pleasures are eagerly pursued until they have squandered away all the grace of God (v. 13). And while these continue, not a serious thought of God can find a place in their minds. And even when afflictions come upon them (v. 14), still they will make hard shifts before they will let the grace of God, concurring with his providence, persuade them to think of a return (vv. 15–16).

When they see themselves naked, indigent, and undone, then they recover the exercise of their reason (v. 17). Then they remember the blessings they have thrown away and attend to the misery they have incurred. And hereupon they resolve to return to the Father and put the resolution immediately in practice (vv. 18–19). Behold with wonder and pleasure the gracious reception they find from divine, injured goodness! When such a prodigal comes to his Father, the Father sees him afar off (v. 20). He pities, meets, embraces him; and interrupts his acknowledgments with the tokens of his returning favor (v. 21). He arrays him with the robe of a Redeemer's righteousness, with inward and outward holiness, adorns him with all his sanctifying graces, and honors him with the tokens of adopting love (v. 22). This he does with unutterable delight in that he who was lost is now found (vv. 23–24).

Let no elder brother murmur at this indulgence, but rather welcome the prodigal back into the family. And let those who have been thus received wander no more, but emulate the strictest piety of those who for many years have served their heavenly Father and not transgressed his commandments.

CHAPTER 16

8. *And the lord commended the unjust steward.* Namely, in this respect, because he had used timely precaution. So that though the dishonesty of such a servant be detestable, yet his foresight, care, and contrivance about the interests of this life deserve our imitation with regard to the more important affairs of another. *The children of this world.* Those who seek no other portion than this world. *Wiser.* Not absolutely, for they are, one and all, flagrant fools.

But they are more consistent with themselves. They are truer to their principles. They more steadily pursue their end. They are wiser *in their generation.* That is, in their own way. *Than the children of light.* The children of God, whose light shines on their hearts.

12. *If ye have not been faithful in that which is another man's.* None of these temporal things are yours; you are only stewards of them, not proprietors. God is the Proprietor of all; he lodges them in your hands for a season, but still they are his property. Rich men, understand and consider this. If your steward uses any part of your estate (so called in the language of men) any further or any otherwise than you direct, he is a knave; he has neither conscience nor honor. Neither have you either one or the other if you use any part of that estate—which is in truth God's, not yours—any otherwise than he directs. *That which is your own.* Heaven; which, when you have it, will be your own for ever.

13. And you cannot be faithful to God if you trim between God and the world, if you do not serve him alone.

15. *Said unto them, Ye are they which justify yourselves before men.* The sense of the whole passage is, That pride wherewith you justify yourselves feeds covetousness, derides the gospel (v. 14), and destroys the law (v. 18); all which is illustrated by a terrible example.

22. *The beggar.* Worn out with hunger and pain and need of all things, *died, and was carried by the angels* (amazing change of the scene!) *into Abraham's bosom.* So the Jews styled paradise, the place where the souls of good men remain from death to the resurrection. *The rich man also died, and was buried.* Doubtless with pomp enough, though we do not read of his lying in state; that stupid, senseless pageantry, that shocking insult on a poor, putrefying carcass, was reserved for our enlightened age!

23. *He . . . seeth Abraham afar off.* And yet knew him at that distance. And shall not Abraham's children, when they are together in paradise, know each other?

24. *Father Abraham, have mercy on me.* It cannot be denied that here is one precedent in Scripture of praying to departed saints. But who is it that prays, and with what success? Will any who considers this be fond of copying after him?

25. *But Abraham said, Son.* According to the flesh. Is it not worthy of observation that Abraham will not revile even a damned soul? Shall living men revile one another? *Thou in thy lifetime receivedst thy good things.* You chose and accepted worldly things as *thy good,* your happiness. And can any be at a loss to know why he was in torments? This damnable idolatry, had there been nothing more, was enough to sink him to the nethermost hell.

26. *Besides all this, . . . there is a great gulf fixed.* Reader, to which side of it will you go?

31. *Neither will they be persuaded* truly to repent; for this implies an entire change of heart. But a thousand apparitions cannot effect this. God only can, applying his word.

CHAPTER 17

1. *It is impossible but that offences will come.* And they ever did, and do, come chiefly by Pharisees; that is, men who trust in themselves that they are righteous, and despise others.

2. *Little ones.* Weak believers.

4. *If he trespass against thee seven times in a day, and seven times in a day turn again to thee, saying, I repent.* That is, if he gives sufficient proof that he does

really repent, after having sinned ever so often, receive him just as if he had never sinned against you. But this forgiveness is due only to real penitents. In a lower sense we are to forgive all, penitent or impenitent (so as to bear them the sincerest good will, and to do them all the good we can); and that not seven times only, but seventy times seven.

6. *And the Lord said, If ye had faith as a grain of mustard seed.* If you had the least measure of true faith, no instance of duty would be too hard for you.

10. *When ye shall have done all, . . . say, We are unprofitable servants.* For a man cannot profit God. Happy is he who judges himself an unprofitable servant; miserable is he whom God pronounces such. But though we are unprofitable to him, our serving him is not unprofitable to us; for he is pleased to give by his grace a value to our good works which, in consequence of his promise, entitles us to an eternal reward.

21. *For, behold, the kingdom of God is within* [or among] *you.* Look not for it in distant times or remote places. It is now in the midst of you; it is come. It is present in the soul of every true believer. It is a spiritual kingdom, an internal principle. Wherever it exists, it exists in the heart.

23. *They shall say to you, See here; or, see there.* Limiting his presence to this or that place.

33. The sense of this and the following verses is, Yet as great as the danger will be, do not seek to save your life by violating your conscience; if you do, you will surely lose it. Whereas if you should lose it for my sake, you shall be paid with life everlasting. But the most probable way of preserving it now is to be always ready to give it up. A peculiar providence shall then watch over you, and put a difference between you and other men.

CHAPTER 18

1. *He spake a parable unto them.* This and the following parable warn us against two fatal extremes with regard to prayer: the former against faintness and weariness, the latter against self-confidence.

12. *I fast twice in the week.* So did all the strict Pharisees, every Monday and Thursday. *I give tithes of all that I possess.* Many of them gave one full tenth of their income in tithes and another tenth in alms. The sum of this plea is, "I do no harm; I use all the means of grace; I do all the good I can."

34. *They understood none of these things.* The literal meaning they could not but understand. But as they could not reconcile this to their preconceived opinion of the Messiah, they were utterly at a loss in what parabolical or figurative sense to take what he said concerning his sufferings, having their thoughts still taken up with the temporal kingdom.

CHAPTER 19

1. *And he was rich.* These words seem to refer to the discourse in the last chapter (vv. 24–27). Zacchaeus is a proof that it is possible, by the power of God, for even a rich man to enter into the kingdom of heaven.

4. *Ran before.* With great earnestness. *Climbed.* Notwithstanding his quality; desire conquering honor and shame.

5. *Jesus . . . said unto him, Zacchaeus, make haste, and come down.* What a strange mixture of passions must Zacchaeus have now felt, hearing one speak as knowing both his name and his heart!

37. *The whole multitude . . . began to rejoice and praise God.* Speaking at once, as it seems, from a divine impulse, words which most of them did not understand.

38. *Peace in heaven.* God being reconciled to man.

40. *If these should hold their peace, the stones which lie before you would cry out.* That is, God would raise up some still more unlikely instruments to declare his praise. For the power of God will not return empty.

CHAPTER 20

9. *A long time.* It was a long time from the entrance of the Israelites into Canaan to the birth of Christ.

17. *He beheld them.* To sharpen their attention.

20. *Just men.* Men of tender conscience.

38. *He is not a God of the dead,* or "There is no God of the dead." That is, the term "God" implies such a relation as cannot possibly subsist between him and the dead, who, in the Sadducees' sense, are extinguished spirits who could neither worship him nor receive good from him. *For all live unto him.* All who have him for their God live to and enjoy him. And the consequence is apparently just. For as all the faithful are the children of Abraham, and the divine promise of being "a God to him and to his seed" is entailed upon them, it implies their continued existence and happiness in a future state as much as Abraham's. And as the body is an essential part of man, it implies both his resurrection, and theirs; and so overthrows the entire scheme of the Sadducean doctrine.

CHAPTER 21

1. *Looked up.* From those on whom his eyes were fixed before (20:17).

11. *Fearful sights and great signs.* Of which Josephus gives a circumstantial account.

18. *Not an hair of your head.* A

proverbial expression. *Perish*. Without the special providence of God. And then not before the time, nor without a full reward.

19. *In your patience possess ye your souls.* Be calm and serene, masters of yourselves, and superior to all irrational and disquieting passions. By keeping the government of your spirits, you will both avoid much misery and guard the better against all dangers.

22. *All things which are written.* Particularly in Daniel.

31. *The kingdom of God is nigh.* The destruction of the Jewish city, temple, and religion to make way for the advancement of my kingdom.

32. *Till all be fulfilled.* All that has been spoken of the destruction of Jerusalem, to which the question (v. 7), relates; and which is treated from the eighth to the twenty-fourth verses.

34. *Take heed . . . , lest at any time your hearts be overcharged with surfeiting,*[6] *and drunkenness.* And was there need to warn the apostles themselves against such sins as these? Then surely there is need to warn even strong Christians against the very grossest sins. Neither are we wise if we think ourselves out of the reach of any sin.

38. *And all the people came early in the morning . . . to hear him.* How much happier were his disciples in these early lectures than the slumbers of the morning could have made them on their beds! Let us not scruple to deny ourselves the indulgence of unnecessary sleep, that we may morning after morning place ourselves at his feet, receiving the instructions of his word and seeking those of his Spirit.

CHAPTER 22

3. *Then entered Satan.* Who is never lacking to assist those whose heart is bent upon mischief.

15. *With desire I have desired.* That is, I have earnestly desired it. He desired it, both for the sake of his disciples, to whom he desires to manifest himself further at this solemn parting; and for the sake of his whole church, that he might institute the grand memorial of his death.

16. *I will not any more eat thereof.* That is, it will be the last I shall eat with you before I die. *The kingdom of God* did not properly commence until his resurrection. Then was fulfilled what was typified by the Passover.

19. *This is my body.* As he had just now celebrated the paschal supper, which was called the Passover, so in the like figurative language he calls this bread his body. And this circumstance of itself was sufficient to prevent any mistake, as if this bread was his real body any more than the paschal lamb was really the Passover.

20. *This cup is the new testament.* Here is an undeniable figure, whereby the cup is put for the wine in the cup. And this is called *the new testament in my blood,* which could not possibly mean that it was the new testament itself, but only the seal of it and the sign of that blood which was shed to confirm it.

21. *The hand of him that betrayeth me is with me on the table.* It is evident that Christ spoke these words before he instituted the Lord's Supper; for all the other gospels mention the sop, "immediately after receiving which he went out" (John 13:30). (Nor did Judas return anymore until he came into the

---

[6](21:34) Gluttony.

garden to betray his Master.) Now this could not be dipped or given except while the meat was on the table. But this was all removed before the bread and cup were brought.

24. *There was also a strife among them.* It is highly probable this was the same dispute which is mentioned by Matthew and Mark; and consequently, though it is related here, it happened some time before.

28. *Ye . . . have continued with me in my temptations.* And all his life was nothing else, particularly from his entering on his public ministry.

30. *That ye may eat and drink at my table.* That you may enjoy the highest happiness, as guests, not as servants. These expressions seem to be primarily applicable to the twelve apostles and secondarily to all Christ's servants and disciples; whose spiritual powers, honors, and delights are here represented in figurative terms with respect to their advancement both in the kingdom of grace and of glory.

31. *Satan hath desired to have you.* My apostles. *That he may sift you as wheat.* Try you to the uttermost.

32. *But I have prayed for thee.* Who will be in the greatest danger of all. *That thy faith fail not* altogether. *And when thou art returned.*[7] From your flight. *Strengthen thy brethren.* All that are weak in faith, perhaps scandalized at your fall.

38. *Here are two swords.* Many of Galilee carried them when they traveled, to defend themselves against robbers and assassins, who much infested their roads. But did the apostles need to seek such defense? *And he said unto them, It is enough.* I did not mean literally that every one of you must have a sword.

44. *And being in an agony.* Probably just now grappling with the powers of darkness; feeling the weight of the wrath of God, and at the same time surrounded with a mighty host of devils, who exercised all their force and malice to persecute and distract his wounded spirit. *Prayed more earnestly.* Even with stronger cries and tears. *And his sweat.* As cold as the weather was. *Was as it were great drops of blood.* Which, by the vehement distress of his soul, were forced out of the pores in so great a quantity as afterwards united in large, thick, grumous drops and even fell to the ground.

58. *Another* [man] *saw him, and said.* Observe here, in order to reconcile the four Gospels, that several persons concurred in charging Peter with belonging to Christ. (1) The maid that let him in, afterwards seeing him at the fire, first put the question to him and then positively affirmed that he was with Christ. (2) Another maid accused him to the bystanders and gave occasion to the man here mentioned to renew the charge against him, which caused the second denial. (3) Others of the company took notice of his being a Galilean and were seconded by the kinsman of Malchus, who affirmed he had seen him in the garden. And this drew on the third denial.

64. *And when they had blindfolded him, they struck him on the face.* This is placed by Matthew and Mark after the council's condemning him. Probably he was abused in the same manner both before and after his condemnation.

70. *Then said they all, art thou then the Son of God?* Both these, "the Son of God" and "the Son of Man," were known titles of the Messiah; the one taken from his divine, and the other from his human nature.

---

[7] (22:32) KJV: "converted."

CHAPTER 23

16. *I will therefore chastise him.* Here Pilate began to give ground, which only encouraged them to press on.

22. *He said unto them the third time, Why, what evil hath he done?* As Peter, a disciple of Christ, dishonored him by denying him three times, so Pilate, a heathen, honored Christ by three times owning him to be innocent.

31. *If they do these things in a green tree, what shall be done in the dry?* Our Lord makes use of a proverbial expression, frequent among the Jews, who compare a good man to a green tree and a bad man to a dead one. It is as if he had said, If an innocent person suffer thus, what will become of the wicked? What of those who are as ready for destruction as dry wood for the fire?

34. *Then said Jesus.* Our Lord passed most of the time on the cross in silence. Yet seven sentences which he spoke are recorded in the four Gospels, though no one Evangelist has recorded them all. Hence it appears that the four Gospels are as it were four parts which, joined together, make one symphony; sometimes two or three, sometimes all, sound together. *Father.* So he speaks both in the beginning and at the end of his sufferings on the cross. *Forgive them.* How striking is this passage! While they are actually nailing him to the cross, he seems to feel the injury they did to their own souls more than the wounds they gave him; and, as it were, to forget his own anguish out of a concern for their own salvation.

And how eminently was his prayer heard! It procured forgiveness for all that were penitent, and a suspension of vengeance even for the impenitent.

39. *And one of the malefactors . . . railed on him.* Matthew says, "The robbers"; Mark, "They that were cru-cified with him reviled him." Either, therefore, Matthew and Mark put the plural for the singular, as the best authors sometimes do, or both reviled him at the first until one of them felt "the overwhelming power of saving grace."

40. *The other . . . rebuked him.* What a surprising degree was here of repentance, faith, and other graces! And what abundance of good works in his public confession of his sin, reproof of his fellow criminal, his honorable testimony to Christ, and profession of faith in him, while he was in such a disgraceful circumstance, a stumbling even to his disciples! This shows the power of divine grace. But it encourages none to put off their repentance to the last hour; since, as far as appears, this was the first time this criminal had an opportunity of knowing anything of Christ. And his conversion was designed to put a peculiar glory on the Savior in his lowest state, while his enemies derided him and his own disciples either denied or forsook him.

42. *Remember me when thou comest.* From heaven. *Into thy kingdom.* He acknowledged him a king, and such a king as, after he is dead, can profit the dead. The apostles themselves had not then so clear conceptions of the kingdom of Christ.

43. *In paradise.* The place where the souls of the righteous remain from death until the resurrection. As if he had said, "I will not only remember you then, but this very day."

46. *Father, into thy hands.* The Father receives the spirit of Jesus; Jesus himself receives the spirits of the faithful.

CHAPTER 24

4. *Behold, two.* Angels in the form of *men.* Mary had seen them a little before. They had disappeared on these women's coming to the sepulcher, but now appeared again. Matthew and Mark mention only one of them, appearing like a young man.

6–7. *Remember how he spake unto you, . . . Saying, The Son of man must be delivered.* This is only a repetition of the words which our Lord had spoken to them before his Passion. But it is observable, he never styles himself "the Son of Man" after his resurrection.

25. *O foolish.*[8] Not understanding the designs and works of God. *And slow of heart.* Unready to believe what the prophets have so largely spoken.

28. *He made as though he would have gone further.* Walking forward, as if he was going on. And he would have done it, had they not pressed him to stay.

30. *He took bread, and blessed it, and brake.* Just in the same manner as when he instituted his last supper.

31. *Their eyes were opened.* That is, the supernatural cloud was removed.

32. *Did not our heart.* Did not we feel an unusual warmth of love?

34. *The Lord . . . hath appeared to Simon.* Before he was seen of the twelve apostles (I Cor. 15:5). He had, in his wonderful condescension and grace, taken an opportunity on the former part of that day—though where or in what manner is not recorded—to show himself to Peter, that he might early relieve his distresses and fears on account of having so shamefully denied his Master.

---

[8](24:25) KJV: "O fools."

36. *Jesus himself stood in the midst of them.* It was just as easy to his divine power to open a door undiscernibly as it was to come in at a door opened by some other hand.

41. *While they yet believed not for joy.* They did in some sense believe; otherwise they would not have rejoiced. But their excess of joy prevented a clear, rational belief.

45. *Then opened he their understanding, that they might understand the scriptures.* He had explained them before to the two as they went to Emmaus. But still they understood them not until he took off the veil from their hearts by the illumination of his Spirit.

47. *Beginning at Jerusalem.* This was appointed both graciously and wisely: graciously, as it encouraged the greatest sinners to repent when they saw that even the murderers of Christ were not excepted from mercy; and wisely, as hereby Christianity was more abundantly attested, the facts being published first on the very spot where they happened.

51. *And while he blessed them, he was parted from them.* It was much more proper that our Lord should ascend into heaven than that he should rise from the dead in the sight of the apostles. For his resurrection was proved when they saw him alive after his Passion; but they could not see him in heaven while they continued on earth.

the Gospel of John

CHAPTER 1

1. *In the beginning.* Referring to Genesis 1:1 and Proverbs 8:23, when all things began to be made by the Word. In the beginning of heaven and earth and this whole frame of created beings, *the Word* existed without any beginning. He *was* when all things began to be, whatsoever had a beginning. *The Word.* So termed in Psalm 33:6 and frequently by the Septuagint and in the Chaldee Paraphrase, so that John did not borrow this expression from Philo or any heathen writer. He was not yet named "Jesus" or "Christ."

And the Word was with God. Therefore distinct from God the Father. The word rendered "with" denotes a perpetual tendency, as it were, of the Son to the Father in unity of essence. He was with God alone; because nothing beside God had then any being.

And the Word was God. Supreme, eternal, independent. There was no creature in respect of which he could be considered God in a relative sense. Therefore he is considered so in the absolute sense. The Godhead of the Messiah being clearly revealed in the Old Testament (Jer. 23:6; Hos. 1:7; Ps. 23:1), the other Evangelists aim at this to prove that Jesus, a true man, was the Messiah. But when at length some

from hence began to doubt of his Godhead, then John expressly asserted it and wrote in this book, as it were a supplement to the Gospels, as in the Revelation, to the prophets.

3. *All things* besides God were made; and all things which were made, were made by the Word. In the first and second verses is described the state of things before the Creation; in the Creation, verse 3; in the time of man's innocence, verse 4; in the time of man's corruption, verse 5.

4. *In him was life.* He was the foundation of life to every living thing, as well as of being to all that is. *And the life was the light of men.* He who is essential life and the giver of life to all that lives was also the light of men, the fountain of wisdom, holiness, and happiness to man in his original state.

9. *Which lighteth every man.* By what is vulgarly termed "natural conscience," pointing out at least the general lines of good and evil. And this light, if man did not hinder, would shine more and more to the perfect day.

10. *In.* Even from the creation.

11. *He came.* In the fullness of time. *Unto his own.* Country, city, temple.

12. *That believe on his name.* That is, on him. The moment they believe, they are sons; and because they are sons,

God "sendeth forth the Spirit of His Son into their hearts, crying, Abba, Father."

14. The whole verse might be paraphrased thus: "And in order to raise us to this dignity and happiness, the eternal *Word*, by a most amazing condescension, *was made flesh*, united himself to our miserable nature with all its innocent infirmities. He did not make us a transient visit, but tabernacled *among us* on earth, displaying his glory in a more eminent manner than ever of old in the tabernacle of Moses. *And we*, who are now recording these things, *beheld his glory* with so strict an attention that we can testify it was in every respect such a glory as became *the only begotten of the Father.* For it shone forth not only in his transfiguration and in his continual miracles, but in all his tempers, ministrations, and conduct through the whole series of his life. In all he appeared *full of grace and truth.* He was in himself most benevolent and upright; made those ample discoveries of pardon to sinners which the Mosaic dispensation could not do; and really exhibited the most substantial blessing; whereas that was but "a shadow of good things to come."

17. *The law.* Working wrath and containing shadows. *Was given.* No philosopher, poet, or orator ever chose his words so accurately as John. The law, said he, *was given by Moses;* grace was *by Jesus Christ.* Observe the reason for placing each word thus: *The law* of Moses was not his own; the *grace* of Christ was. His grace was opposite to the wrath, his *truth* to the shadowy ceremonies of the law. *Jesus.* John, having once mentioned the Incarnation (v. 14), no more uses that name "the Word" in all his book.

18. *No man hath seen God.* With bodily eyes; yet believers see him with the eye of faith.

23. *I am the voice.* As if he had said, "Far from being Christ, or even Elijah, I am nothing but a voice; a sound that, so soon as it has expressed the thought of which it is the sign, dies into air and is known no more."

29. *John seeth Jesus coming, . . . and saith, Behold the Lamb.* Innocent; to be offered up; prophesied of by Isaiah (53:7); typified by the paschal lamb and by the daily sacrifice.

31. *I knew him not.* Until he came to be baptized. How surprising is this, considering how nearly they were related and how remarkable the conception and birth of both had been! But there was a peculiar providence visible in our Savior's living from his infancy to his baptism at Nazareth; and John living the life of a hermit in the deserts of Judea (Luke 1:80), ninety or more miles from Nazareth. Hereby that acquaintance was prevented which might have made John's testimony of Christ suspect.

46. *Can there any good thing come out of Nazareth?* How cautiously should we guard against such popular prejudices! When these men had once possessed so honest a heart as even that of Nathanael, they led him to suspect the blessed Jesus himself for an impostor, because he had been brought up at Nazareth. But his integrity prevailed over that foolish bias and laid him open to the force of evidence, which a candid inquirer will always be glad to admit even when it brings the most unexpected discoveries.

48. *Under the fig tree, I saw thee.* Perhaps at prayer.

49. *Nathanael answered.* Happy are they that are ready to believe, swift to receive the truth and grace of God.

51. *Hereafter ye shall see.* All of these, as well as you, who believe on me now in my state of humiliation shall hereafter see me come in my glory, and all the angels of God with me. This seems the most natural sense of the words, though they may also refer to his ascension.

CHAPTER 2

2. *Jesus was called, and his disciples, to the marriage.* Christ does not take away human society, but sanctifies it. Water might have quenched thirst; yet our Lord allows wine, especially at a festival gathering. Such was his facility in drawing his disciples at first, who were afterwards to pass through rougher ways.

4. *Jesus saith unto her, Woman.* So our Lord speaks also in John 19:26. It is probable this was the constant appellation which he used for her. Jesus regarded his Father above all, not knowing even his mother "after the flesh." *What have I to do with thee?* A mild reproof of her inordinate concern and untimely interposal. *Mine hour is not yet come.* The time of my working this miracle, or of my going away.

May we not learn that if his mother was rebuked for attempting to direct him in the days of his flesh, how absurd it is to address her as if she had a right to command him on the throne of his glory? Likewise, how indecent it is for us to direct his supreme wisdom as to the time or manner in which he shall appear for us in any of the exigencies of life?

15. *When he had made a scourge of rushes,*[1] which were strewn on the ground, *he drove them all out of the temple* (that is, the court of it), both *the sheep and the oxen.* Though it does not appear that he struck even them and much less any of the men. But a terror from God, it is evident, fell upon them.

19. *This temple.* Doubtless pointing, while he spoke, to his body, the temple and habitation of the Godhead.

24. *Jesus did not trust*[2] *himself unto them.* Let us learn not rashly to put ourselves into the power of others. Let us study a wise and happy medium between universal suspiciousness and that easiness which would make us the property of every pretender to kindness and respect.

CHAPTER 3

3. *Jesus answered.* That knowledge will not avail you, unless you *be born again.* Otherwise you cannot *see*—that is, experience and enjoy—either the inward or the glorious *kingdom of God.*

In this solemn discourse our Lord shows that no external profession, no ceremonial ordinances, or privileges of birth can entitle any to the blessings of the Messiah's kingdom. An entire change of heart as well as of life is necessary for that purpose. This can only be accomplished in man by the almighty power of God. He shows that every man born into the world is by nature in a state of sin, condemnation, and misery, and that the free mercy of God had been given his Son to deliver them from it and to raise them to a blessed immortality. And that all mankind, Gentiles as well as Jews, might share in these benefits, procured by his being lifted up on the cross, and might be received by faith in him. But if they rejected him, their eternal, aggravated condemnation would be the certain consequence.

Except a man be born again. If our Lord by being "born again" means only reformation of life instead of making any new discovery, he has only thrown

---

[1] (2:15) KJV: "a scourge of small cords."
[2] (2:24) KJV: "commit."

a great deal of obscurity on what was before plain and obvious.

5. *Except a man be born of water and of the Spirit.* Except he experience that great inward change by the Spirit and be baptized (wherever baptism can be had) as the outward sign and the means of it.

7. *Ye must be born again.* To be born again is to be inwardly changed from all sinfulness to all holiness. It is fitly so called, because as great a change then passes on the soul as passes on the body when it is born into the world.

12. *Heavenly things.* Such as the eternity of the Son and the unity of the Father, Son, and Spirit.

13. *Hath ascended up to heaven, but he that came down from heaven, . . . which is in heaven.* Therefore he is omnipresent; else he could not be in heaven and on earth at once. This is a plain instance of what is usually termed the communication of properties between the divine and human nature, whereby what is proper to the divine nature is spoken concerning the human, and what is proper to the human is, as here, spoken of the divine.

14–15. *That whosoever.* He must be *lifted up* that hereby he may purchase salvation for all believers. All those who look to him by faith recovering spiritual health, even as all that looked at that serpent recovered bodily health.

16. This was the very design of God's love in sending him into the world. *Whosoever believeth in him.* With that faith which "worketh by love," and "hold fast the beginning of his confidence steadfast to the end." *God so loved the world.* That is, all men under heaven, even those that despise his love and will for that cause finally perish. Otherwise, not to believe would be no

sin to them. For what should they believe? Ought they to believe that Christ was given for them? Then he was given for them. *He gave his only begotten Son.* The Son of God gave himself (Gal. 1:4) truly and seriously.

30. *He must increase, but I must decrease.* So they who are now, like John, "burning and shining lights" must, if not suddenly eclipsed, like him gradually decrease while others are increasing about them. As they, in their turns, grew up amid the decays of the former generation. Let us know how to set as well as how to rise. And let it comfort our declining days to retrace, in those who are likely to succeed us in our work, the openings of yet greater usefulness.

32. *No man.* None comparatively; exceeding few. *Receiveth his testimony.* With true faith.

36. *He that believeth on the Son hath everlasting life.* He has it already. For he loves God; and love is the essence of heaven. *He that obeyeth[3] not.* A consequence of not believing.

CHAPTER 4

7. *Give me to drink.* In this one conversation he brought her to that knowledge which the apostles were so long in attaining.

10. *If thou knewest the gift.* The living water. *And who it is.* He who alone is able to give it. *Thou wouldest have asked of him.* On those words the stress lies. *Water.* In like manner he draws the allegory from bread (John 6:27) and from light (John 8:12); the first, the most simple, necessary, common, and salutary things in nature. *Living water.* The Spirit and its fruits. But she might the more easily mistake his meaning,

---

[3] (3:36) KJV: "believeth."

because "living water" was a common phrase among the Jews for spring water.

14. *Shall never thirst.* Will never (provided he continue to drink thereof) be miserable, dissatisfied, without refreshment. If ever that thirst returns, it will be the fault of the man, not the water. *But the water that I shall give him.* The Spirit of faith working by love. *Shall be in him.* An inward, living principle. *A fountain.*[4] Not merely a well, which is soon exhausted. *Springing up into everlasting life.* Which is a confluence, or rather an ocean, of streams arising from this fountain.

16. *Jesus saith unto her.* He now clears the way that he might give her a better kind of water than she asked for. *Go, call thy husband.* He strikes directly at her deepest sin.

17. *Thou hast well said.* We may observe in all our Lord's discourse the utmost weightiness and yet the utmost courtesy.

18. *Thou hast had five husbands.* Whether they were all dead or not, her own conscience, now awakened, would tell her.

19. *Sir, I perceive.* So soon was her heart touched.

21. *Believe me.* Our Lord uses this expression in this manner but once, and that to a Samaritan. To his own people, the Jews, his usual language is, "I say unto you."

22. *Salvation is of the Jews.* So spoke all the prophets that the Savior should arise out of the Jewish nation; and that from there the knowledge of him should spread to all nations under heaven.

24. *God is a Spirit.* Not only remote from body and all the properties of it, but likewise full of all spiritual perfec-

tions, power, wisdom, love, holiness. And our worship should be suitable to his nature. We should worship him with the truly spiritual worship of faith, love, and holiness, animating all our tempers, thoughts, words, and actions.

26. *Jesus saith.* Hastening to satisfy her desire before his disciples came. *I . . . am he.* Our Lord did not speak this so plainly to the Jews, who were so full of the Messiah's temporal kingdom. If he had, many would doubtless have taken up arms in his favor, and others would have accused him to the Roman governor. Yet he did in effect declare the thing, though he denied the particular title. For in a multitude of places he represented himself both as the Son of Man and as the Son of God, both which were generally understood by the Jews as peculiarly applicable to the Messiah.

27. *His disciples . . . marvelled that he talked with the woman.* Which the Jewish rabbis reckoned scandalous for a man of distinction to do. They marveled likewise at his talking with a woman of that nation, which was so peculiarly hateful to the Jews.

28. *The woman then left her waterpot.* Forgetting smaller things.

29. *A man, which told me all things that ever I did.* Our Lord had told her but a few things. But his words awakened her conscience, which soon told her all the rest.

34. *My meat.* That which satisfies the strongest appetite of my soul.

35. *The fields . . . are white already.* As if he had said, "The spiritual harvest is ripe already.".The Samaritans, ripe for the gospel, covered the ground round about them.

36. *He that reapeth.* Whoever saves souls. *Receiveth wages.* A peculiar bless-

---

[4](4:14) KJV: "a well."

ing to himself. *And gathereth fruit.* Many souls. *That both he that soweth.* Christ, the great sower of the seed. *And he that reapeth may rejoice together.* In heaven.

52. *Enquired he of them the hour when he began to amend.* The more exactly the works of God are considered, the more faith is increased.

CHAPTER 5

2. *There is at Jerusalem.* It appears that John wrote his gospel before Jerusalem was destroyed; supposedly about thirty years after the Ascension.

4. *An angel.* Yet many undoubtedly thought the whole thing to be purely natural. *At a certain season.* Perhaps at a certain hour of the day during this paschal week. *Went down.* The Greek word implies that he had ceased going down before the time of John's writing this. God might design this to raise expectation of the acceptable time approaching, to add a greater luster to his Son's miracles, and to show that his ancient people were not entirely forgotten of him. *Then first.* Whereas the Son of God healed every day not one only, but whole multitudes that resorted to him.

15. *The man departed, and told the Jews that it was Jesus, which had made him whole.* One might have expected that, when he had published the name of his benefactor, crowds would have thronged about Jesus to have heard the words of his mouth and to have received the blessings of the gospel. Instead of this they surround him with a hostile intent. They even conspire against his life and, for an imagined transgression in point of ceremony, would have put out this light of Israel. Let us not wonder, then, if our "good be evil spoken of"; if even candor, benevolence, and usefulness do not

disarm the enmity of those who have been taught to prefer sacrifice to mercy. And who, disrelishing the genuine gospel, naturally seek to slander and persecute the professors, but especially the defenders of it.

17. *My Father worketh hitherto, and I work.* From the Creation until now he has been working without intermission. Jesus affirmed, "I do likewise." This is the proposition which is explained from verses 19 to 30, confirmed and vindicated in the thirty-first and following verses.

18. *Making himself equal with God.* It is evident that all the hearers so understood him and that our Lord never contradicted, but confirmed it.

20. *The Father . . . sheweth him all things that himself doeth.* A proof of the most intimate unity. *And he will shew him.* By doing them. At the same time (not at different times) the Father shows and does, and the Son sees and does.

23. *That all men should honour the Son, even as they honour the Father.* Either willingly, and so escaping condemnation by faith; or unwillingly, when feeling the wrath of the Judge. This demonstrates the equality of the Son with the Father. If our Lord were God only by office or investiture, and not in the unity of the divine essence and in all respects equal in Godhead with the Father, he could not be honored *even as*, that is, with the same honor that they honored the Father. *He that honoureth not the Son* with the same equal honor thus greatly dishonors *the Father which hath sent him.*

24. *And shall not come into condemnation.* Unless he make shipwreck of the faith.

27. *Because he is the Son of man.* He is appointed to judge mankind, because he was made man.

30. *I can of mine own self do nothing.*

It is impossible I should do anything separately from my Father. *As I hear* of the Father and see, so I judge and do, because I am essentially united to him. (See v. 19.)

35. *He was a burning and a shining light.* Inwardly burning with love and zeal; outwardly shining in all holiness.

37. *Hath testified of me.* Namely, at my baptism. I speak not of my supposed father, Joseph. You are utter strangers to him of whom I speak.

39. *Search the scriptures.* A plain command to all men.

42. *But I know you.* With this ray he pierces the hearts of the hearers. And this, doubtless, he spoke with the tenderest compassion.

46. *He wrote of me.* Everywhere; in all his writings; particularly in Deuteronomy 18:15, 18.

CHAPTER 6

1. *After these things.* The history of between ten and eleven months is to be supplied here from the other Evangelists.

26. Our Lord does not satisfy their curiosity, but corrects the wrong motive they had in seeking him. *Because ye did eat.* Merely for temporal advantage. Until now, Christ had been gathering hearers. He now begins to try their sincerity by a figurative discourse concerning his Passion and the fruit of it, to be received by faith.

27. *Labour.* Work for this. *Unto everlasting life.* Our Lord expressly commands, Work for life, as well as from life, from a principle of faith and love. *Him hath God the Father sealed.* By this very miracle, as well as by his whole testimony concerning him. (See John 3:33.)

28. *The works of God.* Works pleasing to God.

30. *What sign shewest thou?* Amazing, after what they had just seen!

34. *Give us this bread.* Meaning it still in a literal sense. Yet they seem now to be not far from believing.

35. *I am the bread of life.* Having and giving life. *He that cometh; . . . he that believeth.* Equivalent expressions. *Shall never hunger; . . . thirst.* Shall be satisfied, happy, for ever.

37. *All that the Father giveth me.* All that feel themselves lost and follow the drawings of the Father, he in a peculiar manner gives to the Son. *Shall come to me.* By faith. *And him that cometh to me I will in no wise cast out.* I will give him pardon, holiness, and heaven if he endure to the end "to rejoice in his light."

39. *Of all which he hath* [already] *given me.* See John 17:6, 12. If they endure to the end. But Judas did not.

40. Here is the sum of the three foregoing verses. *This is the will of him that sent me.* This is the whole of what I have said. This is the eternal, unchangeable will of God. Every one who truly believes shall have everlasting life.

44. Christ, having checked their murmuring, continues in what he was saying (v. 40). *No man can come to me, except the Father . . . draw him.* No man can believe in Christ unless God gives him power. He draws us first by good desires, not by compulsion, not by laying the will under any necessity; but by the strong and sweet, yet still resistible, motions of his heavenly grace.

45. *Every man therefore that hath heard.* The secret voice of God he and he only believes.

50. *Not die.* Not spiritually; not eternally.

51. *If any man eat of this bread.* That is, believe in me. *He shall live for ever.* In other words, He that believes to the end shall be saved. *My flesh, which I will give.* This whole discourse concerning his flesh and blood refers directly to his Passion and but remotely, if at all, to the Lord's Supper.

53. *Except ye eat the flesh of the Son of man.* Spiritually; unless you draw continual virtue from him by faith. "Eating his flesh" is only another expression for believing.

55. *Meat indeed; . . . drink indeed.* With which the soul of a believer is as truly fed as his body with meat and drink.

60. *This is an hard saying.* Hard to the children of the world, but sweet to the children of God. Scarce ever did our Lord speak more sublimely, even to the apostles in private.

63. *It is the spirit.* The spiritual meaning of these words, by which God gives life. *The flesh*—the bare, carnal, literal meaning—*profiteth nothing. The words that I speak, . . . they are spirit.* Are to be taken in a spiritual sense. And when they are so understood, *they are life.* That is, a means of spiritual life to the hearers.

64. *But there are some of you that believe not.* And so receive no life by them, because you take them in a gross, literal sense. *For Jesus knew from the beginning* of his ministry *who should betray him.* Therefore it is plain that God does foresee future contingencies.

66. *From that time many of his disciples went back.* So our Lord now began to purge his floor. The proud and careless were driven away, and those remained who were available for the Master's use.

70. *Have I not chosen* [or elected] *you twelve.* But they might fall from even that election. *And one of you.* On this gracious warning, Judas ought to have repented. *Is a devil.* Is now influenced by one.

CHAPTER 7

15. *How knoweth this man letters, having never learned?* How comes he to be so well acquainted with sacred literature as to be able to thus expound the Scripture with such gracefulness and propriety, seeing he has never learned this at any place of education?

16. *My doctrine is not mine.* Acquired by any labor of learning. *But his that sent me.* Immediately infused by him.

17. *If any man will do his will, he shall know of the doctrine, whether it be of God.* This is a universal rule with regard to all persons and doctrines. He who is thoroughly willing to do it shall certainly know what the will of God is.

22. *Moses therefore gave unto you circumcision.* The sense is, Because he enjoined you circumcision (though indeed it was far more ancient than he), you think it no harm to circumcise a man on the Sabbath. And are you angry at me (which anger had now continued sixteen months) for doing so much greater a good, for healing a man, body and soul, on the Sabbath?

34. *Ye shall seek me.* Whom you now despise. These words are, as it were, the text which is commented upon in this and the following chapter. *Where I am.* Christ's so frequently saying while on earth, "Where I am," when he spoke of his being in heaven, intimates his perpetual presence there in his divine nature; though his going there was a future thing with regard to his human nature.

37. *In the last day, the great day of the feast.* On this day there was the greatest concourse of people, and they readily fetched water from the fountain of Siloam, which the priests poured out on the great altar, singing one to another, "With joy shall you draw water from the wells of salvation." On this day, likewise, they commemorated God's miraculously giving water out of the rock and offered up solemn prayers for seasonable rains.

39. *The Holy Ghost was not yet given.* That is, those fruits of the Spirit were not yet given, even to true believers, in that full measure.

42. *Out of the town of Bethlehem.* And how could they forget that Jesus was born there? Had not Herod given them terrible reason to remember it?

53. *And every man went unto his own house.* So that short, plain question of Nicodemus spoiled all their measures and broke up the council! "A word spoken in season, how good is it," especially when God gives it his blessing!

CHAPTER 8

6. *With his finger wrote.* God wrote once in the Old Testament, Christ once in the New—perhaps the words he afterwards spoke when they continued asking him.

12. *But shall have the light of life.* He that closely, humbly, steadily follows me shall have the divine light continually shining upon him, diffusing over his soul knowledge, holiness, joy, until he is guided by it to life everlasting.

16. *But I and the Father that sent me.* His Father is in him, and he is in the Father (John 14:10–11). And so the Father is no more alone without the Son than the Son is without the Father (Prov. 8:22–23, 30). His Father and he are not one and another God, but one God (though distinct persons) and so inseparable from each other. And though the Son came from the Father to assume human nature and perform his office as the Messiah upon earth, as God is sometimes said to come from heaven for particular manifestations of himself; yet Christ did not leave the Father, nor the Father leave him, any more than God leaves heaven when he is said to come down to the earth.

32. *The truth.* Written in your hearts by the Spirit of God. *Shall make you free.* From guilt, sin, misery, Satan.

44. *From the beginning.* Of his becoming a devil. *And abode not in the truth.* Commencing *murderer* and a liar at the same time. And certainly he was "a killer of men" (as the Greek word properly signifies) *from the beginning* of the world. For from the very Creation he designed and contrived the ruin of men. *When he speaketh a lie, he speaketh of his own.* For he is the proper parent and, as it were, creator of it. See the origin not only of lies, but of evil in general!

51. *If a man keep my saying.* We keep his doctrine by believing; his promises, by hoping; his commands, by obeying. *He shall never see death.* That is, death eternal. He shall live for ever.

56. *He saw it.* By faith, in types, figures, and promises. As particularly in Melchizedek; in the appearance of Jehovah to him in the plains of Mamre (Gen. 18:1); and in the promise that in his "seed all the nations of the earth should be blessed." Possibly he had likewise a peculiar revelation of either Christ's first or second coming.

57. *Thou art not yet fifty years old.* At the most. Perhaps the gravity of our Lord's countenance, together with his afflictions and labors, might make him appear older than he really was.

59. *But Jesus hid himself.* Probably by becoming invisible.

CHAPTER 9

4. *The night cometh.* Christ is the light. When the light is withdrawn, night comes. *When no man can work.* No man can do anything towards working out his salvation after this life is ended. Yet Christ can work always. But he was to work upon earth only during the day or season which was appointed for him.

5. *I am the light of the world.* I teach men inwardly by my Spirit, and outwardly by my preaching, what is the will of God. And I show them by my example how they must do it.

7. *He went, . . . and washed, and came seeing.* He believed and obeyed and found a blessing. Had he been wise in his own eyes and reasoned like Naaman on the impropriety of the means, he had justly been left in darkness. Lord, may our proud hearts be subdued to the methods of your recovering grace! May we leave you to choose how you will bestow favors, which it is our highest interest to receive on any terms!

30. *The man answered.* Utterly illiterate as he was. And with what strength and clearness of reason! So had God opened the eyes of his understanding as well as his bodily eyes.

31. *Know that God heareth not sinners.* Not impenitent sinners, so as to answer their prayers in this manner. The honest courage of this man in adhering to the truth, though he knew the consequence (v. 22), gives him claim to the title of a confessor.

34. *Born in sins.* And therefore, they supposed, born blind. *They cast him out.* From the synagogue; excommunicated him.

38. *Lord, I believe.* What an excellent spirit! He was so deep and strong in understanding (as he had just shown, to the confusion of the Pharisees) and yet so teachable!

CHAPTER 10

3. *And the sheep hear his voice.* The circumstances that follow exactly agree with the customs of the ancient Eastern shepherds. They called their sheep by name, went before them, and the sheep followed them. So real Christians hear, listen to, understand, and obey the voice of a shepherd whom Christ has sent. And he counts them his own, dearer than any friend or brother; calls, advises, directs each "by name, and leadeth them out in the paths of righteousness," beside the waters of comfort.

4. *He goeth before them.* In all the ways of God; teaching them in every point, by example as well as by precept. *And the sheep follow him.* They tread in his steps. *For they know his voice.* Having the witness in themselves that his words are "the wisdom and the power of God." Reader, are you a shepherd of souls? Then answer to God—Is it well with you and your flock?

7. *I am the door.* Christ is both the door and the shepherd and all things.

8. *Whosoever are come.*[5] Independently of me, assuming any part of my character; pretending, like your elders and rabbis, to a power over the consciences of men; attempting to make laws in the church and to teach their own traditions as the way of salvation. All those prophets and expounders of God's Word who enter not by the door of the sheepfold, but run before I have sent them by my Spirit. Our Lord seems in particular to speak of those who had undertaken this office since he began his ministry.

9. *If any man.* As a sheep. *Enter in.* Through faith. *He shall be saved.* From the wolf and from those murdering shepherds. *And shall go in and out.* Shall continually attend on the shepherds whom I have sent. *And find pasture.* Food for his soul in all circumstances.

12. *But he that is an hireling.* It is not the mere receiving of hire which makes a man a hireling (for "the labourer is worthy of his hire," Jesus himself being the judge), but the loving of hire; loving the hire more than the work; working for the sake of the hire. He is a hireling who would not work were it

---

[5] (10:8) KJV: "All that ever came before me."

not for the hire; to whom this is the great if not only motive of working. If a man who works only for hire is such a wretch, a mere thief and a robber, what is he who continually takes the hire and yet does not work at all?

16. *And other sheep I have.* Whom he foreknew.

18. *I lay it down of myself.* By my own free act and deed. *I have power to lay it down, and I have power to take it again.* I have an original power and right of myself, both to lay it down as a ransom and to take it again after full satisfaction is made for the sins of the whole world.

He chiefly spoke of the Father before his suffering; of his own glory after it. Our Lord's receiving this commission as Mediator is not to be considered as the ground of his power to lay down and resume his life. For this he had in himself, as having an original right to dispose thereof, before the Father's commission. But this commission was the reason why he thus used his power in laying down his life. He did it in obedience to his Father.

26. *But ye believe not, because ye are not of my sheep.* Because you do not, will not, follow me. Because you are proud, unholy, lovers of praise, lovers of the world, lovers of pleasure, not of God.

27–29. *My sheep hear my voice, and I know them, and they follow me.* Our Lord still alludes to the discourse he had had before this festival. As if he had said, My sheep are they who (1) hear my voice by faith; (2) are known, that is, approved by me, as loving me; and (3) follow me, keep my commandments, with a believing, loving heart. And to (1) those who truly believe (observe three promises annexed to three conditions), I give *eternal life.* He does not say "I will give," but "I give"; for "he that believeth hath everlasting life." (2) Those whom I know truly to love me *shall never perish,* provided they abide in

my love. (3) Those who follow me, neither men nor devils can *pluck . . . out of my hand. My Father,* who hath, by an unchangeable decree, given me all that believe, love, and obey, *is greater than all* in heaven or earth; *and none is able to pluck them out of* [his] *hand.*

30. *I and my Father are one.* Not by consent of will only, but by unity of power and consequently of nature. *Are.* This word confutes Sabellius, proving the plurality of persons. *One.* This word confutes Arius, proving the unity of nature in God. Never did any prophet before, from the beginning of the world, use any one expression of himself which could possibly be so interpreted as this and other expressions were by all that heard our Lord speak. Therefore, if he was not God he must have been the vilest of men.

CHAPTER 11

11. *Our friend Lazarus sleepeth.* This he spoke just when he died. Such is the death of good men in the language of heaven. But the disciples did not yet understand this language. And the slowness of our understanding makes the Scripture often descend to our barbarous manner of speaking.

16. *With him.* With Jesus, whom he supposed the Jews would kill. It seems to be the language of despair.

33. *He . . . was troubled.* An expression amazingly elegant and full of the highest propriety. For the affections of Jesus were not properly passions, but voluntary emotions, which were wholly in his own power. And this tender trouble, which he now voluntarily sustained, was full of the highest order and reason.

35. *Jesus wept.* Out of sympathy with those who were in tears all around him, as well as from a deep sense of the misery sin had brought upon human nature.

39. *Lord, by this time he stinketh.* Thus did reason and faith struggle together.

41. *Jesus lifted up his eyes.* Not as if he applied to his Father for assistance; there is not the least show of this. He performed the miracle with an air of absolute sovereignty as the Lord of life and death. But it was as if he had said, "I thank you that, by the disposals of your providence, you have granted my desire in this remarkable opportunity of exerting my power and showing forth your praise."

46. *Some of them went their ways to the Pharisees.* What a dreadful confirmation of that weighty truth, "If they hear not Moses and the prophets, neither will they be persuaded, though one rose from the dead"!

CHAPTER 12

2. It seems that Martha was a person of some figure, from the great respect which was paid to her and her sister in visits and condolences on Lazarus' death, as well as from the costly ointment mentioned in the next verse. And probably it was at their house our Lord and his disciples lodged when he returned from Jerusalem to Bethany every evening of the last week of his life, upon which he was now entered.

10. *The chief priests consulted that they might put Lazarus also to death.* Here is the plain reason why the other Evangelists, who wrote while Lazarus was living, did not relate his story.

16. *These things understood not his disciples at the first.* The design of God's providential dispensations is seldom understood at first. We ought therefore to believe, though we understand not, and give ourselves up to the divine disposal. The great work of faith is to embrace those things which "we know not now," but "shall know hereafter."

17. *When he called Lazarus out of his grave.* How admirably does the apostle express as well the greatness of the miracle as the facility with which it was accomplished! The easiness of the Scripture style on the most grand occurrences is more sublime than all the pomp of orators.

27. *Now is my soul troubled.* He had various foretastes of his Passion. *And what shall I say?* Not, What shall I choose? For his heart was fixed in choosing the will of his Father; but he labored for utterance.

29. *The people therefore, that stood by, and heard it.* A sound, but not the distinct words. In the most glorious revelations there may remain something obscure to exercise our faith.

32. *I . . . will draw all men.* Gentiles as well as Jews. And those who follow my drawings Satan shall not be able to keep.

38. *The arm of the Lord.* The power of God, manifested by Christ in his preaching, miracles, and work of redemption.

39. *Therefore they could not believe.* That is, by the just judgment of God, for their obstinacy and willful resistance of the truth they were at length so left to the hardness of their hearts that neither the miracles nor doctrine of our Lord could make any impression on them.

44. *Jesus said with a loud voice.*[6] This which follows to the end of the chapter is, with John, the epilogue of our Lord's public discourses and a kind of recapitulation of them.

CHAPTER 13

7. *What I do thou knowest not now; but thou shalt know hereafter.* We do not

---

[6](12:44) KJV: "Jesus cried and said."

now know perfectly any of his works, either of creation, providence, or grace. It is enough that we can love and obey now and that we shall know hereafter.

8. *If I wash thee not.* If you do not submit to my will. *Thou hast no part with me.* You are not my disciple. In a more general sense, it may mean, If I do not wash you in my blood and purify you by my Spirit, you can have no communion with me, nor any share in the blessings of my kingdom.

14. *Ye also ought to wash one another's feet.* And why did they not? Why do we not read of any one apostle ever washing the feet of any other? Because they understood their Lord better. They knew he never designed that this should be taken literally. He designed to teach them the great lesson of humble love, as well as to confer inward purity upon them. And hereby he teaches us, (1) In every possible way to assist each other in attaining that purity. And (2) To wash each other's feet by performing all sorts of good offices to each other, even those of the lowest kind, when opportunity serves and the necessity of any calls for them.

23. *One of his disciples, whom Jesus loved.* John avoids with great care expressly naming himself. Perhaps our Lord now gave him the first proof of his peculiar love by disclosing this secret to him.

25. *Leaning.*[7] Down, and so asking him privately.

26. *Jesus answered.* In his ear. So careful was he not to offend (if it had been possible) even Judas himself. *He gave it to Judas.* And probably the other disciples thought Judas peculiarly happy. But when even this instance of our Lord's tenderness could not move him, then Satan took full possession.

27. *That thou doest, do quickly.* This is not a permission, much less a command. It is only as if he had said, "If you are determined to do it, why do you delay?" In this way he showed Judas that he could not be hid, and expressed his own readiness to suffer.

34. *A new commandment.* Not new in itself, but new in the school of Christ; for he had never before taught it to them expressly. Likewise new as to the degree of it, *as I have loved you.*

38. *Till thou hast denied me thrice.* His threefold denial was thrice foretold: first, at the time mentioned here; secondly, at that mentioned by Luke; lastly, at that recorded by Matthew and Mark.

CHAPTER 14

1. *Believe.* This is the sum of all his discourse, which is urged until they did believe (John 16:30); and then our Lord prays and departs.

2. *In my Father's house are many mansions.* Enough to receive both the holy angels, your predecessors in the faith, all that now believe, and a great multitude which no man can number.

11. *Believe me.* On my own word. *That I am* God. *The very works.* This respects not merely the miracles themselves, but his sovereign, God-like way of performing them.

12. *Greater works than these shall he do.* So one apostle performed miracles merely by his shadow (Acts 5:15); another, by "handkerchiefs carried from his body" (Acts 19:12); and all spoke with various tongues. But converting one sinner is a greater work than all these.

15. *If you love me, keep my commandments.* Immediately after faith he exhorts to love and good works.

---

[7](13:25) KJV: "Lying."

19. *Because I live, ye shall live also.* Because I am the Living One in my divine nature and shall rise again in my human nature and live for ever in heaven; therefore you shall live the life of faith and love on earth, and hereafter the life of glory.

23. *Jesus answered.* Because you love and obey me, and they do not, therefore I will reveal myself to you and not to them. *My Father will love him.* The more any man loves and obeys, the more God will love him. *And we will come unto him, and make our abode with him.* Which implies such a large manifestation of the divine presence and love that the former, in justification, is as nothing in comparison of it.

26. *He shall teach you all things.* Necessary for you to know. Here is a clear promise to the apostles and their successors in the faith that the Holy Ghost will teach them all that truth which is needful for their salvation.

27. *My peace I give.* Lord, evermore give us this peace! How serenely may we pass through the most turbulent scenes of life when all is quiet and harmonious within! You have made peace through the blood of your cross; may we give all diligence to preserve this inestimable gift until it issues in everlasting peace!

30. *The prince of this world cometh.* To make his grand assault. *And hath nothing in me.* No right, no claim, or power. There is no guilt in me to give him power over me; no corruption to take part with his temptation.

CHAPTER 15

2. *Every branch that beareth fruit, he purgeth it.* "By obeying the truth" (I Peter 1:22) and by inward or outward sufferings (Heb. 12:10–11). So purity and fruitfulness help each other. *That it may bring forth more fruit.* For this is one of the noblest rewards God can bestow on former acts of obedience, to make us yet more holy and fit for further and more eminent service.

3. *Ye are clean.* All of you to whom I now speak are purged from the guilt and power of sin. *Through the word.* Which, applied by the Spirit, is the grand instrument of purifying the soul.

6. *If a man abide not in me.* By living faith; not by church communion only. He may thus abide in Christ and be *withered* all the time, and *cast . . . into the fire* at last. *He is cast forth.* From the vineyard, the invisible church. Therefore he was in it once.

9. *Continue ye in my love.* Keep your place in my affection. See that you do not forfeit that invaluable blessing. How needless a caution, if it were impossible for them not to abide therein!

11. *That my joy might remain in you.* The same joy which I feel in loving the Father and keeping his commandments.

14. *Ye are my friends, if ye do whatsoever I command you.* On this condition, not otherwise. A thunderbolt for Antinomianism. Who then dares assert that God's love does not at all depend on man's works?

16. *Ye.* My apostles. *Have not chosen me, but I have chosen you.* As clearly appears from the sacred history. *And ordained you, that ye may go and bring forth fruit.* I have chosen and appointed you for this end, that you may go and convert sinners. *And that your fruit should remain.* That the fruit of your labors may remain to the end of the world; yes, to eternity. *That whatsoever ye shall ask.* The consequence of your going and bearing fruit will be that all your prayers will be heard.

19. *Because ye are not of the world, . . . therefore the world hateth you.* Because your maxims, tempers, actions are quite opposite to theirs. For the very same reason must the world in all ages hate those who are not of the world.

23. *He that hateth me.* As every unbeliever does. For as the love of God is inseparable from faith, so is the hatred of God from unbelief.

26. *When the Comforter is come, whom I will send unto you from the Father, the Spirit of truth, which proceedeth from the Father, he shall testify of me.* The Spirit's coming and being sent by our Lord from the Father to testify of him are personal characters and plainly distinguish him from the Father and the Son. And his title as *the Spirit of truth,* together with his proceeding from the Father, can agree to none but a divine person. And that he proceeds from the Son as well as from the Father may be fairly argued from his being called "the Spirit of Christ" (I Peter 1:11) and from his being here said to be sent by Christ from the Father, as well as sent by the Father in his name.

CHAPTER 16

2. *The time cometh, that whosoever killeth you will think that he doeth God service.* But blessed be God, the time is so far past that those who bear the name of Christ do not now generally suppose they do him service by killing each other for a difference in opinion or mode of worship.

11. *The prince of this world is judged.* And in consequence, therefore, dethroned, deprived of the power he had so long usurped over men. Yet those who reject the deliverance offered them will remain slaves of Satan still.

13. *When he . . . is come.* It is universally allowed that the Father, Son, and Holy Ghost dwell in all believers. And the internal agency of the Holy Ghost is generally admitted. That of the Father and the Son, as

represented in this Gospel, deserves our deepest consideration.

22. *Ye now therefore have sorrow.* This gives us no manner of authority to assert that all believers must come into a state of darkness. They never need lose either their peace or love or the witness that they are the children of God. They never can lose these but through sin, ignorance, vehement temptation, or bodily disorder.

23. *Whatsoever ye shall ask.* Knowledge, love, or anything else. *He will give it.* Our Lord gives us here a carte blanche. Believer, write down what you will. He had said (John 14:13), "I will do it," where the discourse was of glorifying the Father through the Son. Here, speaking of the love of the Father to believers, he says, *He will give* it.

CHAPTER 17

In this chapter our Lord prays, (1) For himself, verses 1–5. (2) For the apostles, verses 6–19 and again, verses 24–26. (3) For all believers, verses 20–23. (4) For the world, verses 21–23. In this prayer he comprises all he had said from 13:31 and seals, as it were, all he had previously done, beholding all things past, present, and to come. This chapter contains the easiest word and the deepest sense of any in all the Scripture. Yet it is no incoherent rhapsody, but the whole is closely and exactly connected.

2. *To as many as thou hast given him.* To all believers. This is a clear proof that Christ designed his sacrifice to avail for all; yea, that *all flesh,* every man, should partake of everlasting life.

5. *The glory which I had.* He does not say "received." He always had it, until he emptied himself of it in the days of his flesh.

6. *Thine they were.* By creation and by descent from Abraham. *And thou gavest* *them me.* By giving them faith in what I have spoken.

10. *And all mine are thine, and thine are mine.* These are very high and strong expressions, too grand for any mere creature to use; as implying that all things whatever, inclusive of the divine nature, perfections, and operations, are the common property of the Father and the Son.

12. *Those that thou gavest me I have kept, and none of them is lost, but the son of perdition.* So one even of them whom God had given him is lost. So far was even that decree from being unchangeable! *That the scripture might be fulfilled.* That is, whereby the Scripture was fulfilled.

17. *Sanctify.* Consecrate them by the anointing of your Spirit to their office, and perfect them in holiness by means of your word.

19. *I sanctify myself.* I devote myself, as a victim, to be sacrificed.

22. *The glory which thou gavest me I have given them.* The glory of the only begotten shines in all the sons of God. How great is the majesty of Christians!

26. *I have declared unto them thy name.* Your new, best name of love. *That the love wherewith thou hast loved me . . . and I.* That you and your love, and I and my love, *may be in them.* That they may love me with that love.

CHAPTER 18

1. *A garden.* Probably belonging to one of his friends. He might retire to this private place, not only for the advantage of secret devotion, but also that the people might not be alarmed at his arrest; nor attempt, in the first sallies of their zeal, to rescue him in a tumultuous manner.

6. *As soon then as he had said unto them, I am he, they went backward, and fell to the ground.* How amazing it is that they should renew the assault after so sensible an experience both of his power and mercy! But probably the priests among them might persuade themselves and their attendants that this also was done by Beelzebub; and that it was through the providence of God, not the indulgence of Jesus, that they received no further damage.

8. *If . . . ye seek me, let these* [my disciples] *go.* It was an eminent instance of his power over the spirits of men that they so far obeyed this word as not to seize even Peter when he had cut off the ear of Malchus.

10. *Simon Peter.* No other Evangelist names him; nor could they safely. But John, writing after his death, might do it without any such inconvenience.

38. *What is truth?* Said Pilate, a courtier; perhaps meaning, What signifies truth? Is that a thing worth hazarding your life for? So he left him presently to plead with the Jews for him, looking upon him as an innocent but weak man.

CHAPTER 19

20. *It was written in Hebrew.* Because it was the language of the nation. *And Greek.* For the information of the Hellenists, who spoke that language and came in great numbers to the feast. *And Latin.* For the majesty of the Roman Empire.

24. *They parted my raiment among them.* No circumstance of David's life bore any resemblance to this, or to several other passages in the Twenty-second Psalm. So that in this Scripture, as in some others, the prophet seems to have been thrown into a preternatural ecstasy wherein, personating the Messiah, he spoke merely what the Spirit dictated, without any regard to himself.

34. *Blood and water.* It was strange, seeing he was dead, that blood should come out; more strange that water also; and most strange of all that both should come out immediately, at one time, and yet distinctly. It was pure and true water, as well as pure and true blood. The asseveration of the beholder and testifier of it shows both the truth and greatness of the miracle and mystery.

37. *They shall look on him whom they pierced.* He was pierced by the soldier's spear. They who have occasioned his sufferings by their sins (and who has not?) shall either *look on him* in this world with penitential sorrow; or with terror when he comes in the clouds of heaven (Rev. 1:7).

38–39. *Joseph of Arimathaea . . . besought Pilate. And then came also Nicodemus.* Acknowledging the Christ, when even his chosen disciples forsook him. In that extremity Joseph was no longer afraid, Nicodemus no longer ashamed.

CHAPTER 20

6–7. *Peter . . . seeth the linen clothes lie, and the napkin . . . in a place by itself.* The angels, who ministered to him when he rose, undoubtedly folded up the napkin and linen clothes.

8. *He saw.* That the body was not there. *Believed.* That they had taken it away, as Mary said.

17. *Touch me not.* Or rather, Do not cling to me (for she held him by the feet, Matt. 28:9); detain me not now. You will have other opportunities of conversing with me. *For I am not yet ascended to my Father.* I have not yet left the world. *But go* [immediately] *to my brethren.* Thus does he intimate in the strongest manner the forgiveness of their fault, even without ever mentioning it. These exquisite touches, which everywhere abound in the evangelical writings [the Gospels], show how per-

fectly Christ knew our frame. *I ascend.* He anticipates it in his thoughts, and so speaks of it as a thing already present. *Unto my Father, and your Father; and to my God, and your God.* This uncommon expression shows that the only begotten Son has all manner of fellowship with God. And a fellowship with God the Father, some way resembling his own, he bestows upon his brethren. Yet he does not say, "Our God," for no creature can be raised to an equality with him; but "my God, and your God," intimating that the Father is his in a singular and incommunicable manner; and ours, through him, in such a way as a creature is capable of.

21. *Peace be unto you.* This is the foundation of the mission of a true gospel minister—peace in his own soul (II Cor. 4:1). *As my Father hath sent me, even so send I you.* Christ was the Apostle of the Father (Heb. 3:1); Peter and the rest, the apostles of Christ.

22. *He breathed on them.* New life and vigor. *And saith.* As you receive this breath out of my mouth, so *receive ye* the Spirit out of my fullness. *The Holy Ghost.* Influencing you in a peculiar manner to fit you for your great mission. This was an earnest of Pentecost.

31. *These are written, that ye might believe.* That you may be confirmed in believing. Faith comes sometimes by reading, though ordinarily by hearing.

CHAPTER 21

7. *And did cast himself into the sea.* To swim to him immediately. The love of Christ draws men through fire and water.

15. *Thou knowest.* He had now learned by sad experience that Jesus knew his heart.

19. *By what death he should glorify God.* It is not only by acting, but chiefly by suffering that the saints glorify God. *Follow me.* Showing hereby likewise what death he should die.

20. *Peter, turning.* As he was walking with Christ. *Seeth the disciple whom Jesus loved following.* There is a peculiar spirit and tenderness in this plain passage. Christ orders Peter to follow him in token of his readiness to be crucified in his cause. John stays not for the call; he rises and follows him too, but says not a word of his own love or zeal. He chose that the action only should speak this. And even when he records the circumstance, he tells us not what that action meant, but with great simplicity relates the fact only. If here and there a generous heart sees and emulates it, be it so. But he is not solicitous that men would admire it. It was addressed to his beloved Master, and it was enough that he understood it.

24. *This is the disciple which testifieth.* Being still alive after he had written. *And we know that his testimony is true.* The church added these words to John's Gospel, even as Tertius did the words of Paul's Epistle to the Romans (16:22).

25. *If they should be written particularly.*[8] Every fact, and all the circumstances of it. *I suppose.* This expression, which softens the hyperbole, shows that John wrote this verse.

---

[8] (21:25) KJV: "if they should be written every one."

the acts
of the apostles

CHAPTER 1

5. *Ye shall be baptized with the Holy Ghost.* And so are all true believers, to the end of the world. But the extraordinary gifts of the Holy Ghost also are here promised.

8. *But ye shall receive power, . . . and ye shall be witnesses unto me.* That is, you shall be empowered to witness my gospel, both by your preaching and suffering.

18. *And falling headlong.* It seems the rope broke before or as he died.

23. *And they appointed two.* So far the faithful could go by consulting together, but no farther. Therefore here commenced the proper use of the lot, whereby a matter of importance which cannot be determined by any ordinary method is committed to the divine decision.

CHAPTER 2

1. At the Pentecost of Sinai in the Old Testament and the Pentecost of Jerusalem in the New were the two grand manifestations of God, the legal and the evangelical; the one from the mountain, and the other from heaven; the terrible and the merciful one.

2. *And suddenly there came a sound from heaven.* So will the Son of Man come to judgment.

3. *And there appeared unto them cloven tongues like as of fire.* That is, small flames of fire. It might intimate God's touching their tongues, as it were (together with their hearts), with divine fire; his giving them such words as were active and penetrating, even as flaming fire.

4. *And began to speak with other tongues.* The miracle was not in the ears of the hearers (as some have unaccountably supposed), but in the mouth of the speakers. And this family praising God together with the tongues of all the world was an earnest that the whole world should in due time praise God in their various tongues. *As the Spirit gave them utterance.* Moses, the type of the law, was of a slow tongue; but the gospel speaks with a fiery and flaming one.

13. *Others mocking.* The world begins with mocking, then proceeds to cavilling (Acts 4:7); to threats (4:17); to imprisoning (Acts 5:18); to blows (5:40); to slaughter (Acts 7:58). *These men are full of sweet[1] wine.* So the Greek word properly signifies, as there was no

---

[1] (2:13) KJV: "new."

new wine so early in the year as Pentecost. Thus natural men are prone to ascribe supernatural things to mere natural causes; and many times as impudently and unskillfully as in the present case.

14. *But Peter, standing up.* All the gestures, all the words of Peter show the utmost sobriety. *Lifted up his voice.* With cheerfulness and boldness.

17. The times of the Messiah are frequently called *the last days,* the gospel being the last dispensation of divine grace. *I will pour out my Spirit.* Not on the Day of Pentecost only. *Upon all flesh.* On persons of every age, sex, and rank. *And your young men shall see visions.* In young men the outward senses are most vigorous and the bodily strength is entire, whereby they are best qualified to sustain the shock which usually attends the visions of God. In old men the internal senses are most vigorous, suited to divine dreams. Not that the old are wholly excluded from the former, nor the young from the latter.

19. Terrible indeed were those happenings in particular which preceded the destruction of Jerusalem: such as the flaming sword hanging over the city, and the fiery comet pointing down upon it for a year; the light that shone upon the temple and the altar in the night, as if it had been noonday; the opening of the great and heavy gate of the temple without hands; the voice heard from the most holy place, "Let us depart hence"; the admonition of Jesus, the son of Ananus, crying for seven years together, "Woe, woe, woe"; the vision of contending armies in the air and of entrenchments dug against a city there represented; the terrible thunders and lightnings and dreadful earthquakes, which every one considered as portending some great evil; all which through the singular providence of God are particularly recorded by Josephus.

21. *That whosoever shall call on the name of the Lord.* This expression implies the whole of religion, and particularly prayer uttered in faith. *Shall be saved.* From all those plagues; from sin and hell.

23. *Him, being delivered by the determinate counsel and foreknowledge of God.* The apostle here anticipates an objection: Why did God suffer such a person to be so treated? Why did he not know what wicked men intended to do; and had he not power to prevent it? Yes, he knew all that those wicked men intended to do. And he had power to blast all their designs in a moment. But he did not exert that power, because he "so loved the world." It was the determinate counsel of his love to redeem mankind from eternal death, by the death of his only begotten Son.

27. *Thou wilt not leave my soul in hell.* The invisible world. But it does not appear that ever our Lord went into hell. His soul, when it was separated from the body, did not go there, but to paradise (Luke 23:43). The meaning is, You will not leave my soul in its separate state, nor suffer my body to be corrupted.

31. *He seeing this before spake of the resurrection of Christ.* Peter argues thus: It is plain David did not speak this of himself; therefore he spoke of Christ's rising. But how does that promise of a kingdom imply his resurrection? Because he did not receive it before he died, and because his kingdom was to endure for ever (II Sam. 7:13).

38–39. *Repent.* And hereby return to God. *Be baptized,* [believing] *in the name of Jesus Christ, . . . and ye shall receive the gift of the Holy Ghost.* See the Three-One God clearly proved. *The gift of the Holy Ghost* does not mean, in this place, the power of speaking with tongues (for the promise of this was not given *to all that are afar off*, in distant ages and nations); but rather the constant fruits of faith, even right-eousness and peace and joy in the Holy Ghost. *Even as many as the Lord our God shall call.* By his word and by his Spirit, whether they are Jews or Gentiles; and who are not disobedient to the heaven-ly calling.

42. *They continued stedfastly.* So their daily church communion consisted in these four particulars: (1) Hearing the word. (2) Having all things in com-mon. (3) Receiving the Lord's Supper. (4) Prayer.

> "Ye different sects, who all declare,
> Lo, here is Christ, and Christ is
>   there,
> Your stronger proofs divinely give,
> And show me where the Christians
>   live!"

45. *And sold their possessions.* Their lands and houses. *And goods.* Their movables. *Parted them to all men, as every man had need.* To say the Chris-tians did this only until the destruction of Jerusalem is not true; for many did it long after. Not that there was any positive command for so doing; it was not needed, for love constrained them. It was a natural fruit of that love with which each member of the community loved every other as his own soul. And if the whole Christian church had continued in this spirit, this usage would have continued through all ages. To affirm, therefore, that Christ did not design that it should continue is neither more nor less than to affirm that Christ did not design that this measure of love should continue. I see no proof of this.

46. *Did eat their meat with gladness and singleness of heart.* They carried the same happy and holy temper through all their common actions, eating and working with the same spirit with

which they prayed and received the Lord's Supper.

CHAPTER 3

13. *Whom ye delivered up.* When God had given him to you, and when you ought to have received him as a most precious treasure, and to have pre-served him with all your power.

17. *As did also your rulers.* He does not call them "our," but "your" rulers; for as the Jewish dispensation ceased at the death of Christ, consequently so did the authority of its rulers.

22. *A prophet shall the Lord your God raise up, . . . like unto me.* And that in many particulars. Moses instituted the Jewish church; Christ instituted the Christian. With the prophesying of Moses was soon joined the effect, the deliverance of Israel from Egypt; with the prophesying of Christ that grand effect, the deliverance of his people from sin and death. Those who could not bear the voice of God, yet desired to hear that of Moses; much more do those who are wearied with the law desire to hear the voice of Christ. Moses spoke to the people all and only those things which God had com-manded him; so did Christ. But though he was like Moses, yet was Christ infinitely superior to him in person as well as in office.

23. *Every soul, which will not hear that prophet, shall be destroyed from among the people.* One cannot imagine a more masterful address than this to warn the Jews of the dreadful consequence of their infidelity, in the very words of their favorite prophet, out of a pretend-ed zeal for whom they rejected Christ.

CHAPTER 4

1–2. *The priests . . . being grieved.* That the name of Jesus was preached to the people. Especially they were offended at the doctrine of his resurrection; for as they had put him to death, his rising again proved him to be "the Just One," and so brought his blood upon their heads. The priests were grieved, lest their office and temple services should decline and Christianity take root through the preaching of the apostles and their power of working miracles. *The captain of the temple.* Being concerned to prevent all sedition and disorder. *The Sadducees.* Being displeased at the overturning of all their doctrines, particularly with regard to the resurrection.

4. *The number of the men.* Besides women and children. *Was about five thousand.* So many did our Lord now feed at once with the bread from heaven!

8. *Then Peter, filled with the Holy Ghost.* That moment. God moves his instruments, not when they please, but just when he sees it needful.

10. *Whom God raised from the dead.* They knew in their own consciences that it was so; though they had hired the soldiers to tell a most senseless and incredible tale to the contrary (Matt. 28:12–15), yet it is observable they did not, so far as we can learn, dare to plead it before Peter and John.

12. *There is none other name . . . whereby we must be saved.* The apostle uses a beautiful gradation from the temporal deliverance which had been accomplished for the poor cripple by the power of Christ, to that of a much nobler and more important kind, which is accomplished by Christ for impotent and sinful souls. In this he follows the admirable custom of his great Lord and Master, who continually took occasion from the earthly to speak of spiritual things.

17. *But that it spread no further.* For they look upon it as a mere gangrene. *Let us severely[2] threaten them.* Great men, you do nothing. They have one greater than you to flee to.

19. *Whether it be right . . . to hearken unto you more than unto God, judge ye.* Was it not by the same Spirit that Socrates, when they were condemning him to death for teaching the people, said, "O ye Athenians, I embrace and love you; but I will obey God rather than you. And if you would spare my life on condition I should cease to teach my fellow citizens, I would die a thousand times rather than accept the proposal."

31. *They were all filled.* Afresh.

34. *Neither was there any among them that lacked.* We may observe, this is added as the proof that "great grace was upon them all." And it was the immediate, necessary consequence of it; yes, and must be, to the end of the world. In all ages and nations the same cause, the same degree of grace, could not but, in like circumstances, produce the same effect. *For as many as were possessors of lands or houses sold them.* Not that there was any particular command for this. But there was great grace and great love, of which this was the natural fruit.

36. *The son of consolation.* Not only on account of his so largely assisting the poor with his fortune, but also of the peculiar gifts of the Holy Spirit whereby he was so well qualified both to comfort and to exhort.

CHAPTER 5

1. *But a certain man named Ananias.* It is certain, not a believer; for all that believed "were of one heart, and of one

---

[2] (4:17) KJV: "straitly."

soul." Probably not baptized, but intending now to offer himself for baptism.

3. *To lie to the Holy Ghost.* Who is in us. *And to keep back.* Here was the first instance of it. This was the first attempt to bring propriety of goods into the Christian church.

4. *While it remained, was it not thine own?* It was in his own choice to be a Christian or not; and consequently either to sell his land or keep it. *And after it was sold, was it not in thine own power?* For it does not appear that he professed himself to be a Christian when he sold it.

5. *And Ananias . . . fell down, and gave up the ghost.* And this severity was not only just, considering that complication of vain-glory, covetousness, fraud, and impiety which this action contained; but it was also wise and gracious, as it would effectually deter any others from following his example. It was likewise a convincing proof of the upright conduct of the apostles in managing the sums with which they were entrusted; and in general of their divine mission. For none can imagine that Peter would have had the assurance to pronounce, and much less the power to execute, such a sentence if he had been guilty himself of a fraud of the same kind. Or had he been lying to the Holy Ghost in the whole of his pretensions to be under his immediate direction.

7. *About the space of three hours.* How precious a space! The woman had a longer timer for repentance.

11. *The church.* This is the first time it is mentioned. And here is a native specimen of a New Testament church; which is a company of men, called by the gospel, grafted into Christ by baptism, animated by love, united by all manner of fellowship, and disciplined by the death of Ananias and Sapphira.

24. *They doubted . . . whereunto this would grow.* They were even at their wit's end. The world in persecuting the children of God entangle themselves in numberless difficulties.

28. *Did not we straitly command you that ye should not teach?* See the poor cunning of the enemies of the gospel. They make laws and interdicts at their pleasure, which those who obey God cannot but break; and then take occasion thereby to censure and punish the innocent as guilty. *Ye . . . intend to bring this man's blood upon us.* The apostles did not desire to accuse any man. They simply declared the naked truth.

31. *Him hath God exalted.* From the grave to heaven. *To give repentance.* Whereby Jesus is received as a Prince. *And forgiveness of sins.* Whereby he is received as a Savior. Hence some infer that repentance and faith are as mere gifts as remission of sins. Not so; for man cooperates in the former, but not in the latter. God alone forgives sins.

38. *Let them alone.* In a cause which is manifestly good, we should immediately join. In a cause, on the other hand, which is manifestly evil, we should immediately oppose. But in a sudden, new, doubtful occurrence, this advice is eminently useful. *If this counsel or this work.* He seems to correct himself, as if it were some sudden work rather than a counsel or design. And so it was; for the apostles had no counsel, plan, or design of their own. They were but mere instruments in the hand of God, working just as he led them from day to day.

41. *Rejoicing . . . to suffer shame.* This is a sure mark of the truth; joy in affliction, such as is true, deep, pure.

CHAPTER 6

1. *There arose a murmuring.* Here was the first breach made on those who were before "of one heart, and of one soul." Partiality crept in unawares on some, and murmuring on others. Ah, Lord, how short a time did pure, genuine, undefiled Christianity remain in the world! O the depth! How unsearchable are your counsels! Marvelous are your ways, O King of saints!

In this partiality of the Hebrews and murmuring of the Hellenists were the seeds of a general persecution sown. Did God ever, in any age or country, withdraw his restraining providence and let loose the world upon the Christians until there was a cause among themselves? Is not an open, general persecution always both penal and medicinal? A punishment of those that will not accept milder reproofs, as well as a medicine to heal their sickness? And at the same time a means both of purifying and strengthening those whose heart is still right with God?

2. *It is not reason that we should leave the word of God, and serve tables.* In the first church, the primary business of apostles, evangelists, and bishops was to preach the word of God; the secondary, to take a kind of paternal care (the church being in that instance like a family) for the food, especially of the poor, the strangers, and the widows. Afterwards, the deacons of both sexes were constituted for this latter business; and whatever time they had to spare from this they employed in works of spiritual mercy. But their proper office was to take care of the poor. And when some of them afterwards preached the gospel, they did this, not by virtue of their deaconship, but of another commission—that of evangelists, which they probably received not before, but after they were appointed deacons. And it is not unlikely that others were chosen deacons, or stewards, in their place when any of these commenced to be evangelists.

3. *Of honest report.* That there may be no room to suspect them of partiality or injustice. *Full of the Holy Ghost and wisdom.* For it is not a light matter to dispense even the temporal goods of the church. To do even this well, a large measure both of the gifts and grace of God is required. *Whom we may appoint over this business.* It would have been happy for the church had its ordinary ministers in every age taken the same care to act in concert with the people committed to their charge which the apostles themselves, extraordinary as their office was, did on this and other occasions.

4. *We will give ourselves continually to prayer, and to the ministry of the word.* This is doubtless the proper business of a Christian bishop—to speak to God, in prayer; to men, in preaching his word, as ambassador for Christ.

15. *As ... the face of an angel.* Covered with supernatural luster. They reckoned that his preaching of Jesus as the Christ was destroying Moses and the law; and God bears witness to him with the same glory as he did to Moses when he gave the law by him.

CHAPTER 7

This solemn testimony of Stephen is most worthy of his character as "a man full of the Holy Ghost, and of faith, and power"; in which though he does not advance so many regular propositions contradictory to those of his adversaries, yet he closely answers them all. Nor can we doubt but he would from these premises have drawn inferences touching the destruction of the temple, the abrogation of the Mosaic law, the punishment of that rebellious people, and above all, touching Jesus of Nazareth, the true Messiah, had not his discourse been interrupted by the clamors of the multitude, stopping their ears and rushing upon him.

16. *And were carried over into Sychem.* It seems that Stephen, rapidly running over so many circumstances of history, has not leisure (nor was it needful where they were so well known) to recite them all distinctly. Therefore he here contracts into one, two different sepulchers, places, and purchases, so as in the former history to name the buyer, omitting the seller; in the latter, to name the seller, omitting the buyer. This concise manner of speaking, as strange as it seems to us, was common among the Hebrews; particularly when, in a case notoriously known, the speaker mentioned but part of the story and left the rest, which would have interrupted the current of his discourse, to be supplied in the mind of the hearer.

35. This angel who spoke to Moses on Mount Sinai expressly called himself "Jehovah," a name which cannot, without the highest presumption, be assumed by any created angel since "He whose name alone is Jehovah is the Most High over all the earth" (Ps. 83:18). It was therefore the Son of God who delivered the law to Moses, under the character of Jehovah, and who is here spoken of as the Angel of the Covenant in respect of his mediatorial office.

42. *The host of heaven.* The stars are called an army, or host, because of their number, order, and powerful influence.

45. *Brought . . . into the possession of the Gentiles.* All along Stephen intimates two things: (1) That God always loved good men in every land. (2) That he never loved bad men even in this.

55. *But he . . . looked up stedfastly into heaven, and saw the glory of God.* Doubtless he saw such a glorious representation, God miraculously operating on his imagination as on Ezekiel's when he "sat in his house at Babylon" and saw Jerusalem and seemed to himself to be transported there (Ezek. 8:1–4). And probably other martyrs, when called to suffer the last extremity, have had extraordinary assistance of some similar kind.

58. *And the witnesses laid down their clothes at a young man's feet, whose name was Saul.* O Saul, could you have believed, if one had told you, that you yourself should be stoned in the same cause; and should triumph in committing your soul likewise to that Jesus whom you are now blaspheming! His dying prayer reached you, as well as many others. And Stephen the martyr and Saul the persecutor (afterwards his brother both in faith and martyrdom) are now joined in everlasting friendship and dwell together in the happy company of those who "have made their robes white in the blood of the Lamb."

59. *And they stoned Stephen, invoking[3] and saying, Lord Jesus, receive my spirit.* This is the literal translation of the words, the name of God not being in the original. Nevertheless, such a solemn prayer to Christ, in which a departing soul is thus committed into his hands, is such an act of worship as no good man could have paid to a mere creature. Stephen here worships Christ in the very same manner in which Christ worshipped the Father on the cross.

CHAPTER 8

2. *Devout men.* Who feared God more than persecution. And yet were they not of little faith? Else they would not have made so *great lamentation.*

4. *Therefore they that were scattered abroad went every where.* These very

---

[3] (7:59) KJV: "calling upon God."

words are reassumed, after as it were a long parenthesis, in Acts 11:19, and the thread of the story continues.

15. *The Holy Ghost.* In his miraculous gifts, or his sanctifying graces? Probably in both.

21. *For thy heart is not right in the sight of God.* Probably Peter discerned this long before he declared it; although it does not appear that God gave to any of the apostles a universal power of discerning the hearts of all they conversed with, any more than a universal power of healing all the sick they came near. This we are sure Paul had not, though he was not inferior to the chief of the apostles. Otherwise he would not have allowed the illness of Epaphroditus to have brought him so near to death (Phil. 2:25–27); nor have left so useful a fellow laborer as Trophimus sick at Miletus (II Tim. 4:20).

22. *Repent, . . . if perhaps the thought of thine heart may be forgiven thee.* Without all doubt, if he had repented he would have been forgiven. The doubt was whether he would repent.

23. *Thou art in the gall of bitterness.* In the highest degree of wickedness, which is bitterness; that is, misery to the soul.

28. *Sitting in his chariot read the prophet Esaias.* God meets those who remember him in his ways. It is good to read, hear, seek information, even on a journey. Why should we not redeem all our time?

30. *And Philip ran thither to him, . . . and said, Understandest thou what thou readest?* He did not begin about the weather, news, or the like. In speaking for God we may frequently come to the point at once without circumlocution.

36. *And as they went on the way, they came unto a certain water.* Thus even the circumstances of the journey were under the direction of God. The kingdom

of God suits itself to external circumstances without any violence; as air yields to all bodies and yet pervades all. *What doth hinder me to be baptized?* Probably he had been circumcised, otherwise Cornelius would not have been the firstfruits of the Gentiles.

38. *And they went down both.* Out of the chariot. It does not follow that he was baptized by immersion. The text neither affirms nor intimates anything concerning it.

39. *The Spirit of the Lord caught away Philip.* Carried him away with a miraculous swiftness without any action or labor of his own. This had happened to several of the prophets.

CHAPTER 9

3. *And suddenly.* When God suddenly and vehemently attacks a sinner, it is the highest act of mercy. So Saul, when his rage was come to the height, is taught not to "breathe slaughter." And what was wanting in time to confirm him in his discipleship is compensated by the inexpressible terror he sustained. By this also the suddenly constituted apostle was guarded against the grand snare into which novices are apt to fall.

6. *It shall be told thee.* So God himself sends Saul to be taught by a man, as the angel does to Cornelius (Acts 10:5). Admirable condescension, that the Lord deals with us by men like ourselves.

9. *And he was three days.* An important season! So long he seems to have been in the pangs of the new birth. *Without sight.* By scales growing over his eyes, to intimate to him the blindness of the state he had been in, to impress him with a deeper sense of the almighty power of Christ, and to turn his thoughts inward while he was less capable of conversing with outward objects. This was likewise a manifest token to others of what had happened to him on his journey and ought to have humbled and convinced those bigoted Jews to whom he had been sent from the Sanhedrin.

13. *Then Ananias answered.* How natural is it to reason against God!

15. *He is a chosen vessel . . . to bear my name.* That is, to testify of me. It is undeniable that some men are unconditionally chosen or elected to do some works for God.

40. *Peter put them all forth.* That he might have the better opportunity of wrestling with God in prayer. *Said, Tabitha, arise. And she opened her eyes: and when she saw Peter, she sat up.* Who can imagine the surprise of Dorcas when called back to life? Or of her friends when they saw her alive? For the sake of themselves and of the poor, there was cause for rejoicing; and much more for such a confirmation of the gospel. Yet to herself it was a matter of resignation, not joy, to be called back to these scenes of vanity. But doubtless her remaining days were still more zealously spent in the service of her Savior and her God. Thus was a richer treasure laid up for her in heaven, and she afterward returned to a more exceeding weight of glory than that from which so astonishing a providence had recalled her for a season.

CHAPTER 10

4. *Thy prayers and thine alms are come up for a memorial before God.* Dare any man say that these were only splendid sins, or that they were an abomination before God? And yet it is certain that in the Christian sense, Cornelius was then an unbeliever. He had not then faith in Christ. So certain is it that every one who seeks faith in Christ should seek it in prayer and in doing good to all men.

Though in strictness, what is not exactly according to the divine rule must stand in need of divine favor and indulgence.

7. *A devout soldier.* How many such attendants have our modern officers? A devout soldier would now be looked upon as little better than a deserter from his colors.

14. *But Peter said, Not so, Lord.* When God commands a strange or seemingly improper thing, the first objection frequently finds pardon. But it ought not to be repeated. This doubt and delay of Peter had several good effects. Hereby the will of God in this important point was made more evident and incontestable; Peter also, having been so slow of belief himself, could the more easily bear the doubting of his brethren (Acts 11:2ff.).

17. *While Peter doubted in himself, . . . behold, the men.* Frequently those things which befall us within and from without at the same time are a key to each other. The things which thus concur and agree together ought to be diligently attended to.

19–20. *Behold, three men seek thee. Arise therefore, and get thee down, and go with them, doubting nothing.* How gradually was Peter prepared to receive this new admonition of the Spirit! Thus God often leads his children by degree, always giving them light for the present hour.

33. *Now therefore are we all here present before God.* The language of every truly Christian congregation.

34. *That God is no respecter of persons.* Is not partial in his love. The words mean in a particular sense that he does not confine his love to one nation; in a general sense, that he is loving to every man and wills that all men should be saved.

35. *But in every nation he that feareth him, and worketh righteousness.* He that first reverences God as great, wise, good; the Cause, End, and Governor of all things; and secondly, from this awful regard to him, not only avoids all known evil, but endeavors, according to the best light he has, to do all things well. *Is accepted with him.* Through Christ, though he knows him not. Nevertheless, the addition of these is an unspeakable blessing to those who were before, in some measure, accepted. Otherwise God would never have sent an angel from heaven to direct Cornelius to Peter.

38. *How God anointed Jesus.* Particularly at his baptism, thereby inaugurating him to his office. *With the Holy Ghost and with power.* It is worthy our remark that frequently when the Holy Ghost is mentioned, there is added a word particularly adapted to the present circumstance. So the deacons were to be "full of the Holy Ghost and wisdom" (Acts 6:3); Barnabas was "full of the Holy Ghost and faith" (11:24); the disciples were "filled with joy and with the Holy Ghost" (13:52); and here, where his mighty works are mentioned, Christ himself is said to be anointed "with the Holy Ghost and with power."

44. *The Holy Ghost fell on all them which heard the word.* Thus were they consecrated to God as the firstfruits of the Gentiles. And thus did God give a clear and satisfactory evidence that he had accepted them as well as the Jews.

47. *Can any man forbid water, that these should not be baptized, which have received the Holy Ghost.* He does not say, They have the baptism of the Spirit; therefore they do not need baptism with water. But just the contrary: If they have received the Spirit, then baptize them with water.

How easily is this question decided if we will take the Word of God for our judge! Either men have received the Holy Ghost or not. If they have not, "Repent," says God, "and be baptized, and ye shall receive the gift of the Holy Ghost." If they have, if they are already baptized with the Holy Ghost, then, who can *forbid water?*

CHAPTER 11

17. *Unto us, who believed.* The sense is, Because we believed, not because we were circumcised, was the Holy Ghost given to us. *What was I.* A mere instrument in God's hand. And who are we, that we should withstand God? Particularly by laying down rules of Christian communion which exclude any whom he has admitted into the church of the firstborn from worshipping God together. O that all church governors would consider how bold a usurpation this is on the authority of the supreme Lord of the church! O that the sin of thus withstanding God may not be laid to the charge of those who, perhaps with a good intention but in an over-fondness for their own methods, have done and are continually doing it!

20. *Spake unto the Grecians.* As the Greeks were the most celebrated of the gentile nations near Judea, the Jews called all Gentiles by that name. Here we have the first account of preaching the gospel to the idolatrous Gentiles. All those to whom it had been preached before did at least worship one God, the God of Israel.

21. *And the hand of the Lord.* That is, the power of his Spirit.

CHAPTER 12

1. *About that time.* So wisely did God mix rest and persecution in due time and measure succeeding each other.

5. *Prayer was made without ceasing . . . for him.* Yet when their prayer was answered, they could scarce believe it

(v. 15). But why had they not prayed for James also? Because he was put to death as soon as apprehended.

15. *They said, . . . Thou art mad.* As we say, You are not in your senses to talk so. *It is his angel.* It was a common opinion among the Jews that every man had his particular guardian angel, who frequently assumed both his shape and voice. But this is a point on which the Scriptures are silent.

17. *And he said, Go shew these things unto James.* The brother or kinsman of our Lord, and author of the epistle which bears his name. He appears to have been a person of considerable weight and importance, probably the chief overseer of that province, and of the church in Jerusalem in particular.

21. *Herod, arrayed in royal apparel.* In a garment so wrought with silver that the rays of the rising sun striking upon, and being reflected from it, dazzled the eyes of the beholders.

23. *The angel of the Lord smote him.* Of this other historians say nothing. So wide a difference is there between divine and human history! An angel of the Lord brought out Peter; an angel smote Herod. Men did not see the instruments in either case. These were only known to the people of God.

CHAPTER 13

2. *Separate me Barnabas and Saul.* This was not ordaining them. Paul was ordained long before, and that "not of men, neither by man." It was only inducting him to the province for which our Lord had appointed him from the beginning, and which was now revealed to the prophets and teachers. In consequence of this they fasted, prayed, and laid their hands upon them—a rite which was used not in ordination only, but in blessing and on many other occasions.

10. *Thou child of the devil.* A title well suited to a magician, and one who not only was himself unrighteous, but labored to keep others from all goodness.

13. *John departing from them returned.* Tired with the fatigue, or shrinking from danger.

17. *The God.* By such a commemoration of God's favors to their fathers, at once their minds were conciliated to the speaker; they were convinced of their duty to God and invited to believe his promise and the accomplishment of it. The six verses (17–22) contain the whole sum of the Old Testament.

22. *I have found David, . . . a man after mine own heart.* This expression is to be taken in a limited sense. David was such at that time, but not at all times. And he was so in that respect as he performed all God's will in the particulars there mentioned. But he was not a man after God's heart in other respects, wherein he performed his own will. In the matter of Uriah, for instance, he was as far from being a man after God's heart as Saul himself was. It is therefore a very gross, as well as dangerous, mistake to suppose that this is the character of David in every part of his behavior. We must beware of this unless we would recommend adultery and murder as things after God's own heart.

33. *Thou art my Son, this day have I begotten thee.* It is true he was the Son of God from eternity. The meaning therefore is, I have this day declared you to be my Son. As Paul said elsewhere, "Declared to be the Son of God with power, by the resurrection from the dead" (Rom. 1:4). And it is with peculiar propriety and beauty that God is said to "have begotten him" on the day when he raised him from the dead, as he seemed then to be born out of the earth anew.

36. *Served . . . the will of God.* Why

are you here, you who are yet in the world? Is it not that you also may serve the will of God? Are you serving it now? Are you doing his will?

39. *By the law of Moses.* The whole Mosaic institution. The division of the law into moral and ceremonial was not so common among the Jews as it is among us. Nor does the apostle here consider it at all; but Moses and Christ are opposed to each other.

46. *Then Paul and Barnabas waxed bold, and said.* Those who hinder others must be publicly reproved. *It was necessary.* Though you are not worthy. He shows that he had not preached to them from any confidence of their believing.

48. *As many as were ordained to eternal life.* Luke does not say "foreordained." He is not speaking of what was done from eternity, but of what was done through the preaching of the gospel. He is describing that ordination, and that only which was at the very time of hearing it. During this sermon those believed, says the apostle, to whom God then gave power to believe. It is as if he had said, They believed, "whose hearts the Lord opened"; as he expresses it in a clearly parallel place, speaking of the same kind of ordination (Acts 16:14ff.). It is observable, the original word is not once used in Scripture to express eternal predestination of any kind. The sum is, All those and those only who were now ordained now believed. Not that God rejected the rest; it was his will that they also should have been saved; but they thrust salvation from them. Nor were they who then believed constrained to believe. But grace was first copiously offered them. And they did not thrust it away, so that a great multitude even of Gentiles were converted. In a word, the expression properly implies a present operation of divine grace, working faith in the hearers.

CHAPTER 14

11. *The gods are come down.* Which the heathens supposed they frequently did, Jupiter especially. But how amazingly does the prince of darkness blind the minds of them that believe not! The Jews would not own Christ's Godhead, though they saw him work numberless miracles. However, the heathens seeing mere men work one miracle were for deifying them immediately.

17. *He left not himself without witness.* For the heathens had always from God himself a testimony both of his existence and of his providence. *In that he did good.* Even by punishments he testifies of himself; but more peculiarly by benefits. *Gave us rain.* By which air, earth, and sea are, as it were, all joined together. *From heaven.* The seat of God; to which Paul probably pointed while he spoke. *Filling* the body with *food,* the soul with *gladness.*

20. *He rose up, and came into the city.* That he should be able to do this just after he had been left for dead was a miracle little less than a resurrection from the dead; especially considering the manner wherein the Jewish malefactors were stoned. The witnesses first threw as large a stone as they could lift, with all possible violence, upon his head, which alone was sufficient to dash the skull in pieces. All the people then joined, as long as any motion or token of life remained.

CHAPTER 15

2. *They.* The brethren. *Determined that Paul and Barnabas, and certain other of them, should go up to Jerusalem . . . about this question.* This is the journey to which Paul refers (Gal.

2:1–2) when he says he "went up by revelation," which is very consistent with this; for the church in sending them might be directed by a revelation, made either immediately to Paul or to some other person, relating to so important an affair.

5. *But . . . certain . . . Pharisees.* For even believers are apt to retain their former turn of mind, and prejudices derived therefrom.

7. *When there had been much disputing.* It does not appear that this was among the apostles themselves. But if it had, if they themselves had debated at first, yet might their final decision be from an unerring direction. For however they were inspired, we need not suppose their inspiration was always so instantaneous and express as to supersede any deliberation in their own minds or any consultation with each other.

18. *Known unto God are all his works from eternity.*[4] Which the apostle infers from the prophecy itself, and the accomplishment of it. And this conversion of the Gentiles being known to him from eternity we ought not to think a new or strange thing.

It is observable, he does not speak of God's works in the natural world (which had been nothing to his present purpose), but of his dealing with the children of men. Now he could not know these without knowing the characters and actions of particular persons on a correspondence with which the wisdom and goodness of his providential dispensations is founded. For instance, he could not know how he would deal with heathen idolaters (whom he was now calling into his church) without knowing that there would be heathen idolaters; and yet this was a thing purely contingent, a thing as dependent on the freedom of the human mind as any we can imagine. This text, therefore, among a thousand more is an unanswerable proof that God foreknows future contingencies, though there are difficulties relating to this which man cannot solve.

23. *Writing thus* [and sending it] *by their hand.* The whole conduct of this affair plainly shows that the church in those days had no conception of Peter's primacy or of his being the chief judge in controversies. For the decree is drawn up, not according to his, but the apostle James's proposal and direction; and that in the name, not of Peter, but of all the apostles and elders and of the whole church. Peter's name is not mentioned at all, either in the order for sending to Jerusalem on the question (v. 2), or in the address of the messengers concerning it (v. 4), or in the letter which was written in answer.

29. *Blood.* The eating which was never permitted the children of God from the beginning of the world. Nothing can be clearer than this. *From which if ye keep yourselves, ye shall do well.* That is, you will find a blessing. This gentle manner of concluding was worthy the apostolical wisdom and goodness. But how soon did succeeding councils of inferior authority change it into the style of anathemas! Such forms have proved an occasion of consecrating some of the most devilish passions under the most sacred names; and, like some ill-adjusted weapons of war, are most likely to hurt the hand from which they are thrown.

36. *And see how they do.* How their souls prosper; how they grow in faith, hope, love. What else ought to be the grand and constant inquiry in every

---

[4](15:18) KJV: "from the beginning of the world."

ecclesiastical visitation? Reader, how is it with you?

38. *But Paul thought not good.* To trust him again who had deserted them before; who had shrunk from the labor and danger of converting those they were now going to confirm.

39. *And the contention was so sharp.* Literally, a paroxysm, or fit of a fever. But nothing in the text implies that the sharpness was on both sides. It is far more probable that it was not; that Paul, who had the right on his side (as he undoubtedly had), maintained it with love. *And so Barnabas took Mark, and sailed unto Cyprus.* Forsaking the work in which he was engaged, he went away to his own country.

40. *And Paul . . . departed.* Held on his intended course. *Being recommended by the brethren unto the grace of God.* We do not find that Barnabas stayed for this. Oh, how mighty is the grace of God; which, in the midst of the world, in the midst of sin, among so many snares of Satan, and in spite of the incredible weakness and depravity of nature, yet overcomes all opposition, sanctifies, sustains, and preserves us to the end!

It appears not only that Paul and Barnabas were afterwards thoroughly reconciled (I Cor. 9:6; Gal. 2:9), but also that Mark was again admitted by Paul as a companion in his labors (Col. 4:10; Philem. 24; II Tim. 4:11).

CHAPTER 16

7. *But the Spirit suffered them not.* Forbidding them as before. Sometimes a strong impression, for which we are not able to give any account, is not altogether to be despised.

9. *A man of Macedonia.* Probably an angel clothed in the Macedonian habit, or using the language of the country, and representing the inhabitants of it.

Help us. Against Satan, ignorance, and sin.

10. *We endeavored to go into Macedonia.* This is the first place in which Luke intimates his attendance on the apostle. And here he does it only in an oblique manner. Nor does he throughout the history once mention his own name or any one thing which he did or said for the service of Christianity. The same remark may be made on the rest of the sacred historians, who every one of them show the like amiable modesty.

14. *Whose heart the Lord opened.* The Greek word properly refers to the opening of the eyes. And the heart has its eyes (Eph. 1:18). These are closed by nature; and to open them is the peculiar work of God.

15. *She was baptized, and her household.* Who can believe that in so many families there was no infant? Or that the Jews, who were so long accustomed to circumcising their children, would not now devote them to God by baptism? *She constrained us.* The souls of the faithful cleave to those by whom they were gained to God.

21. *And teach customs, which are not lawful for us to receive.* The world has received all the rules and doctrines of all the philosophers that ever were. But this is a property of gospel truth: It has something in it peculiarly intolerable to the world.

25. *Paul and Silas prayed, and sang praises unto God.* In spite of weariness, hunger, stripes, and blood. *And the prisoners heard.* A song to which they were not accustomed.

28. *Do thyself no harm.* Although the Christian faith opens the prospect into another life, yet it absolutely forbids, and effectually prevents, a man's discharging himself from this one.

30. *What must I do to be saved?* From the guilt I feel and the vengeance I fear. Undoubtedly God then set his sins in array before him and convinced him in the clearest and strongest manner that the wrath of God was upon him.

33. *He . . . washed their stripes.* It should not be forgot that the apostles had not the power of working miraculous cures when they pleased, either on themselves or their dearest friends. Nor was it expedient they should, since it would have frustrated many wise designs of God which were answered by their sufferings.

34. *He set meat before them, and rejoiced.* Faith makes a man joyful, prudent, liberal.

37. *They have beaten us openly uncondemned, being Romans.* Paul does not always plead this privilege. But in a country where they were complete strangers, such treatment might have brought upon them a suspicion of having been guilty of some uncommon crime and so have hindered the course of the gospel.

40. *When they had seen the brethren, they comforted them, and departed.* Even though many circumstances now invited their stay, yet they wisely complied with the request of the magistrates, that they might not seem to express any degree of obstinacy or revenge or give any suspicion of a design to stir up the people.

CHAPTER 17

4. *Of the chief women not a few.* Our freethinkers pique themselves upon observing that women are more religious than men; and this, in compliment both to religion and good manners, they impute to the weakness of their understandings. And indeed, as far as nature can go in imitating religion by performing the outward acts of it, this picture of religion may make a fairer show in women than in men, both by reason of their more tender passions and their modesty, which will make those actions appear to more advantage. But in the case of true religion, which always implies taking up the cross, especially in time of persecution, women lie naturally under a great disadvantage as having less courage than men. So that their embracing the gospel was then a stronger evidence of the power of him whose strength is perfected in weakness, as a stronger assistance of the Holy Spirit was needful for them to overcome their natural fearfulness.

11. *These were more ingenuous.*[5] Or generous. To be teachable in the things of God is true generosity of soul. Receiving *the word with all readiness of mind* and the most accurate search into the truth are well consistent.

18. It is easy to see how happily the apostle levels his discourse at some of the most important errors of each, *of the Epicureans, and of the Stoics,* while, without expressly attacking either, he gives a plain summary of his own religious principles. *What will this babbler say?* Such is the language of natural reason, full of and satisfied with itself. Yet even here Paul had some fruit; though nowhere less than at Athens. And no wonder, since this city was a seminary of philosophers, who have ever been the pest of true religion.

22. *Then Paul stood in the midst of Mars' hill.* An ample theater! *Said.* Giving them a lecture of natural divinity with admirable wisdom, acuteness, fullness, and courtesy. They inquire after new things. Paul, in his divinely philosophical discourse, begins with the first and goes on to the last things,

---

[5] (17:11) KJV: "more noble."

both which were new things to them. He points out the origin and the end of all things, concerning which they had so many disputes, and equally refutes both the Epicurean and Stoic.

25. *Life.* In him we live. *And breath.* In him we move. By breathing, life is continued. I breathe this moment; the next is not in my power. *And all things.* For in him we are. So exactly do the parts of this discourse answer each other.

27. *If haply.* The way is open; God is ready to be found, but he will lay no force upon man. *They might feel after him.* This is in the midst between seeking and finding. Feeling, being the lowest and grossest of all our senses, is fitly applied to that low knowledge of God. *Though he be not far from every one of us.* We need not go far to seek or find him. He is very near us; in us. It is only perverse reason which thinks he is afar off.

28. *In him.* Not in ourselves. *We live, and move, and have our being.* This denotes his necessary, intimate, and most efficacious presence. No words can better express the continual and necessary dependence of all created beings, in their existence and all their operations, on the first and almighty Cause, which the truest philosophy as well as divinity teaches.

29. *We ought not to think.* A tender expression, especially in the first person plural. As if he had said, "Can God himself be a less noble being than we who are his offspring?"

30. *God . . . commandeth all men every where to repent.* There is a dignity and grandeur in this expression, being an ambassador from the King of heaven. And this universal demand of repentance declared universal guilt in the strongest manner, and admirably confronted the pride of the haughtiest Stoic of them all. At the same time it bore down the idle plea of fatality. For how could any one repent of doing what he could not but have done?

CHAPTER 18

3. *They were tentmakers.* For it was a rule among the Jews (and why is it not among the Christians?) to bring up all their children to some trade, were they ever so rich or noble.

5. *Paul was pressed in the spirit.* The more, probably, from what Silas and Timothy related. Every Christian ought diligently to observe any such pressure in his own spirit and, if it agree with Scripture, to follow it. If he does not, he will feel great heaviness.

6. *I am clean.* None can say this, but he that has borne a full testimony against sin.

9–10. I am with thee. Therefore fear not all the learning, politeness, grandeur, or power of the inhabitants of this city. *Speak, and hold not thy peace.* For your labor shall not be in vain. *For I have much people in this city.* So he prophetically calls them that afterwards believed.

1. *He continued there a year and six months.* A long time. But how few souls are now gained in a longer time than this! Who is at fault? Generally, both teachers and hearers.

12. *When Gallio was the deputy of Achaia.* Of which Corinth was the chief city. This Gallio, the brother of the famous Seneca, is much commended, both by him and by other writers, for the sweetness and generosity of his temper and easiness of his behavior. Yet one thing he lacked! But he knew it not and had no concern about it.

15. *But if it be.* He speaks with the utmost coolness and contempt. *A question of words.* The names of the heathen gods were fables and shadows. But the question concerning the name of Jesus is of more importance than anything else under heaven. Yet there is this singularity, among a thousand others, in the Christian religion, that human reason, curious as it is in all other things, abhors to inquire into it.

24. *An eloquent man, and mighty in the scriptures.* Of the Old Testament. Every talent may be of use in the kingdom of God if joined with knowledge of the Scriptures and fervor of spirit.

27. *Helped them much . . . through grace.* It is through grace only that any gift of any one is profitable to another. *Them . . . which had believed.* Apollos did not plant, but water. This was the peculiar gift which he had received. And he was better able to convince the Jews than to convert the heathens.

CHAPTER 19

2. *Have ye received the Holy Ghost.* The extraordinary gifts of the Spirit, as well as his sanctifying graces? *We have not so much as heard.* Whether there be any such gifts.

5. *They were baptized.* They were baptized twice, but not with the same baptism. John did not administer that baptism which Christ afterwards commanded; that is, in the name of the Father, Son, and Holy Ghost.

13. *Exorcists.* Several of the Jews about this time pretended to a power of casting out devils, particularly by certain arts or charms, supposed to be derived from Solomon. *Took upon them to call over them.* Vain undertaking! Satan laughs at all those who attempt to expel him either out of the bodies or the souls of men but by divine faith. All the light of reason is nothing to the craft and strength of that subtle spirit.

His craft cannot be known but by the Spirit of God; nor can his strength be conquered but by the power of faith.

18. *And shewed their deeds.* The efficacy of God's word, penetrating the inmost recesses of their soul, wrought that free and open confession to which perhaps even torments would not have compelled them.

19. *Burned them.* Which was far better than selling them, even though the money had been given to the poor.

21. *After these things were ended.* Paul sought not to rest, but pressed on as if he had yet done nothing. He is already possessed of Ephesus and Asia. He purposes for Macedonia and Achaia. He has his eye upon Jerusalem; then upon Rome; and afterwards on Spain (Rom. 15:24). No Caesar, no Alexander the Great, no other hero comes up to the magnanimity of this little Benjamite. Faith and love to God and man had enlarged his heart, even as the sand of the sea.

CHAPTER 20

12. *And they brought the young man alive.* But, alas, how many of those who have allowed themselves to sleep under sermons or, as it were, to dream awake have slept the sleep of eternal death and fallen to rise no more!

19. *With all humility of mind, and with many tears, and trials.*[6] These are the concomitants of it. The service itself is described more particularly in the following verse. This humility he recommends to the Ephesians themselves (Eph. 4:2). His tears are mentioned again, verse 31, as also II Corinthians 2:4 and Philippians 3:18. These passages, laid together, supply us with the genuine character of Paul. Holy tears,

---

[6] (20:19) KJV: "and temptations."

from those who seldom weep on account of natural occurrences, are no mean specimen of the efficacy and proof of the truth of Christianity. Yet joy is well consistent with tears (v. 24). The same person may be "sorrowful, yet always rejoicing."

20. *Taught . . . from house to house.* Else he had not been pure from their blood. For even an apostle could not discharge his duty by public preaching only. How much less can an ordinary pastor!

21. *Repentance toward God.* The very first motion of the soul toward God is a kind of repentance.

24. *Neither count I my life dear.* It adds great force to this and all the other passages of Scripture, in which the apostles express their contempt of the world, that they were not uttered by persons like Seneca and Antoninus, who talked elegantly of despising the world while in the full affluence of all its enjoyments; but by men who daily underwent the greatest calamities and exposed their lives in proof of their assertions.

28. *Over the which the Holy Ghost hath made you overseers.* For no man or number of men upon earth can constitute an overseer, bishop, or any other Christian minister. To do this is the peculiar work of the Holy Ghost.

31. *I ceased not to warn every one night and day.* This was watching indeed! Who copies after this example?

32. *Which is able to build you up.* To confirm and increase your faith, love, holiness. God can thus build us up without any instrument. But he does build us up by them. Oh, beware of dreaming that you have less need of human teachers after you know Christ than before!

35. *Ye ought to support the weak.* Those who are disabled by sickness or any bodily infirmity from maintaining themselves by their own labor.

37. *They all wept.* Of old, men—yes, the best and bravest of men—were easily melted into tears; a thousand instances of which might be produced from profane as well as sacred writers. But now, in spite of the effeminacy which almost universally prevails, we leave those tears to women and children.

38. *Sorrowing most of all for the words which he spake.* What sorrow will be in the great day when God shall speak that word to all who are found on the left hand, that they shall *see his face no more!*

CHAPTER 21

4. *Who said to Paul through the Spirit.* That afflictions awaited him at Jerusalem. This was properly what they said by the Spirit. They themselves advised him not to *go up.* The disciples seemed to understand their prophetic impulse to be an intimation from the Spirit that Paul, if he were so minded, might avoid the danger by not going to Jerusalem.

13. *I am ready not to be bound only, but also to die.* And to him that is ready for it, the burden is light.

14. *And when he would not be persuaded.* This was not obstinacy, but true Christian resolution.

20. *They are all zealous of the law.* For the whole Mosaic dispensation. How astonishing is this! Did none of the apostles beside Paul know that this dispensation was now abolished? And if they did know and testify this, how came their hearers not to believe them?

23. *Do . . . this that we say to thee.* Doubtless they meant this advice well. But could Paul follow it in godly sincerity? Was not the yielding so far to the judgment of others too great a deference to be paid to any mere men?

24. *And all may know . . . that thou thyself also walkest orderly, and keepest the law.* Ought he not, without any reverence to man, where the truth of God was so deeply concerned, to have answered plainly, "I do not keep the Mosaic law; neither need any of you?" Peter does not keep the law. God himself expressly commanded him not to keep it; ordering him to "go in to men uncircumcised, and to eat with them" (Acts 11:3), which the law utterly forbids.

26. *Then Paul took the men.* Yielding his own judgment to their advice, which seemed to flow not out of spiritual, but carnal wisdom; seeming to be what he really was not; making as if he believed the law still in force.

30. *And forthwith the gates were shut.* Both to prevent any further violation of the temple and to prevent Paul's taking sanctuary at the horns of the altar.

33. *Came near, and took him.* And how many great ends of Providence were answered by this imprisonment! This was not only a means of preserving his life after he had suffered severely for worldly prudence, but gave him an opportunity of preaching the gospel safely in spite of all tumult (Acts 22:22); yes, and that in those places to which otherwise he could have had no access (v. 40).

CHAPTER 22

3. *Taught according to the perfect manner of the law.* The learned education which Paul had received was once, no doubt, the matter of his boasting and confidence. Unsanctified learning made his bonds strong and furnished him with numerous arguments against the gospel. Yet, when the grace of God had changed his heart and turned his accomplishments into another channel, he was the fitter instrument to serve God's wise and merciful purposes in the defense and propagation of Christianity.

6. *About noon.* All was done in the face of the sun. *From heaven a great light.* By whatever method God reveals himself to us, we shall have everlasting cause to recollect it with pleasure. Especially when he has gone in any remarkable manner out of his common way for this gracious purpose. If so, we should often dwell on the particular circumstances and be ready, on every proper occasion, to recount those wonders of power and love, for the encouragement and instruction of others.

16. *Be baptized, and wash away thy sins.* Baptism, administered to real penitents, is both a means and seal of pardon. Nor did God ordinarily in the primitive church bestow this on any unless through this means.

19. *And I said.* It is not easy for a servant of Christ, who is himself deeply impressed with divine truths, to imagine to what a degree men are capable of hardening their hearts against them. He is often ready to think, with Paul, that it is impossible for any to resist such evidence. But experience makes him wiser and shows that willful unbelief is proof against all truth and reason.

20. *When the blood of thy martyr Stephen was shed, I also was standing by.* A real convert retains the remembrance of his former sins. He confesses them and is humbled all the days of his life.

28. *I was free born.* We learn here we are under no obligation as Christians to give up our civil privileges (which we are to receive and prize as the gift of God) to every insolent invader. In a thousand circumstances, gratitude to God and duty to men will oblige us to insist upon them and engage us to strive to transmit them improved, rather than impaired, to posterity.

CHAPTER 23

11. *And the night following the Lord Jesus.* What Paul had before purposed in spirit (Acts 19:21), God now in due time confirms. Another declaration to the same effect is made by an angel of God (27:23). From the twenty-third chapter the sum of this book turns on the testimony of Paul to the Romans. How would the defenders of Peter's supremacy triumph, could they find but half as much ascribed to him! *Thou hast testified.* Particular promises are usually given when all things appear desperate. *Also at Rome.* Danger is nothing in the eyes of God; all hindrances further his work. A promise of what is afar off implies all that necessarily lies between. Paul shall testify at Rome; therefore he shall come to Rome; therefore he shall escape the Jews, the sea, the viper.

17. *Then Paul.* Though he had an express promise of it from Christ, he was not to neglect any proper means of safety.

CHAPTER 24

2. *Tertullus began.* A speech how different from Paul's, which is true, modest, solid, and without paint!

4. *That I be not further tedious unto thee.* By trespassing either on your patience or modesty. The eloquence of Tertullus was as bad as his cause: a lame introduction, a lame transition, and a lame conclusion! Did not God confound the orator's language?

10. *I . . . answer for myself.* And it may be observed, his answer exactly corresponds with the three articles of Tertullus's charge: sedition, heresy, and profanation of the temple.

14. *After the way which they call heresy.* This appellation Paul corrects. Not that it was then an odious word; but it was not honorable enough. A party or sect (so that word signifies) is formed by men. This way was prescribed by God. The apostle had now said what was sufficient for his defense;

but, having a fair occasion, he makes an ingenuous confession of his faith in this verse, his hope in the next, his love in the seventeenth.

19. *Who ought to have been here before thee.* But the world never commits greater blunders, even against its own laws, than when it is persecuting the children of God.

25. *And as he reasoned of righteousness, temperance, and judgment to come.* This was the only effectual way of preaching Christ to an unjust, lewd judge. *Felix trembled.* How happily might this conviction have ended, had he been careful to pursue the views which were then opening upon his mind! But, like thousands, he deferred the consideration of these things to a more *convenient season;* a season which, alas, never came! For though he heard again, he was terrified no more.

In the meantime, we do not find Drusilla, though a Jewess, was thus alarmed. She had been used to hearing of a future judgment; perhaps, too, she trusted to being a daughter of Abraham or to the expiation of the law, and so was proof against the convictions which seized on her husband, though a heathen. Let this teach us to guard against all such false dependencies as tend to elude those convictions that might otherwise be produced in us by the faithful preaching of the word of God. Let us stop our ears against those messengers of Satan who appear as angels of light, who would teach us to reconcile the hope of salvation with a corrupt heart or an unholy life. *Go thy way for this time.* O how will every damned soul one day lament his having neglected such a time as this!

27. *Felix, willing to shew the Jews a pleasure, left Paul bound.* Thus men of the world, to gratify one another, stretch forth their hands to the things of God! Yet the wisdom of Felix did not profit him, nor did it satisfy the Jews at all. Their accusations followed him to Rome and had utterly ruined him, but for the interest which his brother Pallas had with Nero.

CHAPTER 25

4. *But Festus answered.* So Festus's care to preserve the imperial privileges was the means of preserving Paul's life. By what invisible springs does God govern the world; with what silence, and yet with what wisdom and energy!

9. *Wilt thou go up to Jerusalem?* Festus could have ordered this without asking Paul; but God secretly overruled the whole that he might have an occasion of appealing to Rome.

16. *It is not the manner of the Romans.* How excellent a rule, to condemn no one unheard! A rule which, as it is common to all nations (courts of inquisition only excepted), so it ought to direct our proceedings in all affairs, not only in public but private life.

19. *And of one Jesus.* Thus does Festus speak of him to whom every knee shall bow! *Whom Paul affirmed to be alive.* And was this a doubtful question? But why, O Festus, did you doubt concerning it? Only because you did not search into the evidence of it. Otherwise, that evidence might have opened to you until it had grown up into full conviction; and your illustrious prisoner would have led you into the glorious liberty of the children of God.

CHAPTER 26

1–29. Nothing can be imagined more suitable or more graceful than this whole discourse of Paul before Agrippa; in which the seriousness of the Christian, the boldness of the apostle, and the politeness of the gentleman and the scholar appear in a most beautiful contrast, or rather a most happy union.

11. *To blaspheme.* This is the most dreadful of all! Repent, you enemies of the gospel. If Spira, who was compelled, suffered so terribly, what will become of those who compel, like Saul, but do not repent like him?

13. *Above the brightness of the sun.* And no marvel. For what is the brightness of this created sun to the Sun of Righteousness, "the brightness of the Father's glory"?

18. *To turn them.* Through the power of the Almighty, from the spiritual *darkness* wherein they are involved, to the *light* of divine knowledge and holiness; *from the power of Satan,* who now holds them in sin, guilt, and misery, to the love and happy service of *God, that they may receive* through faith (he seems to place the same blessings in a fuller light) pardon, holiness, and glory.

19. *I was not disobedient.* I did obey; I used that power (Gal. 1:16). So that even this grace whereby Paul was influenced was not irresistible.

20. *That they should repent.* This repentance, we may observe, is previous both to inward and outward holiness.

24. *Festus said, . . . Paul, thou art beside thyself.* No, Festus, it is you who is beside himself, who strikes quite wide of the mark. And no wonder: he saw that nature did not act in Paul, but the grace that acted in him he did not see. And therefore he took all this ardor which animated the apostle for a mere start of learned frenzy.

25. *I am not mad, most noble Festus.* How inexpressibly beautiful is this reply! How strong! Yet how decent and respectful! Madmen seldom call men by their names and titles of honor. Thus also Paul refutes the charge.

26. *Before whom also I speak freely.* This freedom was probably one circumstance which Festus accounted as madness.

27. *King Agrippa, believest thou the prophets?* He that believes these believes Paul, yes, and Christ. The apostle now comes close to his heart. What did Agrippa feel when he heard this! *I know that thou believest.* Here Paul lays so fast hold on the king that he can scarce make any resistance.

28. *Then Agrippa said to Paul, Almost thou persuadest me to be a Christian.* See here Festus altogether a heathen, Paul altogether a Christian, Agrippa halting between both. Poor Agrippa! Only almost persuaded! So near the mark and yet fall short! Another step, and you are within the veil! Reader, stop not with Agrippa, but go on with Paul.

29. *Were . . . such as I am.* Christians indeed, full of "righteousness, peace, and joy in the Holy Ghost." He speaks from a full sense of his own happiness and an overflowing love to all.

30. And when she had thus spoken, the king rose up. An unspeakably precious moment to Agrippa. Whether he duly improved it or not, we shall see in that day.

31. *This man doeth nothing worthy of death or of bonds.* They speak of his whole life, not of one action only. And could you learn nothing more than this from that discourse? A favorable judgment of such a preacher is not all that God requires.

tian will often advise even better than him.

23. *God, whose I am, and whom I serve.* How short a compendium of religion, yet how full, comprehending faith, hope, and love!

24. *God hath given.* Paul had prayed for them, and God gave him their lives, perhaps their souls also. And the centurion, subserving the providence of God, gave to Paul the lives of the prisoners. How wonderfully does his providence reign in the most contingent things! And rather will many bad men be preserved with a few good (so it frequently happens), than one good man perish with many bad. So it was in this ship; so it is in the world. *All them.* Not only all the prisoners, as Julius afterwards did (v. 43). Ask for souls; they shall be given you, yes, more than you hope for.

31. We learn here to use the most proper means for security and success, even while we depend on divine providence and wait for the accomplishment of God's own promise. He never designed that any promise should encourage rational creatures to act in an irrational manner; or to remain inactive when he has given them natural capacities of doing something, at least, for their own benefit. To expect the accomplishment of any promise without exerting these is at best vain and dangerous presumption, if all pretense of relying upon it be not profane hypocrisy.

CHAPTER 27

11. *The centurion believed the master.* And indeed it is a general rule, Believe an artificer in his own art. Yet when there is the greatest need, a real Chris-

CHAPTER 28

2. *The barbarians.*[7] So the Romans and Greeks termed all nations but their own. But surely the generosity shown by these uncultured inhabitants of Mal-

---

[7](28:2) KJV: "the barbarous people."

ta was far more valuable than all the varnish which the politest education could give, where it taught not humanity and compassion.

4. *And when the barbarians saw.* It is with pleasure we trace among these barbarians the force of conscience and the belief of a particular providence which some people of more learning have stupidly thought it philosophy to despise. But they erred in imagining that calamities must always be interpreted as judgments. Let us guard against this lest, like them, we condemn not only the innocent, but "the excellent of the earth."

6. *They changed their minds, and said that he was a god.* Such is the stability of human reason! A little before, he was a murderer; presently, he is a god. Just as the people of Lystra—one hour sacrificing, and the next stoning. No, but there is a medium. He is neither a murderer nor a god, but a man of God. But natural men never run into greater mistakes than in judging the children of God.

22. *This sect, we know that every where it is spoken against.* This is no proof at all of a bad cause, but a very profitable mark of a good one.

23. *To whom he expounded and testified the kingdom of God, persuading them concerning Jesus.* These were his two grand topics: (1) That the kingdom of the Messiah was of a spiritual, not temporal, nature. (2) That Jesus of Nazareth was the very person foretold as the Lord of that kingdom. On this point he had as much need to persuade as to convince, their will making as strong a resistance as their understanding.

31. *No man forbidding him.* Such was the victory of the word of God. While Paul was preaching at Rome, the gospel shone with its highest luster.

ROMANS

CHAPTER 1

1. *Called to be an apostle.* And made an apostle by that calling. While God calls, he makes what he calls. As the Judaizing teachers disputed Paul's claim to the apostolic office, it is with great propriety that he asserts it in the very entrance of an epistle wherein their principles are entirely overthrown. And various other proper and important thoughts are suggested in the short introduction; particularly the prophecies concerning the gospel, the descent of Jesus from David, the great doctrines of his Godhead and resurrection, the sending of the gospel to the Gentiles, the privileges of Christians, and the obedience and holiness to which they were obliged in virtue of their profession.

3. *Which was made of the seed of David according to the flesh.* That is, with regard to his human nature. Both the natures of our Savior are here mentioned; but the human is mentioned first, because the divine was not manifested in its full evidence until after his resurrection.

4. *By the resurrection from the dead.* For this is both the fountain and the object of our faith; and the preaching of the apostles was the consequence of Christ's resurrection.

7. *Grace.* The peculiar favor of God. *And peace.* All manner of blessings, temporal, spiritual, and eternal. This is both a Christian salutation and an apostolic benediction. *From God our Father, and the Lord Jesus Christ.* This is the usual way wherein the apostles speak, "God the Father," "God our Father." Nor do they often, in speaking of him, use the word *Lord,* as it implies the proper name of God, "Jehovah." In the Old Testament, indeed, the holy men generally stated, "The Lord our God"—for they were then, as it were, servants; whereas now they are sons. And sons so well know their father that they need not frequently mention his proper name. It is one and the same peace, and one and the same grace, which is from God and from Jesus Christ. Our trust and prayer fix on God as he is the Father of Christ; and on Christ as he presents us to the Father.

8. *I thank.* In the very entrance of this one epistle are the traces of all spiritual affections; but of thankfulness above all, with the expression of which almost all of Paul's epistles begin. *Through Jesus Christ.* The gifts of God all pass through Christ to us; and all our petitions and thanksgivings pass through Christ to God.

11. *That I may impart unto you.* Face

to face, by laying on of hands, prayer, preaching the gospel, private conversation. *Some spiritual gift*. With such gifts the Corinthians, who had enjoyed the presence of Paul, abounded (I Cor. 1:7; 12:1; 14:1). So did the Galatians (Gal. 3:5); yes, all the churches which had had the presence of any of the apostles had peculiar advantages of this kind from the laying on of their hands (Acts 19:6; 8:17; II Tim. 1:6). That Peter had no more been at Rome than Paul at the time when this epistle was written appears from the general tenor of it, and from this place in particular. For otherwise, what Paul wishes to impart to the Romans would have been imparted already by Peter.

16. *For I am not ashamed of the gospel.* To the world, indeed, it is folly and weakness (I Cor. 1:18). Therefore, in the judgment of the world he ought to be ashamed of it; especially at Rome, the head and theater of the world. But Paul is not ashamed, knowing *it is the power of God unto salvation to every one that believeth*. The great and gloriously powerful means of saving all who accept salvation in God's own way. As Paul comprises the sum of the gospel in this epistle, so he does the sum of the epistle in this and the following verse.

17. *The righteousness of God.* This expression sometimes means God's eternal, essential righteousness, which includes both justice and mercy and is eminently shown in condemning sin and yet justifying the sinner. Sometimes it means that righteousness by which a man, through the gift of God, is made and is righteous; and that both by receiving Christ through faith and by conformity to the essential righteousness of God. Paul, when speaking of justification, means hereby the righteousness of faith; therefore called *the righteousness of God*, because God found out and prepared, reveals and gives,

approves and crowns it. In this verse the expression means the whole benefit of God through Christ for the salvation of a sinner.

18. *For.* There is no other way of obtaining life and salvation. Having laid down his proposition, the apostle now enters upon the proof of it. His first argument is, The law condemns all men as being under sin. None therefore is justified by the works of the law. This is treated up to chapter 3:20. From then on, he infers, therefore justification is by faith.

21. *In their imaginations.* Various, uncertain, foolish. What a terrible instance have we of this in the writings of Lucretius! What *vain imaginations*, and how dark a heart amid so pompous professions of wisdom!

23. *And changed.* With the utmost folly. Here are three degrees of ungodliness and of punishment. The punishment in each case is expressed by "God . . . gave them up." If a man will not worship God as God, he is so left to himself that he throws away his very manhood.

24. *God also gave them up.* By withdrawing his restraining grace.

30. *Haters of God.* That is, rebels against him, deniers of his providence, or accusers of his justice in their adversities; having an inward heart-enmity to his justice and holiness. *Inventors of evil things.* Of new pleasures, new ways of gain, new arts of hurting, particularly in war.

31. *Without natural affection.* The custom of exposing their own newborn children to perish by cold, hunger, or wild beasts—which so generally prevailed in the heathen world, particularly among the Greeks and Romans—was an amazing instance of this; as is also that of killing their aged and helpless parents, now common among the American heathens.

32. *Not only do the same, but have pleasure in them that do them.* This is the highest degree of wickedness. A man may be hurried by his passions to do the thing he hates; but he who has pleasure in those who do evil loves wickedness for wickedness' sake. And hereby he encourages them in sin and heaps the guilt of others upon his own head.

CHAPTER 2

1. *Therefore.* The apostle now makes a transition from the Gentiles to the Jews until, upon verse 6, he encompasses both.

4. *Of his goodness and forbearance and longsuffering.* Seeing you both have sinned, do sin, and will sin. All these are afterwards comprised in the single word *goodness.*

5. *Treasurest up unto thyself wrath.* Although you think you are treasuring up all good things. O what a treasure may a man lay up either way in this short day of life! *Against the day of wrath and revelation of the righteous judgment of God.* Just opposite to "the goodness and forbearance and longsuffering" of God. When God shall be revealed, then shall also be revealed the secrets of men's hearts (v. 16).

8. *But unto them that are contentious.* Like you, O Jew, who thus fights against God. The character of a false Jew is disobedience, stubbornness, impatience.

9. *Of the Jew first.* Here we have the first express mention of the Jews in this chapter. And it is introduced with great propriety. Their having been trained up in the true religion and having had Christ and his apostles first sent to them will place them in the foremost rank of the criminals who obey not the truth.

11. *There is no respect of persons.* God will reward every one according to his works. But this is well consistent with his distributing advantages and opportunities of improvement, according to his own good pleasure.

14. *For when the Gentiles.* That is, any of them. Paul, having refuted the perverse judgment of the Jews concerning the heathens, proceeds to show the just judgment of God against them. He now speaks directly of the heathens in order to convince the heathens. Yet the concession he makes to these serves all the more strongly to convince the Jews.

15. *Written in their hearts.* By the same hand which wrote the commandments on the tables of stone. *Their conscience.* There is none of all its faculties which the soul has less in its power than this.

16. *God shall judge the secrets of men.* On secret circumstances depends the real quality of actions, frequently unknown to the actors themselves (v. 29). Men generally form their judgments, even of themselves, merely from what is apparent.

21–22. *Teachest thou not thyself?* He does not teach himself who does not practice what he teaches. *Dost thou steal, . . . commit adultery, . . . commit sacrilege?* Sin grievously against your neighbor, yourself, God. Paul had shown the Gentiles first their sins against God, then against themselves, then against their neighbors. He now inverts the order; for sins against God are the most glaring in a heathen, but not in a Jew.

25. *Circumcision verily profiteth.* He does not say "justifies." How far it profited is shown in the third and fourth chapters. *Thy circumcision is made uncircumcision.* Is so already in effect. You will have no more benefit by it than if you had never received it. The very same observation holds with regard to baptism.

28. *For he is not a Jew.* In the most

important sense, that is, one of God's beloved people.

29. *But he is a Jew.* That is, one of God's people. *Which is one inwardly.* In the secret recesses of his soul. And the acceptable *circumcision is that of the heart.* Referring to Deuteronomy 30:6; the putting away of all inward impurity. This is seated *in the spirit,* the inmost soul, renewed by the Spirit of God. *And not in the letter.* Not in the external ceremony.

CHAPTER 3

13. *Their throat.* Is noisome and dangerous as *an open sepulchre.* Observe the progress of evil discourse, proceeding out of the heart, through the throat, tongue, lips, until the whole mouth is filled.

19. *What things soever the law* [the Old Testament] *saith, it saith to them who are under the law.* That is, to those who own its authority; to the Jews and not the Gentiles. Paul quoted no Scripture against them, but pleaded with them only from the light of nature. *May become guilty.* May be fully convicted and apparently liable to most just condemnation. These things were written of old and were quoted by Paul, not to make men criminal, but to prove them so.

23. *For all have sinned.* In Adam and in their own persons; by a sinful nature, sinful tempers, and sinful actions. *And come short of the glory of God.* The supreme end of man; short of his image on earth and the enjoyment of him in heaven.

24. *Freely by his grace.* One of these expressions might have served to convey the apostle's meaning; but he doubles his assertion in order to give us the fullest conviction of the truth and to impress us with a sense of its peculiar importance. It is not possible to find

words that should more absolutely exclude all consideration of our own works and obedience, or more emphatically ascribe the whole of our justification to free, unmerited goodness.

26. The attribute of justice must be preserved inviolate; and inviolate it is preserved if there was a real infliction of punishment on our Savior. On this plan all the attributes harmonize; every attribute is glorified and not one superseded, no, nor so much as clouded.

27. *But by the law of faith.* Since this requires all, without distinction, to apply as guilty and helpless sinners to the free mercy of God in Christ. *The law of faith* is that divine constitution which makes faith, not works, the condition of acceptance.

28. *We conclude that a man is justified by faith.* And even by this, not as it is a work, but as it receives Christ; and consequently has something essentially different from all our works whatever.

31. *We establish the law.* Both the authority, purity, and the end of it; by defending that which the law attests; by pointing out Christ, the end of it; and by showing how it may be fulfilled in its purity.

CHAPTER 4

2. The meaning is, If Abraham had been justified by works, he would have had room to glory. But he had not room to glory. Therefore he was not justified by works.

3. *Abraham believed God.* That promise of God concerning the numerousness of his seed (Gen. 15:5, 7); but especially the promise concerning the Christ (Gen. 12:3), through whom all nations should be blessed.

5. *But to him that worketh not.* It being impossible he should without faith. *But believeth, . . . his faith is counted for righteousness.* Therefore,

God's affirming of Abraham that faith was imputed to him for righteousness plainly shows that he worked not; or, in other words, that he was not justified by works, but by faith only. Hence we see plainly how groundless that opinion is that holiness or sanctification is previous to our justification. For the sinner, being first convinced of his sin and danger by the Spirit of God, stands trembling before the awful tribunal of divine justice; and has nothing to plead but his own guilt and the merits of a Mediator.

Christ here interposes; justice is satisfied; the sin is remitted, and pardon is applied to the soul by a divine faith wrought by the Holy Ghost, who then begins the great work of inward sanctification. Thus God justifies the ungodly and yet remains just and true to all his attributes! But let none presume to continue in sin, for to the impenitent, God is a consuming fire. *On him that justifieth the ungodly.* If a man could possibly be made holy before he was justified, it would entirely set his justification aside, seeing he could not, in the very nature of the thing, be justified if he were not at that very time ungodly.

7. *Happy[1] are they.* If there be indeed such a thing as happiness on earth, it is the portion of that man *whose iniquities are forgiven* and who enjoys the manifestation of that pardon. Well may he endure all the afflictions of life with cheerfulness and look upon death with comfort. O let us not contend against it, but earnestly pray that this happiness may be ours!

9. *Faith was reckoned to Abraham for righteousness.* This is fully consistent with our being justified, that is, pardoned and accepted by God upon our believing, for the sake of what Christ has done and suffered. For though this, and this alone, be the meritorious cause of our acceptance with God, yet faith may be said to be "imputed to [us] for righteousness," as it is the sole condition of our acceptance. We may observe here that forgiveness, not imputing sin, and imputing righteousness are all one.

17. *And calleth those things which be not.* Summoning them to rise into being and appear before him. The seed of Abraham did not then exist; yet God said, *So shall thy seed be.* A man can say to his servant actually existing, "Do this"; and he does it. But God says to the light, while it does not exist, "Go forth"; and it goes.

24. *If we believe on him that raised up Jesus.* God the Father, therefore, is the proper object of justifying faith.

CHAPTER 5

1. *Being justified by faith.* This is the sum of the preceding chapters. *We have peace with God.* We are enemies to God no longer (v. 10), neither do we fear his wrath (v. 9). We have peace, hope, love, and power over sin, the sum of the fifth, sixth, seventh, and eighth chapters. These are the fruits of justifying faith. Where these are not, justifying faith is not.

3. *We glory in tribulations also.* Which we are so far from esteeming a mark of God's displeasure that we receive them as tokens of his fatherly love, whereby we are prepared for a more exalted happiness. The Jews objected to the persecuted state of the Christians as inconsistent with the people of the Messiah. It is therefore with great propriety that the apostle so often mentions the blessings arising from this very thing.

---

[1] (4:7) KJV: "Blessed."

6. *Christ died for the ungodly.* Not only to set them a pattern, but to procure them power to follow it. It does not appear that this expression of dying for any one has any other significance than that of rescuing the life of another by laying down our own.

7. *A just[2] man.* One who gives to all what is strictly their due. *A good man.* One who is eminently holy; full of love, compassion, kindness, mildness, and every heavenly and amiable temper.

9. *We shall be saved from wrath through him.* That is, from all the effects of the wrath of God. But is there then wrath in God? Is not wrath a human passion? And how can this human passion be in God? We may answer this by another question: Is not love a human passion? And how can this human passion be in God? But to answer directly: Wrath in man, and so love in man, is a human passion. But wrath in God is not a human passion; nor is love, as it is in God. Therefore the inspired writers ascribe both the one and the other to God only in an analogical sense.

10. *We shall be saved.* Sanctified and glorified.

12. *Death.* With all its attendants. It *entered into the world* when it entered into being; for until then it did not exist. *All have sinned.* In Adam. These words assign the reason why death came upon *all men,* infants themselves not excepted, *for that all have sinned.*

14. *Death reigned.* And how vast is his kingdom! Scarce can we find any king who has as many subjects as are the kings whom he has conquered.

17. There is a difference between grace and the gift. *Grace* is opposed to the *offence;* the *gift,* to *death,* being the gift of life.

20. *But where sin abounded, grace did much more abound.* Not only in the remission of that sin which Adam brought on us, but of all our own; not only in remission of sins, but infusion of holiness; not only in deliverance from death, but admission to everlasting life, a far more noble and excellent life than that which we lost by Adam's fall.

21. *Through righteousness unto eternal life by Jesus Christ our Lord.* Here is pointed out the source of all our blessings, the rich and free grace of God. The meritorious cause; not any works of righteousness of man, but only the merits of our Lord Jesus Christ. The effect or end of all is not only pardon, but life; divine life, leading to glory.

CHAPTER 6

3. *Baptized into Jesus Christ.* In baptism we, through faith, are ingrafted into Christ; and we draw new spiritual life from this new root through his Spirit, who fashions us like unto him, and particularly with regard to his death and resurrection.

4. *We are buried with him.* Alluding to the ancient manner of baptizing by immersion. As he lives a new life in heaven, *so we also should walk in newness of life.* This, says the apostle, our very baptism represents to us.

6. *Our old man.* Contemporary with our being, and as old as the fall; our evil nature. A strong and beautiful expression for that entire depravity and corruption which by nature spreads itself over the whole man, leaving no part uninfected. This in a believer is *crucified* with Christ, mortified, gradually killed, by virtue of our union with

---

[2] (5:7) KJV: "righteous."

him. *That the body of sin*—all evil tempers, words, and actions which are the members of the old man (Col. 3:5)—*might be destroyed.*

14. *For ye are not under the law.* A dispensation of terror and bondage, which only sows sin without enabling you to conquer it. *But under grace.* Under the merciful dispensation of the gospel, which brings complete victory over it to every one who is under the powerful influences of the Spirit of Christ.

17. *That form of doctrine which was delivered you.* Literally it is, "The mold into which ye have been delivered"; which, as it contains a beautiful allusion, conveys also a very instructive admonition, intimating that our minds, all pliant and ductile, should be conformed to the gospel precepts, as liquid metals take the figure of the mold into which they are cast.

19. *Because of the infirmity of your flesh.* Slowness of understanding flows from the weakness of the flesh, that is, of human nature. *As ye have yielded your members servants to uncleanness and to iniquity unto iniquity; even so now yield your members servants to righteousness unto holiness.* "Iniquity" (whereof uncleanness is an eminent part) is here opposed to "righteousness"; and "unto iniquity" is the opposite of "unto holiness."

Righteousness here is a conformity to the divine will; *holiness,* to the whole divine nature. Observe, they who are *servants of righteousness* go on to *holiness;* but they who are *servants . . . to iniquity* get no further. Righteousness is service, because we live according to the will of another; but also liberty, because of our inclination to it and delight in it.

23. *Death.* Temporal, spiritual, and eternal. The due *wages of sin; but the gift of God is eternal life.* The difference is remarkable. Evil works merit the reward they receive; good works do not. The former demand wages; the latter accept a free gift.

CHAPTER 7

1. The apostle continues the comparison between the former and the present state of the believer and at the same time endeavors to wean the Jewish believers from their fondness for the Mosaic law.

5. *When we were in the flesh.* Carnally minded, in a state of nature, before we believed in Christ. *Of sins, which were by the law.* Accidentally occasioned, or irritated thereby. *Work in our members.* Spread themselves all over the whole man.

7. *What shall we say then?* This is a kind of a digression to the beginning of the next chapter wherein the apostle, in order to show in the most lively manner the weakness and inefficacy of the law, changes the person and speaks as of himself concerning the misery of one under the law. This Paul frequently does when he is not speaking of his own person, but only assuming another character (Rom. 3:5; I Cor. 10:30; 4:6). The character here assumed is that of a man, first ignorant of the law, then under it and sincerely but ineffectually striving to serve God. To have spoken this of himself or any true believer would have been foreign to the whole scope of his discourse; no, utterly contrary thereto as well as to what is expressly asserted (Rom. 8:2).

8–9. *But sin.* My inbred corruption. *Sin revived, and I died.* My inbred sin took fire, and all my virtue and strength died away; and I then saw myself to be dead in sin and liable to death eternal.

11. *Deceived me.* While I expected life by the law, sin came upon me unawares and slew all my hopes.

12. *The commandment.* That is, every

branch of the law is *holy, and just, and good*. It springs from and partakes of the holy nature of God; it is every way just and right in itself; it is designed wholly for the good of man.

14. *I am carnal*. Paul, having compared together the past and present state of believers—that "in the flesh" (v. 5), and that "in the spirit" (v. 6)—in answering two objectives (Is then the law sin?—v. 7; and, Is the law death?—v. 13) interweaves the whole process of a man reasoning, groaning, striving, and escaping from the legal to the evangelical state. This he does from verse seven to the end of this chapter.

18. *In my flesh*. The flesh here signifies the whole man as he is by nature.

21. *I find then a law*. An inward, constraining power flowing from the dictate of corrupt nature.

23. *But I see another law in my members*. Another inward constraining power of evil inclinations and bodily appetites. *Warring against the law of my mind*. The dictate of my mind, which delights in the law of God. *Bringing me into captivity*. In spite of all my resistance.

24. *Wretched man that I am!* The struggle is now come to the height. The man, finding there is no help in himself, begins almost unawares to pray, *Who shall deliver me?* He then seeks and looks for deliverance until God in Christ appears to answer his question. The word which we translate "deliver" implies "force." And indeed without this there can be no deliverance. *The body of this death*. That is, the body of death; this mass of sin leading to death eternal and cleaving as close to me as my body to my soul. We may observe, the deliverance is not accomplished yet.

25. *I thank God through Jesus Christ our Lord*. That is, God will deliver me through Christ. But the apostle, as his frequent manner is, beautifully interweaves his assertion with thanksgiving, the hymn of praise answering in a manner to the voice of sorrow, "Wretched man that I am!"

CHAPTER 8

1. *There is therefore now no condemnation*. Either for things present or past. Now he comes to deliverance and liberty. The apostle here resumes the thread of his discourse which was interrupted at 7:7.

4. *That the righteousness of the law*. The holiness it required, described in verses 5–11. *Might be fulfilled in us, who walk not after the flesh, but after the Spirit*. Who are guided in all our thoughts, words, and actions not by corrupt nature, but by the Spirit of God. From this place Paul describes primarily the state of believers, and that of unbelievers only to illustrate this.

5. *They that are after the flesh*. Who remain under the guidance of corrupt nature. *Mind the things of the flesh*. Have their thoughts and affections fixed on such things as gratifying corrupt nature; namely, on things visible and temporal; on things of the earth, on pleasure (of sense or imagination), praise, or riches. *But they that are after the Spirit*. Who are under his guidance. *The things of the Spirit*. Think of, relish, love things invisible, eternal; the things which the Spirit has revealed, which he works in us, moves us to, and promises to give us.

9. *If any man have not the Spirit of Christ*. Dwelling and governing in him. *He is none of his*. He is not a member of Christ, not a Christian, not in a state of salvation. A plain, express declaration which admits of no exception. He that has ears to hear, let him hear!

15. *Abba, Father*. The latter word explains the former. By using both the

Syriac and the Greek words, Paul seems to point out the joint cry both of the Jewish and Gentile believers. *The spirit of bondage* here seems directly to mean those operations of the Holy Spirit by which the soul, on its first conviction, feels itself in bondage to sin, to the world, to Satan, and obnoxious to the wrath of God. This, therefore, and *the Spirit of adoption* are one and the same Spirit, only manifesting itself in various operations according to the various circumstances of the persons.

16. *The Spirit itself beareth witness with our spirit.* With the spirit of every true believer by a testimony distinct from that of his own spirit, or the testimony of a good conscience. Happy they who enjoy this clear and constant!

23. *The adoption.* Persons who had been privately adopted among the Romans were often brought forth into the forum and publicly owned as their sons by those who adopted them. So at the general resurrection, when the body itself is redeemed from death, the sons of God shall be publicly owned by him in the great assembly of men and angels.

26. *Likewise the Spirit.* No, not only the universe, not only the children of God, but the Spirit of God also himself, as it were, groans while he *helpeth our infirmities,* or weaknesses. Our understandings are weak, particularly in the things of God; our desires are weak; our prayers are weak. *The Spirit itself maketh intercession for us.* In our hearts, even as Christ does in heaven. *With groanings.* The matter of which is from ourselves, but the Spirit forms them, and they are frequently inexpressible, even by the faithful themselves.

29. Here the apostle declares who those are whom he foreknew and predestined to glory; namely, those who are *conformed to the image of his Son.* This is the mark of those who are foreknown and will be glorified (II Tim. 2:19; Phil. 3:10, 21).

30. *Them he.* In due time. *Called.* By his gospel and his Spirit. *And whom he called.* When obedient to the heavenly calling (Acts 26:19). *He also justified.* Forgave and accepted. *And whom he justified,* provided they "continue in his goodness" (Rom. 11:22), he in the end *glorified.* Paul does not affirm, either here or in any other part of his writings, that precisely the same number of men are called, justified, and glorified. He does not deny that a believer may fall away and be cut off between his special calling and his glorification (Rom. 11:22). Neither does he deny that many are called who never are justified. He only affirms that this is the method whereby God leads us step by step toward heaven. *He . . . glorified.* He speaks as one looking back from the goal upon the race of faith. Indeed grace, as it is glory begun, is both an earnest and a foretaste of eternal glory.

33. *God's elect.* It does not appear that even good men were ever termed "God's elect" until above two thousand years from the Creation. God's electing or choosing the nation of Israel, and separating them from the other nations who were sunk in idolatry and all wickedness, gave the first occasion to this sort of language. And as the separating of the Christians from the Jews was a like event, no wonder it was expressed in like words and phrases, only with this difference that the term "elect" was of old applied to all the members of the visible church; whereas in the New Testament it is applied only to the members of the invisible church.

CHAPTER 9

In this chapter Paul, after strongly declaring his love and esteem for them, sets himself to answer the grand objection of his countrymen; namely, that the rejection of the Jews and reception of the Gentiles was contrary to the word of God. That he had not here the least thought of personal election or reprobation is manifest: (1) Because it lay quite wide of his design which was this, to show that God's rejecting the Jews and receiving the Gentiles was consistent with his word. (2) Because such a doctrine would not only have had no tendency to convince, but would have evidently tended to harden the Jews. And (3) Because when he sums up his argument in the close of the chapter he has not one word or the least intimation about it.

2. *I have great heaviness.* A high degree of spiritual sorrow and of spiritual joy may consist together (Rom. 8:39).

3. *I could wish.* Human words cannot fully describe the motions of souls that are full of God. As if he had said, I could wish to suffer in their stead; yes, to be an anathema from Christ in their place. In how high a sense he wished this, who can tell, unless he himself had been asked and had resolved the question? Certainly he did not then consider himself at all, but only others and the glory of God. The thing could not be; yet the wish was pious and solid, though with the tacit condition that it be both right and possible.

6. *Not as though.* The Jews imagined that the word of God must fail if all their nation were not saved. This Paul now refutes and proves that the word itself had foretold their falling away. *They are not all Israel, which are of Israel.* The Jews vehemently maintained the contrary; namely, that all who were born Israelites, and they only, were the people of God. The former part of this assertion is refuted here, the latter in verses 24 and following. The sum is, God accepts all believers, and them only; and this is no way contrary to his word. No, he has declared in his word, both by types and by express testimonies, that believers are accepted as the "children of the promise," while unbelievers are rejected, though they are "children of the flesh."

10. That God's blessing does not belong to all the descendants of Abraham appears not only by this instance, but by that of Esau and Jacob, the latter of whom was chosen to inherit the blessing before either of them had done good or evil. The apostle mentions this to show that neither were their ancestors accepted through any merit of their own.

11. *That the purpose of God according to election might stand.* Whose purpose was to elect or choose the promised seed.

14. *Is there unrighteousness with God?* Is it unrighteous, or unjust, of God to give Jacob the blessing rather than Esau? Or to accept believers, and them only? *God forbid.* In no wise. This is well consistent with justice; for he has a right to fix the terms on which he will show mercy according to his declaration to Moses, petitioning for all the people after they had committed idolatry with the golden calf.

15. *I will have mercy on whom I will have mercy.* According to the terms I myself have fixed. *And I will have compassion on whom I will have compassion.* Namely, on those only who submit to my terms, who accept of it in the way that I have appointed.

16. *So then it is not of him that willeth nor of him that runneth.* It is not the effect either of the will or the works of man, but of the grace and power of God. The will of man is here opposed to the grace of God; and man's running, to the divine operation. And this general declaration refers not only to Isaac and Jacob and the Israelites in the time of Moses, but likewise to all the spiritual children of Abraham, even to the end of the world.

17. *For.* God has an indisputable right to reject those who will not accept the blessings on his own terms.

18. *Therefore.* That is, accordingly he does show mercy on his own terms, namely, on them who believe. *And whom he will.* Namely, them that believe not. *He hardeneth.* He leaves to the hardness of their hearts.

21. *Hath not the potter power over the clay.* And much more has not God power over his creatures to appoint one vessel, namely, the believer, to honor; and another, the unbeliever, to dishonor?

God, as sovereign Lord and Proprietor of all, dispenses his gifts or favors to his creatures with perfect wisdom, but by no rules or methods of proceeding that we are acquainted with. The time when we shall exist, the country where we shall live, our parents, our constitution of body and turn of mind—these and numberless other circumstances are doubtless ordered with perfect wisdom, and by rules that lie quite out of our sight.

But God's methods of dealing with us, as our Governor and Judge, are clearly revealed and perfectly known; namely, that he will finally reward every man according to his works: "He that believeth . . . shall be saved; but he that believeth not shall be damned."

Therefore, although he "hath . . . mercy on whom he will have mercy, and whom he will he hardeneth"—that is, allows to be hardened in consequence of their obstinate wickedness— yet his is not the will of an arbitrary, capricious, or tyrannical being. He wills nothing but what is infinitely wise and good; and therefore his will is a most proper rule of judgment. He will show mercy, as he has assured us, to none but

true believers, nor harden any but such as obstinately refuse his mercy.

22. *What if God, willing.* Referring to verses 18 and 19. That is, although it was now his will because of their obstinate unbelief. *To shew his wrath.* Which necessarily presupposes sin. *Fitted to destruction.* By their own willful and final impenitence. Is there any injustice in this?

24. *Even us.* Here the apostle comes to the other proposition, of grace free for all, whether Jew or Gentile.

30–31. *What shall we say then?* What is to be concluded from all that has been said but this, *That the Gentiles, which followed not after righteousness,* who a while ago had no knowledge of, no care or thought about it, *have attained to righteousness,* or justification. *Even the righteousness which is of faith.*

This is the first conclusion we may draw from the preceding observations. The second is that *Israel*—the Jews— though they *followed after the law of righteousness* (that law which, duly used, would have led them to faith and thereby to righteousness), *hath not attained to the law of righteousness.* To that righteousness or justification which is one great end of the law.

32. And wherefore have they not? Is it because God eternally decreed they should not? There is nothing like this to be met with; but agreeable to his argument the apostle gives us this good reason for it, *Because they sought it not by faith.* Whereby alone it could be attained.

CHAPTER 10

4. *For Christ is the end of the law.* The scope and aim of it. It is the very design of the law to bring men to believe in Christ for justification and salvation.

5. He who perfectly keeps all these precepts in every point, he alone may claim life and salvation by them. But this way of justification is impossible to any who have ever transgressed any one law in any point.

8. *The word is nigh thee.* Within your reach; easy to be understood, remembered, practiced. This is eminently true of *the word of faith.* The gospel. *Which we preach.* The sum of which is, If your heart believes in Christ, and your life confesses him, "thou shalt be saved."

9. *If thou shalt confess with thy mouth.* Even in time of persecution when such a confession may send you to the lions.

10. *For with the heart.* Not the understanding only. *Man believeth unto righteousness.* So as to obtain justification. *And with the mouth confession is made.* So as to obtain final salvation. Confession here implies the whole of outward, as believing does the root of all inward, religion.

12. *The same Lord over all is rich.* So that his blessings are never to be exhausted, nor is he ever constrained to hold his hand. The great truth proposed in the eleventh verse is repeated here, and in the thirteenth, and further confirmed, verses 14–15, as not only to imply that "whosoever shall call upon the name of the Lord shall be saved"; but also that the will of God is that all should savingly call upon him.

19. *Did not Israel know?* They might have known, even from Moses and Isaiah, that many of the Gentiles would be received, and many of the Jews rejected. *I will provoke you to jealousy by them that are no people.* As they followed gods that were not gods, so he accepted in their stead a nation that was not a nation; that is, a nation that was not in covenant with God. *A foolish nation.* Such are all which know not God.

21. *An unbelieving*[3] *and gainsaying*

people. Just opposite to those who believed with their hearts and made confession with their mouths.

CHAPTER 11

2. *God hath not cast away* that part of *his people which he foreknew.* Speaking after the manner of men. For in fact, knowing and foreknowing are the same thing with God, who knows or sees all things at once, from everlasting to everlasting.

5. *According to the election of grace.* According to that gracious purpose of God, "he that believeth . . . shall be saved."

6. There is something so absolutely inconsistent between being justified by grace and being justified by works that if you suppose either, you of necessity exclude the other. For what is given to works is the payment of a debt; whereas grace implies an unmerited favor. So that the same benefit cannot, in the very nature of things, be derived from both.

11. *Have they stumbled that they should fall?* Totally and finally? No. *Through their fall.* Or slip; it is a very soft word in the original.

12. The first part of this verse is treated in verses 13 and following; the latter, *how much more their fulness* (that is, their full conversion), verses 23 and following.

So many prophecies refer to this grand event that it is surprising any Christian can doubt of it. And these are greatly confirmed by the wonderful preservation of the Jews as a distinct people to this day. When it is accomplished, it will be so strong a demonstration both of the Old and New Testament revelations as will doubtless

---

[3] (10:21) KJV: "disobedient."

convince many thousands of Deists in countries nominally Christian; of whom there will, of course, be increasing multitudes among merely nominal Christians. And this will be a means of swiftly propagating the gospel among the Mohammedans and pagans, who would probably have received it long ago had they conversed only with real Christians.

16. *For if the firstfruit be holy, the lump is also holy.* The consecration of them was esteemed the consecration of all; and so the conversion of a few Jews is an earnest of the conversion of all the rest.

25. Paul calls any truth known but to a few a *mystery.* Such had been the calling of the Gentiles; such was now the conversion of the Jews.

32. *For God hath concluded them all in unbelief.* Allowing each in their turn to revolt from him. First, God permitted the Gentiles in the early age to revolt and took the family of Abraham as a peculiar seed to himself. Afterwards he permitted them to fall through unbelief and took in the believing Gentiles. And he did even this to provoke the Jews to jealousy and so to bring them also in the end to faith. This was truly a mystery in the divine conduct which the apostle adores with holy astonishment.

33. *O the depth of the riches both of the wisdom and knowledge of God!* In the ninth chapter Paul had sailed but in a narrow sea; now he is in the ocean. *The depth of the riches* is described in verse 35; the *depth of . . . wisdom,* in verse 34; the *depth of . . . knowledge,* in the latter part of this verse. Wisdom directs all things to the best end; knowledge sees that end. *How unsearchable are his judgments.* With regard to unbelievers. *His ways.* With regard to believers. *His ways* are more upon a level; *his judgments,* a great deep. But his ways we cannot trace.

36. *Amen.* This is a concluding word in which the affection of the apostle, when it is come to the height, shuts up all.

CHAPTER 12

1. *Your bodies.* That is, yourselves; a part is put for the whole; the rather, as in the ancient sacrifices of beasts, the body was the whole. These also are particularly named in opposition to that vile abuse of their bodies mentioned in Romans 1:24. Several expressions follow which have likewise a direct reference to other expressions in the same chapter. *Which is your reasonable service.* The worship of the heathens was utterly unreasonable (Rom. 1:18ff.); so was the glorying of the Jews (Rom. 2:3ff.). But a Christian acts in all things by the highest reason, from the mercy of God inferring his own duty.

2. *That ye may prove.* Know by sure trial; which is easily done by him who has thus presented himself to God.

6. *Whether prophecy.* This, considered as an extraordinary gift, is that whereby heavenly mysteries are declared to men, or things to come foretold. But it seems here to mean the ordinary gift of expounding Scripture. *Let us prophesy according to the proportion of faith.* According to the analogy—Peter expresses it "as the oracles of God"—or general tenor of them; according to that grand scheme of doctrine which is delivered therein, touching original sin, justification by faith, and present, inward salvation. Every article concerning which there is any question should be determined by this rule. Interpret every doubtful Scripture according to the grand truths which run through the whole.

9. Having spoken of faith and its fruits (vv. 3ff.), he comes now to *love.*

Verses 9–11 refer to the seventh chapter; the twelfth verse to chapter 8; the thirteenth verse to chapter 9.

10. *In honour preferring one another.* Which you will do if you habitually consider what is good in others and what is evil in yourselves.

12. *Rejoicing in hope.* Of perfect holiness and of everlasting happiness. Hitherto of faith and love; now of hope also (chaps. 5–6). And afterwards, of duties towards others; towards saints, verse 13; persecutors, verse 14; friends, strangers, enemies, verses 15 and following.

13. *Distributing to the necessity of saints.* Relieve all Christians that are in need. It is remarkable that the apostle, treating expressly of the duties flowing from the communion of saints, yet never says one word about the dead.

20. *Feed him.* With your own hand; if it be needful, even put bread into his mouth. *Heap coals of fire on his head.* That part which is most sensible.

"So artists melt the sullen ore of lead,
By heaping coals of fire upon its
   head;
In the kind warmth the metal learns
   to glow,
And pure from dross the silver runs
   below."

21. *But overcome evil with good.* Conquer your enemies by kindness and patience.

CHAPTER 13

3. *Wilt thou then not be afraid.* There is one fear which precedes evil actions and deters them; this should always remain. There is another fear which follows evil actions; they who do well are free from this.

4. *Sword.* The instrument of capital punishment, which God authorizes him to inflict.

8. *To love one another.* An eternal debt which can never be sufficiently discharged; yet if this be rightly performed, it discharges all the rest. *For he that loveth another.* As he ought. *Hath fulfilled the* [whole] *law.* Toward his neighbor.

10. *Therefore love is the fulfilling of the law.* For the same love which restrains from all evil incites us to all good.

11. *That now it is high time to awake out of sleep.* How beautifully is the metaphor carried on! This life, a night; the resurrection, the day; the gospel shining on the heart is the dawn of this day. We are to awake out of sleep and to rise up and throw away our nightclothes, which are fit only for darkness, and put on new. And being soldiers, we who are encompassed with so many enemies are to arm and prepare for fight.

The day dawns when we receive faith, and then sleep gives place. Then it is time to rise, to arm, to walk, and to work, lest sleep steal upon us again. Final salvation, glory, is nearer to us now *than when we believed.* It is continually advancing, flying forward upon the swiftest wings of time. And that which remains between the present hour and eternity is comparatively but a moment.

14. *But put ye on the Lord Jesus Christ.* Herein is contained the whole of our salvation. It is a strong and beautiful expression for the most intimate union with him, and being clothed with all the graces which were in him. The apostle does not say, "Put on purity and sobriety, peacefulness and benevolence"; but he says all this and a thousand times more at once in saying, "Put ye on the Lord Jesus Christ."

CHAPTER 14

1. *Him that is weak.* Through needless scruples. *Receive.* With all love and courtesy into Christian fellowship. *But not to doubtful disputations*. About questionable points.

10. *But why dost thou judge thy brother?* Hitherto the apostle has addressed the weak brother; now he speaks to the stronger.

11. *As I live.* An oath proper to him because he only possesses life infinite and independent. It is Christ who is here termed both Lord and God; as it is he to whom we live and to whom we die. *Every tongue shall confess to God.* Shall own him as their rightful Lord; which shall then only be accomplished in its full extent. The Lord grant that we may find mercy in that day; and may it also be imparted to those who have differed from us! Yes, to those who have censured and condemned us for things which we have done from a desire to please him, or refused to do from a fear of offending him.

14. *Persuaded by the Lord Jesus.* Perhaps by a particular revelation. *That there is nothing.* Neither flesh nor herbs. *Unclean of itself.* Unlawful under the gospel.

15. *If thy brother be grieved.* That is, wounded, led into sin. *Destroy not him.* So we see that he for whom Christ died may be destroyed. *With thy meat.* Do not value your meat more than Christ valued his life.

17. *For the kingdom of God.* That is, true religion does not consist in external observances. But in *righteousness.* The image of God stamped on the heart; the love of God and man accompanied with the peace that passes all understanding, *and joy in the Holy Ghost.*

22. *Happy is he that condemneth not himself.* By an improper use of even innocent things. And happy is he who is free from a doubting conscience! He who has this may allow the thing, yet condemn himself for it.

23. *Whatsoever is not of faith is sin.* Whatever a man does without a full persuasion of its lawfulness, it is sin to him.

CHAPTER 15

1. *We then that are strong.* Of a clearer judgment, and free from these scruples.

13. *Now the God of hope.* A glorious title of God, but until now unknown to the heathens; for their goddess Hope, like their other idols, was nothing; whose temple at Rome was burned by lightning. It was, indeed, built again not long after, but was again burned to the ground.

14. There are several conclusions of this epistle. The first begins at this verse; the second, Romans 16:1; the third, verse 17; the fourth, verse 21; and the fifth, verse 25.

20. *Lest I should* [only] *build upon another man's foundation.* The providence of God seemed in a special manner generally to prevent this, though not entirely, lest the enemies of the apostle who sought every occasion to set light by him should have had room to say that he was behind other apostles, not being sufficient for planting of churches himself, but only for preaching where others had been already; or that he declined the more difficult part of the ministry.

23. *Having no more place in these parts.* Where Christ has now been preached in every city.

24. *If first I be somewhat filled with your company.* How remarkable is the modesty with which he speaks! They might rather desire to be filled, or satisfied, with his. *Somewhat filled.* Intimating the shortness of his stay; or perhaps, that Christ alone can thoroughly satisfy the soul.

26. *The poor saints which are at*

Jerusalem. It can by no means be inferred from this expression that the community of goods among the Christians had ceased. All that can be gathered from it is that in this time of extreme dearth (Acts 11:28–29), some of the church in Jerusalem were in need; the rest being merely able to subsist themselves, but not to supply the necessities of their brethren.

28. *I will come by you into Spain.* Such was his design; but it does not appear that Paul went into Spain. There are often holy purposes in the minds of good men which are overruled by the providence of God so as never to take effect. And yet they are precious in the sight of God.

30. *I beseech you . . . for the love of the Spirit.* That is, by the love which is the genuine fruit of the Spirit. *Ye strive together with me in your prayers.* He must pray himself who would have others strive together with him in prayer. Of all the apostles, Paul alone is recorded to desire the prayers of the faithful for himself. And this he generally does in the conclusions of his epistles; yet not without making a difference. For he speaks in one manner to them whom he treats as his children, with the gravity or even severity of a father, such as Timothy, Titus, Corinthians, and Galatians; in another, to them whom he treats rather like equals, such as the Romans, Ephesians, Thessalonians, Colossians, Hebrews.

CHAPTER 16

1. *A servant.* The Greek word is a "deaconess." *Of the church which is at Cenchrea.* In the apostolic age there were some grave and pious women appointed deaconesses in every church. It was their office not to teach publicly, but to visit the sick—the women in particular—and to minister to them both in their temporal and spiritual necessities.

5. *Greet the church that is in their house.* Where any Christian had a large house, there they all assembled together; though as yet the Christians at Rome had neither bishops nor deacons. No, there does not appear to have been then in the whole city more than one of these domestic churches. Otherwise there can be no doubt but Paul would have saluted them also.

13. *And his mother and mine.* This expression may only denote the tender care which Rufus's mother had taken of him.

14. *Salute Asyncritus, Phlegon,* etc. He seems to join those together who were joined by kindred, nearness of habitation, or any other circumstance. It could not but encourage the poor especially to be saluted by name who perhaps did not know the apostle had ever heard of them. It is observable that while the apostle forgets none who are worthy, yet he adjusts the nature of his salutation to the degrees of worth in those whom he salutes.

15. *Salute.* Had Peter been then at Rome, Paul would doubtless have saluted him by name, since no one in this numerous catalogue was of an eminence comparable to him. But if he was not then at Rome, the whole Roman tradition with regard to the succession of their bishops fails in the most fundamental article.

25. *Now to him that is of power.* The last words of this epistle exactly answer the first, chapters 1–5. In particular, concerning the power of God, the gospel, Jesus Christ, the Scriptures, the obedience of faith, all nations.

27. *To God only wise, be glory through Jesus Christ for ever.* And let every believer say, *"Amen!"*

I CORINTHIANS

CHAPTER 1

1. *Paul, called to be an apostle.* There is great propriety in every clause of the salutation, particularly in this, as there were some in the church of Corinth who called the authority of his mission in question.

2. *With all that in every place.* Nothing could better suit that universal love which Paul labors to promote in this epistle than such a declaration of his good wishes for every true Christian upon earth. *Call upon the name of Jesus Christ our Lord.* This plainly implies that all Christians pray to Christ as well as to the Father through him.

7. *Waiting.* With earnest desire. *For the* [glorious] *coming of our Lord Jesus Christ.* A sure mark of a true or false Christian is to long for, or dread, this revelation.

8. *In the day of our Lord Jesus Christ.* Now it is our day, wherein we are to work out our salvation; then it will be eminently the day of Christ and of his glory in the saints.

13. *Is Christ divided?* Are not all the members still under one head? Was not he alone crucified for you all; and were you not all baptized in his name? The glory of Christ, then, is not to be divided between him and his servants; neither is the unity of the body to be torn asunder, seeing Christ is one still.

17. *Lest the cross of Christ should be made of none effect.* The whole effect of Paul's preaching was owing to the power of God accompanying the plain declaration of the great truth that Christ bore our sins upon the cross. But this effect might have been imputed to another cause, had he come with that wisdom of speech which they admired.

23. *We go on to preach* in a plain and historical, not rhetorical or philosophical, manner, *Christ crucified, unto the Jews a stumblingblock.* Just opposite to the signs they demand. *And unto the Greeks foolishness.* A silly tale, just opposite to the wisdom they seek.

24. *But unto them which are called.* And obey the heavenly calling. *Christ.* With his cross, his death, his life, his kingdom. And they experience, first, that he is *the power,* then, that he is *the wisdom of God.*

25. *Because the foolishness of God.* The gospel scheme, which the world judges to be mere foolishness, *is wiser than* the wisdom of men; and weak as they account it, *stronger than* all the strength of men.

26. *Ye see your calling.* What manner of men they are whom God calls.

30. *Righteousness.* The sole ground of our justification who were before under the wrath and curse of God. *And sanctification*. A principle of universal holiness, whereas before we were altogether dead in sin. *And redemption*. That is, complete deliverance from all evil, and eternal bliss both of soul and body.

CHAPTER 2

2. *I determined not to know any thing*. To waive all my other knowledge and not to preach anything, except *Jesus Christ, and him crucified*. That is, what he did, suffered, taught. A part is put for the whole.

4. *In demonstration of the Spirit and of power*. With that powerful kind of demonstration which flows from the Holy Spirit; which works on the conscience with the most convincing light and the most persuasive evidence.

6. *Among them that are perfect*. Adult, experienced Christians. By *wisdom* he seems to mean not the whole Christian doctrine, but the most sublime and abstruse parts of it.

8. *The Lord of glory*. In giving Christ this august title, peculiar to the great Jehovah, he plainly shows him to be the supreme God. In like manner the Father is characterized as "the Father of glory" (Eph. 1:17); and the Holy Ghost, "the Spirit of glory" (I Peter 4:14). The application of this title to all three shows that the Father, Son, and Holy Ghost are "the God of glory," as the only true God is called in Psalm 29:3 and Acts 7:2.

12. *Now we have received, not the spirit of the world*. This spirit is not properly received, for the men of the world always had it. But Christians receive the Spirit of God, which before they had not.

13. *Which the Holy Ghost teachest*. Such are all the words of Scripture. How high a regard ought we, then, to retain for them!

14. *But the natural man*. That is, every man who has not the Spirit; who has no other way of obtaining knowledge but by his senses and natural understanding. *Because they are spiritually discerned*. They can only be discerned by the aid of that Spirit and by those spiritual senses which he has not.

CHAPTER 3

2. I *fed you*, as babes, *with milk*. The first and plainest truths of the gospel. So should every preacher suit his doctrine to his hearers.

8. Has not all this reasoning the same force still? Ministers are still barely instruments in God's hand and depend as entirely as ever on his blessing to give the increase to their labors. Without this, they are nothing. With it, their part is so small that they hardly deserve to be mentioned. May their hearts and hands be more united; and, retaining a due sense of the honor God does them in employing them, may they faithfully labor not as for themselves, but for the great Proprietor of all, until the day comes when he will reward them in full proportion to their fidelity and diligence!

12. *Gold, silver, precious stones*. Three sorts of materials which will bear the fire; true and solid doctrines. *Wood, hay, stubble*. Three which will not bear the fire. Such are all doctrines, ceremonies, and forms of human invention; all but the substantial, vital truths of Christianity.

13. The time is coming when *every man's work shall be made manifest: for the day* of the Lord, that great and final day, *shall declare it*. To all the world. *Because it shall be revealed*. What faith beholds as so certain and so near is spoken of as already present. *By fire; and the fire shall try every man's work of what sort it is*. The strict process of that day will try every man's doctrines, whether they come up to the Scripture standard or not. Here is a plain allusion to the flaming light and consuming heat of the general conflagration. But the expression, when applied to the trying of doctrines and consuming of those who are wrong, is evidently figurative; because no material fire can have such an effect on what is of a moral nature.

15. *Yet so as by fire.* Or, as narrowly as a man escapes through the fire when his house is all in flames about him.

This text (vv. 12–15), then, is so far from establishing purgatory that it utterly overthrows it. For the fire here mentioned does not exist until the day of judgment. Therefore, if this be the fire of purgatory, it follows that purgatory does not exist before the day of judgment.

22. *Or the world.* This leap from Peter to "the world" greatly enlarges the thought and argues a kind of impatience of enumerating the rest. Peter and every one in the whole world, however excellent in gifts or grace or office, are also your servants for Christ's sake.

CHAPTER 4

1. *Ministers of Christ.* The original word properly signifies such servants as labored at the oar in rowing vessels; and accordingly intimates the pains which every faithful minister takes in his Lord's work.

8. *Now ye are full.* The Corinthians abounded with spiritual gifts; and so did the apostles. But the apostles, by continual need and sufferings, were kept from self-complacency. The Corinthians, suffering nothing and having plenty of all things, were pleased with and applauded themselves; and they were like children who, being raised in the world, disregard their poor parents.

9. *Appointed to death.* Alluding to the Roman custom of bringing forth those persons last on the stage either to fight with each other or with wild beasts, who were devoted to death; so that if they did escape one day, they were brought out again and again until they were killed.

11. *And are naked.* Who can imagine a more glorious triumph of the truth than that which is gained in these circumstances; when Paul, with an impediment in his speech and a person more contemptible than graceful, appeared in lowly, perhaps tattered dress before persons of the highest distinction, and yet commanded such attention and made such deep impressions upon them!

13. *We are made as the filth of the world, and are the offscouring of all things.* Such were those poor wretches among the heathens who were taken from the dregs of the people to be offered as expiatory sacrifices to the infernal gods. They were loaded with curses, affronts, and injuries all the way to the altars; and when the ashes of those unhappy men were thrown into the sea, these very names were given them in the ceremony.

CHAPTER 5

5. *To deliver such an one.* This was the highest degree of punishment in the Christian church; and we may observe that the passing of this sentence was the act of the apostle, not of the Corinthians. *Unto Satan.* Who was usually permitted in such cases to inflict pain or sickness on the offender. *For the destruction.* Though slowly and gradually. *Of the flesh.* Unless prevented by speedy repentance.

7. *For even Christ our passover is sacrificed for us.* The Jewish passover, about the time when this epistle was written (I Cor. 5:11) was only a type of this. What exquisite skill both here and everywhere conducts the zeal of the inspired writer! How surprising a transition is here, and yet how perfectly natural! The apostle, speaking of the incestuous criminal, slides into his darling topic, a crucified Savior. Who would have expected it on such an occasion? Yet, when it is thus brought in, who does not see and admire both the propriety of the subject and the delicacy of its introduction?

CHAPTER 6

9. *Idolaters* is here placed between *fornicators* and *adulterers,* because they generally accompanied it. *Nor effeminate.* Who live in an easy, indolent way; taking up no cross, enduring no hardship. But how is this? These good-natured, harmless people are ranked with *idolaters* and sodomites! We may learn from this that we are never secure from the greatest sins until we guard against those which are thought to be the least; nor indeed, until we think no sin is little since every one is a step toward hell.

18. *Flee fornication.* Flee all unlawful commerce with women with speed, with abhorrence, with all your might. *But he that committeth fornication sinneth against his own body.* Pollutes, dishonors, and degrades it to a level with brute beasts.

19. And even your body is not, strictly speaking, your own; even this *is the temple of the Holy Ghost.* Dedicated to him and inhabited by him. What the apostle calls elsewhere "the temple of God" (I Cor. 3:16–17) and "the temple of the living God" (II Cor. 6:16) he here calls *the temple of the Holy Ghost,*

plainly showing that the Holy Ghost is the living God.

20. *Glorify God in your body, and in your spirit.* Yield your bodies and all their members, as well as your souls and all their faculties, as instruments of righteousness to God. Devote and employ all you have and all you are, entirely, unreservedly, and for ever to his glory.

CHAPTER 7

1. *Not to touch a woman.* That is, not to marry. So great and many are the advantages of a single life.

3. *The debt.*[1] This ancient reading seems far more natural than the common one.

8. *It is good for them if they abide even as I.* That Paul was then single is certain; and from Acts 7:58, compared with the following parts of the history, it seems probably that he always was so. It does not appear that this declaration, any more than verse 1, has any reference at all to a state of persecution.

12. *Speak I.* By revelation from God, though our Lord has not left any commandment concerning it.

24. *Therein abide with God.* Doing all things as unto God and as in his immediate presence. They who thus *abide with God* preserve an holy indifference with regard to outward things.

25. *Now concerning virgins.* Of either sex. *I have no commandment of the Lord.* By a particular revelation. Nor was it necessary he should; for the apostles wrote nothing which was not divinely inspired. But with this difference: sometimes they had a particular revelation and a special commandment; at other times they wrote from the divine light which abode with them, the

---

[1](7:3) KJV: "due benevolence."

standing treasure of the Spirit of God. And this also was not their private opinion, but a divine rule of faith and practice.

39. *Only in the Lord.* That is, only let Christians marry Christians; a standing direction, and one of utmost importance.

40. *Have the Spirit of God.* Teaching me all things. This does not imply any doubt; but affirms the strongest certainty of it, together with a reproof of them for calling it into question. Whoever would conclude from hence that Paul was not certain he had the Spirit of Christ neither understands the true import of the words nor considers how expressly he lays claim to the Spirit, both in this epistle (2:16; 14:37) and in the other (II Cor. 13:3).

CHAPTER 8

8. *But meat commendeth us not to God.* Neither by eating nor by refraining from it. Eating and not eating are in themselves things merely indifferent.

13. *If meat.* Of any kind. Who will follow this example? What preacher or private Christian will abstain from anything lawful in itself when it offends a weak brother?

CHAPTER 9

2. *The seal of mine apostleship.* Who have received not only faith by my mouth, but all the gifts of the Spirit by my hands.

5. *And Cephas.* Hence we learn: (1) That Peter continued to live with his wife after he became an apostle. (2) That he had no rights as an apostle which were not common to Paul.

17. *Willingly.* He seems to mean "without receiving anything." Paul here speaks in a manner peculiar to himself.

Another might have preached "willingly" and yet have received a maintenance from the Corinthians. But if he had received anything from them, he should have termed it preaching "unwillingly." And so, in the next verse, another might have used that power without abusing it. But his own using it at all he would have termed abuse.

19. *I made myself servant unto all.* I acted with as self-denying a regard to their interest and as much caution not to offend them as if I had been literally their servant or slave. Where is the preacher of the gospel who treads in the same steps?

20. *As under the law.* Observing it myself while I am among them. Not that he declared this to be necessary, or refused to converse with those who did not observe it. This was the very thing which he condemned in Peter (Gal. 2:14).

26. *I therefore so run, not as uncertainly.* I look straight to the goal; I run straight toward it. I cast away every weight, regard not any that stand by. *As one that beateth the air.* This is a proverbial expression for a man's missing his blow and spending his strength not on his enemy, but on empty air.

27. *But I keep under my body.* By all kinds of self-denial. *And bring it into subjection.* To my spirit and to God. The words are strongly figurative and signify the mortification of the "body of sin" by an allusion to the natural bodies of those who were subdued or bruised in combat. *Lest that by any means, when I had preached to others.* The Greek word means "after having discharged the office of a herald" (still carrying on the allusion), whose office it was to proclaim the conditions and to display the prizes.

I myself should be a reprobate.[2] Disapproved by the Judge, and so falling short of the prize. This single text may give us a just notion of the scriptural doctrine of election and reprobation. It clearly shows us that particular persons are not in holy writ represented as elected absolutely and unconditionally to eternal life, or predestined absolutely and unconditionally to eternal death, but that believers in general are elected to enjoy the Christian privileges on earth; which if they abuse, those very elect persons will become reprobate. Paul was certainly an elect person if ever there was one. Yet he declares it was possible that he himself might become "a reprobate." He actually would have become such if he had not thus kept his body "under," even though he had been so long an elect person, a Christian, and an apostle.

CHAPTER 10

2. *And were all,* as it were, *baptized unto Moses.* Initiated into the religion which he taught them. *In the cloud and in the sea.* Perhaps sprinkled here and there with drops of water from the sea or the cloud, by which baptism might be the more evidently signified.

6. *Now these things were our examples.* Showing what we are to expect if, enjoying the like benefits, we commit the like sins. The benefits are set down in the same order as by Moses in Exodus; the sins and punishments in a different order.

7. The other cautions are given in the first person; but these in the second. And with what exquisite propriety does he vary the person! It would have been improper to say, "Neither let *us* be idolaters"; for he was himself in no danger of idolatry, nor probably of murmuring against Christ or the divine providence.

11. *Upon whom the ends of the world are come.* The expression has great force. All things meet together and come to a crisis under the last, the gospel dispensation; both benefits and dangers, punishments and rewards. It remains that Christ come as an avenger and judge. And even these *ends* include various periods, succeeding each other.

16. *The communion of the body of Christ.* The means of our partaking of those benefits which were purchased by *the body of Christ* offered for us.

29. *For why is my liberty judged of another man's conscience?* Another's conscience is not the standard of mine, nor is another's persuasion the measure of *my liberty.*

31. *Therefore.* To close the present point with a general rule, applicable not only in this, but in all cases. *Whatsoever ye do.* In all things whatever, whether of a religious or civil nature, in all the common as well as sacred actions of life, keep the glory of God in view and steadily pursue in all this one end of your being, the planting or advancing of the vital knowledge and love of God, first in your own soul, then in all mankind.

CHAPTER 11

3. *The head of every man.* Particularly every believer. *The head of Christ is God.* Christ, as Mediator, acts in all things subordinately to his Father. But we can no more infer that they are not of the same divine nature because God is said to be *the head of Christ,* than that man and woman are not of the same human nature because the man is said to be *the head of the woman.*

---

[2] (9:27) KJV: "a castaway."

7. *For a man indeed ought not to veil his head,* because *he is the image and glory of God* in the dominion he bears over the creation, representing the supreme dominion of God, which is his glory. *But the woman* is only a matter of *glory* to the man, who has a becoming dominion over her. Therefore she ought not to appear except with her head veiled as a tacit acknowledgment of it.

11. Neither male nor female is excluded; neither is preferred before the other in Christ's kingdom.

13. *Is it comely that a woman pray unto God,* the Most High, with that bold and undaunted air which she must have when, contrary to universal custom, she appears in public with her head *uncovered?*

16. *We have no such custom* here nor in any of the other *churches of God.* The several churches in the apostles' time had different customs in things that were not essential; and that under one and the same apostle, as circumstances, in different places, make it convenient. And in all things merely indifferent, the custom of each place was of sufficient weight as to determine prudent and peaceable men. Yet even this cannot overrule the scrupulous conscience, which really doubts whether the thing be indifferent or not. But those who are referred to here by the apostle were *contentious,* not conscientious, persons.

18. *In the church.* In the public assembly. *I hear that there be divisions among you; and I partly believe it.* That is, I believe it of some of you. It is plain that by divisions, or schisms, is not meant any separation from the church, but uncharitable divisions in it; for the Corinthians continued to be all one church. And in spite of all their strife and contention, there was not separation of any one party from the rest with regard to external communion.

21. *For in eating* what you call the Lord's supper, instead of all partaking of one bread, each person brings his own supper and eats it without staying for the rest. And hereby the poor, who cannot provide for themselves, have nothing; while the rich eat and drink to the full. This is just as the heathens used to do at the feasts on their sacrifices.

23. *I have received.* By an immediate revelation.

24. *This is my body, which is broken for you.* That is, this broken bread is the sign of my body which is even now to be pierced and wounded for your iniquities. Take then, and eat of this bread in a humble, thankful, obedient remembrance of my dying love; of the extremity of my sufferings on your behalf, of the blessings I have thereby procured for you, and of the obligations to love and duty which I have by all this laid upon you.

25. *After supper.*[3] Therefore you ought not to confuse this with a common meal. *In remembrance of me.* The ancient sacrifices were in remembrance of sin. This sacrifice, once offered, is still represented in remembrance of the remission of sins.

27. *Eat . . . and drink . . . unworthily.* That is, in an unworthy, irreverent manner; without regarding either him who appointed it or the design of its appointment.

28. *But let a man examine himself.* Whether he know the nature and design of the institution, and whether it be his own desire and purpose to comply therewith.

---

[3] (11:25) KJV: "when he had supped."

CHAPTER 12

8. *The word of wisdom.* A power to understand and explain the manifold wisdom of God in the grand scheme of gospel salvation. *Word of knowledge.* Perhaps an extraordinary ability to understand and explain the Old Testament types and prophecies.

9. *Faith* may here mean an extraordinary trust in God under the most difficult and dangerous circumstances. *The gifts of healing* need not be wholly confined to healing diseases with a word or a touch. It may exert itself also, though in a lower degree, where natural remedies are applied. And it may often be this, not superior skill, which makes some physicians more successful than others. And thus it may be with regard to other gifts. As, after the golden shields were lost, the king of Judah put brazen in their place; so, after the pure gifts were lost, the power of God exerts itself in a more covert manner, under human studies and helps; and that the more plentifully, according as there is the more room given for it.

10. *Prophecy.* Foretelling things to come. *Discerning.* Whether men be of an upright spirit or not; whether they have natural or supernatural gifts for offices in the church; and whether they who profess to speak by inspiration speak from a divine, a natural, or a diabolical spirit.

15—16. *Is it therefore not of the body.* Is the inference good? Perhaps *the foot* may represent private Christians; *the hand,* officers in the church; *the eye,* teachers; the *ear,* hearers.

22. *Those members of the body, which seem to be more feeble.* Being of a more delicate and tender structure; perhaps the brains and bowels, or the veins, arteries, and other minute channels in the body.

28. *First apostles.* Who plant the gospel in the heathen nations. *Secondarily prophets.* Who either foretell things to come or speak by extraordinary inspiration for the edification of the church. *Thirdly teachers.* Who precede even those who work miracles.

CHAPTER 13

3. *It profiteth me nothing.* Without this, whatever I speak, whatever I have, whatever I know, whatever I do, whatever I suffer is nothing.

4. The *charity* of God and of our neighbor for God's sake is patient towards all men. Love suffers all the weakness, ignorance, errors, and infirmities of the children of God; all the malice and wickedness of the children of the world. And all this not only for a time, but to the end. And in every step toward overcoming evil with good, it is kind, soft, mild, benign. It inspires the sufferer at once with the most amiable sweetness, and the most fervent and tender affection. *Vaunteth not itself.* Does not act rashly. Does not hastily condemn any one; never passes a severe sentence on a slight or sudden view of things. Nor does it ever act or behave in a violent, headstrong, or precipitate manner. *Is not puffed up.* Humbles the soul to the dust.

5. *Doth not behave itself unseemly.* Is not rude or willingly offensive to any. *Seeketh not her own* ease, pleasure, honor, or temporal advantage. No, sometimes the lover of mankind seeks not, in some sense, even his own spiritual advantage; does not think of himself so long as a zeal for the glory of God and the souls of men swallows him up. But, though he is all of fire for these ends, yet he *is not easily provoked.* He is not provoked to sharpness or to unkindness toward any one. Outward provocations indeed will frequently occur; but he triumphs over all.

Love *thinketh no evil*. Indeed it cannot but see and hear evil things, and know that they are so; but it does not willingly think evil of any, neither infer evil where it does not appear. It tears up, root and branch, all imagining of what we have not proof. It casts out all jealousies, all evil surmises, all readiness to believe evil.

6. *Rejoiceth not in iniquity*. Weeps at either the sin or folly of even an enemy; takes not pleasure in hearing or in repeating it, but desires it may be forgotten for ever. *But rejoiceth in the truth*. Bringing forth its proper fruit, holiness of heart and life. Good in general is its glory and joy, wherever diffused in all the world.

7. Love *beareth all things*. Whatever evil the lover of mankind sees, hears, or knows of any one, he mentions it to none; it never goes out of his lips except where absolute duty constrains to speak. *Believeth all things*. Puts the most favorable construction on every thing and is ever ready to believe whatever may tend to the advantage of any one's character. And when it can no longer believe well, it *hopeth* whatever may excuse or extenuate the fault which cannot be denied. Where it cannot even excuse, it hopes God will at length give "repentance unto life." Meantime it *endureth all things*. Whatever the injustice, the malice, the cruelty of men can inflict. He cannot only do, but likewise suffer all things though Christ who strengthens him.

8. *Never faileth*. Love accompanies to and adorns us in eternity; it prepares us for and constitutes heaven. *But whether there be prophecies, they shall fail*. When all things are fulfilled and God is all in all. *Whether there be tongues, they shall cease*. One language shall prevail among all the inhabitants of heaven, and the low and imperfect languages of earth be forgotten. That *knowledge* likewise which we now so eagerly pursue shall then *vanish away*. As starlight is lost in that of the midday sun, so our present knowledge will vanish in the light of eternity.

9. *For we know in part, and we prophesy in part*. The wisest of men have here but short, narrow, imperfect conceptions, even of the things round about them, and much more of the deep things of God. And even the prophecies which men deliver from God are far from taking in the whole of future events, or of that wisdom and knowledge of God which is treasured up in the Scripture revelation.

10. *But when that which is perfect is come*. At death and in the last day. *That which is in part shall be done away*. Both that poor, low, imperfect, glimmering light which is all the knowledge we now can attain to; and these slow and unsatisfactory methods of attaining, as well as of imparting it to others.

11. *As a child*. In our present state we are mere infants in point of knowledge compared to what we shall be hereafter. *I put away childish things*. Of my own accord, willingly, without trouble.

12. *Now we see*. Even the things that surround us. But *through a glass*. Or mirror, which reflects only their imperfect forms in a dim, faint, obscure manner; so that our thoughts about them are puzzling and intricate and everything is a kind of riddle to us. *But then*. We shall see not a faint reflection, but the objects themselves. *Face to face*. Distinctly. *Now I know in part*. Even when God himself reveals things to me, a great part of them is still kept under the veil. *But then shall I know even as also I am known*. In a clear, full, comprehensive manner; in some measure like God, who penetrates the center of every object and sees at one glance through my soul and all things.

CHAPTER 14

1. *Follow after charity* with zeal, vigor, courage, patience; else you can neither attain nor keep it. *But especially[4] that ye may prophesy.* The word here does not mean foretelling things to come; but rather opening and applying the Scripture.

5. *Greater.* That is, more useful. By this alone are we to estimate all our gifts and talents.

14. *For if I pray in an unknown tongue.* The apostle, as he did at the sixth verse, transfers it to himself. *My spirit prayeth.* By the power of the Spirit I understand the words myself. *But my understanding is unfruitful.* The knowledge I have is no benefit to others.

15. *I will pray with the spirit, and I will pray with the understanding also.* I will use my own understanding as well as the power of the Spirit. I will not act so absurdly as to utter in a congregation what can edify none but myself.

16. *How ... say Amen.* Assenting and confirming your words, as it was even then usual for the whole congregation to do.

20. *Be not children in understanding.* This is an admirable stroke of true oratory to bring down the height of their spirit by representing that wherein they prided themselves most as mere folly and childishness.

21. *With men of other tongues and other lips will I speak unto this people.* And so he did. He spoke terribly to them by the Babylonians when they had set at nought what he had spoken by the prophets, who used their own language. These words received a further accomplishment on the Day of Pentecost.

23. *And there come in those that are unlearned.* Men of learning might have understood the tongues in which they spoke. It is observable, Paul says here *those that are unlearned, or unbelievers;* but in the next verse, "one that believeth not, or one unlearned." Several bad men together hinder each other by evil discourse. Single persons are more easily gained.

25. *The secrets of his heart made manifest.* Laid open, clearly described; in a manner which to him is most astonishing and utterly unaccountable. How many instances of it are seen at this day! So does God still point his word.

27. *And let one interpret.* Either himself (v. 13) or, if he have not the gift, some other, into the common tongue. It seems the gift of tongues was an instantaneous knowledge of a tongue until then unknown, which he who received it could afterwards speak when he thought fit, without any new miracle.

32. *And the spirits of the prophets are subject to the prophets.* But what enthusiast considers this? The impulses of the Holy Spirit, even in men really inspired, so suit themselves to their rational faculties as not to divest them of the government of themselves, like the heathen priests under their diabolical possession. Evil spirits threw their prophets into such ungovernable ecstasies as forced them to speak and act like madmen. But the Spirit of God left his prophets the clear use of their judgment as to when and how long it was fit for them to speak, and never hurried them into any improprieties either as to the matter, manner, or time of their speaking.

34. *Let your women keep silence in the churches.* Unless they are under an

---

[4](14:1) KJV: "rather."

extraordinary impulse of the Spirit. For in other cases *it is not permitted unto them to speak.* By way of teaching in public assemblies.

CHAPTER 15

2. *Ye are saved, if ye hold fast.*[5] Your salvation is begun and will be perfected if you continue in the faith. *Unless ye have believed in vain.* Unless indeed your faith was only a delusion.

9. *I persecuted the church.* True believers are humbled all their lives, even for the sins they committed before they believed.

20. *But now.* His proof of the resurrection lies in a narrow compass (vv. 12–19). Almost all the rest of the chapter is taken up in illustrating, vindicating, and applying it.

24. *Then.* After the resurrection and the general judgment. *Cometh the end.* Of the world; the grand period of all those wonderful scenes that have appeared for so many succeeding generations. *When he shall have delivered up the kingdom.* The divine reign both of the Father and Son is from everlasting to everlasting. But this is spoken of the Son's mediatorial kingdom, which will then be delivered up, and of the immediate kingdom or reign of the Father, which will then commence. Till then the Son transacts the business which the Father has given him, for those who are his, and by them as well as by the angels, with the Father and against their enemies. But the glory which he had before the world began (John 17:5; Heb. 1:8) will remain even after this is delivered up. If the citizens of the "new Jerusalem" shall "reign for ever" (Rev. 22:5), how much more shall he?

26. *The last enemy that shall be destroyed is death.* Namely, after Satan (Heb. 2:14) and sin (I Cor. 15:56) are destroyed. In the same order they prevailed. Satan brought in sin, and sin brought forth death. And Christ, when he of old engaged with these enemies, first conquered Satan, then sin, in his death; and lastly death, in his resurrection. In the same order he delivers all the faithful from them, yes, and destroys these enemies themselves. Death he so destroys that it shall be no more. He destroys sin and Satan so that they shall no more hurt his people.

31. *I die daily.* I am daily in the very jaws of death. Beside that I live, as it were, in a daily martyrdom.

32. *I have fought with beasts at Ephesus.* With the savage fury of a lawless multitude (Acts 19:29ff.).

34. *Awake.* An exclamation full of apostolic majesty. Shake off your lethargy!

36. To the inquiry concerning the manner of rising, and the quality of the bodies that rise, the apostle answers first by a similitude (vv. 36–42) and then plainly and directly (vv. 42–43).

42. *It is sown.* A beautiful word; committed, as seed to the ground. *In corruption.* Just ready to putrefy and, by various degrees of corruption and decay, to return to the dust whence it came. *It is raised in incorruption.* Utterly incapable of either dissolution or decay.

43. *It is sown in dishonour.* Shocking to those who loved it best, human nature in disgrace! *It is raised in glory.* Clothed with robes of light, fit for those whom the King of Heaven delights to honor. *It is sown in weakness.* Deprived even of that feeble strength which it once enjoyed. *It is raised in power.* Endued with vigor, strength, and activity, such as we cannot now conceive.

---

[5] (15:2) KJV: "if ye keep in memory."

47. *The second man.* Christ was not the second man in order of time; but in this respect, that as Adam was a public person who acted in the stead of all mankind, so was Christ. As Adam was the first general representative of men, Christ was the second and the last. And what they severally did terminated not in themselves, but affected all whom they represented.

52. *In a moment.* Amazing work of omnipotence! And cannot the same power now change us into saints in a moment? *The trumpet shall sound.* To awaken all who sleep in the dust of the earth.

55. *O death, where is thy sting?* Which once was full of hellish poison. *O grave.* That is, hades, the receptacle of separate souls. *Where is thy victory?* You are now robbed of all your spoils; all your captives are set at liberty. *Grave,* or hades, literally means the invisible world and relates to the soul; *death,* to the body. The Greek words are found in the Septuagint translation of Hosea 13:14.

58. *Be ye stedfast.* In yourselves. *Unmoveable.* By others; continually increasing in the work of faith and labor of love. *Know that your labour is not in vain in the Lord.* Whatever you do for his sake shall have its full reward in that day.

Let us also endeavor, by cultivating holiness in all its branches, to maintain this hope in its full energy; longing for that glorious day when, in the utmost extent of the expression, "death shall be swallowed up" for ever, and millions of voices, after the long silence of the grave, shall burst out at once into that triumphant song, "O death, where is thy sting? O grave, where is thy victory?"

CHAPTER 16

2. *Let every one.* Not the rich only; let him also that has little gladly give of that little. *As God hath prospered him.* Increasing his alms as God increases his substance. According to this lowest rule of Christian prudence, if a man when he has or gains one pound will give a tenth to God, when he has or gains a hundred he will give the tenth of this also. And yet I show unto you a more excellent way. He that has ears to hear, let him hear. Stint yourself to no proportion at all. But lend to God all you can.

13. To conclude. *Watch ye.* Against all your seen and unseen enemies. *Stand fast in the faith.* Seeing and trusting him that is invisible. *Acquit yourselves like men.*[6] With courage and patience, *Be strong.* To do and suffer all his will.

18. *Acknowledge.* With suitable love and respect.

22. *If any man love not the Lord Jesus Christ.* If any be an enemy to his person, offices, doctrines, or commands. *Let him be Anathema Maranatha.* "Anathema" signifies a thing devoted to destruction. It seems to have been customary with the Jews of that age, when they had pronounced any man an "anathema," to add the Syriac expression, "Marana tha," that is, "The Lord comes," namely, to execute vengeance upon him. This weighty sentence the apostle chose to write with his own hand and to insert it between his salutation and solemn benediction, that it might be the more attentively regarded.

---

[6](16:13) KJV: "quit you like men."

II CORINTHIANS

CHAPTER 1

3. *The Father of mercies, and the God of all comfort.* Mercies are the fountain of comfort; comfort is the outward expression of mercy. God shows mercy in the affliction itself. He gives comfort both in and after the affliction. Therefore is he termed, *the God of all comfort.* Blessed be this God!

4. *Who comforteth us in all our tribulation.* He that has experienced one kind of affliction is able to comfort others in that affliction. He that has experienced all kinds of affliction is able to comfort them in all.

20. *For all the promises of God in him are yea, and in him Amen.* Are surely established in and through him. They are *yea* with respect to God promising; *Amen,* with respect to men believing; *yea,* with respect to the apostles; *Amen,* with respect to their hearers.

22. *Who hath also sealed us.* Stamping his image on our hearts, thus marking and sealing us as his own property. *And given the earnest of the Spirit.* There is a difference between an earnest and a pledge. A pledge is to be restored when the debt is paid; but an earnest is not taken away, but completed. Such an earnest is the Spirit. The firstfruits of it we have in Romans 8:23; and we wait for all the fullness.

24. *Not for that we have dominion over your faith.* This is the prerogative of God alone. We see the light in which ministers should always consider themselves and in which they are to be considered by others. Not as having dominion over the faith of the people and having a right to dictate by their authority what they shall believe, or what they shall do; but as *helpers of your joy,* by helping them forward in faith and holiness. In this view, how amiable does their office appear! And how friendly to the happiness of mankind! How far, then, are they from true benevolence who would expose it to ridicule and contempt!

CHAPTER 2

6. *Sufficient to such a man.* With what a remarkable tenderness does Paul treat this offender! He never once mentions his name. Nor does he here so much as mention his crime.

14. *To triumph* implies not only victory, but an open manifestation of it. And as in triumphal processions, especially in the east, incense and perfumes were burned near the conqueror, the apostle beautifully alludes to this circumstance in verse 15. Likewise, Paul alludes to the different effects which strong perfumes have upon different persons; some of whom they revive, while they throw others into the most violent disorders.

CHAPTER 3

6. *Who also hath made us able ministers of the new testament.* Of the new, evangelical dispensation. Not of the law, fitly called *the letter,* from God's literally writing it on the two tables. *But of the spirit.* Of the gospel dispensation which is written on the table of our hearts by the Spirit. *For the letter.* The law, the Mosaic dispensation. *Killeth.* Seals in death those who still cleave to it. *But the Spirit.* The gospel, conveying the Spirit to those who receive it. *Giveth life.* Both spiritual and eternal. Yes, if we adhere to the literal sense even of the moral law, if we regard only the precept and the sanction as they stand in themselves, not as they lead us to Christ, they are doubtless a killing ordinance and bind us down under the sentence of death.

13. *Which put a veil over his face.* Which is to be understood with regard to his writings also. *That the children of Israel could not stedfastly look to the end of that* [dispensation] *which is* [now] *abolished.* The end of this was Christ. The whole Mosaic dispensation tended toward and terminated in him; but the Israelites had only a dim, wavering sight of him, of whom Moses spoke in an obscure, covert manner.

14. *In the* [public] *reading of the old testament.* The veil is not now on the face of Moses or of his writings, but *in the reading* of them, and on the heart of them who believe not.

16. *The veil shall be taken away.* That very moment; and they see with the utmost clearness how all the types and prophecies of the law are fully accomplished in him.

17. *There is liberty.* Not the veil, the emblem of slavery. There is liberty from servile fear, liberty from the guilt and from the power of sin, liberty to behold with open face the glory of the Lord.

18. What a beautiful contrast is here! Moses saw the glory of the Lord, and it rendered his face so bright that he covered it with a veil, Israel not being able to bear the reflected light. We behold his glory in the glass of his word, and our faces shine too; yet we veil them not, but diffuse the luster which is continually increasing as we fix the eye of our mind more and more steadfastly on his glory displayed in the gospel.

CHAPTER 4

4. *The god of this world.* What a sublime and horrible description of Satan! He is indeed the god of all who believe not, and works in them with inconceivable energy. *Who is the image of God.* Hence we may understand how great is the glory of Christ. He who sees the Son sees the Father in the face of Christ. The Son exactly exhibits the Father to us.

6. *For God . . . hath shined in our hearts.* The hearts of all those whom the god of this world no longer blinds. God, who is himself our light; not only the author of light, but also the fountain of it.

7. *In earthen vessels.* In frail, feeble, perishing bodies. He proceeds to show that afflictions, yes, death itself are so far from hindering the ministration of the Spirit that they even further it, sharpen the ministers, and increase the fruit.

8. *We are troubled.* The four articles in this verse respect inward afflictions; the four in the next, outward. In each clause the former part shows the *earthen vessels;* the latter, *the excellency of the power.*

11. *Are alway delivered unto death.* Are perpetually in the very jaws of destruction; which we willingly submit to that we may "obtain a better resurrection."

12. *So then death worketh in us, but life in you.* You live in peace; we die daily.

13–14. *We also . . . speak.* We preach the gospel even in the midst of affliction and death, because we believe that God will *raise up us* from the dead and will *present us,* ministers, *with you,* all his members, "faultless before his presence with exceeding joy."

17. *Our light affliction.* The beauty and sublimity of Paul's expressions here, as descriptive of heavenly glory opposed to temporal affliction, surpass all imagination and cannot be preserved in any translation or paraphrase, which after all must sink infinitely below the astonishing original.

CHAPTER 5

2. *Desiring to be clothed upon.* This body, which is now covered with flesh and blood, with the glorious house which is from heaven. Instead of flesh and blood, which cannot enter heaven, the rising body will be clothed or covered with what is analogous thereto, but incorruptible and immortal.

4. *Do groan, being burdened.* The apostle speaks with exact propriety. A burden naturally expresses groans. And we are here burdened with numberless afflictions, infirmities, temptations.

7. *For* we cannot clearly see him in this life, wherein *we walk by faith* only. An evidence, indeed, that necessarily implies a kind of "seeing him who is invisible"; yet as far beneath what we shall have in eternity as it is above that of bare, unassisted reason.

10. *Must all appear.* Openly, without covering, where all hidden things will be revealed; probably the sins even of the faithful, which were forgiven long before. For many of their good works, such as their repentance, their revenge against sin, cannot otherwise appear. But this will be performed at their own desire without grief and without shame.

14. *For the love of Christ.* To us, and our love to him. *Constraineth us.* Both to the one and the other; bears us on with such a strong, steady, prevailing influence as winds and tides exert when they waft the vessel to its destined harbor.

16. *After the flesh.* According to his former state, country, descent, nobility, riches, power, wisdom. We fear not the great. We regard not the rich or wise. We account not the least less than ourselves. We consider all, only in order to save all. Who is he who thus knows *no man after the flesh?* In what land do these Christians live?

17. *Therefore if any man be in Christ.* A true believer in him. *He is a new creature.* Only the power that makes a world can make a Christian. And when he is so created, *old things are passed away.* Of their own accord, even as snow in spring. *Behold* the present, visible, undeniable change! *All things are become new.* He has new life, new senses, new faculties, new affections, new appetites, new ideas and conceptions. His whole tenor of action and conversation is new, and he lives, as it were, in a new world. God, men, the whole creation, heaven, earth, and all therein appear in a new light and stand related to him in a new manner since he was created anew in Christ Jesus.

20. *We pray you in Christ's stead.* What unparalleled condescension and divinely tender mercies are displayed in this verse! Did the judge ever beseech a condemned criminal to accept a pardon? Does the creditor ever beseech a ruined debtor to receive an acquittance in full? Yet our almighty Lord and our eternal Judge not only vouchsafes to offer these blessings, but invites us, entreats us, and with the most tender importunity solicits us not to reject them.

21. *That we might be made the righteousness of God in him.* Might *in him* be invested with that righteousness, first imputed to us, then implanted in us, which is in every sense *the righteousness of God.*

CHAPTER 6

2. *For he saith.* The sense is, As of old there was a particular time wherein God was pleased to pour out his peculiar blessings, so there is now. And this is the particular time; this is a time of peculiar blessing.

6. *By knowledge.* That is, prudence. Spiritual, divine; not what the world terms so. Worldly prudence is the practical use of worldly wisdom. Divine prudence is the due exercise of grace, making spiritual understanding go as far as possible.

10. *As having nothing, and yet possessing all things.* For all things are ours if we are Christ's. What a magnificence of thought is this!

14. *Be ye not unequally yoked together with unbelievers.* Christians with Jews or with heathens. The apostle specially speaks of marriage. But the reasons he urges equally hold against any needless intimacy with them. Of the five questions that follow, the three former contain the argument; the two latter, the conclusion.

16. *What agreement hath the temple of God with idols?* If God would not endure idols in any part of the land wherein he dwelt, how much less under his own roof!

18. *And ye shall be my sons and daughters, saith the Lord Almighty.* The promise made to Solomon (I Chron. 28:6) is here applied to all believers, as the promise made particularly to Joshua is applied to them (Heb. 13:5). Who can express the worth, who can conceive the dignity, of this divine adoption? Yet it belongs to all who believe the gospel, who have faith in Christ. They have access to the Almighty; such free and welcome access as a beloved child to an indulgent father. To him they may fly for aid in every difficulty, and from him obtain a supply in all their needs.

CHAPTER 7

1. *Let us cleanse ourselves.* This is the latter part of the exhortation which was proposed in II Corinthians 6:1 and resumed in verse 14. *From all filthiness of the flesh.* All outward sin. *And spirit.* All inward sin. Yet let us not rest in negative religion, but in *perfecting holiness.* Carrying it to the height in all its branches and enduring to the end *in the* [loving] *fear of God,* the sure foundation of all holiness.

8. *I did repent.* That is, I felt a tender sorrow for having grieved you, until I saw the happy effect of it.

10. *The sorrow of the world.* Sorrow that arises from worldly considerations.

CHAPTER 8

5. *Not as we hoped.* That is, beyond all we could hope for.

12. *Is accepted.* With God. And the same rule holds universally. Whoever acknowledges himself to be a vile, guilty sinner and, in consequence of this acknowledgment, flies for refuge to the wounds of a crucified Savior and relies on his merits alone for salvation, may in every circumstance of life apply this indulgent declaration to himself.

14. *A supply for your want: that there may be equality.* No lack on one side, no superfluity on the other. It may likewise have a further meaning—that as the temporal bounty of the Corinthians did now supply the temporal needs of their poor brethren in Judea, so the prayers of these might be a means of bringing down many spiritual blessings on their benefactors. So that all the spiritual needs of the one might be amply supplied; all the temporal of the other.

CHAPTER 9

6. A general rule. God will proportion the reward to the work and the temper whence it proceeds.

8. How remarkable are these words! *All grace.* Every kind of blessing. *May abound to every good work.* God gives us everything that we may do good therewith and so receive more blessings. All things in this life, even rewards, are, to the faithful, seeds for a future harvest.

9. *He hath dispersed abroad.* A generous word. With a full hand, without any anxious thought which way each grain falls. *His righteousness.* Beneficence, with the blessed effects of it. *Remaineth for ever.* Unexhausted, God still renewing his store.

15. *His unspeakable gift.* His outward and inward blessings, the number and excellence of which cannot be uttered.

CHAPTER 10

3. *Though we walk in the flesh.* In mortal bodies, and consequently we are not free from human weakness. Yet *we do not war.* Against the world and the devil. *After the flesh.* By any carnal or worldly methods. Though the apostle here, and in several other parts of this epistle, speaks in the plural number for the sake of modesty and decency, yet he principally means himself. On him were

these reflections thrown, and it is his own authority which he is vindicating.

4. *For the weapons of our warfare.* Those we use in this war. *Not carnal.* But are spiritual and therefore *mighty through God to the pulling down of strong holds.* Of all the difficulties which men or devils can raise in our way. Though faith and prayer belong also to the Christian armor (Eph. 6:15ff.), yet the word of God seems to be here chiefly intended.

5. *Into captivity every thought to the obedience of Christ.* Those evil reasonings are destroyed. The mind itself, being overcome and taken captive, lays down all authority of its own and entirely gives itself up to perform, for the time to come, to Christ its conqueror, *the obedience* of faith.

10. *His bodily presence is weak.* His stature, says Chrysostom, was low, his body crooked, and his head bald.

CHAPTER 11

3. *From the simplicity that is in Christ.* That simplicity which is lovingly intent on him alone, seeking no other person or thing.

6. *Though I be rude in speech.* If I speak in a plain, unadorned way, like an unlearned person. So the Greek word properly signifies.

9. *For.* I choose to receive help from the poor Macedonians rather than the rich Corinthians! Were the poor in all ages more generous than the rich?

17. *I speak it not after the Lord.* Not by an express command from him, though still under the direction of his Spirit.

CHAPTER 12

2. *I knew a man in Christ.* It is plain from verses 6 and 7 that he means himself, though in modesty he speaks as of a third person. *Whether in the body . . . or whether out of the body, I cannot tell.* It is equally possible with God to present distant things to the imagination in the body, as if the soul were absent from it and present with them; or to transport both soul and body for what time he pleases to heaven; or to transport the soul only there for a season and in the meantime to preserve the body fit for its re-entrance. But since the apostle himself did not know whether his soul was in the body or whether one or both were actually in heaven, it would be vain curiosity for us to attempt determining it. *The third heaven.* Where God is; far above the aerial and the starry heaven. Some suppose it was here the apostle was let into the mystery of the future state of the church, and received his orders to turn from the Jews and go to the Gentiles.

4. *He was caught up into paradise.* The seat of happy spirits in their separate state between death and the resurrection. *Words, which it is not lawful for a man to utter.* Human language being incapable of expressing them. Here he anticipated the joyous rest of the righteous who die in the Lord. But this rapture did not precede, but followed after, his being caught up to the third heaven. This is a strong intimation that he must first discharge his mission and then enter into glory. And beyond all doubt, such a foretaste of it served to strengthen him in all his later trials, when he could call to mind the very joy that was prepared for him.

6. *But now I forbear.* I speak sparingly of these things, for fear *any man should think* too highly *of me.* O where is this fear now to be found? Who is afraid of this?

7. *There was given to me.* By the wise and gracious providence of God. *A thorn in the flesh.* A visitation more painful than any thorn sticking in the flesh. *The messenger* [or angel] *of Satan to buffet me.* Perhaps both visibly and invisibly; and the word in the original expresses the present time as well as the past. All kinds of affliction had befallen the apostle. Yet none of those did he deprecate. But here he speaks of one, as above all the rest, one that macerated him with weakness, and by the pain and ignominy of it prevented his being lifted up more, or at least not less, than the most vehement headache could have done; which many of the ancients say he labored under. Paul seems to have had a fresh fear of these *buffetings* every moment, when he so frequently represses himself in his boasting, though it was extorted from him by the utmost necessity.

8. *I besought the Lord thrice.* As our Lord besought his Father.

9. *And he said unto me.* In answer to my third request. *My grace is sufficient for thee.* How tender a repulse! We see there may be grace where there is the quickest sense of pain. *My strength* is more illustriously displayed by the *weakness* of the instrument. *Therefore will I rather glory in my infirmitites* than in my revelations, *that the power of Christ may rest upon me.* The Greek word properly means "may cover me all over like a tent." We ought most willingly to accept whatever tends to this end, however contrary to flesh and blood.

10. *Infirmities.* Whether proceeding from Satan or from men. *For when I am weak.* Deeply conscious of my weakness, *then* does the strength of Christ rest upon me.

CHAPTER 13

5. *Know ye not your own selves, how Jesus Christ is in you.* All Christian believers know this by the witness and by the fruit of his Spirit. Some translate the words "Jesus Christ is among you"—that is, in the church of Corinth—and understand them of the miraculous gifts and the power of Christ which attended the censures of the apostle.

11. *Be perfect.* Aspire to the highest degree of holiness.

14. *The grace.* Or favor. *Of the Lord Jesus Christ.* By which alone we can come to the Father. *And the love of God.* Manifested to you and abiding in you. *And the communion.* Or fellowship. *Of the Holy Ghost.* In all his gifts and graces.

It is with great reason that this comprehensive and instructive blessing is pronounced at the close of our solemn assemblies; and it is a very indecent thing to see so many quitting them, or getting into postures of remove, before this short sentence can be ended.

How often have we heard this benediction pronounced! Let us study it more and more that we may value it proportionately; that we may either deliver or receive it with a becoming reverence, with eyes and hearts lifted up to God, who giveth the blessing out of Sion, and life for evermore.

Galatians

CHAPTER 1

1. *Paul, an apostle.* Here it was necessary for Paul to assert his authority; otherwise he is very modest in the use of this title. He seldom mentions it when he mentions others in the salutations with himself, as in the epistles to the Philippians and Thessalonians; or when he writes about secular affairs, as in that to Philemon; nor yet in writing to the Hebrews, because he was not properly their apostle.

4. *According to the will of God.* Without any merit of ours. Paul begins most of his epistles with thanksgiving; but writing to the Galatians, he alters his style and first sets down his main proposition, that by the merits of Christ alone, *who gave himself for our sins,* we are justified.

7. *Which* [indeed] *is not* [properly] *another* gospel. For what you have now received is no gospel at all. It is not glad, but heavy tidings, as setting your acceptance with God upon terms impossible to be performed.

10. *Do I now persuade men . . . ?* Is this what I aim at in preaching or writing? *If I yet.* Since I was an apostle. *Pleased men.* Studied to please them; if this were my motive of actions. No, if I did in fact please the men who know not God, *I should not be the servant of Christ.* Hear this, all you who vainly hope to keep in favor both with God and with the world!

12. *But by the revelation of Jesus Christ.* Our Lord revealed to him at first his resurrection, ascension, and the calling of the Gentiles, and his own apostleship; and told him then that there were other things for which he would appear to him.

15. *Who separated me from my mother's womb.* Who set me apart for an apostle, as he did Jeremiah for a prophet (Jer. 1:5). Such an unconditional predestination as this may consist with both God's justice and mercy.

CHAPTER 2

1. *I went up again to Jerusalem.* This seems to be the journey mentioned in Acts 15, several passages here referring to that great council wherein all the apostles showed that they were of the same judgment with him.

5. With such wonderful prudence did the apostle use his Christian liberty! He circumcised Timothy (Acts 16:3) because of weak brethren, but not Titus because of false brethren.

10. *Remember the poor.* The poor Christians in Judea who had lost all they had for Christ's sake.

11. *But.* The argument here comes

to the height. Paul reproves Peter himself. So far was he from receiving his doctrine from man or from being inferior to the chief of the apostles.

14. *I said unto Peter before them all.* See Paul single against Peter and all the Jews!

16. *But by the faith of Jesus Christ.* That is, by faith in him. The name "Jesus" was first known by the Gentiles; the name "Christ" by the Jews. *Even we.* And how much more must the Gentiles, who have still less pretense to depend on their own works!

18. By no means. *For if I build again.* By my sinful practice. *The things which I destroyed.* By my preaching. *I* [only] *make myself.* Or show myself, not Christ, to be a *transgressor;* the whole blame lies on me, not him or his gospel. As if he had said, The objection was just if the gospel promised justification to men continuing in sin. But it does not. Therefore if any who profess the gospel do not live according to it, they are sinners, it is certain, but not justified; and so the gospel is clear.

19. *For I through the law.* Applied by the Spirit to my heart, deeply convincing me of my utter sinfulness and helplessness. *That I might live unto God.* Not continue in sins. For this very end am I, in this sense, freed from the law that I may be freed from sin.

20. *But Christ liveth in me.* Is a fountain of life in my inmost soul from which all my tempers, words, and actions flow. *I live by the faith of the Son of God.* I derive every moment from that supernatural principle; from a divine evidence and conviction that he *loved me, and gave himself for me.*

CHAPTER 3

6. Doubtless in confirmation of that grand doctrine that we are justified by faith, even *as Abraham* was. Both in this and in the epistle to the Romans, the apostle makes great use of the instance of Abraham. This, because from Abraham the Jews drew their great argument, as they do this day, both for their own continuance in Judaism and for denying the Gentiles to be the church of God.

8. *And the scripture.* So great is the excellence and fullness of the Scripture that all the things which can ever be controverted are therein both foreseen and determined.

11. *The just shall live by faith.* That is, the man who is accounted just or righteous before God shall continue in a state of acceptance, life, and salvation *by faith.* This is the way God has chosen.

19. *It.* The ceremonial law. *Was added.* To the promise. *Because of transgressions.* Probably, the yoke of the ceremonial law was inflicted as a punishment for the national sin of idolatry (Exod. 32:1), at least the more grievous parts of it; and the whole of it was a prophetic type of Christ. The moral law was added to the promise to discover and restrain transgressions, to convince men of their guilt and need of the promise, and to give some check to sin. And this law passes not away; but the ceremonial law was only introduced until Christ should come.

24. *Wherefore the law was our schoolmaster to bring us unto Christ.* It was designed to train us up for Christ. And this it did both by its commands, which showed the need we had of his atonement; and by its ceremonies, which all pointed us to him.

28. *There is neither Jew nor Greek.* That is, there is no difference between them; they both are equally accepted through faith. *There is neither male nor female.* Circumcision being laid aside, which was peculiar to males and was designed to put a difference during that dispensation between Jews and Gentiles.

CHAPTER 4

3. *Under the elements of this world.* Under the typical observances of the law, which were like the first elements of grammar, the ABCs of children; and were of so gross a nature as hardly to carry our thoughts beyond this world.

11. The apostle here, dropping the argument, applies to the affections (vv. 11–20) and humbles himself to the Galatians with an inexpressible tenderness.

19. *My little children.* He speaks as a parent, with both authority and the most tender sympathy, toward weak and sickly children. *Until Christ be formed in you.* Until there be in you all the mind that was in him.

28. *Are the children of promise.* Not born in a natural way, but by the supernatural power of God. And as such we are heirs of the promise made to believing Abraham.

30. *Cast out the bondwoman and her son.* Who mocked Isaac. In like manner will God cast out all who seek to be justified by the law, especially if they persecute them who are his children by faith.

CHAPTER 5

2. *If ye be circumcised.* And seek to be justified thereby. *Christ.* The Christian institution. *Shall profit you nothing.* For you hereby disclaim Christ and all the blessings which are through faith in him.

11. The grand reason why the Jews were so offended at his preaching Christ crucified, and so bitterly persecuted him for it, was that it implied the abolition of the law. Yet Paul did not condemn conforming, out of conde-

scension to the weakness of any one, even to the ceremonial law; but he did absolutely condemn those who taught it as necessary to justification.

14. *For all the law is fulfilled in one word, even in this; Thou shalt love thy neighbour as thyself.* Inasmuch as none can do this without loving God (I John 4:12); and the love of God and man includes all perfection.

19. *Now the works of the flesh.* By which that inward principle is discovered. *Are manifest.* Plain and undeniable. *Works* are mentioned in the plural because they are distinct from and often inconsistent with each other. But "the fruit of the Spirit" is mentioned in the singular (v. 22) as being all consistent and connected together. *Which are these.* He enumerates those *works of the flesh* to which the Galatians were most inclined; and those parts of "the fruit of the Spirit" of which they stood in the greatest need.

21. *Revellings.* Luxurious entertainments. Some of the works here mentioned are wrought principally, if not entirely, in the mind; and yet they are called "works of the flesh." Hence it is clear, the apostle does not by "the flesh" mean the body or sensual appetites and inclinations only, but the corruption of human nature as it spreads through all the powers of the soul, as well as all the members of the body.

22. *Gentleness.* Toward all men; ignorant and wicked men in particular.

23. *Meekness.* Holding all the affections and passions in even balance.

24. *Crucified the flesh.* Nailed it, as it were, to a cross whence it has no power to break loose, but grows continually weaker and weaker.

25. *If we live in the Spirit.* If we are indeed raised from the dead and are alive to God by the operation of his Spirit. *Let us also walk in the Spirit.* Let us follow his guidance in all our tempers, thoughts, words, and actions.

26. *Let us not be desirous of vain glory.* Of the praise or esteem of men. They who do not carefully and closely follow the Spirit easily slide into this. The natural effects of which are *provoking* to envy them that are beneath us, and *envying* them that are above us.

CHAPTER 6

1. *Brethren, if a man be overtaken in a fault.* By surprise, ignorance, or stress of temptation. *Ye which are spiritual.* Who continue to live and work by the Spirit. *Restore such an one.* By reproof, instruction, or exhortation. Every one who can ought to help herein, only *in the spirit of meekness.* This is essential to a spiritual man; and in this lies the whole force of the cure. *Lest thou also be tempted.* Temptation easily and swiftly passes from one to another, especially if a man endeavors to cure another without preserving his own meekness.

2. *Bear ye one another's burdens.* Sympathize with and assist each other in all your weaknesses, grievances, and trials. *And so fulfil the law of Christ.* "The law of Christ" (an uncommon expression) is the law of love. This our Lord peculiarly recommends; this he makes the distinguishing mark of his disciples.

5. *For every man shall bear his own burden.* In that day shall give an account of himself to God.

10. *As we have therefore opportunity.* At whatever time or place and in whatever manner we can. The opportunity in general is our lifetime; but there are also many particular opportunities. Satan is quickened in doing hurt by the shortness of the time (Rev. 12:12). By the same consideration let us be quickened in doing good. *Let us do good.* In every possible kind in every possible degree. *Unto all men.* Good or evil, neighbors or strangers, good or evil, friends or enemies.

14. *But God forbid that I should glory.* Should boast of any thing I have, am, or do; or rely on any thing for my acceptance with God, but what Christ has done and suffered for me. By means of *whom the world is crucified unto me.* All the things and persons in it are to me as nothing. *And I unto the world.* I am dead to all worldly pursuits, cares, desires, and enjoyments.

17. *The marks of the Lord Jesus.* The scars, marks, and brands of my sufferings for him.

ephesians

CHAPTER 1

3. *Blessed be the God and Father of our Lord Jesus Christ, who hath blessed us.* God's blessing us is his bestowing all spiritual and heavenly blessings upon us. Our blessing God is in paying him our solemn and grateful acknowledgments, both on account of his own essential blessedness and of the blessings which he bestows upon us. He is *the God . . . of our Lord Jesus Christ,* as man and Mediator. He is his *Father,* primarily, with respect to his divine nature as his only begotten Son; and secondly, with respect to his human nature as that is personally united to the divine. *With all spiritual blessings in heavenly places.* With all manner of spiritual blessings, which are heavenly in their nature, origin, and tendency, and shall be completed in heaven. Far different from the external privileges of the Jews and the earthly blessings they expected from the Messiah.

4. *As he hath chosen us.* Both Jews and Gentiles, whom he foreknew as believing in Christ (I Peter 1:2).

5. *Having predestinated us unto the adoption of children.* Having foreordained that all who afterwards believed should enjoy the dignity of being sons of God, and joint-heirs with Christ.

According to the good pleasure of his will. According to his free, fixed, unalterable purpose to confer this blessing on all those who should believe in Christ, and those only.

9. *The mystery of his will.* The gracious scheme of salvation by faith, which depends on his own sovereign will alone. This was but darkly discovered under the law; is now totally hid from unbelievers; and has heights and depths which surpass all the knowledge even of true believers.

11. *Predestinated according to the purpose of him who worketh all things after the counsel of his own will.* The unalterable decree, "He that believeth shall be delivered"; which is not arbitrary, but flowing from the rectitude of his nature. Or else, what security would there be that it would be his will to keep his word even with the elect?

13. *Ye were sealed with that holy Spirit of promise.* The sealing seems to imply: (1) A full impression of the image of God on their souls. (2) A full assurance of receiving all the promises, whether relating to time or eternity.

18. *The eyes of your understanding.* It is with these alone that we discern the things of God. Being first opened, and then *enlightened.* By his Spirit. *That ye* *may know what is the hope of his calling.* That you may experimentally[1] and delightfully know what are the blessings which God has called you to hope for by his word and his Spirit. *And what the riches of the glory of his inheritance in the saints.* What an immense treasure of blessedness he has provided as an inheritance for holy souls!

19. *And what is the exceeding greatness of his power to us-ward who believe.* Both in quickening our dead souls and preserving them in spiritual life.

20. *And set him at his own right hand.* That is, he has exalted him in his human nature, as a recompense for his sufferings, to a quiet, everlasting possession of all possible blessedness, majesty, and glory.

21. *Far above all principality, and power, and might, and dominion.* That is, God has invested him with uncontrollable authority over all demons in hell, all angels in heaven, and all the princes and potentates on earth. *And every name that is named.* We know the king is above all, though we cannot name all the officers of his court. So we know that Christ is above all, though we are not able to name all his subjects.

23. *The fulness of him that filleth all in all.* It is hard to say in what sense this can be spoken of the church; but the sense is easy and natural if we refer it to Christ Jesus, who is the fulness of the Father.

CHAPTER 2

1. *And you hath he quickened.* In the nineteenth and twentieth verses of the preceding chapter, Paul spoke of God's working in them by the same almighty power whereby God raised Christ from the dead. On the mention of this Paul, in the fullness of his heart, runs into a flow of thought concerning the glory of Christ's exaltation in the three following verses. He here resumes the thread of his discourse. *Who were dead.* Not only diseased, but dead; absolutely void of all spiritual life; and as incapable of quickening yourselves as persons literally dead.

2. *According to the prince of the power of the air.* The effect of which power all may perceive, though all do not understand the cause of it; a power unspeakably penetrating and widely diffused. But yet, as to its baneful influences, beneath the orb of believers. The evil spirits are united under one head, the seat of whose dominion is in the air. Here he sometimes raises storms, sometimes makes visionary representations, and is continually roving to and fro.

5. *By grace ye are saved.* Grace is both the beginning and end. The apostle speaks indifferently in either the first or second person; the Jews and Gentiles being in the same circumstances, both by nature and by grace. This text lays the axe to the very root of spiritual pride and all glorying in ourselves. Therefore Paul, foreseeing the backwardness of mankind to receive it, yet knowing the absolute necessity of its being received, again asserts the very same truth (v. 8) in the very same words.

6. *And made us* [all] *sit together in heavenly places.* This is spoken by way of anticipation. Believers are not yet possessed of their seats in heaven; but each of them has a place prepared for him.

8. *By grace are ye saved through faith.* Grace, without any respect to human worthiness, confers the glorious gift. Faith, with an empty hand and without any pretense to personal deserving, receives the heavenly blessing.

---

[1] (1:18) That is, "experientially." See also Wesley's note on 6:17.

9. *Not of works.* Neither this faith nor this salvation is owing to any works you ever did, will, or can do.

10. *For we are his workmanship.* Which proves both that salvation is by faith and that faith is the gift of God. *Created . . . unto good works.* That afterwards we might give ourselves to them. *That we should walk in them.* Though not be justified by them.

12. *Having no hope.* Because they had no promise whereon to ground their hope. *Without God.* Wholly ignorant of the true God and so, in effect, atheists. Such in truth are, more or less, all men in all ages until they know God by the teaching of his own Spirit.

14. *And hath broken down the middle wall of partition.* Alluding to that wall of old which separated the court of Israel from the court of the Gentiles. Such a wall was the ceremonial law, which Christ had now taken away.

20. *And are built upon the foundation of the apostles and prophets.* Like the foundation sustaining the building, so the word of God, declared by the apostles and prophets, sustains the faith of all believers. God laid the foundation by them; but *Christ himself being the chief corner stone* of the foundation. Elsewhere he is termed the foundation itself (I Cor. 3:11).

21. *In whom all the building fitly framed together.* The whole fabric of the universal church rises up like a great pile of living materials. *Unto an holy temple in the Lord.* Dedicated to Christ and inhabited by him, in which he displays his presence and is worshipped and glorified. What is the temple of Diana of the Ephesians, whom you formerly worshipped, to this?

the noblest strains of eloquence to paint the exceeding low opinion the apostle had of himself, and the fullness of unfathomable blessings which are treasured up in Christ.

12. *Have boldness.* Unrestrained liberty of speech, such as children use in addressing an indulgent father when, without fear of offending, they disclose all their needs and make known all their requests.

17. *Being rooted and grounded.* That is, deeply fixed and firmly established *in love.*

18–19. *May be able to comprehend.* So far as a human mind is capable. *What is the breadth . . . [of] the love of Christ.* Embracing all mankind. *And length.* From everlasting to everlasting. *And depth.* Not to be fathomed by any creature. *And height.* Not to be reached by any enemy.

And to know. But the apostle corrects himself and immediately observes that it cannot be fully known. This only we know, that the love of Christ *passeth* all *knowledge. With all the fulness of God.* With all his light, love, wisdom, holiness, power, and glory. A perfection far beyond a bare freedom from sin.

20. *Now unto him.* This doxology is admirably adapted to strengthen our faith, that we may not stagger at the great things the apostle has been praying for, as if they were too much for God to give or for us to expect from him. *That is able.* Here is a most beautiful gradation. When he has given us *exceeding,* yes, and above all this. *Above all that we ask.* Above all we can *think.* Yes, exceedingly, abundantly above all that we can either ask or think.

CHAPTER 3

8. *Unto me, who am less than the least of all saints, is this grace given.* Here are

CHAPTER 4

3. *Endeavouring to keep the unity of the Spirit.* That mutual union and harmony which is a fruit of the Spirit. *The bond of peace* is love.

5. *One* outward *baptism.*

8. *When he ascended up on high, he led captivity captive.* He triumphed over all his enemies—Satan, sin, and death—which had before enslaved all the world; alluding to the custom of ancient conquerors who led those they had conquered in chains after them. And as they also used to give donatives to the people at their return from victory, so he *gave gifts unto men.* Both the ordinary and extraordinary gifts of the Spirit.

9. *Now that he ascended, what is it but that he also descended.* That is, does it not imply that he descended first? Certainly it does, on the supposition of his being God. Otherwise it would not; since all the saints will ascend to heaven, though none of them descended thence. *Into the lower parts of the earth.* So the womb is called (Ps. 39:15); the grave (Ps. 63:9).

11. *And some, prophets; and some, evangelists.* A prophet testifies of things to come; an evangelist of things past, and that chiefly by preaching the gospel before or after many of the apostles.

12. In this verse is noted the office of ministers; in the next, the aim of the saints; in verses 14–16, the way of growing in grace. And each of these has three parts, standing in the same order.

13. *Unto the measure of the stature of the fulness of Christ.* To that maturity of age and spiritual stature wherein we shall be filled with Christ, so that he will be all in all.

14. *Tossed to and fro.* From within, even when there is no wind. *And carried about with every wind.* From without; when we are assaulted by others who are unstable as the wind.

16. A beautiful allusion to the human body, composed of different joints and members, knit together by various ligaments, and furnished with vessels of communication from the head to every part.

19. *Who being past feeling.* The original word is peculiarly significant. It properly means "past feeling pain." Pain urges the sick to seek a remedy which, where there is no pain, is little considered.

21. *If so be that ye have heard him.* Teaching you inwardly by his Spirit. *As the truth is in Jesus.* According to his own gospel.

26. *Be ye angry, and sin not.* That is, if you are angry, take heed you sin not. Anger at sin is not evil; but we should feel only pity to the sinner. If we are angry at the person as well as the fault, we sin. And how hardly do we avoid it! *Let not the sun go down upon your wrath.* Reprove your brother and be reconciled immediately. Lose not one day. A clear, express command. Reader, do you keep it?

30. *Grieve not the holy Spirit.* By any disobedience. Particularly by corrupt discourse or by any of the following sins. Do not force him to withdraw from you, as a friend does whom you grieve by unkind behavior.

31. *Let all bitterness.* The height of settled anger, opposite to kindness (v. 32). *And wrath.* Lasting displeasure towards the ignorant and them who are out of the way, opposite to tenderheartedness. *And anger.* The very first risings of disgust at those who injure you, opposite to forgiving one another. *Clamour.* Or bawling. "I am not angry," says one, "but it is my way to speak so." Then unlearn that way; it is the way to hell. *And evil speaking.* Be it in ever so mild and soft a tone, or with ever such professions of kindness. Here is a beautiful retrogradation, beginning with the highest and descending to the lowest degree of the lack of love.

32. *As God,* showing himself *kind*

and *tenderhearted* in the highest degree, *hath forgiven you.*

CHAPTER 5

1. *Be ye therefore followers.* Imitators. *Of God.* In forgiving and loving. O how much more honorable and more happy to be an imitator of God than of Homer, Virgil, or Alexander the Great!

4. *Nor foolish talking.* Tittle-tattle, talking of nothing, the weather, fashions, meat and drink.

6. *Because of these things.* As innocent as the heathens esteem them and as those dealers in *vain words* would persuade you to think them.

15. *Circumspectly.* Exactly, with the utmost accuracy, getting to the highest pitch of every point of holiness. *Not as fools.* Who think not where they are going or do not make the best of their way.

16. With all possible care *redeeming the time.* Saving all you can for the best purposes; buying every possible moment out of the hands of sin and Satan; out of the hands of sloth, ease, pleasure, worldly business; the more diligently, because the present *days are evil,* days of the grossest ignorance, immorality, and profaneness.

19. *And spiritual songs.* On any divine subject. By there being no inspired songs peculiarly adapted to the Christian dispensation, as there were to the Jewish, it is evident that the promise of the Holy Ghost to believers in the last days was by his larger effusion to supply the lack of it.

20. *Giving thanks.* At all times and places. And *for all things.* Prosperous or adverse, since all work together for good.

22. In the following directions concerning relative duties, the inferiors are all along placed before the superiors, because the general proposition concerns submission; inferiors ought to do their duty, whatever their superiors do. *Wives, submit yourselves unto your own husbands.* Unless where God forbids. *As unto the Lord.* The obedience a wife pays to her husband is at the same time paid to Christ himself.

24. *In every thing.* Which is not contrary to any command of God.

25. *Even as Christ also loved the church.* Here is the true model of conjugal affection. With this kind of affection, with this degree of it, and to this end should husbands love their wives.

30. *Are members.* And as intimately united to Christ, in a spiritual sense, as if we were literally "bone of [his] bones, and flesh of his [flesh]."

CHAPTER 6

1. *Children, obey your parents.* In all things lawful the will of the parent is a law to the child.

2. *Honour.* That is, love, reverence, obey, assist in all things. The mother is particularly mentioned, as being more liable to be slighted than the father.

3. *And thou mayest live long on the earth.* This is usually fulfilled to eminently dutiful children; and he who lives long and well has a long seed-time for the eternal harvest. But this promise, in the Christian dispensation, is to be understood chiefly in a more exalted and spiritual sense.

4. *Provoke not your children to wrath.* Do not needlessly fret or exasperate them.

7. *As to the Lord, and not to men.* That is, rather than to men; and by making every action of common life a sacrifice to God, having an eye to him in all things, even as if there were no other master.

11. *The whole armour.* As if the armor would scarce do, it must be the *whole* armor. This is repeated in verse 13 because of the strength and subtlety of our adversaries, and because of an "evil day" of sore trial being at hand.

12. *For we wrestle not* only, not chiefly, *against flesh and blood.* Weak men, or fleshly appetites. *But against principalities, against powers.* The mighty princes of all the infernal legions. And great is their power, and that likewise of those legions whom they command. *Against the rulers of the darkness of this world.* Perhaps these principalities and powers remain mostly in the citadel of their kingdom of darkness. But there are other evil spirits who range abroad, to whom the provinces of the world are committed. *Of the darkness.* This is chiefly spiritual darkness. *Of this world.* Or this age which prevails during the present state of things. *Against spiritual wickedness.* That is, against wicked spirits, who continually oppose faith, love, holiness, either by force or fraud; and labor to infuse unbelief, pride, idolatry, malice, envy, anger, hatred. *In high places.* Which were once their abode and which they still aspire to as far as they are permitted.

13. *In the evil day.* The war is perpetual; but the fight is one day less violent, another more so. *The evil day* is either at the approach of death, or in life; may be longer or shorter; and admits of numberless varieties. *And having done all, to stand.* That you may still keep on your armor, still stand upon your guard, still watch and pray; and thus you will be enabled to endure unto the end and stand with joy before the face of the Son of Man.

14. *Having your loins girt about.* That you may be ready for every motion. *With truth.* Not only with the truths of the gospel, but with "truth in the inward parts"; for without this all our knowledge of divine truth will prove but a poor girdle in *the evil day.* So our

Lord is described in Isaiah 11:5. And as a girded man is always ready to go on, so this seems to intimate an obedient heart, a ready will. Our Lord adds to the loins girded, the lights burning (Luke 12:35); showing that watching and ready obedience are the inseparable companions of faith and love. *And having on the breastplate of righteousness.* The righteousness of a spotless purity, in which Christ will present us faultless before God through the merit of his own blood. With this breastplate our Lord is described in Isaiah 59:17. In the breast is the seat of conscience, which is guarded by righteousness. No armor for the back is mentioned; we are always to face our enemies.

15. *And your feet shod with the preparation of the gospel.* Let this be always ready to direct and confirm you in every step. This part of the armor for the feet is needful, considering what a journey we have to go, what a race to run. Our feet must be so shod that our footsteps slip not. To order our life and conversation aright, we are prepared by the gospel blessing, the peace and love of God ruling in the heart (Col. 3:14–15). By this only can we tread the rough ways, surmount our difficulties, and hold out to the end.

16. *Above* or over *all.* As a sort of universal covering to every other part of the armor itself, continually exercise a strong and lively *faith.* This you may use as a *shield,* which will *quench all the fiery darts,* the furious temptations, violent and sudden injections *of the wicked.*

17. *And take the helmet* of the hope *of salvation.* (I Thess. 5:8.) The head is that part which is most carefully to be defended. One stroke here may prove fatal. The armor for this is "the hope of salvation." The lowest degree of this hope is a confidence that God will work the whole work of faith in us; the highest is a full assurance of future glory, added to the experimental knowledge of pardoning love. Armed with this *helmet,* the hope of the joy set before him, Christ "endured the cross, despising the shame" (Heb. 12:2).

And the sword of the Spirit, which is the word of God. This Satan cannot withstand when it is edged and wielded by faith. Until now our armor has been only defensive. But we are to attack Satan as well as secure ourselves, the shield in one hand and the sword in the other. Whoever fights with the powers of hell will need both. He who is covered with armor from head to foot and neglects this will be foiled after all. This whole description shows us how great a thing it is to be a Christian. The lack of any one thing makes him incomplete. Though he has his loins girt with truth, righteousness for a breastplate, his feet shod with the preparation of the gospel, the shield of faith, the helmet of salvation, and the sword of the Spirit, yet one thing he lacks after all. What is that? It follows:

18. *Praying always.* At all times, on every occasion, in the midst of all employments, inwardly *praying always. In the Spirit.* Through the influence of the Holy Spirit. *With all prayer.* With all sort of prayer, public, private, mental, vocal. Some are careful in respect of one kind of prayer and negligent in others. If we would have the petitions we ask, let us use all. Some there are who use only mental prayer and think they are in a state of grace, and use a way of worship far superior to any other. But such only fancy themselves to be above what is really above them; it requiring far more grace to be enabled to pour out a fervent and continued prayer than to offer up mental aspirations. *And supplication.* Repeating and urging our prayer, as Christ did in the garden. *And watching.* Inwardly attending on God to know his will, to gain power to do it, and to attain to the blessings we desire. *With all perseverance.* Continuing to the end in this holy exercise. *And supplication for all saints.* Wrestling in fervent, continued intercession for others, especially for the faithful that they may do all the will of God, steadfast to the end. Perhaps we receive few answers to prayer because we do not intercede enough for others.

20. *An ambassador in bonds.* The ambassadors of men usually appear in great pomp. How differently does the ambassador of Christ appear!

philippians

CHAPTER 1

1. *Servants.* Paul, writing familiarly to the Philippians, does not style himself an apostle. And under the common title of *servants* he tenderly and modestly joins with himself his son[1] *Timotheus,* who had come to Philippi not long after Paul had received him (Acts 16:3, 12). *To all the saints.* The apostolic epistles were sent more directly to the churches than to the pastors of them.

4. *With joy.* After the Epistle to the Ephesians, wherein love reigns, follows this, wherein there is perpetual mention of joy. "The fruit of the Spirit is love, joy. . . ." And joy peculiarly enlivens prayer. The sum of the whole epistle is "I rejoice. You rejoice."

6. He, having justified you, has begun to sanctify you and will carry on this work until it issue in glory.

8. *I long after you all in the bowels of Jesus Christ.* In Paul, not Paul lives, but Jesus Christ.

9. *And this I pray, that your love.* Which they had already shown. *May abound yet more and more.* The fire which burned in the apostle never says, It is enough. *In knowledge and in all judgment.* Which is the ground of all spiritual knowledge. We must be inwardly sensible of divine peace, joy, love; otherwise, we cannot know what they are.

10. *Things that are excellent.* Not only good, but the very best; the superior excellence of which is hardly discerned but by the adult Christian.

11. *Being filled with the fruits of righteousness, which are by Jesus Christ, unto the glory and praise of God.* Here are three properties of that sincerity which is acceptable to God. (1) It must bear fruits, *the fruits of righteousness,* all inward and outward holiness, all good tempers, words, and works; and that so abundantly that we may be *filled* with them. (2) The branch and the fruits must derive both their virtue and their very being from the all-supporting, all-supplying root, *Jesus Christ.* (3) As all these flow from the grace of Christ, so they must issue in *the glory and praise of God.*

19. *This shall turn to my salvation.* Shall procure me a higher degree of glory.

20. *In my body.* However it may be disposed of. How that might be, he did not yet know. For the apostles did not

---

[1](1:1) Figuratively and spiritually, not genealogically. See I Timothy 1:2: "My own son in the faith." Cf. I Timothy 1:18 and II Timothy 1:2.

know all things; particularly in things pertaining to themselves they had room to exercise faith and patience.

21. *To me to live is Christ.* To know, to love, to follow Christ is my life, my glory, my joy.

22. *But if I live in the flesh, this is the fruit of my labour.* This is the fruit of my living longer, that I can labor more. Glorious labor! Desirable fruit! In this view, long life is indeed a blessing.

25. *I know.* By a prophetic notice given him while he was writing this. *That I shall abide and continue* some time long *with you.* And doubtless he did see them after this confinement.

CHAPTER 2

3. *Let each esteem other better than themselves.* (For every one knows more evil of himself than he can of another.) Which is a glorious fruit of the Spirit, and an admirable help to our continuing "of one mind."

6. *Who, being in the* [essential] *form.* The incommunicable nature. *Of God.* From eternity, as he was afterward in the form of man; real God, as real man. *Counted it no act of robbery.*[2] That is the precise meaning of the words—no invasion of another's prerogative, but his own strict and unquestionable right. *To be equal with God.* The word here translated "equal" occurs in the adjective form five or six times in the New Testament (Matt. 20:12; Luke 6:34; John 5:18; Acts 11:17; Rev. 21:16). In all these places it expresses not a mere resemblance, but a real and proper equality. It here implies both the fullness and the supreme height of the Godhead.

7. *But.* Christ was so far from tenaciously insisting upon his claim that he

willingly relinquished it. He was content to forego the glories of the Creator and to appear in the form of a creature; nay, to be made in the likeness of the fallen creatures; and not only to share the disgrace, but to suffer the punishment due to the meanest and vilest among them all. He *made himself of no reputation.* That is, he emptied himself of that divine fullness which he received again at his exaltation. Though he remained "full" (John 1:14), yet he appeared as if he had been empty; for he veiled his fullness from the sight of men and angels. Yes, he not only veiled, but in some sense renounced the glory which he had before the world began.

Took. And by that very act he emptied himself. *The form of a servant.* The *form,* the *likeness,* the "fashion" (v. 8), though not exactly the same, are yet nearly related to each other. *The form* expresses something absolute; *the likeness* refers to other things of the same kind; "the fashion" respects what appears to sight and sense. *And was made in the likeness of men.* A real man, like other men. Hereby he took *the form of a servant.*

8. *And being found in fashion as a man.* A common man, without any peculiar excellence or comeliness. *He humbled himself.* To a still greater depth. *And became obedient.* To God, though equal with him. *Unto death.* The greatest instance both of humiliation and obedience. *Even the death of the cross.* Inflicted on few but servants or slaves.

10. *Should bow.* Either with love or trembling.

11. *That every tongue.* Even of his enemies.

12–13. *For it is God which worketh in you both to will and to do of his good*

---

[2](2:6) KJV: "thought it not robbery."

pleasure. Not for any merit of yours. Yet his influences are not to supersede, but to encourage our own efforts. *Work out your own salvation.* Here is our duty. *For it is God which worketh in you.* Here is our encouragement. And O what a glorious encouragement, to have the arm of Omnipotence stretched out for our support and our encouragement!

14. *Do all things.* Not only without contention (v. 3), but even *without murmurings and disputings.* Which are real, though smaller, hindrances of love.

17. *Upon the sacrifice and service of your faith.* The Philippians, like the other converted heathens, were a sacrifice to God through Paul's ministry (Rom. 15:16). And as in a sacrificing wine was poured at the foot of the altar, so he was willing that his blood should be poured out. The expression well agrees with that kind of martyrdom by which he was afterwards offered up to God.

21. *For all seek their own.* Ease, safety, pleasure, or profit. Amazing! In that golden age of the church, could Paul thoroughly approve of one only, among all the laborers who were with him? (Phil. 1:14, 17.) And how many do we think can now approve themselves to God? *Not the things which are Jesus Christ's.* They who seek these alone will sadly experience this. They will find few helpers like-minded with themselves.

CHAPTER 3

2. *Beware of dogs.* Unclean, unholy, rapacious men. The title which the Jews usually gave the Gentiles he returns upon themselves.

7. *But* all these *things* I then account-

ed *gain,* which were once my confidence, my glory, and joy; *those,* ever since I have believed, *I counted loss,* worth nothing in comparison to Christ.

8. *Yea,* I still *count* both all these and *all things* else to be mere *loss,* compared to the inward, experimental[3] *knowledge of Christ,* as *my Lord,* as my prophet, priest, and king, as teaching me wisdom, atoning for my sins, and reigning in my heart. To refer this to justification only is miserably to pervert the whole scope of the words. They manifestly relate to sanctification also; yes, to that chiefly.

For whom I have [actually] *suffered the loss of all things.* Which the world loves, esteems, or admires; of which I am so far from repenting that I still *count them but dung.* The discourse rises. *Loss* is sustained with patience, but *dung* is cast away with abhorrence. The Greek word signifies the vilest refuse of things, the dross of metals, the dregs of liquors, the excrements of animals, the most worthless scraps of meat, the basest offals fit only for dogs. *That I may win Christ.* He who loses all things, not excepting himself, gains Christ and is gained by Christ. And still there is more; which even Paul speaks of his having not yet gained.

9. *And be found* by God ingrafted *in him, not having mine own righteousness, which is of the law.* Not that outward righteousness prescribed by the law and performed by my own strength. *But that* inward righteousness *which is through the faith.* Which can flow from no other fountain. *The righteousness which is of God.* From his almighty Spirit, not by my own strength, but *by faith* alone. Here also the apostle is far from speaking of justification only.

10. The knowledge of Christ, men-

---

[3] (3:8) "Experimental" is British usage for "experiential."

tioned in the eighth verse, is here more largely explained. *That I may know him.* As my complete Savior. *And the power of his resurrection.* Raising me from the death of sin into all the life of love. *And the fellowship of his sufferings.* Being crucified with him. *Being made conformable unto his death.* So as to be dead to all things here below.

11. *The resurrection of the dead.* That is, the resurrection to glory.

12. *Not as though I had already attained* the prize. He here enters on a new set of metaphors, taken from a race. But observe how, in the utmost fervor, he retains his sobriety of spirit. *Either were already perfect.* There is a difference between one who is perfect and one who is perfected. The one is fitted for the race (v. 15); the other, ready to receive the prize. *But I follow after, if that I may apprehend* perfect holiness, preparatory to glory. *For which also I am apprehended of Christ Jesus.* Appearing to me in the way (Acts 26:14). In speaking conditionally both here and in the preceding verse, Paul implies no uncertainty, but only the difficulty of attaining.

13. *I count not myself to have apprehended* this already; to be already possessed of perfect holiness. *Forgetting those things which are behind.* Even that part of the race which is already run. *And reaching forth unto.* Literally, "stretched out over the things that are before." Pursuing with the whole bent and vigor of my soul, perfect holiness and eternal glory.

14. *In Christ Jesus.* The author and finisher of every good thing.

15. *Let us therefore, as many as be perfect.* Fit for the race, strong in faith; so it means here. *Be thus minded.* Apply wholly to this one thing. *And if in any thing ye,* who are not perfect, who are weak in faith, *be otherwise minded,* pursuing other things. God, if you

desire it, *shall reveal even this unto you.* Will convince you of it.

18. *Enemies of the cross of Christ.* Such are all cowardly, all shamefaced, all delicate Christians.

19. *Whose god is their belly.* Whose supreme happiness lies in gratifying their sensual appetites.

21. *Who shall change our vile body.* Into the most perfect state and the most beauteous form. It will then be purer than the unspotted parallel, which comprehends all perfection, *like unto his glorious body.* Like that wonderfully glorious body which he wears in his heavenly kingdom and on his triumphant throne.

CHAPTER 4

3. *And I intreat thee also, true yokefellow.* Paul had many *fellow-laborers,* but not many yokefellows. In this number there were Barnabas first, and then Silas, whom he probably addresses here; for Silas had been his yokefellow at the very place (Acts 16:19). *Whose names,* although not set down here, *are in the book of life.* As are those of all believers. This is an allusion to the wrestlers in the Olympic games whose names were all enrolled in a book. Reader, is your name there? Then walk circumspectly, lest the Lord blot you out of his book!

5. *All men.* Good and bad, gentle and froward. Those of the roughest tempers are good-natured to some from natural sympathy and various motives; a Christian is good to all.

6. *Let your requests be made known.* They who by a preposterous shame or distrustful modesty cover, stifle, or keep in their desires, as if they were either too small or too great, must be racked with care; from which they are entirely delivered who pour them out with a free and filial confidence. *With* *thanksgiving.* The surest mark of a soul free from care and of prayer joined with true resignation. This is always followed by peace. Peace and thanksgiving are coupled together (Col. 3:15).

7. *And the peace of God.* That calm, heavenly repose, that tranquillity of spirit which God only can give. *Shall keep.* Shall guard, as a garrison does a city. *Your hearts.* Your affections. *And minds.* Your understandings and all the various workings of them; through the Spirit and power of *Christ Jesus,* in the knowledge and love of God. Without a guard set on these, the purity and vigor of our affections cannot long be preserved.

8. *Whatsoever things are true.* Here are eight particulars placed in two fourfold rows—the former containing their duty; the latter, the commendation of it. The first word in the former row answers the first in the latter; the second word, the second; and so on.

9. *Those things . . . do: and the God of peace shall be with you.* Not only the peace of God, but God himself, the fountain of peace.

10. *I rejoiced in the Lord greatly.* Paul was no Stoic; he had strong passions, but all devoted to God.

11. *I have learned.* From God. He alone can teach this. *In whatsoever state I am, therewith to be content.* Joyfully and thankfully patient. Nothing less is Christian contentment. We may observe a beautiful gradation in the expressions, *I have learned;* "I know"; "I am instructed"; "I can."

13. *I can do all things.* Even fulfill all the will of God.

18. *An odour of a sweet smell.* More pleasing to God than the sweetest perfumes to men.

COLOSSIANS

CHAPTER 1

2. *The saints*. This word expresses their union with God. *Brethren*. This, their union with their fellow Christians.

9. *And spiritual understanding*. To discern by that light whatever agrees with or differs from his will.

11. *Strengthened with . . . all patience and longsuffering with joyfulness*. This is the highest point: not only to know, to do, and to suffer the whole will of God; but to suffer it to the end, not merely with *patience,* but with thankful joy.

14. *In whom we have redemption*. The voluntary Passion of our Lord appeased the Father's wrath, obtained pardon and acceptance for us, and consequently dissolved the dominion and power which Satan had over us through our sins. So that *forgiveness* is the beginning of redemption, as the resurrection is the completion of it.

15. *Who is*. By describing the glory of Christ and his preeminence over the highest angels, the apostle here lays a foundation for the reproof of all worshippers of angels. *The image of the invisible God*. Whom none can represent but his only begotten Son; in his divine nature the invisible image, in his human nature the visible image, of the Father. *The firstborn of every creature*. That is, begotten before every creature; subsisting before all worlds, before all time, from all eternity.

16. *For*. This explains the latter part of the preceding verse. *Him*. This word, frequently repeated, signifies his supreme majesty and excludes every creature. *That are in heaven*. And heaven itself. But the inhabitants are named, because more noble than the house. *Invisible*. The several species of which are subjoined. *Thrones* are superior to *dominions; principalities* are superior to *powers*. Perhaps the two latter may express their office with regard to other creatures. The two former may refer to God, who makes them his chariots and, as it were, rides upon their wings.

17. *And he is before all things*. It is not said, he "was"; he *is* from everlasting to everlasting. *And by him all things consist*. The original expression not only implies that he sustains all things in being, but more directly, all things were and are compacted in him into one system. He is the cement as well as support of the universe. And is he less than the supreme God?

18. *And*. From the whole he now descends to the most eminent part, the church. *He is the head of . . . the church*. Universal; the supreme and only head both of influence and of government to the whole body of believers. *Who is.* The repetition of the expression (see v. 15) points out the entrance on a new paragraph. *The beginning.* Absolutely, the Eternal. *The firstborn from the dead.* From whose resurrection flows all the life, spiritual and eternal, of all his brethren. *That in all things.* Whether of nature or of grace. *He might have the preeminence.* And who can sound this depth?

19. *In him should all fulness dwell.* Constantly, as in a temple; and always ready for our approach to him.

22. *In the body of his flesh.* So distinguished from his body, the church. The body here denotes his entire manhood.

23. *If ye continue in the faith.* Otherwise you will lose all the blessings which you have already begun to enjoy. *And be not moved away from the hope of the gospel.* The glorious hope of perfect love.

24. *That which is behind of the afflictions of Christ.* That which remains to be suffered by his members. These are termed the sufferings of Christ: (1) Because the suffering of any member is the suffering of the whole, yes, and of the head especially, which supplies strength, spirits, sense, and motion to all. (2) Because they are for his sake, for the testimony of his truth. And these also are necessary for the church; not to reconcile it to God, or satisfy for sin (for that Christ did perfectly), but for example to others, perfecting of the saints and increasing their reward.

CHAPTER 2

8. *Through philosophy and vain deceit.* That is, through the empty deceit of philosophy blended with Christianity. This the apostle condemns: (1) Because it was empty and deceitful, promising happiness, but giving none. (2) Because it was grounded, not on solid reason, but on *the tradition of men,* Zeno, Epicurus, and the rest. And (3) Because it was shallow and superficial, not advancing beyond the knowledge of sensible things; no, not beyond the first *rudiments* of them.

10. *And ye.* Who believe. *Are complete in him.* That is, filled with him (John 1:16). Christ is filled with God, and you are filled with Christ. And you are filled by him. The fullness of Christ overflows his church (Ps. 133:3). He is originally full. We are filled by him with wisdom and holiness.

12. Which he wrought in you when you were, as it were, *buried with him in baptism.* The ancient manner of baptizing by immersion is as plainly alluded to here as the other manner of baptizing by sprinkling or pouring of water is in Hebrews 10:22. But no stress is laid on the age of the baptized or the manner of performing it, in one or the other; but only on our being risen with Christ through the powerful operation of God in the soul; which we cannot but know assuredly if it really is so. And if we do not experience this, our baptism has not answered the end of its institution. *Wherein also ye are risen with him.* From the death of sin to the life of holiness. It does not appear that in all this Paul speaks of justification at all, but of sanctification altogether.

13. *And you, being dead.* Doubly dead to God, not only wallowing in *trespasses,* outward sins, but also in *the uncircumcision of your flesh.* A beautiful expression for original sin, the inbred corruption of your nature, your uncircumcised heart and affections. *Quickened together with him.* Making you partakers of the power of his resurrection. It is evident the apostle thus far speaks not of justification, but of sanctification only.

14. *The handwriting . . . against us.* Where a debt is contracted, it is usually testified by some handwriting; and when the debt is forgiven, the handwriting is destroyed, either by blotting it out, taking it away, or tearing it.

23. *Neglecting of the body.* Denying it many gratifications and putting it to many inconveniences. Yet they have no real value before God, nor do they upon the whole mortify, but satisfy *the flesh.* They indulge our corrupt nature, self-will, pride, and desire of being distinguished from others.

CHAPTER 3

5. *Mortify therefore.* Put to death, slay with a continued stroke.

8. *Filthy communication.* And was there need to warn even these saints of God against so gross and palpable a sin as this? O what is man, until perfect love casts out both fear and sin!

12. All who are thus renewed are *elect of God, holy* and therefore the more *beloved* of him. Holiness is the consequence of their election, and God's superior love, of their holiness.

14. The love of God contains the whole of Christian perfection and connects all the parts of it together.

15. *And* then shall *the peace of God rule in your hearts.* Shall sway every temper, affection, thought, as the *reward* (so the Greek word implies) of your preceding love and obedience.

16. *Let the word of Christ.* So the apostle calls the whole Scripture and thereby asserts the divinity of his Master. *Dwell.* Not make a short stay or an occasional visit, but take up its stated residence.

18. *Wives, submit.* Or be subject to. It is properly a military term alluding to that entire submission that soldiers pay to their general.

21. *Lest they be discouraged.* Which may occasion their turning either desperate or stupid.

CHAPTER 4

10. *Ye have received commandments.* Namely, by Tychicus bringing this letter. The ancients adapted their language to the time of reading the letter; not, as we do, to the time when it was written. It is not improbable that they might have scrupled to receive him without this fresh direction after he had left Paul and departed from the work.

12. *Perfect.* Endued with every Christian grace. *Complete.* That is, filled. As no longer being babes, but grown up to the measure of the stature of Christ; being full of his light, grace, wisdom, holiness.

17. *The ministry.* Not a lordship, but a service; a laborious and painful work; an obligation to do and suffer all things; to be the least and the servant of all. *In the Lord.* Christ; by whom and for whose sake we receive the various gifts of the Holy Spirit.

1 thessalonians

CHAPTER 1

1. There is a peculiar sweetness in the epistle, unmixed with any sharpness or reproof; those evils which the apostle afterward reproved having not yet crept into the church.

4. *Knowing . . . your election.* Which is through faith, by these plain proofs.

5. *In much assurance.* Literally, "with full assurance," and much of it; the Spirit bearing witness by shedding the love of God abroad in your hearts, which is the highest testimony that can be given. And these signs, if not the miraculous gifts, always attend the preaching of the gospel, unless it be in vain. Neither are the extraordinary operations of the Holy Ghost ever wholly withheld where the gospel is preached with power and men are alive to God.

10. *Whom he raised from the dead.* In proof of his future coming to judgment. *Which delivered us.* He redeemed us once; he delivers us continually; and will deliver all who believe from *wrath,* the eternal vengeance, which will then *come* upon the ungodly.

CHAPTER 2

11. By exhorting, we are moved to do a thing willingly; by comforting, to do it joyfully; by charging, to do it carefully.

17. In this verse we have a remarkable instance, not so much of the transient affections of holy grief, desire, or joy, as of that abiding tenderness, that loving temper, which is so apparent in all Paul's writings toward those he considers his children in the faith. This is the more carefully to be observed because the passions, occasionally exercising themselves and flowing like a torrent in the apostle, are observable to every reader; whereas it requires closer attention to discern those calm standing tempers, that fixed posture of his soul, whence the others only flow out and which more peculiarly distinguish his character.

CHAPTER 3

3. *We are appointed thereunto.* Are in every respect laid in a fit posture for it by the very design and contrivance of God himself, for the trial and increase of our faith and all other graces. He gives riches to the world, but stores up his treasure of wholesome afflictions for his children.

8. *Now we live.* Indeed, we enjoy life, so great is our affection for you.

11. *Direct our way.* This prayer is addressed to Christ as well as to the Father.

CHAPTER 4

3. *Sanctification.* Entire holiness of heart and life; particular branches of it are subjoined. *That ye should abstain from fornication.* A beautiful transition from sanctification to a single branch of the contrary; and this shows that nothing is so seemingly distant or below our thoughts but we have need to guard against it.

5. *Not in the lust of concupiscence.* That is, passionate desire, which had no place in man when in a state of innocence. *Which know not God.* And so many naturally seek happiness in a creature. What seemingly accidental words slide in; and yet how fine, and how vastly important!

8. What naked majesty of words! How oratorical, and yet with what great simplicity! Here is a simplicity that does not impair but improve the understanding to the utmost; that, like the rays of heat through a glass, collects all the powers of reason into one orderly point from being scattered abroad in utter confusion.

11. *That ye study.* Literally, "that you be ambitious"; and ambition worthy of a Christian. *To work with your own hands.* Not a needless caution; for temporal concerns are often a cross to them who are newly filled with the love of God.

13. *But.* Herein the efficacy of Christianity greatly appears, that it neither takes away nor embitters, but sweetly tempers that most refined of all affections, our desire of or love to the dead.

15. *By the word of the Lord.* By a particular revelation. *We which are alive and remain.* This intimates the fewness of those who will be then alive compared with the multitude of the dead.

Believers of all ages and nations make up, as it were, one body; in consideration of which the believers of that age might put themselves in the place and speak in the person of them who were to live until the coming of the Lord. Not that Paul hereby asserted (though some seem to have imagined so) that the day of the Lord was at hand.

17. *In the air.* The wicked will remain beneath, while the righteous, being absolved, shall be assessors with their Lord in the judgment.

CHAPTER 5

4. *Are not in darkness.* Sleeping secure in sin.

6. *Let us awake, and keep awake.*[1] Being awakened, let us have all our spiritual senses about us.

12. *Know.* See, mark, take knowledge of them and their work. Sometimes the same person may both *labour,* that is, preach; be *over,* or govern; and *admonish* the flock by particular application to each; sometimes two or more different persons, according as God variously dispenses his gifts. But O what a misery it is when a man undertakes this whole work without either gifts or graces for any part of it! Why, then, will he undertake it? For pay? What! Will he sell both his own soul and all the souls of the flock? What words can describe such a wretch as this? And yet even this may be "an honorable man"!

13. *Esteem them very highly.* Literally, "more than abundantly." The inexpressible sympathy that is between true pastors and their flock is intimated not only here, but also in many other places of this epistle (see 2:7–8).

16. *Rejoice evermore.* In uninterrupted happiness in God.

---

[1](5:6) KJV: "let us watch and be sober."

17. *Pray without ceasing.* Which is the fruit of always rejoicing in the Lord.

18. *In every thing give thanks.* Which is the fruit of both the former. This is Christian perfection. Further than this we cannot go; and we need not stop short of it. Our Lord has purchased joy as well as righteousness for us. It is the very design of the gospel that, being saved from guilt, we should be happy in the love of Christ.

Prayer may be said to be the breath of our spiritual life. He who lives cannot possibly cease breathing. So much as we really enjoy of the presence of God, so much prayer and praise do we offer up "without ceasing"; else our rejoicing is but delusion. Thanksgiving is inseparable from true prayer. He who always prays is ever giving praise, whether in ease or pain, both for prosperity and for the great adversity. He blesses God for all things, looks on them as coming from him, and receives them only for his sake; not choosing nor refusing, liking nor disliking any thing, but only as it is agreeable or disagreeable to his perfect will.

19. *Quench not the Spirit.* Wherever it is, it burns; it flames in holy love, in joy, prayer, thanksgiving. O quench it not, dampen it not in yourself or others, either by neglecting to do good or by doing evil.

20. *Despise not prophesyings.* That is, preaching; for the apostle is not here speaking of extraordinary gifts. It seems, one means of grace for all; and whoever despises any of these, under whatever pretense, will surely (though perhaps gradually and almost insensibly) "quench the Spirit."

23. *Spirit and soul and body.* Only the last two are the natural constituent parts of man. The first is the supernatural gift of God, to be found in Christians only. That man cannot possibly consist of three parts appears hence: the soul is either matter or not matter; there is no medium. But if it is matter, it is part of the body; if not matter, it coincides with the spirit.

II thessalonians

CHAPTER 1

3. It is highly observable that the apostle wraps up his praise of men in praise to God, giving him the glory. *Aboundeth*. Like water that overflows its banks and yet increases still.

9. *Everlasting destruction*. As there can be no end of their sins (the same enmity against God continuing), so neither of their punishment; sin and its punishment running parallel throughout eternity itself. They must of necessity, therefore, be cut off from all good and all possibility of it. *From the presence of the Lord*. Wherein chiefly consists the salvation of the righteous. What unspeakable punishment is implied even in falling short of this, supposing that nothing more were implied in his taking vengeance!

11. *All the good pleasure of his goodness*. Which is no less than perfect holiness.

CHAPTER 2

2. *Be not soon shaken in mind*. In judgment. *Or be terrified*.[1] As those easily are who are immoderately fond of knowing future things. *Neither by* any pretended revelation from the *spirit, nor by* pretence of of any *word* spoken by me.

3. *A falling away*. From the pure faith of the gospel. This began even in the apostolic age. *That man of sin, . . . the son of perdition*. Eminently so called, is not come yet. However, in many respects the pope has an indisputable claim to those titles. He is, in an emphatic sense, *that man of sin* as he increases all manner of sin above measure. And he is, too, properly characterized *the son of perdition* as he has caused the death of numberless multitudes, both of his opposers and followers, destroyed innumerable souls, and will himself perish everlastingly.

7. He will surely be revealed; *for the mystery*, the deep, secret power *of iniquity* just opposite to the power of godliness, already works. It began with the love of honor and the desire of power; and is completed in the entire subversion of the gospel of Christ. This *mystery of iniquity* is not wholly confined to the Roman church, but extends itself to others also. It seems to consist of: (1) Human inventions added to the written word. (2) Mere outside performances put in the room

---

[1](2:2) KJV: "or be troubled."

552

of faith and love. (3) Other mediators besides the man Christ Jesus. The two last branches, together with idolatry and bloodshed, are the direct consequences of the former, namely, adding to the word of God.

13. *God hath from the beginning.* Of your hearing the gospel. *Chosen you to salvation.* Taken you out of the world and placed you in the way to glory.

15. *Hold.* Without adding to or diminishing from *the traditions which ye have been taught.* The truths which I have delivered to you.

CHAPTER 3

4. *We trust in the Lord concerning you.*[2] Thus only should we trust in any man.

5. *And the Lord.* The Spirit, whose proper work this is. *Direct.* Lead you straight forward. *Into the patience of Christ.*[3] Of which he set you a pattern.

6. *That walketh disorderly.* Particularly by not working. *Not after the tradition which he received of us.* The admonition we gave, both by word of mouth and in our former epistle.

10. *Neither should he eat.* Do not maintain him in idleness.

12. *With quietness they work.* Work quietly, letting the concerns of other people alone.

14. *Have no company with him.* No intimacy, no familiarity, no needless correspondence.

15. *Admonish him as a brother.* Tell him lovingly of the reason why you shun him.

---

[2] (3:4) KJV: "we have confidence in the Lord touching you."
[3] (3:5) KJV: "into the patient waiting for Christ."

1 timothy

CHAPTER 1

1. *Paul, an apostle.* Familiarity is to be set aside where the things of God are concerned.

5. *Is charity.* The foundation is faith; the end, love. But this can only subsist in a heart purified by faith and is always attended with a *good conscience.*

10. *Menstealers.* The worst of all thieves, in comparison of whom highwaymen and housebreakers are innocent. What then are most traders in negroes, procurers of servants for America, and all who enlist soldiers by lies, tricks, or enticements?

13. *But I obtained mercy.* He does not say, "Because I was unconditionally elected," but *because I did it ignorantly.* Not that his ignorance took away his sin; but it left him capable of mercy; which he would hardly have been had he acted thus contrary to his own conviction.

15. *Came into the world to save sinners.* All sinners, without exception.

17. *The King eternal.* Or, the King of eternity. A phrase frequent with the Hebrews. How unspeakably sweet is the thought of eternity to believers!

19. *Some having put away.* Or, thrust away. It goes away unwillingly; it always says, "Do not hurt me." And they who retain this do not make shipwreck of their faith. Indeed, none can make shipwreck of faith who never had it. These, therefore, were once true believers. Yet they fell not only foully, but finally; for ships once wrecked cannot be afterwards saved.

CHAPTER 2

1. *Supplications* are here the imploring help in time of need; *prayers* are any kind of offering up of our desires to God. But true prayer is the vehemence of holy zeal, the ardor of divine love, arising from a calm, undisturbed soul moved upon by the Spirit of God. *Intercessions* are prayers for others. We may likewise give *thanks . . . for all men,* in the full sense of the word, for God "will have all men to be saved," and Christ is the Mediator of all.

2. *For all that are in authority.* Seeing even the lowest country magistrates frequently do much good or much harm. God supports the power of magistracy for the sake of his own people when, in the present state of men, it could not otherwise be kept up in any nation whatever.

3. *For this.* That we pray for all men. Do you ask, "Why are not more converted?" We do not pray enough. *Is good and acceptable in the sight of God our Saviour.* Who has actually saved us who believe, and *will have all men to be saved.* It is strange that any whom he has actually saved should doubt the universality of his grace!

5. *One mediator.* We could not rejoice that there is a God were there not a mediator also, one who stands between God and men to reconcile man to God and to transact the whole affair of our salvation. This excludes all other mediators, as saints and angels, whom the Roman church sets up and idolatrously worships as such; just as the heathens of old set up many mediators to pacify their superior gods.

6. *Who gave himself a ransom for all.* Such a ransom, the word signifies, wherein a like or equal is given; as an eye for an eye, or life for life. And this ransom, from the dignity of the person redeeming, was more than equivalent to all mankind.

8. *Without wrath.* In any kind, against any creature. And every temper or motion of our soul that is not according to love is *wrath.*

And doubting. Which is contrary to faith. Wrath and unholy actions and lack of faith in him we call upon are the three grand hindrances of God's hearing our petitions. Christianity consists of faith and love, embracing truth and grace. Therefore the sum of our wishes should be to pray, live, and die without any wrath or doubt.

9. *With . . . sobriety.* Which, in Paul's sense, is the virtue which governs our whole life according to true wisdom. These four are expressly forbidden by name to all *women* (here is no exception) *professing godliness,* and no art of man can reconcile with the Christian profession the willful violation of an express command.

14. *And Adam was not deceived.* The serpent deceived Eve, and Eve did not deceive Adam but persuaded him. "Thou hast hearkened unto the voice of thy wife" (Gen. 3:17). The preceding verse showed why a woman should not "usurp authority over the man." This verse shows why she ought not "to teach." She is more easily deceived, and more easily deceives.

15. *Shall be saved in childbearing.* Carried safe through the pain and danger which that sentence entails on them for the transgression; yes, and finally saved, *if they continue* in loving faith and holy wisdom.

CHAPTER 3

2. *A bishop.* Or pastor of a congregation. *The husband of one wife.* This means neither that a bishop must be married nor that he may not marry a second wife; which it is just as lawful for him to do as to marry a first, and may in some cases be his bounded duty.

8. *Not greedy of filthy lucre.* With what abhorrence does he every where speak of this! All that is gained (above food and raiment) by ministering in holy things is filthy gain indeed; far more filthy than what is honestly gained by raking kennels or emptying common sewers.

11. *Faithful in all things.* Both to God, their husbands, and the poor.

CHAPTER 4

3. *Forbidding* priests, monks, and nuns *to marry, and commanding* all men *to abstain from* such and such *meats* at such and such times. *Which . . . know the truth.* That all meats are now clean. *With thanksgiving.* Which supposes a pure conscience.

5. *And prayer.* The children of God are to pray for the sanctification of all the creatures which they use. And not only the Christians, but even the Jews, yes, the very heathens used to consecrate their table by prayer.

7. Train yourself up in holiness of heart and life with the utmost labor, vigor, and diligence.

13. *Give attendance to reading.* Both publicly and privately. Enthusiasts, observe this! Expect no end without the means.

15. *Meditate.* The Bible makes no distinction between this and to contemplate. True meditation is no other than faith, hope, love, joy melted down together, as it were, by the fire of God's Holy Spirit and offered up to God in secret. He who is *wholly* [in] them, will be little in worldly company, in other studies, in collecting books, medals, or butterflies; wherein many pastors drone away so considerable a part of their lives.

CHAPTER 5

6. *She that liveth in pleasure.* Voluptuously, delicately, in elegant, regular sensuality, though not in the use of any such pleasures as are unlawful in themselves.

8. *Denied the faith.* Which does not destroy, but perfect natural duties. What has this to do with heaping up money for our children, for which it is often so impertinently alleged? But all men have their reasons for laying up money. One will go to hell for fear of want; another acts like a heathen, lest he should be *worse than an infidel.*

12. *They have cast off their first faith.* Have deserted their trust in God and have acted contrary to the first conviction, namely, that wholly to devote themselves to his service was the most excellent way. When we first receive power to believe, does not the Spirit of God generally point out what are the most excellent things; and at the same time, give us a holy resolution to walk in the highest degree of Christian severity? And how unwise are we even to sink into anything below it!

17. *Be counted worthy of double honour.* A more abundant provision, seeing that such will employ it all to the glory of God. As it was the most laborious and disinterested men who were put into these offices, so whatever any one had to bestow, in his life or death, was generally lodged in their hands for the poor. By this means the churchmen became very rich in after ages; but as the design of the donors was something else, there is the highest reason why it should be disposed of according to their pious intent.

22. *Lay hands suddenly on no man.* That is, appoint no man to church offices without full trial and examination; else you will be accessary to and accountable for his misbehavior in his office.

CHAPTER 6

2. *Let them not despise them.* Pay them the less honor or obedience. *Because they are brethren.* And in that respect on a level with them. They who live in a religious community know the danger of this, and that greater grace is requisite to bear with the faults of a brother than of an infidel or man of the world. *These things.* Paul, the aged, gives young Timothy a charge to dwell upon practical holiness. Less experienced teachers are apt to neglect the superstructure while they lay the foundation; but of so great importance did Paul see it to enforce obedience to Christ, as well as to preach faith in his blood, that after strongly urging the life of faith on professors, he even adds another charge for the strict observance of it.

4. *Knowing nothing.* As he ought to know. *Doting about questions.* Dotingly fond of dispute—an evil, but common, disease, especially where practice is forgotten. Such, indeed, contend earnestly for singular phrases and favorite points of their own. Everything else, however, like the preaching of Christ and his apostles, is all "law" and "bondage" and "carnal reasoning."

5. *Supposing that gain is godliness.* Thinking that the best religion is the getting of money; a far more common case than is usually supposed.

6. *But godliness with contentment.* The inseparable companion of true, vital religion. *Is great gain.* Brings unspeakable profit in time as well as eternity.

7. *It is certain we can carry nothing out.* To what purpose, then, do we heap together so many things? O, give me one thing—a safe and ready passage to my own country!

8. *Raiment.* That is, covering. Both raiment and a house to cover us. This is all that a Christian needs and all that his religion allows him to desire.

9. *They that will be rich.* To have more than these; for then they would be so far rich; and the desire banishes contentment and exposes them to ruin. *Fall.* That is, plunge. A sad gradation! *Into temptation.* Miserable food for the soul! *And a snare.* Or trap. Dreadful "covering"! *And into many foolish and hurtful lusts.* Which are sown and fed by having more than we need. Then farewell all hope of contentment! What remains but *destruction* for the body and *perdition* for the soul?

10. *And pierced themselves through with many sorrows.* From a guilty conscience, tormenting passions, desires contrary to reason, religion, and one another. How cruel are worldly men to themselves!

11. *But thou, O man of God.* Whatever all the world else do. A *man of God* is either a prophet, a messenger of God, or a man devoted to God; a man of another world. *Flee.* As from a serpent, instead of coveting *these things.*

Follow after righteousness. The whole image of God; though sometimes this word is used, not in the general, but in the particular, meaning only that single branch of it which is termed "justice." *Faith.* Which is also taken here in the general and full sense; namely, a divine, supernatural sight of God, chiefly in respect of his mercy in Christ. This *faith* is the foundation of *righteousness,* the support of *godliness,* the root of every grace of the Spirit. *Love.* This Paul intermixes with everything that is good. He, as it were, penetrates whatever he treats of with *love,* the glorious spring of all inward and outward holiness.

17. What follows seems to be a kind of postscript. *Charge them that are rich.* Rich in such beggarly riches as *this world* affords. Not to be *high-minded.* O who regards this! Not to think better of themselves for their money or anything it can purchase. Neither to *trust in uncertain riches,* which they may lose in an hour, either for happiness or defense. *But in the living God.* All the rest is dead clay. *Who giveth us,* as it were, holding them out to us in his hand. *All things* which we have. *Richly.* Freely, abundantly. *To enjoy,* as his gift, in him and for him. When we use them thus, we do indeed *enjoy* all things. Where else is there any notice taken of the *rich* in all the apostolic writings, save to denounce woes and vengeance upon them?

19. *They may lay hold on eternal life.* This cannot be done by alms-deeds; yet they "come up for a memorial before God" (Acts 10:4). The lack even of this may be the cause why God will withhold grace and salvation from us.

20. *Science falsely so called.* Most of the ancient heretics were great pretenders to knowledge.

ıı tımothy

CHAPTER 1

3. *Whom I serve from my forefathers.* That is, whom both I and my ancestors served. *With pure conscience.* He always worshipped God according to his conscience, both before and after his conversion. One who stands on the verge of life is much refreshed by the remembrance of his predecessors, to whom he is going.

7. *Power* and *a sound mind* are two good extremes. *Love* is between, the tie and temperament of both, preventing the two bad extremes of fearfulness and rashness.

9. *Who hath saved us.* By faith. The love of the Father, the grace of our Savior, and the whole economy of salvation are here admirably described.

15. *Turned away from me.* What, from Paul the aged, the faithful soldier, and now prisoner of Christ! This was a glorious trial and wisely reserved for that time when he was on the borders of immortality.

CHAPTER 2

4. *That.* Minding war only, *he may please* his captain. In this and the next verse there is a plain allusion to the Roman law of arms and to that of the Grecian games. According to the for-mer, no soldier was to engage in any civil employment; according to the latter, none could be crowned as conqueror who did not keep strictly to the rules of the game.

10. *I endure all things.* See the spirit of a real Christian! Who would not wish to be like-minded? *Salvation* is deliverance from all evil; *glory,* the enjoyment of all good.

13. *If we believe not.* That is, though some believe not, God will make good all his promises to them that do believe.

14. *Put them in remembrance.* Remind them who are under your charge. O how many unnecessary things are thus unprofitably, no, hurtfully contended for.

15. *Rightly dividing the word of truth.* Properly explaining and applying the whole Scripture so as to give each hearer his due portion. But they who give one part of the gospel to all (the promises and comforts to unawakened, hardened scoffing men) have real need to be ashamed.

19. *Standeth sure.* Can never be overthrown, being, as it were, sealed with a seal which has an inscription on each side. On the one side it has *The Lord knoweth them that are his;* on the other side, *Let every one that nameth the name of Christ* [as his Lord] *depart from* *iniquity.* Indeed, they only are his who depart from iniquity. To all others he will say, "I never knew you" (Matt. 7:22–23).

22. *Out of a pure heart.* But *youthful lusts* destroy this purity; *righteousness, faith, charity, peace,* accompany it.

CHAPTER 3

1. *In the last days.* The time of the gospel dispensation, commencing at the time of our Lord's death, is peculiarly described as "the last days."

2. *Lovers of their own selves.* Only, not their neighbors'. The first root of evil; lovers of money, the second.

4. *Lovers of* [sensual] *pleasures.* Which naturally extinguish all love and sense of God.

5. *Having a form.* An appearance of godliness, but not regarding, no, even *denying* and blaspheming, the inward power and reality of it. Is not this eminently fulfilled at this day?

12. *All that will live godly.* Therefore count the cost. Are you resolved? *In Christ.* Out of Christ there is no godliness. *Shall suffer persecution.* More or less. There is no exception. Either the truth of Scripture fails, or those who think they are religious and are not persecuted in some shape or other, on that very account, deceive themselves.

13. *Deceiving, and being deceived.* He who has once begun to deceive others is both the less likely to recover from his own error, and the more ready to embrace the errors of other men.

16. *Given by inspiration of God.* The Spirit of God not only once inspired those who wrote it, but continually inspires and supernaturally assists those who read it with earnest prayer.

17. *Throughly furnished.* By Scripture, either to teach, reprove, correct, or train up others.

CHAPTER 4

3. *Having itching ears.* Fond of novelty and variety, which the number of new teachers and their empty, soft, or philosophical discourses pleased. Such teachers and such hearers seldom are much concerned with what is strict or to the purpose.

5. *Watch.* An earnest, constant, persevering exercise. In Scripture, watching or waiting implies steadfast faith, patient hope, laboring love, unceasing prayer; yes, the mighty exertion of all the affections of the soul that a man is capable of.

6. *I am now ready to be offered.* Literally, "to be poured out," as the wine and oil were on the ancient sacrifices.

8. *A crown of* that *righteousness* which God has imputed to me and wrought in me. *That love his appearing.* Which only a real Christian can do. I say "a real Christian" to comply with the mode of the times. Otherwise they would not understand, although the word "Christian" necessarily implies whatever is holy, as God is holy. Strictly speaking, to join "real" or "sincere" to a word of so complete an import is grievously to debase its noble significance and is like adding "long" to "eternity," or "wide" to "immensity."

16. *All.* My friends and companions. *Forsook me.* And do we expect to find such as will not forsake us?

18. *And the Lord shall deliver me from every evil work.* Which is far more than delivering me from death. Yes, *and,* over and above, *preserve me unto his heavenly kingdom.* Far better than that of Nero.

20. *Trophimus have I left . . . sick.* Not having power (as neither had any of the apostles) to work miracles when he pleased, but only when God pleased.

titus

CHAPTER 1

1–2. *A servant of God.* According to the faith of the elect. *An apostle of Jesus Christ.* According to the knowledge of the truth. We serve God according to the measure of our faith. We fulfill our public office according to the measure of our knowledge. *The truth which is after godliness.* Which in every point runs parallel with and supports the vital, spiritual worship of God and, indeed, has no other end or scope. These two verses contain the sum of Christianity, which Titus was always to have in his eye. *God's elect.* All real Christians.

5. *Ordain elders.* Appoint the most faithful, zealous men to watch over the rest. Their character follows, verses 6–9. These were the *elders,* or bishops, that Paul approved of; men who had living faith, a pure conscience, a blameless life.

6. *The husband of one wife.* Surely the Holy Ghost, by repeating this so often, designed to leave the Romanists without excuse.

11. *Be stopped.* The word properly means "to put a bit into the mouth" of an unruly horse.

15. *Unto the pure.* Those whose hearts are purified by faith; this we allow. *All things are pure.* All kinds of meat, the Mosaic distinction between clean and unclean meats being now taken away. *But unto them that are defiled and unbelieving is nothing pure.* The apostle joins "defiled" and "unbelieving" to intimate that nothing can be clean without a true faith; for both the understanding and conscience, those leading powers of the soul, are polluted. Consequently, so is the man and all he does.

CHAPTER 2

4. *To love their husbands, . . . to love their children.* With a tender, temperate, holy, wise affection. O how hard a lesson!

5. *Discreet.* Particularly in the love of their children. *Chaste.* Particularly in the love of their husbands. *Keepers at home.* Whenever they are not called out by works of necessity, piety, and mercy. *Good.* Well-tempered, sweet, soft, and obliging. *Obedient to their own husbands.* Whose will, in all things lawful, is a rule to the wise. *That the word of God be not blasphemed.* Or evil spoken of; particularly by unbelieving husbands who lay all the blame on the religion of their wives.

10. *Shewing all good fidelity.* Soft, obliging faithfulness. *That they may adorn the doctrine of God our Saviour.*

More than Paul says of kings. How he raises the lowness of his subject! So may they, the lowness of their condition.

12. *We should live soberly.* In all purity and holiness. Sobriety, in the Scripture sense, is rather the whole temper of a man than a single virtue in him. It comprehends all that is opposite to the drowsiness of sin, the folly of ignorance, the unholiness of disorderly passions. Sobriety is no less than all the powers of the soul being consistently and constantly awake, duly governed by heavenly prudence, and entirely conformable to holy affections.

13. *Of the great God and our Saviour Jesus Christ.* So that, if there be (according to the Arian scheme) a great God and a little God, Christ is not the little God, but the great one.

14. *That he might redeem us* miserable bondslaves as much from the power and the very being as from the guilt of all our sins.

15. *Let no man despise thee.* That is, let none have any just cause to despise you. Yet they surely will. Men who know not God will despise a true minister of his word.

CHAPTER 3

4–7. *Not by works,* In this important passage the apostle presents us with a delightful view of our redemption. (1) We have the cause of it; not our *works* or *righteousness,* but *the kindness and love of God our Saviour.* (2) We have the effects: which are, (a) justification; *being justified,* pardoned, and accepted through the merits alone of Christ, not from any desert in us, *but according to his mercy,* by his grace, his free, unmerited goodness; (b) sanctification, expressed by *the washing of regeneration* (that is, baptism, the thing signified as well as the outward sign) and the renewal *of the Holy Ghost;* which purifies the soul, as water cleanses the body, and renews it in the whole image of God. (3) The consummation of all; that *we should be made heirs according to the hope of eternal life,* and live now in the joyful hope of it.

8. *Be careful to maintain good works.* Though the apostle does not lay these for the foundation, yet he brings them in at their proper place and then mentions them, not slightly, but as affairs of great importance. He desires that all believers should be *careful.* Have their thoughts upon them; use their best contrivance, their utmost endeavors, not merely to practice, but *to maintain,* that is, to excel, to be eminent and distinguished in this. Because, though they are not the ground of our reconciliation with God, yet they are amiable and honorable to the Christian profession. *And profitable unto men.* Means of increasing the everlasting happiness both of ourselves and others.

10. *An heretic.* This is the first place in the whole Scripture where this word "heretic" occurs. And here it evidently means a man who obstinately persists in contending about foolish questions and thereby occasions strife and animosities, schisms and parties in the church. This, and this alone, is a heretic in the Scripture sense. And his punishment likewise is here fixed: shun, avoid him, leave him to himself. As for the Catholic sense, "A man that errs in fundamentals," although it crept, with many other things, early into the church, yet it has no shadow of foundation either in the Old or New Testament.

philemon

CHAPTER 1

1. This single epistle infinitely transcends all the wisdom of the world. It gives us a specimen of how Christians ought to treat secular matters from higher principles.

6. I pray *that the communication of thy faith may become effectual*. That is, that your faith may be effectually communicated to others who see and acknowledge our piety and charity.

9. *Yet for love's sake I rather beseech thee.* In how handsome a manner does the apostle just hint at, and immediately drop, the consideration of his power to command, and tenderly entreat Philemon to hearken to his friend, his aged friend, and now prisoner for Christ!

With what endearment, in the next verse, does he call Onesimus his "son" before he names his name! And as soon as he had mentioned it, with what fine address does he just touch on his former faults and instantly pass on to the happy change that was now made upon him; so disposing Philemon to attend to his request and the motives wherewith he was going to enforce it.

11. *Now profitable.* None should be expected to be a good servant before he is a good man.

12. *Receive him, that is, mine own bowels.* Whom I love as my own soul. Such is the natural affection of a father in Christ toward his spiritual children.

13. *In thy stead.* To do those services for me which you, if present, would gladly have done yourself.

17. *If thou count me therefore a partner.* So that your things are mine, and mine are yours.

19. *Not say to thee how thou owest unto me even thine own self.* It cannot be expressed how great our obligation is to those who have gained our souls to Christ.

hebrews

CHAPTER 1

1. *By the prophets.* The mention of whom is a virtual declaration that the apostle accepted the whole Old Testament and was not about to advance any doctrine in contradiction to it.

2. *Whom he hath appointed heir of all things.* After the name of "Son," his inheritance is mentioned. God had *appointed* him the *heir* long before he made the worlds (Eph. 2:11; Prov. 8:22). The Son is the firstborn, born before all things; the *heir* is a term relating to the creation which followed (v. 6). *By whom also he made the worlds.* Therefore the Son was before all worlds. His glory reaches from everlasting to everlasting, though God spoke by him to us only *in these last days.*

3. *Express image.* That is, stamp. Whatever the Father is, is exhibited in the Son, as a seal in the stamp on wax. *Purged our sins.* In order to which it was necessary he should for a time divest himself of his glory. In this chapter Paul describes his glory chiefly as he is the Son of God; afterwards in Hebrews 2:6, as the glory of the man Christ Jesus. He speaks, indeed, briefly of the former before his humiliation, but copiously after his exaltation; as from hence the glory he had from eternity began to be evidently seen. Both his purging our sins and his sitting on the right hand of God are largely treated in the seven following chapters. *Sat down.* The priests stood while they ministered; sitting, therefore, denotes the consummation of his sacrifice. These words "sat down" contain the scope, the theme, and the sum of the epistle.

4. *So much better than the angels.* It was extremely proper to observe this, because the Jews gloried in their law, as it was delivered by the ministration of angels. How much more may we glory in the gospel which was given not by the ministry of angels, but by the very Son of God!

5. *Thou art my Son.* God of God, Light of Light. *This day have I begotten thee.* I have begotten you from eternity, which, by its unalterable permanence of duration, is one continued, unsuccessive day. *I will be to him a Father, and he shall be to me a Son.* I will own myself to be his Father, and him to be my Son, by eminent tokens of my peculiar love. The former clause relates to his natural Sonship by an eternal, inconceivable generation; the other, to his Father's acknowledgment and treatment of him as his incarnate Son. Indeed, this promise related immediately to Solomon, but in a far higher sense to the Messiah.

7. *Who maketh his angels.* This implies they are only creatures, whereas the Son is eternal (v. 8) and the Creator himself (v. 10). *Spirits, . . . a flame of fire.* Which intimates not only their office, but also their nature; which is excellent indeed—the metaphor being taken from the most swift, subtle, and efficacious things on earth—but nevertheless infinitely below the majesty of the Son.

CHAPTER 2

3. *So great salvation.* A deliverance from so great wickedness and misery into so great holiness and happiness.

6. *What is man?* To the vast expanse of heaven, to "the moon and the stars, which thou hast ordained"! Psalm 8 seems to have been composed by David in a clear and moonshiny and starlight night while he was contemplating the wonderful fabric of heaven; because in his magnificent description of its luminaries he takes no notice of the sun, the most glorious of them all. The words here cited concerning dominion were, doubtless, in some sense applicable to Adam; although in their complete and highest sense they belong to none but the Second Adam.

7. *Thou madest him.* Adam. *A little lower than the angels.* The Hebrew is "a little lower than [that is, 'next to'] God." Such was man as he came out of the hands of his Creator. It seems he was the highest of all created beings. But these words are also in a further sense, as the apostle here shows, applicable to the Son of God. It should be remembered that the apostles constantly cited the Septuagint translation, very frequently without any variation. It was not their business in writing to the Jews, who at that time held it in high esteem, to amend or alter this, which would of consequence have occasioned disputes without end.

10. *For it became him.* The apostle in this verse expresses in his own words what he expressed before in those of the psalmist. What is here said of our Lord's being made *perfect through sufferings* has no relation to our being saved or sanctified by sufferings. Even he himself was perfect as God and as man before ever he suffered. By his sufferings in his life and death he was made a perfect or complete sin offering. But unless we were to be made the same sacrifice and to atone for sin, what is said of him in this respect is as much out of our sphere as his ascension into heaven. It is his atonement and his Spirit carrying "the work of faith with power" in our hearts that alone can sanctify us. Various afflictions indeed may be made subservient to this; and so far as they are blessed to weaning us from sin and causing our affection to be set on things above, so far they do indirectly help on our sanctification.

15. *And deliver them.* Every man who fears death is subject to bondage, is in a slavish, uncomfortable state. And every man fears death, more or less, who knows not Christ. Death is unwelcome to him if he knows what death is. But Christ delivers all true believers from this bondage.

CHAPTER 3

1. *Partakers of the heavenly calling.* God calls from heaven and to heaven by the gospel.

12. *An evil heart of unbelief.* Unbelief is the parent of all evil, and the very essence of unbelief lies in *departing from . . . God* as *the living God,* the fountain of all our life, holiness, happiness.

14. *If.* But not else; and a supposition made by the Holy Ghost is equal to the strongest assertion. Both the sentiment and the manner of expression are the same as verse 6.

16. The whole elect people of God (a very few excepted) did *provoke* God presently after their great deliverance, continued to grieve his Spirit for forty years, and perished in their sin!

CHAPTER 4

3. *For we* [only] *which have believed do enter into rest.* The proposition is, There remains a rest for us. This is proved (vv. 3–11) thus: Psalm 95 mentions a rest; yet it does not mean: (1) God's rest from creating, for this was long before the time of Moses. Therefore in his time another rest was expected, of which they who then heard fell short. Nor is it (2) The rest which Israel obtained through Joshua; for the psalmist wrote after him. Therefore, it is (3) The eternal rest in heaven. *As he said.* Clearly showing that there is a further rest than that which followed the finishing of the Creation.

12. *For the word of God.* Preached (v. 2) and armed with threatenings (v. 3). *Is quick, and powerful.* Attended with the power of the living God, and conveying either life or death to the hearers.

14. *We have a great high priest.* Great indeed, being *the* eternal *Son of God, . . . that is passed into the heavens.* As the Jewish high priest passed through the veil into the holy of holies, carrying with him the blood of the sacrifices, on the yearly day of atonement; so our great high priest went once for all through the visible heavens with the virtue of his own blood into the immediate presence of God.

15. He sympathized with us even in *our* [innocent] *infirmities,* needs, weaknesses, miseries, dangers.

16. *Throne of grace.* Grace erected it and reigns there, and dispenses all blessings in a way of mere unmerited favor.

CHAPTER 5

4. The apostle begins here to treat the priesthood of Christ. The sum of what he observes concerning it is, Whatever is excellent in the Levitical priesthood is in Christ, and in a more eminent manner; and whatever is lacking in those priests is in him.

7. The sum of the things treated in the seventh and following chapters is contained in verses 7–10; and in this sum is admirably comprised the process of his Passion, with its inmost causes, in the very terms used by the Evangelists.

To him that was able to save him from death. Which yet he endured in obedience to the will of his Father. *And was heard in that* which he particularly *feared.* When the cup was offered him first, there was set before him that horrible image of a painful, shameful, accursed death which moved him to pray conditionally against it. For if he had desired it, his heavenly Father would have sent him more than twelve legions of angels to deliver him. But what he most exceedingly feared was the weight of infinite justice; the being "bruised" and "put to grief" by the hand of God himself.

Compared with this, everything else was a mere nothing. And yet, so greatly did he even thirst to be obedient to the righteous will of his Father and even to "lay down his life for the sheep," that he vehemently longed to be baptized with this baptism (Luke 12:50). Indeed, his human nature needed the support of Omnipotence; and for this he sent up *strong crying and tears.* But throughout his whole life he showed that it was not the sufferings he was to undergo, but rather the dishonor that sin had done to so holy a God that grieved his spotless soul. The consideration of its being the will of God tempered his fear and afterwards swallowed it up; and he was *heard,* not so that the cup should pass away, but so that he drank it without any fear.

8. *Though he were a Son.* This is interposed, lest any should be offended at all these instances of our human weakness. In the garden, how frequently did he call God his Father (Matt. 26:39ff.)! And therefore it most evidently appears that his being the Son of God did not arise merely from his resurrection. *Yet learned he.* The word *learned,* premised to the word *suffered,* elegantly shows how willingly he learned. He learned *obedience* when he began to suffer, when he applied himself to drink that cup; obedience in suffering and dying.

9. *And being made perfect.* By sufferings (2:10); brought through all to glory.

10. The Holy Ghost seems to have concealed who Melchizedek was on purpose that he might be the more eminent type of Christ. This only we know, that he was a priest and king of Salem, or Jerusalem.

13. *Is unskilful in the word of righteousness.* The sublimer truths of the gospel. Such are all who desire and can digest nothing but the doctrine of justification and imputed righteousness.

14. *But strong meat.* These sublimer truths relating to "perfection" (6:1).

CHAPTER 6

5. *And have tasted the good word of God.* Have had a relish for and a delight in it. *And the powers of the world to come.* Which every one tastes, who has a hope full of immortality. Every child who is naturally born first sees the light, then receives and tastes proper nourishment, and partakes of the things of this world. In like manner, the apostle, comparing spiritual with natural things, speaks of one born of the Spirit as seeing the light, tasting the sweetness, and partaking of the things *of the world to come.*

6. *They shall fall away.* Here is not a supposition, but a plain relation of fact. The apostle here describes the case of those who have cast away both the power and the form of godliness; who have lost both their faith and hope and love (vv. 10ff.), and that willingly (10:26). Of these willful, total apostates he declares that it is impossible to renew them again unto repentance (though they were renewed once), either to the foundation or anything built thereon.

11. *To the full assurance of hope.* Which you cannot expect if you abate your diligence. The full assurance of faith relates to present pardon; the full assurance of hope, to future glory. The former is the highest degree of divine evidence that God is reconciled to me in the Son of his love; and the latter is the same degree of divine evidence (wrought in the soul by the same immediate inspiration of the Holy Ghost) of persevering grace and of eternal glory. So much, and no more, as faith every moment beholds "with open face," so much does hope see to all eternity. But this assurance of faith and hope is not an opinion, not a mere construction of Scripture, but is given immediately by the power of the Holy Ghost; and what none can have for another, but for himself only.

17. *God . . . confirmed it by an oath.* Amazing condescension! He who is greatest of all acts as if he were a middle person; as if while he swears, he were less than himself, by whom he swears! You who hear the promise, do you not yet believe?

20. A *forerunner* is usually less in dignity than those who are to follow him. But it is not so here, for Christ, who is gone before us, is infinitely superior to us. What an honor is it to believers to have so glorious a forerunner, now appearing in the presence of God for them!

CHAPTER 7

1. The sum of the chapter is that the Christ—as appears from his type, Melchizedek, who was greater than Abraham himself, from whom Levi descended—has a priesthood altogether excellent, new, firm, perpetual.

4. The greatness of Melchizedek is described in all the preceding and following particulars. But the most manifest proof of it was that Abraham gave him tithes as to a priest of God and a superior; though he was himself a patriarch, greater than a king, and a progenitor of many kings.

11. *Another priest.* The apostle now demonstrates that *the Levitical priesthood* must yield to the priesthood of Christ, because Melchizedek, after whose order he is a priest, (1) is opposed to Aaron (vv. 11–14); (2) has no end of life (vv. 15–19), but remains a priest continually.

22. *A better covenant.*[1] This word *covenant* frequently occurs in the remaining part of this epistle. The original word means either a covenant or a last will and testament. Paul takes it sometimes in the former sense, sometimes in the latter; sometimes he includes both.

25. *Wherefore he is able also to save them to the uttermost.* From all the guilt, power, root, and consequence of sin.

CHAPTER 8

1. *We have such an high priest.* Having finished his description of the type in Melchizedek, the apostle begins to treat directly the excellence of Christ's priesthood beyond the Levitical.

5. *The pattern.* Somewhat like the strokes penciled out upon a piece of fine linen which exhibit the figures of leaves and flowers, but have not yet received their splendid colors and curious shades. *Shadow.* Or shadowy representation, which gives you some dim and imperfect idea of the body, but not the fine features, not the distinguishing air; none of those living graces which adorn the real person. Yet both the pattern and shadow lead our minds to something nobler than themselves: the *pattern,* to that holiness and glory which complete; the *shadow,* to that which occasions it.

8. *I will make a new covenant with the house of Israel.* With all the Israel of God, in all ages and nations. It is new in many respects, though not as to the substance of it: (1) Being ratified by the death of Christ. (2) Freed from those burdensome rites and ceremonies. (3) Containing a more full and clear account of spiritual religion. (4) Attended with larger influences of the Spirit. (5) Extended to all men. (6) Never to be abolished.

11. *From the least to the greatest.* In this order the saving knowledge of God ever did and ever will proceed; not first to the greatest and then to the least.

12. *For I will* justify them, which is the root of all true knowledge of God. This therefore is God's method. First, a sinner is pardoned. Then he knows God as gracious and merciful. Then God's laws are written on his heart; he is God's and God is his.

CHAPTER 9

2. *Wherein was the candlestick, and the table, and the shewbread.* The bread,

---

[1](7:22) KJV: "testament."

shown continually before God and all the people, consisting of twelve loaves according to the number of the tribes, was placed on this table in two rows, six upon one another in each row. This candlestick and bread seem to have typified the light and the life which are more largely dispensed under the gospel by him who is the Light of the World and the Bread of Life.

14. *Who through the eternal Spirit.* The work of redemption being the work of the whole Trinity. Neither is the Second Person alone concerned even in the amazing condescension that was needful to complete it. The Father delivers up the kingdom to the Son; and the Holy Ghost becomes the gift of the Messiah, being sent, as it were, according to his good pleasure. *From dead works.* From all the inward and outward works of the devil, which spring from spiritual death in the soul and lead to death everlasting. *To serve the living God.* In the life of faith, in perfect love and spotless holiness.

26. *In the end of the world.* The sacrifice of Christ divides the whole age or duration of the world into two parts and extends its virtue backward and forward from this middle point, in which they meet to *put away* both the guilt and power of *sin.*

27. *After this the judgment.* Of the great day. At the moment of death every man's final state is determined. But there is not a word in Scripture of a particular judgment immediately after death.

CHAPTER 10

5. *When he cometh into the world.* In the Fortieth Psalm the Messiah's coming into the world is represented. It is said *into the world,* not into the tabernacle (Heb. 9:1), because all the world is interested in his sacrifice.

14. *He hath perfected for ever them.* That is, has done all that was needful in order to gain their full reconciliation with God.

15. In this and the three following verses the apostle winds up his argument concerning the excellence and perfection of the priesthood and sacrifice of Christ. He had proved this before by a quotation from Jeremiah; which he here repeats, describing the new covenant as now completely ratified, and all the blessings of it secured to us by the one offering of Christ Jesus, which renders all other expiatory sacrifices and any repetition of his own utterly needless.

20. *Through the veil, that is to say, his flesh.* As by rending the veil in the temple, the holy of holies became visible and accessible; so by wounding the body of Christ, the God of heaven was manifested and the way to heaven opened.

22. *And our bodies washed with pure water.* All our conversation spotless and holy, which is far more acceptable to God than all the legal sprinklings and washings.

25. *As the manner of some is.* Either through fear of persecution, or from a vain imagination that they were above external ordinances.

26. *For if we.* Any of us Christians. *Sin wilfully.* By total apostasy from God, which is termed "drawing back" in verse 38.

CHAPTER 11

1. The definition of faith given in this verse and exemplified in the various instances following undoubtedly includes justifying faith, but not directly as justifying. For faith justifies only as it refers to and depends on Christ. But here is no mention of him as the object of faith; and in several of the instances that follow, no notice is taken of him or his salvation, but only of temporal blessings obtained by faith. And yet they may all be considered as evidences of the power of justifying faith in Christ, and of its extensive exercise in a course of steady obedience amid difficulties and dangers of every kind.

Now faith is the substance of things hoped for, the evidence [or conviction] *of things not seen.* Things hoped for are not so extensive as things not seen. The former are only things future and joyful to us; the latter are either future, past, or present, and those either good or evil, whether to us or others. *The substance of things hoped for.* Giving a kind of present substance to the good things which God has promised. The divine supernatural *evidence* exhibited to, and the conviction hereby produced in, a believer *of things not seen,* whether past, future, or spiritual; particularly of God and the things of God.

3. *By the word.* The sole command *of God,* without any instrument or preceding matter. And as Creation is the foundation and specimen of the whole divine economy, so faith in the Creation is the foundation and specimen of all faith. *Were not made of things which do appear.* Out of the dark, unapparent chaos (Gen. 1:2). And this very chaos was created by the divine power; for before it was thus created it had no existence in nature.

4. *By faith.* In the future Redeemer. *Abel offered . . . a more excellent sacrifice.* The firstlings of his flock, implying both a confession of what his own sins deserved, and a desire of sharing in the great atonement. *Than Cain.* Whose offering testified no such faith, but a mere acknowledgment of God the Creator.

13. *These all.* Mentioned in verses 7–11. *Died in faith.* In death faith acts most vigorously. *Embraced.* As one does a dear friend when he meets him.

26. *The reproach of Christ.* That which he bore for believing in the Messiah to come, and acting accordingly. *Unto the recompence of the reward.* Not to an inheritance in Canaan; he had no warrant from God to look for this, nor did he ever attain it; but what his believing ancestors looked for—a future state of happiness in heaven.

33–34. Faith animates to the most heroic enterprises, both civil and military. Faith overcomes all impediments; effects the greatest things; attains to the very best; and inverts, by its miraculous power, the very course of nature.

40. *That they without us should not be made perfect.* That is, that we might all be perfected together in heaven.

CHAPTER 12

1. *Let us lay aside every weight.* As all who run a race take care to do. Let us throw off whatever weighs us down or damps the vigor of our soul. *And the sin which doth so easily beset us.* As does the sin of our constitution, the sin of our education, the sin of our profession.

2. *Unto Jesus.* As the wounded Israelites looked to the brazen serpent. Our crucified Lord was prefigured by the lifting up of this; our guilt, by the stings of the fiery serpents; and our faith, by their looking up to the miraculous remedy. *The author and finisher of our faith.* Who begins it in us, carries it on, and perfects it.

3. *Consider.* Draw the comparison and think. The Lord bore all this; and shall his servants bear nothing?

9. *Unto the Father of spirits.* That we may *live* with him for ever. Perhaps these expressions, *fathers of our flesh* and *Father of spirits,* intimate that our earthly fathers are only the parents of our bodies, our souls not being originally derived from them but all created by the immediate power of God; perhaps, at the beginning of the world.

12. *Wherefore lift up the hands.* Whether your own or your brethren's. *Which hang down.* Unable to continue the combat. *And the feeble knees.* Unable to continue the race.

14. *Follow peace with all men.* This second branch of the exhortation concerns our neighbors; the third, God. *And holiness.* Not following after all holiness is the direct way to fall into sin of every kind.

15. *Springing up.* Destroy the sweet peace; lest any, not following after holiness, fall into profaneness or fornication. In general any corruption, either in doctrine or in practice, is a *root of bitterness* and may pollute many.

18. *For.* A strong reason why they ought the more to regard the whole exhortation drawn from the priesthood of Christ; because both salvation and vengeance are now nearer at hand.

19. *The sound of a trumpet.* Formed, without doubt, by the ministry of angels, and preparatory to the *words,* that is, the Ten Commandments, which were uttered with a loud *voice* (Deut. 5:22).

22. *But ye.* Who believe in Christ. *Are come.* The apostle does not here speak of their coming to the church militant, but of that glorious privilege of New Testament believers, their communion with the church triumphant. But this is far more apparent to the eyes of celestial spirits than to ours, which are yet veiled. Paul here shows an excellent knowledge of the heavenly economy, worthy of him who had been caught up into the third heaven.

23. *To the general assembly.* The word properly signifies a stated convention on some festival occasion. *And church.* The whole body of true believers, whether on earth or in paradise. *Of the firstborn.* The firstborn of Israel were enrolled by Moses; but these are *written in heaven* as citizens there. It is observ-

able that in this beautiful gradation, these firstborn are placed nearer to God than the angels. (See James 1:18.)

24. *And to the blood of sprinkling.* To all the virtue of his precious blood shed for you, whereby you are sprinkled from an evil conscience. This blood of sprinkling was the foundation of our Lord's mediatorial office. Here the gradation is at the highest point.

25. *Him that speaketh.* And whose speaking even now is a prelude to the final scene. The same voice which spoke both by the law and in the gospel, when heard from heaven, will shake heaven and earth.

26. *Yet once more I shake not the earth only, but also heaven.* These words may refer in a lower sense to the dissolution of the Jewish church and state; but in their full sense they undoubtedly look much further, even to the end of all things. This universal shaking began at the first coming of Christ; it will be consummated at his second coming.

29. *For our God is a consuming fire.* In the strictness of his justice and the purity of his holiness.

CHAPTER 13

4. *Marriage is honourable in* [or for] *all* sorts of men, clergy as well as laity; though the Romanists teach otherwise.

8. Men may die; but *Jesus Christ,* yes, and his gospel, is *the same* from everlasting to everlasting.

11. *For.* According to their own law, the sin offerings were wholly consumed, and no Jew ever ate thereof. But Christ was a sin offering. Therefore they cannot feed upon him, as we do who are freed from the Mosaic law.

13. *Let us go forth therefore unto him without the camp.* Out of the Jewish dispensation.

14. *No continuing city.* All things here are but for a moment; and Jerusalem itself was just then on the point of being destroyed.

17. *Obey them that have the rule over you.* The word implies also "that lead or guide you"; namely, in truth and holiness. *And submit yourselves.* Give up (not your conscience or judgment, but) your own will, in all things purely indifferent. *As they that must give account.* To the great Shepherd, for every part of their behavior towards you. How vigilant then ought every pastor to be! How careful of every soul committed to his charge! *With joy, and not with grief.* He is not a good shepherd who does not either rejoice over them or groan for them. The groans of other creatures are heard; how much more shall these come up in the ears of God! Whoever answers this character of a Christian pastor may undoubtedly demand this obedience.

25. *Grace be with you all.* Paul's usual benediction. God apply it to our hearts!

JAMES

CHAPTER 1

1. *A servant of . . . Jesus Christ.* Whose name the apostle mentions but once more in the whole epistle (2:1). And not at all in his other discourses (Acts 15:14ff.; 21:20–25). It might have seemed, if he mentioned him often, that he did it out of vanity, as being the brother of the Lord.

5. *If any of you lack.* The connection between the first and following verses, both here and in the fourth chapter, will be easily discerned by him who reads them while he is suffering wrongfully. He will then readily perceive why the apostle mentions all those various affections of the mind. *Wisdom.* To understand whence and why temptations come and how they are to be improved. Patience is in every pious man already. Let him exercise this and ask for wisdom. The sum of wisdom, both in the temptation of poverty and of riches, is described in the ninth and tenth verses.

6. *But let him ask in faith.* A firm confidence in God. James both begins and ends with faith (5:15), the hindrances of which he removes in the middle part of his epistle.

8. *A double-minded man.* Who has, as it were, two souls; whose heart is not simply given up to God.

11. *For the sun is no sooner risen, . . . but it withereth the grass.* There is an unspeakable beauty and elegance, both in the comparison itself and in the very manner of expressing it, intimating both the certainty and the suddenness of the event. *So also shall the rich man fade away in his ways.* In the midst of his various pleasures and employments.

14. *Drawn away of his own lust.* We are therefore to look for the cause of every sin in, not out of, ourselves. Even the injections of the devil cannot hurt before we make them our own. And every one has desires arising from his own constitution, tempers, habits, and way of life.

15. *Then when lust hath conceived.* By our own will joining therewith. *Bringeth forth* [actual] *sin.* It does not follow that the desire itself is not sin. He that begets a man is himself a man.

17. He is the Father of all light, material or spiritual, in the kingdom of grace and of glory. *With whom is no variableness.* No change in his understanding. *Neither shadow of turning* in his will. He infallibly discerns all good and evil, and invariably loves one and hates the other. There is, in both the Greek words, a metaphor taken from the stars, particularly proper where the *Father of lights* is mentioned. Both are applicable to any celestial body, which has a daily vicissitude of day and night, and sometimes longer days, sometimes longer nights. In God is nothing of this kind. He is mere light. If there is any such vicissitude, it is in ourselves, not in him.

19. *Let every man be swift to hear.* This is treated from verse 21 to the end of the next chapter. *Slow to wrath.* Neither murmuring at God, nor angry at his neighbor. This is treated in the third and throughout the fourth and fifth chapters.

21. *Wherefore lay apart,* as a dirty garment, *all filthiness and superfluity of naughtiness.* For however specious or necessary it may appear to worldly wisdom, all wickedness is vile, hateful, contemptible, and really superfluous. Every reasonable end may be effectually answered without any kind or degree of it. Lay this, every known sin, aside or all your hearing is vain.

23. *Beholding his natural face in a glass.* How exactly does the Scripture glass show a man the face of his soul!

25. *But whoso looketh . . . and continueth therein.* That is, not with a transient glance, but bending down, fixing eyes, and searching all to the bottom. *Into the perfect law* of love as established by faith. James here guards us against misunderstanding what Paul says concerning the yoke and bondage of the law. He who keeps the law of love is free (John 8:31ff.). He who does not keep it is not free, but is a slave to sin and a criminal before God (James 2:10).

27. The only true *religion* in the sight of God *is this, To visit,* with counsel, comfort, and relief, *the fatherless and widows,* —those who need it most—*in their affliction,* in their most helpless and hopeless state. *And to keep himself unspotted from the world.* From the maxims, tempers, and customs of it.

But this cannot be done until we have given our hearts to God and love our neighbor as ourselves.

CHAPTER 2

7. *Do not they blaspheme that worthy name.* Of God and of Christ. The apostle speaks chiefly of rich heathens. But are Christians, so called, a whit behind them?

12. *By the law of liberty.* The gospel; the law of universal love, which alone is perfect freedom.

14. From James 1:22, the apostle has been enforcing Christian practice. He now applies to those who neglect this under the pretense of faith. Paul had taught that "a man is justified by faith without the deeds of the law." This some began already to twist to their own destruction. Wherefore James, purposely repeating (vv. 21, 23, 25) the same phrases, testimonies, and examples which Paul had used (Rom. 4:3; Heb. 11:17, 31), refutes not the doctrine of Paul, but the error of those who abused it. There is, therefore, no contradiction between the apostles; they both delivered the truth of God, but in a different manner, as having to do with different kinds of men. On another occasion, James himself pleaded the cause of faith (Acts 15:13–21); and Paul himself strenuously pleads for works, particularly in his latter epistles.

This verse is a summary of what follows. *What doth it profit?* is enlarged on in verses 15–17; *though a man say* in verses 18–19; *can faith save him?* in verse 20. It is not "though a man have faith," but *though a man say he hath faith.* Here, therefore, true, living faith is meant. But in other parts of the argument the apostle speaks of a dead, imaginary faith. He does not therefore teach that true faith can, but that it cannot, subsist without works. Nor does he oppose faith to works, but that empty name of faith to real faith working by love. *Can faith* "which is without works" *save him?* No more than it can profit his neighbor.

21. *Was not Abraham . . . justified by works?* Paul says that he was justified by faith (Rom. 4:2ff.). Yet James does not contradict him; for he does not speak of the same justification. Paul speaks of that which Abraham received many years before Isaac was born (Gen. 15:6); James, of that which he did not receive until *he had offered Isaac his son upon the altar.* He was justified, therefore, in Paul's sense (that is, accounted righteous) by faith antecedent to his works. He was justified in James's sense (that is, made righteous) by works consequent to his faith. So that James's justification by works is the fruit of Paul's justification by faith.

22. *Seest thou how faith?* For by faith Abraham offered him (Heb. 11:17). *Wrought with his works.* Therefore faith has one energy and operation; works, another. And the energy and operation of faith are before works and together *with* them. Works do not give life to faith, but faith begets works and then is perfected by them. *And by works was faith made perfect?* Here James fixes the sense wherein he uses the word "justified," so that no shadow of contradiction remains between his assertion and Paul's. Abraham returned from that sacrifice perfected in faith and far higher in the favor of God. Faith has not its being from works (for it is before them), but its perfection. That vigor of faith which begets works is then excited and increased thereby, as the natural heat of the body begets motion, whereby itself is then excited and increased. (See I John 3:22.)

24. *Ye see then how that by works a man is justified, and not by faith only.* Paul, on the other hand, declares, "A man is justified by faith" and not by works (Rom. 3:28). And yet there is no contradiction between the apostles, because: (1) They do not speak of the same faith (Paul speaking of "living" faith; James speaking here of "dead" faith). (2) They did not speak of the same works (Paul speaking of works antecedent to faith; James speaking of works subsequent to it).

25. After Abraham, the father of the Jews, the apostle cites Rahab, a woman and a sinner of the Gentiles, to show that in every nation and sex true faith produces works and is perfected by them; that is, by the grace of God working in the believer while he is showing his faith by his works.

CHAPTER 3

1. *Be not many teachers.*[1] Let no more of you take this upon you than God thrusts out, seeing it is so hard not to offend in speaking much. *Knowing that we.* That all who thrust themselves into the office. *Shall receive the greater condemnation.* For more offenses. James here, as in several of the following verses, by a common figure of speech includes himself: *we shall receive,* "we offend," "we put bits," "we curse." None of which, as common sense shows, are to be interpreted either of him or of the other apostles.

6. *And setteth on fire the course of nature.* All the passions, every wheel of his soul.

8. *But the tongue can no man tame.* Of another; no, nor his own without peculiar help from God.

9. *Men which are made after the*

---

[1](3:1) KJV: "masters."

similitude of God. Indeed, although we have now lost this likeness, yet there remains from thence an indelible nobleness which we ought to reverence both in ourselves and others.

13. *Let him shew* his wisdom as well as his faith by *his works,* not by words only.

17. *But the wisdom that is from above is first pure.* From all that is earthly, natural, devilish. *Then peaceable.* True peace attending purity, it is quiet, inoffensive. *Gentle.* Soft, mild, yielding, not rigid. *Easy to be intreated.* To be persuaded, or convinced; not stubborn, sour, or morose. *Full of . . . good fruits.* Both in the heart and in the life, two of which are immediately specified. *Without partiality.* Loving all, without respect of persons; embracing all good things, rejecting all evil.

CHAPTER 4

2. *Ye ask not.* And no marvel; for a man full of evil desire, of envy or hatred, cannot pray.

4. *Know ye not that the friendship* [or love] *of the world*—the desire of the flesh, the desire of the eye, and the pride of life, or courting the favor of worldly men—*is enmity with God? Whosoever therefore will be a friend of the world*—whoever seeks either the happiness or favor of it—does thereby constitute himself *the enemy of God;* and can he expect to obtain anything of him?

8. Then *draw nigh to God* in prayer, *and he will draw nigh to you,* will hear you; which, so that nothing may hinder, *cleanse your hands,* cease from doing evil. *And purify your hearts.* From all spiritual adultery. Be no more *double-minded,* vainly endeavoring to serve both God and mammon.

9. *Be afflicted.* for your past unfaithfulness to God.

11. *Speak not evil one of another.* This is a grand hindrance of peace. O who is sufficiently aware of it!

17. *To him it is sin.* His knowledge does not prevent, but increase, his condemnation.

CHAPTER 5

1. The apostle does not speak this so much for the sake of the rich themselves, as of the poor children of God who were then groaning under their cruel oppression.

3. *Shall be a witness against you.* Of your having buried those talents in the earth, instead of improving them according to your Lord's will.

4. *The hire of the labourers . . . crieth.* Those sins chiefly cry to God concerning which human laws are silent. Such are luxury, unchastity, and various kinds of injustice. The *labourers* themselves also cry to God, who is just coming to avenge their cause.

6. *Ye have . . . killed the just.* Many just men; in particular, that Just One (Acts 3:14). They afterwards killed James, surnamed the Just, the writer of this epistle.

8. *For the coming of the Lord.* To destroy Jerusalem.

11. *We count them happy which endure.* Who suffer patiently. The more they suffer, the greater is their present happiness.

12. *Swear not.* However provoked. The Jews were notoriously guilty of common swearing, though not so much by God himself as by some of his creatures. The apostle here particularly forbids these oaths as well as all swearing in common conversation. It is very observable how solemnly the apostle introduces this command, *above all things, . . . swear not.* As if he had said, "Whatever you forget, do not forget this." This abundantly demonstrates the horrible iniquity of the crime. But he does not forbid the taking of a solemn oath before a magistrate.

14. *Anointing him with oil.* This single conspicuous gift, which Christ committed to his apostles (Mark 6:13), remained in the church long after the other miraculous gifts were withdrawn. Indeed, it seems to have been designed to remain always; and James directs the elders, who were the most—if not the only—gifted men, to administer it. This was the whole process of physic in the Christian church until it was lost through unbelief. That novel invention, extreme unction, practiced not for cure, but where life is despaired of, bears no manner of resemblance to this.

15. *And the prayer* [offered in] *faith shall save the sick.* From his sickness; *and if* any sin be the occasion of his sickness, it *shall be forgiven him.*

16. *Confess your faults.* Whether you are sick or in health. *One to another.* He does not say, to the elders. This may or may not be done, for it is nowhere commanded. We may confess them to any who can pray in faith. He will then know how to pray for us and be more stirred up so to do. *And pray one for another, that ye may be healed.* Of all our spiritual diseases.

19. As if he had said, I have now warned you of those sins to which you are most liable; and in all these respects, watch not only over yourselves, but every one over his brother also. Labor, in particular, to recover those that are fallen. *If any of you do err from the truth.* Practically, by sin.

20. *Shall save a soul.* Of how much more value than the body (v. 14).

1 peter

CHAPTER 1

2. *According to the foreknowledge of God.* Speaking after the manner of men. For, strictly speaking, there is no foreknowledge, any more than there is afterknowledge, with God. All things are known to him as present from eternity to eternity. This is therefore no other than an instance of the divine condescension to our low capacities. *Elect.* By the free love and almighty power of God taken out of, separated from, the world. Election, in the Scripture sense, is God's doing any thing that our merit or power have no part in. The true predestination, or foreappointment of God is: (1) He who believes shall be saved from the guilt and power of sin. (2) He who endures to the end shall be saved eternally. (3) They who receive the precious gift of faith thereby become the sons of God; and, being sons, they shall receive the Spirit of holiness to walk as Christ also walked.

Throughout every part of this appointment of God, promise and duty go hand in hand. All is free gift; and yet such is the gift that the final issue depends on our future obedience to the heavenly call. But of other predestination than this, either to life or death eternal, the Scripture knows not. Moreover, it is: (1) Cruel respect of persons; an unjust regard of one, and an unjust disregard of another. It is mere creature partiality and not infinite justice. (2) It is not plain Scripture doctrine, if true; but rather, inconsistent with the express written word that speaks of God's universal offers of grace; his invitations, promises, threatenings being all general. (3) We are bid to choose life, and reprehended for not doing it. (4) It is inconsistent with a state of probation in those who must be saved or must be lost. (5) It is of fatal consequence; all men are ready, on very slight grounds, to fancy themselves of the elect number.

But the doctrine of predestination is entirely changed from what it formerly was. Now it implies neither faith, peace, nor purity. It is something that will do without them all. Faith is no longer, according to the modern predestinarian scheme, a divine "evidence of things not seen" wrought in the soul by the immediate power of the Holy Ghost; not an evidence at all, but a mere notion. Neither is faith made any longer a means of holiness, but something that will do without it. Christ is no more a Savior from sin, but a defense, a countenancer of it. He is no more a fountain of spiritual life in the soul of believers, but leaves his elect inwardly dry and outwardly unfruitful; and is made little more than a refuge from the image of the heavenly, even from righteousness, peace, and joy in the Holy Ghost.

3. *Blessed be the God and Father of our Lord Jesus Christ.* His Father, with respect to his divine nature; his God, with respect to his human. *By the resurrection of Jesus Christ.* Which is not only a pledge of ours, but a part of the purchase price. It has also a close connection with our rising from spiritual death, that as he lives, so shall we live with him. He was acknowledged to be the Christ, but usually called "Jesus" until his resurrection; then he was also called "Christ."

5. *Through faith.* Through which alone salvation is both received and retained.

9. *Salvation.* From all sin into all holiness, which is the qualification for, the forerunner and pledge of, eternal salvation.

10. *And searched diligently.* Like miners searching after precious ore, after the meaning of the prophecies which they delivered.

13. *Gird up the loins of your mind.* As persons in the Eastern countries used to do, in traveling or running, to gird up their long garments, so gather you up all your thoughts and affections and keep your mind always disencumbered and prepared to run the race which is set before you.

22. *Seeing ye have purified your souls in obeying the truth through the Spirit,* who bestows upon you freely both obedience and purity of heart and *unfeigned love of the brethren,* go on to still higher degrees of love.

CHAPTER 2

2. *Milk of the word.* That word of God which nourishes the soul as milk does the body, and which is *sincere,* pure from all guile, so that none are deceived who cleave to it.

4. *As unto a living stone.* Living from eternity; alive from the dead. There is a wonderful beauty and energy in these expressions, which describe Christ as a spiritual foundation, solid, firm, durable; and believers as a building erected upon it, in preference to that temple which the Jews accounted their highest glory. And Peter, speaking of him thus, shows he did not judge himself, but Christ to be the rock on which the church was built. *Disallowed indeed of men.* He is rejected even at this day, not only by Jews, Turks, heathens, infidels; but by all Christians, so called, who live in sin or who hope to be saved by their own works.

7. *Unto you therefore which believe, he . . . is made the head of the corner.* The chief cornerstone, on which the whole building rests. Unbelievers, too, will at length find him such to their sorrow (Matt. 21:44).

11. *Strangers and pilgrims.* The first word properly means those who are in a strange house; the second, those who are in a strange country. You sojourn in the body; you are pilgrims in this world.

22–23. In all these instances the example of Christ is peculiarly adapted to the state of servants, who easily slide either into *sin* or *guile,* reviling their fellow servants or threatening them, the natural result of anger without power.

CHAPTER 3

4. *The hidden man of the heart.* Complete inward holiness, which implies *a meek and quiet spirit.* A meek spirit gives no trouble willingly to any; a quiet spirit bears all wrongs without being troubled. *In the sight of God.* Who looks at the heart. All superfluity of dress contributes more to pride and anger than is generally supposed. The apostle seems to have his eye to this by substituting meekness and quietness in the room of the ornaments he forbids. "I do not regard these things" is often said by those whose hearts are wrapped up in them. But offer to take them away and you touch the very idol of their soul. Some indeed only dress elegantly that they may be looked on; that is, they squander away their Lord's talent to gain applause; thus making sin to beget sin, and then plead one in excuse of the other.

7. *Dwell with* [the women] *according to knowledge.* Knowing they are weak and therefore to be used with all tenderness. Yet do not despise them for this, but give them *honour,* both in heart, in word, and in action; as those who are called to be *heirs together of* that eternal *life* which you and they hope to receive by the free *grace* of God. *That your prayers be not hindered.* On the one part or the other. All sin hinders prayer; particularly anger. Any thing at which we are angry is never more apt to come into our mind than when we are at prayer; and those who do not forgive will find no forgiveness from God.

12. *The eyes of the Lord are over the righteous.* For good. Anger appears in the whole face; love, chiefly in the eyes.

16. *Having a good conscience.* So much the more beware of anger, to which the very consciousness of your innocence may betray you. Join with good conscience meekness and fear, and you obtain a complete victory. *Your good conversation in Christ.* That is, which flows from faith in him.

19. *By which* Spirit *he went and preached.* Through the ministry of Noah. *Unto the spirits in prison.* The

unholy men before the Flood, who were then reserved by the justice of God as in a prison, until he executed the sentence upon them all; and are now also reserved to the judgment of the great day.

21. *The antitype whereof.*[1] The thing typified by the ark, even *baptism doth also now save us.* That is, through the water of baptism we are saved from the sin which overwhelms the word as a flood. *Not,* indeed, the bare outward sign, but the inward grace; a divine consciousness that both our persons and our actions are accepted through him who died and rose again for us.

CHAPTER 4

7. *Be ye therefore sober, and watch unto prayer.* Temperance helps watchfulness, and both of them help prayer. Watch, that you may pray; and pray, that you may watch.

8. *Charity shall cover the multitude of sins.* He who loves another covers his faults, however many they be. He turns away his own eyes from them and, as far as is possible, hides them from others. And he continually prays that all the sinner's iniquities may be forgiven and his sins covered. Meantime, the God of love measures to him with the same measure into his heart.

11. *Speak . . . as the oracles of God.* Let all his words be according to this pattern, both as to matter and manner, more especially in public. By this mark we may always know who are so far the true or false prophets. *The oracles of God* teach that men should repent, believe, obey. He who treats faith and leaves out repentance, or does not enjoin practical holiness to believers, does not speak as the oracles of God; he does not

---

[1](3:21) KJV: "The like figure whereunto."

preach Christ, let him think as highly of himself as he will.

12. *Wonder not at the burning which is among you.*[2] The literal meaning of the expression. It seems to include both martyrdom itself, which so frequently was by fire, and all the other sufferings joined with or previous to it; *which is* permitted by the wisdom of God *to try you.* Be not surprised at this.

17. *What shall the end be of them that obey not the gospel.* How terribly will he visit them! The judgments which are milder at the beginning grow more and more severe. But good men, having already sustained their part, are only spectators of the miseries of the wicked.

CHAPTER 5

2. *Feed the flock.* Both by doctrine and discipline. *Not for filthy lucre.* Which, if it be the motive of acting, is *filthy* beyond expression. O consider this you who leave one flock and go to another merely because there is more gain, a larger salary! Is it not astonishing that men can see no harm in this? That it is not only practiced, but avowed, all over the nation?

5. *Be subject one to another.* Let every one be ready, upon all occasions, to give up his own will. *And be clothed with humility.* Bind it on (so the word signifies) so that no force may be able to tear it from you.

8. But in the mean time, watch. There is a close connection between this and "casting your care" (v. 7) upon him. How deeply had Peter himself suffered for lack of watching! *Be vigilant.* As if he had said, "Awake, and keep awake. Sleep no more; be this your care."

---

[2] (4:12) KJV: "Think it not strange concerning the fiery trial which is to try you."

II peter

CHAPTER 1

1. *To them that have obtained.* Not by their own works, but by the free grace of God.

5. In this most beautiful connection, each preceding grace leads to the following; each following tempers and perfects the preceding. They are set down in the order of nature rather than the order of time. For though every grace bears a relation to every other, yet here they are so nicely ranged that those which have the closest dependence on each other are placed together.

6. *And to your knowledge temperance; and to temperance patience.* Bear and forbear; sustain and abstain; deny yourself and take up your cross daily. The more knowledge you have, the more renounce your own will; indulge yourself the less. "Knowledge puffeth up," and the great boasters of knowledge (the Gnostics) were those who turned the grace of God into wantonness. But see that your knowledge be attended with *temperance*. Christian temperance implies the voluntary abstaining from all pleasure which does not lead to God. It extends to all things inward and outward; the due government of every thought, as well as affection. It is using the world, so to use all outward and so to restrain all inward things, that they may become a means of what is spiritual; a scaling ladder to ascend to what is above. Intemperance is to abuse the world. He who uses anything below, looking no higher, and getting no further, is intemperate. He who uses the creature only so as to attain to more of the Creator is alone temperate and walks as Christ himself walked.

7. *And to godliness brotherly kindness.* No sullenness, sternness, moroseness. "Sour godliness," so called, is of the devil. *And to brotherly kindness charity.* The pure and perfect love of God and of all mankind. The apostle here makes an advance upon the preceding article, *brotherly kindness,* which seems only to relate to the love of Christians toward one another.

8. *Make you . . . neither . . . barren* [slothful] *nor unfruitful.* Do not allow you to be faint in your mind or without fruit in your lives. If there is less faithfulness, less care and watchfulness, since we were pardoned than there was before, and less diligence, less outward obedience, than when we were seeking remission of sin, we are both slothful and unfruitful in the knowledge of Christ, that is, in the faith, which then cannot work by love.

10. *To make your calling and election sure.* God has called you by his word and his Spirit; he has elected you, separated you from the world, through sanctification of the Spirit. O cast not away these inestimable benefits! *If ye are thus diligent to make your calling and election sure . . . ye shall never* finally *fall.*

13. *In this tabernacle.* Or tent. How short is our abode in the body! How easily does a believer pass out of it!

16. If what they advanced of Christ was not true, if it was of their own invention, then to impose such a lie on the world as it was (in the very nature of things above all human power to defend) and to do this at the expense of life and of all things only to enrage the whole world (Jews and Gentiles) against them was no cunning, but was the greatest folly of which men could have been guilty.

19. *Have also a more sure the word of prophecy.* The words of Moses, Isaiah, and all the prophets are one and the same word, every way consistent with itself. *Until the day dawn.* Until the full light of the gospel should break through the darkness. As is the difference between the light of a lamp and that of the day, such is that between the light of the Old Testament and of the New.

CHAPTER 2

1. *Bring in damnable heresies.* They first, by denying the Lord, introduced destructive heresies, that is, divisions; or they occasioned first these divisions and then were given up to a reprobate mind, even to deny the Lord who bought them. Either the heresies are the effect of denying the Lord, or the denying the Lord was the consequence of the heresies.

4. *Delivered them.* Like condemned criminals to safe custody, as if bound with the strongest chains in a dungeon *of darkness, to be reserved unto judgment,* that of the great day. Though still those chains do not hinder their often walking up and down seeking whom they may devour.

13. *They that count it pleasure to riot in the day time.* They glory in doing it in the face of the sun. They are *spots* in themselves, *blemishes* to any church. *Sporting themselves with their own deceivings.* Making a jest of those whom they deceive, and even jesting while they are deceiving their own souls.

22. *The dog; . . . the sow.* Such are all men in the sight of God before they receive his grace and after they have made shipwreck of the faith.

CHAPTER 3

5. *The* [aerial] *heavens were . . . and the earth.* Not as it is now, but *standing out of the water and in the water.* Perhaps the interior globe of earth was fixed in the midst of the great deep, the abyss of *water;* the shell or exterior globe *standing out of the water,* covering the great deep. This or some other great and manifest difference between the original and present constitution of the globe seems then to have been so generally known that Peter charges their ignorance of it totally upon their willfulness.

8–9. *That one day is with the Lord as a thousand years, and a thousand years as one day.* Moses had said (Ps. 90:4), "A thousand years in thy sight are but as" one day; which Peter applies with regard to the last day so as to denote God's eternity, whereby he exceeds all measure of time in his essence and in his operation; his knowledge, to which all things past or to come are present every moment; his power, which needs no long delay in order to bring its work to perfection; and his longsuffering, which excludes all impatience of expectation and desire of making haste.

One day is with the Lord as a thousand years. That is, in one day, in one moment, he can do the work of a thousand years. Therefore he *is not slack;* he is always equally ready to fulfill his promise. *And a thousand years* [are] *as one day.* That is, no delay is long to the eternal God. Therefore he *is longsuffering;* he gives us space for repentance, without any inconvenience to himself. In a word, with God time passes neither slower nor swifter than is suitable to him and his economy; nor can there be any reason why it should be necessary for him either to delay or hasten the end of all things. How can we comprehend this? If we could comprehend it, Peter needed not to have added, *with the Lord.*

10. *The elements shall melt with fervent heat.* "The elements" seems to mean the sun, moon, and stars; not the four commonly so called;[1] for air and water cannot melt, and the earth is mentioned immediately after. *That are therein shall be burned up.* And has not God already abundantly provided for this? (1) By the stores of subterranean fire which are so frequently bursting out at Aetna, Vesuvius, Hecla, and many other burning mountains. (2) By the ethereal (commonly called electrical) fire, diffused through the whole globe; which, if the secret chain that now binds it up were loosed, would immediately dissolve the whole frame of nature. (3) By comets, one of which, if it touch the earth in its course toward the sun, must needs strike it into that abyss of fire; if in its return from the sun, when it is heated, as a great man computes, two thousand times hotter than a red-hot cannonball, it must destroy all vegetables and animals long before their contact and soon after burn it up.

11. *Seeing then that all these things shall be dissolved.* To the eye of faith it appears as done already. *All these things.* Those mentioned before; all that are included in that Scriptural expression "the heavens and the earth"; that is, the universe. On the fourth day God made the stars (Gen. 1:16), which will be dissolved together with the earth. They are deceived, therefore, who restrain either the history of the Creation or this description of the destruction of the world to the earth and lower heavens; imagining the stars to be more ancient than the earth and to survive it. Both the dissolution and renovation are ascribed, not to the one heaven which surrounds the earth, but to the heavens in general (vv. 10, 13), without any restriction or limitation.

15. *As our beloved brother Paul also . . . hath written unto you.* This refers not only to the single sentence preceding, but to all that went before. Paul had written to the same effect concerning the end of the world, in several parts of his epistles and particularly in his Epistle to the Hebrews.

16. *As also in all his epistles.* Peter wrote this a little before his own and Paul's martyrdom. Paul therefore had now written all his epistles; and even from this expression we may learn that Peter had read them all, perhaps sent to him by Paul himself. Nor was he at all disgusted by what Paul had written concerning him in the Epistle to the Galatians. *As they do also the other scriptures.* Therefore Paul's writings were now part of the Scriptures.

18. *But grow in grace.* That is, in every Christian temper. There may be, for a time, grace without growth, as there may be natural life without growth. But such sickly life of soul or

---

[1] (3:10) A reference to the ancient Greeks' classifying of matter into the four elements of earth, air, water, and fire.

body will end in death and every day draw nigher to it. Health is the means of both natural and spiritual growth. If the remaining evil of our fallen nature be not daily mortified, it will, like an evil tumor in the body, destroy the whole man. But "if ye through the Spirit do mortify the deeds of the body" (only so far as we do this), "ye shall live" the life of faith, holiness, happiness. The end and design of grace, being purchased and bestowed on us, is to destroy the image of the earthy and restore us to that of the heavenly. And so far as it does this, it truly profits us; and also makes way for more of the heavenly gift, that we may at last be filled with all the fullness of God.

The strength and well-being of a Christian depend on what his soul feeds on, as the health of the body depends on whatever we make our daily food. If we feed on what is according to our nature, we grow; if not, we pine away and die. The soul is of the nature of God, and nothing but what is according to his holiness can agree with it. Sin, of every kind, starves the soul and makes it consume away. Let us not try to invert the order of God in his new creation; we shall only deceive ourselves.

It is easy to forsake the will of God and follow our own; but this will bring leanness into the soul. It is easy to satisfy ourselves without being possessed of the holiness and happiness of the gospel. It is easy to call these frames and feelings, and then to oppose faith to one and Christ to the other. Frames (allowing the expression) are no other than heavenly tempers, the mind that was in Christ. Feelings are the divine consolations of the Holy Ghost shed abroad in the heart of him who truly believes. And wherever faith is, and wherever Christ is, there are these blessed frames and feelings. If they are not in us, it is a sure sign that though the wilderness became a pool, the pool is become a wilderness again.

To him be glory both now and for ever. An expression naturally flowing from that sense which the apostle had felt in his soul throughout this whole chapter. Eternity is a day without night, without interruption, without end.

1 John

CHAPTER 1

1. *Of the Word of life.* He is termed "the Word" (John 1:1); "the Life" (John 1:4); as he is the living Word of God, who, with the Father and the Spirit, is the fountain of life to all creatures, particularly of spiritual and eternal life.

2. *That eternal life,* which always was, and afterward *was manifested unto us.* This is mentioned in the beginning of the epistle. In the end of it is mentioned the same *eternal life,* which we shall always enjoy.

4. *That your joy may be full.* So our Lord also in John 15:11; 16:22. There is a joy of hope, a joy of faith, and a joy of love. Here the joy of faith is directly intended. It is a concise expression. *Your joy.* That is, your faith and the joy arising from it. But it likewise implies the joy of hope and love.

5. *That God is light.* The light of wisdom, love, holiness, glory. What light is to the natural eye, God is to the spiritual eye. *And in him is no darkness at all.* No contrary principle. He is pure, unmixed light.

7. *But if we walk in the light.* In all holiness. *As he is* [a deeper word than walk, and more worthy of God] *in the light,* then we may truly say, *we have fellowship one with another.* We who have seen, and you who have not seen, do alike enjoy that fellowship with God; the imitation of God being the only sure proof of our having fellowship with him. *Cleanseth us from all sin.* Both original and actual, taking away all the guilt and all the power.

9. But *if,* with a penitent and believing heart, *we confess our sins, he is faithful.* Because he had promised this blessing by the unanimous voice of all his prophets. *Just.* Surely then he will punish. No, for this very reason he will pardon. This may seem strange; but upon the evangelical principle of atonement and redemption, it is undoubtedly true, because, when the debt is paid or the purchase made, it is the part of equity to cancel the bond and consign over the purchased possession. *To forgive us our sins.* To take away all the guilt of them. *And to cleanse us from all unrighteousness.* To purify our souls from every kind and every degree of it.

CHAPTER 2

These things write I unto you, that ye sin not. Thus he guards them beforehand against abusing the doctrine of reconciliation. All the words, institutions, and judgments of God are leveled against sin, either that it may not be committed or that it may be abolished.

And if any man sin. Let him not lie in sin, despairing of help. *We have an advocate.* We have for our advocate not a meager person, but him of whom it was said, "This is my beloved son." Not a guilty person, who stands in need of pardon for himself, but *Jesus Christ the righteous;* not a mere petitioner, who relies purely upon liberality, but one who has merited, fully merited, whatever he asks.

3. *If we keep his commandments.* Particularly those of faith and love.

5. *Know we that we are in him.* So is the tree known by its fruits. To "know him," to be *in him,* to "abide in him" are nearly synonymous terms; only with a gradation: knowledge, communion, constancy.

8. *Again, a new commandment I write unto you.* Namely, with regard to loving one another. A commandment which, though it also was given long ago, yet *is* [truly new] *in him and in you.* It was exemplified *in him* and is now fulfilled by you in such a manner as it never was before. For there is no comparison between the state of the Old Testament believers and that which you now enjoy; the *darkness* of that dispensation *is past,* and Christ *the true light now shineth* in your hearts.

10. *And there is none occasion of stumbling in him.* Whereas he who hates his brother is an occasion of stumbling to himself. He stumbles against himself and against all things within and without; while he who loves his brother has a free, disencumbered journey.

11. *He that hateth his brother.* And he must hate if he does not love him. There is no medium.

16. *The lust of the flesh.* Of the pleasure of the outward senses, whether of the taste, smell, or touch. *The lust of the eyes.* Of the pleasures of imagination, to which the eye chiefly is subservient; of that internal sense whereby we relish whatever is grand, new, or beautiful. *The pride of life.* All that pomp in clothes, houses, furniture, equipment, manner of living, which generally procure honor from the bulk of mankind and so gratify pride and vanity. It therefore directly includes the desire of praise and, remotely, covetousness. All these desires are not from God, but from the prince of this world.

18. *Ye have heard that antichrist shall come.* Under the term "antichrist" or "the spirit of antichrist" he includes all false teachers and enemies to the truth; yes, whatever doctrines or men are contrary to Christ. It seems to have been long after this that the name of antichrist was appropriated to that grand adversary of Christ, "the man of sin" (II Thess. 2:3). The antichrist, in John's sense—that is, "antichristianism"—has been spreading from his time until now, and will do so until that great adversary arises and is destroyed by Christ's coming.

22. *Who is a liar.* Who is guilty of that lying but he who denies that truth which is the sum of all Christianity? That Jesus is the Christ, that he is the Son of God, that he came in the flesh, is one undivided truth; and he who denies any part of this in effect denies the whole. *He is antichrist.* And the spirit of antichrist, who in denying the Son denies the Father also.

CHAPTER 3

4. *Whosoever committeth sin* thereby transgresses the holy, just, and good law of God and so sets his authority at nought; for this is implied in the very nature of sin.

8. *He that committeth sin is* [a child] *of the devil; for the devil sinneth from the beginning.* That is, was the first sinner in the universe and has continued to sin ever since. *The Son of God was mani-*

fested, that he might destroy the works of the devil. All sin. And will he not perform this in all who trust in him?

9. *Whosoever is born of God,* by living faith, whereby God is continually breathing spiritual life into his soul, and his soul is continually breathing out love and prayer to God, *doth not commit sin.*

15. *Whosoever hateth his brother—* and there is no medium between loving and hating him—is, in God's account, *a murderer.* Every degree of hatred is a degree of the same temper which moved Cain to murder his brother.

16. The word "God" is not in the original. It was omitted by the apostle just as the particular name is omitted by Mary when she says to the gardener, "Sir, if thou hast borne him hence" (John 20:15); and by the church, when she says, "Let him kiss me with the kisses of his mouth" (Song of Sol. 1:2). In both places there is a language, a very emphatic language, even in silence. It declares how totally the thoughts were possessed by the blessed and glorious subject. It expresses also the superlative dignity and amiableness of the person meant, as though he and he alone was or deserved to be both known and admired by all.

19. The word "heart" in John's language is the conscience. The word "conscience" is not found in the writings of John.

21–22. *If our heart condemn us not.* If our conscience, duly enlightened by the word and Spirit of God and comparing all our thoughts, words, and works with that word, pronounce that they agree therewith, *then have we confidence toward God.* Not only our consciousness of his favor continues and increases, but we have a full persuasion that *whatsoever we ask, we* [shall] *receive of him.*

23. *And this is his commandment.* All

his commandments in one word. *That we should believe . . . and love.* In the manner and degree which he has taught. This is the greatest and most important command that ever issued from the throne of glory. If this be neglected, no other can be kept; if this be observed, all others are easy.

CHAPTER 4

7. *Let us love one another.* From the doctrine he has just been defending he draws this exhortation. It is by the Spirit that the love of God is shed abroad in our hearts.

8. *God is love.* This little sentence brought John more sweetness, even in the time he was writing it, than the whole world can bring. God is often characterized as holy, righteous, wise; but not holiness, righteousness, or wisdom in the abstract, as he is said to be love; intimating that this is his darling, his reigning attribute, the attribute that shed an amiable glory on all his other perfections.

18. *There is no fear in love.* No slavish fear can be where love reigns. *But perfect* [adult] *love casteth out* [slavish] *fear; because* [such] *fear hath torment* and so is inconsistent with the happiness of love. A natural man has neither fear nor love; one who is awakened, fear without love; a babe in Christ, love and fear; a father in Christ, love without fear.

19. *We love him, because he first loved us.* This is the sum of all religion, the genuine model of Christianity. None can say more; why should any one say less, or less intelligibly?

21. *That he who loveth God love his brother.* Every one, whatever his opinions or mode of worship be, purely because he is the child and bears the image of God. Bigotry is properly the lack of this pure and universal love. A bigot only loves those who embrace his opinions and receive his way of worship; and he loves them for that, and not for Christ's sake.

CHAPTER 5

1. *Whosoever believeth.* The scope and sum of this whole paragraph appears from the conclusion of it (v. 13), "These things have I written to you that believe; . . . that ye may know that ye have eternal life." So faith is the first and last point with John also.

4. *Is born of God overcometh the world.* Conquers whatever it can lay in the way, either to allure or frighten the children of God from keeping his commandments.

5. *Who is he that overcometh the world . . . ?* That is superior to all worldly care, desire, fear? Every believer, and none else. The seventh verse (usually so reckoned) is a brief recapitulation of all which has been before advanced concerning the Father, the Son, and the Spirit. It is cited in conjunction with the sixth and eighth by Tertullian, Cyprian, and an uninterrupted train of Fathers. And indeed, what the sun is in the world, what the heart is in a man, what the needle is in the mariner's compass, this verse is in the epistle. By this the sixth, eighth, and ninth verses are indissolubly connected.

6. *This is he.* John here shows the immovable foundation of that faith that Jesus is the Son of God; not only the testimony of man, but the firm, indubitable testimony of God. *That came.* Jesus is he of whom it was promised that he should come; and so, accordingly, *is* come. And this the Spirit, and the water, and the blood testify. *Even Jesus.* Who, coming by water and blood, is by this very thing demonstrated to be the *Christ.*

Not by water only. Wherein he was baptized. *But by water and blood.* Which he shed when he had finished the work his Father had given him to do. He not only undertook at his baptism "to fulfil all righteousness," but on the cross accomplished what he had undertaken; in token whereof, when it all was finished, blood and water came out of his side. *And it is the Spirit that* [likewise] *beareth witness* of Jesus Christ, namely, by Moses and all the prophets, by John the Baptist, by all the apostles, and in all the writings of the New Testament. And against his testimony there can be no exception, *because the Spirit is truth.* The very God of truth.

16. *Sin a sin which is not unto death.* That is, any sin but total apostasy from both the power and form of godliness.

19. *And the whole world.* All who have not the Spirit of God not only are "touched" by the evil one, but by idolatry, fraud, violence, lasciviousness, impiety, all manner of wickedness. *Lieth in wickedness.* Void of life, void of sense. In this short expression the horrible state of the world is painted in the most lively colors; a comment on which we have in the actions, conversations, contracts, quarrels, and friendships of worldly men.

20. *And we are in him that is true.* As branches in the vine, even in Jesus Christ, the eternal Son of God. *This* [Jesus] *is the* [only living and] *true God,* together with the Father and the Spirit, and the original fountain of *eternal life.* So the beginning and the end of the epistle agree.

21. *Keep yourselves from idols.* From all worship of false gods, from all worship of images or of any creature, and from every inward idol; from loving, desiring, fearing anything more than God. Seek all help and defense from evil, all happiness in the true God alone.

II John

1. *Unto the elect.* That is, Christian. *Kuria*[1] is undoubtedly a proper name, both here and in verse 5; for it was not then usual to apply the title of lady to any but the Roman empress. Neither would such a manner of speaking have been suitable to the simplicity and dignity of the apostle.

3. *Grace* takes away guilt; *mercy,* misery. *Peace* implies the abiding in grace and mercy. It includes the testimony of God's Spirit, both that we are his children and that all our ways are acceptable to him. This is the very foretaste of heaven itself, where it is perfected.

5. *That which we had from the beginning.* Of our Lord's ministry. Indeed it was in some sense from the beginning of the world.

6. *And this is* [the proof of true] *love,* universal obedience built on the love of God.

7. Carefully keep what you have heard from the beginning, *for many deceivers are entered into the world, who confess not that Jesus Christ is come in the flesh.* Who disbelieve either his prophetic, priestly, or kingly office. Whoever does *this is a deceiver.* Or, seducer from God. *And an antichrist.* Fighting against Christ.

8. *But . . . receive a full reward.* Having fully employed all our talents to the glory of him who gave them. Here again the apostle modestly transfers it to himself.

12. *Having many things to write, . . . I would not write* now. Only these, which were then peculiarly needful.

---

[1](V. 1) KJV: "lady."

III John

1. *Gaius* was probably that Gaius of Corinth whom Paul mentions in Romans 16:23.

4. *I have no greater joy.* Such is the spirit of every true Christian pastor. *To hear that my children walk in truth.* Gaius probably was converted by Paul. Therefore when John speaks of him with the other believers as his children, it may be considered as the tender style of paternal love, whoever were the instruments of their conversion. And his using this appellation, when writing under the character of "the elder," has its peculiar beauty.

6. *Thou shalt do well.* How tenderly does the apostle enjoin this!

11. *Follow not that which is evil.* In Diotrephes. *But that which is good.* In Demetrius.

14. *Greet the friends by name.* That is, in the same manner as if I had named them one by one. The word "friend" does not often occur in the New Testament, being swallowed up in the more endearing one of "brother."

JUDE

4. *Certain men crept in unawares, who were before of old.* Even as early as Enoch; of whom it was foretold that by their willful sins they would incur *this condemnation.*

6. *And the angels which kept not their first estate.* Once assigned them under the Son of God. *But* [voluntarily] *left their own habitation.* Then properly their own, by the free gift of God. *In everlasting chains under darkness.* O how unlike their own habitation! When these fallen angels came out of the hands of God, they were holy; else God made that which was evil. And being holy, they were beloved of God; else he hated the image of his own spotless purity. But now he loves them no more; they are doomed to endless destruction (for if he loved them still, he would love what is sinful). And both his former love and his present righteous and eternal displeasure towards the same work of his own hands are because he changes not; because he invariably loves righteousness and hates iniquity.

9. *Yet Michael.* It does not appear whether Jude learned this by any revelation or from ancient tradition. It suffices that these things were not only true, but acknowledged as such by them to whom he wrote. *The archangel.* This word occurs but once more in the sacred writings (I Thess. 4:16). So that whether there be one archangel only, or more, it is not possible for us to determine. *When contending with the devil.* At what time we know not. *About the body of Moses.* Possibly the devil would have discovered the place where it was buried, which God for wise reasons had concealed.

11. *Woe unto them!* Of all the apostles, Jude alone, and that in this single place, pronounces a woe.

13. *Wandering stars.* In the Greek, "planets," which shine for a time, but have no light in themselves and will be soon cast into utter darkness. Thus the apostle illustrates their desperate wickedness by comparisons drawn from the air, earth, sea, and heavens.

19. *These be they who separate themselves, sensual, having not the Spirit.* Having natural senses and understanding only, not the Spirit of God; otherwise they could not *separate.* For that it is a sin, and a very heinous one, to separate from the church is beyond all question.

20. *Praying in the Holy Ghost.* Who alone is able to build you up, as he alone laid the foundation. In this and the following verse Jude mentions the Father, Son, and Spirit together with faith, love, and hope.

21. By these means, through his grace, *keep yourselves in the love of God,* and in the confident expectation of that *eternal life* which is purchased for you and conferred upon you through the *mercy of our Lord Jesus Christ.*

22–23. In the meantime, watch over others, as well as yourselves, and give them such help as their various needs require. For instance: (1) Some who are wavering in judgment, staggered by others' or by their own evil reasoning, endeavor more deeply to convince of the whole truth as it is in Jesus. (2) Some snatch with a swift and strong hand "out of the fire" of sin and temptation. (3) On others show *compassion* in a milder and gentler way; though still with a jealous *fear,* lest you be infected with the disease you endeavor to cure. See that while you love the sinners, you retain the utmost abhorrence of their sins, and of any the least degree of or approach to them.

Revelation

INTRODUCTION

It is scarce possible for any who either love or fear God not to feel their hearts extremely affected in seriously reading either the beginning or the latter part of the Revelation. These, it is evident, we cannot consider too much; but the intermediate parts I did not study at all for many years, as utterly despairing of understanding them after the fruitless attempts of so many wise and good men. And perhaps I should have lived and died in this sentiment had I not seen the works of the great Bengelius. But these revived my hopes of understanding even the prophecies of this book; at least many of them in some good degree, for perhaps some will not be opened but in eternity. Let us, however, bless God for the measure of light we may enjoy, and improve it to his glory.

The following notes are mostly those of that excellent man; a few of which are taken from his *Gnomon Novi Testamenti,* but far more from his *Ekklarte Offenbarung,* which is a full and regular comment on the Revelation. Every part of this I do not undertake to defend. But none should condemn him without reading his proofs at large. It did not suit my design to insert these; they are above the capacity of ordinary readers. Nor had I room to insert the entire translation of a book which contains nearly twelve hundred pages.

All I can do is partly to translate, partly abridge the most necessary of his observations; allowing myself the liberty to alter some of them, and to add a few notes where he is not full. His text, it may be observed, I have taken almost throughout, which I apprehend he has abundantly defended both in the *Gnomon* itself and in his *Apparatus* and *Crisis in Apocalypsin.*

Yet I by no means pretend to understand or explain all that is contained in this mysterious book. I only offer what help I can to the serious inquirer, and shall rejoice if any be moved thereby more carefully to read and more deeply to consider the words of this prophecy. Blessed is he who does this with a single eye. His labor shall not be in vain.

CHAPTER 1

3. *Happy*[1] is he that readeth, and they that hear the words of this prophecy. Some have miserably handled this book. Hence others are afraid to touch it and, while they desire to know all things else, reject only the knowledge of those which God has shown. They inquire after any thing rather than this; as if it were written, "Happy is he that doth *not* read this prophecy." No, but *happy is he that readeth, and they that hear . . . and keep those things which are written therein.* Especially at this time when so considerable a part of them is on the point of being fulfilled.

Nor are helps lacking whereby any sincere and diligent inquirer may understand what he reads therein. The book itself is written in the most accurate manner possible. It distinguishes the several things whereof it treats by seven epistles, seven seals, seven trumpets, seven vials; each of which sevens is divided into four and three. Many things the book itself explains: the seven stars; the seven candlesticks; the lamb and his seven horns and seven eyes; the incense; the dragon; the heads and horns of the beasts; the fine linen; the testimony of Jesus. And much light arises from comparing it with the ancient prophecies and the predictions in the other books of the New Testament.

In this book our Lord has comprised what was lacking in those prophecies touching the time which followed his ascension and the end of the Jewish polity. Accordingly, it reaches from the old Jerusalem to the new, reducing all things into one sum, in the exactest order, and with a near resemblance to the ancient prophets. The introduction and conclusion agree with Daniel; the description of the man-child and the promises to Zion, with Isaiah; the judgment of Babylon, with Jeremiah; again, the determination of times, with Daniel; the architecture of the holy city, with Ezekiel; the emblems of the horses, candlesticks, with Zechariah.

Many things largely described by the prophets are here summarily repeated, and frequently in the same words. To them we may then usefully have recourse. Yet the Revelation suffices for the explaining of itself, even if we do not yet understand those prophecies; yes, it casts much light upon them. Frequently, likewise, where there is a resemblance between them, there is a difference also; the Revelation, as it were, taking a stock from one of the old prophets, and inserting a new graft into it. Thus Zechariah speaks of two olive trees; and so does John, but with a different meaning. Daniel has a beast with ten horns; so has John; but not with quite the same significance. And here the difference of words, emblems, things, and times ought studiously to be observed.

Our Lord foretold many things before his Passion; but not all things, for it was not yet seasonable. Many things, likewise, his Spirit foretold in the writings of the apostles, so far as the necessities of those times required. Now he comprises them all in one short book; therein presupposing all the other prophecies and at the same time explaining, continuing, and perfecting them in one thread. It is right therefore to compare them; but not to measure the fullness of these by the scantiness of those preceding.

Christ, when on earth, foretold what would come to pass in a short time,

---

[1](1:3) KJV: "Blessed."

adding a brief description of the last things. Here he foretells the intermediate things; so that both put together constitute one complete chain of prophecy. This book is therefore not only the sum and the key of all the prophecies which preceded, but likewise a supplement to all; the seals being closed before. Of consequence, it contains many particulars not revealed in any other part of Scripture. They have therefore little gratitude to God for such a revelation reserved for the exaltation of Christ, who boldly reject whatever they find here which was not revealed, or not so clearly, in other parts of Scripture.

He that readeth, and they that hear. John probably sent this book by a single person into Asia, who read it in the churches, while many heard. But this, likewise, in a secondary sense refers to all that shall duly read or hear it in all ages. *The words of this prophecy.* It is a revelation with regard to Christ, who gives it; a prophecy with regard to John, who delivers it to the churches. *And keep those things which are written therein.* In such a manner as the nature of them requires; namely, with repentance, faith, patience, prayer, obedience, watchfulness, constancy. It behooves every Christian, at all opportunities, to read what is written in the oracles of God; and to read this precious book in particular, frequently, reverently, and attentively.

10. *I was in the Spirit.* That is, in a trance, a prophetic vision; so overwhelmed with the power and filled with the light of the Holy Spirit as to be insensible of outward things and wholly taken up with spiritual and divine. What follows is one single, connected vision which John saw in one day; and therefore he who would understand it should carry his thought straight on through the whole, without an interruption. The other prophetic books are collections of distinct prophecies, given upon various occasions; but here is one single treatise, whereof all the parts exactly depend on each other.

Chapter 4:1 is connected with chapter 1:19; and what is delivered in the fourth chapter goes on directly to the twenty-second.

11. *Saying, . . . What thou seest.* And hear. He both saw and heard. This command extends to the whole book. All the books of the New Testament were written by the will of God, but none were so expressly commanded to be written. *In a book.* So all the Revelation is but one book. Nor did the letter to the angel of each church belong to him or his church only; but the whole book was sent to them all.

17. *I fell at his feet as dead,* human nature not being able to sustain so glorious an appearance. Thus was he prepared (like Daniel of old, whom he peculiarly resembles) for receiving so weighty a prophecy. A great sinking of nature usually precedes a large communication of heavenly things. John, before our Lord suffered, was so intimate with him as to lean on his breast, to lie in his bosom. Yet now, near seventy years after, the aged apostle is by one glance struck to the ground. What a glory must this be! You sinners, be afraid; cleanse your hands; purify your hearts. You saints, be humble; prepare; rejoice. But rejoice unto him with reverence; an increase of reverence towards this awful majesty can be no prejudice to our faith. Let all petulance, with all vain curiosity, be far away while you are thinking or reading of these things.

CHAPTER 2

Of the letters to the angels of the churches it may be necessary to speak first in general, and then particularly.

In general we may observe that when the Israelites were to receive the law at Mount Sinai, they were first to be purified; and when the kingdom of God was at hand, John the Baptist prepared men for it by repentance. In like manner we are prepared by these letters for the worthy reception of this glorious revelation. By following the directions given herein, by expelling incorrigibly wicked men and putting away all wickedness, those churches were prepared to receive this precious depositum. And whoever in any age would profitably read or hear it must observe the same admonitions.

These letters are a kind of sevenfold preface to the book. It is not until Revelation 4:1 that John enters upon that grand vision which takes up the residue of the book.

The address in each letter is expressed in plain words; the promise, in figurative. In the address our Lord speaks to the angel of each church which then was, and to the members thereof directly; whereas in the promise he speaks of all that should overcome, in whatever church or age, and deals out to them one of the precious promises (by way of anticipation) from the last chapters of the book.

2. *I know.* Jesus knows all the good and all the evil which his servants and his enemies suffer and do. Weighty word, "I know"—how dreadful will it one day sound to the wicked, how sweet to the righteous! The churches and their angels must have been astonished to find their several states so exactly described, even in the absence of the apostle, and could not but acknowledge the all-seeing eye of the Christ and of his Spirit. With regard to us, to every one of us also he says, *I know thy works.* Happy is he that conceives less good of himself than Christ knows concerning him.

5. It is not possible for any to recover the "first love," but by taking these three steps: (1) Remember. (2) Repent. (3) Do the first works. *Remember therefore from whence thou art fallen.* From what degree of faith, love, holiness, though perhaps insensibly.

There can be no state, either of any pastor, church, or single person, which has not here suitable instructions. All, whether ministers or hearers, together with their secret or open enemies, in all places and all ages, may draw hence the necessary self-knowledge, reproof, commendation, warning, or confirmation. Whether any be as dead as the angel at Sardis, or as much alive as the angel at Philadelphia, this book is sent to him, and the Lord Jesus has something to say to him therein. For the seven churches with their angels represent the whole Christian church, dispersed throughout the whole world, as it subsists not, as some have imagined, in one age after another, but in every age. This is a point of deep importance, and always necessary to be remembered: that these seven churches are, as it were, a sample of the whole church of Christ, as it was then, as it is now, and as it will be in all ages.

7. In these seven letters twelve promises are contained, which are an extract of all the promises of God. In these promises sometimes the enjoyment of the highest goods, sometimes deliverances from the greatest evils, is mentioned. And each implies the other, so that where either part is expressed, the whole is to be understood. That part is expressed which has the most resemblance to the virtues or works of him spoken to in the letter preceding.

19. *I know thy . . . charity.* How different a character is this from that of the angel of the church at Ephesus! *And service, and faith, and thy patience.* Love is shown, exercised, and improved by serving God and our neighbor; so is faith by patience and good works.

28. *I will give him the morning star.* You, O Jesus, are the morning star! O give yourself to me! Then will I desire no sun, only you, who is the sun also. He whom this star enlightens has always morning and no evening. He that, after having conquered his enemies, keeps the works of Christ to the end shall have the morning star, an unspeakable brightness and peaceable dominion in him.

CHAPTER 3

7. *The holy one, the true one.*[2] Two great and glorious names. *He that hath the key of David.* A master of a family, or a prince, has one or more keys wherewith he can open and shut all the doors of his house or palace. So had David a key, a token of right and sovereignty, which was afterwards adjudged to Eliakim (Isa. 22:22). Then much more has Christ, the Son of David, the key of the spiritual city of David, the new Jerusalem; the supreme right, power, and authority, as in his own house.

22. *He that hath an ear, let him hear.* This stands in the three former letters before the promise; in the four latter, after it; clearly dividing the seven into two parts. The titles given our Lord in the three former letters peculiarly respect his power after his resurrection and ascension, particularly over his church; those in the four latter, his divine glory, and unity with the Father and the Holy Spirit. Again, this word being placed before the promises in the three former letters excludes the false prophets at Ephesus, the false Jews at Smyrna, and the partakers with the heathens at Pergamos from having any share therein. In the four latter, being placed after them, it leaves the promises immediately joined with Christ's address to the angel of the church, to show that the fulfilling of these was near; whereas the others reach beyond the end of the world.

It should be observed that the overcoming, or victory (to which alone these peculiar promises are annexed), is not the ordinary victory obtained by every believer; but a special victory over great and peculiar temptations by those that are strong in faith.

CHAPTER 4

We are now entering upon the main prophecy. The whole Revelation may be divided thus:

The first, second, and third chapters contain the introduction;

The fourth and fifth, the proposition;

The sixth, seventh, eighth, and ninth describe the things which are already fulfilled;

The tenth to the fourteenth, things which are now fulfilling;

The fifteenth to the nineteenth, things which will be fulfilled shortly;

The twentieth to twenty-second, things at a greater distance.

2. *And immediately I was in the spirit.* Even in a higher degree than before (Rev. 1:10). *And, behold, a throne was set in heaven.* Here commentators divide: and some proceed theologically; others, historically; whereas the right way is to join both together.

The court of heaven is here laid open; and the throne of God is, as it were, the center from which every thing in the visible world goes forth,

---

[2](3:7) KJV: "he that is holy, he that is true."

and to which every thing returns. Here, also, the kingdom of Satan to us disclosed; and hence we may extract the most important things out of the most comprehensive and, at the same time, most secret history of the kingdom of hell and heaven. But herein we must be content to know only what is expressly revealed in this book. This describes, not merely what good or evil is successively transacted on earth, but how each springs from the kingdom of light or darkness, and continually tends to the source whence it sprung; so that no man can explain all that is contained therein from the history of the church militant only.

And yet the histories of the past ages have their use, as this book is properly prophetical. The more, therefore, we observe the accomplishment of it, so much the more may we praise God, in his truth, wisdom, justice, and almighty power, and learn to suit ourselves to the time, according to the remarkable directions contained in the prophecy.

8. *Saying, Holy, holy, holy.* Is the Three-One God. There are two words in the original, very different from each other; both which we translate "holy." The one means properly "merciful"; but the other, which occurs here, implies much more. This holiness is the sum of all praise which is given to the almighty Creator for all that he does and reveals concerning himself until the new song brings with it new matter of glory. This word properly signifies "separated," both in Hebrew and other languages. God is separate from all things. He is and works from himself, out of himself, in himself, through himself, for himself. Therefore he is the first and the last, the only one and the Eternal, living and happy, endless and unchangeable, almighty, omniscient, wise and true, just and faithful, gracious and merciful. Hence it is that

"holy" and "holiness" mean the same as "god" and "Godhead"; and as we say of a king, "His Majesty," so the Scripture says of God, "His Holiness" (Heb. 12:10).

This holiness is often styled "glory." That is also termed "holy" which is consecrated to him, and for that end separated from other things; and so is that wherein we may be like God, or united to him.

In the hymn resembling this, recorded by Isaiah (6:3), is added, "The whole earth is full of his glory." But this is deferred in the Revelation until the glory of the Lord (his enemies being destroyed) fills the earth.

11. *Thou art worthy.* This he receives not only when he is thus praised, but also when he destroys his enemies and glorifies himself anew. *Glory and honour and power.* Answering the thrice-holy of the living creatures (v. 9). *For thou hast created all things.* Creation is the ground of all the works of God; therefore for this, as well as for his other works, will he be praised to all eternity.

CHAPTER 5

1. It is scarce needful to observe that there is not in heaven any real book of parchment or paper or that Christ does not really stand there in the shape of a lion or of a lamb. Neither is there on earth any monstrous beast with seven heads and ten horns. But as there is upon earth something which, in its kind, answers such a representation; so there are in heaven divine counsels and transactions answerable to these figurative expressions. All this was represented to John at Patmos in one day by way of vision, but the accomplishment of it extends from that time throughout all ages.

The *book* and its *seals* represent all power in heaven and earth given to

Christ. A copy of this book is contained in the following chapters. By "the trumpets," contained under the seventh seal, the kingdom of this world is shaken, that it may at length become the kingdom of Christ. By "the vials," under the seventh trumpet, the power of the beast, and whatsoever is connected with it, is broken. This sum of all we should have continually before our eyes; so the whole Revelation flows in its natural order.

13. What is *in heaven* says *blessing;* what is *on the earth, . . . honour;* what is *under the earth, . . . glory;* what is *in the sea, . . . power.* This praise from all creatures begins before the opening of the first seal; but it continues from that time to eternity, according to the capacity of each. His enemies must acknowledge his *glory;* but those in heaven say, "Blessed be God and the Lamb."

This royal manifesto is, as it were, a proclamation that shows how Christ fulfills all things, and "every knee shall bow." It inspires the attentive and intelligent reader with such a magnanimity that he accounts nothing in this world great; no, not the whole frame of visible nature, compared to the immense greatness of what he is here called to behold, yes, and in part, to inherit.

CHAPTER 6

The seven seals are not distinguished from each other by specifying the time of them. They swiftly follow the letters to the seven churches, and all begin almost at the same time.

Before we proceed, it may be observed, (1) No man should constrain either himself or another to explain every thing in this book. It is sufficient for every one to speak just so far as he understands. (2) We should remember that, although the ancient prophets wrote the occurrences of those kingdoms only with which Israel had to do, yet the Revelation contains what relates to the whole world, through which the Christian church is extended. Yet, (3) We should not prescribe to this prophecy as if it must needs admit or exclude this or that history, according as we judge one or the other to be of great or small importance. "God seeth not as a man seeth"; therefore what we think great is often omitted, what we think little inserted, in Scripture history or prophecy. (4) We must take care not to overlook what is already fulfilled; and not to describe as fulfilled what is still to come.

We are to look in history for the fulfilling of the four first seals, quickly after the date of the prophecy. In each of these appears a different horseman.

2. *A white horse.* Trajan's accession to the empire seems to be the dawning of these seven seals. *And he went forth conquering, and to conquer.* That is, from one victory to another. We find no emperor like Trajan for making conquests. He aimed at nothing else; he lived only to conquer. Meantime, in him was eminently fulfilled what had been prophesied of the fourth empire (Dan. 2:40; 7:23), that he should "devour, . . . tread down, . . . and break in pieces . . . the whole earth." As soon as Trajan ascended the throne, peace was taken from the earth.

5-6. *And lo a black horse.* A fit emblem of mourning and distress; particularly of "black famine," as the ancient poets term it. This was also fulfilled in the reign of Trajan, especially in Egypt, which lay southward from Patmos. In this country, which used to be the granary of the empire, there was an uncommon dearth at the very beginning of his reign; so that he was obliged to supply Egypt itself with corn from other countries. The same scarcity there was in the thirteenth year of his reign, the harvest failing for lack of the rising of the Nile.

8. The first seal brought victory with it; in the second was "a great sword"; but here a *scimitar*.[3] In the third was moderate dearth; here famine and plague and wild *beasts* beside. And it may well be that from the time of Trajan downwards, the fourth part of men upon the earth, that is, within the Roman Empire, died by sword, famine, pestilence, and wild beasts. It is observable that war brings on scarcity, and scarcity pestilence through want of wholesome sustenance; and pestilence, by depopulating the country, leaves the few survivors an easier prey to the wild beasts. And this these judgments make way for one another in the order wherein they are here represented.

10. *O Lord.* The Greek word properly signifies the master of a family; it is therefore beautifully used by these, who are peculiarly of the household of God. *Dost thou not judge and avenge our blood.* There is no impure affection in heaven; therefore this desire of theirs is pure and suitable to the will of God. The martyrs are concerned for the praise of their Master, of his holiness and truth; and the praise is given him (Rev. 19:2) where the prayer of the martyrs is changed into a thanksgiving.

CHAPTER 7

4. *Of the children of Israel.* To these will afterwards be joined a multitude out of all nations. But it may be observed, this is not the number of all the Israelites who are saved from Abraham or Moses to the end of all things; but only of those who were secured from the plagues which were then ready to fall on the earth. It seems as if this book had, in many places, a special view to the people of Israel.

9. *A great multitude.* Of those who had happily finished their course. Such multitudes are afterwards described, and still higher degrees of glory which they attain after a sharp fight and magnificent victory (Rev. 14:1; 15:2; 19:1; 20:4). There is an inconceivable variety in the degrees of reward in the other world. Let not any slothful one say, "If I get to heaven at all, I will be content!" Such a one may let heaven go altogether. In worldly things, men are ambitious to get as high as they can. Christians have a far more noble ambition. The difference between the very highest and the lowest state in the world is nothing to the smallest difference between the degrees of glory. But who has time to think of this? Who is at all concerned about it?

10. *Salvation to our God.* Who has saved us from all evil into all the happiness of heaven. The salvation for which they praise God is described, verse 15; that for which they praise the Lamb, verse 14; and both, in the sixteenth and seventeenth verses.

17. *For the Lamb . . . shall feed them.* With eternal peace and joy; so that they shall hunger no more. *And shall lead them unto living fountains of waters.* The comforts of the Holy Ghost; so that they shall thirst no more. Neither shall they suffer or grieve any more, for *God shall wipe away all tears from their eyes.*

CHAPTER 8

2. *To them were given seven trumpets.* When men desire to make known openly a thing of public concern, they give a token that may be seen or heard

---

[3](6:8) KJV: "sword."

far and wide; and among such, none are more ancient than trumpets (Lev. 25:9; Num. 10:2; Amos 3:6). The Israelites in particular used them, both in the warship of God and in war; therewith openly praising the power of God before, after, and in the battle (Josh. 6:4; II Chron. 13:14). And the angels here made known by these trumpets the wonderful works of God, whereby all opposing powers are successively shaken, until the kingdom of the world becomes the kingdom of God and his Anointed.

These trumpets reach nearly from the time of John to the end of the world.

7. *The first angel sounded.* Thus vengeance began at the Jewish enemies of Christ's kingdom; though even then the Romans did not quite escape. But afterwards it came upon them more and more violently: the second trumpet affects the Roman heathens in particular; the third, the dead, unholy Christians; the fourth, the empire itself.

9. *And the third part of the ships were destroyed.* It is a frequent thing to resemble a state or republic to a ship, wherein many people are embarked together and share in the same dangers. And how many states were utterly destroyed by those inhuman conquerors! Much likewise of this was literally fulfilled. How often was the sea tinged with blood! How many of those who dwelt mostly upon it were killed! And what number of ships destroyed!

10. *A great star.* Arianism was the inlet to all heresies and calamities, and at length to Mohammedanism itself. This *great star* was not an angel, but a teacher of the church, one of the stars in the right hand of Christ. Such was Arius. He fell from on high, as it were *from heaven,* into the most pernicious doctrines, and made in his fall a gazing on all sides, being *great* and now *burning* as a torch.

12. *And the third part of the sun was smitten.* Or, struck. An eclipse of the sun or moon is termed by the Hebrews a "stroke." Now, as such a darkness does not come all at once, but by degrees, so likewise did the darkness which fell on the Roman, particularly the Western, Empire. One province was lost after another until, in the year 476, Odoacer seized upon Rome, deposed the emperor, and put an end to the empire itself.

CHAPTER 9

2–3. *And there arose a smoke out of the pit.* The locusts, who afterwards rise out of it, seem to be the Persians; agreeable to which, this smoke is their detestable, idolatrous doctrine, and false zeal for it, which now broke out in an uncommon paroxysm. *And the sun and the air were darkened.* A figurative expression denoting heavy affliction. This smoke occasioned more and more such darkness over the Jews in Persia. *There came out of the smoke locusts.* A known emblem of a numerous, hostile, hurtful people. Such were the Persians, from whom the Jews in the sixth century suffered beyond expression.

12. *One woe is past.* The Persian power, under which was the first woe, was now broken by the Saracens.

15. The power of the Saracens so increased that within fourscore years after Mohammed's death they had extended their conquests farther than the warlike Romans did in four hundred years.

20. *That they should not worship devils.* The invocation of departed saints, whether true or false or doubtful or forged, crept early into the Christian church and was carried farther and farther; and who knows how many who are invoked as saints are among evil, not good, angels; or how far devils have mingled with such blind worship and with the wonders wrought on those occasions?

21. *Neither repented they of their murders, nor of their sorceries.* Whoever reads the histories of the seventh, eighth, and ninth centuries will find numberless instances of these in every part of the Christian world. But though God cut off so many of the scandals to the Christian name, yet the rest went on in the same course. Some of them, however, might repent under the plagues which follow.

CHAPTER 10

7. *The mystery of God should be finished.* It is said (Rev. 17:17), "The words of God shall be fulfilled." The word of God is fulfilled by the destruction of the beast; *the mystery,* by the removal of the dragon. But these great events are so near together that they are here mentioned as one. The beginning of them is in heaven, as soon as the seventh trumpet sounds; the end is on the earth and the sea. *As he hath declared to his servants the prophets.* The accomplishment exactly answering the prediction. The ancient prophecies relate partly to that grand period from the birth of Christ to the destruction of Jerusalem; partly to the time of the seventh angel, wherein they will be fully accomplished. To the seventh trumpet belongs all that occurs from Revelation 11:15 to 22:5.

11. *Thou must prophesy again.* Of the mystery of God; of which the ancient prophets had prophesied before. And he did prophesy, by "measuring the temple" (Rev. 11:1); as a prophecy may be delivered either by words or actions. *Many peoples, and nations, and tongues, and kings.* The people, nations, and tongues are contemporary; but the kings, being many, succeed one an-

other. These kings are not mentioned for their own sake, but with a view to the "holy city" (Rev. 11:2). Here is a reference to the great kingdoms in Spain, England, Italy, etc., which arose from the eighth century; or at least underwent a considerable change, as France and Germany in particular; to the Christian, afterward Turkish, empire in the East; and especially to the various potentates who have successively reigned at or over Jerusalem and do now, at least titularly, reign over it.

CHAPTER 11

1. In this chapter is shown how it will fare with the "holy city" until the mystery of God is fulfilled; in the twelfth, what will befall the woman who is delivered of the man-child; in the thirteenth, how it will be with the kingdom of Christ while the "two beasts" are in the height of their power. *And measure the temple of God.* At Jerusalem, where John was placed in the vision. Of this we have a large description by Ezekiel (chs. 40–48).

2. *Shall they tread under foot.* Inhabit. So they began to do before John wrote. And it has been trodden almost ever since by the Romans, Persians, Saracens, and Turks. But that severe kind of treading which is here peculiarly spoken of will not be until the trumpet of the seventh angel and towards the end of the troublous times.

3. *My two witnesses.* These seem to be two prophets; two select, eminent instruments. Some have supposed (though without foundation) that they are Moses and Elijah, whom they resemble in several respects. *And they shall prophesy a thousand two hundred and threescore days.* Common days, that is, an hundred and eighty weeks. So long will they *prophesy* (even while the last and sharp treading of the holy city continues), both by word and deed, witnessing that Jesus is the Son of God, the heir of all things, and exhorting all men to repent and fear and glorify God.

4. *These are the two olive trees.* That is, as Zerubbabel and Joshua, the two olive trees spoken of by Zechariah (3:9; 4:10), were then the two chosen instruments in God's hand, even so shall these be in their season. Being themselves full of the unction of the Holy One, they shall continually transmit the same to others also. *Standing before the God of the earth.* Always waiting on God, without the help of man, and asserting his right over the earth and all things therein.

9. *Three days and a half.* So exactly are the times set down in this prophecy. If we suppose this time began in the evening and ended in the morning and included (which is no way impossible) Friday, Saturday, and Sunday, the weekly festival of the Turkish people, the Jewish tribes, and the Christian tongues; then all these together, with the heathen nations, would have full leisure to gaze upon and rejoice over them.

13. *Was there a great earthquake, and the tenth part of the city fell.* We have here an unanswerable proof that this city is not Babylon or Rome, but Jerusalem. For Babylon shall be wholly burned before the fulfilling of the mystery of God. *And the remnant.* The remaining sixty-three thousand were converted; a grand step toward the fulfilling of the mystery of God. Such a conversion we no where else read of. So there shall be a larger as well as holier church at Jerusalem than ever was yet.

15. *The kingdoms of this world.* That is, the royal government over the whole world, and all its kingdoms (Zech. 14:9). *Are become the kingdoms of our Lord.* This province has been in the enemy's hands; it now returns to its rightful Master. In the Old Testament, from Moses to Samuel, God himself was the King of his own people. And the same will be in the New Testament; he will himself reign over the Israel of God. *And of his Christ.* This appellation is now first given him since the introduction of the book, on the mention of the kingdom devolving upon him, under the seventh trumpet. Prophets and priests were anointed, but more especially kings; wherefore that term, "anointed," is applied only to a king. Accordingly, whenever the Messiah is mentioned in Scripture, his kingdom is implied. *Are become.* In reality, all things (and so the kingdom of this world) are God's in all ages; yet Satan and the present world, with its kings and lords, are risen against the Lord and against his Anointed. God now puts an end to this monstrous rebellion and maintains his right to all things.

CHAPTER 12

1. *A great wonder in heaven.* A *wonder,* or sign, means something that has an uncommon appearance and from which we infer that some unusual thing will follow. *A woman.* The emblem of the church of Christ, as she is originally of Israel, though built and enlarged on all sides by the addition of heathen converts; and as she will hereafter appear, when all her "natural branches" are again "grafted in." She is at present on earth; and yet, with regard to her union with Christ, she may be said to be in heaven (Eph. 2:6). Accordingly, she is described as both assaulted and defended in heaven (vv. 4, 7).

Clothed with the sun, and the moon under her feet. These figurative expressions must be so interpreted as to preserve a due proportion between them. So, in Joseph's dream, the sun betokened his father; the moon, his mother; the stars, their children. There may be some such resemblance here; and as the prophecy points out the "power over all nations," perhaps the sun may betoken the Christian world; the moon, the Mohammedans, who also carry the moon in their ensigns; and the *crown of twelve stars,* the twelve tribes of Israel, which are smaller than the sun and the moon. This chapter answers the state of the church from the ninth century to this time.

2. *And she being with child cried, travailing in birth.* The very pain, without any outward opposition, would constrain a woman in travail to cry out. These cries, throes, and pains to be delivered were the painful longings, the sighs, and prayers of the saints for the coming of the kingdom of God. The woman groaned and travailed in spirit, that Christ might appear as the Shepherd and King of all nations.

6. *And the woman fled into the wilderness.* This wilderness is undoubtedly on earth, where the woman also herself is now supposed to be. It betokens that part of the earth where, after having brought forth, she found a new abode. And this must be in Europe; as Asia and Africa were wholly in the hands of the Turks and Saracens; and in a part of it where the woman had not been before. In this wilderness, God had already *prepared . . . a place,* that is, made it safe and convenient for her. The wilderness is those countries of Europe which lie on this side of the Danube; for the countries which lie beyond it had received Christianity before.

That they should feed her. That the people of that place may provide all things needful for her. *A thousand two hundred and threescore days.* So many

prophetic days, which are not, as some have proposed, twelve hundred and sixty, but seven hundred and seventy-seven, common years. This Bengelius has shown at large in his German introduction. These we may compute from the year 847 to 1524. So long the woman enjoyed a safe and convenient place in Europe, which was chiefly Bohemia; where she was fed until God provided for her more plentifully at the Reformation.

7. *And there was war in heaven.* Here Satan makes his grand opposition to the kingdom of God; but an end is now put to his accusing the saints before God. The cause goes against him (vv. 10–11), and Michael executes the sentence. Satan would be like God; the very name of Michael asks, "Who is like God?" Not Satan; not the highest archangel. It is he likewise that is afterward employed to seize, bind, and imprison that proud spirit.

12. We are now come to a most important period of time. We live in the *short time* wherein Satan has great wrath; and this *short time* is now upon the decline. We are in the "time, times, and half a time" wherein the woman is "fed in the wilderness"; yes, the last part of it, the "half time," is begun. We are towards the close of the "forty-two months" of the beast; and when his number is fulfilled, grievous things will come to pass.

God has not given this prophecy in so solemn a manner only to show his providence over his church, but also that his servants may know at all times in what particular period they are. The more dangerous any time is, the greater is the help which it affords.

CHAPTER 13

1. O reader, this is a subject wherein we also are deeply concerned and which must be treated, not as a point of curiosity, but as a solemn warning from God! The danger is near. Be armed both against force and fraud, even with the whole armor of God. *Out of the sea.* That is, Europe. This beast is the Roman papacy, as it came to a point six hundred years since, stands now, and will for some time longer. To this, and to no other power of earth, agrees the whole text, and every part of it in every point. This beast is a spiritually secular power, opposite to the kingdom of Christ. A power not merely spiritual or ecclesiastical, nor merely secular or political; but a mixture of both.

7. *To make war with the saints.* With the Waldenses and the Albigenses. Against these many of the popes made open war. Until now the blood of Christians had been shed only by the heathens or Arians; from this time, by scarce any but the papacy.

CHAPTER 14

1. *An hundred forty and four thousand.* Either those out of all mankind who had been the most eminently holy, or the most holy out of the twelve tribes of Israel; the same that were mentioned in Revelation 7:4 and perhaps also in Revelation 15:2. They are now in safety and have the *name* of the Lamb and of his Father *written in their foreheads* as being the redeemed of God and of the Lamb, his now inalienable property. This prophecy often introduces the inhabitants of heaven as a kind of chorus with great propriety and elegance. The church above, making suitable reflections on the grand events which are foretold in this book, greatly serves to raise the attention of real Christians and to teach the high concern they have in them. Thus is the church on earth instructed, animated, and encouraged by the sentiments,

temper, and devotion of the church in heaven.

8. *Saying, Babylon is fallen.* With the overthrow of Babylon, that of all the enemies of Christ and, consequently, happier times are connected. *Babylon* "the Great." So the city of Rome is called upon many accounts. Babylon was magnificent, strong, proud, powerful; so is Rome also. Babylon was first, Rome afterwards, the residence of the emperors of the world. What Babylon was to Israel of old, Rome has been to the literal and spiritual "Israel of God." Hence the liberty of the ancient Jews was connected with the overthrow of the Babylonian Empire. And when Rome is finally overthrown, then the people of God will be at liberty.

Whenever Babylon is mentioned in this book, "the Great" is added, to teach us that Rome then commenced Babylon when it commenced the great city. Its spiritual greatness began in the fifth century and increased from age to age. It seems it will come to its utmost height just before its final overthrow.

Her *fornication* is her idolatry; invocation of saints and angels; worship of images; human traditions; with all that outward pomp, yes, and that fierce and bloody zeal wherewith she pretends to serve God.

12. *Here is the patience of the saints.* Seen in suffering all things rather than receive this mark. *That keep the commandments of God.* The character of all true saints; and particularly the great command to believe in Jesus.

15. *Thrust in thy sickle, . . . for the harvest . . . is ripe.* This implies a high degree of holiness in those good men, and an earnest desire to be with God.

CHAPTER 15

3–4. *And they sing the song of Moses.* So called, partly from its near agreement with the words of that song which he sung after passing the Red Sea (Exod. 15:11) and of that which he taught the children of Israel a little before his death (Deut. 32:3–4). But chiefly because Moses was the minister and representative of the Jewish church, as Christ is of the church universal. Therefore it is also termed *the song of the Lamb*. It consist of six parts, which answer each other:

(1) *Great and marvellous are thy works,*
  (2) *for thou only art gracious.*[4]
(3) *Just and true are thy ways,* (4) *for all nations shall come and worship before thee.*
(5) *Who shall not fear thee . . . and glorify thy name?* (6) *For thy judgments are made manifest.*

For thou only art gracious. And this grace is the spring of all those wonderful works, even of his destroying the enemies of his people. Accordingly in Psalm 136, that clause "For his mercy endureth for ever" is subjoined to the thanksgiving for his works of vengeance as well as for his delivering the righteous. *For all nations.* This is a glorious testimony of the future conversion of all the heathens. The Christians are now a little flock; they who do not worship God, an immense multitude. But *all nations shall come,* from all parts of the earth, to *worship* him and *glorify* his name. And then the inhabitants of the earth will at length learn to fear him.

8. *And the temple was filled with smoke.* The cloud of glory was the visible manifestation of God's presence in the tabernacle and temple. It was a sign of protection at erecting the tabernacle and at the dedication of the temple. But in the judgment of Korah

the glory of the Lord appeared, when he and his companions were swallowed up by the earth. So proper is the emblem of smoke from the glory of God, or from the cloud of glory, to express the execution of judgment as well as to be a sign of favor. Both proceed from the power of God, and in both he is glorified.

CHAPTER 16

1. *Pour out the vials.* The epistles to the seven churches are divided into three and four; the seven seals, and so the trumpets and vials, into four and three. The trumpets gradually, and in a long tract of time, overthrow the kingdoms of the world; the vials destroy chiefly the beast and his followers, with a swift and impetuous force. The four first affect the earth, the sea, the rivers, the sun; the rest fall elsewhere and are much more terrible.

5. *The Gracious one.*[5] So he is styled when his judgments are abroad, and that with a peculiar propriety. In the beginning of the book he is termed "the Almighty." In the time of his patience he is praised for his power, which otherwise might then be less regarded; in the time of his taking vengeance, for his mercy. Of his power there could be no doubt.

10. The four first vials are closely connected together; the fifth concerns the throne of the beast, the sixth the Mohammedans, the seventh chiefly the heathens.

15. *Behold, I come as a thief.* Suddenly, unexpectedly. Observe the beautiful abruptness. *Blessed is he that watcheth.* Looking continually for him that "comes quickly." *And keepeth his gar-*

---

[4] (15:3–4) KJV: "holy."
[5] (16:5) Wesley's version renders the verse: "Righteous art thou, who art, and who wast, the Gracious one, because thou hast judged thus."

ments. Which men use to put off when they sleep. *Lest he walk naked, and they see his shame.* Lest he lose the graces which he takes care to keep, and others see his sin and punishment.

CHAPTER 17

3. *I saw a woman.* Both the Scripture and other writers frequently represent a city under this emblem. This woman is the city of Rome, with its buildings and inhabitants, especially the nobles.

5. *And upon her forehead was a name written.* Whereas the saints have the name of God and the lamb on their foreheads.

12. *The ten horns . . . are ten kings.* They are ten secular potentates contemporary with, not succeeding, each other, who receive authority *with the beast,* probably in some convention, which, after a very short space, they will deliver up to the beast. Because of their short continuance, only *power as kings,* not a kingdom, is ascribed to them. While they retain this authority, or power, together with the beast, he will be stronger than ever before; but far stronger still, when their power is also transferred to him.

CHAPTER 18

1. *And the earth was lightened with his glory.* To make his coming more conspicuous. If such be the luster of the servant, what images can display the majesty of the Lord, who has "thousands of thousands" of those glorious attendants ministering to him, and "ten thousand times ten thousand" standing before him?

13. *And chariots.* A purely Latin word is here inserted in the Greek. This John undoubtedly used on purpose in describing the luxury of Rome.

22. Arts of every kind, particularly music, sculpture, painting, and statuary, were there carried to their greatest height. *Shall be heard no more at all in thee.* Not only the arts that adorn life, but even those employments without which it cannot subsist, will cease from you for ever. All these expressions denote absolute and eternal desolation. *The voice of harpers.* Music was the entertainment of the rich and great; trade, the business of men of middle rank; preparing bread and the necessities of life, the employment of the lowest people; marriages, in which lamps and songs were known ceremonies, are the means of peopling cities, as new births supply the place of those that die. The desolation of Rome is therefore described in such a manner as to show that neither rich nor poor, neither persons of middle rank nor those of the lowest condition, should be able to live there any more. Neither shall it be repeopled by new marriages, but remain desolate and uninhabited for ever.

CHAPTER 19

1. *Saying, Alleluia.* This Hebrew word signifies "Praise Jah," or "Him that is." God named himself to Moses, "Eheieh," that is, "I will be" (Exod. 3:14); and at the same time, "Jehovah," that is, "He that is, and was, and is to come." During the trumpet of the seventh angel he is styled "He that is and was" (Rev. 16:5), and not "He that is to come"; because his long-expected coming is under this trumpet actually present. At length he is styled "Jah," "He that is," the past together with the future being swallowed up in the present, the former things being no more mentioned, for the greatness of those that now are. The title is of all others the most peculiar to the everlasting God.

7. *The marriage of the Lamb is come.* Is near at hand, to be solemnized speedily. What this implies, none of "the spirits of just men," even in paradise yet know. O what things are those which are yet behind! And what purity of heart should there be to meditate upon them. *And his wife hath made herself ready.* Even upon earth; but in a far higher sense, in that world. After a time allowed for this, the new Jerusalem comes down, both made ready and adorned (Rev. 21:2).

8. The bride is all holy men, the whole invisible church. *Arrayed in fine linen, clean and white.* This is an emblem of *the righteousness of saints,* both of their justification and sanctification.

9. *Write.* John seems to have been so amazed at these glorious sights that he needed to be reminded of this.

11. *And I saw the heaven opened.* This is a new and peculiar opening of it in order to show the magnificent expedition of Christ and his attendants against his great adversary. *And behold a white horse.* Many little regarded Christ when he came meek, "riding upon an ass"; but what will they say when he goes forth upon his white horse, with the sword of his mouth?

15. This ruler of the nations was born (or appeared as such) immediately after the seventh angel began to sound. He now appears, not as a child, but as a victorious warrior. The nations have long ago felt his *rod of iron,* partly while the heathen Romans, after their savage persecution of the Christians, themselves anguished under numberless plagues and calamities, by his righteous vengeance; partly, while other heathens have been broken in pieces by those who bore the Christian name. For although the cruelty, for example, of the Spaniards in America, was unrighteous and detestable, yet did God therein execute his righteous judgment on the unbelieving nations; but they shall experience his iron rod as they never did yet, and then will they all return to their rightful Lord.

20. Here is the last of *the beast.* After several repeated strokes of omnipotence, he is gone alive into hell. There were two that went alive into heaven; perhaps there are two that go alive into hell. It may be, Enoch and Elijah entered at once into glory without first waiting in paradise; *the beast* and *the false prophet* plunge at once into the extremest degree of torment without being reserved in chains of darkness until the judgment of the great day.

21. *The remnant were slain.* A like difference is afterwards made between the devil, and Gog and Magog (Rev. 20:9–10).

Here is a most magnificent description of the overthrow of the beast and his adherents. It has, in particular, one exquisite beauty that, after exhibiting the two opposite armies and all the apparatus for a battle (vv. 11–19), then follows immediately (v. 20) the account of the victory without one word of an engagement or fighting. Here is the most exact propriety; for what struggle can there be between omnipotence and the power of all the creation united against it! Every description must have fallen short of this admirable silence.

CHAPTER 20

2. *And bound him a thousand years.* That these thousand do not precede or run parallel with, but wholly follow, the times of the beast may manifestly appear, (1) From the series of the whole book, representing one continued chain of events. (2) From the circumstances which precede. The woman's bringing forth is followed by the casting of the dragon out of heaven to the earth. With this is connected the third woe, under which the dragon through, and with, the beast rages horribly. At the conclusion of the third woe the beast is overthrown and cast "into a lake of fire." At the same time the other grand enemy, the dragon, shall be bound and shut up. (3) These thousand years bring a new, full, and lasting immunity from all outward and inward evils, the authors of which are now removed, and an affluence of all blessings. But such a time the church has never yet seen.

(4) These thousand years are followed by the last times of the world, the letting loose of Satan, who gathers together Gog and Magog and is thrown to the beast and false prophet into the lake of fire. Now Satan's accusing the saints in heaven, his rage on earth, his imprisonment in the abyss, his seducing Gog and Magog, and being cast into the lake of fire evidently succeed each other. (5) What occurs from 20:11 to 22:5 manifestly follows the things related in the nineteenth chapter. The thousand years came between; whereas if they were past, neither the beginning nor the end of them would fall within this period. In a short time those who assert that they are now at hand will appear to have spoken the truth.

Meantime, let every man consider what kind of happiness he expects therein. The danger does not lie in maintaining that the thousand years are yet to come; but in interpreting them, whether past or to come, in a gross and carnal sense. The doctrine of the Son of God is a mystery. So is his cross; and so is his glory. In all these he is a sign that is spoken against. Happy they who believe and confess him in all!

3. *That he should deceive the nations no more.* One benefit only is here expressed as resulting from the confinement of Satan. But how many and great bless-ings are implied! For the grand enemy being removed, the kingdom of God holds on its uninterrupted course among the nations; and the great mystery of God, so long foretold, is at length fulfilled; namely, when the beast is destroyed and Satan bound.

This fulfillment approaches nearer and nearer; and contains things of the utmost importance, the knowledge of which becomes every day more distinct and easy. In the meantime it is highly necessary to guard against the present rage and subtlety of the devil. Quickly he will be bound. When he is loosed again, the martyrs will live and reign with Christ. Then follow his coming in glory, the new heaven, new earth, and new Jerusalem. *The bottomless pit* is properly the devil's prison; afterwards he is cast into the lake of fire. He can *deceive the nations no more, till the thousand years* [v. 2] *are fulfilled.* Then *he must be loosed.* So does the mysterious wisdom of God permit. *A little season.* Small comparatively; although upon the whole it cannot be very short, because the things which are to be transacted therein (vv. 8–9) must take up a considerable space.

We are very shortly to expect, one after another, the calamities occasioned by the second beast, the harvest and the vintage, the pouring out of the vials, the judgment of Babylon, the last raging of the beast and his destruction, the imprisonment of Satan. How great these things be! And how short the time! What is needful for us? Wisdom, patience, faithfulness, watchfulness. It is no time to settle upon our lees. This is not, if it be rightly understood, an acceptable message to the wise, the mighty, the honourable of this world. Yet that which is to be done shall be done; there is no counsel against the Lord.

4. *And they lived.* Their souls and

bodies being reunited. *And reigned with Christ.* Not on earth, but in heaven. The "reigning on earth" mentioned (Rev. 11:15) is quite different from this. *A thousand years.* It must be observed that two distinct thousand years are mentioned throughout this whole passage. Each is mentioned thrice; the thousand wherein Satan is bound, verses 2–3, 7; the thousand wherein the saints shall reign, verses 4–6. The former end before the end of the world; the latter reach to the general resurrection. So that the beginning and end of the former thousand is before the beginning and end of the latter. Therefore as in the second verse at the first mention of the former, so in the fourth verse at the first mention of the latter, it is only said, "*a* thousand years"; in the other places (vv. 3, 5, 7), "*the* thousand," that is, the thousand mentioned before. During the former, the promises concerning the flourishing state of the church (Rev. 10:7) shall be fulfilled; during the latter, while the saints reign with Christ in heaven, men on earth will be careless and secure.

5. *The rest of the dead lived.* Mentioned in verse 4. *Were finished.* The thousand years during which Satan is bound begin and end much sooner.

The small time, and the second thousand years, begin at the same point, immediately after the first thousand. But neither the beginning of the first nor of the second thousand will be known to the men upon earth, as both the imprisonment of Satan and his loosing are transacted in the invisible world.

By observing these two distinct thousand years, many difficulties are avoided. There is room enough for the fulfilling of all the prophecies, and those which before seemed to clash are reconciled; particularly those which speak, on the one hand, of a most flourishing state of the church as yet to come; and, on the other, of the fatal security of men in the last days of the world.

7. *And when the* [former] *thousand years are expired, Satan shall be loosed out of his prison.* At the same time that the first resurrection begins. There is a great resemblance between this passage and Revelation 12:12. As at the casting out of the dragon there was joy in heaven, but there was woe upon earth; so at the loosing of Satan, the saints begin to reign with Christ; but the nations on earth are deceived.

11. *A great white throne.* How great, who can say? *White* with the glory of God, of him that sat upon it, Jesus Christ. The apostle does not attempt to describe him here; only adds that circumstance, far above all description, *from whose face the earth and the heaven fled away.* Probably both the aerial and the starry heaven, which "shall pass away with a great noise." *And there was found no place for them.* But they were wholly dissolved, the very elements melting "with fervent heat." And all this, not at the strict command of the Lord Jesus; not at his awful presence, or before his fiery indignation; but at the mere presence of his Majesty, sitting with severe but adorable dignity on his throne.

12. *And I saw the dead.* Of every age and condition. This includes also those who undergo a change equivalent to death (I Cor. 15:51). *And the books.* Human judges have their books written with pen and ink. How different is the nature of these books! *Were opened.* O how many hidden things will then come to light; and how many will have quite another appearance than they had before in the sight of men! With the book of God's omniscience, that of conscience will then exactly tally. The book of natural law, as well as of revealed, will then also be displayed. It is not said, "The books will be read"; the light of that day will make them visible to all. Then, particularly, shall every man know himself, and that with the last exactness. This will be the first true, full, impartial, universal history.

And another book. Wherein are enrolled all that are accepted through the Beloved; all who lived and died in the faith that worketh by love. *Which is the book of life.* What manner of expectation will then be, with regard to the issue of the whole!

CHAPTER 21

1. *A new heaven and a new earth.* After the resurrection and the general judgment. John is not now describing a flourishing state of the church, but a new and eternal state of all things.

2. *And I . . . saw the holy city.* The new heaven, the new earth, and the new Jerusalem are closely connected. This city is wholly new, belonging not to this world, not to the millennium, but to eternity. This appears from the series of the vision, the magnificence of the description, and the opposition of this city to the second death.

3. *They shall be his people.* So shall the covenant between God and his people be executed in the most glorious manner.

4. *And there shall be no more death.* This is a full proof that this whole description belongs not to time, but eternity. The saints have everlasting life and joy.

10. *And he carried me away in the spirit.* The same expression as before (Rev. 17:3). *And shewed me that great city, the holy Jerusalem.* The old city is now forgotten, so that this is no longer termed the "new," but absolutely Jerusalem. O how did John long to enter in! But the time was not yet come.

Ezekiel also describes "the holy city," and what pertains thereto (40–48); but a city quite different from the old Jerusalem, as it was either before or after the Babylonian captivity. The descriptions of the prophet and of the apostle agree in many particulars; but in many more they differ. Ezekiel expressly describes the temple, and the worship of God therein, closely alluding to the Levitical service. But John saw no temple and describes the city far more large, glorious, and heavenly than the prophet. Yet that which he describes is the same city; but as it subsisted soon after the destruction of the beast. This being observed, both the prophecies agree together, and one may explain the other.

17. It is said, *The measure of a man.* In treating all of these things, a deep reverence is necessary; and so is a measure of spiritual wisdom; that we may neither understand them too literally and grossly, nor go too far from the natural force of the words. The "gold," the "pearls," the "precious stones," the "walls," "foundations," "gates" are undoubtedly figurative expressions; seeing the city itself is in glory, and the inhabitants have spiritual bodies; yet these spiritual bodies are also real bodies, and the city is an abode distinct from its inhabitants and proportioned to them who take up a finite and a determinate space. Those measures, therefore, above mentioned are real and determinate.

CHAPTER 22

1. *And he shewed me a pure river of water of life.* The ever fresh and fruitful effluence of the Spirit. See Ezekiel 47:1–12, where also the trees are mentioned which "bear fruit every month," that is, perpetually. *Proceeding out of the throne of God and of the lamb.*

"All that the Father hath," said the Son of God, "is mine"; even the throne of his glory.

4. *And they shall see his face.* Which was not granted to Moses. They shall have the nearest access to, and thence the highest resemblance of, him. This is the highest expression in the language of Scripture to denote the most perfect happiness of the heavenly state (I John 3:2). *And his name shall be in their foreheads.* Each of them shall be openly acknowledged as God's own property, and his glorious nature shall most visibly shine forth in them.

5. *And they shall reign.* But who are the subjects of these kings? The other inhabitants of the new earth. For there must needs be an everlasting difference between those who when on earth excelled in virtue, and those comparatively slothful and unprofitable servants who were just saved "as by fire." The kingdom of God is taken by force; but the prize is worth all the labor. Whatever of high, lovely, or excellent is in all the monarchies of the earth is all together not a grain of dust, compared to the glory of the children of God. God is "not ashamed to be called their God, for whom he hath prepared this city." But who shall come up into his holy place? "They that do his commandments" (v. 14).

For ever and ever. What encouragement is this to the patience and faithfulness of the saints that, whatever their sufferings are, they will work out for them "an eternal weight of glory"! Thus ends the doctrine of this Revelation, in the everlasting happiness of all the faithful. The mysterious ways of Providence are cleared up, and all things issue in an eternal Sabbath, an everlasting state of perfect peace and happiness, reserved for all who endure to the end.

13. *I am Alpha and Omega.* Who exist from everlasting to everlasting. How clear, incontestable a proof does our Lord here give of his divine glory!

14. *May have right.* Through his gracious covenant. *To the tree of life.* To all the blessings signified by it. When Adam broke his commandment, he was driven from *the tree of life.* They *that do his commandments* shall eat thereof.

18–19. *I testify unto every man.* From the fullness of his heart, the apostle utters this testimony, this weighty admonition, not only to the churches of Asia, but to all who should ever hear this book. He that adds, all the plagues shall be added to him; he that takes from it, all blessings shall be taken from him; and doubtless, this guilt is incurred by all those who lay hindrances in the way of the faithful, which prevent them from hearing the Lord's "I come," and answering, "Come, Lord Jesus." This may likewise be considered as an awful sanction, given to the whole New Testament; in like manner as Moses guarded the law (Deut. 4:2; 12:32); and as God himself did (Mal. 4:4) in closing the canon of the Old Testament.

21. *The grace.* The free love. *Of our Lord Jesus.* And all its fruits. *Be with you all.* Who thus long for his appearing!